Marketing
Theory

Marketing Theory

Evolution and Evaluation of Schools of Marketing Thought

Global Expanded Edition

Jagdish N. Sheth
Emory University

Atul Parvatiyar
Texas Tech University

Can Uslay
Rutgers University

WILEY

VICE PRESIDENT, ACADEMIC PUBLISHING	Amanada Miller
DIRECTOR	Justin Vaughan
EDITOR	Jennifer Manias
MANAGING EDITOR	Pascal Raj Francois
PRODUCTION EDITOR	Mahalakshmi Babu
MARKETING MANAGER	Alex Tasic
COVER PHOTO CREDIT	© GeorgePeters/Getty Images

This book was set in 10.5/12.5pt Times Ten LT Std by Straive™.

Founded in 1807, John Wiley & Sons, Inc. has been a valued source of knowledge and understanding for more than 200 years, helping people around the world meet their needs and fulfill their aspirations. Our company is built on a foundation of principles that include responsibility to the communities we serve and where we live and work. In 2008, we launched a Corporate Citizenship Initiative, a global effort to address the environmental, social, economic, and ethical challenges we face in our business. Among the issues we are addressing are carbon impact, paper specifications and procurement, ethical conduct within our business and among our vendors, and community and charitable support. For more information, please visit our website: www.wiley .com/go/citizenship.

ISBN: 978-1-394-31054-8 (PBK)

Library of Congress Cataloging-in-Publication Data:

LCCN: 2024044262

The inside back cover will contain printing identification and country of origin if omitted from this page. In addition, if the ISBN on the back cover differs from the ISBN on this page, the one on the back cover is correct.

SKY10086279_092724

To my advisor and mentor (late) John A. Howard, who gave me the opportunity and the inspiration to study the history of marketing thought.
—Jagdish N. Sheth

To my incredible mentor, Professor Jagdish Sheth, and Mrs. Madhu Sheth. They have taught me most of what I know and made a remarkable difference in my family's lives.
—Atul Parvatiyar

To my esteemed mentor Jagdish Sheth and the three most inspirational women in my life – my amazing mother Nezihe (and her memory), sister Arseli, and my better-half Banu.
—Can Uslay

Praise for the Book

"This impressive redrawing of the theoretical foundations of marketing, by marketing experts Jag Sheth, Atul Parvatiyar, and Can Uslay, has been updated to take account of the dynamic environmental changes of the modern era. Its thesis that there are now four dominant schools of marketing is truly thought-provoking. To be in the know, buy your copy now!"

Paul R. Baines
Professor of Political Marketing
University of Leicester, United Kingdom

"*Marketing Theory: Evolution and Evaluation of Schools of Marketing Thought* is a wonderfully researched, written, and seminal 'tour de force' of the theoretical origins, development, and contours of the marketing discipline. It is an impressive demonstration of scholarship at its best."

Leonard Berry
University Distinguished Professor of Marketing
Mays Business School, Texas A&M University

"There have been many important developments in marketing theory over the past two decades. Hence, established scholars and doctoral students will welcome this newly revised and expanded book that explores the evolution of marketing theory. It is especially valuable to have a comprehensive and up-to-date volume that brings together different streams of marketing thought in our burgeoning field."

Ruth N. Bolton
Emerita Professor of Marketing
W. P. Carey School of Business, Arizona State University

"A comprehensive source of insights into the continuously evolving field of marketing, through the lens of the prevailing frameworks, paradigms, and theories. It will be a valuable resource for marketing scholars of all levels of all ages, interests, and theoretical inclinations."

George Day
Geoffrey T. Boisi Professor Emeritus
The Wharton School, The University of Pennsylvania

"This revision of *Marketing Theory* by Sheth, Parvatiyar, and Uslay is important to a discipline that has few theory courses in doctoral programs. Understanding schools of thought can advance a resurgence of interest in marketing theory. The marketing discipline is facing an identity crisis, and this excellent contribution will improve marketing knowledge."

O. C. Ferrell
James T. Pursell, Sr. Eminent Scholar in Ethics &
Director of the Center for Ethical Organizational Cultures
Raymond J. Herbert College of Business, Auburn University

"Because an academic discipline's continuing existence requires faculty who know the discipline's theoretical, empirical, and historical knowledge-content, *Marketing Theory: Evolution and Evaluation of Schools of Marketing Thought* should be required reading in all marketing doctoral programs. Indeed, all those who profess to be professors of marketing can benefit from reading this admirably revised edition of *Marketing Theory*."

Shelby D. Hunt
The Jerry S. Rawls and P.W. Horn Distinguished Professor of Marketing
Rawls College of Business Administration, Texas Tech University

"This book is a must-read for anyone interested in the evolution of marketing thought. In this updated edition, Sheth, Parvatiyar, and Uslay take the reader on an exciting intellectual journey, punctuated by insightful commentary and evaluations of sixteen schools of marketing thought."

Ajay Kohli
Gary T. and Elizabeth R. Jones Chair in Management & Regents Professor
Scheller College of Business, Georgia Tech

"I am often asked: Does Marketing Have a Theory? I used to reply that we have 12 theory schools in marketing! Thanks for the new edition of *Marketing Theory*. I will now say that we have 16 theory schools in marketing, thanks to the work of Jagdish Sheth, Atul Parvatiyar, and Can Uslay."

Philip Kotler
Professor Emeritus of Marketing & S.C. Johnson &
Son Distinguished Professor of International Marketing
Kellogg School of Management, Northwestern University

"I am glad to see this revised and expanded version of the *Marketing Theory* book. The book has been a classic over the years, and this revision ensures it will continue to be an important reading for doctoral students and academics worldwide. Kudos to the authors!"

Nirmalya Kumar
Lee Kong Chian Professor of Marketing at Singapore Management University &
Distinguished Academic Fellow at INSEAD Emerging Markets Institute

"I'm excited to see this new edition and the addition of separate chapters on Marketing Strategy, Services Marketing, International Marketing, and Relationship Marketing. It is indeed a welcome and significant resource for those of us who regularly offer Ph.D. seminars in *Marketing Theory*. It will be a critical aid in helping marketing scholars integrate thinking and understanding across these multiple schools for marketing thought and will likely generate many thoughtful classroom discussions. In my mind, helping our next generation of marketing scholars to think theoretically is our most critical mission."

Linda L. Price
Dick and Maggie Scarlett Chair of Business Administration & Professor of Marketing
Director- Ph.D. Program in Marketing and Sustainable Business Practices
College of Business, University of Wyoming

"The first edition of *Marketing Theory: Evolution and Evaluation* was a classic. The second edition is a fitting revision that retains the strengths of the first edition while providing a thorough review of new developments over the past three decades. Marketers, whether practicing professionals or academic scholars, will benefit from this insightful review of marketing's theoretical history and current foundations. And, as they read this volume, they should take pride in the contributions of the marketing discipline to the consumer, the firm, and society at large."

David W. Stewart
President's Professor of Marketing and Business Law (Emeritus)
College of Business Administration, Loyola Marymount University

"Research in marketing has flourished in identifying numerous rich and fascinating phenomena. However, research has been less successful in identifying rigorous theories to explain these phenomena and unify them into a body of useful disciplinary knowledge. Sheth, Parvatiyar, and Uslay have done a tremendous service to the field by uncovering the history of marketing theory, setting the criteria for future theory construction, and identifying promising candidates for a general theory of marketing."

Gerard J. Tellis
Neely Chaired Professor of American Enterprise, and
Director of the Institute of Outlier Research in Business &
Director of the Center for Global Innovation
Marshall School of Business, University of Southern California

"*Marketing Theory* by Sheth, Parvatiyar, and Uslay is a timely and important contribution to the advancement of the marketing discipline in multiple ways. It is an instructional resource for a doctoral seminar in marketing theory and a reference resource on marketing theories and schools of thought for researchers in marketing. Several of the questions posed by and addressed by the authors in this book (e.g., What Is, or Should Be, the Dominant Perspective of Marketing? Is It Really Possible to Create a General Theory of Marketing?) can set the stage for interesting and insightful doctoral seminar sessions."

Rajan Varadarajan
University Distinguished Professor, Regents Professor, and
Ford Chair in Marketing & E-Commerce
Mays Business School, Texas A&M University

"A much-needed update of a classical account of historical and contemporary schools of thought in the dynamic, continuing evolution of market and marketing theory. It should be an essential addition to the personal library of all serious marketing scholars."

Stephen L. Vargo
Shidler Distinguished Professor & Professor of Marketing
Shidler College of Business, The University of Hawai'i at Mānoa

"The field of Marketing is fascinating, complex, and continually evolving as society advances. This updated classic, from an extraordinary scholarly team led by Jagdish Sheth, describes the development of this young field and evaluates its key schools of thought. It is very well written: readers will surely enjoy the coverage and learn much from it."

William L. Wilkie
Nathe Professor of Marketing, Emeritus
Mendoza College of Business, University of Notre Dame

"An insightful analysis of 16 established schools of thought in marketing that offer the readers a unique opportunity to create their own integrated marketing theory. Now, as a discipline, we can move closer to the ideal of a general theory of marketing for the digital age."

Yoram (Jerry) Wind
The Lauder Professor Emeritus and Professor of Marketing
The Wharton School, The University of Pennsylvania

"In recent years, there have been numerous calls for an increased focus on theory development in the marketing discipline. This book provides a valuable commentary on theoretical progress and advances thoughtful perspectives on how our field can move forward."

Manjit Yadav
JC Penney Chair in Marketing & Retailing Studies
Mays Business School, Texas A&M University

"I loved the first edition of this book. The new edition is even better! It is a penetrating, thoughtful assessment of past, current, and even future marketing thought and practice. The authors' use of the term "school" is appropriate for practitioners and scholars. The "schools" of thought they identify and enrich through their observations and assessment invoke varied ways of thinking. They offer an array of pathways for recognizing, diagnosing, and addressing marketing problems. And marketing problems are what unite academic and practitioner-scholars. A must-read for all marketers."

Gerald Zaltman
The Joseph C. Wilson Professor of Business Administration Emeritus
Harvard Business School, Harvard University, and
Partner, Olson Zaltman Associates

Foreword

All disciplines that have empirical content as part of their subject matter attempt to explain physical phenomena in their fields, often aiming for better grounding practice in scientific principles. But many gaps exist, making the functioning of such disciplines problematic. Marketing is no exception.

One set of gaps persists between theory and method and between findings and policy implications. A common belief is that a linear sequence occurs from theory to method and from findings to implications. Develop a theory and hypotheses, then apply a method to test hypotheses; achieve results, then infer what they mean. Such logic can be limiting and overlook interrelationships between the constituents in the research process. Thus, researchers have recently asked whether some of the presumed linkages mentioned above can be bidirectional or harbor mutuality. Certainly, theory often guides the choice of methods. But the methods one considers and chooses can shape theory, either constraining too much of what we can learn or liberating us from narrow thinking. Likewise, findings need to be interpreted. But such interpretation can lead one to reconsider and redefine the findings, their meaning, and even method and theory. There seems to be a need for a more holistic, nonlinear, and bidirectional, even joint, reconceptualization of the relationships between theory and method and between findings and implications.

Another set of gaps occurs through (over) specialization and segregation of roles in the field. Via tastes, training, how one defines one's approach to marketing, where one publishes, how one conceives of marketing, etc., marketers gravitate to one point of view or another, one practice or another. Many marketers define themselves by methodologies or technologies they use in their daily lives. They might see themselves as survey researchers, experimentalists, qualitative researchers, game theorists, statisticians, methodologists, and so on. Some marketers view themselves as problem solvers, others as empiricists or scientists. A few are theorists. The gaps that evolve out of such specialties deepen the knowledge and skills involved in each but at the expense of preventing synergy amongst them, which affects the quality of research and its application.

Theory can be a catalyst or guiding principle for overcoming the above-mentioned gaps if it is complex and rich enough to weave together profound philosophical and scientific ideas to undergird the marketing phenomena under study. Yet, there is a reason for concern in marketing that we are in a phase of fragmentation and overarching purposelessness, rather than experiencing discerning and judicious leadership, defining what marketing is and can become. Not enough marketers are concerned with marketing theory, and too few schools teach marketing thought or even the foundations of theories from other fields upon which marketers regularly draw. To compound matters further, new graduates lack knowledge of the history and nature of marketing thought. Sometimes, they focus only on narrow theories used in their research to secure their first job. The systemic competitive process currently practiced for new jobs has led to a funneling of effort early on in doctoral education to produce papers for publication before the job interview process has begun. Achieving such publications typically leads to a lack of exposure to other theories, even those close to the one guiding the dissertation. One consequence is that if the stream of research from the dissertation fizzles out, then the basis for generating new ideas grounded in new theories is made difficult because the immersion needed to learn and develop research from new theories is a challenge when one has to do so while teaching and participating in the life of one's department and school. There is little foundation to draw upon because of the breadth and depth foregone as a doctoral student. Riding on the coattails of one's advisor helps in the short-run but invariably leads to opportunity costs due to missed growth in a broader theoretical education needed to sustain a career throughout its course. All students must address the conflict between dependence and interdependence and between the short and long run if they are to have positive career outcomes.

This new edition by Sheth, Parvatiyar, and Uslay directly addresses the second and third gaps noted above and has important implications for the first. Before I comment on this below, I want to say how extraordinary a role model Jag Sheth has been to me personally. I missed the opportunity to work with Jag and be on the same faculty, which was a significant loss to me. Jag exemplified at least three qualities throughout his career that directly confront the gaps noted above. First, Jag is an incredible theorist. He knows and draws upon basic and applied research across a wide range of content yet creates new theories to address unique issues in marketing. Secondly, Jag uses state-of-the-art methods in his empirical work. From the very beginning of his career, Jag has employed many sophisticated statistical procedures particularly attuned to the phenomena he studies. Third, Jag is a transformational thinker and has made many fundamental contributions to marketing strategies at the highest levels of corporate leadership and scholarship. These three characteristics of Jag's life as a scholar have provided me and many others with ideals for which to strive. I do not know of anyone in the field who has exceeded in all three areas as Jag has, which is what it means to be an exemplar and role model.

Now back to the book. Marketing education and research by the late 1950s had become marginalized. Path-breaking reports by the Carnegie Foundation (Pierson, 1959) and the Ford Foundation (Gordon and Howell, 1960) maintained that business schools lost their way and were too vocational and not enough theory-driven. It resulted in a change in direction where the emphasis was placed on hiring faculty members from such basic disciplines as economics, psychology, statistics, and sociology. Then in 1969, the landmark book, *The Howard-Sheth Theory of Buyer Behavior*, was published, which raised the consciousness of the need for theoretical thinking in marketing. This book was exceptional in its theorizing yet, at the same time, drove home the realization that marketing must craft skills in its researchers, teachers, and students to practice marketing management itself.

Many business school curricula and professors have neglected the need to integrate theory and practice of concepts and tools. But Sheth, Parvatiyar, and Uslay, in this new edition of *Marketing Theory,* have uncovered and articulated the core of our field. A big part of the paradigm represented throughout the book is the tension between the various schools of thought that the authors nurture. Readers must constantly struggle and come to a temporary resolution with each school of thought and build a worldview cutting across the schools of thought as they progress through the chapters. Each reader will resolve the tension in different ways. Some will embrace one school of thought while rejecting the other schools. Some will conclude that there doesn't need to be one school of thought that one must embrace, but instead, two or more might be combined creatively. Still, others will come to see that context drives the validity of one school of thought or another and that they will come to flexibly apply the most appropriate school to the context at hand. If readers buckle down, the result will be a living synthesis of the principles bespoken in the book, which will equip readers with a conceptual foundation to understand and apply theory at the highest levels.

Nowhere else in the field can one find such a historical, integrated, comprehensive, and challenging treatment of marketing theory as in this book. It gives us a much-needed resurgence of theoretical discourse in the field.

Richard Bagozzi
Dwight F. Benton Professor of
Behavioral Science in Management
Stephen M. Ross School of Business
University of Michigan

Preface

The first edition of *Marketing Theory: Evolution and Evaluation* was published in 1988 and was received very well by marketing scholars. It was also used as a textbook in doctoral seminars on marketing theory. The first edition's preface stated "*This book is both a chronicle of the evolution of marketing thought and its metatheory evaluation as a discipline. The evolution of marketing thought over the past 75 years is both fascinating and impressive. Indeed, exploring the writings of early marketing scholars and wondering about the rationale behind their thinking has been as exciting and nerve-wracking as exploring the wonders of nature!*" We have experienced the same excitement and wonder in updating the first edition. Over the last 30 years, marketing as a discipline has grown exponentially.

Out of the 12 schools of thought identified and evaluated in the first edition, several of them have become part of the history books, and others have been transformed by digital technology. For example, the commodity school has evolved into branding, and the institutional school has evolved into e-commerce and electronic marketplaces. The buyer behavior school has become a stand-alone discipline as consumer behavior with a strong focus on behavioral sciences. Finally, the managerial school has morphed into strategic marketing.

We have identified four new schools of marketing thought that developed in the past 30 years: (a) relationship marketing, (b) marketing strategy, (c) international marketing, and (d) services marketing. We have included separate chapters for each of these new schools of marketing thought in this revised edition. As before, we have evaluated the new schools using the same scientific criteria of syntax (structure and specification), semantics (testability and empirical support), and pragmatics (richness and simplicity). Indicating scientific maturity of the discipline, all new schools of thought have scored well, especially on pragmatism (richness and simplicity).

Marketing is a contextual discipline; therefore, context matters. It is also a dynamic discipline and, therefore, subject to evolutionary changes over time. There are four contextual drivers of change on marketing: (a) rise of the digital economy, (b) changing demographics, (c) globalization, and (d) growth of emerging markets. In our Prologue, we have narrated how these four forces have implicated each of the past 12 schools of marketing.

The first edition of the *Marketing Theory* book discussed if there will be a general theory of marketing that is comprehensive and integrative. In the Epilogue of the revised edition, we have identified four contenders for a general theory of marketing: (a) Market Orientation, (b) Service-Dominant Logic, (c) Rule of Three Theory, and (d) Resource Advantage (R-A) Theory of Competition. We believe that the Resource Advantage Theory of marketing is both comprehensive and integrative. It needs to become required reading in all marketing PhD programs as well as for marketing scholars.

Like the previous edition, we benefited from the generous feedback of the scores of editors, reviewers, and students. Conversations with our students and colleagues at the University of Illinois–Urbana Champaign, University of Southern California, Emory University, Chapman University, Rutgers University, Georgia State University, and Texas Tech University have influenced and shaped our thinking. In particular, we thank Lerzan Aksoy, Kyungwon Lee, Goksel Yalcinkaya, and Sengun Yeniyurt for their valuable feedback regarding the new schools of thought we have added. Their suggestions have greatly improved the manuscript. The ratings and any remaining errors are our own.

We also want to thank the John Wiley team (Jennifer Manias, Liz Wingett, Pascal Raj Francois), who enthusiastically supported this project. Jagdish Sheth thanks Angel Harris and Laura Hilado; Can Uslay thanks Anjana Chandra, Shivani Srivastava, and Rahul Anand for their administrative support; and Atul Parvatiyar thanks Holt Dorris and Claudia Ramirez for their support with chapter references. We also thank Ratan Kumar Pandit for his assistance on this project.

Jagdish N. Sheth
Atul Parvatiyar
Can Uslay

Acknowledgements

During the Christmas holidays in 1977, Professor Ken Uhl, the Head of the Department of Business Administration at the University of Illinois at Urbana-Champaign, had a massive heart attack and died unexpectedly. I was on vacation in the Grand Canyon Valley with my family when I received an urgent call from Ms. Connie Shaw, the Department Executive Secretary. She informed me that Ken was no more, and I must take charge as the Acting Head of the Department within a couple of weeks.

Ken Uhl was a good friend and a mentor to me at Illinois, along with Robert Ferber and Seymour Sudman. I rushed back to the University of Illinois and started the transition, including hosting a memorial for Ken Uhl. Ken had built up the department and also taught a doctoral seminar on Marketing Theory. I was teaching Multivariate Methods and Consumer Behavior classes for doctoral students. I volunteered to teach the Marketing Theory Seminar course in Fall 1979. I was always fascinated by theory building since the development of *The Howard-Sheth Theory of Buyer Behavior,* published in 1969.

I started reading books on Marketing Theory by Robert Bartels and George Schwartz and classical books in marketing by several scholars, mainly from Harvard, Ohio State University, Wharton, and the University of Illinois. There were also a few influential articles in *Harvard Business Review* and the *Journal of Marketing.* There were few more within journals in Agricultural Economics.

During the Fall of 1979, I got the privilege of working with Dennis Garrett, one of the doctoral students at Illinois. Dennis provided invaluable support, and he enrolled in the Seminar on Marketing Theory. We worked together for 4 years on developing course material and teaching Marketing Theory. During that time, the idea of writing the *Marketing Theory: Evolution and Evaluation* book (1988) was conceived.

At the same time, Richard Bagozzi had agreed to be a series editor for John Wiley's InterScience books and encouraged me to sign the contract with Wiley. It took several years before the book was published, mostly because I had moved to the University of Southern California (USC) and was extremely busy ensuring that all the doctoral students I was supervising graduated in time.

Dennis Garrett and I were not comfortable with understanding Wroe Alderson and his theory of transvections. Wroe Alderson was a great thinker, but he invented words and language which were challenging to understand. So, we invited my colleague, David Gardner, to be the third author and provide his perspective on Alderson's functionalist theory.

Marketing Theory: Evolution and Evaluation book was finally published in 1988. It was well-received by our academic peers interested in Marketing Theory. It also became a popular textbook in doctoral seminars on Marketing Theory. Meanwhile, Dennis Garrett switched his career to Marquette University in Milwaukee, where he eventually became the Dean of the Business School. At my end, I became very busy at USC as I had started a Center for Telecommunication Management (CTM) and teaching a doctoral seminar in Marketing Theory and a class in the Executive MBA program. When I moved to Emory University in 1991, I became super busy recruiting new faculty and starting the Center for Relationship Marketing with Atul Parvatiyar. Time just flew by, and the *Marketing Theory* book was kept on the back burner, despite several requests to update.

Well, it has finally happened! I am delighted that Wiley agreed to publish this Expanded Edition, and I have been able to motivate my great colleagues—Atul Parvatiyar and Can Uslay—to be my coauthors for this updated book. My sincere thanks to Dennis Garrett and David Gardner for their coauthorship of the first edition of the book. I would also like to express my special thanks to Barbara Gross, then a doctoral student at the University of Southern California, and Paul Trapp, then a doctoral student at the University of Illinois, who provided superb assistance in collecting and verifying all the references, in ensuring that the quotes are accurate, and in assisting in the final draft of the previous version of the book.

Jagdish N. Sheth

About the Authors

Jagdish N. Sheth is the Charles H. Kellstadt Professor of Business, Goizueta Business School, Emory University. He is globally known for his scholarly contributions in consumer behavior, relationship marketing, competitive strategy, and geopolitical analysis. Over 50 years of experience in teaching and research at University of Southern California, University of Illinois at Urbana-Champaign, Columbia University, MIT, and Emory. He has been advisor to numerous corporations all over the world. He has authored or coauthored more than 350 papers and numerous books.

Dr. Sheth is a recipient of the 2020 Padma Bhushan Award for literature and education, one of the highest civilian awards given by the Government of India. He is a Fellow of the Academy of International Business (AIB); the Association of Consumer Research (ACR); the American Psychological Association (APA); and the American Marketing Association (AMA). He is a Distinguished Fellow of the Academy of Marketing Science (AMS) and the International Engineering Consortium. He is the recipient of all four top awards given by the American Marketing Association (AMA). Additionally, he received the Global Innovation Award and Marion Creekmore Award, both from Emory University.

Atul Parvatiyar is Professor of Practice in Marketing and Supply Chain Management and Director of the Center for Sales and Customer Relationship Excellence at the Rawls College of Business Administration, Texas Tech University. His areas of expertise include relationship marketing, CRM, global marketing, marketing theory, retailer-vendor relationships, and sustainable business practices. His articles are published in *AMS Review, Journal of the Academy of Marketing Science, Journal of Business Research, Journal of Macromarketing, International Marketing Review, International Business Review, Journal of Marketing Channels, Journal of Economic Sociology*, and other journals and books. He is a co-editor of *Legends in Marketing Series* with Dr. Sheth, and his previously published/edited books include the *Handbook on Relationship Marketing* and the *Handbook on Advances in Marketing in an Era of Disruptions.* He has more than 15 years of international entrepreneurial experience and has consulted for numerous Fortune 500 companies. He has also won several teaching awards and recognitions.

Can Uslay (MBA and Ph.D., Georgia Institute of Technology) is Professor of Marketing and Vice Dean for Academic Programs and Innovations for Rutgers Business School at Newark and New Brunswick, New Jersey. His research interests lie broadly within marketing strategy and theory construction. He is a recipient of the Chancellor's Award, the Valerie Scudder Award, MAACBA Teaching Innovation Award, U. Michigan WDI Global Case Writing Competition Award, and several Dean's awards for outstanding scholarship, teaching, and service. His research has been published in the leading academic journals such as the *Journal of Marketing, Journal of the Academy of Marketing Science, European Business Review, International Business Review, International Journal of Technology Management, International Journal of Business Environment, International Journal of Quality and Reliability Management, Journal of Advertising Education, Journal of Business-to-Business Marketing, Journal of Business Research, Journal of Business Strategy, Journal of Macromarketing, Journal of Public Policy and Marketing, Journal of Research in Marketing and*

Entrepreneurship, Journal of Strategic Marketing, Marketing Education Review, Review of Marketing Research, and the *Rutgers Business Review.* He has co-authored four and co-edited another four books, and over fifty articles/book chapters/sections (eight in re-print). He has served as the Chair of the Entrepreneurial Marketing SIG of the American Marketing Association (2014–2021), and currently serves as Area Editor for the *Rutgers Business Review,* and DSEF and AEF VPP Fellow. His work experience prior to academia includes various organizations/functions such as internal consulting at a conglomerate, international marketing of consumer electronics, and assisting the State of Georgia for high-tech based economic development.

Contents

Prologue

Introduction

Since the 1980s, when the first edition of *Marketing Theory: Evolution and Evaluation* was published, marketing discipline has grown exponentially. Marketing is a contextual discipline (Sheth and Sisodia 1999). As the context changes, both marketing practice and marketing theory evolve and advance. This has been even more true since the 1980s as access to and cost of analyzing data have dramatically declined with technological advances such as the personal computer, social media, and online databases. Several external contextual forces that enabled the exponential growth since the 1980s are (a) changing demographics; (b) digital economy; (c) growth of emerging markets; and (d) globalization. Sheth and Sisodia (1999) advocated that the discipline needs to revisit the law-like generalizations in marketing based on location, time, competition, and customer-centric concepts and theories.

Changing Demographics

Five demographic factors have redefined consumption and consumers. Aging populations have shifted market needs to health and wealth preservation, safety and security concerns, as well as dramatic changes in the recreation needs and desires both in active recreation, such as sports, and in passive recreation, such as watching television and family get-togethers. Similarly, working women households have become almost universal. Today, more than 75 percent of women with children work, and a majority of them are working on a full-time basis. What was discretionary (supplemental income) now has become a necessity, especially in most metropolitan cities. As more women work, time has become an even more scarce resource as compared to income. It has led to the outsourcing of many homemaker activities such as cooking, cleaning, and childcare.

Since all marketing is either time-bound or location-bound, there is an increasing gap between when marketers offer their services such as home repairs and maintenance or doctors' appointments and when the consumers have discretionary time to access the services. There are fundamental time shifts and time shortages due to the rise of the dual-income, career-oriented family. For example, Monday through Friday, from 8:00 am to 5:00 pm, there is nobody at home (the 2020–2022 pandemic is an exception). However, the majority of service providers still insist on doing business during office hours. Weekends are no longer a time to relax. They have become a catch-up day to do household chores as well as shopping and service deliveries. Working women households have also led to a blurring of roles between the homemaker and the breadwinner to cope with time scarcity and time shifts in procurement and consumption.

A third demographic change is the steady decline of the middle class in the West since the 1980s. While the manufacturing age created a middle class, the services age creates greater diversity of income ranging from below the minimum wage service workers to certified professionals such as doctors, lawyers, and managerial occupations. It is further compounded by the dual-income households (two service workers compared to two professional workers). As the income diversity (Gini coefficient) grows, so does the price diversity from the lowest-priced goods to the highest-priced luxury products and services across all categories. What was once a one-to-five ratio is now at least one-to-twenty between the lowest-priced and the highest-priced products. It is true for cars, appliances, clothing, and even grocery products. The upper price limits continue to extend as super-premium products become as popular as no-frills low-priced products. The decline of the middle class is often attributed to the fall of the department stores such as Sears and JC Penney, as they catered to middle-class families for over a century. It is also attributed as the real underlying reason for the growth of high-priced luxury products and services.

The fourth demographic is the increasing ethnic mix in the U.S. and, to some extent, worldwide. Mobility has increased since the early nineties due to the emergence of regional blocs such as the European Union.

In the U.S., it is expected that nonwhite minorities collectively will become the majority of the population by 2030 to 2040. The two largest states (California and Texas) are already a non-white majority, and Florida and other states will generally follow this.

Cross-cultural understanding and explanations are no longer critical between nations as they are within a country or jurisdiction. Marketing to different ethnic groups within a market is emerging as a new field of research. It is likely that ethnic markets in the U.S. (such as little Vietnamese, Korean, and Indian) are likely to emerge as lead markets as they become mainstream offerings. It has already happened for Mexican and Italian food.

Finally, the fifth demographic trend is living alone by choice. As the first-time marriage has been shifting from 18 years to 28 years, more young people live alone and often prefer independence and freedom. So is true of the aging population. It is estimated that one-third of the U.S. households will be single adult homes by 2030.

All of these five demographic trends contribute to the growth of the services sector. It has led to a separate services marketing school of thought. We have dedicated a new chapter to this school of thought. The fundamental impact of all five changing demographics is that the average (or mean) is a less useful matrix to measure. Instead, the range (variance) is more and more critical to observe and measure. In other words, there is increasing heterogeneity in domestic markets. It will challenge our traditional concepts of mass consumption and mass production. It will also lead to increased product variety (SKU) with the same efficiency of mass production. Mass customization seems inevitable by targeting micro levels in each retail store location for department stores, fast-food franchises, and services.

Rise of the Digital Economy

Perhaps the most significant change in context is the exponential growth of the digital economy. In less than three decades, Internet has become universal and global with increasing bandwidth (broadband). It is as transformative as electricity, telephony, and television were on consumption, and, consequently, is transforming marketing practice and concepts. Thirty years ago, no one would believe that Amazon could become the largest retailer in the U.S. without any brick-and-mortar stores. The rise of e-commerce has brought about significant changes in the way consumers search for information, shop online, and have the products delivered to the home or office. The lockdown of many businesses due to the COVID-19 pandemic further accelerated it.

The Internet provides global reach. Therefore, the traditional thinking in retailing such as "location, location, and location" and retail laws of gravitation are no longer as relevant as they were in the pre-Internet days. Most brick-and-mortar retailers who did not embrace online ordering and home delivery are struggling to survive.

A second significant aspect of the digital economy is the spectacular and unexpected growth of smartphones. Expectedly, smartphones will replace virtually all feature phones by 2030 and may exceed seven billion users. Smartphones have narrowed the gap between the urban and rural markets in many economies and between the advanced and the emerging economies. In some ways, many emerging economies leapfrogged the personal computer (PC) revolution and have become immersed with smartphones for social media, e-commerce, and online payments without the use of credit cards.

Today, there are more than 10 million mobile and web apps for consumers ranging from online dating to online home services to online prescription drugs and online ridesharing services. Any product or service that can be digitized can be offered on smartphones and tablets, including textbooks, academic journals, newspapers, and magazines.

Finally, the growth of social media, including Facebook, Instagram, WhatsApp, WeChat, and YouTube, has redefined word-of-mouth sharing experiences. Today, users generate more content than marketers, and social media are borderless (Sheth 2020a). Smartphones with broadband Internet have impacted every aspect of marketing and consumer behavior. Below are some of our observations in this context.

1. Wants are becoming necessities. Today, consumers cannot do without a mobile phone. They are becoming as much necessity as electricity.
2. Word-of-mouth is no longer local in the neighborhood. It is global today.
3. Direct-to-consumer (DTC) is exponentially growing to displace traditional channels, intermediaries, and the middlemen.

4. Social media is borderless. The largest nation in the world is neither China nor India. It is what we refer to as the Facebook Nation with more than two billion active users.

5. Consumers are choosing more a subscription model of market transactions. It is impacting the current pricing practices, which are ownership-centric.

6. Online ordering, especially in the B2B markets, is impacting the flow of market operations. Rather than making decisions about what to put on the shelf of retailers and paying the "slotting fees" in online ordering, the shelf space becomes even more strategic.

7. Brick-and-mortar retailing is likely to sell more value-added services above and beyond the merchandise, becoming more like a service center.

As Sheth and Sisodia (1999) also observed, many law-like generalizations of marketing, primarily based on empirical testing of phenomena, have become questionable as the external context changes. The rise of the digital economy is likely to impact the managerial school of thought significantly. The digital age has created a new breed of entrepreneurs with very different views of branding and marketing. For example, who would think of Airbnb, Google, Yahoo, YouTube, and Uber as companies' names? More importantly, they have created enormous shareholder value. They have replaced traditional industrial age companies such as General Electric and General Motors. Consequently, we expect entrepreneurial marketing to emerge as a new school of marketing thought (see sidebar on entrepreneurial marketing).

Entrepreneurial Marketing: An Emerging School of Thought?

Traditional marketing has been criticized for delivering less return while consuming more resources (shrinking ROI over time, for example, see Karniouchina, Uslay, and Erenburg 2011). Hence it is increasingly under pressure to demonstrate value (Sheth and Sisodia 2006). Any remarkable performance gains rendered from adopting the latest mar-tech tools, big data analytics, or even use of e-influencers and social media are dissipated as competitors imitate and catch up. Therefore, a continuous innovation mindset is quickly becoming the ante to succeed in the global arena.

Since innovation is fused deep in its genes (i.e., underlying core constructs), we think that entrepreneurial marketing (and its agility) has the potential to revitalize the marketing discipline in the coming decade, just like market orientation did so in the 1990s.[1] Moreover, increasing market turbulence, systemic shocks, and competitive intensity result in more and more business uncertainty and a landscape that entrepreneurial marketing (EM) was conceived to cope with (Whalen et al. 2016). Innovation, proactiveness, customer intensity, risk-taking, value-creation, opportunity, and resource leveraging have been identified as the conceptual underpinnings of entrepreneurial marketing (Morris, Schindehutte, and LaForge 2002).

Like the managerial marketing school benefited tremendously from adopting transaction cost theory to its context, marketing scholars have benefited from the effectuation theory of entrepreneurship (Sarasvathy 2001, 2008, also see www.effectuation.org) to advance entrepreneurial marketing conceptually. Effectuation theory focuses on the entrepreneur herself—who s/he is, who s/he knows, and her knowledge and expertise. The theory also suggests focus on using existing means and networks (bird in hand principle), leveraging resources and contingencies (lemonade principle), and forming partnerships (crazy quilt principle) to achieve acceptable risk and return applying the worst-case scenario analysis (what can I afford to lose?). It recommends crafting an emergent strategy—different from the traditional marketing strategy approach wherein managers are expected to set (profit-maximizing) goals—of identifying and securing needed resources to implement the chosen and deliberate strategy. Entrepreneurial marketing also embraces intuition and agility in marketing research, favoring quick and dirty customer feedback (or series of A/B experiments) and bootstrapping, compared to elaborate but time-consuming marketing research studies (Eggers et al. 2020; Read et al. 2009).

---

1 Entrepreneurial marketing is defined as "an *agile mindset* that pragmatically *leverages resources*, employs networks, and takes acceptable risks to proactively exploit opportunities for *innovative co-creation and delivery of value to stakeholders*, including customers, employees, and platform allies" (Alqahtani and Uslay 2020, p. 64; italics added for emphasis). Please also see Hills, Hultman, and Miles (2008) for a comprehensive review of the entrepreneurial marketing literature.

While the origins of EM are rooted in the efforts of small enterprises and entrepreneurs trying to compete with larger firms (Hills and Hultman 2011, 2013), it has since evolved to offer a more inclusive high-value conceptualization beneficial for firms of varying size and strategic orientation (Lam and Harker 2015; Sethna, Jones, and Harrigan 2013).

EM scholarship has advanced through a dedicated journal (*Journal of Research in Marketing and Entrepreneurship*) and global research symposia on marketing and entrepreneurship (recently rebranded as Global Research Conference on Marketing and Entrepreneurship [GRCME]) that is now into its fourth decade.[2] Other reputable journals, such as *Journal of Business Research, Journal of Strategic Marketing,* and *Journal of Macromarketing,* have also published special issues on entrepreneurial marketing. Even though the scholarly work on entrepreneurial marketing extends to over four decades, we think that the main reason the domain has not yet come of age is its lack of an established scale instrument. However, we believe that recent efforts (e.g., Eggers et al. 2020; Alqahtani, Uslay, and Yeniyurt 2021) promise to overcome this final hurdle soon. Therefore, we take the liberty of singling out entrepreneurial marketing as one of the top contenders to be recognized as a distinct school of thought within the marketing discipline over the next decade.

---

2   Entrepreneurial Marketing Special Interest Group (EMSIG) was also among the first set of SIGs conceived by the AMA (originally named Marketing and Entrepreneurship SIG) and has been thriving as a mid-sized SIG with global membership. Among its activities, AMA EMSIG also sponsors GRCME and a doctoral consortium annually.

Globalization

The energy crisis in the 1970s resulted in an economic shutdown comparable to the Great Recession in 2008. During the 2020–2021 pandemic, the world's economic growth engines came to a grinding halt in almost all advanced economies, which led to a restructuring of industries and companies. In response, the world leaders concluded that international trade would be the new growth engine. It led to abolishing the protectionist trade barriers and tariffs and led to GATT (General Agreement on Trade and Tariffs). Free trade was encouraged with the establishment of the WTO (World Trade Organization). Simultaneously the 12 Common Market countries of Western Europe established the European Commission, which eventually led to the European Union's formation as a single market in 1993. China ultimately became the manufacturing capital of the world.

The liberalization of trade and signing of free trade agreements (bilateral and multilateral) resulted in trading blocks such as NAFTA in North America, ASEAN in Southeast Asia, and Mercosur in Latin America. This low-tariff liberal trade generated more brands and product choices in consumer electronics, cellular phones, automobiles, appliances, and garments and consumables.

American companies outsourced manufacturing to China and other countries that had cheap labor. Despite the recent use of tariffs to equalize cost advantage, globalization has continued. It is now more apparent in online trade and social media, which, as we mentioned before, are borderless with electronic exchanges. For example, Amazon, Alibaba, and Flipkart can today offer foreign-made products to compete or complement local products worldwide. In fact, most local/regional markets carry global products and brands today. Thus, it has changed the nature of market offerings from local to international competition. The traditional schools of marketing thought, such as the commodity, functional, and institutional schools of thought, have been impacted by globalization and the new digital economy.

Emerging Markets

The rise of emerging markets is one more context that is impacting the future of the marketing discipline. Emerging markets are the growth engines of the world economy. Based on the purchasing power parity (PPP) index, China is now the largest economy and has surpassed the U.S. ahead of schedule. The third-largest economy now is India which is also likely to surpass the U.S. sometime between 2030 and 2040.

There are several reasons why emerging markets are growing faster than advanced economies. First, most consumption in emerging markets were via unbranded products and services. These are now increasingly becoming branded products and services. Also, product distribution was through unorganized retailing. It is

(PPP Based GDP, 2020)	$ Trillion
1. China	$27.80
2. U.S.	$20.29
3. India	$11.32
4. Japan	$ 5.45
5. Russia	$ 4.18
6. Germany	$ 4.16
7. Indonesia	$ 3.78
8. Brazil	$ 3.32
9. U.K.	$ 2.98
10. France	$ 2.86

Source: International Monetary Fund (IMF)

> Purchasing Power Parity (PPP) is a better measure to reflect Gross Domestic Product (GDP). It reflects the importance of consumer markets

Figure 1 GDP of top 10 countries based on 2020 Purchasing Power Parity (PPP).

also becoming more organized retailing. This shift from unbranded to branded products and unorganized to organized retailing is a direct consequence of e-commerce platforms that are more accessible and affordable. Consequently, market growth in smaller townships and cities is happening at a faster pace, in most cases, than the large metropolitan cities.

Second, most young people want to live independently. They are, therefore, first-time buyers of all things, including furniture, automobiles, motorcycles, and mobile phone services. Most young people do not know how to cook or clean, and they need help in raising children, including daycare services. Consumers are eating out more. Out of three meals a day, more than 50 percent of the meal consumption is away from home. And, out of what consumers eat at home, 50 percent is prepared by a commercial restaurant and delivered to the house. It includes Domino's Pizza, Kentucky Fried Chicken (KFC), and Chipotle.

Finally, most consumers in emerging markets have mobile phones, including smartphones. Many of them would like to buy and consume aspirational products, and aspirational brands with these smartphones are easy to access. The modernization of consumers in emerging markets is a fundamental driver and will sustain growth for several decades.

Unfortunately, as emerging market economies transition from agrarian economy to manufacturing and information economy, they cause enormous pressure on the environment. In addition to the 2 billion-plus people in China and India, over a billion people in Africa, plus consumers in Central and Latin America, are all undergoing similar economic transitions, leading to tremendous pressures on societal resources. It will require more than two planets' resources to accommodate this modernization of markets (Apte and Sheth 2016). Thus, overall the field of international marketing has grown dramatically; therefore, we have also decided to include a separate chapter on the International Marketing school of thought in this expanded edition of the book.

Impact on the 12 Schools of Marketing Thought

As a consequence of the changing external environment, each of the 12 schools of thought enumerated in the first edition has gone through or is going through a transformation from their original focus and thought process.

Commodity School

The commodity school has transformed into three new areas of research, and it has gone beyond typology and definition debates. First, the focus has shifted from the product (shopping—specialty—convenience goods) to brands (e.g., Aaker 1991; Keller 1993; Park, Jaworski, and MacInnis 1986; Srivastava, Shervani, and Fahey

1998). How brands create shareholder value has been a critical area of understanding. In particular, marketing scholars have added social and emotional values to the utilitarian value of a brand. Similarly, the intangible value of the brand independent of the product or service has become popular, thanks to the Interbrand and Brand Finance ratings. Over time, traditional consumer brands such as Coca-Cola have given way to Apple's technology brands as the most-valued brands. There has also been research on brand hierarchy (Keller 2002) and the role of master brands and sub-brands (Koschmann and Sheth 2019).

The second area of transformation is the shift of focus from product (commodities) to services. Since the 1980s, the services sector has grown significantly due to changing demographics and the digital economy. This has led to separate services marketing school of thought. As such, we have devoted an entire chapter to the evolution of services marketing.

Finally, the typology and classification of commodities have been replaced by three segments within a product category. They are price—value—premium (or good—better—best) market segments. There are three segments in perishables and dry goods in supermarkets and definitely for automobiles and appliances. As mentioned before, research interest has shifted to understanding market variance or diversity due to age, income, and ethnicity. Of course, market heterogeneity is even more pronounced in emerging markets, characterized by populations from below the poverty level to very affluent and ultra-wealthy consumers.

Regional School

The rise of the digital economy with smartphones, apps, and e-commerce has pretty much made the regional school obsolete. While it may still prevail in parts of the world, what used to be a core definition of the market (bazaars and shopping centers) is becoming peripheral. In other words, the universal reality of trading (buying and selling) at bazaars and trading posts is likely to become a specialty market such as antique markets or book fairs. Consumers are increasingly shifting from the physical to digital exchanges, as evidenced during the 2020–2021 pandemic and beyond. Digital-first is emerging as the new normal when shopping (gathering information) consumer goods and services. Electronic market exchanges have no boundaries. They can be local or global; they can offer convenience as well as shopping goods; they enable services as well as product transactions. In other words, the regional school may be the first casualty in the marketing discipline.

Functional School

In one sense, some functions and viability of the functional school have been divested from marketing and coopted into the supply chain management movement (which now has several dedicated and reputable academic journals) around which many universities have also created thriving departments.

Interestingly, the functional school within marketing is now beginning to experience a resurgence as time, in addition to money, becomes key resource constraints for the consumer. Time scarcity and time shift will bring to the fore the need for more convenience and greater personalization. How does one make marketing frictionless? How can marketing functions optimize consumers' time scarcity even more than money scarcity? What marketing functions in a value chain enable search, purchase, possession, and consumption without effort? What role do bots and robots play? And finally, how can customer support become a competitive advantage (Sheth, Jain, and Ambika 2020)? These are important questions within the purview of functional school of thinking. Thus, we believe the functional school can be a significant opportunity for a conceptual theory or at least some key constructs to be developed.

Institutional School

The institutional school has also gone through a significant transformation since the 1980s, partly due to the digital economy's rise and partly due to the growth of emerging markets.

1. The first significant transformation is the use of transaction cost economics (TCE) advocated by Ronald Coase (1937) and Oliver Williamson (1981, 2002). It suggests that there are three broad categories of costs associated with a market transaction. They are (a) search and information costs, (b) bargaining and

decision costs, and (c) policing and enforcement costs. Markets may not be efficient, and price may not be a good indicator of efficiency and effectiveness. It may be that a hierarchy (inter-organizational linkage or relationship such as a supplier and a customer) may be more efficient. TCE has been heavily used in understanding one-to-one relationships between a customer and a supplier, especially in business-to-business markets. TCE thinking eventually ended up in relationship marketing. As also mentioned in Chapter 6, what matters most in any buyer-seller market is repeated transactions and long-term relationships. In other words, the *raison d'etre* of marketing is not just to acquire customers but to also retain them over time.

Relationship marketing, as a new school of thought, also added the behavioral perspective of organizational dynamics school advocated by Louis Stern and Adel El-Ansary. It also advocated cross-functional integration, coordination, and cooperation between the organizations. For example, consider the cross-functional coordination required across legal, accounting, IT, logistics, and warehousing activities between a large retailer and its manufacturing supplier. Hence, at the Center for Relationship Marketing (CRM) at Emory University, several studies focused on customer business development that enhanced the value for the customer's customer, such as value for Walmart's customer in the Procter and Gamble (P&G) and Walmart relationship. Similar studies and analyses were conducted for the relationship between Coca-Cola and McDonald's (largest customer of Coca-Cola Company) and between Whirlpool and Sears for Kenmore brand owned by the retailer and contract manufactured by Whirlpool. Relationship marketing has become a major new school of marketing thought, and hence we have included a separate chapter on it in this edition.

2. The digital economy made a significant impact on the institutional school of marketing. It collapsed the number of intermediaries from three or more to two, one, or none, with the rise of Amazon. It also integrated the wholesale and the retail functions into one entity; for example, Walmart became a giant brick-and-mortar retailer by focusing on small towns and offering them world-class brands. Today, it is possible for any marketer to reach out directly to customers (DTC) and bypass the intermediaries. Thus, the functional value of delivery, time, and place utility for customers is possible today because we have home delivery logistics and credit card and mobile payments as well as financing systems in place.

3. With the growth of emerging markets, the unorganized distribution system consisting of as many as 10 intermediaries is now getting more organized by mega-retailers such as Carrefour, Walmart, and IKEA. Retailing is getting modernized in most emerging markets, especially in China. Since emerging markets will be the world's growth engines, it will be necessary to continuously watch them as more innovation in channel management are happening in countries like China, India, Brazil, and parts of Africa.

One must pay attention to the use of smartphones and high-speed networks in China and India to understand the evolution of future channels of distribution in emerging markets. For example, Kenya is home to M-PESA, an online payment system anchored to cell phones. Transactions worth almost half of Kenya's GDP are processed on the M-PESA platform, and around 93% of Kenyans use it. Similarly, WeChat in China and Aadhaar digital platform in India both serve tremendous numbers of consumers.

4. The role of institutions is not just delivering form, time, and place utility. It is access and affordability. Market access is critical to reaching the 'Base of the Pyramid' (BoP) in low-income markets (Prahalad 2004). The subsistence market has become a significant area of research interest in marketing. On one hand, you have a direct marketing company such as Avon, that has created a network of more than a million agents to serve even the most remote markets in the Amazon forest. On the other hand, access to rural markets is also a public policy matter in healthcare and education for both developed and emerging markets. The recent Covid vaccine distribution challenges is a good example of the difficulty of institutionalizing such logistics (shipping and storage).

5. Finally, the institutional school needs to focus on non-traditional institutions to reach specific markets where the traditional distribution systems arc unable or unwilling to distribute products and services. It includes faith-based institutions and sociopolitical gatekeepers in urban slums. Overall, the institutional school of thought has morphed into several new research opportunities in the last 30 years.

Functionalist School

Unfortunately, the functionalist school has declined since the 1980s. There are three reasons. First, no one took the baton from Wroe Alderson to further refine and empirically test the propositions from his theory. Second, as mentioned in the first edition, Alderson covered new words and vocabulary which were hard to understand and follow. It required translation into marketing language. Finally, some of the key concepts of differentiation, value-add functions, along with the description of the role of wholesale and retail institutions were diffused within managerial, functional, and institutional schools of marketing thought. It is, in some sense, really tragic for the discipline because Alderson's theory had the potential to evolve into a general theory of marketing.

Managerial School

Since the 1980s, the managerial school has experienced explosive growth for several reasons. First, focus on competition in addition to customer needs became mainstream. Michael Porter (1980) was the most influential scholar, with his five forces of competition and his framework of low-cost versus differentiation strategies for competitive advantage. In the process, managerial marketing has morphed into marketing strategy (Bharadwaj and Varadarajan 2005; Day 1994; Jayachandran, Gimeno, and Varadarajan 1999; Szymanski, Bharadwaj, and Varadarajan 1993; Srivastava, Shervani and Fahey 1998; Uslay, Altintig, and Winsor 2010). While the impetus for this was the PIMS database that originated at General Electric for benchmarking companies across industries, it became a focus of academic research once it was housed at Harvard Business School under the leadership of Robert Buzzell (Buzzell 1981, 2004; Buzzell and Gale 1987). The research focused on quantitatively measuring the elasticity or a positive correlation between market share and profitability. Subsequently, the battle for market share remained the mantra for decades since the world economy and the U.S. economy suffered from a lack of growth due to the energy crisis and what was referred to as stagflation (stagnant growth with high inflation). It led to a decline in the stock market, and many conglomerates became great targets of private equity companies for hostile takeovers. The most publicized was the hostile takeover of Reynolds Tobacco Company (which had diversified through its acquisition of Nabisco) by KKR, a private equity company. *Barbarians at the Gate* (Burrough and Helyar 1989) became a bestseller and was made into a movie with the same title. There was a similar but less hostile investment in the Coca-Cola Company by Berkshire Hathaway (Warren Buffett) which forced the company to divest its water and wine as well as its entertainment business. Focus on competition continued unabated because of foreign competition from Japan, especially in the steel, automobile, and consumer electronics businesses. This was later followed by competition from South Korea and China across many industries.

A second major factor for this transformation was the strategic planning framework developed by the Boston Consulting Group (BCG) (Henderson 1970; Reeves, Moose, and Venema 2014) with its classification of the portfolio of businesses as cash cows, dogs, stars, and question marks. It was anchored to the two dimensions of industry growth and the company's market share.

Finally, as mentioned before, most advanced countries in the 1980s did not generate domestic economic growth partly due to the aging population, which focused on trade as a growth engine. Free trade across the world further intensified competition, this time on a global level. Sheth and Sisodia (2002) propagated the Rule of Three theory of competition to reflect the reality that in any mature and competitive market, there is a convergence toward three dominant players and others either go into the ditch because of competition or become niche players (also see Sheth, Uslay, and Sisodia 2020).

Strategic marketing grew exponentially with the publication of seminal articles on market orientation by Kohli and Jaworski (1990) and Narver and Slater (1990). Therefore, we have dedicated a separate chapter on the evolution and evaluation of strategic marketing in this revised edition.

Buyer Behavior School

Since the 1980s, the buyer behavior school has gained considerably by institutionalization at the Association for Consumer Research (ACR) and publication of the Journal of Consumer Research (JCR). It has grown so significantly that it is now a stand-alone discipline and resembles applied psychology more. The American Psychological Association (APA) had a division called consumer psychology (Division 23), whose members were psychologists working in the advertising field. It was spun out into a separate Society of Consumer Psychology (SCP) with its own journal.

Buyer behavior school of marketing is relabeled as Consumer Behavior (CB). Since the 1980s, CB has moved on beyond the attitude-behavior multi-attribute model as the dominant paradigm. It is today more eclectic in both theory and methodology. For example, there is less use of survey research technique and more use of controlled experiments. Similarly, the perspective has changed from the psychology of choosing to an immersive understanding of the consumer's ecosystem, especially the real world of consumption. It is referred to as odyssey research and resembles the anthropological approach of field study of living with the community and conducting qualitative interviews with individual families.

Consumer behavior has also explored areas of consumption that were neglected in the past: consumption of entertainment (movies), low-income consumers (BoP), and excessive consumption. Finally, there has been focused and specialized research on transformative consumer research (TCR) and consumption culture.

While CB has generated a vast number of publications, it has not yet generated a comprehensive theory of consumer behavior focusing on consumption (as opposed to buyers). We hope CB scholars will develop a grand theory of consumer behavior. One promising area is mindful consumption (Sheth, Sethia, and Srinivas 2011). In other words, a normative theory of consumption aiming to protect the consumer, the community, and the planet from over-consumption by being mindful or conscious about what one eats, wears, and disposes of as waste. Methodologically, CB has gone back to its roots in psychology. The most common methodology is a controlled experiment. We call it the "study one, study two, study three, …" method. Typically, a series of experiments are conducted by manipulating the primary antecedent, controlling for some moderators, and defining a focal construct as the mediator, for example, habit or trust. We have not included a separate chapter on consumer behavior in this edition. The cumulative body of research is so vast that it would require a separate stand-alone monograph or book to capture it.

The Activist School

Since the early 1990s, the activist school of marketing or the consumer movement has gained greater attention among policymakers, marketers, and social activists. This is due to several external factors. First, it seems that every time there is an economic crisis, there is a surge of consumer activism. For example, the spectacular growth of AARP (American Association of Retired Persons) with the aging population became a powerful lobby and political force for the gray power. The collapse of communism, the dot com bust in the early 2000s, the great recession of 2008, and more recently, the populism movement in many parts of the world has fostered equity, diversity, and inclusiveness in many areas of marketing practice.

Second, customer satisfaction measures became universal with the popularity of J.D. Power ratings of products and services. More recently, it was augmented by adopting the simplistic Net Promoter Score (NPS); most large corporations link customer satisfaction to executive compensation.

Third, the spectacular growth of social media and user-generated content have encouraged marketers to be more customer-centric. Even small neighborhood stores today have user experiences and ratings on their website. For example, Yelp has become a powerful social media content platform to access user feedback and customer experiences. Word-of-mouth (WoM) is beyond local neighborhoods. It has gone global due to social media.

Finally, the United Nation's millennium development goals and principles for responsible management education (PRME) have focused on such global issues as poverty, diseases, education, pandemics, and the environment. This is addressed by a social compact between the policymakers, NGOs, and private sector companies. It has led to a transformation of the activist school into focusing on Corporate Social Responsibility (CSR), a growing field of research and teaching.

In India, the government imposes a 2 percent tax on net profits for all for-profit companies above a certain level of assets, revenues, and profits. This has led to the Indian economy generating more than five billion dollars to invest in solving social problems with or without active participation by corporate leadership. Similarly, the Business Council, a group of 200 or more large corporations, announced in August 2019 that the purpose of the corporation is to serve all its stakeholders (investors, employees, suppliers, customers, and community). In other words, the business of business is more than business (Sheth 2020b).

Similarly, Sisodia, Wolfe, and Sheth (2007) advocated conscious capitalism in their book *Firms of Endearment: How World-Class Companies Profit from Passion and Purpose*. The study compared a group of 30 companies that were stakeholder-driven and compared the financial performance (of 19 companies listed on the stock market) against the 11 companies in *Good to Great* (Collins, 2001) and against the benchmark of the S&P 500 index. The firms of endearment companies averaged about 40 percent annual returns over 15 years (the 1990s through 2000s) compared to 20 percent of the 11 Good to Great companies and around 9 percent for the S&P 500 index. Conscious capitalism has since become more mainstream, and as a concept, it is increasingly embraced by large corporations across the world.

In conclusion, as it transforms into corporate social responsibility, the activist school will continue to grow. It will be less episodic (crisis-induced protests and agitation) and a more mainstream research area for business practice and public policy.

Macromarketing School

Over the last 30 years, macromarketing (how marketing impacts society and how society impacts marketing) has become an increasingly important area outside the marketing discipline. For example, issues such as automation, outsourcing of jobs, trade imbalances, great economic recession, and growing epidemic of non-infectious diseases such as obesity, hypertension, heart disease, cancer, and mental health have become societal concerns, in addition to climate change and lifestyles. Similarly, outside the marketing discipline, there is still a debate whether marketing adds value or negatively impacts society's well-being.

Macromarketing is likely to get the centerstage in the new millennium precisely because of the four megatrends we discussed earlier: changing demographics, the rise of the digital economy, growth of emerging markets, and globalization of products and services. Below are key areas of emerging focus in macromarketing:

1. Climate change and environmental sustainability.
2. The well-being of people including happiness and other non-economic indicators of society.
3. Research programs anchored to the United Nations 17 New Millennium goals, which at an aggregate level represent the triple bottom line (People, Planet, and Profit) (Sheth and Parvatiyar 2021).
4. Role of the third leg of the tripod of society (civil institutions): These include foundations and NGOs (non-governmental organizations) or NPOs (non-profit organizations). For example, what role can large foundations such as the Gates Foundation or Azim Premji Foundation or the Rockefeller and Ford Foundations play? Are they likely to own companies similar to Paul Newman Foundation or the Hershey Foundation, where the profit motive is not the purpose of business? Most private universities in the U.S. are non-profit corporations, and their endowment income offers need-based as well as merit-based scholarships.
5. Tri-sector partnerships between Private–Public–Government: While private enterprises tend to avoid the government except when they are bidding for its business, each sector possesses a tremendous amount of un- or under-utilized assets that could be repurposed to solve the world's social problems (see Chapter 8 in Sheth, Uslay and Sisodia 2020; Uslay 2019). For example, the private sector can help consumers better utilize food stamp programs in the U.S. or can co-use its fleet to distribute medicine in Africa.

Finally, macromarketing may be renamed as marketing for a better world. American Marketing Association (AMA) has strongly advocated that marketing can be a positive force for society. The *Journal of Marketing* has a special issue on this topic and has invited a series of papers by top marketing scholars to offer their views on how marketing can serve society. Moreover, AMA has recently inducted a new SIG (special interest group) on sustainability. There are similar interests and emerging focus on mindful and sustainable consumer behavior by members of the Association of Consumer Research (ACR). We are convinced this will be followed by the Academy of Marketing Science (AMS) and INFORMS.

Organizational Dynamics School

As mentioned before, the institutional school's economic perspective and the organizational dynamics school's behavioral perspective have converged in the last 30 years. Both are now part of the relationship marketing school. As Stern and Reve (1980, p. 53) pointed out, "they should be viewed as complementary because the former deals with mainly economic 'outputs' while the latter is concerned with behavioral 'processes'."

We hope the relationship marketing school of thought will revisit the early writings on power, conflict, rewards, and control between channel partners. As mentioned in the original book, the underlying construct is a competitive coalition. It is a balance between competition and cooperation or what was later referred to as co-opetition (Nalebuff and Brandenburger 1996).

The five forces of competition articulated by Porter (1980) can also be extended to the five forces of cooperation or collaboration. Contrary to the conventional thinking of an inverse relationship, the relationship between competition and collaboration is arguably U-shaped. As competition intensifies between the five forces, cooperation among them drops. However, there is an optimal point beyond which too much competition results in greater cooperation through coalitions between the customer and the supplier or between new entrants and sometimes existing rivals (Sheth, Uslay, and Sisodia 2020).

The Systems School

As mentioned in the first edition, the systems school of marketing is intuitively obvious and relevant to the marketing discipline. However, it has failed to realize its potential for several reasons. First, the computation power one needs to operationalize the whole system, its subsystems, and the feedback mechanism was prohibitive. This was often reflected in the software similarities of a game such as Markstrat or beer simulation or pharma industry simulation. There was no computing power in the personal computer at that time, and everything was organized to link back to the centralized processing in the mainframe computer.

Second, there was also a lack of data from the real world to test any systems theory. In fact, General Electric established the Strategic Planning Institute (SPI) to collect data from large enterprises and build the PIMS (Profit Impact of Market Strategies) database. A systems approach was considered valuable since the annual data could be organized for time-series analysis and linked to financial performance.

Third, the systems approach requires large-scale funding from the government or the industry. It also requires a team of interdisciplinary scholars to design and operate the system. These did not materialize and even today, obtaining industry-specific data to comprise a complete system remains difficult.

Finally, the academic reward system changed to publishing articles in top academic journals at the expense of systematic research, which takes longer to generate results. A rare exception to this is the Buyer Behavior Project at Columbia University (Howard and Sheth 1969).

We hope that an organization such as the *Marketing Science Institute* (MSI) may become a catalyst and obtain either a government grant or motivate a syndicate of companies across industries to fund further development. It is more likely to happen in the services sector. Also, we believe it will be more acceptable if the systems approach focuses on the triple bottom line perspective of the United Nations. In today's cloud computing environment, both the cost and the speed will make the systems approach more tractable.

Social Exchange School

Since the 1980s, the social exchange theory has not progressed much. The fundamental axiom of exchange as the foundation of marketing theory is itself under question (Sheth and Uslay 2007). There are several reasons for this eclipse. First is the rise of relationship marketing which advocates ongoing relationships which may go beyond market transaction or exchange. This includes, for example, joint ventures and formal partnerships between the buyer and the seller in the B2B markets.

Second, many market transactions may not be anchored to the exchange of value. For example, gift-giving and charity are not indeed exchanges. Similarly, not all transactions are between the firm or the consumer, and there are many cases where there is no formal buyer and seller relationship. Even within a family, there may be value creation by each parent for their children but no exchange, formal or even informal.

Finally, a household is not just a consuming unit but also a production unit. After purchasing a product or service, the household does a significant amount of value-added transformation to make it consumable. Similarly, in many services, from hair styling, hospitality to health care, the producers and the users co-create the value and not exchange the value. In other words, value creation and co-creation are both better constructs than exchange (Sheth and Uslay 2007; Sheth 2020c). In many ways, the social exchange school has been displaced by the more recent service-dominant logic (Vargo and Lusch 2004; 2017). In other words, it is the capabilities that matter in value creation and value distribution.

We have added an epilogue that focuses on the evolution of marketing theory in recent years. We review developments and suggest how the discipline can advance toward developing a general theory of marketing.

CHAPTER

Introduction

LEARNING OBJECTIVES

After reading this chapter, you will be able to:

- Establish the reasons for the resurgence of interest in marketing theory.
- Classify the 16 major schools of marketing thought.
- Explain the dominant perspectives of marketing.
- Elaborate on the relationship between marketing and society.
- State the domain of marketing theory.
- Evaluate the possibility of creating a general theory of marketing.
- Identify the metatheory criteria for the evaluation of theories.

This book discusses and evaluates various schools of marketing thought that have evolved since the inception of the discipline in the early 1900s. In addition to the more traditional schools of thought, such as the commodity school, the functional school, and the institutional school, the book describes and evaluates the more contemporary schools of thought that emerged in the early 1960s. These include the macro-marketing school, the buyer behavior school, the managerial marketing school, and the systems school of marketing. In this edition of the book, we also discuss and evaluate four new schools of marketing thought that subsequently emerged in the 1980s. These include the marketing strategy school, services marketing school, international marketing school, and relationship marketing school of marketing thought.

There are two reasons for writing this book. First, after an extended period of distraction and neglect, there is a resurgence of interest in theorizing about the discipline. We believe that a contemporary assessment of existing schools of thought will enable scholars to incorporate the existing knowledge in their efforts to generate newer theories and schools of thought in marketing.

Secondly, the discipline of marketing is entering turbulent times as indicated by the following five major controversies:

1. What is, or should be, the dominant perspective in marketing?
2. What is, or should be, the relationship between marketing and society?
3. What is, or should be, the proper domain of marketing theory?
4. Is marketing a science or at best a standardized art?
5. Is it really possible to create a general theory of marketing?

On the one hand, these questions create an identity crisis for the discipline, and on the other hand, they present exciting opportunities to generate more innovative ideas. We hope an appreciation of marketing's rich tradition will provide a sense of security and at the same time enable scholars to improve on our knowledge.

In this chapter, we will examine each of these issues in detail, provide classification of various schools of thought, and suggest metatheory criteria to evaluate each school of thought.

1.1   Resurgence of Interest in Marketing Theory

The strongest signal of the renewed interest in marketing theory was the publication of the Fall 1983 issue of *Journal of Marketing,* which focused exclusively on theoretical issues. Several books have also been published on theory construction and marketing theory (Zaltman et al. 1982, Hunt l976a, Hunt 1983b, Brown and Fisk 1984, Sheth and Garrett 1986b). Finally, the American Marketing Association (AMA) has organized the annual winter educators' conferences that focus exclusively on marketing theory.

While this trend is laudable and was long overdue, our contention is that we must understand our roots and foundations of knowledge as we go forward toward generating new and innovative theories in marketing. Therefore, this book will attempt to provide in one single volume a summary of the development and evolution of marketing thought and evaluate it utilizing metatheory criteria.

Some extant review papers summarize the history of marketing thought. Although dated, the classic is Bartels' excellent review of the development of marketing thought up to the late 1950s (Bartels 1962). His chronicling of marketing history is also summarized in Bartels (1965). Another valuable resource, which is not widely acknowledged, is P. D. Converse's paper that discusses the beginnings of marketing thought in the United States (Converse 1959). Updates of the history of marketing thought are provided by Sheth and Gardner (1982) and Sheth and Gross (1988), chronicling the schools of marketing developed since the early 1960s.

Although these are beneficial reviews, they do not provide a sense of history, because of space limitations. In this book, we hope to provide a much more in-depth summary and discussion of the various schools of thought. Furthermore, we hope to provide a more comparative perspective by bringing together all the major schools of thought in one volume. In addition to identifying and discussing various schools of marketing thought, it is equally important to evaluate each school's contribution to the development of marketing theory. This evaluation may be helpful to future theorists of marketing to capitalize on the strengths and avoid the weaknesses of past theories. We plan to utilize a metatheory approach for this evaluation process. Metatheory has a rich tradition in marketing, starting with Halbert (1964) and Bartels (1970), and subsequently Zaltman et al. (1982) and Hunt (1983b).[1]

1.2   The Era of Turbulent Transition

A second reason for writing this book is to provide a sense of security and heritage during the turbulent stage of transition that marketing is currently experiencing. We have identified five areas or major controversies that impact the discipline, which are likely to become critical issues for further research on marketing theory.

1.2.1   What Is, or Should Be, the Dominant Perspective of Marketing?

Throughout its history as a separate discipline, marketing thought has been generally dominated by one prevailing perspective at any point in time. During the 1960s and 1970s, consumer behavior had been the dominant perspective. Beginning with early scholars such as Katona (1953) and Howard (1963a), the marketing discipline scurried to push consumer behavior to the forefront of academic discussion and research.

During its reign, the consumer behavior perspective generated several notable concepts on such diverse topics as perceived risk (Bauer 1960), information processing (Bettman 1979), reference group influence (Bourne 1965), social class (Martineau 1958), involvement (Krugman 1965), psychographics (Wells 1975), attitudes (Hansen 1972), and situational influences (Belk 1974). However, to borrow terminology from the product life cycle framework, the consumer behavior perspective has begun to move from the maturity stage to the saturation stage during the late 1970s. Scholars have become increasingly frustrated with consumer behavior's inability to fulfill quickly its once-promising potential. Jacoby (1978) caustically wrote that:

> ... judging from papers which continue to be published in our most prestigious journals and from
> research reports which often form the basis for important marketing management and public

---

1   Metatheory perspectives have been also provided by Sheth (1967), Howard and Sheth (1969), and Zaltman et al. (1973) in consumer behavior.

policy decisions, it is all too apparent that too large a proportion of the consumer (including marketing) research literature is not worth the paper it is printed on or the time it takes to read. (p. 87)

Likewise, Sheth (1979b) emphasized consumer behavior's shortcomings by noting:

> It would be simply exhilarating if we can evolve some agreed upon and properly validated laws of consumer behavior. So far, it seems that we have discovered only two obvious laws of consumer behavior: those who don't need the product, consume it and secondly those who need it, do not consume it! (p. 426)

While the marketing discipline still regards consumer behavior as a worthy perspective, a movement is in progress to elevate strategic marketing to dominance once held by consumer behavior. As an indication of the growing importance of, and interest in, strategic marketing, the Spring 1983 issue of *Journal of Marketing* was devoted entirely to papers analyzing strategic issues. Fundamentally, strategic marketing has emerged in response to criticisms that marketing has failed to adequately consider the development of long-term competitive advantage (Wind and Robertson 1983). Thus, we witness in the following definitions that strategy involves the judicious matching of a firm's resources with environmental opportunities and constraints to achieve a long-run competitive advantage:

> Strategy is the match between an organization's resources and skills and the environmental opportunities and risks it faces and the purposes it wishes to accomplish. (Hofer and Schendel 1978, p. 11)

> ... strategic management is a manner of thinking that integrates broadly defined strategic and operating viewpoints and decisions for the purpose of directing resources toward opportunities consistent with enterprise capabilities to achieve a sustainable differential advantage. (Kerin and Peterson 1983, p. 4)

Although the strategic marketing perspective is relatively new, some scholars are already advocating that the optimal basis for future marketing theory development is combining both the strategic marketing perspective and the consumer behavior perspective. This dual focus on competitive and consumer analysis is particularly evident in Anderson's (1982) constituency-based perspective:

> Thus, from a constituency-based perspective, marketing's role in strategic planning reduces to three major activities. First, at both the corporate and divisional levels it must identify the optimal long-term position or positions that will assure customer satisfaction and support ... marketing's second major strategic planning activity involves the development of strategies designed to capture its preferred positions. This will necessarily involve attempts to gain a competitive advantage over firms pursuing similar positioning strategies ... Finally, marketing must negotiate with top management and the other functional areas to implement its strategies. (p. 24)

Similarly, Day and Wensley (1983) reflected this duality of the strategic and consumer behavior perspectives when they asserted:

> ... we foresee a growing consensus around the notion that the marketing function initiates, negotiates, and manages acceptable exchange relationships with key interest groups, or constituencies, in the pursuit of sustainable competitive advantages, within specific markets, on the basis of long run consumer and channel franchises. (p. 83)

Thus, amid this transition from domination by the consumer behavior perspective to an emphasis on the strategic marketing perspective, we can detect the emergence of a viewpoint that posits that marketing should be founded on two pillars—a thorough understanding of the consumer's needs and behavior, and a critical analysis of opportunities for competitive advantage (Day 1984, Bagozzi 1986). The challenge for future marketing theorists is to develop theories that adequately incorporate both of these equally important foundations.

1.2.2 What Is, or Should Be, the Relationship between Marketing and Society?

Because it is a tremendous responsibility to gather resources from the environment, transform these resources into need-satisfying products and services, and then distribute these products and services to consumers in a society, it is probably inevitable that not everyone in society will agree with how marketing performs these functions (e.g., Goble and Shaw 1975, Sethi 1979). Particularly during the second half of the twentieth century, marketing came under sharp criticism for its presumed poor utilization of scarce environmental resources and its alleged disregard for public welfare.

As the world population increased dramatically and marketing struggled to continually advance the general standard of living for this growing populace, many members of society began to realize that some critical resources in the environment were being placed in jeopardy (Kangun 1974). This concern for marketing's impact on the environment focused on three issues. First, in extracting resources from the environment to use in creating products, marketing placed a heavy burden on certain nonrenewable resources such as petroleum. Also, the extensive use of forestry resources caused many critics to wonder about the loss of recreation utility from the forests. Secondly, marketing faced rebuke because the actual use of many products by consumers directly impacted environmental quality. Perhaps the most publicized example in this area concerns the toxic fumes emitted by automobiles and the subsequent lowering of the air purity levels. Finally, the disposal of many products placed a strain on the environment (Zikmund and Stanton 1971). Social analysts were concerned that marketing might be using excessive packaging, making waste collection more difficult and costly. Further, the use of nonreturnable cans and bottles was criticized because this marketing practice supposedly encouraged consumers to litter the highways with refuse (Crosby and Taylor 1982). The primary concern regarding the disposal of products was the adverse impact on water resources. The waterways became increasingly polluted, and even the underground water resources became tainted due to the runoff from garbage disposal sites.

Fortunately, the marketing discipline has responded to the call of society for greater analysis of marketing's impact on the environment. Within the academic community, several outstanding volumes pertaining to the marketing and environment interface were published, including Kangun (1972), Fisk (1974), and Fisk et al. (1978).

In addition to environmental issues, social critics have also taken marketing to task for its treatment of the consumer. One specific focus of concern has been the potentially harmful effects of product consumption, which received early scrutiny with Upton Sinclair's (1906) exposé of the deplorable sanitary conditions in the meatpacking industry. However, it was not until the 1960s that product safety became a paramount issue. During that decade, two major events occurred that riveted the consumers' attention to product effects questions. First, in 1962 it was revealed that thalidomide, a new tranquilizing drug often used by pregnant women, caused congenital disabilities. Second, in 1965, Ralph Nader published his best-selling book, *Unsafe at Any Speed*, which alleged that the General Motors' Corvair was inherently dangerous to drive.

Beyond the grave issue of the adverse effects of product consumption, the marketing discipline has refined its focus to concentrate on marketing's overall treatment of specific consumer groups. Included in this analysis are the following:

1. **The elderly consumer:** Numerous articles have considered the effects of aging on the consumer and how marketing should respond positively to these changes (e.g., Phillips and Sternthal 1977, Schewe 1985, French et al. 1983).

2. **The young consumer:** Marketing's relationship with children as consumers has generated much interest, particularly regarding the persuasive effects of television advertising (McNeal 1987, *FTC Staff Report on Television Advertising to Children* 1978, Popper and Ward 1980).

3. **Ethnic minorities:** Many critics have questioned marketing's treatment of prominent minority groups, such as blacks and Hispanics, who spend large amounts in consumer goods markets (Andreasen 1982, Sexton 1971, Sturdivant 1968).

4. **Foreign consumers:** As marketing becomes more global in perspective, critics have attacked marketers for supposedly taking advantage of consumers in less developed countries. A notable example of this controversy has been the criticism of Nestlé's promotion of infant formula (Post 1985).

Unquestionably, consumer activists have exhorted consumers to adopt a more aggressive stance regarding businesses' marketing tactics (Day and Aaker 1970). As a result, there is increasing interest in consumer complaining behavior (Czepiel, Rosenberg, and Suprenant 1980; Day and Landon 1977). Recently articles have investigated negative word-of-mouth by dissatisfied consumers (Richins 1983) and appropriate managerial responses to consumer complaints (Resnik and Harmon 1983).

In addition to analyzing more assertive consumer responses to marketing activities, marketing discipline is beginning to concentrate more seriously on how governmental regulation attempts to monitor and control the social impacts of the marketing function. Although pricing policies have long been open to governmental scrutiny, greater emphasis is now placed on restrictions on distribution (Cady 1982), product liability issues (Morgan 1982), and advertising regulation (Dunn 1981).

The most significant development in the area of the marketing and society relationship has been the emergence of a separate sector of marketing thought, called *macromarketing*. Although there is some disagreement regarding the precise definition and boundaries of macromarketing (Hunt and Burnett 1982), macromarketing basically analyzes the impacts and consequences of interactions between marketing systems and social systems. The vitality of this relatively new field is reflected in the excellent series of macromarketing seminars (Slater 1977, White and Slater 1978, Fisk and Nason 1979, Fisk et al. 1980) and the launching of the *Journal of Macromarketing*.

For marketing theorists, the challenge is to create theories that adequately incorporate volatile issues of the relationship between marketing and society. As Levitt (1958) did in his classic article, should we conclude that marketing should definitely *not* be responsible to society for any of its activities? Or should we probe for new theoretical foundations that help marketing cope with the social consequences of its functions? In our view, we clearly must accept that marketers must join forces with consumer advocates and public policymakers in government to forge new visions of marketing's responsibility to society and society's responsibility to marketing. To accomplish this admittedly difficult task, we urgently need more robust theories than the haphazard, ad hoc regulatory reaction that has dominated the marketing and society relationship in recent years.

1.2.3 What Is, or Should Be, the Proper Domain of Marketing Theory?

Although it is somewhat embarrassing to admit, marketing discipline must acknowledge that we honestly do not precisely know what should be the proper domain or boundaries of marketing. This indecision and debate are concentrated on two different fronts. First, we are unsure as to the correct external boundaries of marketing. Specifically, should marketing be applied to social, nonprofit, and general exchange situations? Secondly, we are just beginning to rekindle an old controversy regarding the homogeneity of the internal subdivisions within marketing. It raises a series of questions: "Are domestic marketing and international marketing similar or dissimilar?" and "What, if any, are the differences among consumer marketing, industrial marketing, and services marketing?"

In one of the classic articles, Kotler and Levy (1969) proposed that marketing is a pervasive societal activity applicable beyond the traditional business arena. They argued that every organization is involved in marketing whether or not these activities are recognized as such. To advance this perspective even further, Kotler (1972a, p. 49) presented a generic concept of marketing: "Marketing is specifically concerned with how transactions are created, stimulated, facilitated, and valued. This is the generic concept of marketing."

In an attempt to clarify the broadened boundaries of marketing, Kotler (1972a) focused on the importance of transaction:

> The core concept of marketing is the transaction. A transaction is the exchange of values between two parties. The things of value need not be limited to goods, services, and money; they include other resources such as time, energy, and feelings. Transactions occur not only between buyers and sellers, and organizations and clients, but also between any two parties. (p. 48)

Not everyone agrees with this generic concept of marketing. Luck (1969, p. 53) took strong exception to this new perspective. It derisively noted that "if a task is performed, anywhere by anybody, that has some resemblance to a task performed in marketing, that would be marketing." Instead, he counterargued that "a manageable, intelligent and logical definition of marketing can be fashioned when its scope is bounded within those processes or activities whose ultimate result is a market transaction" (p. 54). Although numerous scholars added their viewpoints to the debate (Arndt 1978, Carman 1973, Dawson 1979, Nickels 1974, Robin 1978, Tucker 1974), Bartels (1974) presented one of the more insightful and succinct statements of the nature of the unresolved problem when he wrote:

> The crux of the issue is this: is the identity of marketing determined by the *subject* matter dealt with or by the *technology* with which the subject is handled? Specifically, is marketing the application of certain functions, activities, or techniques to the dissemination of *economic goods* and *services,* including the satisfactions they provide? Or is it the application of those functions and techniques to the dissemination of *any* ideas, programs, or causes — non-economic as well as business? (pp. 74–75)

To make sense of the myriad of conflicting opinions concerning marketing's proper boundaries, Hunt (1976b) suggested that the scope of marketing may be delimited in terms of three dimensions—nonprofit/profit, micro/macro, and positive/normative. Although this framework indeed represents a significant step forward, the controversy is still far from settled.

Most marketing scholars are familiar with this debate about the proper boundaries of marketing. In fact, the American Marketing Association (AMA) has established separate divisions, special conferences, and tracks to accommodate the debate. However, we are not as cognizant of the controversy regarding the homogeneity of the internal subdivisions in the marketing discipline. Specifically, three separate questions, with obvious theoretical implications, must be answered.

The first question focuses on "Is services marketing different from products marketing?" Although discussion of the marketing of services appeared in the marketing literature in the 1960s (Judd 1964), we have witnessed a more rigorous analysis of services marketing's nature and potential uniqueness in the subsequent years. In an excellent review of this area, Uhl and Upah (1983) concluded that there are four major differences between products and services. These differences relate to (1) tangibility, (2) ability to be stored, (3) ability to be transported, and (4) ability to be mass-marketed. Based on these four points, they defined a service thus:

> A service is any task (work) performed by another or the provision of any facility, product, or activity for another's use and not ownership, which arises from an exchange transaction. It is intangible and incapable of being stored or transported. There may be an accompanying sale of a product. (p. 236)

In an attempt to advance our knowledge of services marketing, Lovelock (1983) presented an extensive classification system for services. Drawing from the precedent established in the commodity school of thought (Copeland 1923), Lovelock developed five classification schemes that aim to answer the following five questions:

1. What is the nature of the service act?
2. What type of relationship does the service organization have with its customers?
3. How much room is there for customization and judgment on the part of the service provider?
4. What is the nature of demand and supply for the service?
5. How is the service delivered?

While Lovelock (1983) and Uhl and Upah (1983) focused on the reasons why services marketing should be considered as a distinct area, Levitt (1981) argued strongly against this view:

> Distinguishing between companies according to whether they market services or goods has only limited utility. A more useful way to make the same distinction is to change the words we use. Instead of speaking of services and goods, we should speak of intangibles and tangibles. Everybody sells intangibles in the marketplace, no matter what is produced in the factory. (p. 94)

Enis (1979) and Enis and Roering (1981) have also argued that goods and services share many common characteristics and that marketing of goods and marketing of services may appropriately call for similar strategies. More recently, Zeithaml, Parasuraman, and Berry (1985) developed a conceptual framework suggesting some unique characteristics of services (intangibility, inseparability of production and consumption, heterogeneity, and perishability) and some unique marketing problems and strategic responses that stem from these characteristics. However, they also point out that significant differences exist *among* services and *between* services and goods.

Future marketing theorists must grapple with the issue of the differences and similarities between goods and services. Further, they must decide whether their theories apply to services marketing and product marketing, if indeed they conclude there is a clear distinction between the two classes.

The second question takes the form of "Is there a difference between consumer goods marketing and industrial goods marketing?" Generally, marketing scholars have accepted the notion that there are substantial differences between these two marketing activities. As a reflection of this belief, we have separate books explicitly devoted to industrial marketing (Hill, Alexander, and Cross 1975, Haas 1986) and entire academic courses that concentrate solely on the marketing of industrial products and services. In 1954, an Industrial Marketing Committee Review Board published in the *Journal of Marketing* a classic article entitled "Fundamental Differences Between Industrial and Consumer Marketing." They cited such factors as:

> Rational buying motives appear to predominate in the industrial field (as against emotional motives in the consumer field), but their influence declines with the increase in product similarity. (p. 153)

> Multiple-buying responsibility is commonplace in the industrial field in the purchase of major items of equipment and the establishment of formulas for purchases of raw materials and component parts. (p. 154)

> The channels of distribution for industrial goods are likely to be shorter than channels for consumer goods. There are fewer middlemen in the industrial chain and a much larger percentage of industrial goods is sold direct to the buyer in industrial marketing than the percentage sold direct to the consumer in consumer marketing. (p. 155)

As a further reflection of the fundamental belief in differences between industrial and consumer marketing, the marketing discipline generated a separate research area to explore industrial buying behavior (Webster and Wind 1972, Sheth 1973, Wind and Thomas 1980).

However, it would be premature to conclude at this juncture that there are, in fact, fundamental differences between industrial and consumer marketing (Fern and Brown 1984). Sheth (1979a) has argued that there is a more significant variation in marketing methods *within* industrial marketing and consumer marketing than there is *between*. Thus, he notes that certain consumer goods, such as houses, may require direct marketing techniques, while some industrial goods, like solvents and lubricants, may be mass-marketed.

Therefore, marketing theorists are presented with yet another intellectual challenge. Does the proposed theory relate to both marketing of consumer goods and marketing of industrial goods? If not, how do theorists defend making a distinction between these two categories of marketing?

The third and final question regarding the internal subdivisions within marketing is arguably the most important for the future development of marketing theory. With the increased emphasis on global markets and international trade, we must ask, "Are domestic marketing and international marketing similar or dissimilar?" Numerous anecdotes relate to the follies of companies that failed miserably and often humorously when their marketing managers attempted to employ their successful domestic marketing strategies in foreign markets (Ricks, Arpan, and Fu 1974). Because of these costly mistakes, the marketing profession has questioned whether a company should standardize its international marketing program (Bartels 1968a, Britt 1974, Buzzell 1968, Sorenson and Wiechmann 1975).

There have been numerous advocates of standardization. Fatt in 1967 asserted that some consumer needs are universal:

> The desire to be beautiful is universal...In a sense, the young women in Tokyo and the young women in Berlin are sisters not only "under the skin," but on their skin and on their lips and

fingernails, and even in their hairstyles. If they could, the girls of Moscow would follow suit; and some of them do. (p. 61)

In a less dramatic endorsement of the pro standardization view, Buzzell (1968) wrote:

> My thesis is that although there are many obstacles to the application of common marketing policies in different countries, there are also some very tangible benefits. The relative importance of the pros and cons will, of course, vary from industry to industry and from company to company. But the benefits are sufficiently universal and sufficiently important to merit careful analysis by management in virtually any multinational company. Management should not automatically dismiss the idea of standardizing some parts of the marketing strategy, at least within major regions of the world. (p. 103)

If anything, it appears that the movement toward increased use of standardization has gathered strength in recent years. Levitt (1983) asserted:

> A powerful force drives the world toward a converging commonality, and that force is technology. It has proletarianized communication, transport, and travel. It has made isolated places and impoverished people eager for modernity's allurements. Almost everyone everywhere wants all the things they have heard about, seen or experienced via the new technologies. The result is a new commercial reality—the emergence of global markets for standardized consumer products on a previously unimagined scale of magnitude. (p. 92)

But, once again, we witness a lack of unanimity among marketing scholars regarding this issue. For example, both Kotler (1986a) and Wind (1986) are opposed to Levitt's hypothesis, and Sheth (1986) suggests a contingency framework that identifies situations where standardization will be successful and other situations where customization is necessary.

Beyond debating the wisdom of standardizing marketing programs in the international markets, some critics have even suggested that theory development in marketing is restricted because of the predominance of the American viewpoint. Dholakia, Firat, and Bagozzi (1980) presented five intriguing points for discussion when they asserted that:

1. Marketing concepts are a product of, and contextually bound to, the American industrial system.
2. This fact limits the spatial and temporal validity of marketing concepts.
3. The context boundedness inhibits the emergence of a universal conception of the nature and scope of marketing.
4. Specific biases and barriers are created in terms of theoretical development in the field.
5. Efforts are needed to deconceptualize, reconceptualize and thereby universalize the analytical categories of marketing. (p. 25)

Therefore, marketing theorists must inquire, "Is this theory applicable only to marketing in country X, or is it relevant to marketing in any country?" This is a perplexing issue that remains to be resolved.

The question of defining the proper domain of marketing is a monumental problem that is likely to cause marketing theorists many sleepless nights. Our essential point is that when a scholar proposes a new theory, he or she must explicitly explain the domain to which this theory is relevant. Is it applicable to for-profit marketing, nonprofit marketing, social marketing, industrial goods marketing, or international marketing? If not, why not? Can marketing theorists convince the marketing community that the theory should have only limited applicability? In many ways, the discipline of psychology has faced a similar dilemma. For example, to what extent does social psychology differ from consumer, clinical, community, or cross-cultural psychology? The American Psychological Association (APA) was forced to create more than 40 divisions to accommodate diverse applications-based perspectives and address the more fundamental question: Is this really necessary or desirable for the discipline? Indeed, the APA consolidated divisions into assemblies but also experienced significant opposition.

1.2.4   Is Marketing a Science or, at Best, a Standardized Art?

The disagreement over marketing's possible status as a science has been continuing relatively unabated for almost forty years (O'Shaughnessy and Ryan 1979). Some marketing scholars firmly believe that marketing can never be a science. For example, Hutchinson (1952) argued:

> There is a real reason, however, why the field of marketing has been slow to develop a unique body of theory. It is a simple one: marketing is not a science. It is rather an art or a practice, and as such much more closely resembles engineering, medicine, and architecture than it does physics, chemistry, or biology. (p. 289)

However, most of the discussion has concentrated on defining a science and how well marketing meets these scientific requirements. Bartels (1951), Buzzell (1963), and Hunt (1976b) have all presented views regarding appropriate scientific criteria:

> If marketing is to be so regarded as science then study of it both in form and content must correspond to the standards of science in the social realm. First, the objective of observation and investigation must be the establishment of general laws or broad principles, not merely settled rules of action or operating procedures. Second, prediction made possible through the development of laws should be of social import and not merely institutional application. Third, theory and hypotheses employed in prediction and in the drawing of further inferences should be useful for the extension of knowledge as well as for guiding administrative means toward profitable ends. Fourth, abstractions as well as concrete facts should be used in the explanation of marketing phenomena. (Bartels 1951, pp. 322–323)

> …it is generally agreed that a science is (1) a classified and systemized body of knowledge, (2) organized around one or more central theories and a number of general principles, (3) usually expressed in quantitative terms, (4) knowledge which permits the prediction and, under some circumstances, the control of future events. (Buzzell 1963, p. 33)

> …sciences (1) have a distinct subject matter drawn from the real world which is described and classified, (2) presume underlying uniformities and regularities interrelating the subject matter, and (3) adopt intersubjectively certifiable procedures for studying the subject matter. This perspective can be appropriately described as a consensus composite of philosophy of science views on science. (Hunt 1976b, p. 27)

This topic of marketing and science is particularly relevant now because several scholars writing in the 1983 *Journal of Marketing* special issue on marketing theory attacked marketing's perception of science. In particular, concerns were raised about marketing's reliance on the logical positivism/empiricism perspective. Anderson (1983) maintained:

> …it is clear that positivism's reliance on empirical testing as the sole means of theory justification cannot be maintained as a viable description of the scientific process or as a normative prescription for the conduct of scientific activities. This point is essentially noncontroversial in contemporary philosophy and sociology of science. Despite its prevalence in marketing, positivism has been abandoned by these disciplines over the last two decades in the face of the overwhelming historical and logical arguments that have been raised against it. (p. 25)

Along a similar vein, Peter and Olson (1983) argued:

> While we recognize that no defensible criterion for distinguishing science from nonscience has been found, we believe that the main task of science is to create useful knowledge. To the degree that marketing has done so, then it can be labelled a science. As marketing scientists we should be concerned to make our discipline more effective in creating useful knowledge about our

subject matter. We believe that such improvements are best achieved by adopting the relativistic/ constructionist approach to science, the context specificity of scientific knowledge, and other features of the R/C program that can give marketing scholars the freedom and confidence to create new conceptual schemes and perspectives. This is in contrast to following the outdated rules of the Postivistic/Empiricist approach that focuses only on testing theories we already have. (pp. 123–124)

Thus, this controversy regarding the scientific status of marketing creates a major dilemma for marketing theorists: If the logical empiricism perspective is no longer relevant, how then should theories be created and evaluated? How does a scholar, who was trained to be objective and mastered numerous empirically-based methodologies, go about developing and testing theories given the apparent shift in perspectives within the marketing discipline?

The marketing literature has given considerable attention to these critical questions. In a very influential article, Bagozzi (1984) focused on the structural aspects of theory construction, summarizing the logical empiricist model of theory structure (the Received View), then presenting an alternative, more operationally oriented, approach (the Holistic Construal) whose philosophical roots lie in the realist theory of science. Other scientific orientations recently explored in the marketing literature include criticism and constructivism (Arndt 1985); relativism (Anderson 1983, 1986, Peter and Olson 1983, Cooper 1987, Muncy and Fisk 1987); and humanism (Hirschman 1986). Further, Sternthal, Tybout, and Calder (1987) have advocated that comparative approaches, instead of more traditional confirmatory approaches, be used in judging the rigor of theory tests.

1.2.5   Is It Really Possible to Create a General Theory of Marketing?

The topic of a general theory of marketing has not received sufficient attention from marketing theorists. Unfortunately, in the past, marketing scholars had tended to address only a very limited area of marketing's domain when they sought to develop "new and improved" theories. As a result, the discipline has become almost cluttered with a dizzying array of theories that have considerable depth but also an appalling lack of breadth. El-Ansary (1979) spotlighted this issue by urging the field to seek a general theory of marketing:

> Marketing theory began as a single, rather broad theory. As time passed, marketing practice and viewpoints have changed, and marketing concepts and approaches proliferated. All these changes have altered both the content and the form of marketing thought providing greater diversity of theories. The proliferation of facts, concepts, and theories is forcing integration of knowledge on higher planes of unification and abstraction. A general theory of marketing is needed to unify the diverse theories of marketing. (p. 399)

Does this mean that the marketing discipline has never before proposed a general theory of marketing? Of course not. Several attempts have been made to create a general theory of marketing. Bartels (1968b) proposed a general theory that was composed of several component sub-theories:

1. **Theory of social initiative:** "Society, not the business entrepreneur, is the basic undertaker of all activity. Marketing is that activity undertaken by society at large to meet its consumption needs—the producing, distributing and consuming of products needed for human existence." (p. 32)
2. **Theory of economic (market) separations:** "The reasons that the people of a society need some form of marketing is that producers and consumers are separated... The separation of producers and consumers, however, are of many types: spatial (physical distances), temporal (time difference between production and consumption), financial (buyers not possessing purchasing power at the time they have willingness or need to buy)." (p. 32)
3. **Theory of market roles, expectations, interactions:** Pursuing its economic objectives in removing market separations, society acts in numerous roles, each of which is responsible for part of the process of marketing." (p. 32)
4. **Theory of flows and systems:** "Flows are the movements of elements which resolve market separations. Marketing does not occur as a single movement, but rather as a number of movements, in series, parallel, reciprocal, or duplicatory." (p. 33)

5. **Theory of behavior constraints:** "Action in the marketing system is not determined wholly by any one individual or set of participants. It is governed by many determinants and occurs within constraints defined by society." (p. 33)

6. **Theory of social change and marketing evolution:** "No systems of marketing remain static; all are in stages of adaptation to continuing change, both in the external environment and within the marketing organization itself." (p. 33)

7. **Theory of social control of marketing:** "As society sanctions the emergence of a marketing mechanism, it also evaluates and regulates its appraisal." (p. 33)

However, Hunt (1971) critically examined Bartels' proposed general theory of marketing and concluded that the seven sub-theories did not meet the theory-building criteria to qualify as theories. Instead, Hunt claimed that "they represent an assemblage of classification schemata, some intriguing definitions, and exhortations to fellow marketing students to adopt a particular perspective in attempting to generate marketing theory" (p. 68).

Although Wroe Alderson never formally presented a general theory of marketing, Hunt, Muncy, and Ray (1981) reviewed his extensive writings and compiled their interpretation of an Aldersonian general theory of marketing. They highlighted six major elements in this general theory:

1. "Marketing is the exchange which takes place between consuming groups and supplying groups (Alderson 1957, p. 15)." (p. 268)

2. "The household is one of the two principal organized systems in marketing (Alderson 1965, p. 37)." (p. 268)

3. "The firm is the second primary organized behavior system in marketing (Alderson 1965, p. 38)." (pp. 268–269)

4. "Given heterogeneity of demand and heterogeneity of supply, the fundamental purpose of marketing is to effect exchanges by matching segments of demand with segments of supply (Alderson 1957, pp. 195–199)." (p. 269)

5. "A third organized behavior system in marketing is the channel of distribution." (p. 270)

6. "Given heterogeneity of demand, heterogeneity of supply, and the requisite institutions to effect the sorts and transformations necessary to match segments of demand with segments of supply, the marketing process will take conglomerate resources in the natural state and bring about meaningful assortments of goods in the hands of consumers (Alderson 1965, p. 26)." (p. 271)

A third major general theory of marketing was proposed by El-Ansary (1979). Although the details of this theory are somewhat sketchy, El-Ansary emphasized that the vertical marketing system, composed of consumers and commercial organizations, formed the foundation for his general theory. In addition, El-Ansary indicated the need for supporting theories of consumer behavior, channel institutions, micromarketing, macromarketing, and strategic marketing.

We do not currently have a well-defined and universally accepted general theory of marketing. Hunt (1983a) redirected our attention toward the attainment of this goal. In his article, Hunt provides the distinguishing characteristics of general theories and the fundamental explanada of marketing. As to the nature of general theories, he wrote:

> We may conclude that general theories explain a large number of phenomena and serve to unify the lawlike generalizations of less general theories. Theorists concerned with developing general theories should be alert to the problems involved in empirically testing their theoretical constructions. When key constructs in the theory become highly abstract, in the sense of being too far removed from observable reality or in the sense that relationships among key constructs become too loosely specified, then empirical testability suffers, predictive power declines, and explanatory impotence sets in. Despite these limitations, such theories or models might still serve the useful purpose of "roadmaps" for guiding the theoretical efforts of others. (p. 12)

Regarding the fundamental explanada of marketing, Hunt (1983a) suggested four areas for theory development:

1. The behavior of buyers directed at consummating exchanges.
2. The behavior of sellers directed at consummating exchanges.

3. The institutional frameworks directed at consummating and/or facilitating exchanges.
4. The consequences on society of buyers' behavior, the behavior of sellers, and the institutional framework directed at consummating and/or facilitating exchanges.

Hunt noted that a general theory of marketing would explain all phenomena within all four of these areas. In contrast, a general theory *in* marketing would explain all phenomena within just one of these four areas.

Why should marketing scholars even endeavor to develop a general theory of marketing? We can present at least three reasons why developing a general theory of marketing should be given high priority. First, the marketing discipline, as it gains more breadth and sophistication, is becoming increasingly fragmented. Indeed, some scholars become such "experts" in certain narrow topical areas in marketing that they completely lose sight of the entire scope of the marketing discipline. Some marketing community members openly admit, for example, that as consumer behaviorists, they know nothing about distribution channels, and they do not care to fill this knowledge deficiency. With a general theory as a reference point or "home base," theorists pursuing a limited theory in any particular area would be encouraged to relate their specific theory to the general theory. By doing so, these theorists could draw upon the richness of the propositions suggested by the general theory, and they could also demonstrate how their theory supports or even modifies the general theory.

Second, marketing is undergoing an identity crisis. Consider how difficult it is to answer, briefly and comprehensively, the simple question: "What is marketing?" The fact is that we currently are not very sure just precisely what marketing is and what it should be. A general theory of marketing could help remedy this identity crisis by delineating the nature of the marketing discipline.

Third, in addition to an identity crisis, we are also experiencing a credibility crisis. Marketing practitioners are becoming increasingly disillusioned with the advice offered by their academic counterparts and often regard the knowledge generated by academic researchers as irrelevant to their concerns (Myers, Massy, and Greyser 1980). There are far too many instances in which marketing scholars abandon the pursuit of developing a theory about subject X because (1) they simply lose interest in the task, (2) the debate over the appropriateness of the proposed theory degenerates into a clash of powerful egos, or (3) they have developed a theory that is so convoluted that nobody in the applied or academic community can understand it. If properly designed and communicated, a general theory of marketing could help convince marketing practitioners, and even scholars in other disciplines, that marketing theorists are pursuing worthwhile objectives in a logical and orderly manner.

We hope that the description and evaluation of past schools of marketing thought will provide a sense of security, and guide future scholars during these turbulent times.

1.3 Framework for the Book

This book will describe and evaluate all the major schools of marketing thought that have surfaced since marketing emerged as an independent discipline in the early 1900s. Before discussing each school of marketing thought, it is essential to clarify what we mean by a school of thought and why we have chosen the sixteen schools of marketing as the comprehensive body of knowledge.

A school of marketing thought must possess the following criteria: First, it must have a distinct focus relevant to marketing goals and objectives, specifying *who* will benefit from marketing activities and practices. Second, it must also have a perspective on *why* marketing activities are carried out or should be carried out by the stakeholders. Finally, in addition to a pioneer thinker, a school of thought should be associated with many other scholars who have contributed to the thought process. In other words, there must be group consensus that the viewpoint espoused by the pioneer scholar is interesting and worth pursuing in marketing.

The sixteen schools of thought discussed in this book (including the four new schools of thought that gained prominence in the 1980s and beyond) meet these three criteria. However, we recognize that what we consider to be a "school of thought" may be considered by some of our colleagues to be a "theory" and by others to be a "marketing thought process." Indeed, we have ourselves struggled with this issue. Rather than letting a definitional problem paralyze our research on the evolution of marketing thought, we have followed in the tradition of Bartels (1962, 1965) in referring to the various approaches to the study of marketing as schools of thought.

To denote the similarities between certain schools of thought and enhance the book's contents for the readers' benefit, we use a 2-by-2 matrix to classify the various theories. The foundations for this classificatory framework are the two dimensions of interactive versus non-interactive perspective and economic versus non-economic perspective (see Table 1.1).

The interactive versus non-interactive dimension captures basic assumptions about the role of marketing and its objectives. First, schools of thought based on interactive processes incorporate the concept of balance of power between sellers and buyers in the marketplace. In contrast, this is assumed away in schools of thought based on the non-interactive perspective. The earliest schools of marketing thought typically adopted a non-interactive perspective in which one party in the marketing process, usually the producer, was portrayed as an action agent who impacted buyers' behavior in the marketplace. This non-interactive viewpoint was also predominant among certain marketing theorists in the 1960s and 1970s, who reversed the earlier positions and focused on the consumer as the primary party of importance and action in the marketing process.

Table 1.1 Classification of Marketing Schools

	Non-interactive Perspective	Interactive Perspective
Economic Perspective	Commodity Functional Regional *International Marketing*	Institutional Functionalist Managerial *Relationship Marketing*
Non-economic Perspective	Buyer Behavior Activist Macromarketing *Marketing Strategy*	Organizational Dynamics Systems Social Exchange *Services Marketing*

Note: Marketing schools of thought referred to above in italics are the newer schools of thought, not mentioned in the previous version of the book. They are discussed in detail in Chapters 7–10.

However, other schools of thought have rejected this non-interactive perspective and have instead adopted the position that marketing is best understood as an interactive process involving relations and effects among producers, channel members, and consumers. This interactive viewpoint has advanced two separate but related propositions. First, it is generally acknowledged that basic marketing activities are not necessarily role-bound. Schools of thought predicated on the interactive perspective generally allow for the performance of marketing functions by either the buyer or the seller. For example, the producer, a channel member, or even the consumer may perform the transportation function. One of the earliest supporters of changing roles in the interactive perspective was McInnes (1964), who wrote:

> This conceptual approach also opens the door to considering the consumer as a marketing agent capable of assuming market functions herself and, therefore, capable by her impact of altering marketing institutions. The functions would still exist; it is only the agent performing them that changes. There still has to be transportation, storage, financing, merchandising, assembly, etc. But these may, and have been, shifted to parties other than producers, wholesalers, or retailers. (p. 65)

Second, proponents of the interactive view have also maintained that a marketing actor does not perform in a vacuum. In contrast to the non-interactive perspective, the interactive perspective forces the theorist to think of reactions to a marketing activity by one party and counter-reactions by the other party. Each actor in the marketing process affects, and in turn is affected by, the other actors with whom contact is made. Bonoma, Bagozzi, and Zaltrnan (1978) summarized the distinction between the interactive (dyadic) and non-interactive (unit) perspective:

> ...the behavior of *single* buyers or organizations is considered a direct and usually linear function of the imposition of certain stimuli from the environment. We term this perspective in marketing, in which an "organism" (e.g., industrial buyer, consumer) is presented with a stimulus from without (e.g., advertisement) and the effect of this stimulus on his behavior the "unit paradigm. (p. 51)

... (1) behavior of whatever kind, cannot be analyzed or explained independently of the context in which it occurs; (2) to "reduce" explanations into constructs (however simple) which violate the structure of the interaction under consideration, is to guarantee confusion, and most importantly, (3) since marketing is a *social* activity, marketers should adopt a social perspective for marketing analysis. This perspective assumes that the basic unit of social activity is the dyad. (p. 53)

Expounding on this interactive (dyadic) perspective, Bonoma, Bagozzi, and Zaltman suggested that four main variables should be analyzed when employing this viewpoint:

1. **Relational variables:** "Relational variables are concepts specifying the nature of the connections binding actors in a dyad. They are characteristics of the interaction rather than attributes of the actors or properties of outside forces. Typical relational variables include dependence, power, influence, conflict, reciprocity, exchange, intensity, and competition." (p. 59)
2. **Social structural variables:** "They may be defined as (1) the conditions of the situation within which the dyadic relation occurs and (2) the social positions that actors in the dyad occupy." (p. 60)
3. **Social actor variables:** "Social actor variables refer to the characteristics of individuals that contribute to or hinder the resolution of dyadic relations." (p. 62)
4. **Normative variables:** "Normative variables are concerned with how people, or categories of people, ought to behave." (pp. 62–63)

Therefore, it is evident that the schools of marketing thought that emphasize the interactive perspective are more concerned with the interdependent relationship between marketing actors. Conversely, the non-interactive marketing theories focus on the influence activities of one actor on other marketing actors. In short, persuasion or selling (buying) becomes the primary focus for the non-interactive schools, whereas exchange or relationship becomes the focus for interactive schools of thought.

The second dimension of the matrix framework focuses on the economic versus non-economic orientation of theories and was selected to emphasize the different approaches to achieving marketing's objectives, either from a seller's viewpoint or from a buyer's viewpoint. Some schools of marketing thought (many of the early writings in marketing's history) adopted a strong economic perspective in which the actions of marketing actors were considered to be driven by economic values. From this vantage point, the goal of the marketing system was the fulfillment of basic consumer needs with producers, channel members, and consumers endeavoring to perform their respective functions in the most efficient manner possible to maximize their profits. In these economic theories, the focus is clearly on critical economic variables such as production and distribution efficiency, prices of inputs and outputs, and consumer income levels.

At the other end of this dimension are those schools that heavily reflect a non-economic influence. Scholars working in these areas perceived that the actions of producers, channel members, and consumers could not be adequately explained based on economic analysis alone (Cyert and March 1963, Dichter 1964, Howard 1963a, Katona 1960, Mallen 1963). Instead, they advocated increased investigation of the social and psychological factors that may influence the behavior of marketing actors. Therefore, we perceive a decided shift in which (1) producers were hypothesized to strive for survival and long-term stability rather than maximum short-run performance; (2) distribution channel structure was seen to be the result of the interplay of power, conflict, and channel norms instead of economic efficiency forces; and (3) consumer behavior was perceived to be the result of complex psychological motivations and pervasive social pressures rather than the simple use of finite incomes to satisfy unlimited needs and wants.

In our opinion, the dichotomy of economic versus non-economic perspective is very important in classifying various schools of marketing for the following reasons: First, as compared with non-economic perspectives (such as psychological, sociological, and anthropological), the economic perspective provides a highly focused but probably a narrow perspective about why sellers and buyers behave the way they do in the marketplace. Second, the economic perspective enables the theorist to relate back to the origins of marketing as a sub-discipline of economics, providing a distinct identity for marketing by associating it with a distinct domain of human behavior. This is not true if one takes a psychological, sociological, or anthropological perspective, primarily because those disciplines have not recognized marketing as a subfield of their domains of interest.

Finally, the economic perspective tends to be normative, whereas the non-economic perspectives tend to be descriptive.

Taken together, the two dimensions of interactive versus non-interactive and economic versus non-economic allow us to fully comprehend the differences among the various schools of thought in terms of their values, orientation, and basic philosophies of human motivation and human behavior. Each of the following four chapters of this book will concentrate on one of the four cells in our classification framework. However, the four new schools of marketing thought that have emerged since the 1980s will be dealt with separately in Section III of this book as Chapters 7–10. For the readers' benefit, we will briefly overview the nature of the theories that will be presented and evaluated in the remainder of the book.

1.3.1 Chapter 2: Non-Interactive-Economic Schools of Marketing

In this quadrant are the classic perspectives in marketing that emerged when marketing was first cast as a discipline divorced from the founding field of economics. What is particularly fascinating is that, although many reform movements have swept through the marketing theory arena, these early schools still possess incredible relevance to modern marketing practice and analysis.

The *commodity school* concentrated on the physical characteristics of products and the related consumer buying habits for different categories of products. Although Charles Parlin was the initial proponent of the commodity perspective (Gardner 1945), Melvin Copeland (1923) is generally cited as the most influential early writer in this area because he presented the now-famous tripartite classification of convenience goods, shopping goods, and specialty goods. This classification system has demonstrated remarkable durability, as evidenced by the fact that these terms are still in the vocabulary of present-day marketing practitioners, consumers, and scholars. Our extended analysis of the commodity school will also reveal how several scholars have attempted to challenge and refine Copeland's system and how other scholars, particularly Aspinwall (1958), have launched alternative commodity classification systems.

Whereas the commodity school concentrated on the characteristics of products, the *functional school* pursued a different tack by focusing on the activities that must be performed during the marketing process. Arch Shaw (1912) is generally acknowledged as the founding father of the functional perspective. However, it is intriguing to note as a historical oddity that Shaw's original 1912 article of sixty pages devoted only ten pages to the functional concept. However, this spark was sufficient to ignite widespread interest in this approach. As we will discuss later, one of the fundamental problems with the functional perspective has been the inability of scholars to agree on a standard set of marketing functions. Perhaps because of this unresolved flaw, the functional school has not received much attention from marketing theorists. Ironically, however, we may note that many marketing departments in corporations are organized along functional lines with separate groups devoted to such functions as product management, sales, advertising, market research, and distribution. Also, the academic curricula in many universities' marketing departments reflect the functional influence with separate courses offered in product management, promotion, market research, sales force management, pricing, and distribution. Thus, we might ask, "Should marketing theorists reconsider the possible contributions of the functional school?"

While the commodity and functional schools are both well-known and supported by copious bodies of literature, the *regional school* is often overlooked in discussions of major schools of marketing thought. This regional perspective can be traced back to the writings in the 1930s and 1940s by Reilly (1931) and Converse (1943, 1949), who analyzed, by way of formulas or "laws of gravitation," where consumers were most likely to do their shopping. This concern for shopping patterns is still reflected today in the extra care retailers take in choosing their store locations. The regional school is also founded on the writings of E. T. Grether (1950, 1983), whose influential contributions to the marketing discipline have spanned approximately a half-century. In many respects, Grether's interpretation of regionalism is much richer than the Reilly-Converse view because he focused on the flows of materials and goods among regions of the country that are varied in terms of their resource abundance. As a reflection of the practical importance of the regional perspective, we may point to the current interest in and, in some cases, alarm over the movement of masses of consumers and businesses from the "Snowbelt" to the "Sunbelt," as well as the increasing import and export trade between the United

States and the rest of the world. Further, the regional approach is relevant to issues of geographic market segmentation (Kahle 1986).

1.3.2   Chapter 3: Interactive-Economic Schools of Marketing

The interactive-economic schools of thought generally emerged in the marketing discipline at least a decade later than the non-interactive-economic schools discussed in Chapter 2. Therefore, these schools demonstrate a somewhat more advanced and sophisticated view of the marketing task with their interactive components.

The *institutional school* is generally considered, along with the commodity and functional schools, to be one of the "grand old foundations" of marketing thought. While the commodity school dealt with the characteristics of the product and the functional school concentrated on marketing activities, the institutional school was concerned with analyzing the organizations involved in the marketing process. The early stimulus for this school of thought was the belief, often derisively voiced by consumers, that the "middlemen" between the producer and the consumer added more cost than value to the products. Therefore, marketers were placed on the defensive and forced to evaluate these institutions to determine their contributions to marketing. From this beginning, the institutional school moved forward to investigate the structure and evolution of channel systems. However, the vital point to raise is that scholars in the institutional school consistently sought to explain these structural and evolutionary phenomena through *economic efficiency* criteria. As we shall see, the organizational dynamics school, a direct descendant of the institutional school, pursues marketing institutions analysis from a behavioral rather than economic perspective.

Although the commodity, functional, regional, and institutional schools of thought were all supported and advanced by the writings of numerous marketing scholars, the *functionalist school* is an exception in that this perspective was founded mainly on the work of one person, Wroe Alderson. Based primarily on his two landmark textbooks in 1957 and 1965, Alderson introduced a new and intriguing approach to the intellectual marketing community. The heart of Alderson's conceptualization was the fundamental importance of the exchange process and the heterogeneity of demand and supply. Beyond providing other marketing scholars with a new orientation, Alderson also differed from others with his creative vocabulary, including such terms as transvections, assortments, collections, conglomerates, sorting, and transformations. Although some critics argue that Alderson's work is flawed by his rather undisciplined writing style and his failure to evaluate and integrate prior literature, it is undeniable that his thoughts are still generating considerable interest in marketing theory. Indeed, there have been two excellent reviews of Alderson's contributions published recently (Hunt, Muncy, and Ray 1981, Blair and Uhl 1977) and several other articles presented at the marketing theory conferences sponsored by the American Marketing Association.

The third school in the interactive-economic quadrant is the *managerial school* of thought. While many of Alderson's terms are still ambiguous to even experienced marketing scholars, the terminology of the managerial school is familiar to probably any student who has progressed past the introductory marketing course. The strength and popularity of the managerial school can be traced to its uncomplicated, elegant focus on such concepts as the marketing concept, marketing mix, product life cycle, and market segmentation. These concepts were developed and nurtured by eminent marketing pioneers such as Joel Dean, John Howard, Wendell Smith, Neil Borden, William Lazer, Theodore Levitt, and Philip Kotler. Unfortunately, a significant problem with the emergence and growth of the managerial school of thought with its emphasis on marketing practice was the simultaneous and perhaps inevitable loss of interest in marketing theory. We believe it is imperative to critically examine the managerial perspective and integrate its more worthy elements into the theoretical realm.

1.3.3   Chapter 4: Non-Interactive-Non-Economic Schools of Marketing

The non-interactive-non-economic schools are comparatively new perspectives with origins in the 1960s and 1970s. These schools represent a dramatic shift in orientation because of the emergence of interest in behavioral, or social and psychological influences in marketing.

The one school that has undoubtedly received more attention than any other school ever in the history of marketing is the *buyer behavior school*. Whereas the six schools already mentioned focused almost exclusively on the producer or seller of market goods, the buyer behavior school performed a sharp about-face. It concentrated on the buyer of these goods. The leading scholars in this school, including Ernest Dichter, John Howard, George Katona, James Engel, and Francisco Nicosia, among others, concluded that it was unsatisfactory to accept that the buyer was simply an "economic person" seeking to allocate his/her finite income wisely to satisfy his/her numerous needs. Instead, they suggested that marketing theorists should dig deeper into the consumer's actions and discover more complex and more realistic reasons for their behavior. Thus, these scholars began to borrow concepts developed in other disciplines, especially psychology and sociology, and apply them in marketing. It is well known that the general response to the behavioral school was enthusiastic and optimistic with support finally reaching such proportions that a separate academic organization called *Association for Consumer Research* was formed to focus on research and theory on consumer behavior. Unfortunately, as with other schools of thought that have generated too much interest, the buyer behavior school soon began to lose contact with the broader marketing discipline. This separation between marketing and buyer behavior is currently the subject of heated debate that shows no apparent signs of resolution.

The *macromarketing school* represented another clear shift in perspective when some scholars, notably Robert Holloway and George Fisk, asserted that more consideration should be given to environmental and societal forces. Included among these forces are technology, political regulation, societal trends, and competition. The most significant contribution of this school of thought was the emphasis on analyzing those largely uncontrollable environmental factors that have a tremendous effect on marketing practitioners' activities. Thus, marketing theorists were forced to acknowledge that the marketing process was not conducted in a vacuum devoid of outside influences that may indeed be uncontrollable, bothersome, and detrimental to the pursuit of maximum efficiency. The environmental school has prospered in recent years to the point that we have now coined a new term, macromarketing, for this school of thought. Besides, the interest in macromarketing is verified by the emergence in 1981 of the *Journal of Macromarketing* and the annual macromarketing conferences.

Although the macromarketing school was based primarily on impartial and rational analysis of the impact of environmental variables on marketing, the *activist school* was oriented toward critiquing, often in a highly partisan and emotional manner, the effects of marketing on the environment. It is fascinating to note that the activist school is perhaps the only major school of marketing thought that was initially spawned outside the traditional confines of the marketing discipline. Only after social and environmental "watchdogs," such as Ralph Nader, riveted society's attention on marketing failures did marketing scholars begin to pay attention to the dark side of marketing practice. However, once marketing scholars, such as Norman Kangun, Lee Preston, Fred Sturdivant, Alan Andreasen, Keith Hunt, and others turned their attention to these issues, rapid progress was made. We now have sizable bodies of literature pertaining to product safety, consumer satisfaction/dissatisfaction, disadvantaged consumers, product disposal effects on the environment, and the social responsibility of businesses. The paramount question that we must now ask ourselves is, "Was our concern for the social and environmental effects of marketing only a passing fancy?" Indeed, with the recession of the early 1980s and the return to more conservative values and political leadership, some skeptics suggest that the activist school may be relegated to the annals of marketing history.

1.3.4 Chapter 5: Interactive-Non-Economic Schools of Marketing

In the last of the four cells, we have several schools of thought that utilize the non-economic and interactive orientations. As might be expected with the dual complexity of both the non-economic and interactive facets, these schools have emerged in the marketing discipline only within the past few decades.

The *organizational dynamics school* had generated a rather impressive amount of interest by arguing that interorganizational behavior is the critical focal point for understanding the marketing process. This school is a direct descendant of the institutional school. Still, scholars in the organizational dynamics field have opted to dissect the interplay among marketing institutions using social and psychological concepts rather than economic concepts. Therefore, such early writers as Mallen (1963) and Stern (1969) asserted that the concepts of power, conflict, control, and roles would have great relevance for marketing theorists. To bolster their contentions, scholars in the organizational dynamics school have borrowed heavily from works in organizational behavior, social psychology, and sociology by authors like French and Raven (1959), Emerson (1962), Aldrich (1979), and Pfeffer and Salancik (1978). At one point, this school was very "hot" in the marketing theory arena, with numerous conceptual and empirical articles being published in marketing's leading journals. We must question how long it will retain the intellectual curiosity of marketing scholars and what its long-term contributions will be toward a general theory of marketing.

Another interactive-non-economic school of thought to emerge in recent years is the *systems school*. The most distinguishing tenet of the systems school is the wholistic belief that the total is more than the sum of the parts, and that we are losing something if we do not remain wholistic in our theory and research. Unlike psychology and, to some extent, economics, systems philosophy has been more prevalent in sociology and ecology. It is, therefore, not surprising that the systems school has borrowed heartily from social systems and living systems perspectives. Systems as a word began to enter into the marketing literature in the mid-1960s, and several textbooks in the late 1960s and early 1970s adopted a systems approach (e.g., Fisk 1967, Lazer 1971, Enis 1974). However, it is hard to identify any individual as the pioneer of this school of thought in marketing. Also, too many distinct systems perspectives came into existence in rapid succession. On the one hand, Forrester (1959) and Amstutz (1967) provided the operations research and simulation perspective, and, on the other hand, Bell (1966) offered the social systems perspective. More recently, Reidenbach and Oliva (1981) have proposed the general living systems approach to marketing, while Montgomery and Weinberg (1979) have discussed and developed marketing information systems. Perhaps the marketing discipline jumped on the systems approach too quickly, adopting a loose and superficial interpretation of systems. It is somewhat surprising that the broadest and most generic perspective to developing marketing theory has not found a solid champion to argue for the systems approach forcefully. However, Rethans (1979) has suggested that the systems approach should be adopted as an integrative framework for theory development in marketing.

Finally, the *social exchange school* of marketing thought seems destined to be labeled as the most controversial school in marketing history. Although Alderson (1965) initiated this perspective when he set forth his Law of Exchange, the controversy did not erupt until Kotler and Levy (1969) suggested, quite forcefully, that marketing was applicable to all social transactions, not just economic transactions. While it was pretty evident that marketing techniques were being applied in nontraditional areas, such as politics and religion, the more conservative elements in the marketing community were disturbed by the thought that marketing should broaden its boundaries beyond the friendly confines of the business world. This dispute has now subsided, but it is by no means dead.

Also, there is another side to the volatile nature of the social exchange school. Specifically, marketing scholars are not quite sure how potent the notion of the exchange is. Some scholars (Bagozzi 1979, Kotler 1972a) maintain that the exchange concept forms the foundation for a general theory of marketing. Houston and Gassenheimer (1987) have suggested that exchange should serve as the theoretical hub around which other marketing theories connect but point out that it has yet to fulfill its promise of providing such a coherent structure for the discipline. Although exchange is an important element of marketing, other scholars have argued that it is much too shallow and transparent to sustain a strong theoretical tradition.

1.3.5   Chapters 7–10: New School of Marketing Thought

Beyond the twelve initially identified classical schools of marketing thought in the previous version of this book, four new schools of marketing thought have emerged in recent times. As shown in Table 1.1, the new emergent marketing school of thought on international marketing is classified as economic-non-interactive, whereas marketing strategy is a non-economic, non-interactive school of thought. Relationship marketing is an economic and interactive school of thought, while services marketing is classified as non-economic interactive. Given the extensive body of literature developed on these schools in the last four decades, we have devoted separate chapters on each of these new schools (Chapters 7–9). Below is a brief overview of each one of them.

The concepts of managerial school morphed into a *marketing strategy school* of thought developed in the 1980s and beyond. The impetus for the marketing strategy school came from the growing importance of marketing concepts in developing the firm's strategic plan and Michael Porter's competitive framework. Market characteristics and competitive factors became key dimensions of developing a corporate strategic plan, particularly for decisions on product-market offerings and business portfolios. The relationship between market share and business unit performance became the domain of study and empirical analysis with the availability of the PIMS database in the 1980s. Several leading marketing scholars, such as Derek Abell, David Aaker, Robert Buzzell, George Day, Allen Shocker, Rajendra Srivastava, and Rajan Varadarajan, studied and debated market structures and firm performance relationships. Market orientation and utilization of market intelligence as key aspects of developing firm-level marketing competencies became a focus of study with Benard Jaworski, Ajay Kohli, David Montgomery, Christine Moorman, John Narver, and Stanley Slater. More recently, Shelby Hunt and Robert Morgan put forth a resource-advantage (R-A) theory of competition that has further advanced the marketing strategy school of thought. Furthermore, Jagdish Sheth, Rajendra Sisodia, and Can Uslay have provided global evidence on how market structures and firm success follow the "rule of three" and its strategic implications. The evolution and contributions of the marketing strategy school of thought are discussed in Chapter 7.

The regional school of marketing extended into a more encompassing global thinking as an *international marketing school* of thought, discussed in Chapter 8. From a contextual domain, international marketing has built itself into a new school of thinking. Initially, this school focused more on exports and international trade. However, as multinational business activities grew, more scholars became interested in developing concepts and frameworks for marketing across and within foreign countries. They began to address issues for foreign market selection, entry, and operations strategy, concentration versus diversification strategies for international market expansion, the debate on standardization versus adaptation of international marketing-mix, global branding, cross-cultural marketing, networks, and strategic alliances, and issues related to the effect of country of origin. The core premise of international marketing was determining what strategies and international business arrangements lead to the best economic performance for the focal firm. Many leading scholars have contributed to this school of thinking, including Gerald Albaum, George Balabanis, Rajiv Batra, Daniel Bello, Jean Boddewyn, Philip Caetora, Tamer Cavusgil, Peter Chao, Samuel Craig, Michael Czinkota, Susan Douglas, Admantios Diamantopoulos, David Griffith, Kelly Hewitt, Tomas Hult, Subhash Jain, Johny Johansson, Constantine Katsikeas, Warren Keegan, Masaaki Kotabe, Philip Kotler, Theodore Levitt, Robert Peterson, John Quelch, Saeed Samiee, Coskun Samli, Jagdish Sheth, Jan-Benedict Steenkamp, Hans Thorelli, and Yoram Wind among others.

As discussed in Chapter 9, the *services marketing school* of thought has emerged recently to take center stage within the marketing theory discourse. With the growing dominance of services in the aggregate economy and the intangible, heterogeneous nature of services usually inseparable from consumption, the services marketing school has argued for a different marketing approach than commodities and goods. The focus of this school has been on service assurance, reliability, responsiveness, communication, credibility, competence, interactions, empathy, relationships, experiences, and co-creation processes. The development of SERVQUAL as an instrument of rigorous measurement spurred a stream of research to enrich the service-centered thinking of marketing. This school overlaps considerably with relationship marketing and marketing strategy schools of thought. Prominent academics contributing to this school include Len Berry, Mary Jo Bitner, Ruth Bolton, Steve Brown, Martin Christopher, Christian Gronroos, Evert Gummesson, Theodore Levitt, Christopher Lovelock, Robert Lusch, Richard Oliver, A. Parasuraman, Adrian Payne, Roland Rust, Jagdish Sheth, Kenneth Teas, Steve Vargo, and Valerie Zeithaml.

Finally, in Chapter 10, we discuss another school of thought developed in the 1990s that caught the imagination of marketing scholars worldwide is the *relationship marketing school* of thought. The primary tenet of this school is that long-term, cooperative, and collaborative relationships are better in many circumstances than transactional or adversarial relationships assumed within the neoclassical economic framework. Influenced by transaction cost economics advanced by Ronald Coase and Oliver Williamson and social norms of social exchange theory and principles of social contracting by Ian Macneil, several marketing scholars examined relational orientation and firm performance. Characterized by different levels of repeat exchanges, frequent interactions, shared goals and resources, co-creation, loyalty, and social-psychological bonds, relationships range on a continuum from adversarial and transactional to cooperative and collaborative partnerships. This school of thought attracted the attention of scholars from many areas of marketing, including advertising, channels, consumer behavior, industrial marketing, international marketing, strategy, and services marketing. Therefore, leading scholars from each of these areas contributed to the development of this school of thinking. Prominent among them have been Jim Anderson, Erin Anderson, Richard Bagozzi, Len Berry, David Cravens, Robert Dwyer, Adel El-Ansary, Shankar Ganesan, Christian Gronroos, Thomas Gruen, Evert Gummesson, Hakan Hakansson, Jan Heide, Shelby Hunt, Philip Kotler, V. Kumar, Kristian Moller, Robert Morgan, James Narus,

Robert Palmatier, Atul Parvatiyar, Adrian Payne, Werner Reinart, Donald Schultz, Jagdish Sheth, Rajan Varadarajan, David Wilson, and Barton Weitz. In addition to transaction cost economics and social exchange theory, the relationship marketing school has also considerably leaned upon social and psychological theories applied in consumer behavior research, and lately on the resource-advantage theory proposed by Hunt and Morgan. Morgan and Hunt were also the first to propose a relationship marketing theory based on two intermediate variables of trust and commitment mediating successful relationship arrangements.

1.4   Metatheory Criteria for the Evaluation of Theories

One of the weaknesses in the development of marketing thought has been the lack of metatheory evaluation and non-critical acceptance of previously proposed theories. Marketing theorists do not consistently critique other theories to identify their particular strengths and weaknesses when they formulate their own theories. Thus, we believe that many of us in the marketing theory arena are guilty on two counts. First, we are often unaware of the existence and content of major schools of thought from marketing's past. Secondly, even if we are cognizant of these previous theories, we all too often accept them at face value without subjecting them to careful review to isolate their virtues and flaws.

Although one of our main objectives, as noted in the preceding pages, is to review the major schools of marketing thought and increase the awareness level, we also want to evaluate these theories and suggest what they may offer for future theorizing. For this evaluation phase, we have chosen to utilize a metatheory approach.

As a point of departure, we should first answer a question that many readers may ask: "What exactly is metatheory?" Fortunately, the subject of metatheory has received attention from such notable scholars as Halbert (1964), Bartels (1970), and Zaltman, Pinson, and Angelmar (1973). More recently, it has received attention from Zaltman et al. (1982) and Leong (1985). According to Bartels (1970, p. 4), "metatheory is here understood to pertain to the requirements of theory formulation, with particular reference to the structure of thought and to utilization of language for the communication of meaning." Zaltman et al. (1973) expound a bit further by noting:

> Metatheory is the science of science or the investigation of investigation. Metatheory involves the careful appraisal of the methodology of science and the philosophical issues involved in the conduct of science. It is concerned with such topics as the operationalization of scientific concepts, the logic of testing theories, the use of theory, the nature of causality, and procedures for making predictions. Broadly defined, metatheory is the investigation, analysis and the description of (1) technology of building theory, (2) the theory itself, and (3) the utilization of theory. (p. 4)

The metatheoretical criteria we have chosen to use for our evaluation can be classified into three distinct categories with two criteria in each of these three areas:

1. Syntax	2. Semantics	3. Pragmatics
A. Structure	A. Testability	A. Richness
B. Specification	B. Empirical support	B. Simplicity

The three broad categories of syntax criteria, semantics criteria, and pragmatics criteria were initially discussed in marketing by Halbert (1964).

Syntax (Organization) Criteria: A "good" theory should be structurally sound with a precise *organizational pattern*. As defined by Halbert (1964, p. 32), "syntactics has to do with the legitimacy of the operations that can be performed on the elements that form the theory." Therefore, two essential syntax criteria, structure, and specification, may be used to evaluate theories.

Structure basically questions whether the theoretical concepts are properly defined and integrated to form a solid nomological network. Zaltman et al. (1973) discussed this same basic notion under their criterion of "coherence or systematic structure:"

Thus information gathered or knowledge acquired should not be found in random relationships. Instead, items of knowledge should be grouped together in some logical way. Thus, related concepts should be grouped to form hypotheses and related hypotheses grouped to form theories. (p. 11)

Bartels (1970) also discussed this structure criterion when he proposed a metatheory criterion that he termed "subject identification":

A first requirement which a metatheory makes is that a theory should deal with a specific, definable subject and be related to it throughout. This is a requirement of subject identification and unity. Stated conversely, a theory should not be built upon uncertain or conflicting concepts of a subject, unless to deal with the uncertainty or to resolve the conflict. (p. 5)

The second of the syntax criteria is the *specification* criterion, which states that the relationships among the theoretical concepts must be specified to delimit the hypotheses clearly. In other words, a theory demonstrates weakness on the specification criterion when relationships among the concepts are usually couched in a contingency framework where A is related to B but only if other concepts (C, D, etc.) are absent or present. Bartels (1970) called this requirement the "interconcept relationship" criterion:

A second type of difference in ideas is that between basic conceptual categories, in contrast to that within those categories. Basic concepts are subdivided for the purpose of identifying their concepts, but the differences between dissimilar concepts are noted for the purpose of relating them. The establishment of such relationships is essential to the construction of theory ... A presumption of causality is basic to prediction. The causality presumed in theory, however, is conceptual rather than physical. It is a presumed condition in the relationship between two concepts, whereby one is deemed an independent variable, the other a dependent variable. The dominance of the one and the subordinance of the other defines determinism or causality. (pp. 9–10)

Semantics (Reality) Criteria: Semantics criteria evaluate the theory's relationship to reality by analyzing the *testability* and *empirical support* of the theory. A theory may satisfy the syntax criteria requirements but still fail to meet the test of the semantics criteria, as noted by Halbert (1964):

A theory may fulfill all of the syntactical requirements with complete adequacy, and still have serious faults. The statement of the primitive notions, the operators, and the permissible manipulation of the symbols in which the theory is stated may all be complete and logically correct. The difficulties may lie in the way in which the theory is related to the real world ... If we are to use a theory to tell us what observations to make, then we must be clear, precise, and complete in our description of what constitutes a relevant observation and how to interpret such observation so as to test the theory. This area of the philosophy of science is called semantics. (p. 33)

The *testability* criterion is the first of the two semantics criteria. According to the testability criterion, a strong theory is one in which precise and direct operational definitions of the theory's concepts are provided to ensure testability and intersubjective consensus (Zaltman et al. 1973). Therefore, if a theorist developed a new theory of channel member behavior using the concepts of power, conflict, and cooperation, he or she must indicate how those concepts are to be operationally defined and measured in the "real world" of marketing channels. Suppose the operational definitions are satisfactorily presented in theory. In that case, the theorist should entrust the actual testing of the theory to other scholars without worrying that they will misinterpret how to measure the key theoretical concepts. Thus, often when a theory's originator complains about the poor results that other scholars obtained when testing his or her theory, the blame should be appropriately placed upon the author of the theory for not adequately meeting the testability criterion.

Empirical support, the second of the semantics criteria, evaluates the degree of confirming evidence that has been gathered to support the theory's hypotheses. Regarding this criterion, Zaltman et al. (1973) wrote:

> ...the criterion of reliability is difficult to meet. Apart from establishing that a particular observation is not very likely to have occurred on a random basis, there is the more demanding question concerning the reliability of a particular explanation or interpretation. There will frequently be a competing explanation for the phenomenon observed that has not been ruled out by the particular test. This might be called the problem of interpretative reliability: The larger the number of plausible alternative interpretations, the lower the degree of reliability. (p. 11)

Therefore, any newly proposed theory must inevitably fail on the empirical support criterion, because it has not yet been subjected to empirical verification. However, as more and more theory tests are completed with uniform and positive results, the theory's empirical support becomes more convincing. It should be pointed out that a theory or school of thought may have significant empirical support for its constructs even though the theory itself may not be subjected to empirical research.

Pragmatics (Relevance) Criteria: Simply stated, the pragmatics criteria question the relevance of the theory to the "users." In the case of marketing theories, the users of the theories are marketing practitioners, public policy makers, and consumers who actually function in the marketplace to overcome the separations between producers and consumers. If a theory is not beneficial to them, then the theory does not satisfy the pragmatics criteria. Once again, Halbert (1964) points out that the three categories of syntax, semantics, and pragmatics are fully independent:

> Even if a theory is adequately described in semantic and syntactic aspects, it still may not be a very good theory. The way in which it fails to be good may be because of a lack of attention to the richness or fruitfulness of the theory in terms of the needs, desires, and problems of the people who may have use for it. The aspect of the analysis of theory concerned with the use of theory is called pragmatics. We require of our theories that they be rich, fruitful, and useful and apply to important problems as well as that they be formally adequate and definitionally precise. (p. 35)

The first pragmatics criterion is the *richness* criterion, which asks how comprehensive and generalizable the theory is. Generally, a theory is more useful or relevant to a marketing practitioner, a policymaker, or a consumer if it covers a large expanse of problems or situations typically encountered. Bartels (1970) named this criterion the "generality of relationships":

> ...the greater value of a theory is in its suitability to explanation of experience on a broader scale. Universality is an ideal seldom achieved, especially in the fitting of theories to social or behavioral circumstances. It is nevertheless, a status to which generalization tends in scientific reasoning. (p. 11)

Similarly, Zaltman et al. (1973) note:

> ...comprehensiveness or scope of knowledge is a desirable criterion. It is a goal of science and ultimately an unachievable one in most instances, to develop statements or laws having wide applicability. The larger the number of different contexts a given theory or subtheory can encompass, the more powerful—that is, the more comprehensive—it is. (p. 12)

Finally, we come to the second pragmatics criterion and the last of the six metatheory criteria that we will utilize in this book. The *simplicity* criterion has not received much explicit attention from the marketing scholars who have discussed metatheoretical issues. However, the simplicity criterion is of paramount importance because it evaluates the communication and implementation potential of the theory. That is, can the theory be easily explained to others, and can the theory's recommendations be readily implemented by others?

A theory could perform very well on the richness criterion but still fail to pass minimal acceptance standards for the simplicity criterion. In fact, there may be a counterbalancing effect between these two pragmatics criteria. For example, when the theory becomes richer (is more comprehensive and generalizable), it also becomes more difficult to explain and implement.

In our review of the major schools of marketing thought, we will utilize these six metatheory criteria to evaluate the strengths and weaknesses of each of the sixteen major schools. The potential evaluation scores range from 1 (poor) to 10 (excellent). The ratings represent our personal viewpoints regarding each school's performance on the metatheory criteria. While we recognize that our process is subjective, we have attempted to provide a rationale for our ratings. Of course, we do not expect that all our readers will agree with our judgments and, if anything, we view differences of opinion as a positive sign, demonstrating that more and more marketing scholars are taking the time and effort to critique seriously the merits of our discipline's diverse storehouse of marketing theories. Therefore, we encourage the reader to debate our ratings.

At the same time, we acknowledge that a more logical-positivist approach would be to ask a representative sample of scholars to rate each school of thought on the six metatheory criteria and then present a statistical analysis of their viewpoints. This approach was taken by Hunt and Burnett (1982) in defining macromarketing.

 ## Summary

This chapter has provided the introduction to the book. It has suggested two main reasons for writing this book on marketing theories. First, a resurgence of interest in marketing theory has generated a need to review and evaluate known theories and schools of thought in marketing. Secondly, the discipline of marketing is going through an identity crisis due to several critical shifts and changes. Indeed, marketing is on the verge of becoming fragmented into sub-disciplines unless marketing scholars attempt to bring together various perspectives and domains of marketing under one roof. A review of past theories in this book may become highly useful in providing both a sense of security and richness to build future marketing theories.

In this book, we have identified sixteen major schools of thought that have emerged from the inception of marketing in the early nineteen hundreds to the most recent times. Utilizing a two-dimensional map anchored to interactive-non-interactive perspectives and economic-non-economic perspectives, we have classified these sixteen schools of thought as follows:

1. **Non-interactive-Economic** perspectives dominate in the classical commodity, functional, regional, and international marketing schools of thought.
2. **Interactive-Economic** perspectives are more commonly found in the institutional, functionalist, managerial, and relationship marketing schools of thought.
3. **Non-interactive-Non-economic** perspectives underlie the buyer behavior, activist, macromarketing, and marketing strategy schools of thought.
4. **Interactive-Non-economic** perspectives, the most complex approaches, are the underlying processes for the organizational dynamics, systems, social exchange, and services marketing schools of marketing theory.

In addition to providing a substantive and historical perspective of these sixteen major schools of thought, we will also undertake a metatheory evaluation of each school of thought so that future marketing scholars can assess how to build new theories of marketing. We have selected six metatheory criteria that reflect the syntax (organization), the semantics (reality), and the pragmatics (relevance) criteria of judging a theory.

The criteria chosen for organizational aspects are *structure* and *specification*. Structure refers to the definition and integration of concepts into a nomological network. Specification refers to the lack of contingent relationships between two or more concepts.

The two criteria selected for the reality aspects of a theory are *testability* and *empirical support*. Testability means the operational definitions of the theory's constructs are provided to ensure adequate empirical testing and intersubjective consensus. Empirical support refers to the amount of empirical research that has been carried out in support of the theory.

The last two criteria, *richness* and *simplicity*, are selected to measure the relevance of a theory. Richness, as the name implies, means the comprehensiveness of the theory in terms of the domain of marketing it is able to describe, explain, and predict. On the other hand, simplicity refers to the communication and implementation of the theory to users such as marketing practitioners, policymakers, and consumers.

Questions for Analysis and Discussion

1. Does the marketing discipline still face an identity crisis? Why? How can it be resolved?

2. What is marketing's societal role in the current context of ESG (economic, social, and governance) parameters? How can marketing help achieve triple-bottom-line results concerning people, the planet, and profits?

3. What is the dominant perspective of marketing today – consumer behavior, strategic marketing, macromarketing, or quantitative modeling and analytics? How would this dominant marketing perspective evolve in the next 10 to 20 years? Why?

4. What is the importance of the question, "Is marketing a science?" What are its implications for teaching and research in marketing? Does it have a bearing on the standards set by marketing journals for accepting or rejecting manuscripts? How does it impact marketing practice?

5. Which scientific marketing perspective would you favor – logical positivism/empiricism or the normative, prescriptive approach to theory building? Instead, would you follow alternative views, such as holistic construal, relativism, humanism, criticism and constructivism, or theory-in-use? If so, why?

6. What is the need for a general theory of marketing? Despite several attempts, why is there still no commonly accepted general theory of marketing?

7. What can be accomplished by evaluating the schools of marketing thought on the three categories of metatheory criteria – syntax, semantics, and pragmatics? What questions can it help us address about the knowledge structure in the marketing discipline?

CHAPTER

Non-Interactive Economic Schools of Marketing

LEARNING OBJECTIVES

After reading this chapter, you will be able to:

- Explain the three non-interactive economic schools of marketing thought – commodity school, functional school, and the regional school of marketing.

- Critically examine the rationale of focus on objects of the transaction, namely products, and their specific characteristics for classification, by the commodity school scholars.

- Draw implications for managerial decision-making and marketing strategy based on product classification scheme.

- Evaluate the value and risks of focusing on marketing as a set of functions proposed by the functional school of marketing thought.

- Describe how the breakthrough Four Ps of marketing thinking were derivatives of the earlier classification systems presented by the functional school theorists.

- Explain how the geographic and economic perspectives influenced regional marketing scholars in developing theories of "law of retail gravitation," "boundaries of retail trading centers," and the "theory of the wholesale area structure."

- Assimilate metatheoretical evaluation of non-interactive economic schools of marketing thought.

This chapter will describe, summarize, and evaluate the following three schools of marketing thought: the commodity school, the functional school, and the regional school. As stated before, these three schools of thought are all based on economic concepts and, therefore, contain very little behavioral (social or psychological) perspective in theory building. At the same time, all three schools of thought exclusively focus on the marketer's perspective rather than on the interaction between marketers and buyers. In other words, all three schools of thought were created to provide a theoretical foundation for marketing practitioners.

 ## 2.1 The Commodity School of Thought

As marketing emerged as a separate discipline in the early 1900s, the pioneering scholars in the embryonic stage of the discipline were interested in the question: "How do we make sense of this new field of marketing?" After having argued that marketing was sufficiently important and unique to be worthy of a separate and distinct discipline, these pioneers were under pressure to come up with a logical and compelling system for describing and advancing the field of marketing.

While there was certainly no unanimity among these pioneering scholars regarding what to pursue, a sizable group emerged to form the foundation for what came to be referred to as the "commodity" school of marketing. Their rationale was deceptively simple. Given that marketing is concerned with the movement of goods from producers to consumers, the commodity theorists proposed that marketing scholars should concentrate on the *objects* of transactions, namely the products. Because the marketing discipline largely emerged from agricultural economics and agricultural marketing, the approach came to be known as the commodity school, even though its proponents primarily discussed manufactured packaged goods, not agricultural commodities.

As we reflect back on their advocacy for products as the focus of attention, we can appreciate why this approach was so attractive to these early scholars. As these commodity school proponents surveyed the content of other disciplines that were well-respected, they realized that these more advanced disciplines all were based on a comprehensive classification system. As E. L. Rhoades (1927), one of the early supporters of the commodity approach, wrote:

> In the learned fields, scholars are primarily interested in behavior and classify their materials in the way most satisfactory to furnish proper comparisons of behavior. In the marketing field we are primarily interested in behavior, or market functions (how commodities behave in the market). We may then take our cue from the biologist and work back from behavior or functions to a system of classifications of commodities which will be most helpful in a systematic study of the range and variety of those functions. (p. 8)

Thus, these scholars believed that, if the goods exchanged in the marketing process could be classified into some sort of a rational system, marketing would take a giant stride toward gaining scientific legitimacy. However, these early proponents of the commodity school were not only looking inward to the scientific community, they were also peering outward to the applied world of marketing practice. They realized that, even if marketing was accepted within the academic realm, it still would not survive unless it was appreciated by marketing practitioners. In other words, what can marketing theorists tell the producer of paint in Cleveland that will help him do a better job of selling his product to paint stores in Ohio?

The commodity theorists believed that, once a commodity classification system was developed and refined, it would become clear that each market commodity is *not* unique. They wanted to demonstrate that many commodities are really very closely related to each other. So closely related, in fact, that they may be combined into one relatively homogeneous category in which the same marketing procedures and techniques could be utilized for all products in that particular category. This notion of a fairly limited number of categories that are internally homogeneous and externally heterogeneous created a great deal of excitement among the commodity school scholars because they began to have visions of a grand "marketing cookbook." They believed that, when a marketing practitioner was in need of advice regarding the marketing of a specific product, he could simply find which category his product was in and then follow the prescribed marketing recipe for that category. As evidence of this optimism, Melvin Copeland (1925) asserted:

> The classification of a product into one of these groups facilitates the determination of the kind of store through which the market for a specific product should be sought, the density of distribution required, the methods of wholesale distribution to be preferred, the relations to be established with dealers, and in general the sole burden which the advertising must carry. (p. 14)

Therefore, members of the commodity school vanguard were exceedingly upbeat about their perspective because a classification system for products would establish academic respectability and also generate practitioner benefits. However, it is one thing to say that a classification system is the solution to the problems, and it is quite a different matter to actually create this classification system.

As might be expected, a plethora of classification systems were proposed for consideration and adoption during the first few years of the commodity school's ascendency. Charles Parlin should be given the credit for generating in 1912 the initial classification system that captured much attention (Gardner 1945). Parlin and his classification system are intriguing for at least three reasons. First, Parlin was not a member of marketing's academic fraternity. Instead, he was the Manager of Research for the Curtis Publishing Company. Second, his proposed system was published in the *Department Store Report,* Volume B, in October 1912 (Gardner, 1945), and for this reason, it is not readily accessible to present marketing scholars. Finally, if you ask most marketing students who is the founder of the commodity school, they usually cite Melvin Copeland (1923). For a variety of reasons, Parlin has never received due credit for being the creator of the first true commodity classification system. As to the actual content of Parlin's proposal, he suggested that there were three categories of "women's purchases":

Convenience goods are articles of daily purchase such as groceries, apron gingham, children's stockings and, in general, those purchases which are insignificant in value or are needed for immediate use. These goods are, to a considerable extent, bought at the most convenient place without a comparison of values and the fact that they are bought as a matter of convenience rather than of shopping makes possible the suburban dry goods stores, grocery stores and the cross roads general stores. An examination of the stock of one of the suburban stores will give one who is interested in pushing the inquiry further, an exact list of convenience goods.

Emergency goods comprise medicines and supplies which some unexpected happening has rendered immediately necessary. These lines enable a suburban drug store to be something more than a peddler of candy and other convenience goods. Shopping lines include all those purchases which are of sufficient importance to require thought and which will permit of delay, such as suits, dresses, high grade dry goods of all kinds. These things a woman lists on her mental shopping tablet which she never forgets, and when next she visits the city, the articles, one by one, are investigated; values are compared and a serious effort is made to secure the best value for the money. (Parlin 1912, portions reprinted in Gardner 1945, pp. 275–276)

The next prominent classification was offered by Melvin Copeland in 1923. Writing in the *Harvard Business Review*, Copeland made reference to Parlin's earlier work and suggested how his proposed system was an improvement. Also employing three broad categories, Copeland argued that all consumer goods could be labeled as either convenience goods, shopping goods, or specialty goods:

Convenience goods are those customarily purchased at easily accessible stores ... the consumer is familiar with these articles; and as soon as he recognizes the want, the demand usually becomes clearly defined in his mind. Furthermore, he usually desires the prompt satisfaction of the want ... The consumer is in the habit of purchasing convenience goods at stores located conveniently near his residence, near his place of employment, at a point that can be visited easily on the road to and from his place of employment, or on a route traveled regularly for purposes other than buying trips. (p. 282)

Shopping goods are those for which the consumer desires to compare prices, quality, and style at the time of purchase. Usually the consumer wishes to make this comparison in several stores ... The exact nature of the merchandise wanted may not be clearly defined in advance in the mind of the shopper; this is in contrast to the usual attitude in purchasing convenience goods. The purchase of shopping goods, furthermore, usually can be delayed for a time after the existence of the need has been recognized; the immediate satisfaction of the want is not so essential as in the case of most convenience goods. (p. 283)

Specialty goods are those which have some particular attraction for the consumer, other than price, which induces him to put forth special effort to visit the store in which they are sold and to make the purchase without shopping ... For specialty goods the manufacturer's brand, the retailer's brand, or the general reputation of the retail store for quality and service stands out prominently in the mind of the consumer. (p. 284)

It is imperative to note that Copeland's classification system basically relied on the consumers' needs, knowledge of need-satisfying alternatives, and willingness to delay need satisfaction. In this respect, Copeland's approach shows signs of being a distant ancestor of the more recent buyer behavior school of thought. However, Copeland stopped far short of ever questioning exactly *why* the consumers acted as they did. Rather, he was content to accept the behavior of consumers as a given state of affairs and use it as a foundation for grouping the wide variety of marketing goods.

While Copeland based his method of classifying on the needs and actions of consumers, Rhoades (1927) presented a commodity classification system founded on three factors. Although Rhoades agreed that "characteristics of the use of the commodity" were important, he argued that commodities could also be classified based on "physical characteristics of the commodity" (relative degree of perishability, concentration of value, size of the physical unit) and "characteristics of the production of the commodity" (scale of production, place of production, concentration of production, method of production, length of production period). Even though his scheme seems to have its merits, rarely is Rhoades' work mentioned when the commodity school is discussed.

Other than Copeland, the most prominent scholar in the commodity school has been Leo Aspinwall (1958), who launched a classification system using five characteristics to differentiate three types of goods. What immediately strikes the reader of Aspinwall's work is that, unlike Parlin and Copeland, who used terms like convenience goods and shopping goods to describe their categories, Aspinwall named his three categories the red goods, the orange goods, and the yellow goods. Although this seems strange, Aspinwall (1958) had an answer:

> The choice of color names may be inept in some respects, but the idea of an array of goods, based upon the sum of relative values of characteristics of goods, is important. The length of light rays for red, orange, and yellow, in that order, is an array of light rays representing a portion of the spectrum. For our present purpose it is more convenient to use the three colors only, rather than the seven of the full spectrum. The idea of an infinite graduation of values can be envisioned by blending these colors from red to yellow with orange in between. This is the idea we wish to convey as concerning all goods. (p. 441)

For the selection of the classifying characteristics, Aspinwall established several explicit guidelines. First, every characteristic selected must be applicable to every good. Second, every characteristic selected must be relatively measurable in terms of its relationship to every good. And, finally, every characteristic must be logically related to all the other characteristics. Given these parameters, Aspinwall (1958) chose five characteristics for classifying goods:

1. **Replacement rate:** "The rate at which a good is purchased and consumed by users in order to provide the satisfaction a consumer expects from the product" (p. 437).
2. **Gross margin:** "The money sum which is the difference between the laid in cost and the final realized sales price" (p. 438).
3. **Adjustment:** "The services applied to goods in order to meet the exact needs of the consumer" (p. 439).
4. **Time of consumption:** "The measured time of consumption during which the good gives up the utility desired" (p. 440).
5. **Searching time:** "The measure of average time and distance from the retail store" (p. 440).

As a final result, Aspinwall (1958) produced the following system, which he called the "Characteristics of Goods Theory":

	Color Classification		
Characteristics	**Red Goods**	**Orange Goods**	**Yellow Goods**
Replacement rate	High	Medium	Low
Gross margin	Low	Medium	High
Adjustment	Low	Medium	High
Time of consumption	Low	Medium	High
Searching time	Low	Medium	High

In comparing the Copeland and Aspinwall classification systems, it appears that Copeland's "convenience goods" matches very well with Aspinwall's "red goods." Although the remaining matches are not as tight, "specialty goods" are similar to "yellow goods" and "shopping goods" are somewhat related to "orange goods."

Aspinwall, as did many of his predecessors in the commodity school, firmly believed that this approach would be the panacea for most of the marketing practitioners' problems. All that was required was the rather simple task of plugging the product into the classification system and then following the standard marketing directions for that category of goods. As Aspinwall (1958) wrote:

> The marketing characteristics of a product determine the most appropriate and economical method for distributing it. To fix its position on the scale, representing the variation in these characteristics, is to take the first major step toward understanding its marketing requirements. To know these characteristics is to be able to predict with a high degree of reliability how a product will be distributed, since most products conform to the pattern. Serious departure from the theoretical expectations will almost certainly indicate the need for change and improvement in distribution methods. These considerations apply both to physical distribution and to the parallel problem of communications including the choice of promotional media and appeals. (pp. 435–436)

Although Aspinwall's classification system has not received as much scholarly support as the Parlin-Copeland system, Miracle (1965) did attempt to advance and refine Aspinwall's approach. Whereas Aspinwall delineated only the distribution and promotional implications of his classification system, Miracle proposed a modification to Aspinwall's original system and then discussed the product and pricing implications of this revised system.

As we review the history of the marketing discipline, we have noticed that debates among several marketing scholars emerge periodically in the academic literature. Usually, these debates focus on a rather narrow, but nonetheless significant, conceptual point. Such a debate surfaced in the commodity school during the late 1950s and early 1960s. The catalyst of this particular controversy was Richard Holton (1958), who maintained that the definitions of the categories of convenience goods, shopping goods, and specialty goods were in need of revision. According to Holton (1958), greater emphasis should be placed. on the role of the consumer in order to differentiate between convenience goods and shopping goods:

> Since items which are shopping goods for some consumers may be convenience goods for others, convenience goods and shopping goods can be defined accurately only from the standpoint of the individual consumer. It may be sufficient to say that, for the individual consumer, convenience goods are those goods for which the probable gain from making price and quality comparison among alternative sellers is thought to be small relative to the consumer's appraisal of the searching costs in terms of time, money, and effort. Shopping goods then, are for the individual consumer, those goods for which the probable gain from making price and quality comparisons among alternative sellers is thought to be large relative to the consumer's appraisal of the searching costs in terms of time, money, and effort. (pp. 53–54)

The perceptive reader will undoubtedly note that Holton's emphasis on the consumer carefully weighing the benefits and costs of additional search for information is closely related to many of the later "search theories" that were developed in the consumer behavior literature (Newman 1977, Punj and Staelin 1983).

Holton also argued that specialty goods, in essence, were not a discrete category that could be clearly differentiated from the other two categories:

> Can specialty goods be distinguished from convenience goods and shopping goods on the basis of the individual consumer's outlook toward the good? ... Here one must distinguish between the willingness to make a special effort, on the one hand, and the necessity of making that effort on the other ... Would it not follow, then, that a distinguishing feature of the specialty good is the necessity of making a special purchasing effort, rather than just the willingness? The fact that it is necessary to make a special effort to buy the good in question must stem from a limited market

> demand ... Specialty goods, if the above reasoning is justified, are the convenience or shopping goods which face such a limited market that outlets are relatively few, necessitating a "special purchasing effort" on the part of the buyers ... Therefore, it would seem that the specialty-good classification overlaps both the other groups and cannot be distinguished either from the shopping goods or from convenience goods. (Holton 1958, pp. 55–56)

Therefore, Holton was suggesting that one of Copeland's original three categories, the specialty goods, should be demoted to a secondary status in the classification system. It will probably come as no great surprise to the reader to hear that not everyone in the marketing theory community was enthralled with Holton's suggestion. After all, Copeland's three categories had survived for thirty-five years and had developed numerous devotees before Holton challenged it.

The sharpest counterattack was mounted by David Luck (1959), who believed that Holton should have placed more emphasis on the consumer's willingness to make a special effort and less emphasis on the necessity of this effort:

> The theory that Holton puts forth comprehends only the existing distribution of a good and the necessity of consumer shopping, both static phenomena. His theory does not explain the dynamics of consumer behavior or of marketers' objectives.

> In contrast, a theory that recognizes the willingness of consumers to make special purchasing efforts is explanatory, consumer oriented, and useful. Advertising and merchandising commonly are dedicated to creating specialty goods characteristics for a given brand or good. It would indeed be folly to exclude the "specialty" type of good from marketing theory and literature. (p. 64)

The next major entrant into this definitional dispute was Bucklin (1962), who sought to resolve the disagreement by proposing his own, somewhat modified, interpretation of Copeland's original system. Bucklin suggested that, as a first point of differentiation, a distinction should be made between "shopping goods" and "nonshopping goods":

> Shopping goods are those for which the consumer regularly formulates a new solution to his need each time it is aroused. They are goods whose suitability is determined through search before the consumer commits himself to each purchase. (p. 52)

> Turning now to nonshopping goods, one may define these as products for which the consumer is both willing and able to use stored solutions to the problem of finding a product to answer a need. (p. 52)

Then, according to Bucklin, the nonshopping goods may be further subdivided into convenience goods and specialty goods. To clarify the difference between convenience and specialty goods and to support the inclusion of specialty goods as a unique category, he offered the following rationale:

> Clearly, where the consumer is indifferent to the precise item among a number of substitutes which he could buy, he will purchase the most accessible one and look no further. This is a convenience good. On the other hand, where the consumer recognizes only one brand of a product as capable of satisfying his needs, he will be willing to bypass more readily accessible substitutes in order to secure the wanted item. This is a specialty good. (p. 52)

As a result of Bucklin's influence, the three-pronged classification system of convenience, shopping, and specialty goods was once again firmly entrenched as the dominant perspective for commodity school theorists. However, as new concepts and theories evolved in marketing and also in other allied disciplines, marketing scholars continued to reanalyze and challenge this classification system. For example, Kaish (1967) attempted to apply Festinger's theory of cognitive dissonance from psychology to the commodity school in marketing. What captured Kaish's interest was the prior emphasis on the consumer's shopping effort. He perceived a potential flaw because:

... in singling out shopping effort as the prime consideration, these definitions fail to distinguish explicitly between two types of effort. There is the special physical effort that purchasers of specialty goods are willing to make in going out of their way to insist on a particular good, and there is the mental effort of pricing, comparing, and distinguishing among shopping goods. (pp. 28–29)

By incorporating the implications of the theory of cognitive dissonance, Kaish proposed yet another set of definitions for the three basic categories:

Convenience goods are goods in which purchase is not important to the consumer, either because of low price, low durability, or low ego-involvement. Usually, there is consumer acceptance of a number of suitable substitutes for the utilities sought, and, as a result, there is a minimum of prepurchase anxiety that the purchase decision will later prove to be inappropriate and another would have been better.

Shopping goods are goods that arouse high levels of prepurchase anxiety about the possible inappropriateness of the purchase. This anxiety can be allayed by the consumer through information-gathering and subsequent decision-making. These goods are high in economic and psychological importance, contain significant performance differences, and have physical qualities that are readily related to the performance characteristics ...

Specialty goods are goods that are economically or psychologically important enough and have different enough performance characteristics to qualify as shopping goods, but have physical qualities that are not readily related to the performance characteristics sought. In addition, the alternatives may be so limited that the consumer is forced to purchase a good that will be potentially unsatisfying. Prepurchase anxiety is high here also, but not readily reducible by shopping behavior. (p. 31)

The commodity school is particularly fascinating because marketing scholars seemingly never lose interest in it. After the flurry of activity in the decade of 1958–1967 by Holton, Luck, Bucklin, Kaish, and others, the outside observer might expect an extended, if not permanent, avoidance of this school of thought by marketing theorists. However, such was not the case because significant articles concerning the commodity school continued to surface during the 1970s and even into the 1980s.

Ramond and Assael (1974) suggested that the prior classification systems all had significant deficiencies. As an improvement, they proposed that three different approaches to product classification should be explored as fertile ground for future theorizing:

All three find it necessary to define a product as a relation between two kinds of information. First, they must view the product as a relation between physical ingredients and psychological responses (a psychophysical definition). Here a measure of classification might be developed by clustering techniques. Second, they must define the product in terms of consumer actions and channel response (or what might be termed a distributive velocity definition). We later propose that such measures might be the lag between factory shipment and retail sales. Third, they need a relation between awareness, attitude change or other communication effects, and purchase behavior (or what might be defined as a mental velocity measure). (pp. 348–349)

By concentrating on these three approaches, Ramond and Assael reiterated the uncertainty among commodity theorists regarding exactly what dimensions should be used to classify products. Should it be from the perspective of the consumer or the producer/distributor? If from the consumer's viewpoint, should it be based on physical shopping effort or mental effort devoted to brand comparison and dissonance reduction?

The next significant step forward was provided by Holbrook and Howard in 1977 when they challenged the traditional three categories originally proposed by Copeland. Although other scholars had disagreed about the definitions of these three categories of convenience, shopping, and specialty goods, Holbrook and Howard suggested that a fourth category, preference goods, should be added to the basic classification system. They combined three dimensions: (1) product characteristics (magnitude of purchase and clarity of characteristics), (2) consumer characteristics (egoinvolvement and specific self-confidence), and (3) consumer responses (physical shopping and mental effort) to create the following classification of goods diagram.

Holbrook–Howard Commodity Classification System		
	High clarity High self-confidence Mental effort during shopping via brand comparisons No brand insistence	Low clarity Low specific self-confidence Mental effort prior to shopping via information seeking Brand insistence
Low magnitude Low ego-involvement Low physical shopping effort	CONVENIENCE GOODS	PREFERENCE GOODS
High magnitude High ego-involvement High physical shopping effort	SHOPPING GOODS	SPECIALTY GOODS

Clearly, the intention of Holbrook and Howard was to reconstruct the classification system by stressing the importance of the linkage between consumer actions and marketers' activities. Referring to their revised categories, they wrote:

> In particular, it distinguishes between two dimensions representing the consumer's utilization of marketing inputs. The top-bottom split continues to represent the degree to which the consumer saves his physical shopping effort by relying on intensive patterns of distribution to make the product readily available ... But the left-right distinction refers to the timing of mental effort in arriving at a brand choice. To the extent that a product falls on the right-hand side of this breakdown, a consumer may seek information from advertising, word of mouth, or other sources prior to the shopping trip. This implies reliance by the consumer on the seller's promotional efforts and the existence of this reliance for both durables (specialty goods) and nondurables (preference goods). (pp. 214–215)

Enis and Roering (1980) adopted the four-category system proposed by Holbrook and Howard, but they sought to improve it by addressing more explicitly the question of consumer perspective versus marketer perspective. Given the emergence of the interactive or dyadic viewpoint in marketing, they asserted that "a classification scheme that incorporates both the buyer's and the seller's perspective holds the greatest promise for illuminating the exchange process, since exchange only occurs when there is sufficient congruence between these perspectives" (1980, p. 187). Therefore, from the marketer's perspective, they said the four categories could be formed based on the two dimensions of product offering differentiation (the capacity to develop perceived variation among products) and marketing program differentiation (the capacity to individualize the elements of a marketing program to better serve divergent groups within a market). Likewise, from the consumer's perspective, the two relevant dimensions are perceived risk (the belief that the consequences of a purchase decision may be more unpleasant or unfavorable than the buyer perceives them to be) and expected effort (the amount of effort the buyer must exert to complete the exchange transaction).

By combining the marketer's and consumer's perspectives, Enis and Roering developed a new set of definitions for the four categories:

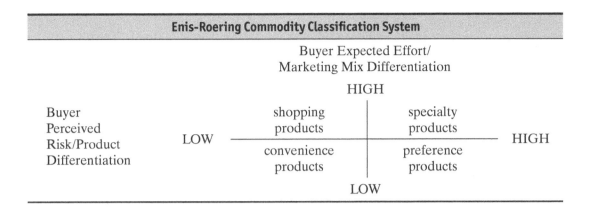

Specialty products are those bundles of attributes which the buyer perceives might involve high risk with respect to performance and/or interpersonal influence, and are worthy of significant shopping effort; thus the marketer of such products can differentiate both the product offering and its marketing program.

Shopping products are those attribute bundles which the buyer perceives are not likely to involve high performance or interpersonal risks, but are worth considerable shopping effort; thus the marketer's task is to differentiate via the marketing program a commodity—a core concept and product offering rather similar to that of competitors.

Convenience products are those attribute bundles perceived to be low risk and expected to be worth little effort, thus the marketer must efficiently produce and distribute a product which is difficult to differentiate in terms of either product offering or marketing program.

Preference products are those attribute bundles which the buyer perceives to possibly involve high risk, but expects to exert only limited shopping effort; thus the marketer can differentiate the product offering, but must then mass market that offering efficiently. (1980, p. 188)

The four-category commodity classification system (shopping, convenience, specialty, and preference) was clarified in a subsequent article by Murphy and Enis (1986). Using the dimensions of effort and risk related to price, Murphy and Enis argued that their classification system could be applied to all marketing transactions: products, services, or ideas. They provided the following definitions for their four categories:

1. **Convenience products:** "... convenience products are defined as lowest in terms of both effort and risk. That is, the consumer will not spend much money or time in purchasing these products, nor does he/she perceive significant levels of risk in making a selection" (p. 25).

2. **Preference products:** "These products are slightly higher on the effort dimension and much higher on risk. In fact, the distinction between convenience and preference products is primarily one of buyer perceived risk. The reason that the consumer perceives this higher level of risk is often through the efforts of the marketer, particularly branding and advertising" (p. 26).

3. **Shopping products:** "The name implies much about the characteristics of these products. Buyers are willing to spend a significant amount of time and money in searching for and evaluating these products. Increased levels of risk are also perceived by consumers for these high involvement products" (p. 26).

4. **Specialty products:** "Those products that are defined to be highest on both the risk and effort dimensions ... are called specialty products. The major distinction between shopping and specialty products is on the basis of effort, not risk. The monetary price is usually higher, as is the time ... At the limit, the buyer will accept no substitutes" (p. 29).

A particularly fascinating aspect of the commodity school is that scholars in this *area* always emphasize the potential managerial importance of developing a "marketing management cookbook." Murphy and Enis (1986) are no exception:

> One purpose of any product classification scheme is to guide managerial decision making. A comprehensive and consistent marketing strategy should be based upon product characteristics as perceived by buyers. The product classification suggested here provides a managerial road map for strategy development: buyers' perceptions, marketers' objectives and basic strategy, and specific strategies for each element of the marketing mix. (p. 35)

In summary, the commodity school has been one of the most robust schools of marketing thought. The possible development of a comprehensive framework that links marketing mix decisions to product categories is intriguing to marketing scholars and practitioners. Even though some critical definitional issues are unresolved, this school has generated many stimulating concepts that continue to interest current marketing theorists.

2.1.1 Evaluation of the Commodity School

STRUCTURE: **Are the concepts properly defined and integrated to form a strong nomological network?**

Although the basic categories first proposed by Copeland in 1923 have undergone remarkably little revision in over sixty years, we are still searching for definitional clarity for the terms of convenience, shopping, specialty, and preference goods. Should these definitions be based on the physical properties of the goods, or on the behavior of the consumers? If the latter option is preferable, should the focus be on the consumer's mental effort or on his/her physical effort?

In recent years there is a movement toward adopting four categories by adding preference goods to the original three categories. However, are we likely to witness an "intellectual battle" for the inclusion of this new category, much like what we saw in the late 1950s with the dispute over the suggested removal of the specialty goods category?

The commodity school seems to have the potential to establish good structure, but it is not there yet. Perhaps what is needed to firmly establish the definitions of the commodity categories is a special session at one of the marketing discipline's major academic conferences highlighted by several papers that specifically scrutinize the vitality of these definitions. If a reasonable level of agreement is achieved at this type of session, the commodity school will have a stronger foundation for future theorizing.

Our score on structure = 3.

SPECIFICATION: **Are the relationships specified in a manner to delimit hypotheses or are they highly contingent?**

This metatheory criterion presents major problems for the commodity school because if the categories of goods are defined based on consumers' behaviors, how should a good be classified if Person A's behavior suggests that it is a convenience good and Person B's behavior indicates it is a specialty good? In other words, the specification of hypotheses becomes *contingent* upon the diversity and individual differences among consumers. If only the majority or average behaviors are used for the good's classification, do we simply ignore the behavior of the minority or the "outlier" consumers and hope they will respond to the marketing programs designed for the majority? This is certainly not a new issue because Converse and Huegy in 1940 noted:

> The line of demarcation between the various types of goods is not always clear cut ... However, the fact that the two classes of goods are not clearly differentiated does not mean that the distinction is useless. The great majority of people buy many articles in the same way. (p. 145)

Beyond the potential variability among consumers, there is also the question of the possible change in any one consumer's behavior over time. For example, a consumer may regard a product, such as jogging shoes, as a shopping good for the first purchase of that product. However, over time, loyalties may develop and the consumer may treat the purchase of jogging shoes as a specialty goods task. This common movement of a consumer through stages based on increased learning and experience is closely related to the Howard and Sheth (1969) categories of extensive problem solving, limited problem solving, and routinized response behavior. Thus, it is possible, assuming the acceptance of the four basic categories of commodities, that *all* products could be classified in *all* four categories. That is, any product would have to be placed in all four categories if some consumers regard it as a convenience good, other consumers treat it as a specialty good, still, others believe it is a shopping good, and finally, some consumers see the product as a preference good. As a result of this potentiality, it is fairly obvious that the hypotheses for marketing of any product must be highly contingent based on the specific targeted group of consumers.

It may, therefore, be necessary to specify classifications with criteria that are invariant or noncontingent. This may require abandoning the consumer perspective and utilizing some other perspective such as physical flow of goods, turnover ratios, store locations, and profit margins. For example, products that demand a high degree of shopping effort for consumers will have a low turnover ratio. At the same time, products with a high degree of perceived risk will require the retailers to perform a number of value-added services resulting in high margin ratios. In other words, it may be possible to classify products into specialty, shopping, convenience, and preference goods based on less contingent but highly correlated surrogates such as turnover and margin ratios.

Our score on specification = 4.

TESTABILITY: **Are the operational definitions provided to ensure testability and intersubjective consensus?**

Although numerous scholars have debated extensively the proper conceptual definitions of the various commodity categories, very little attention, except for Aspinwall's efforts, has been directed at establishing operational definitions for these categories. Specifically, how do we measure "shopping effort" and distinguish between "limited" and "considerable" levels of this shopping effort? Also, how do we measure "risk"? Unfortunately, most writers in the commodity school have apparently presumed that the inclusion of examples of products that fit into each category is a sufficient demonstration of the categories' operational definitions. Examples are helpful, but they clearly do not satisfy the requirement for operational definitions.

Obviously, what is needed are fairly structured measurement scales with which to quantify the indicators of each underlying force that differentiates one commodity from the other. For example, physical shopping effort might be measured by the number of stores customers visit before making a purchase decision and the time spent at each store. Similarly, we might measure perceived risk toward a product class by creating a psychometric scale that measures risk toward the product class.

Our score on testability = 3.

EMPIRICAL SUPPORT: **What is the degree of confirmation in terms of empirical support?**

Apparently, there has been little, if any, attempt to actually test the commodity theory. Several excellent research studies would be feasible in this area. First, a researcher interested in the commodity school could develop a set of operational definitions for the goods categories and then test the validity and reliability of these definitions using a cross-sectional study of products and consumers. Second, a theory related to the managerial relevance of the commodity classification system could be created and then used to modify the marketing mix for a test product to determine whether market performance for the product could be enhanced.

At the same time, there is ample empirical evidence of the use of the commodity approach in marketing practice at both the manufacturing and the retail distribution levels. Furthermore, the classification is as commonly prevalent in practice as the concept of upper-middle-lower socio-economic classes is in social stratification. In short, there is considerable empirical support but it is not scientifically tested or validated.

Our score on empirical support = 6.

RICHNESS: **How comprehensive and generalizable is the theory?**

As noted earlier, the commodity theory has demonstrated remarkable vitality with over seventy years of rather consistent attention from marketing theorists. A strong argument for this enduring interest can be found in the potential richness of the theory. Many scholars have apparently felt that, once the rough edges are removed, the commodity school could be truly robust. However, while the possible richness of the commodity school is undeniable, several rather formidable obstacles remain that must be dealt with before this criterion is satisfied. First, the main emphasis in the previous theorizing has been consistently on consumer goods. Very little attention has been directed at the applicability of the commodity theory to other categories of goods, such as industrial goods, services, and social goods.

Second, if the basis for category definition is to be the behavior of consumers, most scholars implicitly assume that this is typical "American" behavior. However, it is probable that the behavior of consumers varies across diverse cultures, suggesting that the classifications must be adjusted accordingly. As global markets become increasingly critical for corporate survival, this issue must be addressed to ensure greater richness for the commodity school.

Third, can the commodity school cope with changes in behavior based on the introduction of new technology, such as the growth of electronic shopping? The richness of the theory will be substantially improved if it can be shown that the theory can accommodate the impact of new technology and still maintain the tripartite classification.

Fourth, how generalizable are the results that are obtained from the extensive study of just one specific product class? This is a question that has long perplexed marketing scholars, as evidenced by C. S. Duncan's comment in 1921:

> Thus, one may trace the course of cotton, or wheat, or corn, or cattle, or steel, or leather, or any other commodity bought and sold on the market from its source to the consumer, and study the commercial problems connected with it. This will give a specialized knowledge that is invaluable so far as the specific commodity is concerned. Such as analysis will not, however, demonstrate broad principles. From such a basis of knowledge, one cannot know for himself why there is an organized exchange for cotton and wheat and not for wool; he cannot know whether staple goods can be advertised as well as style goods. One may know thoroughly that one subject, but he cannot generalize from it. A single commodity is only an illustration, and it may be a pertinent and vivid one, too, but it will not establish a principle. (p. 8)

What seems to be needed is a conscious effort to extend the traditional classification into industrial products, services, and social programs. Perhaps this may be easier to do by utilizing the more generic classification and the underlying criteria proposed by Aspinwall. In other words, can we classify industrial products, services, and social programs into red, orange, and yellow categories based on such criteria as replacement rate, gross margin, adjustment, time of consumption, and searching time? A little reflection suggests that except for gross margin, it is possible to apply Aspinwall's generic classification to all these sectors of the economy.

Our score on richness = 8.

SIMPLICITY: **How easy is it to communicate and implement the theory?**

This criterion may be the commodity school's strongest point. As mentioned previously, commodity theorists have always been enthusiastic about the possibility of creating a "marketing cookbook" based on a commodity classification system. The leading proponent of this trend was Aspinwall (1958), who suggested what specific forms of distribution and promotion should accompany various types of goods. Of course, in recent years, much less attention has been given to developing a set of marketing guidelines directly related to product categories. But if such a "cookbook" could be developed, it could be very beneficial to marketing practitioners who seem to be generally more interested in "how to do" than in "why to do" issues.

Our score on simplicity = 8.

Table 2.1 gives a summary of scores we have given to the commodity school and our rationale for them. As can be seen, the commodity school performs the best in terms of relevance (pragmatics), next best in terms of reality (semantics), and very poorly with respect to the organization (syntax). Therefore, scholars interested in the commodity school of thought may want to apply their talents toward the syntax aspects of the theory.

Table 2.1 Evaluation of the Commodity School*

Criterion	Rationale	Score
Structure	What criterion to use for classification is the biggest weakness	3
Specification	Highly contingent at present but has the potential to be specified on a noncontingent basis	4
Testability	Extremely weak on operational definitions except Aspinwall	3
Empirical support	Good empirical support but not scientifically tested for its validity	6
Richness	Extremely rich and capable of encompassing all areas of marketing	8
Simplicity	Very easy to communicate and implement in general	8
	TOTAL	32

* Scores range from 1 (poor) to 10 (excellent).

2.2   The Functional School of Thought

The commodity school proved to be extremely popular, especially with many of the earlier marketing theorists. However, not everyone who was actively involved in shaping the discipline of marketing in the early 1900s was a hearty supporter of the commodity school. In fact, a formidable group of scholars, probably equal in size, if not larger, convened to form what came to be known as the functional school of marketing. Like the commodity theorists, the functional theorists also appreciated the need for marketing to attain academic legitimacy and to demonstrate the practical applicability of marketing. However, while the commodity school chose to develop a classification system based on products or the objects of exchange, the functional school decided instead to focus on the activities needed to execute marketing transactions. Thus, these two early schools stand in sharp contrast, with the commodity school based on the "what" element of marketing, while the functional school founded on the "how" element of marketing.

While there is some confusion over who should be deemed the "father" of the functional school, marketing historians generally credit Arch Shaw (1912) with launching the functional perspective in an article in the *Quarterly Journal of Economics*. This article is particularly interesting because stylistically it is dramatically different from the typical article published in modem marketing journals. Although Shaw attacked a variety of issues in the sixty pages of the article, he actually devoted only about ten pages to the discussion of marketing functions. Shaw introduced the first classification of marketing functions by writing:

To understand what seems to be a present tendency to go around the middleman as well as to consider the problem of the merchant-producer with reference to the use of middlemen in distribution, it is necessary to analyze the functions performed by the middleman. Roughly the general functions may be listed as follows:

1. Sharing the risk.
2. Transporting the goods.
3. Financing the operations.
4. Selling (communication of ideas about the goods).
5. Assembling, assorting, and reshipping. (Shaw 1912, p. 731)

L. D. H. Weld, an early marketing scholar who published numerous influential books and articles during the emerging years of marketing, wrote an article in 1917 in which he offered an alternative classification of functions. According to Weld (1917), these functions are not necessarily performed only by middlemen as suggested by Shaw:

1. **Assembling:** "The term 'assembling,' as used here, does not mean the actual physical transportation of commodities from one place to another, but rather the seeking out of sources, the making of business connections whereby commodities may be bought, and the study of market conditions so that they may be bought at the lowest prices possible. Assembling, therefore, involves all the services connected with buying" (p. 307).

2. **Storing:** "Storing, in its broad sense, means the holding of stocks of goods at convenient points" (p. 308).

3. **Assumption of risks:** "Inasmuch as commission merchants, brokers, and agents do not take title to goods, they assume very few of the merchandising risks; but practically every other middleman, as well as the manufacturer, especially when he produces for stock, has to consider the element of risk. The principal kinds of merchandising risks may be enumerated as follows: (1) price fluctuation, (2) destruction by fire, (3) deterioration in quality, (4) style changes, and (5) financial risks" (p. 311).

4. **Rearrangement:** "Rearrangement of commodities involves sorting, grading, breaking up large quantities into small units, packing, etc." (p. 311).

5. **Selling:** "Selling is the most important of the marketing functions, as well as the most costly one to perform. Salaries of salesmen (plus traveling expenses in many cases) constitute the most important single item in merchant's expense account. Selling involves both creating a demand for the goods and getting the goods into the hands of the purchaser. Though both of these phases of selling are performed largely by personal salesmen, demand creation is being accomplished more and more by means of advertising" (p. 312).

6. **Transportation:** "As explained by Shaw, merchandise middlemen formerly attended to the actual carriage of goods from one place to another more than they do now; but this function has been largely taken over by railroads and other transportation agencies that are specialized middlemen in this field. Transportation, however, is still an important function of merchants" (p. 313).

As with most other schools of thought, critics surfaced in the functional school to *offer* critiques of prior contributions from such writers as Shaw (1912) and Weld (1917). One such critic was H.B. Vanderblue, who, in 1921, suggested that there was a potential risk of isolating each functional component, when in fact the functions were often interdependent:

> Sale is frequently dependent upon standardization; finance upon storing; risk upon selling and financing; and there is the close interrelationship of transporting, risking, storing, and financing, illustrated in the use of the order bill of lading and the warehouse receipt as collateral. (Vanderblue 1921, p. 683)

The functional school proved to be very popular. Franklin Ryan in 1935 produced a review of the writings in the functional area and discovered that at least twenty-six books and articles had been published that dealt extensively with marketing functions. As evidence of the disparity of opinions regarding the selection of appropriate functions among these early scholars, Ryan found that fifty-two different functions had been proposed by various authors. Ryan summarized the state of art in the functional school as follows:

> ... the lists of functions presented by most of these writers on marketing are usually meant to be brief summaries of functional categories and are not organized to give a complete and detailed picture of the distributive process. Most of these lists seek to find answers to two implied general questions in regard to the productive-distributive process. These two implied questions are:
>
> 1. What general functions add time, place, ownership, possession, and other kinds of utilities (want-satisfying powers) to physical goods as they gradually move toward the point where they are sold to final customers?
>
> 2. What distinctive functions are performed by entrepreneurs or business executives and their employees who carry on the work of distribution?

In answer to the first questions, these books and articles typically list five functions, as follows: (1) assembling, (2) storing, (3) standardization, (4) transportation, and (5) selling. The distinctive functions of the functionaries in the productive-distributive process are usually listed as (6) the assumption of risks, and (7) financing, which is the providing of capital for the marketing enterprise. (Ryan 1935, pp. 211–212)

The next major contribution to the functional school following Ryan's review article was provided by Earl Fullbrook in 1940. Fullbrook (1940) was rather critical of what had been accomplished in the functional school:

> In spite of the length of time the functional concept has been in use and in spite of its wide currency at the present time, it appears that little has been accomplished since the early years toward any significant refining of the concept. It is apparent from any careful survey of the material in the field that there is no very clear-cut and generally accepted interpretation of, or method of handling, marketing functions. The writer believes the functional approach can be a very useful device but contends that a great deal must be done in further developing it before its real possibilities can be realized. (p. 299)

Fullbrook's main goal in this article was to argue that the functional school should recognize the distinction between a functional requirement and the actual performance of that function:

> A function of marketing should be regarded strictly as a step, task, or service to be performed in getting goods from producers to consumers. This is in accord with the usual definition. That the performance of a function requires activity is granted. That it is logical to regard a function as an activity to be performed is also granted. To so regard it, however, increases the probability that attention will center upon the activities performed instead of upon the nature and extent of the job which has to be done and gives rise to the activities... By regarding a function solely as a task or service that requires performance, it can be analyzed entirely distinct from its actual performance and if the functional treatment is to yield significant results, such procedure is essential... Only after gaining a clear understanding of the nature of a task and of what its performance requires, can one evaluate agencies or methods that are used, or might be used, in doing the job. (p. 234)

Ten years after the Fullbrook article, Edmund McGarry (1950) offered yet another review of previous classification systems for the functional school. And, like his predecessors, he maintained that improvement was still needed before marketing theorists could be satisfied with the content of the functional school:

> From the beginning of the systematic study of marketing, a great deal of attention has been given to the analysis of marketing functions. A large number of articles have been published on the subject in various professional journals, and practically every textbook on marketing attempts to make some use of such an analysis in its presentation. Yet, despite all these writings, there is little agreement as to what the functions are or as to the purpose of defining them. (p. 263)

To remedy these shortcomings, McGarry presented his own recommended classification system, which was composed of the following six functions:

1. The *contactual function,* which has to do with the searching-out of potential customers or suppliers and the making of contact with them.

2. The *merchandising function,* which comprises the various activities undertaken to adapt the product to the users' ideas of what is wanted.

3. The *pricing function,* which has to do with the prices at which goods are offered or at which they will be accepted.

4. The *propaganda function,* which includes all the methods used to persuade the potential users to select the particular product and to make them like the product once they have it.

5. The *physical distribution function,* which comprises the transportation and storage of goods.

6. The *termination function,* which has to do with the actual change in custody of and responsibility for the goods and is the culmination of the process. (p. 279)

At this point, we will briefly pursue a tangential point closely related to the development of the functional school. Many marketing students tend to believe that the so-called Four Ps of marketing, which were popularized by McCarthy (1960), were a revolutionary breakthrough for the marketing discipline. Obviously, however, the Four Ps of product, price, promotion, and place are actually only derivatives from earlier classification systems presented by functional school theorists, such as Shaw, Weld, Ryan, and especially McGarry.

Unlike the commodity school, which has been the subject of several excellent papers in the past decade, the functional school has received very little attention since McGarry's 1950 article. The one noteworthy exception is an article by Lewis and Erickson (1969) in which they attempted to link together the functional and systems perspectives. As to the classification of marketing functions, Lewis and Erickson maintained that marketing had really only two broad functions—to obtain demand and to service demand. Then, as subsets of each of these functions, they argued there were several activities. Under the obtaining demand function, they listed the activities of advertising, personal selling, sales promotion, product planning, and pricing. Activities connected to the servicing demand function were warehousing, inventory management, transportation, and order processing and handling. With respect to the systems approach to marketing, they concluded:

> ... marketing is a system within the total system of a firm. It is a man-made, open system which attempts to move toward a closed system by feedback control. It faces internal restrictions of policy, goals, and finances from within the total system of the firm and external restrictions from the environment in such forms as governments, competitors, and customers. (p. 13)

Combining the functional and systems perspectives, they asserted that the functions of obtaining and servicing demand are actually the output objects of the marketing system, while the previously mentioned activities are the input objects of the marketing system. Although their article could have benefited from a more extensive explanation of the most salient points, Lewis and Erickson should be commended for attempting to reveal the relationships between two distinct perspectives. Perhaps if more scholars endeavored to review the similarities and dissimilarities of two or more schools of thought, it would serve to open up new ways of thinking about these various perspectives. Quite often the marketing discipline suffers not from a paucity of interest in theory, but from a lack of cross-disciplinary viewpoints.

2.2.1   Evaluation of the Functional School

STRUCTURE: **Are the concepts properly defined and integrated to form a strong nomological network?**

The functional school's major strength with respect to structure is identification, listing, and classification of various functions to be performed by marketing. These functional lists do tend to identify value-added services that provide time, place, and possession utilities to the product or service. Although the functional school seems strong on the definitions, it is weak in forming a nomological network among the concepts. In other words, it does not go beyond the listing and categorization of functions. For example, what functions can be eliminated because they are redundant or do not add values in proportion to the incremental costs of performing them? Similarly, what are the interdependent or complementary relationships among various functions? Do they behave like the domino effect, or are they capable of standing on their own? Finally, how can one shift functions from the manufacturer to the middleman to the consumer or vice versa?

Perhaps it might be advantageous to do a historical investigation of the consolidation and shifting of functions in specific product categories and assess how functions relate to one another as an interdependent system. For example, how far is the shift toward self-service or "do it yourself" likely to go before the pendulum begins to shift the other way? Or how much of time, place, and possession utilities can be integrated in product design and manufacturing to eliminate the need for any middlemen?

Our score on structure = 5.

SPECIFICATION: **Are the relationships specified in a manner to delimit hypotheses or are they highly contingent?**

It is interesting to note that specification issues in the functional school of thought have been limited to understanding the impact of each function rather than the relationships between functions. For example, we have a number of hypotheses related to price elasticity, advertising effectiveness, and salesforce management, but we have no hypotheses for such issues as which promotional activities or functions are better suited with a particular distribution system. This is in sharp contrast to the commodity school of thought, which has at least attempted to suggest hypotheses across marketing activities once a product is categorized as a specialty, shopping, or convenience good. Also, it is important to remember that most hypotheses at the functional level have been generated more through the managerial school proponents rather than directly by the functional school proponents. In our opinion, the more exciting aspects of future research in the functional school of thought remain with issues such as the interdependence and shifting of functions.

Our score on specification = 3.

TESTABILITY: **Are the operational definitions provided to ensure testability and intersubjective consensus?**

The functional school ranks higher on this criterion. Most of the functions can be operationally measured and the methods used to measure reality have strong face validity. For example, functions such as assembling, sorting, transportation, storing, financing, and so on are overt behavior measures that result in less disagreement than more psychological variables such as risk and effort proposed in the commodity school. Indeed, this criterion may be the strong point for the functional school's popularity; it is measurable and functions can be cataloged with agreed-on measures.

Our score on testability = 7.

EMPIRICAL SUPPORT: **What is the degree of confirmation in terms of empirical support?**

Similar to the commodity school, the empirical support for the functional school comes from observations, case histories, and anecdotes. Marketing organizations do tend to be configured to perform various tasks identified as marketing functions. At the same time, there is no strong scientific evidence about the impact of shifting or consolidation of functions on market behavior. What is scientifically tested and known are the findings related to each specialized function such as advertising, promotion, financing, shipping, insurance, and the like.

Our score on empirical support = 7.

RICHNESS: **How comprehensive and generalizable is the theory?**

The functional school is very rich. It has identified major categories of functions as well as individual subsets in each major category applicable across all products, services, and markets. Although functions such as storing and transportation may not be appropriate for intangible services, the functional classification is still fundamentally relevant. In other words, the six major functions (contactual, merchandising, pricing, propaganda, physical distribution, and termination) proposed by McGarry (1950) seem to be relevant across all products and services. Therefore, we must conclude that the functional school of thought is very strong on the richness dimension.

Our score on richness = 8.

SIMPLICITY: **How easy is it to communicate and implement the theory?**

The functional school is extremely easy to communicate because it is highly descriptive and has a strong reality base, and readers can personally relate to their own experiences. A functional marketing organization is also simple to implement. In fact, most marketing organizations tend to be functional. It is rumored that at Procter and Gamble, the functional organization generated the title "marketing manager" for the person in charge of coordinating and integrating specialized marketing functions such as advertising, physical distribution, and sales force.

However, the functional school has not attempted to provide guidelines or hypotheses about how these functions ought to be organized or implemented. Each marketing organization has tended to learn on a trial and error or ad hoc basis rather than being driven by a well-tested recipe.

Our score on simplicity = 8.

Table 2.2 provides a summary of scores given to the functional school and the rationale for them. As can be easily noted, the functional school performs much better with respect to the relevance (pragmatic) and reality (semantic) criteria but performs poorly on the organization (syntax) criterion.

In that respect, the functional school is similar to the commodity school. Indeed, this similarity makes sense because both theories were based on extensive observation of marketing practice. They were, therefore, inductively driven rather than deductively driven, resulting in better scores on the pragmatic side but lower scores on the syntax side.

Table 2.2 Evaluation of the Functional School*

Criterion	Rationale	Score
Structure	Strong on definitions but weak on interrelationships among functions	5
Specification	Some specifications at each functional level but lacking in shifting and consolidation of functions	3
Testability	Good on testability because operational measures are overt behavioral scales	7
Empirical support	Very good empirical support in general but lacking in scientific validation	7
Richness	Very rich and can easily encompass all domains of marketing	8
Simplicity	Very easy to communicate and implement within a function but the relationship between functions is more difficult	8
	TOTAL	38

* Scores range from 1 (poor) to 10 (excellent).

2.3   The Regional School of Thought

The regional school of thought is often overlooked when the subject of marketing theory is discussed. The reasons for this school's lack of popularity are difficult to identify, but it does appear that, with E.T. Grether's 1983 article in the *Journal of Marketing* special theory issue, there may be an increased awareness of and interest in this intriguing theoretical perspective.

To provide the uninitiated reader with a quick introduction to the regional school of thought, we may say that regional theorists perceived marketing as a form of economic activity designed to bridge the geographic, or spatial, gaps between buyers and sellers. While regional theorists certainly agreed that the goods being exchanged were important to study (the commodity school) and the activities used to facilitate exchanges were worthy of investigation (the functional school), they felt more attention should be paid to the role of the physical separations between buyers and sellers. Thus, they were fascinated by questions such as "What role does distance play in a consumer's decision to patronize store A rather than store B?" and "How can we explain the flow of goods among various geographical regions that have diverse resources and needs?"

In some ways, the regional school of thought is difficult to encapsulate. On the whole, however, the regional perspective has, throughout its history, been rather quantitatively driven with extensive utilization of mathematical formulas and data. Also, the regional school has been promoted and nurtured by a rather small group of scholars who have tended to remain closely affiliated with this perspective for most of their academic careers. Finally, the regional school is not really a creation of the marketing discipline but is instead an offshoot from earlier work done in the fields of geography and economics that examined the interplay between economic activity and physical space.

Whereas the commodity and the functional schools surfaced in the second decade of the twentieth century, the regional school did not emerge until the 1930s. Although E. T. Grether had begun to adopt the regional perspective in his economics course entitled "Theory of Domestic Trade" at the University of California, Berkeley, in the 1930s (Grether 1983), the publication of William J. Reilly's book *Law of Retail Gravitation* in 1931 was probably the main stimulus for the growth of the regional approach in marketing.

Reilly's goal was to explain the relative attractiveness of two different cities' shopping areas for those consumers who lived in a town between these two cities. According to Reilly, the following formula provided the solution:

$$\frac{B_a}{B_b} = \left(\frac{P_a}{P_b}\right)\left(\frac{D_b}{D_a}\right)^2$$

where

B_a = the proportion of the trade from the intermediate city attracted by city A

B_b = the proportion attracted by city B

P_a = the population of city A

P_b = the population of city B

D_a = the distance from the intermediate town to city A

D_b = the distance from the intermediate town to city B

Therefore, based on this formula, a consumer forms a choice of desirable shopping areas using the two factors of population of the alternative cities (a surrogate measure of the number and quality of retail stores) and the distance from the two cities.

Reilly's method captured the interest of P. D. Converse, who actually conducted numerous tests of Reilly's so-called law of retail gravitation. Although Converse found Reilly's approach quite useful, he also proposed his own modifications in the form of "new laws of retail gravitation." One of Converse's (1949) main contributions was the development of a formula to determine the boundaries of a trading center's trade area:

$$D_b = \frac{D_{ab}}{1 + \sqrt{\frac{P_a}{P_b}}}$$

where

D_b = the breaking point between city A and city B in miles from B

D_{ab} = the distance separating city A from city B

P_b = the population of city B

P_a = the population of city A

As to the usefulness of identifying a town's trade area, Converse (1949, p. 380) wrote:

> Once the trade area is determined, the merchants know where to concentrate their merchandising efforts, and the newspapers know the territories which they should cultivate intensively. To illustrate, a department store was advertising over a considerable area. Its attention was called to the formula for determining the town's trade area. The area was computed and the store found that it was spending much of its advertising appropriation outside its trade area. By concentrating its advertising inside the trade area, it experienced a considerable increase in sales with no increase in advertising expenditures.

This stream of research generated by Reilly and Converse received still more attention from David Huff (1964). Like his predecessors, Huff proposed another model to predict shopping patterns:

$$P_{ij} = \frac{\dfrac{S_j}{T_{ij}^{\lambda}}}{\sum\limits_{j=1}^{n}\dfrac{S_j}{T_{ij}^{\lambda}}}$$

where

P_{ij} = the probability of a consumer at a given point of origin i traveling to a particular shopping center j

S_j = the size of a shopping center j (measured in terms of square footage of selling area devoted to the sale of a particular class of goods)

T_{ij} = the travel time involved in getting from a consumer's travel base i to a given shopping center j

λ = a parameter to be estimated empirically to reflect the effect of travel time on various kinds of shopping trips

In comparing the later work of Huff to the earlier works of Reilly and Converse, we can highlight specific advances that demonstrate a greater degree of sophistication in this analysis of retail trading areas. First, Huff moved to eliminate the surrogate measure of population and instead focus on the actual size of the shopping center for that particular good. Second, Huff recognized that, given the complexity of modern metropolitan transportation systems, consumers concentrated more on travel time rather than on actual distance from alternative shopping sites.

Within the regional school, some scholars chose to shift the focus from the retailing sector to the wholesaling sector. Probably the leading theorist who considered the effects of physical space on wholesaling institutions was David A. Revzan. In his 1961 book, *Wholesaling in Marketing Organization,* he provided the following overview of his approach to regional variable analysis:

> Area structure, in its present content, has reference to the extent to which there are to be found systematic patterns of relationships between the various components of the wholesaling sector and the pertinent spatial units. The initial impact arises from the spatial gaps between where supplies of basic raw materials can be made commercially accessible and the locational patterns of the using manufacturing industries and related business. These initial impacts are enhanced further by the geographic layout of the transportation system by means of which such gaps are bridged. A second level of structure arises in the patterning of spatial arrangements between various components of the wholesale middlemen agency structure. Further spatial arrangements of retailing agencies and of ultimate consumers act as modifying influences at the other end of the commodity flows. (pp. 74–75)

In an effort to move closer to a theory of wholesale area structure, Revzan (1961) proposed that eight factors affect the size of a wholesale market area:

1. **Product weight relative to value:** "Where transportation costs are a small percentage of the total value of the product because the products' value is high relative to its bulk and weight, the supply and distribution areas may be expected to have wider boundaries than if the reverse were the case." (p. 98)

2. **Relative perishability:** "Where such protective devices as canning, fast freezing, and storage are not available or are differentially available, perishability restricts the size of both the supply and distribution areas." (p. 98)

3. **Product differentiation techniques:** "To the extent that manufacturers are successful through their marketing programs in establishing strong national brands for their products, to that extent will the areas of distribution for these products be widened." (p. 98)

4. **Factors affecting plant location:** "The net resultant of the operation of such factors is the differentiation of the orientation of plant locations at sites accessible to raw materials sources because of perishability, labor supply, and transportation cost factors, for example; to consuming marketing sites because of cost factors, size of market, customer preferences for freshness, or for similar reasons; at intermediate locations because of the balancing of inbound and outbound cost factors against the advantages of an intermediate location; or on the so-called footloose

basis because of the desire to maximize the amenities aspect of location against the economic factors". (p. 99)

5. **Price and price policies:** "In uncontrolled, organized markets, differential prices become ... the primary determinants of potential supply and distribution areas. For unorganized markets, price and price differentials are much more difficult to determine, the competitive structure of the industry has a marked effect upon the boundaries of the wholesale trading area". (p. 99)

6. **Transportation rates and services:** "The structure of freight rates in terms of the presence or absence of special commodity rates, the type and amount of progression of rates with distance, the relationship between rail and truck rates, the relationship by quantity levels, the relationship between raw materials and finished product rates, and the differential between rates and transit privileges, all affect the differential relationships between competing markets". (p. 99)

7. **Individual firm's marketing methods:** " ... the decisions of the individual firms as to marketing functions and channels of distribution either enhance or reduce the significance of particular trade centers". (p. 99)

8. **Auxiliary services:** "Finally, the influence of organized wholesale markets is expanded by the use of methods of systematic circulation of price and related market information; by providing specialized physical facilities in which the activities of middlemen may be housed; and *by providing for* specialized financial and other types of institutions and services". (p. 100)

Besides discussing the theoretical aspects of the regional perspective as it relates to wholesaling, Revzan also produced two volumes in 1965 and 1967 in which he analyzed, by means of data from sources such as the U.S. Census, the geographical variations in wholesale/retail sales ratios.

The scholar most closely associated with the regional school of thought is E. T. Grether because he sought to use the regional approach to generate a fairly broad theory of marketing, unlike the narrower theorizing spawned by Reilly, Converse, Huff, and, to some extent, Revzan. Grether's contributions to the regional perspective span approximately a half-century beginning with his teaching of the regional approach in the 1930s at the University of California, Berkeley, and marked most recently by his 1983 *Journal of Marketing* article.

In a 1950 article, Grether described his viewpoint on marketing:

One of the reasons why much of current marketing analysis is considered sterile is that it has been cut loose from the full investigation of the behavior of the firm as a whole, as well as from the economy. Specialization in courses has developed its counterpart in the highly artificial, separate treatment of marketing and selling activities. We forget too easily that business, economic, and social phenomena are organic in nature. Market analysis should be integrated with the other aspects of functional behavior. The behavior of the firm should be investigated not only in a price and marketing sense, but, under the conditions of its physical and social environment, in its determination of its location, its spatial outreach in selling and in buying and its relationships in the marketing channel with suppliers on the one hand and the buyers on the other. (pp. 116–117)

Then, in the classic 1952 textbook entitled *Marketing in the American Economy*, Grether, along with his co-authors Roland Vaile and Reavis Cox, further explained the concept of interregional marketing (Vaile, Grether, and Cox 1952):

Space, like time, is omnipresent. Its impact upon buyers and sellers and commodities is not uniform, however, for the amount occupied by a firm or by a process varies enormously. Space provides opportunities for production, marketing, or other activities at various sites and locations. It also erects obstacles in the form of costs of movement that must be borne by buyers and sellers. (p. 487)

Among the hypotheses proposed by Vaile, Grether, and Cox (1952) was a set of hypotheses designed to explain why some goods are produced and consumed within the same economic region whereas other goods are consumed outside of the region in which they are produced. Using their terminology, "home-market goods" may be restricted to their home regions because of:

1. Lack of transportability.
2. Inability to obtain them separately from the person or business establishment supplying them.
3. A degree of perishability sufficient to hold normal distribution within small areas.
4. High costs of movement.
5. The absence of advantages in obtaining goods from exterior sources sufficient to lead to their importation, as is true of most commodities produced in regions with diversified resources. (p. 491)

Vaile, Grether, and Cox (1952) also drew upon the previous work of Bertil Ohlin (1931) in economics to present a set of hypotheses to explain the volume of interregional marketing. According to their theory, the volume of goods entering trade among regions is determined primarily by:

1. The relative inequality of regions as regards the supplies of agents of production. Regions will tend to export products based upon their abundant, cheap resources.
2. The relative prosperity of regions. Other things being equal, regions with high total and per capita incomes will tend to generate more trade than poor regions.
3. The direction of the reciprocal demands among regions. There will be a larger total volume of trade if two trading regions have a strong demand for each other's characteristic products.
4. The relative effectiveness of competition. The basis for interregional exchange should normally be stronger when competition within regions is active and effective, although there may be individual exceptions. Restraints upon competition would be expected to reflect themselves in smaller interregional movements as well as in a lower total output within a region. (p. 509)

As mentioned earlier, Grether produced a paper for the 1983 *Journal of Marketing* special issue on marketing theory in which he summarized his views on the regional perspective. In this paper, he took great care to demonstrate how the regional approach could be particularly beneficial to the study of marketing strategy:

> Often the identity, number and importance of the competitors vary as between regions. This factor alone may assist in the delineation of regions for purposes of analysis and control. And demands, whether ultimately those of consumer, business, or government, despite the alleged homogenization of markets, can and do vary widely between regions. For many years Revzan has stressed the "myth of the national market." It is not that enterprises do not sell throughout the national market or world markets, but that results often vary widely between regions and even subregions. From the standpoint of a given enterprise, this in itself may be a reasonable basis for regional delineation. Planning marketing strategy is tremendously improved when related to regional breakdowns of both competition and demand. (pp. 40–41)

For those readers who desire to delve deeper into the regional school of thought, we refer them to Ronald Savitt's (1981) review article, "The Theory of Interregional Marketing." Savitt does a particularly fine job of synthesizing Grether's contributions to this theoretical perspective. Another useful article is Goldstucker's (1965) review of the earlier literature pertaining to retail and wholesale trading areas.

In recent years a promising movement is underway among a small group of marketing scholars who are intent on enhancing the mathematical sophistication of trading area models. For example, Huff and Rust (1984) developed methods for assessing the boundary coincidence of two market areas. Similarly, Black, Ostlund, and Westbrook (1985) formulated a set of models relating to retail store location issues. This continued interest in defining geographic influences in marketing suggests that the regional school is still a fertile area for theoretical development.

2.3.1 Evaluation of the Regional School

STRUCTURE: **Are the concepts properly defined and integrated to form a strong nomological network?**

Among the three schools presented in this chapter, there is no question that the regional school performs better on the structure criterion. It has attempted to define most of the terms in as precise a manner as possible. For example, Vaile et al. (1952) define an economic region as follows:

For purposes of formal analysis, an economic region may be defined as a relatively large geographical area with the following four characteristics: (1) it has more than one center of economic control, (2) it has greater internal homogeneity than would be present if it were merged with other contingent areas, (3) it exports a characteristic group of products to other areas, (4) it imports the characteristic products of other areas. (p. 488)

Part of the reason for generating more precise definitions and relationships among concepts is clearly due to the mathematical approach taken by this school of thought. Another reason seems to be the strong influence of the disciplines of economics and geography. Finally, the phenomenon under study, namely the market or the region, is much more amenable to a precise definition because it is based on economic rather than behavioral characteristics.

At the same time, we must point out that there are several other concepts in this school of thought that remain ill-defined and, therefore, highly controversial. These include "characteristic products," "internal homogeneity," "product differentiation," and "centers of economic control." Overall, however, the regional school of thought is more rigorous in its structure than either the commodity or the functional school.

Our score on structure = 7.

SPECIFICATION: Are the relationships specified in a manner to delimit hypotheses or are they highly contingent?

The major hypotheses suggested by Revzan (1961) and Vaile et al. (1952) are highly delimited in nature. Similarly, the hypotheses generated by Reilly (1931), Converse (1949), and Huff (1964) related to retail location are extremely precise and highly specified. As we stated earlier, part of the reason is the quantitative orientation present in this school of thought, and the other part of the reason probably lies in their interest in prediction rather than explanation of a given phenomenon.

At the same time, we do feel that there is some degree of contingency inherent in their theories. For example, what effects do such exogenous factors as a product's weight to value ratio (granite stones), perishability (fresh fish), and product differentiation (digital PBX) have on the size and structure of economic areas in addition to geographical distances? Similarly, is it not reasonable to expect that factors that have an impact on the consumer's choice of a shopping center may be also contingent on whether the product in question is a convenience, shopping, or specialty good? However, there is no question that despite these concerns, the regional school scores well on the specification criterion.

Our score on specification = 6.

TESTABILITY: Are the operational definitions provided to ensure testability and intersubjective consensus?

Specific theories related to retail or wholesale trading areas have done a very good job on the testability criterion. For example, laws of retail gravitation have utilized published data from government sources, and the operational definitions of population sizes and geographic distances are less subject to measurement errors.

On the other hand, the regional school exemplified by Grether and his colleagues suffers from inadequate operationalization of variables. In fact, they have often ended up using surrogate measures, following the tradition in economics, for such constructs as "characteristic products" and "internal homogeneity."

This does not mean that the concepts of the regional school are not testable. However, they may require data banks that were not available in the early history of marketing. Indeed, it should be much easier to score high on the testability criterion today in light of online electronic data banks that are easily available.

Our score on testability = 7.

EMPIRICAL SUPPORT: What is the degree of confirmation in terms of empirical support?

Once again, empirical research carried out by Reilly, Converse, and Revzan has generated strong confirmation of the regional school concepts. Indeed, Reilly has elevated these to the category of a "law of retail gravitation." Similarly, Grether and his colleagues, as well as international trade researchers, have provided good empirical support to the basic propositions of the regional school.

The recent empirical research by Huff and Rust (1984) and Black, Ostlund, and Westbrook (1985) clearly indicates that the body of empirical support for the regional school is growing. In addition, the level of mathematical sophistication introduced by these most recent efforts is light years beyond the simplistic formulations originally offered by early scholars such as Reilly and Converse. However, in comparison to many of the other major schools of marketing thought, the empirical work in the regional school has been confined to a fairly small group of researchers.

In summary, although there is a relatively limited degree of empirical support for the regional school, whatever has been tested has been confirmatory in nature.

Our score on empirical support = 7.

RICHNESS: **How comprehensive and generalizable is the theory?**

The regional school may be the weakest with respect to the dimension of richness. This is primarily due to the narrow area of study chosen by the school, namely the spatial separation between buyers and sellers. But what about the psychological separation or the post-purchase separation that may exist between the two parties? Unfortunately, the regional school apparently cannot accommodate the broader and more pervasive issues of marketing.

Similarly, the regional school has sacrificed richness for the sake of formal precision. This is particularly visible in the mathematical orientation in testing the proposed hypotheses.

Our score on richness = 4.

SIMPLICITY: **How easy is it to communicate and implement the theory?**

The regional theory is somewhat uncomplicated because it focuses on the spatial separation between sellers and buyers. Thus, the practitioner is urged to analyze geographically where his supply markets are located and where his demand markets are located. Such analysis may be very instructive for practitioners in terms of improving the efficiency of their operations.

Unfortunately, the regional school is heavy on analysis but light on prescriptions. It is not a cookbook for marketing practice.

Our score on simplicity = 7.

Table 2.3 summarizes our evaluation of the regional school of thought. Unlike the functional and the commodity schools of thought, the regional school gets much higher scores on the syntax or organizational dimensions and somewhat lower scores on the pragmatic or relevance dimensions. This makes sense in that the regional school has been deductively driven based on some accepted concepts and principles in geography and economics.

Table 2.3 Evaluation of the Regional School*

Criterion	Rationale	Score
Structure	Very good definitions and relationships among concepts	7
Specification	Very well specified hypotheses especially in the retailing area	6
Testability	Very well tested propositions due to excellent operational measures	7
Empirical support	Limited number of studies but good support for the theory	7
Richness	Too narrow because of focus on only spatial separation	4
Simplicity	Relatively easy to communicate and use but not prescriptive enough	7
	TOTAL	38

* Scores range from 1 (poor) to 10 (excellent).

Summary

This chapter has summarized the three non-interactive economic schools of marketing thought. They are the commodity, the functional, and the regional schools of marketing thought.

The commodity school pioneered by Parlin and Copeland focused on the objects of market transactions and has provided the classification of goods into specialty, shopping, and convenience goods. This classification has been questioned by some and further refined by others. Perhaps the most thoughtful work has been by Aspinwall, who has provided a color-based classification of products and services into red, orange, and yellow goods.

The commodity school is based on the inductive process of observing market realities and case histories. It is a highly relevant school of thought with strong empirical support, at least in terms of marketing practice. Unfortunately, it is very weak with respect to the organization dimensions of structure and specification.

The functional school of marketing pioneered by Shaw and Weld has been researched by many more scholars. The primary emphasis has been on identification, listing, and classification of marketing functions that must be performed in market transactions. Although the specific list of activities varies from author to author, it seems that there is a consensus on several fundamental types of functions to be performed by the producer, the middlemen, or the consumers. Perhaps the most comprehensive and meaningful classification is attributed to McGarry, who suggests six functions: contactual, merchandising, pricing, propaganda, physical distribution, and termination functions. It is unfortunate that the functional school has received only limited attention in recent years.

The functional school is also based on the inductive process of case histories and observations. Therefore, it has a high degree of relevance and strong empirical support, at least in terms of marketing practice. It is probably more practical than the commodity school because of the prevalence of the functional structures of marketing organizations. Unfortunately, the functional school also suffers from a very weak syntax with respect to structure and specificity.

The last school of marketing thought described in this chapter is the regional school. Instead of focusing on the objects and activities inherent in market transactions, it has concentrated on the narrower area of spatial separations between sellers and buyers. The regional school has been influenced by geography and economics. The main areas of understanding have been retail locations, wholesale markets, and centers of economic activity such as regions or nations. The regional school has been surprisingly mathematical in orientation with a strong drive to quantify and measure its constructs. Unfortunately, the theory has had only a handful of scholars committed to its ideas.

The regional theory is based on the deductive process of borrowing concepts from well-established disciplines and applying them to the marketing arena. Therefore, it is very good in its organization or syntax, moderate in its empirical support, and somewhat limited in relevance.

Questions for Analysis and Discussion

1. As the advanced countries shift from products to services, can you develop a classification of services? Is it possible to extend the product-based classification (shopping, convenience, and specialty) to services industries?

2. With the growth of NFT (non-fungible tokens), a new type of commodity is emerging. How will the evolution of digital products alter the commodity school of marketing?

3. The growth of online shopping through market exchanges such as Amazon, Flipkart, and Alibaba, is disrupting the brick-and-mortar retailers and blurring the boundaries of wholesalers and retailers. Develop a new theory of the institutional school of marketing.

4. Direct to consumers (DTC) is enabling even small producers of products to bypass the wholesalers and the retailers. How will DTC marketing impact product offerings and prices?

5. The functional school of thought ultimately classified all marketing functions into the following five functions: (a) assembling, (b) storing, (c) standardization, (d) transportation, and (e) selling. Please rank order the five functions in terms of their contribution to the economy and justify your reasoning.

6. Considering the ongoing digital transformation of enterprises, what new marketing functions are likely to emerge?

CHAPTER

Interactive Economic Schools of Marketing

LEARNING OBJECTIVES

After reading this chapter, you will be able to:

- Describe the three interactive-economic schools of marketing thought – the institutional, functionalist, and managerial school.
- Explain the intellectual development of the institutional approach to marketing thought.
- Evaluate the basic tenets of Wroe Alderson's functionalist approach to marketing and how it relates to the organized behavior system and heterogeneous markets.
- Contrast the concepts of transvection and transactions related to marketing efficiency and effectiveness.

- Trace the development of the managerial school of marketing thought and why marketing scholars proposed a shift in focus to consumer needs and desires instead of production efficiencies.
- Explain the emergence of core marketing concepts related to market segmentation, targeting, positioning, brand image, marketing mix, product lifecycles, pricing strategies, and competitive advertising and sales management influences.
- Assess the theoretical contributions of the institutional, functionalist, and managerial schools of marketing thought.

We have identified three schools of marketing that fit the description of economic but interactive perspectives. They are the institutional school, the functionalist school, and the managerial school. These three schools of thought are all based on economic principles and concepts and are influenced very little by the social and psychological variables inherent in market transactions. To that extent, they are similar to the commodity, the functional, and the regional schools of thought.

At the same time, these three schools of thought acknowledge the interdependent relationships between the sellers and the buyers, and, therefore, take the interactive perspective. This belief in the interdependent relationship, as opposed to the dominance of the suppliers in a transaction, makes these schools different from the functional, the commodity, and the regional schools of thought.

3.1 The Institutional School of Thought

The institutional school of marketing thought holds a central position in the development and growth of the marketing discipline. In the earliest days of the emergence of marketing as a separate discipline, the institutional school shared center stage along with the commodity school and the functional school. As discussed in Chapter 2, the commodity school proposed that marketing could be best understood by analyzing the types of goods being exchanged, while the functional school asserted that the focus of analysis should be on the activities conducted in the course of the exchange. While institutional theorists appreciated the arguments advanced by their colleagues in these other two schools, they nonetheless believed that the marketing discipline could benefit by paying greater scholarly attention to the *organizations* that actually perform the functions required to move the goods from the producer to the consumer.

The role of the institutional school is further enhanced when one notes the current interest in the organizational dynamics school of thought. As the direct descendent of the institutional school, the organizational dynamics school is attempting to analyze the relationships among channel members using a behavioral orientation. Thus, the clear distinction between these two related schools is the institutional school's concentration on economic, rather than behavioral, concepts as explanations for the actions of organizations involved in marketing.

The institutional school emerged in the 1910s largely because of a perception among consumers that the prices they were paying at retail stores for agricultural products were unjustifiably high. Specifically, consumers could not understand the necessity for the size of the markup between the prices paid to the farmer and the retail prices in stores. This feeling of mistrust and confusion is understandable when one realizes the rapid and extreme sociological transitions occurring during the early decades of the twentieth century. Many consumers were moving away from the rural areas of the United States, taking jobs and establishing residences in the booming urban areas. These new city dwellers were accustomed to very short and direct marketing channels, where they either produced their own food products or bought them directly from the producers. They were unprepared for the higher prices attendant with the more elaborate marketing channels needed to bring the same food products to their new homes in the cities of America.

In response to this growing dissatisfaction with the perceived wastefulness of the marketing channel members, several marketing scholars decided to evaluate the functions and efficiency of the organizations involved in transporting and transforming goods from the producer to the consumer. Although it is certainly open to debate, a strong case can be made that L. D. H. Weld deserves credit as the founding father of the institutional school. In his 1916 book, *The Marketing of Farm Products,* Weld addressed the issue of marketing channel efficiency:

> When the statement is made that there are too many middlemen, it may mean one of two things: either that the process of subdivision already described has gone too far so that there are too many successive steps, or that there are too many of each class, such as too many country buyers, too many wholesalers, or too many retailers.

> The discussion in the preceding paragraphs bears directly on the question as to whether there are too many successive steps, and this is what most people mean when they glibly state that there are too many middlemen. It was pointed out that such subdivision is merely an example of the well-known doctrine of division of labor, and that economies result from specialization by functions. Although it is perhaps impossible to say definitely whether there are too many middlemen in this sense, it is at least true that there is ample economic justification for a subdivision of the marketing process among specialized classes of dealers; that in some cases lower cost and greater efficiency may be gained by further specialization; and that in other cases it may be possible to reduce the cost by combining the functions of two or more middlemen into the hands of one single middleman. The functions of marketing have to be performed, however many separate middlemen there are; the problem is to find the most economical combination of functions.

> This is a matter that can be determined only by careful investigation in each separate trade. Those who have really made firsthand studies of the marketing system in an impartial and unprejudiced way realize that on the whole the system of marketing that has developed is efficient, rather than "extremely cumbersome and wasteful," and that there are very good practical reasons for the form of organization that has developed. It is necessary to realize these fundamental facts before the reader can approach a study of the marketing problem with a sane point of view. (pp. 21–22)

In 1923, Ralph Starr Butler, who at the time was the advertising manager for the United States Rubber Company, made a significant contribution to the early development of the institutional school when he authored *Marketing and Merchandising.* Like Weld, he took considerable care to justify the role of middlemen in the modem marketing system. His approach was to emphasize the utilities that middlemen create for producers and consumers:

> Another great function of middlemen is to create utilities. There are four kinds of utilities. Elementary utility is illustrated by the qualities in wheat which enable it to support life. Form utility is given to wheat when it is ground into flour in order to make it palatable. Although these two kinds of utility are essential to everyone, the fact that flour, possessing both elementary and form utility, is in the miller's warehouse in Minneapolis, is of little interest to the hungry man in New Orleans. Place utility must be added to it. Even with the addition of place utility, however, the New Orleans man may not be able to use it. If it is brought to his place in January and he needs it in July, it is of no use to him unless it is stored by someone so it will be available to satisfy his July needs. Even possessing elementary, form, and place utility, the flour cannot be used unless it also has time utility—the quality of being available for use when it is needed. With elementary and form utility the market organization has nothing to do, but with place and time utility it has very much to do. Middlemen produce place and time utility; they carry things from the place where they are produced to the place where they are needed, and put them at the disposal of consumers at the time when they are needed. (Butler 1923, pp. 20–21)

Many other scholars joined the ranks of the institutional school and offered their views on marketing. However, we will jump forward in time to the 1930s and 1940s to highlight the contributions of Ralph F. Breyer, Paul D. Converse, Edward Duddy, Harvey W. Huegy, and David Revzan. Breyer, a faculty member at the Wharton School at the University of Pennsylvania, wrote an influential book entitled *The Marketing Institution* in which he chronicled the historical evolution of the marketing process to demonstrate how the current marketing structure came into existence. In the third and fourth chapters of his book, Breyer (1934) persuasively explained the need for marketing institutions:

> To perform the work involved in carrying out the marketing functions demands the construction of a huge, highly complicated piece of business machinery. We have already seen that the functions of marketing have to do with overcoming obstacles and resistances to the exchange of goods. This requires a vast expenditure of time and effort which calls for considerable drafts upon our land, labor, capital, and enterprise resources. These factors must be assembled, apportioned in quality and quantity, and coordinated and correlated into a working machine. The parts of this machine are the various business concerns having to do with marketing. (p. 24)

In addition, Breyer (1934) stressed the importance of markets as the foundation of marketing and the institutional approach:

> The need for marketing depends upon the existence of a market. The amount, nature, and combination of services marketing must perform, and the kind, quantity, and coordination of marketing machinery required are conditional upon the nature of the potentialities which any one market may present. And these vary widely. Hence, the marketing problem, as a whole and in all its details, is colored, conditioned, and hedged about by markets. It is also true that the marketing institution itself reacts upon markets and thus changes the aspects of them. For instance, marketers are able to stimulate the desires of people for their respective products by persuasive and apt salesmanship and advertising. Thus they are actually shaping the potentials that go to make up their markets. It is just this interplay of forces between markets and marketing that constitutes the most purposeful and fruitful vantage point from which to attack an analysis of the marketing institution ... (p. 55)

Paul D. Converse and Harvey W. Huegy were among the first marketing scholars to consider critically the potential benefits and risks of vertical integration in the marketing channel. In their popular textbook *Elements of Marketing,* they wrote (1940):

Vertical integration means the joint operation of two or more stages in production or distribution by one company. It has two advantages: a reduction in marketing expenses and the assurance of a supply of materials or an outlet for the goods. Marketing expenses may be reduced by the elimination of successive buying and selling operations between what otherwise would be separate companies ... Integration offers one of the most hopeful and most successful methods of reducing marketing costs, but it introduces serious problems of management and coordination. Integration is difficult when the attempt is made to produce a variety of raw materials for a finishing mill, or when a factory attempts to operate retail stores. Retailing is a highly competitive business and one that seems to require specialized management for success. Experience appears to indicate that retail and wholesale functions can be successfully combined but that basic manufacturing operations cannot be combined successfully with retailing. (pp. 800–801)

Duddy and Revzan (1947) added a slightly different perspective to the institutional school of thought, and in a sense foreshadowed the emergence of the organizational dynamics school, when they advocated that marketing managers should be sensitive to environmental influences, as well as economic forces that had been traditionally stressed by earlier institutional scholars:

The institutional approach views the economic order as an organic whole made up of a great variety of economic structures, whose functioning is coordinated not only by prices and profit margins, but by management using authoritarian and persuasive techniques, by government regulation, and by social convention and custom. The phenomena of value determination through exchange are only part of the scope included in the view of the institutionalist. For him the changing patterns of institutional organization and the cultural environment within which exchange takes place are of equal interest with any laws of price or any idea of economic equilibrium. (p. 14)

The institutional school reached its peak in terms of intellectual advancement and popularity among marketing scholars during the twenty-year period of approximately 1954 to 1973. During this era, marketing scholars began in earnest to utilize economic theories to analyze critical issues such as the emergence of marketing channels, the evolution of channel structure, and the design of effective and efficient institutional frameworks.

Among his many other contributions to marketing theory, in 1954 Wroe Alderson wrote an influential article on "Factors Governing the Development of Marketing Channels." He summarized his views on the purpose and importance of channels of distribution by stating:

... intermediaries arise in the process of exchange because they can increase the efficiency of the process. The justification for the middleman rests on specialized skill in a variety of activities and particularly in various aspects of sorting. The principle of the discrepancy of assortments explains why the successive stages in marketing are so commonly operated as independent agencies. While economists assume for certain purposes that exchange is costless, transactions occupy time and utilize resources in the real world. Intermediary traders are said to create time, place, and possession utility because transactions can be carried out at lower cost through them than through direct exchange. In our modern economy, the distribution network makes possible specialized mass production on the one hand and the satisfaction of the differentiated tastes of consumers on the other. (Alderson 1954b, pp. 13–14)

As shown in this particular quotation, Alderson clearly demonstrates the view of most institutional theorists that economic efficiency criteria are the primary factors affecting channel design and evolution. However, in 1963 Bert McCammon, one of the leaders of the institutional school during this era, argued that several factors, not all of which were based on economic efficiency criteria, should be considered as possible determinants of channel evolution. Specifically, McCammon asserted (1963):

Economic analysis of institutional change can be and has been carried much further. This type of analysis, however modified, inevitably assumes that the firm's behavior is determined by cost/revenue considerations, and thus it leaves unanswered some or all of the following questions:

Why is change resisted by marketing institutions even though it appears to offer economic advantages?

Why do "uneconomic channels of distribution" persist over extended periods of time?

Why do some firms accept change rapidly, while others lag in their adaptation or refuse to change at all? (p. 479)

To answer those perplexing questions, McCammon suggested that institutional scholars should investigate various sociological and psychological variables. For example, he offered the following hypotheses:

1. The rate of diffusion depends upon the innovation itself. Innovations that involve a substantial capital investment, a major restructuring of a firm's relationship with its customers, and a sizable number of internal realignments are more likely to be accepted slowly than those that involve relatively minor intra- or inter-firm changes ...

2. The innovator is likely to be an "outsider" in the sense that he occupies a marginal role in a given line of trade and is on the outskirts of the prevailing sociometric network. Such individuals are interested in innovation because they have the most to gain and the least to lose by disrupting the status quo ...

3. A firm will respond incrementally to innovation unless its core market is threatened. If the latter is the case, the response to innovation will proceed swiftly ...

4. The higher the entrepreneur's aspirations, the more likely he is to initiate or accept innovation ...

5. The acceptance of innovation is not always permanent ...

6. Innovation will be accepted most rapidly when it can be fitted into existing decision-making habits ...

7. Influentials and innovators are not always the same firms. Institutional innovators, since they tend to be "outsiders," have relatively little influence among their entrepreneurial colleagues ...

8. Greater energy is required to transmit an innovation from one channel to another than is required to transmit it within a channel. (pp. 489–490)

Because he advocated the inclusion of behavioral variables in the analysis of channel evolution, McCammon attempted to pull his fellow institutional theorists away from their attachment to the economic perspective. For this reason, a strong case can be made for including McCammon among those very few scholars who successfully bridged the gulf between the institutional and organizational dynamics schools of thought.

Chronologically, the next noteworthy contribution to the institutional school was provided by F. E. Balderston (1964). He pursued a more normatively based approach to the institutional school by seeking to explain how marketing channels should be designed for optimal benefit to marketing practitioners. Discussing the special problems of channel design for the individual firm, Balderston stated:

The individual firm faces the channel problem in three ways, which differ from the preceding efforts at "global" analysis of an entire marketing channel as a system. First, the goals or objectives of one firm, no matter how far one chooses to complicate these beyond the assumed goal of simple profit maximization, are nevertheless simpler to identify, and simpler to apply in the evolution of alternatives, than is the channel criterion problem when designing channels. Second, if the firm operates, or can operate, as a multi-establishment enterprise, some of the channel alternatives need evaluation in light of the relative efficiency of market participation and internal administration controls ... The third difference between the single-firm channel problem and that of the "global" channel design is, however, a complicating rather than a simplifying difference. As was shown in a preceding section, models of a marketing channel system are generated by (1) identifying commodities or commodity groups to study and then (2) examining the various issues that arise in assigning functional activities to the participating entities. The single firm, however, is not necessarily restricted to participation in a single channel system. It may — to make matters most difficult of all — use the same facilities and manpower, at one or more establishments, to participate simultaneously in several marketing channels. (p. 184)

In 1965, McCammon picked up the theme of integration advanced earlier by Converse and Huegy (1940). In this article he stated that there are three types of centrally coordinated channel systems:

Corporate marketing systems ... combine successive stages of production and distribution under a single ownership ... (p. 497)

Administrative strategies, as opposed to ownership, can also be used to coordinate the flow of goods and services and thereby achieve systemic economies. Individual enterprises, by exerting leadership, can often influence or otherwise control the behavior of adjacent firms within the channel ... (p. 498)

Finally, and most significantly, channel coordination can be effected through the use of contractual agreements. That is, independent firms at different levels can coordinate their activities on a contractual basis to obtain systemic economies and market impact that could not be achieved through individual action. (p. 499)

McCammon listed four major reasons for the emergence and growth of centrally coordinated marketing systems:

1. Increased capital requirements and higher fixed costs.
2. Declining profit margins and rates of return on investment.
3. Growing complexity of marketing processes.
4. Potential economies in centrally coordinated marketing systems.

With the possible exception of McCammon's 1963 article, none of the prior writings in the institutional school proposed a theory of channel structure. However, Bucklin (1965) and Mallen (1973) addressed this weakness in the institutional school by offering two separate theories to explain and predict the structure of channels. Bucklin's theory focused on the concepts of postponement and speculation, which he defined as follows:

If one views postponement from the view of the distribution channel as a whole, it may be seen as a device for individual institutions to shift the risk of owning goods to another. The manufacturer who postpones by refusing to produce except to order is shifting the risk toward to the buyer. The middleman postpones by either refusing to buy except from a seller who provides next day delivery (backward postponement), or by purchasing only when he has made a sale (forward postponement). The consumer postpones by buying from those retail facilities which permit him to take immediate possession directly from the store shelf. (p. 27)

[The] converse may be labelled the principle of speculation. It represents a shift of risk to the institution, rather than away from it. The principle of speculation holds that changes in form, and the movement of goods to forward inventories, should be made at the earliest possible time in the marketing flow in order to reduce the costs of the marketing system. (p. 27)

By combining these principles of postponement and speculation, Bucklin (1965) argued that the creation of stages of inventories in a marketing channel could be explained:

The minimum cost and type of channel are determined by balancing the costs of alternative delivery times against the cost of using an intermediate, speculative inventory. The appearance of such an inventory in the channel occurs whenever its additional costs are more than offset by net savings in postponement to the buyer and seller. (p. 311)

Borrowing from the earlier work of George Stigler (1951), an economist, Mallen (1973) proposed that the concept of functional spinoff could be employed to evaluate and predict changes in distribution structure. Specifically, he suggested eight hypotheses founded on the functional spinoff concept:

1. A producer will spin off a marketing function to a marketing intermediary(s) if the latter can perform the function more efficiently than the former ...

2. If there are continual economies to be obtained within a wide range of volume changes, the middleman portion of the industry (and perhaps individual middlemen) will become bigger and bigger ...

3. A producer will keep or resume a marketing function from a marketing intermediary(s) if the former can perform the function at least as efficiently as the latter ...

4. If in performing a marketing function a marketing intermediary finds that for a part of that function (i.e., a subfunction) another perhaps more specialized marketing intermediary can perform it more efficiently, then he will spin off that subfunction to the latter ...

5. If a producer finds that in marketing to one (or more) of his markets a middleman can perform a given marketing function more efficiently for the reasons noted in hypothesis 1 above, and for another (or others) of his markets he can perform the same function at least as efficiently for the reasons noted in hypothesis 3 above, he will spin off that function in marketing to the first market(s) and keep or resume the function in marketing to the second ...

6. If marketing intermediaries characterize an industry, their nature will be determined by the mix of functions and subfunctions spun off ...

7. The greater the market size is in relation to optimum scale size (at each channel level), the greater the number of channel members that will come into being ...

8. With a change in technology and the growth of optimum scale size, firms may be expected to leave the channel if there is no corresponding change in market size and vice versa. (p. 24)

Since the early 1970s, there has been little significant work done in the institutional school of thought. The primary reason for this decline in activity is the emergence of the organizational dynamics school, which sought to employ the basic institutional perspective but with a behavioral orientation. As clearly reflected in the writings of Bucklin (1965) and Mallen (1973), the institutional school relied heavily on economic concepts related to efficiency with almost no acknowledgment given to behavioral variables that may contribute to our understanding of channel structure and performance. Led primarily by Louis Stern (1969), other scholars suggested that behavioral concepts, such as power, cooperation, and conflict, could assist in the development of more valid and reliable theories of marketing channels. As will be shown in a later section devoted to the organizational dynamics school, a promising movement has been underway in recent years to merge the best elements of the economically based institutional school and the behaviorally based organizational dynamics school.

As we progress toward the development of a more robust theory of marketing based on the analysis of institutions, five issues must receive consideration. First, this theory must explain why the performance of a marketing function may be passed from one channel member to another channel member. More specifically, the impact of technological evolution deserves greater attention as a causal variable in this functional transfer process. For example, the current introduction of sophisticated electronic and computerized communications systems into our society makes it easier for consumers to interact directly with producers or wholesale distributors. As a result, the functions formerly performed by retailers are now sometimes undertaken by either the consumers or the producers and the wholesalers.

Second, marketing theorists have tended over the years to myopically assume that the same set of marketing functions must always be performed, although the actual performance may be conducted by various institutions. However, given the recent dramatic technological strides, it appears that some functions may indeed be entirely eliminated in some channels. For instance, the "just in time" inventory system, made possible by the real-time transportation and communication systems now available, allows a producer to eliminate the need for an intermediate inventory-holding institution between itself and its suppliers. Therefore, any future theory of marketing institutions must consider when and how certain marketing functions may be bypassed by marketing institutions to improve the effectiveness and efficiency of the total marketing system.

Third, vertical marketing systems, which have become standard practice in many industries, require closer scrutiny. A theory of marketing institutions must be capable of predicting the situations in which a vertical marketing system should be implemented. Further, there is a need to explain when a corporate, contractual, or administered system is likely to be most effective. Each of these three alternatives offers unique advantages and liabilities that must be fully tied to a theoretical framework.

Fourth, comparatively little interest has been shown for the variance of channel structures across cultures. As marketing becomes increasingly international in its orientation, more questions are being raised about the problems associated with using marketing institutions in foreign cultures. A comprehensive theory of marketing institutions must address these managerially relevant problems and offer some theory-based solutions. Although it is tempting to conclude immediately that the level of economic development is the main determinant of variable channel structure across cultures, such a conclusion may be unwarranted. Instead, the analysis of the powerful influence of sociocultural values and traditional norms may be helpful in explaining channel structure variability. For instance, open-air markets composed of numerous small-volume dealers persist in many cultures, not because more efficient systems are not available, but rather because tradition dictates that commercial and social interaction should be conducted in this manner.

Finally, marketing institutions have been traditionally defined as including those agents who perform functions that bridge the gap between the producer and the consumer. Thus, from this linear perspective, the producer is the starting point and the consumer is the ending point for theoretical evaluation. With the advent in the 1960s of the concern for environmental quality, there is now a need to develop a circular perspective and analyze those institutions that serve to recycle or dispose of products discarded by consumers. A strong theory of marketing institutions could help to guide the development of the rapidly growing waste management industry and also assist public policymakers as they attempt to regulate these environmentally critical institutions.

3.1.1   Evaluation of the Institutional School

STRUCTURE: **Are the concepts properly defined and integrated to form a strong nomological network?**

The institutional school of thought has done a good job of defining the institutions, their value-adding roles, and their interrelationships between the producers and the consumers. Furthermore, more recent writers such as Bucklin (1965), Mallen (1973), and McCammon (1963) have provided good axiomatic propositions derived from a strong nomological network of concepts. Of course, the basic philosophy is economic rather than behavioral, but the use of functional spinoff principles, diffusion of innovation concepts, and inventory management issues, all indicate that the institutional school has performed better on the structure criterion than either the commodity or the functional schools of thought.

Our score on structure = 7.

SPECIFICATION: **Are the relationships specified in a manner to delimit hypotheses or are**
they highly contingent?

The institutional school also scores well on the specification dimension. The hypotheses are precisely specified and stated to allow for relatively few contingent propositions. They can be easily questioned if you are not an economist and do not believe in the economic propositions, but this should not deter the specification provided by the institutional theorists.

Our score on specification = 7.

TESTABILITY: **Are the operational definitions provided to ensure testability and intersubjective consensus?**

The institutional theory is surprisingly weak on this dimension. Most authors have taken a very careful approach at defining and specifying the concepts and their relationships but have failed to provide good operational definitions. For example, how should the concepts of "speculation" and "postponement" be measured and will there be intersubject consensus on these measures? Similarly, how do we measure the concept of functional efficiency so crucial to functional spinoffs? Although the authors have tried to utilize the concepts of economies of scale and marginal cost principles, these concepts are easy to criticize and must be replaced by better concepts to measure efficiency and productivity.

Our score on testability = 4.

EMPIRICAL SUPPORT: **What is the degree of confirmation in terms of empirical support?**

Unfortunately, there is a very limited degree of scientific support for the propositions generated by the more recent authors including Bucklin, Mallen, and McCammon. At the same time, there is a significant amount of observational validity as well as case histories to the concepts of the institutional school. For example, the role of the middlemen as valueadding institutions providing time, place, and possession utilities and the concept of vertical distribution systems (corporate, administered, or contractual) have a great deal of face validity.

Our score on empirical support = 5.

RICHNESS: **How comprehensive and generalizable is the theory?**

The institutional school initially concentrated on the marketing of agricultural products. Later, institutional theorists also included the distribution of industrial and consumer goods in their analysis.

Unfortunately, the institutional school has not focused on other and perhaps richer dimensions of market satisfaction, product innovations, and conflict and power issues among the channels of distribution. To that extent, the institutional school is not as rich as the functional school. Unless the institutional theorists build more comprehensive frameworks that integrate both behavioral and economic concepts, and treat producers and consumers also as institutions, it is not likely to produce more comprehensive theories.

Our score on richness = 5.

SIMPLICITY: **How easy is it to communicate and implement the theory?**

The institutional school is fairly simple to communicate and implement, especially concepts such as functional spinoffs and vertical distribution systems. It is also easy to communicate and implement the fundamental concepts of value-added functions performed by the middlemen.

Our score on simplicity = 8.

Table 3.1 summarizes our evaluation of the institutional school. It is interesting to note that it scores high on the organization criteria of structure and specification. To that extent, it is similar to the regional school. This is again understandable in view of the fact that the recent theorists have tended to borrow well-defined concepts from economics and diffusion of innovation disciplines. The institutional school, however, is weak with respect to the reality criteria of testability and empirical support. Finally, while it is relatively simple to understand, it is not a very rich school of thought.

Table 3.1 Evaluation of the Institutional School*

Criterion	Rationale	Score
Structure	Well-conceived structures and good definitions of the concepts	7
Specification	Good specification of relationships but limited to economic concepts	7
Testability	Very weak in operational definitions	4

(*Continued*)

Table 3.1 (*Continued*)

Criterion	Rationale	Score
Empirical support	Limited scientific support although good case history and practice oriented validation	5
Richness	Limited by a narrow focus on middlemen and by economic emphasis	5
Simplicity	Very easy to understand and implement	8
	TOTAL	36

* Scores range from 1 (poor) to 10 (excellent).

3.2 The Functionalist School of Thought

This school of thought is radically different from the other schools of thought that preceded it. While it shares many of the perspectives of the institutional school of thought, it differs in two substantially different ways from the commodity, the functional, and the regional schools. It is, first of all, conceptual as opposed to the largely descriptive nature of earlier schools, and, second, it conceives of marketing as a system of interrelated structural and interdependent dynamic relationships.

A broad generalization of the commodity, functional, and regional schools of thought is that they were fostered by researchers whose formal training was in economics and saw marketing as applied economics. While the main proponent of the functionalist approach was trained as an economist, he certainly did not see marketing as applied economics. Rather he saw marketing from a systems perspective where economic processes worked on an interdependent basis. This is not the same as the systems school of thought discussed in Chapter 5. However, the functionalist view of marketing science espoused by Wroe Alderson is certainly consistent with systems analysis as later developed by Amstutz and others in marketing.

This school of thought also differs from most of the others discussed because it is primarily the work of a single scholar. Wroe Alderson was clearly the major intellectual driving force behind the emergence of this school of thought. In a brief review of Alderson and his contributions to marketing, Barksdale (1980) points out the major impact this single individual had on marketing thought. He also points out that Alderson was both a skilled practitioner and a gifted scholar. He started his career in 1925 with the United States Department of Commerce and then with Curtis Publishing Company in the mid-1930s. After a World War II assignment in Washington, he set up his own consulting firm of Alderson and Sessions. He was equally at home in the academic environment and in 1953 served as a visiting professor at MIT. He joined the marketing faculty at the University of Pennsylvania in 1959 and in 1963 was a Ford Foundation Visiting Professor at New York University.

Alderson shaped this school of thought, not only through his writings (1945, 1948, 1949, 1954a, 1956, 1957, 1958, 1965), but also through his active involvement in what were called "Marketing Theory Seminars" (see Wales and Dawson 1979). These seminars were held at the University of Colorado each summer from 1951 to 1963. These "invitation only" seminars were used by Alderson to both encourage those present to think of marketing in conceptual ways and develop marketing theory, and also to develop and explain the functionalist approach to marketing. By his own powerful intellect and his dominating personality, he was clearly "in charge" of these seminars and put his stamp on the introduction of a formal theory approach to marketing science. Since his untimely death in 1965, these seminars have not been a part of the marketing scene and no one has emerged as a spokesperson for the functionalist school of thought.

The work of Alderson is not easy to summarize. Not only does it present the functionalist approach, but often simultaneously, it presents the logic of the formal theory approach to marketing science. It is also no secret that Alderson's writings were often difficult to read. In addition, he often coined terms that many times added to the confusion, rather than clarifying the issue. Nonetheless, the contributions of Alderson to marketing thought are considerable. Alderson has had his critics as well as his devotees. But as Barksdale (1980, p. 3) points out, the number of references to his work has declined sharply. From our perspective, this is most unfortunate as

Alderson was not only a creative scholar, but the incorporation of his thinking and the functionalist approach into current marketing science has the potential to greatly enrich our understanding.

Several attempts have been made to summarize and interpret Alderson's functionalist approach. Nicosia (1962) undertook the task in an article that has been widely reprinted. Nicosia's work was very comprehensive and helped clarify many of the issues presented by Alderson. Unfortunately, his review preceded the publication of Alderson's *Dynamic Marketing Behavior* by several years and therefore misses some of the richness that comes from that work. Rethans (1979) also attempted the task but made only modest additional contributions to our understanding of this school of thought. Of some significance, however, is the contribution of Hunt, Muncy, and Ray (1981), who attempted to clarify and integrate the work of Alderson by "formalizing" his functionalist theory. In addition to defining Alderson's three primitive elements (sets, behaviors, and expectations), these authors articulated Alderson's primary propositions:

1. "Marketing is the exchange which takes place between consuming groups and supplying groups." (p. 268)

2. "The household is one of the two principal organized behavior systems in marketing." (p. 268)

3. "The firm is the second primary organized behavior system in marketing." (pp. 268–269)

4. "Given heterogeneity of demand and heterogeneity of supply, the fundamental purpose of marketing is to effect exchanges by matching segments of demand with segments of supply." (p. 269)

5. "A third organized behavior system in marketing is the channel of distribution." (p. 270)

6. "Given heterogeneity of demand, heterogeneity of supply, and the requisite institutions to effect the sorts and transformations necessary to match segments of demand with segments of supply, the marketing process will take conglomerate resources in the natural state and bring about meaningful assortments of goods in the hands of consumers." (p. 271)

For the reader unacquainted with functionalism as presented by Alderson, it is important to understand the basic tenets of this school and how it differs from the functional school of thought discussed in Chapter 2. While the functional school looks at the functions performed in the practice of marketing, "functionalism" looks at a systemic structure, determining the present relationship between inputs and outputs, and laying the groundwork for bringing about an improvement in these relationships (Alderson 1965). This is not a normative approach. It takes the system as given and tries to improve it, similar to the functionalist approach in other fields of inquiry.

An important aspect of the functionalist approach is the systemic structure or the structure of the system within which marketing both operates and influences. In Alderson's (1954a) own words:

> For any subject under investigation it begins with the pragmatic questions "How does it work?" "What human purposes can it serve?" "How can its effectiveness in serving these purposes be improved?" Functionalism is boldly eclectic rather than rigidly systematic. It does not hesitate to draw upon economics, psychology, or any other discipline for facts or conceptual models which will help in finding the solution of a problem. (p. 40)

Two years later, he added:

> An initial word is also required with respect to the term "functionalism." Too often its use in marketing circles has implied scarcely more than identifying and describing the functions of marketing. The classification of marketing activities is worthwhile but it is only one step in the application of the versatile tool which functional analysis should be. Functionalism always starts by trying to understand the goals or functions of a whole system of action and how it operates in discharging these functions. (Alderson 1956, p. 7)

According to Nicosia (1962):

> Alderson's functionalism merits consideration as an approach or frame of reference which ... offers an all-encompassing integrating perspective of marketing entities and their interrelations — in short, of a marketing system. (p. 404)

Alderson was not the only one to recognize that marketing was a system and the necessity of determining how the total system worked. As discussed earlier in this chapter, Duddy and Revzan conceived marketing as an "organic" whole. Likewise, Breyer focused on the marketing channel and viewed it as a system within the larger marketing system. But Alderson's view was unique in that it drew heavily on the behavioral sciences for many of its conceptualizations of relations between various units in the marketing system. It builds on the commodity, institutional, and functional approaches, but positioned them in a larger totality.

To properly understand this school of thought, it is necessary to appreciate Alderson's key concepts. Alderson clearly states that "the two advanced concepts which project the essence of functionalist theory are the organized behavior system and the heterogeneous market" (Alderson 1965, p. 25). Nicosia (1962, p. 407) had suggested that the two most important concepts of Alderson's functionalism were the organized behavior system and the marketing process. The apparent reason for this discrepancy is that the concept of the heterogeneous market was introduced in Alderson's 1965 work to improve the understanding of the marketing process originally discussed in his 1957 work.

3.2.1 Organized Behavior System

Although this concept was given only brief attention in Alderson's *Marketing Behavior and Executive Action* (1957), it was obviously a key, if unstated, concept. The concept of the organized behavior system was more fully developed in *Dynamic Marketing Behavior* (1965). As pointed out by Monieson and Shapiro (1980), Alderson appears to have been heavily influenced by the thinking of Talcott Parsons. Parsons' theory of social action was intended to be a general theory of action rather than just a psychological or sociological theory of action. His cohesive system emphasizes the interaction of the individual with many factors within a dynamic social environment.

Alderson defines organized behavior systems as "the entities which operate in the marketing environment" (1965, p. 26). "In an organized behavior system the organizing element is the expectation of the members that they as members of the system will achieve a surplus beyond what they could attain through individual and independent action" (1965, p. 25).

The major test proposed by Alderson to determine the boundaries of an organized behavior system is "a common stake in survival" (Alderson 1965, p. 44). This implies that members of an organized behavior system should act to preserve the system if one part of the system or the entire system is threatened. In addition, an organized behavior system has "rules" for determining membership, a rule for determining the assignment of duties within the system, and a criterion for judging the outputs of the system.

Alderson lists the following five major systems that meet this test:

1. Public or political systems
2. Households as systems
3. Enterprise systems
4. Undercover systems
5. Charitable and educational systems

Fundamental to this concept is a system, in which interactions take the form of human behavior. As organized behavior systems interact with the market, they "provide the motive power which keeps the marketing process going" (1965, p. 37). They do so by behaving in a manner that maximizes their best interests and survival.

The two organized behavior systems that were the major focus of Alderson's thinking were the household and the firm. Whereas households are a major organized behavior system, the firm seems to be a major subcomponent of enterprise systems.

The household persists over time because of its expectations concerning future behavior. These expectations must, on the whole, have a positive value for the individuals making up the household. Their expectations concerning the desired patterns of behavior are higher as members of the household than they would be otherwise. The behavior system offers a surplus to its participants which they would not expect to enjoy outside the system. These expectations of desired behavior patterns may not be fully realized. The theory only requires that these anticipations should persist, perhaps with occasional reinforcement, to show that conditions would be no better outside the system.

The household accumulates goods to sustain the expected patterns of behavior. The household today, or its primary purchasing agent, is engaged in creating or replenishing an assortment of goods to sustain expected patterns of future behavior. Items are added to the assortment because they increased the potency of the assortment. Potency may be described as the quality of the assortment which protects the household against unpleasant surprises. (Alderson 1965, pp. 37–38)

Alderson characterizes the household as the ultimate target of the marketing effort. Therefore, it can easily be argued that this is the most important organized behavior system for Alderson. One has only to compare this thought with the earlier schools of marketing thought to see how different the perspective becomes when an integrated approach such as Alderson's functionalism is taken.

The firm as an organized behavior system is directly related to the heterogeneous market according to Alderson. As markets became more complex and diverse, firms developed specialized skills and knowledge that facilitated exchange and the matching of needs with resources.

Heterogeneity provided the immediate basis for exchange. There was no possible route for passing directly to anything resembling the homogeneous markets of pure and perfect competition. The underlying principle of market dynamics is that the existence of a market encourages the growth of a technology which gradually causes all products to flow through the market. (Alderson 1965, p. 39)

Of particular interest is the fact that Alderson did not consider the marketing channel an organized behavior system. He did not deny that a marketing channel could be an organized behavior system, but he argues that it generally lacks a common stake in survival, and he raises the question of "whether either side would assume any substantial costs or risks to ensure the survival of the other side" (Alderson 1965, p. 44)

The marketing channel exists but it would be stretching the point to call it an organized behavior system with a tendency to persist over a long period of time. At best it is a pseudo-system in which there is a fair amount of cooperation over a short interval but with no commitments over the longer run. (Alderson 1965, p. 44)

3.2.2 Heterogeneous Market

Progressive differentiation of products and services is the key to defining the values created by marketing. This approach is based on the assumption that each individual's need is different from every other individual's need in one or more respects. Thus the basic economic process is the gradual differentiation of goods up to the point at which they pass into the hands of consumers. (Alderson 1957, p. 69)

This is a considerably richer and more comprehensive statement than those that suggest that marketing creates time, place, and possession utilities. It is so because, as Barksdale points out (1980, p. 2) "in contrast to economic models of perfect competition, which assume homogeneous markets, Alderson postulated heterogeneity on both the supply and demand sides of markets."

If, in fact, markets are heterogeneous, then the marketing process is the mechanism by which heterogeneous supplies are matched with heterogeneous demands. Key to the marketing process, for Alderson, is the series of sorts and *transformations* by which the matching is accomplished.

Alderson viewed sorting as the basic function of marketing (Alderson 1965):

> Sorting is the decision aspect of marketing whether seen from the standpoint of the supplier or the consumer. The supplier assigns items to classes which are to be treated in different ways thereafter. The consumer selects an item into her assortment in relation to what the assortment already contains. While the marketing specialist is interested in all of the transformations which take place as goods move to market, including production transformations, his most vital concern is with the sorts intervening between successive transformations. (p. 34)

The term sorting includes four types of sorts. In the following, we see that Alderson saw the process as both "breaking down" and "building up" collections:

	Breaking Down	**Building Up**
Heterogeneous	Sorting out	Assorting
Homogeneous	Allocating	Accumulation

Adapted from Alderson (1965, p. 34)

Sorting out is used to describe that situation where a heterogeneous collection is broken into several homogeneous groups, that is, all the 2-by-4s from a tree are put in one pile, the 4-by-6s in another pile, and the 2-by-10s in yet another pile. Accumulation is building up of larger homogeneous collections, that is, putting all the 2-by-4s from many trees into a single large pile of 2-by-4s. Allocation is the assignment or dispersal of goods to intermediaries, that is, sending part of the pile of 2-by-4s to a lumber yard in Chicago. Assorting is the building up of a heterogenous collection or assortment, that is, an individual purchases some 2-by-4s along with other sizes of lumber and nails to build a picnic table that will be used to entertain guests.

> The aspect of sorting of greatest interest is assorting or the building of assortments. Assorting is the final step in taking products off the market. The other three aspects of sorting are not unimportant, but their significance lies in what they can contribute to the final building of assortments. The marketing specialist must look at all the earlier sorts to make sure they were necessary for the end result. (Alderson 1965, p. 35)

The ideal or perfect market would perfectly match each element of supply with each element of demand. For Alderson, markets are not perfect. He suggests (Alderson 1965) that imperfections in the market are the result of a failure in communication. Because of this failure, there may be an excess of some products in the channel of distribution and lesser demand for others. This mismatch in the market can be corrected by information. Information needs to be given to the customer, but also information needs to be gathered about the assortments that customers desire to build to enhance their potency.

In the more traditional economics approach of the homogeneous market, the market is matched by price adjustment. Information is taken for granted. Alderson argues that price is only one piece of information, primarily because his concept of the market is that of a highly segmented or heterogeneous market. While some small segments of the heterogeneous market may respond to price as the only necessary information, other segments may not consider price to be important or use it in conjunction with other information variables.

Consequently, markets are dyadic. There is a constant attempt to better match the marketing process against the heterogeneous market. Advantages are gained and lost in this quest. Alderson captures this in the title of his last book, *Dynamic Marketing Behavior.*

3.2.3 Transvection

While sorts and transformations are the key concepts for understanding the heterogeneous market, the key concept for analysis is the *transvection.* In an attempt to explain the concept of a transvection, Alderson (1965) contrasts the transvection with transactions.

> A transaction is a product of the double search in which customers are looking for goods and suppliers are looking for customers. It is an exchange of information leading to an agreement concerning the marketing of goods. This agreement is a joint decision in which the customer agrees to take the goods offered and the supplier agrees to sell at the stated price and terms. (p. 75)

> A transvection is the unit of action for the system by which a single end product such as a pair of shoes is placed in the hands of the consumer after moving through all the intermediate sorts and transformations from the original raw materials in the state of nature. A transvection is in a sense the outcome of a series of transactions, but a transvection is obviously more than this. A transvection includes the complete sequence of exchanges, but it also includes the various transformations which take place along the way. (p. 86)

The concept of the transvection is undoubtedly the richest of those brought forth by Alderson. It incorporates most, if not all, of the other concepts that Alderson talks about within the framework of functionalism. While the concept of the heterogeneous market focuses on successive differentiation, it is the concept of the transvection that allows analysis of both the efficiency and effectiveness of the process of matching achieved by successive sorts and transformations. For instance, this concept suggests that the best or shortest route to market is some optimal combination of sorts and transformations. Striving for an optimal combination of sorts and transformations allows one to focus on adding or subtracting sorts and transformations, and the consequent homogeneous and heterogeneous collections, using some weighting of cost, time, and risk.

For Alderson, a formal theory should develop a precise language, using primitive terms and definitions.

> The initial task is to develop a terminology which depends on as few primitive terms as possible, is consistent, and exhaustive in the sense of being capable of describing every kind of system relevant to marketing analysis, and which is complete in the sense of allowing for the formulation of theorems concerning transactions and transvections. The three primitive terms adopted here are sets, behavior and expectations. (Alderson and Martin 1965, p. 118–119)

Before his death, Alderson started the process. By using these primitive terms to define other terms, he advanced the complex concepts of the organized behavior system, the heterogeneous market, and the sorting function (Alderson 1965). Although we can only infer the logical process by which Alderson arrived at the point of assembling the elements from which he hoped to develop marketing theory, he did expand on these elements in his 1965 work.

3.2.4 Evaluation of the Functionalist School

STRUCTURE: **Are the concepts properly defined and integrated to form a strong nomological network?**

Perhaps the biggest strength of Wroe Alderson's functionalist school is its structure. Alderson is able to define the basic concepts including market heterogeneity, sorting, transformation, and transvection. Furthermore, he has done an outstanding job of integrating them to create a theory of marketing that makes sense.

Unfortunately, Alderson's theory has evolved over time. Therefore, concept definitions have changed over time, perhaps as a function of testing his ideas with colleagues at the conferences he used to organize.

Our score on structure = 7.

SPECIFICATION: **Are the relationships specified in a manner to delimit hypotheses or are they highly contingent?**

Alderson's functionalist theory also scores high on the specification dimension. He has attempted to provide several basic constructs and utilize them to build a theory that has few contingent hypotheses. Indeed, the functionalist theory is able to accommodate the market dynamics without impact on the four basic concepts of market heterogeneity, sorting, transformations, and transvections.

Our score on specification = 7.

TESTABILITY: **Are the operational definitions provided to ensure testability and intersubjective consensus?**

The weakest aspect of Alderson's theory is the testability dimension. He has failed to provide any operational definitions of his basic concepts. Furthermore, there is considerable disagreement among his followers as to the specific measures for the constructs in his theory.

It is unfortunate that Alderson, like so many brilliant theorists, paid little attention to testing the theory or providing operational definitions so that others could test it without misrepresenting the theory. Therefore, it is no surprise that Alderson's theory has remained untested so far, despite its organizational elegance in terms of structure and specification.

Our score on testability = 2.

EMPIRICAL SUPPORT: **What is the degree of confirmation in terms of empirical support?**

Since the theory has not been put to a test, it has no real scientific empirical support. Some of the concepts, especially associated with market heterogeneity and sorting, are real in that there is observational evidence for them in the real world. However, unlike the functional, the commodity, or the institutional schools, the transvectional theory is basically a conceptual framework devoid of empirical support.

Our score on empirical support = 3.

RICHNESS: **How comprehensive and generalizable is the theory?**

The functionalist theory is extremely rich. It is able to encompass the marketing domain and all of its aspects with no more than three to four basic concepts. Furthermore, the theory is generic enough to accommodate all specialized domains of marketing such as industrial marketing, services marketing, and social marketing. It appears to us that Alderson's theory is also capable of providing a framework for cross-national marketing. For example, concepts of market heterogeneity, as well as sorting and transformation, may easily explain cross-national similarities or differences and how to cope with them in terms of creating the proper assortment.

Our score on richness = 8.

SIMPLICITY: **How easy is it to communicate and implement the theory?**

Another major weakness of Alderson's theory is the difficulty of understanding the basic concepts. Indeed, a number of researchers have criticized and remained skeptical about the relevance of the functionalist theory because of Alderson's passion to create new words and phrases rather than use common terminology.

Similarly, in our opinion, Alderson's theory may *be* very useful as an analytical tool, but it is very hard to implement the concepts in terms of the organization structures and functional responsibilities in marketing departments. In that respect, the functional, the commodity, and the institutional schools are much stronger.

Our score on simplicity = 2.

Table 3.2 summarizes our evaluation of Alderson's functionalist theory. It is an extremely rich theory with good structure and specification. Unfortunately, it suffers from lack *of* simplicity and empirical content. Perhaps the theory can make an excellent contribution if someone attempts formally to test it in a marketing situation.

Table 3.2 Evaluation of the Functionalist School*

Criterion	Rationale	Score
Structure	Very well-structured definitions and good integration of basic concepts	7
Specification	Highly specified and devoid of contingent hypotheses	7
Testability	Poor on operational definitions and a clear disagreement on how to measure his concepts	2
Empirical support	No formal test of the theory and most evidence is anecdotal	3

(Continued)

Table 3.2 (*Continued*)

Criterion	Rationale	Score
Richness	Extremely rich and capable of becoming one of the few general theories of marketing	8
Simplicity	Extremely difficult to understand due to strange vocabulary and impossible to implement in practice	2
	TOTAL	29

* Scores range from 1 (poor) to 10 (excellent).

 ## 3.3 The Managerial School of Thought

In the late 1940s and the early 1950s, several scholars in economics struck off in a bold new direction. Sensing that economics scholars had generally become too isolated from the practical world of business, scholars such as Joel Dean and William Baumol developed the area of "managerial economics." Their goal, quite simply, was to translate the often abstract theories of economics spawned by academicians into principles of business practice that could be readily used by executives in their everyday managerial tasks.

In his classic textbook, *Managerial Economics*, published in 1951, Joel Dean clearly articulated his views on the importance of managerial economics:

> The purpose of this book is to show how economic analysis can be used in formulating business policies. It is therefore a departure from the main stream of economic writings on the theory of the firm, much of which is too simple in its assumptions and too complicated in its logical development to be managerially useful. The big gap between the problems of logic that intrigue economic theorists and the problems of policy that plague practical management needs to be bridged in order to give executives access to the practical contributions that economic thinking can make to top-management policies. (Dean 1951, p. vii)

Following the lead established by the managerial economists, some marketing theorists in the 1950s also began to advocate a more managerially based approach to marketing. For example, in 1957 John Howard published his widely accepted textbook entitled *Marketing Management* (revised in 1963b) and in 1958 Eugene Kelley and William Lazer edited the popular readings book *Managerial Marketing: Perspectives and Viewpoints*.

The real core of the managerial school of thought in marketing, however, emerged in a series of influential articles written during the late 1950s and early 1960s. In these works, scholars like Ted Levitt, Neil Borden, and Wendell Smith introduced such concepts as "marketing myopia," "marketing mix," and "market segmentation" for application by marketing executives. Interestingly, these concepts of marketing management have proven to be remarkably resilient, as demonstrated by their prominent inclusion in current marketing management textbooks.

Although space limitations prohibit a complete review of all of the writings in the managerial school published during its formative era, the following few pages will highlight those articles that registered the greatest impact. In addition, some of the more recent scholarly contributions in the managerial school will be highlighted.

One of the most important conceptual breakthroughs during this school's development was the emergence of the so-called marketing mix. Pioneered by scholars such as Ed Lewis, Neil Borden, and E. Jerome McCarthy, the concept of the marketing mix focused on the need for marketing managers to view the marketing task as the process of mixing or integrating several different functions simultaneously. Writing from the perspective of a theorist mainly concerned with advertising effectiveness, Borden (1964) described the marketing mix philosophy:

> Relatively early in my study of advertising, it had become evident that understanding of advertising usage by manufacturers in any case had to come from an analysis of advertising's place as one element in the total marketing program of the firm. I came to realize that it is essential always to

> ask: what overall marketing strategy has been or might be employed to bring about a profitable operation in light of the circumstances faced by the management? What combination of marketing procedures and policies has been or might be adopted to bring about desired behavior of trade and consumers at costs that will permit a profit? Specifically, how can advertising, personal selling, pricing, packaging, channels, warehousing, and other elements of a marketing program be manipulated and fitted together in a way that will give a profitable operation? (p. 3)

During this particular time period, some scholars began to argue that the pursuit of production efficiencies was perhaps rather shortsighted. Instead, they proposed that marketers should pay greater attention to the ascertainment of the consumers' needs and desires before decisions are made regarding production. Of course, this fundamental principle of the "marketing concept" is probably the most famous axiom developed in modern marketing history. As stated by J.B. McKitterick in his 1957 paper:

> Turning the issue around, if business enterprises are to compete successfully in the quicksilver of modem markets, something more than sophistication in means of doing marketing work is going to be required. Indeed, to plan at all, and think adequately of what competition might do and its possible effects before committing multi-million dollar resources, requires knowledge of the customer which penetrates to the level of theory. So the principal task of the marketing function in a management concept is not so much to be skillful in making the customer do what suits the interests of the business as to be skillful in conceiving and then making the business do what suits the interests of the customer. (p. 78)

Three years later, Robert J. Keith (1960), then president of the Pillsbury Company, also expressed the requirement for marketers to place the consumers' needs before the production abilities of the company:

> In much the same way American business in general—and Pillsbury in particular—is undergoing a revolution of its own today: a marketing revolution.
>
> The revolution stems from the same idea stated in the opening sentence of this article. No longer is the company at the center of the business universe. Today the customer is at the center.
>
> Our attention has shifted from problems of production to problems of marketing, from the product we can make to the product the consumer wants us to make, from the company itself to the marketplace. (p. 35)

More recently, Franklin Houston (1986) critiqued the marketing concept and concluded that marketers have lost sight of the original orientation of this basic concept:

> The marketing concept has suffered in two ways: first, it has been established as the optimal management philosophy when it is not necessarily so in all instances, and second, we can see many examples of poor marketing practices which have been adopted in the name of the marketing concept. It is time that we relearn that the marketing concept is one of a set of three concepts— marketing, sales, and production—that form the basis for understanding the management of marketing. And it is time that we remember that, under differing circumstances, each can be the orientation that best furthers the objectives of the organization. (p. 86)

Closely aligned to the marketing concept is the phenomenon of "marketing myopia," which was originated by Ted Levitt (1960) in a classic article in *Harvard Business Review*. Levitt warned that marketers often naively believe that, just because the current situation is profitable, there will always be a market for their particular products that extends indefinitely into the future. According to Levitt, every industry must warily scan the horizon for signs of corporate vulnerability:

> In truth, there is no such thing as a growth industry, I believe. There are only companies organized and operated to create and capitalize on growth opportunities. Industries that assume themselves to be riding some automatic growth escalator invariably descend into stagnation. The history of

every dead and dying "growth" industry shows a self-deceiving cycle of bountiful expansions and undetected decay. There are four conditions that usually guarantee this cycle:

1. The belief that growth is assured by an expanding and more affluent population.

2. The belief that there is no competitive substitute for the industry's major product.

3. Too much faith in mass production and in the advantages of rapidly declining unit costs as output rises.

4. Preoccupation with a product that lends itself to carefully controlled scientific experimentation, improvement, and manufacturing cost reduction. (pp. 47–48)

With this call for increased sensitivity to the needs of consumers as the basic motivation for marketing effort, there also emerged an awareness that not all consumers possess the same drives and goals. The notion that marketers should segment the market and strive to develop several different marketing mixes to more closely match the diverse needs of the consumers was first proposed by Wendell Smith in 1956. As originally stated by Smith, market segmentation is intuitively appealing:

Market segmentation ... consists of viewing a heterogeneous market (one characterized by divergent demand) as a number of smaller homogeneous markets in response to differing product preferences among important market segments. It is attributable to the desires of consumers or users for more precise satisfaction of their varying wants. (p. 6)

Over the years, the concept of market segmentation has proven to be a rich and sometimes controversial area for marketing theorists. As noted recently by Winter (1984), some marketers have misinterpreted Smith's original writing and have unfortunately focused on the diversity in consumers' levels of demand, stated usually in terms of the "heavy half and light half" of the market, rather than the diversity in the type of demand among consumers. Also, Winter argues that obsession with demographic identification of consumer segments and preoccupation with product forms instead of product needs have detracted from the original concept of market segmentation proposed in 1956.

The concept of market segmentation continues to be attractive to the current generation of marketing scholars. Dickson and Ginter (1987) demonstrated the similarities and contrasts between market segmentation and product differentiation. Recognizing the increased emphasis on industrial marketing, Doyle and Saunders (1985) discussed the application of market segmentation in industrial markets. Finally, quantitative approaches to market segmentation have recently been considered by Grover and Srinivasan (1987) and Blozan and Prabhaker (1984).

In addition, numerous other scholars in the managerial school proposed principles or theories that concentrated on how marketing managers should deal with specific elements of the marketing mix, such as products, price, promotion, and distribution decisions.

In the area of product decisions, one of the most significant developments was the introduction of the "product life cycle" concept. According to Levitt (1965):

Most alert and thoughtful senior marketing executives are by now familiar with the concept of the product life cycle. Even a handful of uniquely cosmopolitan and up-to-date corporate presidents have familiarized themselves with this tantalizing concept. Yet a recent survey I took of such executives found none who used the concept in any strategic way whatever, and pitifully few who used it [in] any kind of tactical way. It has remained—as have so many fascinating theories in economics, physics, and sex—a remarkably durable but almost totally unemployed and seemingly unemployable piece of professional baggage whose presence in the rhetoric of professional discussions adds a much coveted but apparently unattainable legitimacy to the idea that marketing management is somehow a profession. There is, furthermore, a persistent feeling that the life cycle concept adds luster and believability to the insistent claim in certain circles that marketing is close to being some sort of science.

> The concept of the product life cycle is today at about the stage that the Copernican view of the universe was 300 years ago; a lot of people knew about it, but hardly anybody seemed to use it in any effective or productive way.

> Now that so many people know and in some fashion understand the product life cycle, it seems time to put it to work. (p. 8)

More recently, the *Journal of Marketing* devoted its Fall 1981 issue to a series of articles concerning the product life cycle concept. Although the product life cycle is appealing, George Day (1981), the guest editor for the issue, noted the existence of certain conceptual problems:

> There is tremendous ambivalence toward the product life cycle concept within marketing. On the one hand, the concept has an enduring appeal because of the intuitive logic of the product birth → growth → maturity → decline sequence based on a biological analogy. As such it has considerable descriptive value when used as a systematic framework for explaining market dynamics.

> However, the simplicity of the product life cycle makes it vulnerable to criticism, especially when it is used as a predictive model for anticipating when changes will occur and one stage will succeed another, or as a normative model which attempts to prescribe what alternative strategies should be considered at each stage. (p. 60)·

Also, Gardner (1987) examined the product life cycle literature published since 1975. He concluded that the product life cycle is not a theory and has many serious shortcomings. Gardner recommended that a major reconceptualization of the life cycle phenomenon is needed to generate a prescriptive, rather than descriptive, concept.

Within the pricing area, Joel Dean (1950) and Alfred Oxenfeldt (1960) strove to translate economic theories of pricing into normative policy guidelines that could be understood and readily implemented by marketing managers. Of Dean's many contributions to the pricing literature, perhaps his most significant effort was the articulation of the pricing policies of "skimming" and "penetration":

> The strategic decision in pricing a new product is the choice between (1) a policy of high initial prices that skim the cream of demand and (2) a policy of low prices from the outset serving as an active agent for market penetration. Although the actual range of choice is much wider than this, a sharp dichotomy clarifies the issues for consideration. (1950, p. 49)

> *Skimming Prices.* For products that represent a drastic departure from accepted ways of performing a service, a policy of relatively high prices coupled with heavy promotional expenditures in the early stages of market development (and lower prices at later stages) has proved successful for many products. (1950, pp. 49–50)

> *Penetration Price.* The alternative policy is to use low prices as the principal instrument for penetrating mass markets early. This policy is the reverse of the skimming policy in which the price is lowered only as short-run competition forces it. The passive skimming policy has the virtue of safeguarding some profits at every stage of market penetration. But it prevents quick sales to the many buyers who are at a lower end of the income scale or the lower end of the preference scale, and who therefore are unwilling to pay any substantial premium for product reputation superiority. The active approach in probing possibilities for market expansion by early penetration pricing requires research, forecasting, and courage. (1950, p. 50)

Oxenfeldt (1960) may be best remembered for advocating that marketers use a "multistage approach" to pricing:

> In order to organize the various pieces of information and considerations that bear on price decisions, a multi-stage approach to pricing can be a very helpful tool. This method sorts the major elements in a pricing decision into six successive stages:

1. Selection of market targets.

2. Choosing a brand "image."

3. Composing a marketing mix.

4. Selecting a pricing policy.

5. Determining a pricing strategy.

6. Arriving at a specific price. (pp. 125–126)

The sequence of the stages is an essential part of the method, for each step is calculated to simplify the succeeding stage and to reduce the likelihood of error. One might say that this method divides the price decision into manageable parts, each one logically antecedent to the next. In this way, the decision at each stage facilitates all subsequent decisions. This approach might also be regarded as a process of selective search, where the number of alternatives deserving close consideration is reduced drastically by making the decision in successive stages.

In recent years the topic of pricing has been the subject of three major review articles (Nagle 1984, Rao 1984, Tellis 1986). In addition, a number of articles have addressed a variety of pricing issues, such as price negotiations (Evans and Beltramini 1987), price sensitivity (Huber, Holbrook, and Kahn 1986), and product line pricing (Reibstein and Gatignon 1984, Petroshius and Monroe 1987).

The classic article related to the distribution area was authored by John F. Magee in 1960. Magee, and other scholars like Davidson (1961), were instrumental in encouraging marketing managers to elevate distribution decisions to an equal importance with product, pricing, and promotion decisions. According to Magee (1960):

> Grappling with all of these problems is like untangling a tangled skein of yarn. Each decision has an impact on other choices and for this reason is hard to pin down. The distribution problem is a system problem, and it must be looked at as such. If it is examined in total and if the experience and methods available for studying it are used, the issues just mentioned can be resolved in an orderly, mutually compatible way.
>
> In my experience, three key conditions have, when present, made for a sound distribution system study and an effective implementation program:
>
> 1. Recognition by company management that improving distribution means examining the full physical distribution system.
>
> 2. Use of quantitative systems analysis or operations research methods to show clearly the nature of trade-offs and the relation between system operation and company policies.
>
> 3. Cooperative work by men knowledgeable in sales and marketing, transportation, materials handling, materials control, and information handling. (p. 96)

An example of more recent thinking in the distribution management area is Frazier and Sheth's (1985) discussion of the roles of attitude and behavior in the coordination of the distribution channel. By employing these behavioral concepts, they demonstrated the potential application of the organizational dynamics school to the managerial school.

Within the promotion area, marketing scholars in the managerial school offered suggestions to marketing practitioners regarding personal selling and advertising decision-making. In a highly influential article in the Journal of Marketing, Robert J. Lavidge and Gary A. Steiner (1961) argued that the goal of advertising should be to move consumers through a series of stages that eventually result in product purchase:

> Advertising may be thought of as a force, which must move people up a series of steps:
>
> 1. Near the bottom of the steps stand potential purchasers who are completely unaware of the existence of the product or service in question.

2. Closer to purchasing, but still a long way from the cash register, are those who are merely aware of its existence.

3. Up a step are prospects who know what the product has to offer.

4. Still closer to purchasing are those who have favorable attitudes toward the product—those who like the product.

5. Those whose favorable attitudes have developed to the point of preference over all other possibilities are up still another step.

6. Even closer to purchasing are consumers who couple preference with a desire to buy and the conviction that the purchase would be wise.

7. Finally, of course, is the step which translates this attitude into actual purchase. (p. 59)

The topic of advertising continues to be the subject of a significant number of scholarly articles. Recently, emphasis has been placed on the competitive influences in advertising (Erickson 1985, Gatignon 1984), decision making in advertising (Tull et al. 1986), and determinants of advertising effectiveness (MacKenzie, Lutz, and Belch 1986; Preston 1982).

Marketing has always taken a considerable amount of abuse for the supposedly inconsiderate and deceitful tactics employed by salespeople. During the peak of the managerial school, serious attempts were made to reduce the likelihood that salespeople would feel the need to resort to coercive methods of personal selling. For example, Cash and Crissy (1958) advocated the adoption of the "need-satisfaction theory of personal selling":

In this theory it is assumed that purchases are made to satisfy needs. Therefore, in order to make a sale the salesman must discover the prospect's needs and show how his products or services will fill those needs. This is a customeroriented approach as compared with the two previous theories which are, primarily, salesman-oriented approaches.

To be useful in application this theory requires greater skill and maturity on the part of the salesman because he is prevented from talking about his product until he has discovered the customer's needs. This is a sharp contrast to the selling formula, where the salesman is encouraged to point out all the important features of his product. It also requires that the salesman be sufficiently self-confident to undertake control of the sales interview through questioning rather than by dominating the conversation. (p. 14)

For more serious and complex sales situations, this approach is preferred to the two previously described theories. It is obviously more time-consuming, but the increased likelihood of making a sale by matching the customer's needs with the appropriate product features and benefits makes this approach more attractive, particularly in situations where the potential commissions and/or profits are great enough to warrant the extra expenditure of time.

A considerable amount of scholarly attention has been devoted recently to the subjects of personal selling and sales management. In the personal selling area, Weitz (1981) and Weitz, Sujan, and Sujan (1986) presented conceptual frameworks for understanding selling effectiveness. Along a similar line, Dwyer, Schurr, and Oh (1987) considered the development of buyer–seller relationships, and Williams and Spiro (1985) discussed communication issues in salesperson–customer dyads. In the sales management area, recent articles have addressed the impact of supervisory behaviors on the salesforce (Kohli 1985), salesforce turnover (Lucas et al. 1987), salesperson motivation (Sujan 1986), salesforce socialization (Dubinsky et al. 1986), and stages in a salesperson's career (Cron and Slocum 1986).

As noted earlier, a full review of the managerial school is impossible for obvious reasons. A tremendous volume of conceptual articles, empirical studies, and case studies has been written in the past thirty years concerning this school's key concepts (product life cycle, market segmentation, marketing mix, marketing concept, etc.). Additionally, the managerial school encompasses literature on other topics, including product positioning (Shugan 1987) and the interface of marketing with other functional units within the organization (Ruekert and

Walker 1987). In fact, a strong argument can be made for positioning the managerial school as the most comprehensive school among the galaxy of marketing schools of thought. Readers who desire additional information about the managerial school may consult Sheth and Garrett's (1986a) readings book, *Marketing Management: A Comprehensive Reader,* or any recent marketing management textbook, such as Bagozzi (1986) or Kotler and Armstrong (1987).

In summary, the managerial school has had tremendous influence on the marketing profession. Its central concepts continue to be utilized heavily by marketing practitioners in corporate offices and by marketing professors in academic classrooms. In addition to this school's resiliency, another major contribution has been its integrative ability. By emphasizing (1) the marketing concept (which urged practitioners to analyze consumer needs) and (2) the marketing mix (which integrated the functional tasks of marketing), the managerial school established itself as a comprehensive school of thought.

3.3.1 Evaluation of the Managerial School

STRUCTURE: **Are the concepts properly defined and integrated to form a strong nomological network?**

The managerial school is remarkably good on the structure dimension. It has identified the key policy issues of marketing practice, provided adequate definitions to fundamental concepts such as the product life cycle, the marketing mix and market segmentation, and has even attempted to integrate these concepts into one theory of marketing management, such as by Levitt and Kotler.

Indeed, the managerial school seems even more robust than either the regional or the functionalist schools in terms of structure. This can probably be explained by the fact that "there is nothing more practical than a good theory." In other words, there is a considerable payoff to theorists in terms of recognition and income from industry when they generate a good theory of marketing practice.

Our score on structure = 8.

SPECIFICATION: **Are the relationships specified in a manner to delimit hypotheses or are they highly contingent?**

The managerial school also scores well on the specification criterion if we examine each marketing function individually. For example, the managerial school has provided excellent hypotheses for advertising effectiveness, sales force management, distribution efficiency, and product life cycle management. Although many of these hypotheses are contingent on exogenous market forces of competition and customers, the managerial school has attempted to incorporate them either by a covariate analysis or by controlled experiments.

The only area where the managerial school seems weak with respect to the specification criterion is the interdependent relationships among various elements of marketing mix. For example, we still do not have well-established hypotheses to determine whether advertising and distribution are complementary or substitute marketing forces to generate a desirable market response. Similarly, we still do not know whether product and price are related by some underlying process such as value.

Our score on specification = 7.

TESTABILITY: **Are the operational definitions provided to ensure testability and intersubjective consensus?**

The managerial school clearly ranks highest on the testability criterion among all the schools reviewed so far. This is not surprising in view of the fact that the managerial school is anchored to marketing practice and marketing realities. There are excellent operational definitions for each functional area of marketing practice so that both field experiments and survey research can be carried out. This has been particularly true for the price and promotion areas of marketing.

Furthermore, there is good intersubjective consensus about the testability of specific relationships, perhaps due to industry-wide measures and standards created by market research companies, such as A. C. Nielsen and M.R.C.A.

Our score on testability = 8.

EMPIRICAL SUPPORT: **What is the degree of confirmation in terms of empirical support?**

The managerial school has generated by far the greatest amount of scientific studies to test its hypotheses. Although there are strong controversies on specific issues such as how advertising works or which promotional deal generates more sales, it is undeniable that the managerial school has more empirical support for its basic concepts than all the previous five schools of thought put together. At the same time, the managerial school has also generated an enormous amount of empirical support in the world of marketing practice.

Our score on empirical support = 9.

RICHNESS: **How comprehensive and generalizable is the theory?**

The managerial school also scores high on richness because it encompasses all areas of marketing. Its concepts transcend specialized areas such as industrial, international, services, and social marketing. In other words, the basic concepts of product life cycle, market segmentation, marketing mix, and the like seem equally applicable to any specialized area of marketing activity.

The managerial school has only one weakness. It is managerial in its orientation and, therefore, is likely to provide a biased perspective on such areas as consumerism and environmental side effects of marketing activities.

Our score on richness = 9.

SIMPLICITY: **How easy is it to communicate and implement the theory?**

The managerial school is extremely simple to understand. Its concepts are easy to communicate as evidenced by their dissemination in introductory marketing management classes.

Similarly, the managerial school has been implemented in most organizations, although probably not to the same extent as the functional concept. Unfortunately, many corporations do not fully appreciate the marketing concept and still equate marketing with selling.

Our score on simplicity = 9.

Table 3.3 summarizes our evaluation of the managerial school of marketing. It is impressive to note that the managerial school scores well across all the three areas of metatheory: organization, reality, and relevance. This suggests that the reputation of the marketing discipline is likely to be enhanced more by the managerial school than by the functional, institutional, commodity, or even functionalist schools of thought. It is also not surprising to note that the managerial school has attracted more scholars and researchers than any other school of marketing thought, except perhaps the buyer behavior school.

Table 3.3 Evaluation of the Managerial School*

Criterion	Rationale	Score
Structure	Extremely well-defined concepts and relationships	8
Specification	Excellent specification of relationships at the elemental level but not at the marketing mix level	7
Testability	Excellent operational definitions at the functional level	8
Empirical support	Very comprehensive testing at both the scientific and practice levels	9
Richness	Extremely rich so that it transcends all areas of marketing	9
Simplicity	Very easy to understand and implement in practice	9
	TOTAL	50

* Scores range from 1 (poor) to 10 (excellent).

Summary

This chapter has reviewed the institutional, the functionalist, and the managerial schools of thought. All of them are basically economic perspectives but they do acknowledge the interactive processes between the producers, the middlemen, and the consumers. In other words, they believe in interdependence among various marketing actors.

The institutional school has focused on the role of middlemen in marketing and not on the products or the functions of marketing. It began with Weld, Butler, and Breyer but has been enriched significantly by more contemporary scholars including McCammon, Mallen, and Bucklin. The institutional school has generated some intriguing concepts such as the structure of vertical distribution systems, functional spinoff, and the principles of speculation versus postponement. Although the institutional school is very good in structure and specification, it has been lacking in testability and empirical support. However, it has good relevance in terms of richness and simplicity.

The functionalist school proposed by Wroe Alderson is extremely rich. Based on a very few concepts such as market heterogeneity, sorting, transformation, and transvections, Alderson has provided a theory that is generic to all areas of marketing. Unfortunately, the theory has never been tested. Furthermore, Alderson's obsession with coining new phrases and words has compounded the problem of carrying out operationally defined studies to test his theory. Of course, there is no question that Alderson will always be remembered as a major contributor to the development of marketing thought.

The managerial school has focused on marketing practice. In the process, it has generated such widely accepted concepts as the product life cycle, market segmentation, and the marketing mix. The managerial school scores high on all of the six metatheory criteria, which is somewhat surprising in view of the fact that it is a practice- or application-driven school of thought.

Questions for Analysis and Discussion

1. How has Transaction Cost Economics (TCE) impacted the institutional school of marketing?

2. Why did the early institutional literature fail to develop a theory of channel structure? Is it possible to trace this gap in the literature to the emergence of supply chain management as a new discipline?

3. What should be done to build trust in marketing institutions?

4. Wroe Alderson emphasized the household as a principal organized behavior system. Discuss the relevance of his views today. In what contexts is he still very much on target? In what contexts may his view no longer apply?

5. (In what ways) Can Alderson's notion of transvections be extended to advance our understanding of the customer journey?

6. Many think that marketing academia is lagging in the current digital era. In your assessment, did the potential of theory development inherent in the managerial school of marketing diminish as it transitioned into the marketing strategy school of thought?

CHAPTER

Non-Interactive - Non-Economic Schools of Marketing

LEARNING OBJECTIVES

After reading this chapter, you will be able to:

- Explain the three non-interactive and non-economic schools of marketing – Buyer Behavior, Activist, and the Macromarketing schools of marketing thought.
- Identify the academic pioneers in each school of thought.
- Describe the progress in each of the three schools of thought chronologically.

- Highlight the distinct characteristics of these schools of marketing thought and how they influenced the overall marketing discipline.
- Assimilate each school of thought evaluation based on metatheoretical parameters of syntax, semantics, and pragmatics.

This chapter describes and evaluates three non-interactive and non-economic schools of marketing. As pointed out in Chapter 1, the three schools of thought that fit this categorization are the buyer behavior, activist, and macromarketing schools of thought. All of them take the perspective of the recipients of marketing practice, including consumers and society at large. At the same time, they provide conceptual frameworks, hypotheses, and empirical evidence based on behavioral and social sciences rather than economic theories.

The non-interactive-non-economic schools of thought represent a significant shift in the history of marketing thought. First, the traditional and time-honored normative concepts of economics about how markets *should behave* gave way to the more descriptive concepts of the behavioral and social sciences about how markets *actually behave*. This represents a shift from the normative to the positive sciences.

Second, the emphasis also begins to shift away from an earlier focus on more aggregate markets and toward a focus on individual customers in the market or segments of consumers. In that respect, the unit of analysis becomes increasingly microlevel.

In many ways, this two-dimensional shift (economic to behavioral and markets to customers) seems to have resulted in a discontinuity between the older schools and the newer schools of marketing thought. Consequently, all the knowledge and thinking generated by the previous six schools of marketing thought seem to be relegated in importance. Indeed, the emergence of the noneconomic schools of marketing thought seem to fit Kuhn's (1962) paradigm of radical shift as the basis for the revolution of a discipline. Only in recent years have several scholars begun to comment that this discontinuity in marketing thought may have resulted in the loss of valuable heritage and richness of knowledge generated by the commodity, functional, institutional, regional, and managerial schools of thought (Sheth 1979b, 1985a).

4.1 The Buyer Behavior School of Thought

As the name implies, the buyer behavior school has focused on customers in the marketplace. In addition to the demographic information on how many and who are the customers, the buyer behavior school of marketing has attempted to address the question of *why* customers behave the way they do in the marketplace. This emphasis on the why aspect of consumer behavior has resulted in several unique characteristics of the buyer behavior school.

First, consumer behavior is considered a subset of human behavior rather than treated as a unique phenomenon similar to abnormal or deviant behavior. In the process, there has been a strong tendency to borrow explanations of human behavior as possible clues to understanding consumer behavior. As we will demonstrate later, this has resulted in numerous partial theories of consumer behavior, each one based on a unique or specific proposition in psychology, sociology, and anthropology. As Sheth (1967) has amply demonstrated in his review of the field, this pluralistic but parallel borrowing from diverse disciplines of behavioral sciences has generated the phenomenon of the proverbial seven blind men touching the elephant and providing very plausible but different explanations as to why the consumer behaves the way he or she does.

Second, the emphasis in the buyer behavior school has been overwhelmingly on consumer products such as packaged goods and consumer durables. Although there is increasing interest in industrial and services buying behavior, the discipline of buyer behavior is still focused on consumer products. This is partly due to the operational case with which empirical research may be conducted, but we believe it is also rooted in the presumption that buying behavior is a subset of human behavior.

Finally, the buyer behavior school has also delimited itself to understanding brand choice behavior as opposed to other types of choices such as product class, volume, or timing of choices. Furthermore, it has also limited itself to understanding purchase behavior as opposed to consumption and disposal behavior (Holbrook 1985, Sheth 1985b).

It is no exaggeration to state that among all schools of marketing thought, the buyer behavior school has had the greatest impact on the discipline of marketing with the possible exception of the managerial school of marketing. Consequently, this school of thought has attracted numerous scholars both from within and outside of the marketing discipline. It is, therefore, extremely difficult to provide a chronological and detailed evolution of this school of thought as we did with the other schools of marketing thought. Literally, hundreds of scholars and thousands of research papers are in this area. Therefore, we will attempt to provide major highlights of the historical evolution of buyer behavior in marketing and leave it up to the reader to obtain more detailed information from other sources such as proceedings of the Association for Consumer Research (ACR), the *Journal of Consumer Research*, and several books of readings as well as textbooks (e.g., Kassarjian and Robertson 1981; Engel, Blackwell, and Miniard 1986).

The evolution and description of the buyer behavior school of thought is organized as follows:

1. Why did the buyer behavior school become so popular in marketing?
2. Who were the pioneers in the behavioral sciences to make an impact on this emerging field?
3. How did the buyer behavior school evolve and where is it today?
4. What are the major tenets, findings, and generalizations provided by the buyer behavior school?
5. What impact has the buyer behavior school had on the discipline and practice of marketing?

Of course, we will evaluate the buyer behavior school with the same six metatheory criteria as before.

4.1.1 Popularity of the Buyer Behavior School

Our analysis suggests two major reasons for the evolution and rapid popularity of the buyer behavior school: (1) the emergence of the marketing concept; and (2) the established body of knowledge in behavioral science.

Emergence of the Marketing Concept: Soon after the World War II, the American economy along with the Western European economy had begun to shift from a sellers' economy to a buyers' economy. The extraordinary installation of manufacturing capacity had generated excess capacity and it was becoming harder and harder to sell what was produced. This was further compounded by intense competition in the marketplace as several large competitors began to emerge in each industry.

Both marketing practitioners and marketing scholars began to question the traditional supply-oriented marketing practices including the concept of push marketing. For example, Robert Keith (1960) at Pillsbury represented the sentiment of the practitioners when he stated:

> In today's economy the consumer, the man or the woman who buys the product, is at the absolute dead center of the business universe. Companies revolve around the customers, not the other way around. Growing acceptance of this consumer concept has had, and will have, far-reaching implications for business, achieving a virtual revolution in economic thinking. As the concept gains ever greater acceptance, marketing is emerging as the most important single function in business (p. 35).

Similar views were also expressed by several marketing scholars, most notably Philip Kotler. In the first edition of the most popular textbook in marketing, Kotler (1967) sharply contrasted the production, selling, and customer-oriented marketing philosophies with a strong advocacy toward the latter orientation in marketing practice. This academic sentiment was eloquently expressed by Markin (1969):

> [The marketing manager] recognizes at the outset that the success or failure of his marketing strategy rests ultimately with the consumer as market for which his strategy has been designed. Consequently, most strategy formulations are based on the assumption that consumer behavior can be either (i) analyzed and understood, or (ii) analyzed, understood and modified. Both assumptions strongly dictate that marketing managers know and learn how consumer impressions, opinions, and images can be modified and how firms can successfully communicate their marketing programs to the consumer. (p. 7)

Although the customer orientation in marketing was at its infancy in the late 1950s and early 1960s and was limited to packaged goods companies such as Pillsbury, Procter and Gamble, and General Foods, it is important to recognize that customer orientation is today considered vital to the survival of corporations in virtually every sector of the economy (Peters and Waterman 1982, Lele and Sheth 1987).

Established Body of Knowledge: At the same time, there was also a growing realization that a host of disciplines in the behavioral sciences had generated a body of knowledge that may be very useful to business functions in general and marketing in particular. Indeed, the Ford Foundation allocated large sums of grant money to schools of business for the explicit purpose of increasing the competency in behavioral and mathematical sciences. Consequently, the pure disciplines began to apply their expertise and ideas to the unexplored areas of business, and a number of scholars in the behavioral and social sciences began to shift their research to the business arena.

It is beyond the scope of this book to provide an exhaustive list of the applications of behavioral and mathematical sciences to marketing and business. However, we will provide some illustrative examples to sensitize the reader.

From cultural anthropology, Hall (1960) proposed five silent languages that create barriers in overseas business and marketing negotiations. These included languages of time, space, friendship, material possessions, and nature of agreements. From the field of cognitive psychology, March and Simon (1958) and Edwards (1961) provided a number of concepts that are often in conflict with economic propositions. These include such concepts as subjective utility, bounded rationality, satisficing goals and objectives, and organizational conflicts due to differences in perceptions and goals among corporate employees.

We also began to borrow concepts from cognitive psychology such as cognitive dissonance (Festinger 1957) and cognitive conflict in consumer and organizational behavior. From the field of clinical psychology and personality, the business discipline began to learn the concepts of group dynamics, emotional versus rational behavior, and the more humanistic theories of managing and motivating employees (Maslow 1954, Heider 1958, McGregor 1960, Allport 1961, Homans 1961, McClelland 1961). In the area of sociology, we borrowed such concepts as social stratification, social class, and diffusion of innovations including theories of opinion leadership and personal influence (Warner, Meeker, and Eells 1949, Katz and Lazarsfeld 1955, Rogers 1962).

Along with the substantive body of knowledge, business disciplines including marketing began to apply the methodologies of the behavioral sciences. For example, focus group interviews and unstructured personal interviews became very popular in market research. At the same time, we began to collect data based on longitudinal panels of consumers following the traditions established in sociology, political science, and public opinion research. Finally, we also started the use of experiments as a scientific way to test behavioral hypotheses, especially as they related to cognitive and learning theories in psychology. In marketing, for example, Holloway (1967a) published a bibliography on experiments in marketing (updated by Gardner and Belk 1980). We also began to apply the laboratory methods associated with physiological psychology including sensory stimulation and perceptions of physical realities. This resulted in the use of pupil dilation, galvanic skin pressure, and other physiological measures of consumer responses (see Ferber 1974 for a good review in market research).

In addition to the behavioral sciences, marketing began to borrow from the mathematical sciences. Operations research and management science techniques such as stochastic process, linear programming, and optimization theory began to be applied to buyer behavior research (Bass et al. 1961, Massy, Montgomery, and Morrison 1970).

In short, the buyer behavior school of marketing emerged and mushroomed because marketing practitioners perceived a need to understand the customer. Further, an available body of knowledge was appropriate for that understanding.

4.1.2   Early Pioneers from Behavioral Sciences

As mentioned before, numerous scholars from many disciplines of the behavioral sciences generated enthusiasm among marketing scholars who were interested in buyer behavior research. It is again impossible to provide an exhaustive list. However, we will discuss the contributions of a few scholars to illustrate the scope and process of their influence in shaping buyer behavior theory and research traditions.

Among the earliest pioneers from the behavioral sciences was George Katona. His classic paper (Katona 1953) on the differences between economic and psychological behavior generated strong interest in buyer behavior. Katona also pioneered the techniques of consumer intentions and sentiments as a way of forecasting their behavior (Katona and Mueller 1953, 1956). His theories of consumption (1960) and focus on the consumer (1964) are still considered major contributions in economic psychology and consumer psychology.

A second pioneer from the behavioral sciences to make a major impact in marketing and buyer behavior was Paul Lazarsfeld. His research on opinion leadership and personal influence (Katz and Lazarsfeld 1955); generated the tradition of research on word of mouth communication in consumer behavior. He also contributed toward the research methodology of longitudinal panels as a method of collecting data and hierarchical crosstabulations as a method of analyzing data.

The third pioneer from the behavioral sciences was Everett Rogers. His book on diffusion of innovations (Rogers 1962), immediately became popular in marketing, and a number of empirical studies were carried out on the diffusion of new products and brands. Rogers' work is still popular in consumer behavior and marketing, inspiring major works such as those by Arndt (1967) and Robertson (1971), as well as numerous research papers. His recent work (Rogers 1983) serves as a review of well over a thousand research studies on the diffusion concept. More recently; Gatignon and Robertson (1985), have offered twenty-nine theoretical propositions to guide future research in this area, as well as to provide a foundation for those who wish to model various aspects of the diffusion process.

A fourth pioneer for the behavioral sciences was Leon Festinger. His theory of cognitive dissonance (Festinger 1957) began to be applied in the early 1960s, resulting in a stream of publications for the next two decades. Today, cognitive dissonance theory is an integral part of buyer behavior theory.

Similarly, the theories of several other well-known psychologists were applied to understand consumer behavior. These included Sigmund Freud (1953), Clark Hull (1952), Charles Osgood (1957a, 1957b), Daniel Katz (Katz and Stotland 1959, Katz 1960), Neal Miller (1959), Carl Hovland (1954), and Martin Fishbein (1963, 1967; Fishbein and Ajzen 1975). However, their work has received segmented rather than universal attention in marketing.

Finally, March and Simon (1958) and Cyert and March (1963) must be acknowledged for their influence on marketing scholars who were focused more on organizational buying behavior. Their work on organizational psychology was directly applied in understanding and modeling industrial buying behavior.

4.1.3   Evolution of the Buyer Behavior School

Unlike the previous schools of marketing thought, it is extremely difficult to identify any one individual as the father of the buyer behavior school of marketing. Furthermore, it is equally difficult to suggest that at any one time period there was only one thought process dominant in the evolution of the buyer behavior school. Instead, several marketing scholars were simultaneously developing separate research efforts often in conflict with one another. In light of this diversity, we have chosen to provide a chronological perspective.

Decade of the Fifties: The buyer behavior school of thought, especially with the behavioral emphasis, really began in the early 1950s. In the decade of the 1950s, we have identified three separate areas of research.

The first area of research focused on emotional and irrational psychological determinants of consumer behavior. This research tradition was pioneered by Ernest Dichter (1947, 1964) and it is often referred to as motivation research. The basic assumption underlying this research tradition was that consumers make product or brand choices for emotional and deep-seated reasons they are neither willing to discuss nor aware of. The only way to understand these motivations is to use the methodology and concepts of clinical psychology. Motivation research thus began to rely on focus group interviews and personal nonstructured interviews that needed to be analyzed and interpreted by trained clinical psychologists.

There has been considerable criticism of motivation research on basically two grounds. First, its heavy reliance on Freudian psychology and unconscious motivations has been criticized as more an exception rather than a rule in consumer motivations. It is argued that most consumer behavior is conscious rather than unconscious and most consumers are normal rather than abnormal in their behavior. Second, the interpretation of consumer information is regarded as highly subjective and lacking in consensus validation.

Motivation research responded to these criticisms by utilizing psychometrically developed and numerically measurable personality tests such as the MMPI. These personality tests also broadened the motivational determinants of consumer behavior from abnormal to normal motivations. Unfortunately, most research utilizing personality traits as the basis of consumer choice behavior has remained inconclusive and conflicting in its findings. For an excellent review of personality research in consumer behavior, the reader is urged to read Kassarjian (1971).

A second research tradition focused on the social determinants of consumer behavior. Popular concepts from sociology including conspicuous consumption and reference group influence resulted in a series of empirical studies in buyer behavior. While the results of conspicuous consumption research have been somewhat interesting in terms of products and brands that are visible symbols of social class, they have provided less conclusive results for other products and services.

Perhaps the most popular area of research has been the influence of reference groups on both product and brand choice behavior (Bourne 1957). For example, reference groups were found to determine whether a person will be a smoker or not, as well as what brand of cigarettes he will smoke. On the other hand, reference groups apparently do not determine whether a person will read magazines or buy furniture. However, reference groups were found to be highly influential on what type of magazines or furniture the person bought.

A related area of research that began in the 1950s was on the power of word of mouth communication. Katz and Lazarsfeld (1955) as well as Whyte (1955) had demonstrated that personal influence was more critical than mass media in social choices. This resulted in the examining of the role of advertising, personal influence, and opinion leadership in consumer behavior (Arndt 1967).

The third area of research in the 1950s focused on household decision making. The interest in this area was generated by the DuPont Corporation, which conducted surveys of grocery shopping including the shopping list the homemaker prepared before entering the supermarket. At the same time, Katona (1964) and his colleagues at the Institute for Social Research had developed consumer intentions as a leading indicator of spending behavior for the U.S. economy. This generated significant amounts of research on family buying behavior by home economists and marketing scholars (Sheth 1974b). Perhaps the best summary of this area of research tradition can be found in the four volumes edited by Lincoln Clark (1954, 1955, 1958) and Nelson Foote (1961).

Decade of the Sixties: The decade of the 1960s can be characterized as the sunrise of the buyer behavior school. A large number of scholars with very different academic backgrounds began to devote their time and energy to the area of consumer behavior. Out of their efforts, a number of new and innovative research traditions began to emerge in the 1960s.

Perhaps the most incisive and exciting research focused on brand loyalty among consumer grocery products. With the availability of panel diary data from the *Chicago Tribune* and M.R.C.A., a number of scholars began to analyze the purchase patterns of households over time. The early efforts by Ross Cunningham (1956) and George Brown (1952–53) attracted a number of management science experts to the field. This led to the development of brand loyalty models based on the Bernoulli, the Markovian, and other stochastic processes.

Alfred Kuehn (1962) led the way followed by others including Ronald Howard (1963), Ronald Frank (1962), and William Massy (1969) and his students at Stanford University. This research tradition reached its peak in the late 1960s and culminated in the publication of a major book by Massy, Montgomery, and Morrison (1970). Although the application of stochastic and econometric modeling to understand brand buying behavior still continues, it has not been as explosive since the late 1960s.

A second research tradition began to emerge in the early 1960s. This was founded on the use of experimental designs and laboratory-based experiments in a number of different areas of buyer behavior. For example, Robert Holloway (1967b) and his students at the University of Minnesota carried out a series of experiments on the application of Festinger's cognitive dissonance theory in brand choice behavior. At the same time, many advertising practitioners began to use laboratory methods to measure the physiological responses of consumers by such electromechanical apparatus as pupil dilation and galvanic skin pressure. Also, the DuPont Corporation developed a top market research department that conducted numerous field experiments on the effects of advertising media and exposure. Finally, it would be a serious error of omission not to recognize some of the best field experiments conducted by the United States Department of Agriculture on consumer preferences for oranges and apples.

A third stream of research began at Harvard University under the leadership of Raymond Bauer (1960), who proposed a theory of perceived risk in consumer behavior. The basic tenets underlying his theory were based on Simon's concepts of bounded rationality and satisficing. Bauer proposed that consumers do not maximize utilities as suggested by economists but instead minimize risks associated with making consumer choices. This simple but elegant theory became very popular in the same manner as Festinger's cognitive dissonance theory. A number of research studies and doctoral dissertations were carried out in order to test various components and perceived risk implications of Bauer's theory. A good summary of these research findings can be found in Cox (1967).

A fourth stream of research in buyer behavior focused on the development of comprehensive theories of consumer behavior. It was agreed that buyer behavior is too complex and highly dynamic to be fully explained by unidimensional and cross-sectional models. What is needed is a process-oriented theory that allows for learning over time because buyer behavior is repetitive, and consumers can easily generalize their experiences from one choice situation to another.

A number of marketing scholars proposed their own comprehensive theories of buyer behavior. These included Howard (1963a), Andreasen (1965), Nicosia (1966), and Engel, Kollat, and Blackwell (1968). The latter was more an attempt to provide a conceptual integrative framework for their first textbook in consumer behavior, although eventually it came to be recognized as a theory of consumer behavior. Even though there were some differences among these models of buyer behavior, they all have the same two basic characteristics: process orientation and feedback through learning and experiences.

Perhaps the most well-known comprehensive theory of buyer behavior was proposed by Howard and Sheth (1969). For the first time, Howard and Sheth utilized the metatheory criteria in buyer behavior and began to create a comprehensive theory based on several well-known concepts in psychology. These included learning theory, exploratory behavior, and symbolic representations underlying languages and concept formation. The fundamental axioms of the theory were as follows:

I. Consumers like to simplify complex choice situations by a process of learning over time. This results in a psychology of simplification consisting of extensive problem solving, limited problem solving, and, eventually, routinized response behavior.

2. Consumers like to complicate choice situations when the choices are highly routinized and non-challenging. This results in a psychology of complication consisting of novelty and curiosity behavior, as well as active search for new alternatives.

3. Compared to information, experience with products and brands is a more important determinant of future choice. Only when there is no prior experience is the consumer likely to rely on information.

4. Information from the physical product (significative information) is less filtered through perceptual mechanisms of exposure, attention, and retention than information from advertising and personal selling (symbolic information) sources. Also, information from social and neutral sources is perceptually filtered less than information from commercial sources.

5. Consumer satisfaction is psychological and is directly a function of the discrepancy between prior expectations and subsequent experiences. It will, therefore, vary over time for the same consumer as well as across consumers at a point in time. This makes it very difficult for the marketer to achieve universal consumer satisfaction in the marketplace.

6. A number of exogenous factors influence as well as control the process of simplication and complication. These include the consumer's personal characteristics, his/her social environment, as well as his/her scarce resources of money and time. Also, the process of simplification and complication is likely to be different for product categories that vary in their importance or involvement and perceived risks associated with wrong choices.

In our evaluation, the Howard-Sheth theory of buyer behavior became more popular than others for at least three reasons. First, as Zaltman et al. (1973) pointed out, it was more rigorously developed in terms of theory building criteria a la philosophy of science. Second, it attempted to provide construct validity and face validity by consistently incorporating prior research findings from marketing, psychology, and other behavioral sciences. Finally, and perhaps most importantly, the theory was tested in the real world in several large-scale research projects at Columbia University (Farley, Howard, and Ring 1974). Although the results were not conclusive, these empirical tests demonstrated that the theory was testable.

Decade of the Seventies: The decade of the 1970s can be characterized as the coming of age in the buyer behavior field. For the first time, the buyer behavior school began to emerge as a distinct discipline rather than one more school of marketing thought. A number of institutional events occurred in the 1970s that elevated the buyer behavior school to the status of a separate discipline.

The most dramatic was the formation of a separate organization called the Association for Consumer Research (ACR) in 1969. What began as an American Marketing Association (AMA) sponsored workshop on consumer behavior at Ohio State University under the leadership of James Engel turned into the start of a separate organization for scholars, practitioners, and policymakers interested in consumer behavior. According to Gardner (1971), ACR was organized to serve the following purposes:

1. To provide a forum for exchange of ideas among those interested in consumer behavior research in academic disciplines, in government at all levels from local through national, in private business, and in other sectors such as nonprofit organizations and foundations.

2. To stimulate research focusing on a better understanding of consumer behavior from a variety of perspectives.

3. To disseminate research findings and other contributions to the understanding of consumer behavior through professional seminars, conferences, and publications (p. i).

ACR continued to grow throughout the 1970s and today has become an alternative to the American Marketing Association for researchers interested in consumer behavior. Since 1970, ACR has provided a major avenue of publications through its annual conference proceedings, which are respected as scholarly papers.

Another institutional event that reflected the coming of age in buyer behavior was the start of a scholarly journal. The *Journal of Consumer Research* (JCR), organized in 1974, was intended to be an interdisciplinary journal and not just a marketing oriented journal. According to its first editor, JCR was created as a "medium for interdisciplinary exchange over an exceedingly broad range of topics, the common denominator of which is their relationship to the study of consumer behavior" (Frank 1974, p. v).

The decade of the 1970s generated several research trends, some of which reflected the continuation of the 1960s, and others reflected new thinking. For example, the testing of the comprehensive theories of buyer behavior, especially the Howard-Sheth theory, continued into the 1970s (Farley et al. 1974, Howard and Hulbert 1973, Howard 1977, 1988). Similarly, the applications of operations research techniques to buying behavior were also continued by scholars including Blattberg and Sen (1976). Also, the diffusion of innovations research tradition continued under the leadership of more mathematically oriented scholars such as Bass (1969) and Peterson and Mahajan (1978). In fact, it is quite accurate to state that research on personal influence, social class, household decision making, and perceived risk all continued in the decade of the 1970s. Most of this research was published in the *Journal of Consumer Research* and in Association for Consumer Research (ACR) proceedings.

At the same time, several new research streams began to emerge during the decade of the 1970s. The first research area focused on industrial or organizational buying behavior. The groundwork was already established with the publication of a major book by Robinson, Faris, and Wind (1967). Sheth (1973) published a comprehensive model of industrial buying behavior that attempted to integrate and reconcile existing knowledge. Others such as Webster and Wind (1972), Woodside, Sheth, and Bennett (1977), Bonoma and Zaltman (1978), and Johnston and Bonoma (1981) also were active in defining this area. This interest in understanding and empirically researching organizational buying behavior has continued even today.

This area of research has recently been characterized as "still at the conceptual stage" (Anderson, Chu, and Weitz 1987, p. 71). While a research tradition seems to be developing, most of the existing research falls into one of two categories. These categories are clearly not independent, but overlap one another. One category of research pertains to the organizational buying center. It focuses on organizational members who have significant involvement in the decision-making process for a particular purchase. As an example of work in this area, Jackson, Keith, and Burdick (1984) studied the relative influence of buying center members across product categories. They found that influence was generally relatively constant across different buyclasses but varied across product types and decision types. As another example, Krapfel (1985) developed and tested a model to explain the behavior of buying center boundary role persons who take on the additional role of advocate.

A second category of research pertains to organizational buying behavior. This broad category has a general focus on how organizations approach the buying process, without a specific focus on the buying center. As examples of work in this area, Puto, Patton, and King (1985) explored risk handling strategies in the industrial vendor selection process; and Anderson and Chambers (1985) proposed a model of the organizational buying process based on the assumption that "... purchasing process participants are motivated to engage in purchasing behavior by the expectation of both intrinsic and extrinsic rewards" (p. 9). Anderson, Chu, and Weitz (1987) conducted an empirical study of the buyclass theory proposed by Robinson, Faris, and Wind (1967). By querying salesforce managers, they found that:

> Much of what salespeople observe is found to correspond closely to the buyclass theory of organizational buyer behavior. Also the "problem newness" and "information needs" dimensions are found to be strongly related, as expected. However, "seriousness of consideration of alternatives" seems to be a separate dimension that does not operate entirely as predicted by the buyclass framework (p. 71).

Typical of other studies in organizational buying behavior is research by Leigh and Rethans (1984), who focus on a more limited area, applying cognitive script theory to the analysis of industrial purchasing behavior.

A second major area of research in buyer behavior focused on social and public services such as population control, education, health care, transportation, and nutrition (Sheth and Wright 1974). This was a direct result of the emerging interest in applying marketing practice and concepts to nonprofit organizations (Kotler 1975). To a large extent, this focus in buyer behavior toward socially desirable behaviors resulted in increased respect for scholars in marketing. Other disciplines began to realize that buyer behavior can be researched for the benefit of consumers as well as marketers. Consequently, a number of scholars from social psychology and sociology began to notice the field of buyer behavior as a relevant domain for the application of their research concepts and methods. The emphasis toward nonprofit services has now broadened to the services sector in general including the health care, financial, information, and entertainment industries (e.g., Gelb and Gilly 1979).

A third area of research in buyer behavior began to focus on cross-cultural issues. Although Dichter (1962) had tried to sensitize marketing practitioners to the importance of cross-cultural differences in international marketing, conceptual thinking and empirical research did not begin until the early 1970s. The interest was perhaps due to the increased global competition, especially from Japan and Korea, as well as the increasing volume of international trade between the advanced and the lesser developed nations. Despite attempts at developing comprehensive theories of cross-cultural buyer behavior (Sheth and Sethi 1977), cross-cultural buyer behavior was in its infancy in the 1970s and is likely to intensify and grow in the eighties and the nineties.

A fourth area of research to emerge in the 1970s was family buying behavior, including joint decision-making behavior between husbands and wives. Sheth (1974b) generated a comprehensive theory of family buying behavior that was process oriented and somewhat similar to his theory of industrial buying behavior. However, Davis and Rigaux (1974) triggered considerable interest in this area with their insightful research. In particular, the joint decision-making processes and conflict-resolution strategies among family members became an interesting and important area of understanding. This research on family buying behavior also continues to flourish in the 1980s.

The fifth and perhaps the strongest research stream emerged in the area of attitude–behavior relationship and attitude formation and structure. Howard and Sheth (1969) generated a strong theoretical base for suggesting that prior attitudes toward brands become good predictors of future behavior *if there are no inhibitors*. However, Martin Fishbein (1963, 1967; Fishbein and Ajzen 1975) and his theory of behavioral intentions generated strong enthusiasm in consumer behavior. The Fishbein model was simple; but elegant, with precise operational measures for its variables. The basic thesis of the model was that a person's intention to perform a specific behavioral act (BI) is a function of two factors: the person's personal beliefs about the consequences arising from performing that act and/or the person's beliefs about his/her reference group's norms whether he/she should or should not perform that act. In short, personal beliefs or normative beliefs and their respective saliencies determine individual actions. The Fishbein model generated numerous research studies in consumer behavior, some of which even attempted to extend or modify the Fishbein model. At the same time, several other attitude models in social psychology began to be applied in consumer behavior (Wilkie and Pessemier 1973, Sheth 1974a).

A related area that emerged as a separate stream of research is called information processing. How consumers utilize information, assimilate it, and make evaluative judgments toward products and brands became fascinating to several scholars in marketing (Jacoby, Speller, and Kohn 1974, Wright 1973, Bettman 1979). This resulted in at least three distinct controversies. First, can there be an information overload? In other words, are consumers worse off with too much information when making choice judgments? The second area of controversy related to the issue of whether consumers use compensatory versus non-compensatory approaches to making judgments. Several alternative models such as compensatory, disjunctive, conjunctive, and lexicographic models of information processing were competing against one another. Finally, a third area of controversy was related to the methodology of information collection. More specifically, whether to use protocols (verbal descriptions) or to use scaled statements for gathering data became a hot topic of interest and debate.

Although attitude research overwhelmed other research streams in the 1970s, it also generated strong negative reactions. Several scholars began to object to the narrow focus and cognitive base underlying the multi-attribute models (Sheth 1979b, Hirschman 1980, Zielinski and Robertson 1982, Holbrook and Hirschman 1982). It was argued that a number of buyer behavior phenomena may be experiential, emotional, and otherwise noncognitive in nature. Furthermore, the discipline of buyer behavior had many other interesting areas of research (novelty seeking, crowd behavior, deviancy, etc.) that were being neglected by this exclusive focus on cognitive models.

Decade of the Eighties: The decade of the 1980s can be characterized as the new dawn of consumer behavior. The backlash against information processing and multi-attribute models has generated interesting and highly interactive research interests. These include rituals and symbolism (Rook and Levy 1983, Rook 1985), experiential and fantasy behavior (Holbrook and Hirschman 1982), and the impact of religion in consumer behavior (Hirschman 1983). This has also generated a backlash against the quantitative measurements and a preference for more qualitative research traditions prevalent during the era of motivation research. Finally, there is a strong emerging interest in cross-cultural and subcultural issues in consumer behavior (McCracken 1986). Some even argue that the buyer behavior school of marketing is coming back home after running away from the discipline of marketing.

The diversity of research within this school of thought is both a blessing and a problem. However, more and more, this school of thought is moving toward developing and extending already specified constructs and concepts rather than generating isolated findings. To list but a few examples of recent research, Bloch, Sherrell, and Ridgway (1986) have offered an extended framework for consumer search behavior; Havlena and Holbrook (1986) have explored two competing typologies of emotion; and Pessemier and Handelsman (1984) have empirically examined temporal variety in consumer behavior. Further, Laurent and Kapferer (1985) have extended the thinking in the area of consumer involvement; Hauser (1986) has looked at selecting or eliminating choice alternatives; and Westbrook (1987) has explored dimensions of product/consumption-based affective responses and post-purchase behavior.

Of course, the richness of this school of thought, by its very nature, encourages new ideas. As one example, Alba and Hutchinson (1987) have recently examined consumer expertise. They have argued that consumer expertise differs from product-related expertise and have identified five dimensions of expertise (cognitive effort, cognitive structure, analysis, elaboration, and memory), exploring the interrelationships among these dimensions. They also have offered an extensive appendix that discusses the issues involved in this new approach and have listed over four hundred fifty bibliographic references to guide others interested in this area.

Another new research area in buyer behavior is that of semiotics. As described by Zakia and Nadin (1987, p. 5) semiotics is "… a discipline that provides a structure for studying and analyzing how signs function within a particular environment." As an example of research in semiotics, Mick (1986) explored how consumers comprehend symbolism in the marketplace. Further, a special conference on semiotics, co-sponsored by Northwestern University (Kellogg Graduate School of Management) and Indiana University (Research Center for Language and Semiotic Studies), was held at Northwestern University in the summer of 1986.

Numerous other new areas of research have also appeared. As examples, Rook (1985) has expanded on the ritual construct as a vehicle for interpreting consumer behavior, presenting the results of two studies that investigate the personal grooming rituals of young adults; and Gardner (1985) has presented a conceptual framework pertaining to consumer mood states, depicting the mediating role of mood states and their potential importance for consumer behavior. Biehal and Chakravarti (1986) have examined eight issues relevant to consumers' use of memory and external information in making brand choices. Their study forms the basis for a set of propositions about memory processes in consumer behavior.

4.1.4   Evaluation of the Buyer Behavior School

It is difficult to evaluate the buyer behavior school for several reasons. First, there is enormous diversity of research within the buyer behavior school, which makes it difficult to evaluate without averaging and suggesting exceptions to the average. Second, the buyer behavior school has produced the largest amount of research. The sheer volume of research and concepts in this school makes the job more difficult. Finally, the buyer behavior school has been more interdisciplinary than most other schools of marketing. There are several research traditions embedded in the discipline ranging from highly qualitative to highly quantitative methods. We will provide our evaluation of this school, but we urge the reader to keep in mind the difficulties associated with the evaluative task.

STRUCTURE: **Are the concepts properly defined and integrated to form a strong nomological network?**

The buyer behavior school has several levels of integration. At the one extreme, it consists of straight applications and replication of specific concepts, hypotheses, and research techniques of the behavioral and mathematical sciences. These include personality research, attitude research, and stochastic processes. In the middle are several midrange theories such as perceived risk, information processing, and reference group influences. Finally, at the other extreme are the comprehensive theories of buyer behavior.

The buyer behavior school has generated several specific constructs such as brand loyalty, attitudes, involvement, perceived risk, joint decision making, and buying centers. These are all well-defined and properly integrated as needed.

Our score on structure = 8.

SPECIFICATION: Are the relationships specified in a manner to delimit hypotheses or are they highly contingent?

The buyer behavior school scores well in this regard. Even the most comprehensive theories of buyer behavior have provided specific hypotheses that delimit their scope. This is, of course, more true of midrange theories such as the perceived risk theory. Finally, many of the direct applications of behavioral sciences concepts have been based on well-formulated hypotheses. For example, in personality research, certain personality types or traits are hypothesized to produce certain types of buying behavior.

Our score on specifications = 8.

TESTABILITY: Are the operational definitions provided to ensure testability and intersubjective consensus?

On this criterion, the buyer behavior school gets mixed reviews. The operational definitions are excellent when researchers have borrowed standardized and well-tested instruments from other disciplines. These include personality tests and attitude models. Similarly, some of the midrange theories have consciously attempted to evolve toward standardized definitions based on empirical research. These include perceived risk and attitude-intention research. However, there are problems with testability in areas such as motivation research, information processing, involvement, and many of the constructs included in the grand theories of buyer behavior. This is especially true in the areas of organizational, family, and cross-cultural buyer behavior.

Our score on testability = 6.

EMPIRICAL SUPPORT: What is the degree of confirmation in terms of empirical support?

The buyer behavior school has generated the largest amount of empirical research in marketing. There are literally thousands of empirical research studies by both academics and professionals. However, unlike the managerial school of marketing, this school's empirical support has more conflicting results than confirmatory results. In other words, despite the vast amount of research, the degree of confirmation of various research streams is still inconclusive and subject to further testing.

Our score on empirical support = 8.

RICHNESS: How comprehensive and generalizable is the theory?

In this regard, the buyer behavior school scores high. Not only has this school produced comprehensive theories of buyer behavior, but even the midrange theories are regarded as highly generalizable. Furthermore, the buyer behavior school has generated concepts that are usually relevant to both public policymakers and marketing practitioners. Similarly, these concepts are generalizable to both products and services as well as to both consumer and organizational buyer behavior.

Our score on richness = 9.

SIMPLICITY: How easy is it to communicate and implement the theory?

The buyer behavior school gets mixed reviews on this criterion. On the one hand, theories such as perceived risk and attitude models are highly simple to communicate and implement. On the other hand, the process-oriented comprehensive theories such as the Howard-Sheth theory are very complex and difficult to implement in practice. At the same time, consumer behavior is intuitively very appealing since all of us are also consumers and can relate to the concepts based on our own personal experiences.

Our score on simplicity = 8.

Table 4.1 summarizes our evaluation of the buyer behavior school of marketing. It is promising to note that it scores well on all the criteria at least when compared to other schools of thought.

Table 4.1 Evaluation of the Buyer Behavior School*

Criterion	Rationale	Score
Structure	Several specific constructs that are well defined and properly integrated	8
Specification	Theories provide specific hypotheses that delimit their scope	8
Testability	Problems with several midrange theories	6
Empirical support	Much empirical research, but often conflicting results	8
Richness	Produced comprehensive theories and highly generalizable midrange theories	9
Simplicity	Mixed reviews	8
	TOTAL	47

* Scores range from 1 (poor) to 10 (excellent).

4.2 The Activist School of Thought

The activist school of marketing thought represents both empirical research and conceptual thinking related to the issues of consumer welfare and consumer satisfaction. More specifically, it focuses on the imbalance of power between buyers and sellers and on the malpractices of marketing by individual firms in the marketplace.

The activist school is similar to both the buyer behavior school and the macromarketing school in that they all take the perspective of the consumer in the marketplace rather than the marketer. In that respect, they are in sharp contrast to the commodity, functional, and regional schools of thought.

At the same time, the activist school differs from the macrormarketing school by focusing on individual consumers and specific industries or companies rather than taking a more macro or institutional perspective. It also differs from the buyer behavior school by taking a more normative and pro-consumer perspective.

The activist school emerged only after several years of efforts by consumer advocates to remedy the imbalance of power. In an excellent summary of the history of the consumer movement, Beem (1973) defines it as follows:

> The expression, the *Consumer Movement*, may be used provisionally in either of two ways. In its more inclusive sense, the term refers historically to the efforts of individuals and groups acting more or less in concert, to solve consumer problems. In this sense, the Consumer Movement refers to activities from the earliest time to the present, and includes the organized activities of consumers themselves, and of other groups and individuals such as teachers, writers, private business and government activities that have worked in the consumer interest. In a second sense, the Consumer Movement refers more particularly to the great burst of activities on behalf of consumers that began in the 1930s and has continued at an accelerated pace (p. 13).

Beem identifies several institutions and individuals responsible in creating and sustaining the consumer movement:

1. Consumers' cooperatives, which began in the late eighteen hundreds and continued to flourish until the World War II.
2. Interested organizations such as the American Home Economics Association and pressure groups such as women's clubs, labor unions, and educational institutions.
3. Business agencies such as the Better Business Bureau, the American Standards Association, and many trade associations including the American Medical Association and the American Dental Association.

4. Government agencies such as the Food and Drug Administration, the Federal Trade Commission, and the Department of Agriculture. In addition, a number of other federal and state regulatory agencies invited consumer representatives to join their advisory boards.

5. Publication of books that depicted consumers as guinea pigs had a strong impact on arousing public attention toward the problems inherent in marketing practices. These include Upton Sinclair's best seller *The Jungle* (1906); *Your Money's Worth,* by Chase and Schlink (1927); 100,000,000 *Guinea Pigs,* by Kallet and Schlink (1933); *Skin Deep,* by Phillips (1934); *Eat, Drink and Be Wary,* by Schlink (1935); *Counterfeit,* by Kallet (1935); *Partners in Plunder,* by Mathews and Shallcross (1935); and *American Chamber of Horrors,* by Lamb (1936).

However, the rapid rise of the movement in recent years is more directly attributed to consumers and politicians. For example, John Kenneth Galbraith (1958), Vance Packard (1960), and Rachel Carson (1962) pointed out problems of affluent societies. Similarly, President Kennedy in 1963 attempted to establish the rights of consumers to be informed, to choose, to have safe products, and to be heard (Executive Office of the President, 1963). Also, Senator Warren Magnuson not only introduced a number of bills in Congress, but wrote about the dark side of the marketplace (Magnuson and Carper 1968). But undoubtedly the most influential consumer advocate was Ralph Nader.

> It may be said that one man, Ralph Nader, was really responsible for setting off the new Consumer Movement in 1966 with the publication of his study of the safety of automobiles. His concept of the consumer advocate, of a man well trained in the law, devoting his time and great energies to the public interest was indeed unique. Initially, it inspired cynical disbelief, especially in the corporate boardrooms (what's Nader's angle?) which gave way in time to grudging admiration, if not acceptance (he seems for real!). Indeed, amongst the teenage population and college crowd, Nader took on the dimension of a folk hero, and his panache and influence was strong and persistent and is to this day. (Kelly 1973, p. 49)

As we pointed out in Chapter 1, it is important to recognize that very few marketing practitioners or scholars were interested in this area until the late 1960s, when the consumerism movement became nationally important. Indeed, the early efforts by the marketing practitioners to respond to this movement resulted in the setting up of "hot lines" in their public relations departments. Similarly, only some scholars began to focus on consumerism and develop a stream of research and conceptual thinking.

4.2.1 Empirical Research

The empirical research in marketing regarding consumerism issues can be divided into several distinct areas. Perhaps the largest number of research studies has focused on the malpractices of marketing, especially related to product safety and consumer information. Product safety research has been largely carried out by various federal regulatory agencies including the FDA, FTC, and USDA. Academic researchers have focused on such issues as deceptive advertising and product-labeling information (Gardner 1976, Russo 1976, Jacoby and Small 1975, Preston 1976, Armstrong, Kendall, and Russ 1975, Armstrong, Gurol, and Russ 1979, Ford and Calfee 1986).

A second area of empirical research has focused on disadvantaged consumers including the blacks, the Hispanics, the disabled, the poor, and other minority consumers. The classic studies by sociologist David Caplovitz (1963) on the ghetto consumer and his findings that the poor pay more for the same products generated strong interest among several marketing scholars (Andreasen 1975, Ashby 1973, Kassarjian 1969, Bauer and Cunningham 1970, Bullock 1961).

A third area of empirical research has focused on consumer satisfaction and dissatisfaction. Andreasen (1977) provides a rationale for the study of consumer satisfaction as follows:

> Business and nonprofit organizations need measures of how well products and services are meeting client needs and wants so that these organizations can enhance their own and their client's well-being. The government also needs such measures to determine whether the marketplace is functioning well or whether further intervention in the consumer's interest is needed. The

extent to which consumer needs and wants are met has come to be called consumer satisfaction/dissatisfaction (p. 11).

Several conferences were organized in the area of consumer satisfaction/dissatisfaction (Hunt 1977, Day 1977, Hunt and Day 1979, Day and Hunt 1983). Furthermore, many research papers have been published in the Association for Consumer Research (ACR) proceedings. In this area of research, the focus has been largely on empirical studies that measure complaint behavior especially among disadvantaged consumers, such as senior citizens and disabled consumers. At the same time, a considerable number of papers have grappled with the issue of defining and operationalizing measures of consumer satisfaction/dissatisfaction. For example, Cadotte, Woodruff, and Jenkins (1987) compared disconfirmation models of customer satisfaction using causal modeling.

4.2.2 Conceptual Thinking

Only a handful of marketing scholars have attempted to conceptualize the activist school of thought including the role of consumerism in marketing practice. Peter Drucker (1969) defines consumerism as the shame of marketing:

> Consumerism means that the consumer looks upon the manufacturer as somebody who is interested, but who really doesn't know what the consumer's realities are. He regards the manufacturer as somebody who has not made the effort to find out, and who expects the consumer to be able to make distinctions which the consumer is neither able nor willing to make (p. 60).

Drucker, therefore, conceptualizes the activist approach as looking at marketing practice from the buyer's viewpoint rather than from the seller's viewpoint. He shows how advertising, product quality, and other marketing mix elements have very different perceptions in the minds of consumers:

> It is our job to make things simple so that they fit the reality of the consumer, not the ego of our engineers. I've long ago learned that when most manufacturers say "quality," they use the engineers' definition, which is "something that's very hard to make and costs a lot of money." That's not quality, that's incompetence. We have not realized that the very abundance, the very multiplicity of choices creates very real problems of information and understanding for the consumer. We have not looked at our business from his, the consumer's, point of view (p. 61).

Bauer and Greyser (1967) provide a perceptual bias framework for the lack of dialog between business executives and government advocates:

> Why do business and government spokesmen talk past each other in discussing ostensibly the same marketplace? We think it is because each has a basically different model of the consumer world in which marketing operates. This misunderstanding grows from different perceptions about a number of key words (p. 2).

Bauer and Greyser then summarize these differences as follows:

Two Different Models of the Consumer World

Key Words	Critic's View	Businessman's View
Competition	Price competition	Product differentiation
Product	Primary function only	Differentiation through secondary function
Consumer needs	Correspond pointfor-point to primary functions	Any customer desire on which the product can be differentiated
Rationality	Efficient matching of product to customer needs	Any customer decision that serves the customer's own perceived self-interest

(Continued)

Key Words	Critic's View	Businessman's View
Information	Any data that facilitate the fit of a product's proper function with the customer's needs	Any data that will (truthfully) put forth the attractiveness of the product in the eyes of the customer

Adapted from Bauer and Greyser (1967).

Similar to Peter Drucker, Bauer and Greyser also suggest that the best way to reconcile these perceptual differences is for both parties to take the consumer's viewpoint:

> What we propose as a worthwhile endeavor is an independent assessment of the consumer's view of the marketing process, focusing on information needs from his point of view. Thus, rather than businessmen lamenting the critic's proposals for product-rating systems and the critics bemoaning what seems to be obvious abuses of marketing tools, both sides ought to move toward proposing an information system for the consumer that takes into account *his* needs and *his* information-handling capacities while still adhering to the realities of the marketing process (p. 188).

The most thought-provoking and cogent thinking in this area is provided by Kotler (1972b). Kotler believes that the practice of the marketing concept with its customer orientation is necessary to mesh the actions of business with the interests of consumers:

> Consumerism has come as a shock to many businessmen because deep in their hearts they believe that they have been serving the consumer extraordinarily well. Do businessmen deserve the treatment that they are getting at the hands of consumerists?

> It is possible that the business sector has deluded itself into thinking that it has been serving the consumer well. Although the marketing concept is the professed philosophy of a majority of U.S. companies, perhaps it is more honored in the breach than in the observance. Although top management professes the concept, the line executives, who are rewarded for ringing up sales, may not practice it faithfully (p. 55).

Kotler suggests that customer satisfaction is not sufficient to create a win-win situation between consumers and producers for two reasons. First, it is very difficult to define objectively customer satisfaction. Second, what is desired by consumers may not be good for them. Therefore, the marketer may create a happy customer in the short run but in the long run, both the consumer and society at large may suffer in satisfying the customer. He cites several examples such as cigarette smoking and non-nutritious foods to prove his point. He suggests that it is the responsibility of marketing to generate new products that provide *both* immediate customer satisfaction *and* protect the long-term welfare of the consumers.

Kotler provides a paradigm to classify all current product offerings based on the two dimensions of immediate satisfaction and long-term consumer welfare:

Kotler's Paradigm of Product Categories

		Immediate Satisfaction	
		Low	High
Long run consumer welfare	High	Salutary products	Desirable products
	Low	Deficient products	Pleasing products

> ... *desirable products* are those which combine high immediate satisfaction and high long-run benefit, such as tasty, nutritious breakfast foods. *Pleasing products* are those which give high immediate satisfaction but which may hurt consumer interests in the long run, such as cigarettes. *Salutary products* are those which have low appeal but which are also highly beneficial to the consumer in the long run, such as low phosphate detergents. Finally, *deficient products* are those which have neither immediate appeal nor salutary qualities, such as a bad tasting patent medicine.
>
> The manufacturer might as well forget about deficient products because too much work would be required to build in pleasing and salutary qualities. On the other hand, the manufacturer should invest his greatest effort in developing desirable products—e.g., new foods, textiles, appliances, and building materials—which combine intrinsic appeal and long-run beneficiality ... The challenge posed by pleasing products is that they sell extremely well, but they ultimately hurt the consumer's interests. The product opportunity is therefore to formulate some alteration of the product that adds salutary qualities without diminishing any or too many of the pleasing qualities. Salutary products, such as nonflammable draperies and many health foods, are considered "good for the customer" but somehow lack pleasing qualities. The challenge to the marketer is to incorporate satisfying qualities in the product without sacrificing the salutary qualities (pp. 56–57).

Kotler's fourfold classification of products based on the two criteria of long-run consumer welfare and immediate customer satisfaction has considerable merit. It is possible to suggest that long-run consumer welfare measures marketing effectiveness, whereas immediate customer satisfaction measures marketing efficiency. Thus, an industry with many desirable products will be both effective and efficient and, in the process, balance the interests of the company and the public. On the other hand, an industry full of pleasing products will be very efficient or profitable, but may not be effective from society's viewpoint; therefore, it may require social regulation. Finally, an industry full of salutary products may be very effective, but not efficient or profitable; therefore, it may require government incentives or public sector ownership.

In recent years, the activist school has focused its attention on the specific subject of marketing ethics. Although sporadic studies of unethical marketing practices by marketing scholars had appeared for many years, in the 1980s a concerted effort has been made to evaluate conceptually the nature and role of marketing ethics. A major development in this regard was the publication of *Marketing Ethics: Guidelines for Managers*, edited by Gene Laczniak and Patrick Murphy (1985). Chapters in this volume focused on ethical issues in advertising, personal selling, marketing research, pricing, and multinational marketing.

Hunt and Chonko (1984), in a survey of nearly 4300 marketing practitioners, found that the marketing profession is definitely *not* considered Machiavellian. Their study suggests that, while there are individuals who are Machiavellian in their orientation toward marketing activities, marketing people are no more Machiavellian than others in society at large. Also, Hunt, Chonko, and Wilcox (1984) have empirically examined the ethical problems faced by marketing researchers.

Laczniak (1983) has suggested a framework for analyzing marketing ethics and reviewed the "ethical maxims" of the golden rule, the utilitarian principle, Kant's categorical imperative, the professional ethic, and the TV test. However, after evaluating these maxims, he concluded (p. 8):

> While not without value, these limited ethical frameworks have hampered the ethical analysis of marketing managers. They have also caused marketing educators some discomfort when discussing ethical issues in the classroom. In short, many marketing educators have shied away from lecturing on the topics of marketing ethics because of the perception that existing frameworks for analyzing marketing ethics are simplistic and lack theoretical rigor. The net result is that the seeming absence of theoretical frameworks for ethical decision-making has retarded the teaching, practice, and research of marketing ethics.

Ferrell and Gresham (1985) offered a contingency framework with which to evaluate ethical decision making in a marketing organization:

> The proposed framework for examining ethical/unethical decision making is multidimensional, process oriented, and contingent in nature. The variables in the model can be categorized into

individuals and organizational contingencies. The individual variables consist of personal background and socialization characteristics, such as educational and business experiences. The organizational characteristics consist of the effects of organizations external to the employing organization (customers, other firms) and intraorganizational influences (e.g., peers and supervisors). These variables are interdependent as well as ultimately affecting, either directly or indirectly, the dependent variable—ethical/unethical marketing behavior (p. 88).

Robin and Reidenbach (1987) have recently considered the challenge of integrating ethics and social responsibility concerns into the strategic marketing process:

> Without the integration of concerns about ethics and social responsibility at the very beginning of the marketing planning process, as well as throughout the process, the organizational culture may not provide the checks and balances needed to develop ethical and socially responsible marketing programs. Corporate values of profit and efficiency tend to dominate most organizational cultures, particularly in the absence of the overt addition of counterbalancing ethical and socially responsible values. This situation arises because the organization reinforces its members at all levels on the basis of achieving profitability or efficiency objectives. Though profit and efficiency must remain central values within the culture, they must be balanced by other values that help define the limits of activities designed to achieve those objectives and by values describing other important ethical and socially responsible behaviors (p. 52).

Several researchers have recently explored the impact of marketing and advertising on consumers, attempting to offer guidelines for managers and policymakers. For instance, Aaker and Bruzzone (1985) have attempted to identify product categories and advertising copy characteristics that result in higher or lower levels of irritation with advertising. Pollay (1986) went outside the marketing literature to examine the thoughts and theories about advertising proposed by scholars in the humanities and social sciences. He concluded that:

> In brief, they view advertising as intrusive and environmental and its effects as inescapable and profound. They see it as reinforcing materialism, cynicism, irrationality, selfishness, anxiety, social competitiveness, sexual preoccupation, powerlessness, and/or a loss of self-respect (p. 18).

Gaski and Etzel (1986), using the Market Facts mail panel, examined consumer sentiment toward marketing, finding it to be slightly unfavorable. They suggest that consumer sentiment toward marketing should be measured on a regular basis. Finally, Garrett (1987) has studied consumer boycotts, pointing out that boycotting in the 1960s was an early signal of the emergence of the consumerism movement. Based on a study of thirty consumer boycotts, as well as an extensive literature review, he proposed a theory of boycott effectiveness positing three determinants of such effectiveness: economic pressure, image pressure, and policy commitment.

In our review of the activist school, several interesting trends are apparent. First, even though consumer activists not affiliated with the marketing discipline launched the activist perspective, in recent years marketing scholars have taken the lead in the conceptual development of this school. Second, a greater sense of realism has emerged in the activist school. While early writings tended to conclude that unethical marketing practices were perpetrated by greedy and insensitive marketing practitioners, more recent writings have suggested that a complex set of variables may lead even highly responsible and honest individuals to commit ethically questionable acts. Finally, the activist school has moved beyond a simple criticism of improper behavior and has now begun to consider how ethical behavior can be encouraged in an organizational structure through the use of ethical training, guidelines, managerial example, and incentives.

4.2.3   Evaluation of the Activist School

STRUCTURE: **Are the concepts properly defined and integrated to form a strong nomological network?**

Although the activist school was originally very weak on this criterion, progress has been made in recent years to focus attention on the concepts of ethics and social responsibility. Further, some scholars have drawn from the writings in philosophy to introduce to marketing such basic ethical concepts as deontology, utilitarianism, proportionality, social justice, and so on. As a result, the marketing discipline now has a much clearer notion of the parameters that philosophers have utilized to define ethical behavior. However, we still have not developed a conclusive and precise definition of *marketing* ethics. Nonetheless, all signs suggest that this definitional problem may be resolved within the near future.

Perhaps of even more concern is the still unresolved debate regarding marketing's social responsibility. What *exactly* is marketing's social responsibility? And, perhaps more importantly, *who* should answer this thorny question? Almost certainly a precise definition of ethical marketing behavior will be offered before marketing's social responsibility is delineated.

Our score on structure = .5.

SPECIFICATION: Are the relationships specified in a manner to delimit hypotheses or are they highly contingent?

On the positive side, much progress has been made in identifying the variables that may influence a marketer's ethical decision making, such as personal beliefs, organizational pressures, reward systems, and so on.

However, on the negative side, these influencing variables have been combined into contingency frameworks, such as the framework by Ferrell and Gresham (1985). As a result, the relationships among the variables that influence ethical decision making have not been clearly specified. Once again, given the rather dramatic progress achieved in recent years, this major deficiency may be remedied soon.

Our score on specification = 5.

TESTABILITY: Are the operational definitions provided to ensure testability and intersubjective consensus?

Not surprisingly, the activist school encounters critical problems on this criterion. Foremost among these problems is the highly subjective nature of defining ethical behavior. Even with philosophical principles such as the golden rule and utilitarianism as benchmarks, outside evaluators are likely to vary widely in their judgments concerning the ethics of a specific marketing practice. For example, in the highly publicized case in which Nestle was accused of marketing infant formula improperly in Third World countries (Garrett 1986, Post 1985), opinion was sharply divided regarded the ethics of the company's marketing program. Thus, we are still left with the formidable task of determining what exactly is the demarcation line between ethical and unethical behavior in marketing.

Our score on testability = 4.

EMPIRICAL SUPPORT: What is the degree of confirmation in terms of empirical support?

Numerous case studies have been written by marketing professors that chronicle companies' ethical dilemmas. Also, many news reports in the popular press have detailed, and sometimes sensationalized, the supposedly unethical marketing behavior of corporations. In addition, some studies have evaluated how practitioners of marketing would respond to hypothetical situations that involve ethical judgments. Therefore, a substantial body of empirical data confirms that many marketing practices raise ethical issues. However, a glaring vacuum in the empirical data base is the lack of confirmatory research to support the recent theories of ethical decision making suggested by Laczniak (1983), Robin and Reidenbach (1987), and Hunt and Vitell (1986).

Our score on empirical support = 7.

RICHNESS: How comprehensive and generalizable is the theory?

The activist school suffers on the richness criterion because consumer activists have traditionally focused only on preventing unethical marketing practices. They have been unconcerned with the marketing manager's need to realize certain levels of economic effectiveness and efficiency from his/her marketing program. For this reason, the activist school, at least as portrayed by consumer activists, addresses only a minor portion of the concerns that confront marketing managers.

Conversely, the activist school, as envisioned by marketing scholars in the 1980s, has explicitly accepted the fact that marketing managers are constrained by their corporations' needs to realize economic profits. The next step, which has not yet been accomplished, requires these scholars to develop theories of marketing decision making that *simultaneously* satisfy both ethical criteria and economic criteria. If that can be achieved, then the activist school will be immeasurably richer.

Our score on richness = 5.

SIMPLICITY: **How easy is it to communicate and implement the theory?**

Because judgments regarding the ethics of any particular action must be related to circumstances surrounding the action, ethical decision making is very complex. Indeed, in many case examples of supposedly unethical marketing behavior, the allegedly guilty marketing practitioners have quite sincerely stated that they honestly did not realize that their actions could possibly create ethical problems. The use of marketing codes of ethics and increased ethical training has helped to make ethical decision making easier for practitioners. However, these general guidelines will be of only limited assistance when practitioners are confronted with situations with specific circumstances.

Our score on simplicity = 6.

Table 4.2 summarizes our evaluation of the activist school of marketing thought. It suffers weaknesses on all the criteria, especially testability, but is the strongest in terms of empirical support.

Table 4.2 Evaluation of the Activist School*

Criterion	Rationale	Score
Structure	Unresolved debate as to marketing's social responsibility	5
Specification	Many contingency frameworks	5
Testability	Highly subjective nature of defining ethical behavior	4
Empirical support	Lack of confirmatory research in support of theories of ethical decision making	7
Richness	Need for theories that simultaneously satisfy both ethical and economic criteria	5
Simplicity	Limited usefulness to practitioners	6
	TOTAL	32

* Scores range from 1 (poor) to 10 (excellent).

4.3   The Macromarketing School of Thought

The macromarketing school of marketing refers to the role and impact of marketing activities and institutions on society and vice versa. During the early 1960s there was a growing concern about the role of business institutions in society. Public opinion, which considered business as a viable and necessary institution in a society founded on the free enterprise system, had begun to doubt its intentions and activities. Phrases such as price fixing, industrial-military complex, and monopoly powers were gaining increasing attention in the 1960s. As the society began to critically examine business activities soon after the incidents of thalidomide and defective automobiles, business schools began to encourage seminars on business ethics and stakeholder analysis. Macromarketing emerged as a school of marketing directly as a consequence of the growing interest in the role of business in society.

With the exception of the managerial school of marketing, little consideration was given to the environment of marketing by other schools of marketing thought. Although the managerial school of marketing recognized the presence of exogenous variables, it treated them as uncontrollable factors within which marketing functions and practices must operate. Conversely, the macromarketing school began to analyze and understand societal needs and concerns and their impact on marketing as a social institution.

Although understanding the role of marketing in society began in the 1960s, it was not uncommon to find statements to that effect in earlier writings. For example, Vaile, Grether, and Cox expressed this sentiment as early as 1952:

> The authors of this book on marketing came to the subject from different fields of interest. We have a common meeting ground, however, in our conviction that students can best be introduced to marketing by a textbook whose primary point of view is the transcendent importance of this social institution as a vast and complex function of our free enterprise economy. We believe that students must be given a clear understanding of why marketing exists as well as how it is carved out in the American economy's dynamic mixture of public and private enterprise, and that they must be able to come to some judgment as to how well it discharges both its social and economic tasks (p. v).

In some sense, marketing practice has been subjected to social scrutiny even before the industrial age (Steiner 1976). In fact, even today, marketing's image among the average public is that it is a selling activity that entails numerous malpractices of marketing such as deceptive advertising, bait and switch tactics, and pushy salespeople.

However, what is unique about the macromarketing school is the serious and scientific attempts at understanding the role of marketing in society and providing a framework with which to explain the negative perceptions among the average ·public. In particular, we credit two individuals for their early and pioneering work in this area. They are Robert Holloway at the University of Minnesota and George Fisk at Syracuse University.

Holloway visualized marketing as an activity of society. Consequently, marketing both was influenced by and influenced its society. Together with his colleague Robert Hancock, Holloway conceptualized a "rough schema" to depict "the environment of marketing" (Holloway and Hancock 1964, p. 1). The first statement of this "rough schema" was a collection of readings organized around the broad exogenous environments of sociological, political, economic, legal, ethical, competitive, and technological forces. Further revisions of this popular readings book eventually allocated one fifth of their space to articles raising questions about the performance of marketing in society (Holloway and Hancock 1974).

George Fisk, on the other hand, used a general systems perspective to understand the role of marketing in society. Fisk was heavily influenced by the pioneer thinking of Wroe Alderson and Reavis Cox. His first major book was explicitly based on a systems perspective in which he attempted to describe the interrelationships between "the economics of equalization, the strategy and mechanisms of marketing management, and the social consequences of marketing activity" (Fisk 1967, p. xvii). Fisk makes a distinction between microsystems and macrosystems: "Microsystem behavior consists of directly observable goal-motivated activities of individuals, groups, and organizations, whereas macrosystem behavior consists of statistical aggregations of microsystem behavior" (Fisk 1967, p. 77). In particular, Fisk focused on the social performance of marketing and continued to shape this school of thought in his capacity as the first editor of the *Journal of Macromarketing*.

The macromarketing school became dormant soon after the initial writings by Holloway and Fisk. Holloway became more interested in consumerism and the role of business in society, while Fisk shifted his interests to international marketing. At the same time, many other scholars interested in the area got carried away with the more visible and immediate areas of consumerism and malpractices of marketing for which a great deal of impetus came from the Federal Trade Commission (FTC) and other governmental agencies.

Even during this dormant time period, some work appeared, notably by Reed Moyer (1972), which represented a bridge between the broader issues of macromarketing and the more focused issues of the activist school of thought. Moyer (1972) focused on the larger societal issues and on evaluation of marketing performance from his more macro perspective. Moyer suggested that macromarketing issues should be studied from a societal viewpoint unlike the micromarketing issues. As such, macromarketing refers to the *aggregate* performance of marketing as an element of the entire economic system. Therefore, its performance can be judged, at least at the aggregate level, comparable to the performance of other economic systems such as income distribution (taxation), welfare, and productivity. Furthermore, marketing should be held accountable like all other economic systems for achieving certain social objectives.

The macromarketing school of marketing got a new life when the University of Colorado organized the first macromarketing seminar in 1977 under the leadership of Charles Slater. With his vast experience in applying marketing principles to economic problems of the lesser developed countries, Slater was acutely aware of the interaction between marketing and society. His goal in organizing the annual conference at the University of Colorado was to encourage research and development of marketing systems and institutions with the proper interface with society.

It soon became apparent at these conferences that one of the necessary initial steps was to define the boundaries of macromarketing. In view of the fact that conceivably all marketing aspects could be relevant for study and research, this school of thought consciously attempted to define the nature and scope of macromarketing. Thus, unlike the other schools of thought, there was less evolution and more planned direction in defining the school. One of the earlier and still very relevant definitions of macromarketing was provided by Shelby Hunt (1977):

> Macromarketing is a multi-dimensional construct and a complete specification would (should) include the following: Macromarketing refers to the study of (1) marketing systems, (2) the impact and consequences of marketing systems on society and (3) the impact and consequences of society on marketing systems (p. 56).

Several papers have since appeared to clarify the boundaries of macromarketing. For example, Shawver and Nickels (1979) suggested that "when the objective is to describe or enhance aspects of social welfare related to exchange systems the study is macro-marketing" (p. 41).

While there is still some disagreement regarding the exact boundaries of macromarketing, the publication of the *Journal of Macromarketing* has served to define the field, at least for a while. Two alternative approaches are taken to resolve this definitional dilemma. The first is to define what macromarketing is not. For instance, it is not "decision making to produce an intended result for an individual household, business, or public organization" (Fisk 1981, p. 4). In that sense, macromarketing is neither a managerial nor a policy-oriented school of thought.

The second approach is to list topic areas that define "marketing behavior that affects a larger community of society" (Fisk 1981, p. 3). Fisk lists the following topic areas as appropriate for macromarketing:

1. Marketing as a life supply support provisioning technology.

2. The quality and quantity of life goods served by marketing.

3. Marketing as a technology for mobilizing and allocating economic resources.

4. Societal consequences of marketing in learning societies (p. 3).

More recently, Hunt and Burnett (1982) carefully reviewed all prior writings on the dichotomy of macromarketing versus micromarketing. Based on this assessment, they generated the following nine propositions to separate the domains of macromarketing from micromarketing (p. 15):

1. Studies of marketing systems are macro (Moyer 1972).

2. Studies of networks of exchange relationships are macro (Bagozzi 1977).

3. Studies adopting the perspective of society are macro (Shawver and Nickels 1979).

4. Studies examining the consequences of marketing on society are macro (Hunt 1977).

5. Studies examining the consequences of society on marketing are macro.

6. Studies of the marketing activities of industrial, profit-sector organizations are micro (Moyer 1972), as are studies that adopt the perspective of individual profit-sector organizations (Shawver and Nickels 1979).

7. Studies of the marketing activities of individual, nonprofit sector organizations are micro (Hunt 1976b).

8. Studies adopting the perspective of an individual industry are micro (Hunt 1976b).

9. Studies of the marketing activities of consumers are micro (Hunt 1976b).

These propositions were tested by preparing a standardized questionnaire sent to a large sample of academic scholars still active in research. As expected, the perceptions of the marketing scholars as measured by the questionnaire reflected the face validity of the nine propositions. Hunt and Burnett (1982) concluded:

> In conclusion, marketers can and do categorize marketing phenomena, issues and research by way of the macromarketing/micromarketing dichotomy. Using the three criteria of level of aggregation, perspectives of and consequences on, a taxonomical model can completely specify the various kinds of marketing studies (p. 24).

In contrast to Hunt and Burnett's efforts to separate and differentiate macromarketing from micromarketing, Zif (1980) attempted to demonstrate that the managerial approach inherent in micromarketing is equally applicable to macromarketing situations and problems. According to Zif, managers in the public sector and in charge of societal issues and problems can and do behave in a parallel manner with their counterparts in the private sector who are in charge of commercial products and services. The major variables of the managerial approach are familiar from studies of micromarketing: (a) managerial responsibilities, (b) managerial objectives, (c) managerial orientations and strategies, and (d) decision making variables. With some adjustment and redefinition, these variables can be adapted to apply to macro phenomena.

Zif (1980) applied the managerial concepts of micromarketing to macromarketing situations and insightfully demonstrated that the process of management is very similar, although the inputs and outputs may differ significantly between micromarketing and macromarketing situations. Zif does suggest some differences. For example, in comparison with micromarketing, most macromarketing situations show a significant decrease in direct competition and an increase in cooperation in the regulation of consumption and in product-line planning. The concept of the marketing manager as a strategist competing against adversaries shifts to that of an integrator concerned with the development of a whole market working with a centralized data bank and affected only by indirect competition.

The literature generated by the macromarketing school is highly diverse, and it is not yet clear what particular areas of interest are emerging. In the 1970s, considerable interest was fostered in social marketing, or the role of marketing in effecting social change (e.g., Kotler and Zaltman 1971). Typical of recent work, however, is the argument by Zeithaml and Zeithaml (1984) that marketing does have an important role to play in the management of its own environment. Related to this argument, Greene and Miesing (1984) have explored the public policy, technological, and ethical issues relevant to marketing decisions for NASA's space shuttle; Enis and Sullivan (1985) have explored the marketing implications of the AT&T settlement; and Heath and Nelson (1985) have examined the corporate and public policy issues surrounding image and issue advertising, with their primary focus on issues addressed by the Federal Trade Commission (FTC), the Federal Communications Commission (FCC), and the Internal Revenue Service (IRS). Further Hutt, Mokwa, and Shapiro (1986) have examined politics of marketing, suggesting that parallel to the distribution channel is a political "network." Their thinking is an extension of the political economy framework:

> ... economic and political forces coalesce into "organized behavior systems" or "domesticated market domains." Accordingly, market systems can be defined in terms of parties, relationships, and actions which enhance and facilitate both the performance and prevention or prohibition of marketing exchanges (p. 41).

The authors offer a careful discussion of the implications for clarifying marketing's role in the political market domain, as well as a discussion of associated public policy issues.

Both Arndt (1979) and Kotler (1986b) have argued that marketers must acquire political skills if they hope to operate successfully in today's market environment. Arndt (1979) has discussed the increasing prevalence of "internal" or "domesticated" markets, arguing that:

> ... the competitive, open market is in the process of being tamed, regulated, and closed. To an increasing degree, transactions are occurring in "internal" markets within the framework of long-term relationships, not on an ad hoc basis (p. 69).

He describes domesticated markets, and compares them with traditional competitive markets, as follows:

> [In domesticated markets] transactions are moved inside a company (when for instance buyers and sellers actually merge) or inside the boundaries of a group of companies committed to long-term cooperation. Transactions in domesticated markets are usually handled by administrative processes on the basis of negotiated rules of exchange. In open, competitive markets, coordination is implemented ex post through the workings of autonomous, spontaneous, centralized decision processes. Domesticated markets, on the other hand, are coordinated ex ante by centralized control procedures. Information is consciously and directly managed (p. 70).

Arndt points out that domesticated markets offer the advantage of reducing uncertainty in an increasingly turbulent environment. However, operating in domesticated markets also calls for more imaginative marketing, with more attention to the political aspects of economic decision making and more attention to the design, implementation, and maintenance of effective interorganizational marketing systems. This is in contrast to the traditional concentration on the marketing mix or Four Ps (product, price, place, and promotion).

Kotler (1986b) has proposed a broadened view of marketing, explicitly focusing on problems associated with entering blocked or protected markets (markets characterized by high entry barriers). Given the existence of blocked or protected markets, Kotler suggests that marketing is increasingly becoming a political exercise:

> There is a growing need for companies that want to operate in certain markets to master the art of supplying benefits to parties other-than target consumers. This need extends beyond the requirements to serve and satisfy normal intermediaries like agents, distributors, and dealers. I am talking about third parties—governments, labor unions, and other interest groups—that, singly or collectively, can block profitable entry into a market (p. 119).

Kotler goes on to argue that, faced with blocked or protected markets, marketers must engage in "megamarketing" in which the concepts of power and public relations are given emphasis:

> In addition to the four Ps of marketing strategy-product, price, place, and promotion-executives must add two more—power and public relations. I call such strategic thinking *megamarketing*.

> Marketing is the task of arranging need-satisfying and profitable offers to target buyers. Sometimes, however, it is necessary to create additional incentives and pressures at the right times and in the right amounts to noncustomers. Megamarketing thus takes an enlarged view of the skills and resources needed to enter and operate in certain markets. In addition to preparing attractive offers for customers, megamarketing may use inducements and sanctions to gain the desired responses from gatekeepers (p. 119).

There is every reason to believe that the macromarketing school of thought will continue to grow, but its exact direction and overall contribution to marketing has yet to be determined. However, evidence of the maturation of this school of thought is provided by recent attention to methodological issues in conducting macromarketing research (Venkatesh and Dholakia 1986).

4.3.1 Evaluation of the Macromarketing School

STRUCTURE: **Are the concepts properly defined and integrated to form a strong nomological network?**

The macromarketing school is weak on this criterion. It is unfortunate that most scholars in the area have not worked together or organized a conference explicitly to resolve (as opposed to express) differences about the definition of macromarketing. Granted, Hunt and Burnett (1982) make a gallant effort to show that there is a consensus among academic scholars as to what is macromarketing and what is micromarketing. However, it must be pointed out that it is limited to five *specific* domains of macromarketing and four *specific* domains of micromarketing. We really do not know whether one would obtain highly agreed-on definitions if the same respondents were asked to freely describe their own views of macromarketing.

Even if there was a consensus on the definition, it is important to recognize that the structure criterion requires establishment of relationships among the definitional concepts of a theory or school of thought. In other words, we need more than a typology or classification to score high on this criterion.

It is, of course, our hope that scholars interested in macromarketing will generate a theory of macromarketing with explicit propositions similar to what is attempted in the buyer behavior and organizational dynamics schools of thought.

Our score on structure = 4.

SPECIFICATION: Are the relationships specified in a manner to delimit hypotheses or are they highly contingent?

It is unfortunate that the scope and complexity of the macromarketing school forces it to be more contingent than invariant. For example, as an economic subsystem of society, it must coexist in harmony with societal values and concerns, and according to the advocates of this school, it must also serve society's values and concerns. However, societal values and concerns are dynamic, and very few theories of social values can be borrowed to predict the future. This contingency forces the macromarketing school to change its domain, definitions, and relationships as social values changes. Furthermore, at a point in time there are likely to be divergent social values and concerns especially between industrial, preindustrial, and postindustrial societies. The macromarketing school has not articulated the role of marketing (definitions and relationships) in divergent economic societies.

Our score on specification = 4.

TESTABILITY: Are the operational definitions provided to ensure testability and intersubjective consensus?

The Hunt and Burnett (1982) study has strongly indicated that the specific definitions can be empirically tested. Furthermore, they clearly demonstrate that there is a consensus, at least among marketing scholars, as to what is macromarketing and what is micromarketing. Therefore, it is safe to say that the concepts of macromarketing are testable, although the Hunt and Burnett study is a lonely exception.

We also believe that there is an emerging consensus about the domain of macromarketing. As Hunt (1977) has suggested, macromarketing consists of the study of consequences of marketing on society and vice versa. Most scholars tend to agree with this conceptualization. At the same time, it is difficult to go beyond this statement and obtain consensus about the marketing and society interface. For example, social activists such as Sethi (1971) would take a sharply different perspective than practitioner-oriented people such as Levitt (1958). We believe that as we evolve toward a theory of business policy, we will also evolve toward a theory of marketing policy.

Our score on testability = 6.

EMPIRICAL SUPPORT: What is the degree of confirmation in terms of empirical support?

Similar to most of the older schools of thought, the empirical support for the macromarketing school comes from observations, case histories, and anecdotes. This includes, on the one hand, use of marketing techniques to solve social problems such as alcoholism, traffic congestion, and population control; and, on the other hand, regulatory and legislative normative approaches to make marketing more socially responsive. Both types of observations and case histories have good empirical support for the domain of macromarketing. Unfortunately, it is not generalizable, or at least no one has as yet attempted empirical generalizations to support the macromarketing school.

Our score on empirical support = 6.

RICHNESS: How comprehensive and generalizable is the theory?

By definition, the macromarketing school is very comprehensive in its scope and nature. It focuses on the "raison d'être" of marketing as a social institution. Furthermore, it is an important enough social institution to invite comments and criticisms from stakeholders outside the discipline. Finally, as we pointed out earlier, macromarketing issues are ancient and predate the modern industrial states. The inherent danger of the pervasive nature of macromarketing is that it begins to blur its own boundaries. For example, it is not an easy task to separate macromarketing from business policy or from political economy.

Our score on richness = 7.

SIMPLICITY: **How easy is it to communicate and implement the theory?**

The concepts of macromarketing are difficult to communicate to others and implement in practice for several reasons. First, the macromarketing school is a value-laden school and the divergent values of others result in perceptual biases of selective attention and selective retention. Second, it is extremely difficult to get a consensus on the methods to solve social problems and concerns. Furthermore, as Zaltman and Duncan (1977) and Sheth and Frazier (1982) have pointed out, it is not easy to choose between public education, economic incentives, or mandatory rules to bring about harmony between marketing and society. Finally, the issues to be dealt with in macromarketing are not only far reaching in their impact, but often tend to be long term and intangible. All of these forces make macromarketing concepts difficult to communicate and also difficult to implement.

Our score on simplicity = 4.

Table 4.3 summarizes our evaluation of the macromarketing school of thought. It is fairly weak on syntax criteria and simplicity but stronger on semantics criteria and richness.

Table 4.3 Evaluation of the Macromarketing School*

Criterion	Rationale	Score
Structure	Consensus on definition lacking	4
Specification	More contingent than invariant	4
Testability	Specific definitions can be empirically tested. No consensus on marketing and society interface	6
Empirical support	Mainly based on observations, case histories, and anecdotes	6
Richness	Comprehensive, but blurred boundaries	7
Simplicity	Concepts difficult to communicate	4
	TOTAL	31

* Scores range from 1 (poor) to 10 (excellent).

Summary

In this chapter, we have reviewed and evaluated the three non-economic non-interactive schools of marketing thought: the buyer behavior school, the activist school, and the macromarketing school.

The buyer behavior school has a number of distinct characteristics not matched by any other school. First, it generated a paradigm shift in marketing to the extent that it has emerged as a separate, stand-alone discipline. Second, it generated the largest amount of empirical research and theory building. Indeed, the more scientific approaches to developing a discipline both in conceptualizing and testing have been inherent in the buyer behavior school. Finally, the buyer behavior school has elevated the image of marketing as a more respectable discipline whose tools and techniques can be used for the good of society in such socially desirable behaviors as population control and social programs.

Not surprisingly, the buyer behavior school's evaluation on the metatheory criteria comes out high. It scores well on all three criteria: the organization (syntax), the reality (semantics), and the relevance (pragmatics) dimensions.

The activist school of thought gained momentum in the 1960s, although it has a long tradition going back to the late eighteen hundreds and early nineteen hundreds. Unfortunately, the activist school focused more on ad hoc industry- or product-specific issues of protecting the interests of the consumer and therefore did not develop good conceptual frameworks until very recently. It seems to have limited future promise because the interest of the public policy has shifted from consumerism to international competitiveness. This is unfortunate in timing, because a lot can be accomplished now that some good conceptual frameworks have been proposed.

The activist school scores low on the metatheory criteria on all dimensions except empirical support and simplicity. This is not surprising in view of the fact that it began by focusing on specific consumer problems and proposed highly action-oriented recommendations.

The macromarketing school examines the relationship between marketing and society. It is a relatively new school of thought and is the consequence of a broader interest in the role of business as a social institution. Almost in direct contrast to the activist school, the macromarketing school is richer in concepts and poorer in empirical support. This is of course understandable. As one moves away from the specifics of an issue it is harder to generate and analyze reality. We do expect the macromarketing school to enrich its conceptual base with the recent focus on technology and megamarketing concepts of politics and public relations. It seems that macromarketing may finally create the same excitement as the buyer behavior school did in the early 1960s as we shift national public policy concerns away from consumerism and toward international competitiveness.

Questions for Analysis and Discussion

1. How and why did the Buyer Behavior School evolve into the Consumer Behavior School?

2. Do you agree that managerial relevance is irrelevant to consumer research? Why or why not?

3. Should research sponsored by business schools be relevant to the business community? And more specifically, should research of consumer behavior scholars housed in the marketing departments be expected to advance the marketing discipline?

4. Explain how theory development could have helped mitigate the replication crisis in psychology and consumer behavior literature. How can the field move forward in terms of general consumer theory development?

5. Explain how the UN's Principles of Responsible Management Education (unprme.org) have revived the Activist School of Thought in business schools and research agendas. Which of the 17 UN Sustainable Development Goals offer the most promise for theory construction for the Activist School of Marketing Thought?

6. Explain how the UN's Principles of Responsible Management Education (unprme.org) have revived the Macromarketing School of Thought in business schools and research agendas. Which of the 17 Sustainable Development Goals offer the most promise for theory construction for the Macromarketing School of Thought?

7. What are some non-intuitive ways the tri-sector (private-public-government) partnerships can be utilized? What are its marketing theory implications?

Interactive-Non-Economic Schools of Marketing

LEARNING OBJECTIVES

After reading this chapter, you will be able to:

- Describe the critical tenets of the three interactive, non-economic schools of marketing – organizational dynamics school, systems school, and the social exchange school.

- Explain the intricate behavioral dimensions of distribution channels, including their sources of power and the nature of inter-organizational cooperation and conflict.

- Comprehend the application of general systems theory to marketing across contexts.

- Articulate the relationship between marketing and its environment and the linkages and networks of marketing ingredients that integrate to achieve a total action system.

- Critically evaluate the theoretical contributions of the social exchange theory and related concepts in the development of a formal theory of marketing.

In this chapter, we review three more schools of marketing thought. They are the organizational dynamics, the systems, and the social exchange schools. As mentioned in Chapter 1, the two common characteristics of these three schools of marketing thought are as follows:

1. They all take an interactive perspective with respect to market transactions, in which both buyers and sellers are regarded as equally important to understand and analyze. Unlike the economic schools of marketing thought (commodity, functional, and regional), which examine market transactions from the supplier's viewpoint, or the non-economic schools of marketing thought (buyer behavior, macromarketing, and activist), which examine market transactions from the buyer's perspective, these three schools examine the mutual interdependence and integrated relationships inherent between the sellers and the buyers in market transactions.

2. At the same time, these three schools of thought primarily rely on the behavioral sciences rather than economic sciences. Therefore, the underlying concepts borrowed or developed are significantly different from the classical schools (commodity, regional, and functional) as well as the managerial, institutional, and functionalist schools of thought. In that respect, the organizational dynamics, social exchange, and systems schools are much closer to the non-economic schools of buyer behavior, macromarketing, and activist.

These three schools of marketing thought are more recent in their development. Furthermore, they have remained as the specialized interest of a few scholars in marketing, unlike the buyer behavior. school, for example, which attracted attention from many scholars. Consequently, our review of these schools will be somewhat limited. Indeed, we have the opposite experience as compared to the buyer behavior where we had a difficult time incorporating all the contributions within the page limits of this book.

5.1   The Organizational Dynamics School of Thought

As discussed in Chapter 3, the organizational dynamics school of marketing thought is the direct descendant of the institutional school in the sense that both of these schools seek to explain the intricate workings of the channels of distribution. However, the fundamental difference between these two schools is their underlying perspectives. The institutional school utilized economic foundations to analyze how a distribution channel could be structured more efficiently for the eventual benefit of the ultimate consumer. In contrast, the advocates of the organizational dynamics school shifted their attention from the welfare of the consumer to the analysis of the goals and needs of the members of the distribution channel, such as the manufacturers, wholesalers, and retailers.

For this reason, the organizational dynamics theorists began to view the distribution channel as a competitive coalition that was based on self-interest. Although, for example, a wholesaler and retailer must cooperate and coordinate their efforts if they wish to have an effective relationship, these two actors also compete with each other to determine who will gamer the lion's share of the rewards from their cooperative venture. Thus, these theorists sought to understand how channel members could effectively interact in a complex and seemingly contradictory setting of competitive and cooperative drives.

The organizational dynamics school is a relatively new school of marketing thought with the bulk of the scholarly writings in this area published in the 1970s and 1980s. However, the seeds of this school were actually planted in the late 1950s and early 1960s. One of the first articles written about distribution channel relationships using a behavioral orientation was Valentine Ridgeway's article entitled "Administration of Manufacturer-Dealer Systems." According to Ridgeway (1957):

> A manufacturer and his dealers make up a competitive system which is in need of administration much as is a single organization. Some activities can best be performed centrally, and some are carried out best on a decentralized basis but with a need to coordinate the decentralized activities of numerous dealers. The manufacturer is in the most logical position to perform this administration of the system because of his acquaintance with the products, his operations in the larger market, and his contact with the numerous dealers. Despite the separation of ownership of the dealers' facilities and the break in the chain of command, the manufacturer seeks power to administer the system by means of rewards and punishments which he can apply to dealers (p. 483).

After Ridgeway helped to plant the seed for the organizational dynamics school, the next major contribution was made by Bruce Mallen (1963, 1967). Mallen (1963) stressed the interplay of conflict, control, and cooperation in channel member relations:

> This paper will show that between channel members a dynamic field of conflicting and cooperating objective exists; also that if the conflicting objectives outweigh the cooperating ones, the effectiveness of the channel will be reduced. Thus, the efficient distribution of consumer goods will be impeded.

> The channel members can meet this problem in three distinct ways. First, they can have a leader (one of the channel members) who "forces" members to cooperate; this is an autocratic relationship. Second, they can have a leader who "helps" members to cooperate, creating a democratic relationship. Finally, they can do nothing, and so have an anarchistic relationship (p. 24).

Although the efforts by Ridgeway and Mallen set the stage for the emergence of the organizational dynamics school, it was not until 1969 that this school began to truly capture the interest and attention of a large number of marketing scholars. The event in 1969 that thrust the organizational dynamics school into the spotlight in marketing theory was the publication of Louis Stern's readings book, *Distribution Channels: Behavioral Dimensions.* In the introduction to this volume, Stern clearly addresses the inadequacies of the economic perspective formerly proposed by the institutional school:

> The concept of channels of distribution is one of the most original, enduring, and fundamental concepts in the marketing literature. Attempts to understand interfirm relationships within these

channels and to generate strategies for their management have traditionally been cast in terms of economic theory. From this perspective, firms join together in trading arrangements because of cost and revenue considerations; their strategies are conditioned by the type of competition extant in the various markets in which they act. This analytical treatment suffices as long as the tools of economics are thought to be wholly adequate in depicting the realities of behavior in marketing channels. It is becoming more and more apparent, however, that conceptualization beyond that supplied by economic theory is needed if marketing students, academicians, and practitioners alike are to gain further insights into the increasingly complex and diverse nature of such channels. (p. 1)

Of the many influential articles contained in this book, two original articles stand out as having laid the groundwork for later theorists in marketing. First, in a paper co-authored by Frederick Beier and Stern, the concept of power, particularly as developed by social scientists such as Emerson (1962) and French and Raven (1959), is analyzed:

The concepts of dependency and commitment are key to an understanding of power relationships in marketing channels. A channel is generally composed of a set of marketing specialists. The effective linking and coordination of the specialists are prerequisites to the efficient and successful distribution. However, the more extensive is the division of labor among the components of any system in the performance of its functions, the more interdependent the components become. Thus, power is pervasive in the channel, because each member is dependent, at least to some extent, on the others. As one channel member's dependence upon another increases, the greater becomes the power of the latter. On the other hand, as a member's commitment to the system diminishes, the ability of other system members to influence him decreases (Beier and Stern 1969, p. 112).

The second influential article focused on the concept of conflict in distribution channels. Stern and his co-author of this article, Ronald H. Gorman, again stressed the pivotal function of dependency as a cause of conflict:

When a channel of distribution is viewed as a social system, the members of such a channel are, by definition, caught up in a web of interdependency. The actions or behavior of any one member have consequences for the level of output (measured in terms of individual goals) achieved by the others. This dependency relationship represents the root of conflict in channels of distribution. In any social system, when a component perceives the behavior of another component to be impeding the attainment of its goals or the effective performance of its instrumental behavior patterns, an atmosphere of frustration prevails (Stem and Gorman 1969, p. 156).

Following the framework established by Stern, other marketing theorists quickly entered the organizational dynamics school and began to explore more critically the topical subjects of power, conflict, cooperation, and bargaining. Although a complete review of the extensive literature in these areas is clearly beyond the scope of this book, a few of the more compelling research questions will be highlighted.

1. ***What are the sources of power?*** Hunt and Nevin (1974), relying on the work of French and Raven (1959), proposed that a channel member may possess coercive and noncoercive sources of power:

In an empirical case, coercive power can be differentiated from the others because it, alone, involves potential punishment. For all the other noncoercive sources of power, i.e., reward, legitimate, expert, and referent, the individual willingly (rather than begrudgingly) yields power to another (Hunt and Nevin, 1974, p. 187).

Expanding on the Hunt and Nevin framework for coercive and non-coercive power sources, Lusch and Brown (1982) suggested that the use of certain power sources may have a direct impact on the channel members' perceptions of the power relationships:

The categorization and consequences of various power sources may not be as originally posited by Hunt and Nevin (1974). We develop the logic for categorizing power sources as economic (coercion, reward, legal legitimate) and noneconomic (referent, expertise, traditional legitimate, and informational). As we move from economic to noneconomic sources of power we move from direct outcome control to indirect outcome control. If a channel leader successfully implements noneconomic sources of power, the influenced channel member attributes less, not more, power to the powerholder. This outcome occurs because the channel members adopt the channel leader's norms and values as their own and therefore believe that they are acting independently of the powerholder. Consequently, the higher the quality of assistances (a noneconomic source of power), the lower the influenced channel members' perceptions of channel leader's power (p. 187).

Gaski (1987) proposed an alternative explanation for what he deemed the "rather counter-theoretical finding" (p.145) that an inverse relationship exists between a channel member's reward power sources and its actual power. Building on the work of Lusch and Brown (1982), Gaski devised a test for the hypothesis that this "anomaly" can be explained by the interaction between the use of reward and the power subject's attitude. Since his empirical evidence did not support the Lusch and Brown hypothesis, Gaski proposed an alternative explanation — that power had not been validly measured.

2. *How should channel members utilize their available power?* Kasulis and Spekman (1980) added a new normative perspective to the power literature by suggesting how marketing managers should utilize their power sources:

> Channel relations provide frequent opportunities for one member to influence another's behavior. The ultimate objective of any channel management strategy is to develop a degree of cooperation in channel participant behavior. The efficiencies gained from a coordinated channel effort are expected to improve the channel's competitive stance vis-a-vis other distribution networks. This means that the channel administrator should not myopically view half-hearted and forced complicity among channel members as a successful power outcome: but should, instead, strive to cultivate those power bases which tend to elicit an internalization of, and an identification with the system's goals and values. While in some instances firms must rely on coercion, rewards, or contractual agreements, firms should develop, and more extensively use, those bases of power which produce the greatest amount of long run cooperation (p. 190).

Frazier and Summers (1984) explored the use of various influence strategies by boundary personnel within distribution channel relationships. Gaski and Nevin (1985), in a study using an existing distribution system, reported:

> The results support the proposition that exercise of the coercive power source by a supplier has a stronger effect on dealer satisfaction and channel conflict than the mere presence of that power source. In contrast, exercise of the reward power source seems to have only a marginal impact on these dependent variables (p. 139).

McAlister, Bazerrnan, and Fader (1986) have explored the use of a moderately high externally set profitability constraint as a goal-setting mechanism for controlling channel negotiators. In an experimental market situation they found:

> Equal and high power channel members are shown to be made more profitable by the constraint. Low power channel members are shown to be made less profitable by the same constraint behavior (p. 228).

3. *How should power be measured?* Some of the latest work in the power area has focused on the need to develop valid and reliable measures of the power construct. In this regard, Frazier (1983b) has argued that power is directly linked to role performance:

When the level of a source firm's role performance is perceived as being high, the target should be highly motivated to maintain the exchange relationship. Furthermore, the higher the perceived role performance of a source, the fewer the alternatives that should be available to the target to replace it sufficiently. By specifying the primary elements of a source firm's channel role, one can identify the domain of elements needed to represent a target firm's dependence in the relationship (p. 159).

4. ***What is the relationship between power and conflict?*** Lusch (1976), in an empirical study of the automobile distribution channel, concentrated on the possible causal link between power and conflict:

> It can be concluded that noncoercive and coercive sources of power have significant impacts on intrachannel conflict, at least for the distribution of automobiles in the United States. Noncoercive sources tend to reduce intrachannel conflict whereas coercive sources tend to increase it (p. 388).

Lusch's provocative conclusions were challenged by Etgar (1978), who questioned the purported cause and effect relationship between power and conflict:

> If one recognizes that the use of power in a distribution channel is often an end result rather than a cause of conflict, Lusch's results are viewed in a different light. They imply that use of coercive power is linked with high levels of channel conflict. That is, channel leaders use coercive power when basic rivalries and differences divide the channel members. Such differences apparently cannot be solved by "soft" treatment and by convincing channel members to cooperate. Instead, compliance is achieved through the use of threats, denials of resources, etc. (p. 273–274).

Frazier and Summers (1986) report empirical research to support Lusch's (1976) position:

> The results of our field study support the position of those channel theorists who have emphasized the positive role of interfirm power in promoting the effective coordination of channel relationships. Manufacturers' representatives appear to use coercion with great reluctance, only when other types of influence strategies have failed to produce a satisfactory response on an important issue (p. 175).

They also report in this same study (Frazier and Summers 1986) that:

> ... the negative relationship found between dealers' perceptions of their manufacturers' power and the manufacturers' use of coercion may be primarily due to two factors.
>
> 1. The positions of the manufacturer and its dealers tend to be more congruent when the manufacturer has high power based on the dealer's dependence in the interfirm relationship. Furthermore, the manufacturer is able to make more effective use of information exchange under these conditions. These factors tend to reduce the manufacturer's need to engage in overt influence attempts (both coercive and noncoercive) with its dealers.
>
> 2. Manufacturers with high power are better able to utilize noncoercive influence strategies (e.g., requests) effectively when overt influence attempts seem appropriate, and thereby avoid the use of coercion (p.175).

The question of the relationship between power and conflict has also been addressed by Gaski (1984). Based on a major review of the literature, he developed an integrated overview of the status of this area. Gaski's outline of the conceptual foundations and empirical content of this area is used to point toward unresolved issues. Further, Gaski (1986) found a compound effect of the use of certain sources of power.

5. ***How should conflict be measured?*** Just as the measurement of power has been an area of scholarly research, the optimal measures of conflict have received some attention recently by organizational

dynamics theorists. The most rigorous effort to date was provided by Brown and Day (1981), who analyzed the validity of several different measures of manifest conflict:

> Conflict in channels of distribution was conceptualized as a dynamic process in which conflict progresses from a latent state of incompatibility to perceived conflict to felt conflict to the behavioral stage of manifest conflict. In manifest conflict the parties interact with each other to cope with frustrating behaviors. The most promising way to measure manifest conflict in field studies appears to be to monitor the frequency with which disagreements occur about different aspects of the channel relationship and the typical strength or intensity of conflictful behavior which occurs when the disagreements are discussed in written or oral communications (p. 272).

6. *What is cooperation in an interorganizational system?* Although the organizational dynamics literature has been dominated by articles focusing on the topics of power and conflict, some theorists are now beginning to address the issue of cooperation. Childers and Ruekert (1982), drawing on previous definitions of cooperation, proposed a new definition of cooperation within a channel network:

> ... cooperation is the expectation of a balanced exchange of the resources required to achieve both intraorganizational and interorganizational goals through joint action among two or more actors. Important to this definition are the ideas that cooperation stems from mutual effort (joint action) and that underlying this action is the expectation of a balanced exchange (p. 117).

7. *How does power affect the bargaining process?* Because channel members must often negotiate the levels of their inputs and rewards from an interorganizational relationship, the subject of bargaining behavior has become more relevant in recent years. Dwyer and Walker (1981) attempted to manipulate the balance of power between bargainers in a laboratory study to determine how this would affect bargaining activities:

> Despite the contrived setting, several specific conclusions can be drawn from this study on the nature of bargaining in an asymmetrical power condition. First, compared to a more balanced power setting, the negotiation process in an asymmetric market is more "efficient." Bargainers tend to reach agreement at the Pareto optimal solution and divide the total rewards equally when power is symmetrically distributed. However, in the unbalanced condition, while the specific terms of agreement are much less predictable, the bargainers tended to take a more "direct" negotiating approach. Their initial offers were closer to the ultimate agreement and, as a result, they yielded less and sent fewer bids before attaining a solution (p. 111).

In addition to these attempts to clarify specific concepts of power, conflict, cooperation, and bargaining, other organizational dynamics theorists have endeavored to create general models of interorganizational relations. The leading contributors to this general models perspective have been Robicheaux and El-Ansary (1975–76), Cadotte and Stem (1979), Stern and Reve (1980), Achrol, Reve, and Stern (1983), Frazier (1983a), and Gaski (1984). More specialized aspects of these models have been investigated by Anderson and Narus (1984), Anand and Stern (1985), Eliashberg et al. (1986), Anand (1987), and Anderson, Lodish, and Weitz (1987).

Two significant movements have recently emerged in the writings of these general models theorists that deserve special attention. First, Stern and Reve (1980) and Achrol et al. (1983) have advocated that distribution channels be classified as political economies. According to Stern and Reve (1980):

> Basically, the political economy approach views a social system as comprising interacting sets of major economic and sociopolitical forces which affect collective behavior and performance (p. 53).

The most intriguing claim made by proponents of the political economy perspective is that it will bridge the gulf between the institutional school, and the organizational dynamics school:

> ... channel theory is fragmented into two seemingly disparate disciplinary orientations: an economic approach and a behavioral approach. The former attempts to apply microeconomic theory and industrial organization analysis to the study of distribution systems and has been essentially "efficiency" oriented, focusing on costs, functional differentiation, and channel design (cf. Baligh and Richartz 1967, Bucklin 1966, Bucklin and Carman 1974, Cox, Goodman, and Fichandler 1965). The latter borrows heavily from social psychology and organization theory and has been essentially "socially" oriented, focusing on power and conflict phenomena (cf. Alderson 1957, Stern 1969). Rarely have there been attempts to integrate these two perspectives. Indeed, they should be viewed as complementary, because the former deals mainly with economic "outputs" while the latter is concerned with behavioral "processes." (Stern and Reve 1980, p. 53).

Dwyer and Welsh (1985) developed a theoretical model based on the belief that the political economy framework illuminates the interaction between the internal and external sociopolitical and economic forces of marketing channels. Their model should be useful "for explaining interorganizational responses to uncertainty and dependence constraints of the channel environment" (p. 397).

The second noteworthy movement has been launched by Frazier's (1983a) article suggesting that organizational dynamics theorists have been unnecessarily restrictive in their view of the interorganizational relationship. Specifically, Frazier (1983a) posits that the exchanges among channel members can be divided into a three-stage process involving initiating, implementation, and review:

> Previous research in the marketing channels literature has focused on the implementation or coordination of interorganizational exchange relationships and the constructs of interfirm power and conflict. The framework presented herein clearly suggests that a broadening of research effort is required to aid future progress and understanding in the marketing channels area. Attention is especially warranted on why and how exchange relationships are initiated, and how the rewards or losses from the exchange are reviewed and evaluated by each channel member. Indeed, because constructs within the initiation, implementation, and review processes are so highly interrelated with one another, a clear understanding of attempts to coordinate ongoing exchange relationships, including the constructs of power and conflict, is not possible without some understanding of the other two processes, and vice versa. This suggests it would be beneficial for channel researchers to examine both distal and immediate antecedents of existing exchange relationships, analyzing the "history of each exchange" so to speak, in examining and explaining their current nature (p. 75).

Finally, Graham (1987) has offered a theory to explain the outcomes of negotiations between representatives of buying and selling firms. Graham takes a social psychological perspective, proposing that situational constraints (power relationships) and bargaining characteristics (culture/nationality, interpersonal orientation, and listening skills) influence the process of negotiation (use of questions, initial demands, procedural discipline, impression formation accuracy, and topical control), and that the process of negotiation affects negotiation outcomes (economic rewards, satisfaction, and interpersonal attraction).

5.1.1 Evaluation of the Organizational Dynamics School

Our evaluation of the organizational dynamics school must be interpreted with the conscious thought that this is a young and emerging school whose full life cycle is yet to evolve. In some ways, it is even unfair to compare the organizational dynamics school with the same set of criteria as, for example, the classical schools or the buyer behavior school. We will provide an evaluatory summary, but the reader is cautioned to keep the foregoing comments in mind.

STRUCTURE: Are the concepts properly defined and integrated to form a strong nomological network?

Because the organizational dynamics school has heavily relied on well-known concepts from the behavioral sciences especially as they relate to power, conflict, and cooperation, it has reaped the benefit of thinking and development in these borrowed disciplines. Therefore, the basic tenets of the organizational dynamics school seem to be well defined, despite some controversy about the classification or taxonomy of power sources.

On the other hand, it is harder to find agreed on definitions for the outcomes of channel power, conflict, and cooperation. For example, it is not clear whether the outcomes should be measured in behavioral terms or psychological terms. Also, most of the outcomes are non-economic measures, even though the ultimate goals of competitive coalition are the economic goals of profits and growth.

Most hypotheses and proposed theories do have good integration to generate a strong nomological network. Indeed, in this respect, the organizational dynamic school is as good as the buyer behavior and the managerial schools of marketing thought.

Our score on structure = 8.

SPECIFICATION: Are the relationships specified in a manner to delimit hypotheses or are they highly contingent?

It is refreshing to note that the organizational dynamics school has deliberately focused on one aspect of marketing practice, namely the channels relationship. To that extent, most of the hypotheses have been stated in very specific terms. On the other hand, many of the theories and concepts borrowed from organizational psychology are based on a contingency theory approach. In other words, it is possible that channel behavior may be driven by other forces than those hypothesized by the organizational dynamics school. This is particularly true with the comprehensive theories proposed in the area.

Overall, however, we believe that most publications in the organizational dynamics school provide a good deal of specificity, especially in view of the fact that behavioral sciences in general have limitations of their own with regard to specificity.

Our score on specification = 8.

TESTABILITY: Are the operational definitions provided to ensure testability and intersubjective consensus?

It would appear that the organizational dynamics school is relatively weak on this criterion. Partly, this is due to the lack of empirical studies, at least as compared to the buyer behavior and the managerial schools or marketing. However, it is also true that different scholars have proposed different operational measures for both the independent and the dependent variables. As mentioned before, there is no real consensus on whether the outcomes should be measured in behavioral or psychological terms. Similarly, there is no standardized set of scales to measure the independent variables such as power and conflict.

We believe that this relative lack of testability is largely due to the infancy of the school. In due course, some scholars in the field will develop standardized scales similar to attitude and personality research in order to improve testability and replication. However, even though it may be unfair, we must evaluate the school at this point in its life cycle.

Our score on testability = 4.

EMPIRICAL SUPPORT: What is the degree of confirmation in terms of empirical support?

The organizational dynamics school is probably weakest on this criterion. This is primarily due to its specialized nature within marketing. Unlike the managerial and the buyer behavior schools, it has attracted relatively fewer scholars to conduct research and testing. In fact, it is not an exaggeration to state that the organizational dynamics school has more concepts and theories than empirical testing and support This is somewhat contrary to a more typical trend indiscipline development, wherein empirical observations precede theory development. We believe this is due to the heavy reliance by this school on borrowed concepts from the behavioral sciences.

It is obvious that what is needed now is to generate large-scale empirical research comparable to what happened with the buyer behavior and the managerial schools of marketing.

Our score on empirical support = 3.

RICHNESS: **How comprehensive and generalizable is the theory?**

The organizational dynamics school is very comprehensive in explaining the behavioral outcomes of channel members (such as motivation, satisfaction, resentment, and the like). However, it seems to have very limited usefulness in terms of explaining and manipulating the economic behavior of the channel members (such as shifting functions, improving productivity by elimination of functions, or sharing of profits). For example, the organizational dynamics school is not directly linked to the concept of the value chain, and who performs what functions in the chain. Perhaps this is not the intent of the organizational dynamics school. However, it has explicitly rejected most economic concepts as being inadequate to explain channel behavior. Therefore, it should be capable of providing alternative explanations for the same behavior.

Our score on richness = 5.

SIMPLICITY: **How easy is it to communicate and implement the theory?**

The original concepts proposed by Louis Stem and his students are fairly simple and elegant. The fundamental concepts of power, conflict, and cooperation are everyday experiences in both the organizational and the personal worlds of most readers. They are, therefore, easy to relate to, and also easy to implement or apply in the real world.

However, the more recent efforts at developing comprehensive theories of channel behavior remind us of a similar effort at developing comprehensive theories in the buyer behavior school. They are more abstract, harder to relate to, and have too many variables. Furthermore, they are process-oriented rather than outcome oriented, which also makes them more difficult to communicate and implement in practice.

Our score on simplicity = 4.

Table 5.1 summarizes our evaluation of the organizational dynamics schools of marketing. It appears that this school is good in the syntax aspects, but weak in the semantic and pragmatic aspects of theory building.

Table 5.1 Evaluation of the Organizational Dynamics School*

Criterion	Rationale	Score
Structure	Has benefited from the well-defined concepts of the behavioral sciences from which it has borrowed	8
Specification	Has strongly focused on channel relationships and, to that extent, it is well specified	8
Testability	Operational definitions of power, conflict, and outcome variables are highly divergent	4
Empirical support	There are more concepts and propositions than there are empirical tests	3
Richness	Rich in behavioral outcomes but poor in economic or functional outcomes	5
Simplicity	Basic concepts of power, conflict, and cooperation are simple, but the recent process-oriented models are hard to understand	4
	TOTAL	32

* Scores range from 1 (poor) to 10 (excellent).

5.2 The Systems School of Thought

Like many other schools of thought, the systems school of thought emerged in response to the changing environment. However, we observe that many early writers in marketing recognized that marketing must be viewed as a system, even though the systems school did not really emerge until the 1960s. In the 1960s, the systems school of thought in marketing became visible due to the influence of operations research techniques in other disciplines of business. This gave impetus to examining marketing and marketing activities from a systems perspective. Furthermore, widespread use of powerful mainframe computers popularized the word "system" in the management literature.

A review of the proceedings of the educator's conferences of the American Marketing Association points to the popularity of at least the tern "systems." As will be pointed out later, systems and the systems school of thought are not necessarily the same. The 1965 AMA Conference Proceedings (Bennett 1965) does not contain a single paper with "systems" in the title. However, in 1966 (Hass 1966), there are at least five papers with "systems" in their title. By 1967, the theme of the entire conference was "Changing Marketing Systems" (Moyer 1968). For the next several years, "systems" was a common noun in paper titles and at least one marketing textbook was called *Marketing Systems* (Fisk 1967).

To properly evaluate this school of thought, it is important to have some feel of the basic tenets of the systems school. There is a surprising degree of agreement on this. The reason can easily be traced to the pioneering work of Forrester (1958), Boulding (1956), Kuhn (1963), and Bertalanffy (1968).

The work of Forrester is a direct outgrowth of the operations research approach fostered during the World War II. This approach took a multidisciplinary view of problems and viewed the blending of the behavioral and quantitative sciences as necessary for the solution of complex problems. Forrester believed that:

> The company will come to be recognized not as a collection of separate functions, but as a system in which the flows of information, materials, manpower, capital equipment, and money set up forces that determine the basic tendency toward growth, fluctuations, and decline (Forrester 1958, p. 52).

Boulding (1956) posits in his *General Systems Theory* that the often bewildering and confusing relationships between production, marketing, and consumption can be organized into a coherent and unified perspective using the analytical framework of systems, especially systems levels for classifying problems. For Boulding, marketing problems belong to a class of systems characterized by communication and adaptation in social organizations.

Similarly, Ludvig von Bertalanffy (1968), in his *General System Theory,* proposed a theory to explain all systems across contexts. He discussed open systems that interact with their environment, receiving inputs, processing these inputs, exporting outputs to the environment, and exchanging information and energy with the environment.

George Fisk (1967), in commenting on the application of general systems theory to marketing, writes:

> By viewing marketing problems in a system context, decision-makers can find a set of problems of which a particular problem is a member sharing at least some common properties. For many sets of problems much is known about acceptable solutions so that if a decision-maker is dissatisfied with his own solution or if he cannot find any solution he can refer to the set of problems to see if existing solutions apply. In this way, a tremendous body of information becomes more accessible (p. 12).

Kuhn (1963) broadened systems thinking to a more macro perspective with his application of system concepts to society. For Kuhn, marketing is a subsystem within society, with its own further subsystems such as the market and channels of distribution.

Systems, for these and subsequent writers, were made up of two classes of variables: the components or elements and the relationships among these components. These elements are generally thought of as interacting within a set of limited conditions usually referred to as the environment.

Elements are simply the components of the system, and for any particular system they will range over a limited domain. Attributes are properties of elements, and relationships are those things that tie the elements of a system together. It is these relationships that make the notion of a system useful. The environment of any system can be defined as the set of all objects a change in whose attributes are changed by the behavior of the system. Any given system may be further subdivided into systems of a lower order. A system is also a part of a supersystem. That is, there exists a hierarchy of systems. (Dowling 1983, p. 23)

Katz and Kahn did much to familiarize management academics with the systems perspective through their now classic book *The Social Psychology of Organizations* (Katz and Kahn 1966). For them, organizational systems are complex, open, and behavioral. They also suggest that open systems are indeterminant and are frequently referred to as probabilistic systems. In defining complex, open, and behavioral systems, they identify nine characteristics of these systems:

1. *Importation of Energy*: open systems import some form of energy from the environment.

2. *The Throughput*: open systems transform the energy available to them. Work gets done in the system that in some manner reorganizes the input.

3. *The Output*: open systems export some product into the environment.

4. *Systems as Cycles of Events*: the pattern of activities of the energy exchange has a cyclic character. The product exported into the environment furnishes the sources of energy for the repetition of the cycle of activities.

5. *Negative Entropy*: a universal law of nature is entropy, i.e., all forms of organization move toward disorganization or death. To survive, open systems must acquire negative entropy by importing more energy from the environment than expended.

6. *Information Input, Negative Feedback, and the Coding Process*: in addition to energy, the open system also imports information to furnish signals to the structure about the environment and about its own functioning in relation to the environment. The simplest type of information input is negative feedback that allows the system to correct deviations from course. However, the reception of inputs is selected as systems react only to those inputs to which they are attuned. Coding is the term for the selective mechanisms of a system by which incoming information is rejected or accepted and translated.

7. *The Steady-State and Dynamic Homeostasis*: any internal or external factor making for disruption of the system is countered by forces which restore the system as closely as possible to its previous state.

8. *Differentiation*: open systems move in the direction of differentiation and elaboration. Generalized patterns are replaced by more specialized functions.

9. *Equifinality*: a system can reach the same final state from differing initial conditions and by a variety of paths (Katz and Kahn 1966, pp. 14–29).

Relating the thinking of Katz and Kahn to marketing, Dowling (1983) states:

> The marketing subsystem exhibits many of the characteristics of a complex homeostatic mechanism because it helps the business enterprise attain a dynamic equilibrium and preserve its character. For example, one traditional function of marketing is to gather information from certain sections of the environment (customers) and transmit this to other parts of the enterprise. In carrying out this function, information is decoded and then reorganized according to the marketing system's perception of the needs of the enterprise. The decoding/recording phase of this operation is crucial to how the information will be used to change the behavior of the enterprise. Obviously, there are limits to the degree to which marketing can act as a homeostatic mechanism. These limits are defined in terms of the enterprise's other internal subsystems, its environment, and the type and number of system/environment exchange relationships (p. 24).

Even before the more formal statements of systems, marketing scholars understood that the various elements of marketing were of necessity related to and interdependent on each other. Such were the lessons of the commodity, functional, regional, and institutional schools of thought. As Mackenzie and Nicosia (1968) point out, in the period from 1920 to the late 1950s, "Major efforts were given to the problem of obtaining a picture of the whole marketing system" (p. 16). The most visible of these attempts were Clark (1922), Stewart and Dewhust (1939), Duddy and Revzan (1947), Vaile et al. (1952), and Alderson (1957).

As marketing scholars explored systems theory for relevance to marketing, the richness of this approach became evident. Bell (1966) provides an excellent discussion of social systems as they relate to marketing. In this discussion, he lays out the characteristics and requirements of social systems and social systems analysis, regarding marketing systems as special types of social systems. This discussion is summarized as follows:

1. A system is a group of interrelated components. All elements outside this relationship are outside the boundaries of the system and are components of the environment.

2. The behavior of a system is affected by the condition of its components. Similarly, system components are affected by environmental conditions.

3. The condition of a system component is variable. A change in the condition of a component or a change in environmental conditions necessitates an adjustment in the behavior of the system.

4. Closed systems can be completely isolated from the environment for analysis. In analyzing marketing systems, perhaps the best that can be hoped for is to temporarily maintain environmental conditions in an unchanged state.

5. In systems analysis, it is desirable to observe relations between a system and its environment under controlled conditions. Thus, it is advisable to use controlled experimentation in marketing research.

6. In systems analysis, attention is primarily focused on dynamics. This is the process whereby a system adapts to change and moves toward a new equilibrium after experiencing imbalance.

7. Systems are dynamic, composed only of variables. A component that does not change is not part of the system. In the analysis of marketing systems, almost everything is included in the analysis because almost everything is dynamic.

Exploring what the systems approach to marketing means, Lazer and Kelley (1962) discussed in some depth the component elements of marketing systems:

1. A set of functionally interdependent marketing relationships among people and institutions in the system-manufacturers, wholesalers, retailers, facilitating agencies, and consumers.

2. Interaction between individuals and firms necessary to maintain relationships including adjustment to change, innovation, cooperation, competition, linkages and blockages.

3. The establishment of objectives, goals, targets, beliefs, symbols, and sentiments which evolve from and reinforce the interaction. This results in determining realistic marketing objectives and instituting favorable programs, images, attitudes, opinions, and practices.

4. A consumer-oriented environment within which interactions take place subject to the constraints of a competitive market economy, a recognized legal and socio-economic climate, and the accepted relationships and practices of marketing functionaries.

5. Technology of marketing including communications media, credit facilities, standardization and grading techniques, marketing research and physical distribution techniques. (Lazer and Kelley 1962, p. 193).

As mentioned in Chapter 3, the functionalist school as advocated by Alderson is heavily dependent on systems thinking and analysis. For Alderson (1957), there were three types of systems: the atomistic, the mechanical, and the ecological. The atomistic system is usually closed with no one of the components important enough to influence the entire system. The components are free to move and interact, but similar to the pure or perfect market structure, no one component emerges as the leader. Since there are few, if any, marketing systems that could be described as atomistic, this type of system has not been of much interest.

Alderson dismissed the mechanical system because it tends to be even more closed than the atomistic system. However, he recognized that some aspects of marketing appear to be mechanical systems, especially some aspects of warehousing and distribution. However, by pointing out that a system must be in touch with its environment, he almost dismissed mechanical systems as having much relevance to marketing.

Ecology is the study of an organism in relation to its environment. For Alderson, the organized behavior system is the expression of the ecological concept in marketing. While the organized behavior system has some definite limitations as pointed out in Chapter 3, it appears to have value to explain certain types of marketing phenomena.

We are unable to identify a stream of research similar to what we have found in previous schools of thought. Given the promise of this school of thought to both theory development and the practice of marketing, we had anticipated more. In an attempt to classify and organize the writings on systems thought in marketing, we have taken Dowling's (1983) suggestion and organized the literature into what Hall and Fagan (1968) have called macroscopic and microscopic analysis.

> Microscopic analysis focuses on the minute structure of certain subsystems of interest; e.g., advertising and distribution (the traditional marketing perspective). Macroscopic analysis, on the other hand, focuses on the behavior of the system as a whole. Macroscopic analysis does not completely ignore specific marketing phenomena, rather it focuses attention on the patterns of behavior of a system under differing environmental conditions (Dowling 1983, p. 23).

What follows is not an exhaustive review of the literature. However, it is very typical of the thought to date.

5.2.1 Macroscopic Marketing Systems

While we have discussed the approach of Wroe Alderson under the functionalist school of thought, much of Alderson's work could also be considered as relevant to this school of thought. He definitely viewed marketing from a total systems perspective. His work (1957, 1965) is the only major work directly relating systems to marketing thinking.

Also focusing on the system as a whole, Mackenzie and Nicosia (1968) pointed out that marketing literature had progressively adopted a systems point of view.

> Our view and interpretation of marketing literature shows a fund of knowledge which, although almost exclusively verbal, is very rich and amenable to more precise and analytical treatment. This knowledge can be summarized in three separate but conceptually related groups.

> First, consider a group of ideas that points to the existence of certain dimensions of any marketing system. These dimensions can be called "elementary" in that they ought to be there for any marketing system to exist. They are the objectives, objects and subjects of marketing activities, the marketing activities themselves, and all other entities such as laws, regulatory agencies, customs, social institutions, human and other resources, etc.

> A second group of ideas concerning marketing consists of attempts to conceptualize how the morphology of a system produced by its elementary dimensions leads to the system's behavior through dynamic interactions.

> The final group of ideas ... consists of attempts to conceptualize and observe empirically the relationships that may exist within and/or across the elementary dimensions mentioned in the first group (Mackenzie and Nicosia 1968, p. 17).

They also proposed a formal definition of a marketing system in a three-dimensional space: "The three main dimensions of agency, activity, and product define the traditionally more important dimensions of the behavior space known as marketing" (Mackenzie and Nicosia 1968, p. 21).

Amstutz (1967) contributed to the systems approach by developing a computer simulation of competitive market response. Various functions of marketing were operationalized and integrated to simulate the marketing system. Amstutz's model of marketing is the most generic yet developed. Unfortunately, it has not enjoyed further development and refinement.

Farley (1967), using simultaneous equation estimation techniques, demonstrated how marketing systems analysis can be used. He discussed several statistical techniques for estimating parameters of the Jamaican distribution structure. He concludes:

> While the theory in these areas is relatively well-developed, it turns out that there are a number of practical problems—particularly those posed by intercorrelations in explanatory variables of such systems—which lead us to consider less-than-best procedures to deal with the problems. Larger data banks and improved computational procedures may combine to improve the situation. However, in this area, as in many others where branches of technology are brought to bear on marketing problems; a variety of quite practical problems remain to be solved before we can be satisfied with research results (p. 321).

More recently, Howard (1983) has taken a systems approach in integrating descriptive concepts of demand and supply cycle, product hierarchy, competitive structure, and a customer decision model to form a marketing theory of the firm. According to Howard, marketing management has suffered from the lack of a systematic body of knowledge to guide decisions. He maintains that to be useful to managers, the "bits and pieces" of marketing knowledge must be organized into a superstructure. Thus, he advocates viewing marketing as a system.

Dowling (1983), in an attempt to formulate propositions about the future of marketing, examines the evolution of marketing systems. In what could become a classic article, he classified the four marketing management philosophies of production, selling, marketing, and societal marketing concepts into four environments originally proposed in the work of Emery and Trist (1965). Emery and Trist used a two-dimensional framework for outlining the characteristics of an enterprise's environment.

> Each level of environmental complexity relies on (a) a different *organization* of the objects within the environment, and (b) various rates of change over time of these objects. Objects can be described as having either positive attributes; i.e., they represent goals or negative attributes; i.e., they are regarded as noxiants or things to be avoided (Dowling 1983, p. 25).

Based on his conclusions (Dowling 1983, p. 30) that "the evolution of marketing can best be described in terms of the attempt by business enterprises to become more aware of, and to react to, the requirements of their various relevant external publics," he proposes the following observations about the future:

> The future environments of all social systems will be characterized by increasing levels of relevant uncertainty.

> The marketing (sub)system is best conceptualized as carrying out a complex homeostatic function for its parent system, the business enterprise. This boundary role makes it ideally suited to help monitor environmental change and where necessary to provide information which will help initiate change within the structure of its parent enterprise.

> The ability of the marketing system to fulfill its homeostatic functions will determine, in part, how an enterprise perceives and reacts to its environment (Dowling 1983, p. 30).

Relationship Between Marketing and Its Environment

	Environment	Relevant Uncertainty	The Normative Response of the Enterprise (System)	Analogous Marketing Management Philosophies
I	Placid random	Low	Automatic reaction	Production concept
II	Placid clustered	Low-medium	Strategy	Selling concept
III	Disturbed reactive	Medium-high	Strategy, tactics, and operations	Marketing concept
IV	Turbulent	High	Initiate systems changes	Societal marketing concept

Adapted from Dowling (1983).

As an example of another approach classified as macroscopic analysis, Reidenbach and Oliva (1983) apply the open system characteristics of entropy to an examination of marketing. They conclude, using indifference analysis, that as a society, we face major trade-offs between the macro and micro levels of the environments. They argue that marketing must shift from an emphasis on demand creation to that of synchronizing, maintaining, and even reducing and destroying demand in order to slow down the entropic process of pollution and resource diminution.

> The consequence of not assuming a more aggressively responsible posture is proliferations of government-controlled macro agencies charged with the responsibility of regulating the transformation processes. This brings with it a concomitant reduction in social and economic freedom (Reidenbach and Oliva 1983, p. 39).

5.2.2 Microscopic Marketing Systems

There are more examples of microscopic systems analysis. A sample of these would include Ridgeway (1957), Staudt (1958), Goldstucker (1966), Uhl (1968), McNiven (1968), Brien (1968), Gardner (1973), and Reidenbach and Oliva (1981).

For instance, Ridgeway (1957) suggested that a manufacturer and its dealers be considered as a single organization and be administered as a system. Staudt (1958) observed that the firm should be viewed as an integrated system with the market (environment) holding veto power over all its activities. Goldstucker (1966) presented the case for developing a systems framework for retail location. Uhl (1968) commented on the need for marketing information systems. He argued that three general information subsystems appear appropriate: (a) selective dissemination, (b) retrospective, and (c) unsolicited. McNiven (1968) discussed several reasons why marketing information systems are counted as failures and suggested a forward-looking approach. Brien and Stafford (1968) discussed marketing information systems and marketing research, and Brien (1968) chided management for mistaking computers for marketing information systems before management is really systems oriented. Gardner (1973) offered the hypothesis that the concept of "dynamic homeostasis" explains the research tradition and its future use in marketing cases that are brought before regulatory bodies. Reidenbach and Oliva (1981) discussed the application of a "general living systems theory" to marketing and its adaptation to the needs of society.

In the mid-1960s, systems were thought to be one of the most important trends in marketing courses. For example, Lazer (1966) wrote:

> Systems-thinking has affected developments in several disciplines, particularly operations research and engineering. Emphasized are the integration of elements and activities into wholes or total systems, and networks, linkages, interactions, feedback, system-adjustment, survival, and growth. This has led to the widely hailed marketing-management philosophy and the marketing concept, both of which emphasize the coordination, integration, and linkage of marketing ingredients in order to achieve a total system of action. The systems-approach has encouraged the acceptance of functionalism—with its emphasis on adjustment, survival, and growth—and has stimulated the study of input-output and open and closed systems. The systems approach will affect future marketing knowledge in even another way. Systems engineers are now developing new mathematical techniques for modeling and analyzing complex systems. Some of these techniques are applicable to marketing systems, and will result in new conceptual and analytical approaches (p. 35).

But just two years later, Seymour Banks speculated that the systems concept as applied to marketing may be just another fad that will eventually fade away (Banks 1968). After surveying leading marketing firms, he found very few firms using the systems concept in marketing. From the few positive responses, however, he predicted "a gradual expansion of the application of the systems concept to marketing since the requirements are not too rare and the benefits substantial, at least for early adopters" (Banks 1968, p. 28).

Amstutz (1968), in an excellent appraisal of "systems analysis," discussed the misapplication of the term to a wide range of procedures that are neither systematic nor analytic. For Amstutz, "valid systems analysis separates the complex market environment into constituent elements and describes interactions among elements with empirically verifiable assertions" (p. 305).

There are several reasons why the potential of a systems perspective in marketing is not likely to materialize in the short run. The first relates to its global, all-encompassing nature. To date, with the exception of writers like Alderson (1957, 1965), Mackenzie and Nicosia (1968), Dowling (1983), and Reidenbach and Oliva (1983), most writers seem to associate systems with each function of marketing such as product, communication, marketing research, and distribution. It seems apparent that we need to devote considerable conceptual research to marketing as a system versus marketing systems.

The second reason relates to the problems of "doing research" on systems, especially macromarketing systems. We have not yet classified our knowledge into sufficient categories for systems analysis at the macro level. Even if we had our knowledge organized, we lack the appropriate analytic techniques for dealing with the highly probabilistic relationships that are likely to be involved. And if that isn't problem enough, the publish or perish environment in which many researchers find themselves makes it difficult to devote the large block of time necessary to engage in acceptable systems research, especially at the macromarketing level.

There is no question that the systems approach still offers much to the development of marketing thought. Will it ever reach its potential? While the outlook in the immediate future is not encouraging, the recent work of Michael Porter (1980, 1985) offers hope that we can classify marketing knowledge and postulate tentative systems relationships in marketing.

5.2.3   Evaluation of the Systems School

If the organizational dynamics school is in its infancy, then the systems school must be considered in the embryonic stage of development. Therefore, it is unfair to subject the systems school to the meta theory criteria used in this book. Although we will go ahead and evaluate it, the reader is urged to remember that some of the evaluative comments are made in the hopes of encouraging further research in this area.

STRUCTURE: **Are the concepts properly defined and integrated to form a strong nomological network?**

By definition, a systems perspective is taken to integrate various components or elements into a strong network. Therefore, the systems school must be scored high on this criterion. However, the problem lies with the definition of the elements of marketing. There is no real consensus among the systems school scholars about various elements of marketing. 'This is not new'. We commented on a similar problem encountered by the functional school of marketing. Unless the systems school provides a conceptually rigorous classification of marketing functions that can be operationally organized by marketing practitioners, it is unlikely that we will have a generic marketing system. The only exception to this has been Arnstutz (1967) and his simulation of the marketing system. Unfortunately, it has not been adopted by others for further development and refinement.

> *Our score on structure = 5.*

SPECIFICATION: **Are the relationships specified in a manner to delimit hypotheses or are they highly contingent?**

The systems school of thought scores well on specification. Although various scholars of this school do not agree on a common definition, each one has formulated the relationships among the chosen constructs to specify directionality and sometimes even the magnitude of relationships. It is, therefore, possible to attempt a simulation of the systems perspective and provide certain answers based on "what if" changes in the input variables. Indeed, the systems school has even attempted to quantify its relationships so that one can also attempt to optimize market responses. This is especially true at the microscopic marketing subsystems level.

> *Our score on specification= 8.*

TESTABILITY: **Are the operational definitions provided to ensure testability and intersubjective consensus?**

Once again, we must reiterate that many systems perspectives have provided operational definitions to test the outputs as a function of inputs. Again, this has been particularly true of the managerially oriented microscopic systems such as new products, advertising, and distribution models. On the other hand, the more generic macroscopic systems that attempt to interface the external noncontrollable societal environment with the internal controllable marketing environment have not provided operational definitions rigorous enough to make the systems testable. Perhaps the recent efforts by Howard (1983) to incorporate the life cycle as the fundamental concept underlying the demand and the supply side of marketing is a good attempt in the right direction.

Our score on testability = 6.

EMPIRICAL SUPPORT: **What is the degree of confirmation in terms of empirical support?**

On this dimension, the systems school scores low. There are too few attempts to empirically test marketing systems. Some industry efforts, such as measuring advertising effectiveness (DAGMAR model) or new product introduction (DEMON model), generated hope for developing strong empirical support, but it has not fully materialized. This is understandable because it takes a lot money and long-term commitment to develop and implement marketing systems in the real world.

Our score on empirical support = 5.

RICHNESS: **How comprehensive and generalizable is the theory?**

It scores very well on this dimension. Whatever the level of analysis (micro versus macro), scholars of this school have consciously taken a comprehensive perspective to generate richness of ideas and hypotheses. For example, Amstutz's (1967) model of marketing is the most generic system yet developed by anyone. Similarly, Forrester's industrial dynamics can accommodate any number of marketing functions with infinite possible relationships. Even the econometric approaches to systems have proven to be fairly robust and rich.

Our score on richness = 8.

SIMPLICITY: **How easy is it to communicate and implement the theory?**

In our opinion, the systems school is relatively simple since it attempts to describe and depict reality by breaking it up into components or subsystems. The only complication inherent in the systems school is that it is more difficult to implement, not because it is complex but because it requires a significant degree of top management commitment.

Our score on simplicity = 8.

Table 5.2 summarizes our evaluation of the systems school of marketing thought. It is relatively weak in structure and empirical support, but scores relatively high on all other dimensions. As we stated earlier, the systems school holds great promise for the advancement of marketing as a discipline. It is quantifiable and testable. Also, marketing practitioners have a vested interest in using its concepts because they are likely to enhance marketing efficiency and productivity. We urge our colleagues to devote more time to this school of thought.

Table 5.2   Evaluation of the Systems School*

Criterion	Rationale	Score
Structure	Systems orientation should generate well-defined structure, but lack of consensus on what to focus on in defining the marketing system is a major weakness	5
Specification	Good specification due to functional and sequential decomposition of subsystems of marketing	8
Testability	Good operational definitions for microscopic systems but weak for macroscopic systems	6

(Continued)

Table 5.2 (*Continued*)

Criterion	Rationale	Score
Empirical support	Excellent support for each functional marketing system such as new products, advertising, and distribution, but none at the total systems level	5
Richness	Very robust and comprehensive at both micro and macro levels	8
Simplicity	Very easy to understand and implement at subsystem level	8
	TOTAL	40

* Scores range from 1 (poor) to 10 (excellent).

5.3   The Social Exchange School of Thought

Although marketing scholars from various theoretical perspectives long acknowledged that the fundamental purpose of marketing was to facilitate exchanges between buyers and sellers, it was not until the mid-1960s that a group of theorists began to advocate a more explicit emphasis on the social exchange school of marketing thought. The honor for launching this exchange perspective in marketing should be rightly shared by Wroe Alderson and William McInnes.

In a paper in the highly influential volume *Theory in Marketing* published in 1964, McInnes argued that greater attention should be given to the role of the market as the focal point of exchanges between buyers and sellers. According to McInnes, "markets result from the social intercourse of men when the makers and users of economic goods and services seek to satisfy their needs and wants through exchange" (p. 53). Using this foundation of market exchanges, he further argued that:

> Marketing is any "motion" or activity that actualizes the potential relation of producer and consumer. The essential task of marketing is, therefore, always related primarily to the market. The work of marketing always begins with the discovery of market potential ... A concept of marketing in its widest sense, therefore, is any activity which actualizes the potential market relationship between the makers and users of economic goods and services (p. 57).

Among his many contributions to marketing, Wroe Alderson, writing along with Miles W. Martin (Alderson and Martin 1965), proposed "The Law of Exchange" to explain why two parties decide to enter into a transaction. His "Law of Exchange" was defined as:

> Given that x is an element of assortment A1 and y is an element of the assortment of A2, x is exchangeable for y if and only if these three conditions hold:
>
> **(a)** x is different from y
>
> **(b)** The potency of the assortment A1 is increased by dropping x and adding y
>
> **(c)** The potency of the assortment A2 is increased by adding x and dropping y (p. 121).

A critical feature of Alderson's concept of exchange was the pivotal role played by the *perceptions and preferences* of the exchange actors in determining the optimality of the exchange transaction:

> Viewing exchange from the stand point of one of the decision makers, we can say that exchange is optimal if he prefers it to any available alternative. Similarly, for the decision maker on the other side of the transaction, it will be optimal for him if he prefers it to any available alternative. It is assumed that if a concrete situation offers an exchange opportunity, the number of alternatives realistically available to either side is not infinite in number but limited to only a few. Faced with a decision, an individual must be guided by his present knowledge of alternatives and the ordering according to his preferences within that set (p. 122).

The next major boost to the exchange school of thought occurred in 1972 when Philip Kotler presented his "generic concept of marketing." In light of the turmoil during the early 1970s regarding the scope and nature of marketing, Kotler (1972a) sought to clarify his perception of the basic focus of marketing:

> What then is the disciplinary focus of marketing? The core concept of marketing is the transaction. A transaction is the exchange of values between two parties. The things-of-values need not be limited to goods, services, and money; they include other resources such as time, energy, and feelings (p. 48).

To further fortify his view that transaction or exchange is the core concept of marketing, Kotler discussed how marketers seek to facilitate and mold exchange relationships:

> Marketing is a particular way of looking at the problem of achieving a valued response from a target market. It essentially holds that exchange values must be identified, and the marketing program must be based on these exchange values ... The marketer attempts to find ways to increase the person's perceived rate of exchange between what he would receive and what he would give up in freely adopting that behavior. The marketer is a specialist at understanding human wants and values and knows what it takes for someone to act (p. 53).

In the mid-1970s, Richard Bagozzi assumed the leadership position in the social exchange school of thought. In a series of related articles (1974, 1975, 1978, 1979), Bagozzi refined and elaborated on his conception of exchange as the fundamental foundation of marketing. Beginning in his 1974 article, Bagozzi defined the exchange system as "a set of social actors, their relationships to each other, and the endogenous and exogenous variables affecting the behavior of the social actors in those relationships" (p. 78).

One of the major contributions of his 1974 paper was his assault on the prior conceptualization of exchange that had failed to identify the causal relationships:

> Unfortunately, the traditional notion of exchange says little about the theoretical cause-and-effect relations determining the exchange. To say that X will be exchanged for Y when both actors perceive their assortment to be improved is not sufficient for a theory. Marketers want to know why and when an individual will take a particular course of action (p. 79).

In the 1975 article, Bagozzi continued his advocacy of the exchange concept by stating that "it is assumed that marketing theory is concerned with two questions: (1) Why do people and organizations engage in exchange relationships? and (2) How are exchanges created, resolved, or avoided?" (p. 32). In addition, he proposed that a general theory of marketing could be established on the exchange concept:

> Although marketing seems to defy simple definition and circumscription, it is essential that marketers locate the distinctive focus (or foci) of the discipline. Failure to do so impedes both the growth of the discipline and the character of its performance. Exchange is a central concept in marketing, and it may well serve as the foundation for that elusive "general theory of marketing" (p. 39).

Bagozzi's 1978 article, which appeared in *American Behavioral Scientist,* presented several new thoughts that served to advance and realign the exchange concept. First, Bagozzi asserted that the exchange process should be viewed as a social activity rather than as insulated individuals making solitary decisions:

> No longer are buyers and sellers treated solely as isolated actors emitting or responding to stimuli. Rather, marketing behavior is now regarded as an inherently social activity where the outcomes of exchange depend on bargaining, negotiation, power, conflict, and the shared meaning existing between buyer and seller (p. 536).

Second, he suggested that exchange relationships are a function of three broad determinants:

1. Social actor variables: including attraction, similarity, expertise, prestige, etc.
2. Social influence variables: the specific actions, communications, and information transmitted between the parties.

3. Situational variables: including the availability of alternative sources of satisfaction, the physical and psychological setting, and the legal and normative setting.

Bagozzi's 1979 paper, entitled "Toward a Formal Theory of Marketing Exchanges," generally served to clarify and reiterate the current status of the exchange perspective. Perhaps the highlight of this paper is Bagozzi's presentation of a category system for evaluating exchanges:

> If the concept of exchanges is to be used in an explanatory — as opposed to a purely descriptive — sense, then it will have to be conceptualized as a phenomenon capable of variation in one or more ways. This author believes that exchanges might be fruitfully conceived as a threefold categorization of *outcomes, experiences,* and *actions,* each varying in degree and occurring to the actors as individuals, jointly or shared, or both. Outcomes in an exchange refer to physical, social or symbolic objects or events accruing to the actors as a consequence of their relationship ... Experiences are psychological states and consist of affective, cognitive, or moral dimensions. They typically are conveyed symbolically through the objects exchanged, the functions performed by the exchange, or the meanings attributed to the exchange ... The final variable with which to represent an exchange is the actions performed by the actors as a product of their interchange. Actions might represent individual choices and responses or joining commitments (pp. 435–436).

Bagozzi's conceptualization of exchange was critiqued by Ferrell and Perrachione in 1980. They generally applauded Bagozzi for his efforts to advance the theory of marketing, but they strongly argued that his utilization of the exchange concept left much to be desired:

> Bagozzi has restated the exchange theories of other disciplines. He has also drawn many potentially useful and relevant concepts from other disciplines. Thus, what he has accomplished is not enough to qualify as a formal theory (or even the basis for a formal theory) of marketing exchanges.

> It is dangerous to borrow exchange theory concepts from economics and psychology and sociology, and apply them directly in marketing. It was their inadequacy that gave rise to the development of a distinct discipline of marketing in the first place. A return to these theories and concepts can at best be only of limited utility in developing a formal theory of exchange for marketing, and reliance on them to the extent Bagozzi docs may well be counter-productive. Many aspects of a marketing exchange theory will and must borrow from and/or be related to those areas; a good theory will have to be eclectic. We do not believe that what Bagozzi gives is sufficiently eclectic enough to provide the necessary bridge between marketing and related disciplines (Ferrell and Perrachione 1980, p. 159).

Perhaps the most elegant statement related to exchange or transaction as the fundamental proposition on which to build marketing theory comes from Shelby Hunt (1976b, 1983a). After reviewing the debate about whether marketing is a science or an art, as well as different philosophies of science, Hunt (1983a) argued:

> Consistent with the perspective of most marketing theorists (Alderson 1965; Bagozzi 1974, 1978, 1979; Kotler 1972) this writer has proposed that the basic subject matter of marketing is the exchange relationship or transaction (p. 12).

He further suggested:

> The preceding discussion implies that *marketing science is the behavioral science that seeks to explain exchange relationships.* Given this perspective of marketing science, and adopting the customary (albeit somewhat arbitrary) convention of designating one party to the exchange as the "buyer" and one party as the "seller" the fundamental explanada of marketing can be logically derived. The four interrelated sets of fundamental explanada of marketing science are:

> The behaviors of buyers directed at consummating exchanges. The behaviors of sellers directed at consummating exchanges.

> The institutional framework directed at consummating and/or facilitating exchanges.

The consequences on society of the behaviors of buyers, the behaviors of sellers, and the institutional framework directed at consummating and/or facilitating exchanges (p. 13).

A recent article by Houston and Gassenheimer (1987) has contributed a systematic examination of the literature on exchange, maintaining that exchange is the core concept of marketing and should have a role in distinguishing it from other disciplines. Based on their review of the literature, the authors discuss exchange as the result of goal-seeking behavior, occurring under specified conditions (as discussed by Alderson, Kotler, and Bagozzi), and consisting of the passing of value or utility. Further, they discuss the exchange relationship as a richer concept than exchange as an isolated act and identify social distance as an important characteristic associated with the variation seen in exchange relationships.

The social exchange school of thought seems to be one of the few in marketing that has a wide degree of consensus. At the same time, it must be recognized that despite Bagozzi's gallant efforts and Hunt's eloquent pleas, the social exchange school of thought has yet to provide propositions as to why exchange takes place between a buyer and a seller. McInnes (1964) and Houston and Gassenheimer (1987) seem to provide the best explanations of why an exchange takes place. According to McInnes (1964):

> Thus, the basic model of a market consists of a set of real but potential relationships in five dimensions: space, time, perception, evaluation, and ownership ... Since market potentiality is measured by the extent of separation of the parties to an exchange in each of these five dimensions, the greater the separation, the greater the market potential ... These dimensions form the basic pattern that makes a market; they are the five dimensions of market potential that confront every marketing agent and determine every marketing institution (p. 59).

More recently, Houston and Gassenheimer (1987) have offered the following explanation:

> The driving force behind exchange is need satisfaction. We express it as the realization of utility where a utility function is a description of what "commodities" are used to satisfy needs ... (p. 16).

Marketing is the study of potency variation resulting from exchange, and exchange is engaged in by an individual for the enhancement of the potency of his or her assortment. Several ways other than exchange can be used to enhance the potency of one's own assortment. They include, but are not limited to, self-production and certain forms of theft.

5.3.1 Evaluation of the Social Exchange School

STRUCTURE: Are the concepts properly defined and integrated to form a strong nomological network?

Both the generic concept of marketing developed by Kotler (1972a) and the formal theory of marketing exchanges proposed by Bagozzi (1979) clearly meet the structural criterion of theory building. Unfortunately, the social exchange school of thought is a single construct theory that provides good normative rules for the marketing practitioner but does not provide any explanation as to why and how values are created and what motivates the buyer and the seller to engage in an exchange. Nonetheless, the concepts are well defined and properly structured, at least with more consistency than most other schools of thought.

Our score on structure = 8.

SPECIFICATION: Are the relationships specified in a manner to delimit hypotheses or are they highly contingent?

The older definitions of market transaction as the exchange of economic values provided a good demarcation of the domain of marketing. Unfortunately, the generic concept of marketing, which generalized market transaction as the exchange of any value, has created ambiguity as to the boundary of marketing. Indeed, Luck (1969) and others have vehemently argued that the broadening of the marketing concept to the exchange of any values results in the possibility of marketing losing its identity. To that extent, specification is weak.

Our score on specification = 4.

TESTABILITY: **Are the operational definitions provided to ensure testability and intersubjective consensus?**

The social exchange school has failed to provide operational definitions. Indeed, there seems to be no interest in empirical testing of the basic propositions. At the same time, it must be pointed out that, based on anecdotal case histories as well as personal experiences, it is possible to generate intersubjective consensus for the basic tenets of this school of thought. We believe, however, this type of face validity is not sufficient to score high on testability.

Our score on testability = 5.

EMPIRICAL SUPPORT: **What is the degree of confirmation in terms of empirical support?**

Because there has been virtually no interest in scientifically testing the basic propositions of the social exchange school, there exists little formal empirical support. However, this school of marketing thought is well supported by case histories and anecdotal evidence.

Our score on empirical support = 5.

RICHNESS: **How comprehensive and generalizable is the theory?**

The social exchange school is perhaps the most generalizable school among all we have studied in this book. It even surpasses the systems school, especially after Kotler's (1972a) brilliant attempt to develop a generic concept of marketing based on the exchange construct. Indeed, this school is so comprehensive that it begins to blur the boundaries of marketing and other behavioral sciences.

Our score on richness = 9.

SIMPLICITY: **How easy is it to communicate and implement the theory?**

The social exchange school is not only rich but also extremely simple. Perhaps this may be the reason why it has universal appeal. It is as easy to communicate because everyone has experiences to relate to its ideas and implications. Furthermore, it is easy to implement. For example, it is obvious to the marketing practitioner that he/she should channel his/her marketing efforts toward that aspect of exchange that has the highest separation between buyers and sellers. This results in enhancing the effectiveness of marketing. Also, he/she should use that element of the marketing mix that is best in bridging the gap. This results in improved efficiency and effectiveness of marketing.

Our score on simplicity = 9.

Table 5.3 summarizes our evaluation of the social exchange school of thought. It scores very well on the dimensions of structure, richness, and simplicity, but lower on the dimensions of specification, testability, and empirical support.

Table 5.3 Evaluation of the Social Exchange School*

Criterion	Rationale	Score
Structure	Limited construct results in good structure	8
Specification	Broadening the definition of exchange to any value has caused confusion between marketing and social exchange	4
Testability	Good face validity but no consensus or standard definitions of exchange	5
Empirical support	Ample case histories but no formal test of the exchange school	5
Richness	Perhaps the richest of all schools of thought in terms of generalizability	9
Simplicity	Extremely simple to understand and implement	9
	TOTAL	40

* Scores range from 1 (poor) to 10 (excellent).

Summary

The three schools of thought reviewed in this chapter are the organizational dynamics, the systems, and the social exchange schools of marketing. The organizational dynamics school is highly focused on the behavior of channel members in marketing. Furthermore, it has limited itself toward understanding psychological aspects as opposed to economic aspects of channel cooperation and conflict.

On the other hand, the systems school is more comprehensive and encompasses all functions and institutions of marketing as well as marketing as an institution within a society. Although the macroscopic systems have been more abstract and non-tested, the microscopic systems, especially related to each element of the marketing mix (product, promotion, price, distribution) have received strong empirical support by marketing practitioners. At the same time, the systems school has also attempted to utilize quantitative tools and methods, including mathematical and simulation models. To that extent, it is closer to the buyer behavior school of marketing thought.

Finally, the social exchange school of marketing thought seems most promising in developing a general theory of marketing. This is because its constructs are simple but very comprehensive. Furthermore, they are actionable by both public policymakers and marketing practitioners. Unfortunately, there is very little formal testing of the propositions developed by the social exchange school even though there is considerable intuitive, experiential, and historical evidence to support its concepts.

Questions for Analysis and Discussion

1. What distinguishes the interactive-noneconomic schools of thought from the economic schools of thought? From whose perspective do they view market transactions, and what disciplines of social sciences do they essentially borrow their theories from?

2. Why did the interactive-noneconomic schools of marketing remain less popular than other schools such as institutional and buyer behavior schools of thought until the early 1990s? Has its popularity increased with the emergence of relationship marketing and services marketing schools of thought? If yes, in what ways?

3. To what extent did Macneil's (1980) "relational contracting" impact the key considerations, constructs, and theoretical propositions of the interactive-noneconomic schools of marketing, particularly the social-exchange school?

4. How did the study of social norms, agency issues, distributive and procedural justice, and resource-dependence perspectives in business-to-business relationships enrich the knowledge foundation of the interactive-noneconomic schools of marketing thought since the early nineties? What were its consequent effects on this school of thought's syntax, semantics, and pragmatics?

5. Marketing faces tremendous disruptions due to rapid changes in technology, media, and organizational processes. Suppose you were to design a study to investigate the marketing response capabilities of firms within this dynamic disruptive setting. What research questions and hypotheses can you develop anchored on interactive-noneconomic schools of marketing thought?

6. Previously, market exchanges and transactions were the focal aspects of marketing, even for organizational dynamics, systems, and social-exchange schools. However, alternative thinking has emerged more recently, emphasizing value creation and value co-creation as the focal aspects of marketing instead of exchanges. In this context, what theoretical constructs and propositions could be applied to study and model value creation processes based on interactive-noneconomic schools of thought?

CHAPTER

What We Have Learned

LEARNING OBJECTIVES

After reading this chapter, you will be able to:

- Recapitulate whether marketing is a science or, at best, a standardized art.
- Delineate the proper domain of marketing theory – what it is or what it should be.
- Establish what is, or should be, the dominant perspective in marketing.

- Contrast the humanistic versus positivistic research philosophy applications in marketing.
- Explain the relationship between marketing and society.
- Enumerate the requisite ingredients for constructing a general theory of marketing.

Based on our historical review of marketing, we can reach several conclusions regarding the current health and welfare of the marketing discipline:

1. Marketing is now perceived as a legitimate scholarly discipline by our colleagues in related fields, such as economics, psychology, sociology, public administration, social work, political science, and mass communications. Although marketing scholars continue to adopt and apply theories from these other disciplines, marketing has begun to develop its own rather impressive library of internally generated theories. In fact, theories originated by marketing scholars are now being increasingly cited by researchers in these allied disciplines. In addition, the leading journals in marketing, such as the *Journal of Marketing,* the *Journal of Marketing Research,* and the *Journal of Consumer Research,* are widely respected and reviewed outside of the narrow confines of the marketing discipline.

2. Marketing is becoming increasingly disassociated from the negative stereotypes that once dominated the perceptions of most consumers. As consumers became more knowledgeable of the true purpose of marketing and as professional marketing organizations acted decisively to discipline unethical practitioners, many consumers gradually gained confidence in marketing's function in society. To be sure, some consumers continue to be victimized by unscrupulous marketers. However, when compared to marketing's performance in earlier years, modern marketing is dramatically more socially responsible.

3. Marketing has demonstrated impressive versatility and vitality by moving beyond the narrow bounds of traditional business arenas and finding applications in nontraditional fields, such as health care, social services, telecommunications, and political science. This movement suggests that marketing has theories and principles that are applicable to a broader range of exchange relationships. Although marketing philosophers continue to debate the desirable boundaries of the marketing discipline, this controversy has become by default a moot point. While these philosophers debated, practitioners outside the traditional business boundaries decided that marketing could assist them in maximizing their exchange relationships.

4. Marketing has a rich heritage that too many marketing scholars and practitioners do not study or appreciate. In many instances, marketing scholars attempt to publish "new" theoretical research that fails to

incorporate the theoretical principles first spawned in earlier schools of marketing thought, such as the commodity, the functional, and the institutional schools. Unfortunately, too few doctoral programs in marketing explicitly stress coursework in marketing history. Furthermore, doctoral dissertations concerning marketing history are exceedingly rare. However, recent efforts by Ronald Savitt (1980), who has discussed the value of historical research in marketing and suggested a methodological framework for conducting it, and Stanley Hollander at Michigan State University, who has hosted regular (every other year) conferences on marketing history, may focus more attention on the history of marketing.

In this chapter, we will take stock of what we have learned from our review of the evolution of marketing thought, as well as begin to address the following issues raised in Chapter 1:

1. Is marketing a science or, at best, a standardized art?
2. What is, or should be, the proper domain of marketing theory?
3. What is, or should be, the dominant perspective in marketing?
4. What is, or should be, the relationship between marketing and society?
5. Is it really possible to create a general theory of marketing?

6.1   Is Marketing a Science or, at Best, a Standardized Art?

This question is still difficult to answer because a vigorous debate is currently raging in marketing regarding the metatheoretical criteria. While some notable scholars, led by Shelby Hunt (1983b), maintain that logical positivism is the proper foundation for theory development, another growing group, led by Paul Anderson (1983), has recently begun to argue that marketing theories should be judged with relativistic criteria. This controversy certainly bears directly on the distinction of science versus art.

In this book, we utilized a metatheoretical evaluation system with six criteria that bridges the gap between the logical positivist perspective and the relativism perspective. The syntax criteria of structure and specification evaluate the consistency of the nomological network of constructs in a theory. Semantics criteria evaluate a theory's relationship to reality by analyzing its testability and empirical support. Finally, the pragmatics or relevance criteria of richness and simplicity scrutinize the applicability of a theory to those who are actively involved in marketing practice.

In short, the emphasis on syntax and semantics represents preference for logical positivism whereas the emphasis on pragmatics represents preference for relativism. In some sense, this is really a debate as to which is more important — rigor or relevance. It is argued that in our quest to become more scientific and, therefore, respected by traditional disciplines, we have emphasized too much rigor at the expense of relevance. Indeed, the same journals that have enhanced the respectability of marketing have come under some criticism with respect to relevance. Too many papers published in *the Journal of Consumer Research, the Journal of Marketing Research,* and even *the Journal of Marketing* are regarded as irrelevant to the advancement of marketing discipline and marketing practice. In fact, a backlash to this crisis in relevance has resulted in a proliferation of new journals with an emphasis toward balancing rigor and relevance (Luke and Doke 1987).

In addition to the dichotomy of logical positivism versus relativism as the appropriate foundation for theory development, there is a growing debate over appropriate methodology for empirical research and theory testing. This debate has largely focused on the dichotomy between the methods suggested by the tradition of logical positivism and the methods suggested by the philosophy of humanism. Most notably, Elizabeth Hirschman (1986) has argued that, because marketing is a socially constructed enterprise, research in marketing is in need of inputs from humanistic modes of inquiry. In contrast to the experimental and survey methodologies characterizing the logical positivist approach, the humanistic approach advocates more naturalistic forms of inquiry:

> ... it advocates *in-dwelling* of the researcher with the phenomena under investigation. Rather than standing apart from the system being studied, the researcher immerses the self within it. Researcher understanding, therefore, is deemed within the humanistic perspective to arise from direct personal experience, rather than by the manipulation of experimental variables. (p. 238)

According to Hirschman, the different research methodologies advocated by the humanistic approach and the positivist approach result from differences in their basic philosophies, with the humanistic philosophy being virtually the converse of the logical positivist philosophy:

Humanistic Versus Positivistic Research Philosophies

The Humanistic Metaphysic	The Positivistic Metaphysic
1. Human beings construct reality multiple realities.	1. There is a single composed of discrete elements.
2. Researcher and phenomenon are mutually interactive.	2. The researcher and phenomenon are independent.
3. Research inquiry is directed toward the development of idiographic knowledge.	3. It is possible and desirable to develop statements of truth that are generalizable across time and context.
4. Phenomenal aspects cannot be segregated into "causes and effects."	4. Elements of reality can be segregated into causes and effects.
5. Inquiry is inherently value-laden	5. It is possible and desirable to discover value-free objective knowledge.

Adapted from Hirschman (1986, p. 239).

Similarly, in a recent address as an Association for Consumer Research (ACR) Fellow, Everett Rogers has suggested the critical school paradigm as appropriate for guiding theory development and testing within marketing and consumer behavior. According to Rogers (1987), the critical school is more philosophical in its emphasis than is the traditional empirical school based on logical positivism; and it is based on a greater attention to context, an early Marxist orientation, and a concern with who controls a system. In contrast to the empirical school, which is strongest in the United States, the critical school tends to be concentrated in Europe. Advocating that consumer researchers can benefit from the insights of the critical school, Rogers (1987) listed four implications for consumer research:

1. "Consumer scholars should focus on the ownership and control of systems affecting individual consumer behavior." (p. 9)

2. "Consumer research should be cast in a wider scope, both in recognizing (1) that research questions of a global significance should be emphasized over culture-bound inquiries of national systems, and (2) that to understand consumer behavior is to understand society ... " (p. 9)

3. "The critical school suggests to empirical scholars of consumer behavior that they should broaden the range of methodological tools they employ in their investigations." (p. 10)

4. "Ethical aspects of the consumer behavior they investigate should not be ignored by empirical scholars, even if these aspects cannot be studied with their usual research methods." (p. 10)

Table 6.1 provides a summary of the ratings we have given to the twelve schools of thought reviewed in this book. An analysis of the summary provides some interesting insights.

6.1.1 Borrowed Constructs versus Our Own

The early schools of marketing thought, including the commodity and functional schools, were highly relevant and based on empirical observations. However, these schools failed to develop a rich syntax or conceptual base. But as marketing evolved over the past seventy-five years, the conceptual foundation has improved considerably. This movement is clearly a reflection of marketing theorists borrowing well-conceptualized constructs from other disciplines. For example, the managerial school borrowed economic concepts such as elasticity and

Table 6.1 Summary of Evaluations*

Schools of Thought	Metatheory Criteria						
	Structure	Specification	Testability	Empirical Support	Richness	Simplicity	Total
Commodity	3	4	3	6	8	8	32
Functional	5	3	7	7	8	8	38
Regional	7	6	7	7	4	7	38
Institutional	7	7	4	5	5	8	36
Functionalist	7	7	2	3	8	2	29
Managerial	8	7	8	9	9	9	50
Buyer behavior	8	8	6	8	9	8	47
Activist	5	5	4	7	5	6	32
Macromarketing	4	4	6	6	7	4	31
Organizational dynamics	8	8	4	3	5	4	32
Systems	5	8	6	5	8	8	40
Social exchange	8	4	5	5	9	9	40

* Scores range from 1 (poor) to 10 (excellent).

marginal analysis, the regional school adopted concepts like spatial gravitation from geography, and, of course, the buyer behavior school borrowed heavily from psychology, sociology, and communications.

Although the adoption of well-defined theories from other disciplines is desirable, this activity may create a crisis of relevance. More precisely, most schools of marketing thought that relied extensively on borrowed concepts have generally scored low on the richness and the simplicity criteria. This weakness suggests that marketing theorists must place greater emphasis on developing *our own constructs and theories* that are fundamentally strong in all metatheoretical criteria. As we noted in the introduction to this chapter, marketing has begun to gain a measure of respect for some theories and concepts developed internally in recent years. Now we must continue this trend and not be content to merely borrow externally developed theories.

A few examples will illustrate this point. The functional school of thought was probably the earliest predecessor of the concept of value chain popularized by Porter (1985). Values added by different marketing functions such as place, time, and possession values are becoming increasingly important in market-driven industries. We hope that younger scholars in the discipline will add considerable rigor to these functional school concepts with proper codification, modeling, and empirical testing.

Similarly, the classification of products and services into three or four classes based on customer or market characteristics a la the commodity school has the promise of becoming more meaningful than the traditional standard industrial classification of industries based on product characteristics. Additionally, the concepts of "wheel of retailing" and "laws of retail gravitation" from the regional school are our own and should be nurtured and developed rather than abandoned for borrowed concepts from economics, psychology, or sociology.

Finally, the managerial school has generated several unique concepts of which we can be proud. These include the concepts of product life cycle, marketing myopia, marketing mix, and the marketing concept itself. Perhaps the single most unique contribution is the development of the concept of market segmentation and its corollaries of product differentiation and market differentiation. Indeed, it is a pleasant surprise to learn that the "hot" new concepts of business strategy and policy such as differentiation and focus are really based on concepts developed in marketing.

We strongly urge younger marketing scholars to enhance the rich concepts of marketing by developing better syntax (structure and specification). We believe this is preferable to borrowing concepts from other disciplines that may have better syntax but may be low in relevance or pragmatism (richness and simplicity).

6.1.2   Respectability Through the Buyer Behavior School

Not surprisingly, the buyer behavior school ranks very high on most of the metatheoretical criteria. Indeed, many scholars suggest that the respectability of the marketing discipline was enhanced significantly with the emergence of the buyer behavior school. First, by focusing on the consumer rather than the producer, the buyer behavior school gained a measure of independence and legitimacy by not appearing to serve the direct interests of profit-oriented marketing institutions. Second, this school utilized a broader variety of research methods than any previous school of marketing. These research methods ranged from such highly quantitative techniques as stochastic processes, multivariate statistics, and laboratory and field experiments, to such highly qualitative techniques as focus groups and motivation research. Finally, by using rigorous methods and producing research that advanced the theoretical boundaries of borrowed concepts, marketing researchers gained respect from colleagues in allied social sciences and quantitative disciplines. Researchers in these allied disciplines now have increasingly begun to use consumers as test subjects in field experiments to evaluate their theories.

However, even though the buyer behavior school added immeasurably to marketing's stature in the academic community, this school has lost sight, to some extent, of its marketing roots. As a result, many marketing practitioners and even some marketing academicians have suggested that buyer behavior researchers are contributing very little to the improvement of marketing practice (Engel, Blackwell, and Kollat 1978, Sheth 1979b). In response to this criticism, some scholars in this field have begun recently to emphasize the relevance of their research to marketing practitioners and scholars in other subareas of marketing, particularly marketing strategy, pricing, and advertising.

6.1.3   Dominance of the Managerial School

The robustness of the managerial school, in terms of its ratings on the metatheoretical criteria, is perhaps somewhat surprising. Indeed, our relatively high ranking of the managerial school may help to revive scholarly interest in this school. In the past, the managerial school has been generally perceived as a hodgepodge of applied principles that are relevant for training marketing practitioners, but of little value to rigorous marketing theorists.

In our opinion, several factors indicate that the managerial school deserves more serious theoretical attention. First, as mentioned before, the managerial school of marketing has generated several constructs that legitimately can be declared as our own. These include the marketing mix, market segmentation, and possibly the product life cycle and strategic market planning. Except for the earliest schools of marketing thought (commodity, functional, and institutional), the managerial school is the only school that is likely to demarcate the boundaries of marketing.

Second, the managerial school has clearly demonstrated that it can accommodate the knowledge base from a broad blend of competing schools of thought, from the traditional commodity, functional, and institutional schools to the contemporary buyer behavior and organizational dynamics schools. As such, the managerial school may serve as an excellent foundation for the creation of the elusive "general theory" of marketing, or at least for the creation of several good "middle-range" theories of marketing.

Finally, the managerial school has shown that, like the buyer behavior school, it can use a variety of research methods and techniques, including econometrics, psychometrics, biometrics, and computer simulation. In addition, this school has employed both field and laboratory experiments.

In summary, even though the question of marketing's status as an art or a science is contentious, we believe that the buyer behavior and managerial schools have clearly moved the marketing discipline away from a standardized art and toward the establishment of a science of marketing. While the identification of a set of "marketing laws" would presently be premature, we believe in the near future some marketing concepts will be accorded the stature of laws. To facilitate and legitimize this process, perhaps the marketing discipline should convene a special convention to nominate certain marketing concepts for designation as marketing laws. In our judgment, these would include the 20:80 ratio (20 percent of customers buying 80 percent of volume), the product life cycle, the psychology of complication and simplification, market segmentation, and balance of power.

 ## 6.2 What Is, or Should Be, the Proper Domain of Marketing Theory?

The twelve schools of marketing thought have differing perspectives on this issue. The earlier schools tended to treat the marketing domain very narrowly so that primary attention was focused on basic commodity products, especially agricultural commodities (wheat, cotton, milk, cattle, etc.), manufacturing materials (steel, wire, cloth, etc.), and consumer necessities (housing, food, clothing, etc.). From this narrow concentration on basic commodity products, commodity theorists studied the products themselves, functional theorists evaluated the functions needed to market these commodity products, and institutional theorists analyzed the types of agents required to move these commodities from the producers to the consumers.

In contrast, within the past two decades, many marketing scholars have accepted that marketing is applicable to a much broader range of exchange relationships. Nonetheless, like the earlier schools, the more modern schools have still usually concentrated on only one aspect of this broader domain of marketing. For instance, buyer behavior theorists have focused on the consumers, managerial theorists have analyzed the sellers, and organizational dynamics theorists have studied the institutions. Thus, even though the domain of marketing has broadened to include a variety of exchange relationships (services, industrial, social, international, nonprofit, etc.), individual schools of marketing thought have continued to study only one particular agent of these exchange relationships. In our opinion, several basic tenets of marketing can be used to define the proper domain of marketing:

6.2.1 Market Behavior as the Domain of Marketing

Marketing is the study of market behavior, just as psychology is the study of individual human behavior and sociology is the study of group or social behavior. Market behavior includes the behavior of buyers, sellers, intermediaries, and regulators in exchange relationships. To that extent, marketing is broader than any one school of marketing thought. Just as psychology has numerous subdivisions (social psychology, group dynamics, child psychology, clinical psychology, community psychology, organizational psychology, etc.), marketing also has many subdivisions, including services marketing, industrial marketing, international marketing, direct marketing, nonprofit marketing, and so on. Similarly, as psychology has several explanations or perspectives of human behavior (learning, conditioning, motivation, perception, information processing, etc.), marketing also has several explanations or perspectives of market behavior (commodity, functional, institutional, managerial, buyer behavior, etc.).

The principal point is that marketing is delimited as the study of market behavior. Market behavior as the central focus of marketing is more explicit in the earlier schools of thought and more implicit in more recent schools of marketing thought. Whether explicit or implicit, we agree with McInnes (1964), who pointed out that:

> Markets result from the social intercourse of men when the makers and users of economic goods and services seek to satisfy their needs and wants through exchange. (p. 53)

McInnes went on to suggest that:

> In an exchange economy, the relationship of producer and consumer—i.e., the market—is a universal fact. The mere fact of relationship, however, is insufficient to generate an exchange. The existence of a market relation is the foundation for exchange not a substitute for it ... Producers and consumers are related by a market, but no exchange occurs until some force or agent brings them into actual contact. This force, making a potential market contact into a real market contact, is what is generally known as marketing. (pp. 56–57)

We believe that a market exists where there is potential for exchange. From this perspective, it makes little difference whether the market is viewed as a geographic area, a group of institutions, a process, or a classification of activities. From this perspective, a market exists when there are buyers and sellers in any combination of numbers, with or without face-to-face contact.

Marketing thought has usually assumed many sellers and many buyers, or at least a number of buyers and sellers. This is the more prevalent representation of marketing in which sellers are competing against one another for customers and customers are choosing between sellers and evaluating the trade-offs between making versus buying. The fundamental principles of market behavior in this situation are *competition and selection,* with a strong emphasis on promotion and differentiation.

Yet a single buyer and a single seller can constitute a market. Vertically integrated industries such as oil, steel, and telecommunications are examples. Marketing consists of internal marketing with an emphasis on transfer pricing and functional delineation between the internal or captive seller and the internal or dedicated buyer. In stark contrast to the competitive orientation, *cooperation and coordination* are the fundamental tenets of market behavior in this type of market.

A third market situation is where there are many customers but only a single supplier. This is often common in a market monopoly or a regulated monopoly. The supplier is primarily concerned with the allocation of products and service resources among customers, while the customers are primarily concerned with their dependence on the single supplier. The fundamental principles of *allocation and dependence* are necessary to understand market behavior in this situation. Therefore concepts of public interest (dependence) and universal service (allocation) become more relevant than competition, differentiation, and promotion.

Finally, it is possible that there is only one buyer and many suppliers. This is clearly true in the defense industry or when the government is the only buyer in the marketplace. In this situation, the market behavior is likely to be based on *strategic alliances and politics.* Planned selling and networking are much more important than other marketing activities.

The four combinations discussed above are summarized below:

		Buyers	
		One	**Many**
Sellers	**One**	Cooperation and coordination (Vertically integrated industry)	Allocation and dependence (Regulated industry)
	Many	Strategic alliance and politics (Defense industry)	Competition and selection (Competitive industry)

Our colleagues will notice that we are suggesting a level of richness in thinking that is not evident in present schools of marketing thought. By defining the domain of marketing as the study of market behavior, we are able to transcend the aforementioned specific actors, processes, and functions prevalent in separate schools of marketing thought. At the same time, the new definition clearly allows the existing schools to continue to research and theorize in their areas of interest.

6.2.2   Market Transaction as Unit of Analysis

The fundamental unit of analysis in marketing is, or should be, the market interaction between two or more parties. Not all interactions are market transactions. For an interaction to become a market transaction as opposed to a social, psychic, or charitable interaction, we must limit the domain of marketing to those interactions that have clearly identified the roles of the parties to the transaction as providers (sellers) and customers (buyers). In other words, it is the *role definition of the parties* to an interaction that makes it a market transaction and not the object or the process of transaction.

While the great majority of market transactions will be characterized as exchange of value between two or more parties, we must include nonexchange-based transactions in our understanding of markets. Nonexchange-based mechanisms for market transactions include mandatory rules and regulations; transfer of products or services without exchange, such as in gift-giving and charitable contributing; and many derived transactions, such as value-added services, parts, repairs, and maintenance created as a consequence of primary market behaviors.

In our opinion, the marketing discipline has unnecessarily emphasized voluntary exchange as the only mechanism to create markets. Indeed, Sheth (1985c) has enumerated numerous case histories in which markets have been created for products and services by mandatory laws, for example, lead-free gasoline and smoke detectors.

6.2.3   Need for Time Dynamics in Marketing

It is interesting to note that except for a few introduced by the managerial and the buyer behavior schools of marketing thought, the majority of marketing concepts are not specifically dynamic over time. The concepts of product life cycle and brand loyalty are probably the only concepts that have explicitly included time as a dimension.

It is obvious that marketing is a dynamic process and must be treated as such. Therefore, it is essential that dynamics of time be inherent in any conceptualization of marketing. Perhaps the popularity of the product life cycle is due to its inherent time-sensitive and time-shifting characteristics. Consequently, it is very likely that the domain of marketing will be defined around, not only the market, but also the concept of *repeated market transactions* or what is more popularly called "relationship marketing." This should strongly suggest that the focus is not on a single market transaction or on selling, but on a continued relationship between the buyer and the seller.

6.2.4   Constraints in Market Behavior

Market behavior is constrained by a number of forces. For example, the customer has resource constraints such as time, money, and expertise in creating market opportunities. The supplier has similar resource constraints (technology, people, and money) in providing market opportunities. Finally, there are likely to be social and legal normative constraints imposed on market behavior. Just as Freud had to develop the concept of the super-ego as the regulating mechanism between the ego and the id, we must formally conceptualize the normative mechanisms that regulate the market behavior of buyers and sellers.

This is really not as new a concept as it might at first appear. In Chapter 3 we found that the managerial school recognized the presence of exogenous variables. However, that school of thought often treated them as uncontrollable factors within which marketing functions and practices were carried out. In Chapter 4, we noted that the macromarketing school was concerned with societal needs and concerns and their impact on marketing as a social institution. In addition, this concept is inherently included in the study of economics on both the buyer side (utility theory) and the supplier side (theory of the firm).

However, the role of these exogenous variables, to date, has largely gone unexplored. Consequently, the richness and inherent usefulness of present schools of marketing thought are often limited. There are few mechanisms that currently allow us to assess developments regarding these exogenous variables (resource constraints of buyers and sellers and normative constraints from social and legal institutions), let alone incorporate them into marketing thought.

While the foregoing discussion of the basic tenets of marketing is not necessarily exhaustive, it does point out the often narrow approaches to marketing thought contained in the existing schools of marketing. It logically follows that we need to expand our understanding of marketing to incorporate the basic tenets of marketing, that is, market behavior, market transactions as the unit of analysis, marketing as a dynamic process of relationships between buyers and sellers, and the exogenous variables that influence market behavior.

6.3   What Is, or Should Be, the Dominant Perspective in Marketing?

As we presented in the last four chapters, each school of thought has its own perspective. The commodity school focuses on the product, the functional school on the activities, the institutional school on the actors, and the regional school on the market arena. Similarly, the managerial school focuses on the seller, the buyer behavior school on the consumer, and the activist and macromarketing schools on the public interest. While marketing thought has been richly enhanced by these various perspectives, we believe that this diversity resembles the proverbial seven blind men and the elephant. Each perspective seems to define and structure marketing in a manner that, at best, represents only a partial picture. What is needed is a perspective that reflects the raison d'être of marketing, a perspective that is the common cause that no stakeholder (consumer, seller, government, or social critic) can question. Indeed, that perspective should really reflect what marketing is all about.

6.3.1   Values as Marketing Perspective

In our opinion, the main purpose of marketing is to create and distribute values among the market parties through the process of market transactions and market relationships. This concept of creating and distributing value inherently implies that marketing objects, functions, and institutions must create "win-win" market behavior. In game theory language, marketing should be a *positive sum game* rather than a zero sum (or a negative sum) game. Even though this is a simple concept and most scholars are likely to agree to its importance, it is often not manifested in marketing practice. Indeed, if we agree that the role of marketing is to create and distribute values through market transactions and relationships, this concept immediately calls into question earlier concepts of selling and negotiating (win-lose), as well as the self-interest concept as the driving forces of marketing. We believe that the concept of win-win between market parties will go a long way in minimizing the negative stereotypes of marketing created by the concepts of selling and promoting.

It is our belief that we need a theory of marketing that identifies what values are or can be created by marketing, who creates them, and how they are distributed so that all parties benefit from market behavior. We have borrowed some concepts from economics and the behavioral sciences to address these issues. For example, several older schools of marketing thought have suggested form, possession, time, and place values as the domain of marketing. McInnes (1964) adds perception or information as one more value. We can also expand on the possession value by redefining it as possession and consumption value in order to include several psychological theories including conspicuous consumption, epistemic (novelty-curiosity) value, and emotional values inherent in products and services.

6.3.2   Government versus Self-Regulation Perspective

It is obvious that if both customers and suppliers (including intermediaries) truly behave from the win-win perspective of marketing, it is very likely that the external regulation of marketing may become less relevant. In other words, market behavior becomes more and more self-regulated and the role of public policy, including legislation, regulation, and advocacy, becomes less and less meaningful. However, this is more an idealistic view rather than a realistic view of marketing for a number of reasons. First, human nature is documented to be driven by self-interest. Therefore, the win-win concept often requires behavior contrary to human instincts. Although this can be overcome by education and information, it is not likely to be manifested universally. Second, in order to create a win-win situation in a market transaction, it is critical that all parties concerned know what they want and communicate it freely to one another. This is also not likely to happen without conscious learning and education. Finally, even if the two parties know what they want and communicate it to each other, it may not be technologically or economically possible to create a market transaction that results in a surplus of value that then can be distributed among the parties. In short, the realistic constraints are too many for this utopian perspective of marketing.

However, it does not mean that we cannot set creation and distribution of values as the normative goal of marketing and measure performance of actors, functions, and institutions against this normative standard. We urge that this concept become the "test" of future marketing thought just as the results of "pure" or "perfect" competition are the test of economic market behavior, even though such market structures are largely nonexistent.

6.4 What Is, or Should Be, the Relationship Between Marketing and Society?

The relationship between marketing and society has been an issue since the early days of merchant trades. Indeed, it predates industrialization. However, different schools of marketing thought have put different levels of emphasis on this issue. For example, the commodity, the functional, the institutional, and the regional schools of thought are practically silent on this issue. On the other hand, the activist and the macromarketing schools have emerged in order to focus almost exclusively on the relationship between marketing and society. In the middle are the buyer behavior and the managerial schools of marketing thought.

The most common understanding of the relationship between society and business in general and marketing, in particular, is that it is an advocacy or an adversary relationship. In other words, society through legislation and regulation acts as a watchdog to ensure that the marketing process will serve the public interest. Similarly, the marketer, through political action committees as well as public opinion, wants to ensure that the government does not abuse its authority.

The advocacy position is based on the assumption that the objectives, processes, and tools of the business institution are radically different from those of the society. For example, the profit motive of the business is considered incompatible with the public interest motive of the society. The process of market transactions, with its focus on creating and distributing economic values between buyers and sellers, is considered incompatible with the broader issues of resource utilization and noneconomic motives as well as present versus future generation perspectives inherent in society. Finally, the marketer utilizes tools and techniques of influence, competitive behavior, and managerial control through such practices as the Four Ps of marketing, which are often regarded as antisocial. There is even a deep-rooted concern that business, if it succeeds in creating values, may align the consumer on its side and in the process jeopardize the relationship of government by the people, of the people, and for the people.

6.4.1 National Marketing Policy

What should then be the relationship between marketing and society? We believe that the concept of advocacy must be displaced with the concept of partnership behavior between marketing and society. If both institutions behave as partners, it is very likely that we can generate an overall *national marketing policy* comparable to a national industrial or economic policy. The concept of partnership between business and government is not new. It was successfully practiced by the British during the colonial days; it is still practiced widely among many European nations, notably France; and more recently, it has been raised to a level of science in Japan.

What are the advantages of a national marketing policy based on the concept of partnership behavior between government and business? First, it will improve efficiency of market behavior by minimizing the watchdog process inherent in the advocacy philosophy. In short, costs associated with creation and distribution of values will be significantly reduced, which in turn will enhance the raison d'être of marketing.

Second, it will standardize and streamline the regulatory process in marketing. The conflicting laws and "Catch 22" phenomena currently inherent among different regulatory agencies (state versus federal, antitrust versus FTC, industry-specific versus general regulation, as well as self-regulation) often act as inhibitors to creating and distributing values. Hopefully, a national marketing policy will become a facilitating process rather than an inhibitory process in marketing.

Third, a national marketing policy is likely to provide better continuity over time because it reflects what business and society believe they must do. This continuity over time will go a long way toward encouraging relationship marketing instead of marketing as selling and promotion. This, in turn, will disassociate marketing from its negative stereotypes.

While the discussion of specific content and structure of a national marketing policy is beyond the scope of this book, we do believe it must focus on the following issues: First, the role of the government should be to *provide incentives to both customers and suppliers* that will enhance creation and distribution of values. Second, the government must safeguard interests of both the consumers and suppliers. We strongly believe that just as there are marketing malpractices, there are also consumer malpractices that must be openly addressed and managed. These include such deviant behaviors as shoplifting, credit card fraud, vandalism, and emotional or physical abuse of marketing employees. Finally, the national marketing policy must address the issues of international marketing similar to what GATI (General Agreements on Trade and Tariffs) does for international trade.

We believe that pieces of national marketing policy are already in place. For example, there are laws and regulations with respect to product safety, product packaging, trade practices, advertising, and physical distribution of products and services. However, what we do not have is the partnership attitude as well as an integrated relationship between marketing and society.

 ## 6.5   Is It Really Possible to Create a General Theory of Marketing?

It is obvious from the preceding four chapters that we do not have "a," let alone "the" general theory of marketing. Rather, we have a collection of theories, each looking at marketing from a unique perspective. Copeland's trichotomy of goods is still well accepted by the commodity school; the wheel of retailing is firmly established in the institutional school; the Four Ps of marketing seems unshakable in the managerial school; and such theories as perceived risk and the Howard-Sheth theory of buyer behavior are still considered useful and relevant in the buyer behavior school.

But adding to the confusion is the semi-slippery understanding of what a general or master theory of marketing is or might be. Merton (1957) makes a distinction between isolated empirical findings, middle-range theories, and full-blown or master theories.

> I attempt to focus attention on what might be called theories of the middle range: theories intermediate to the minor working hypotheses evolved in abundance during the day-by-day routines of research, and the all-inclusive speculations comprising a master conceptual scheme from which it is hoped to derive a very large number of empirically observed uniformities of social behavior (pp. 5–6).

In marketing, we are able to identify several attempts at devising a master conceptual scheme or master theory. We also observe a number of theories of the middle range. In fact, several schools of marketing thought may be more adequately described as theories of the middle range. But what we really have in marketing theory are literally hundreds of minor working hypotheses.

6.5.1   Some General Theories of Marketing

Although he fell short of a general or master theory of marketing, Wroe Alderson (Alderson and Cox 1948, Alderson 1957, 1965) clearly intended to develop such a theory. Alderson's general theory as restated by Hunt, Muncy, and Ray (1981) is interesting and comprehensive. However, it is seemingly focused on and designed for packaged goods. Also, it seems to have largely ignored the international dimension as well as not fully incorporating the influence of exogenous systems and variables such as technology, government, cultural traditions, and even marketing infrastructures.

In a somewhat less ambitious work than that of Alderson, McInnes (1964) provides a beautiful view of the role of marketing and how marketing can realize its potential in creating perception (information), ownership, time, place, and functional values. However, he is also largely silent on exogenous systems and their impact on marketing. Furthermore, the role of resellers and intermediaries is very lightly treated. Perhaps the biggest weakness of both Alderson's and McInnes' theories of marketing is that they are highly descriptive. They provide very little normative value in terms of control of market behavior.

More recently, John Howard's (1983) marketing theory of the firm shows good promise. It is perhaps the only theory that explicitly brings together the managerial and the buyer behavior schools of marketing thought. Furthermore, it is based on the concept of the product life cycle, and therefore it is time-sensitive and dynamic. Finally, it incorporates both the normative aspect as well as exogenous forces, and marketing within and outside of the organization of a firm.

Although Howard's theory has the potential to become a general theory of marketing, the potential has yet to be realized. First of all, it is based on secondary evidence. It needs to be tested as a general theory of marketing comparable to the testing of the Howard-Sheth theory of buyer behavior. Second, it is much more a theory of the firm rather than a true theory of marketing. It is more managerial in that sense. Finally, it needs considerable integration between the buyer side and the supplier side of the equation, especially with a focus on competitive behavior and competitive strategies.

6.5.2   Ingredients for a General Theory of Marketing

Do we believe that a general theory of marketing is possible? Our answer is a definite "yes," especially as measured by Hunt's criteria of a general theory: lawlike generalizations, unification of middle-range theories, and explanation of large numbers of working hypotheses. We believe that some of the ideas expressed in this chapter may become the building blocks for the development of a general theory of marketing. These include:

1. Marketing is a study of market behavior rather than marketer behavior or buyer behavior.
2. Market behavior is measured by a fundamental unit of analysis called the market transaction. It is a more specified type of interaction between two or more parties in which they take the roles of customers and suppliers.
3. We must focus on the dynamic nature of marketing. This can be achieved by understanding and explaining how *repeated* market transactions take place between two or more parties. The emphasis on repeated transactions will shift the focus of marketing away from marketing equals selling and toward the concept of relationship marketing.
4. Marketing as a study of market behavior must include constraints on that behavior. These constraints can reside with the buyers, with the suppliers, or with such external institutions as the government and other societal stakeholders.
5. The raison d'être of marketing is to create and distribute values. This can be achieved by ensuring that the process of marketing results in a positive sum or a win-win situation between two or more parties to a market transaction. Although it is difficult to enumerate the precise nature of values, it is safe to include function, perception, possession, time, and place values that bridge the gap between supplier resources and consumer needs.
6. In order to ensure that the general theory of marketing gains the respect of the scientific community, it must be strong on the syntax, the semantics, and the pragmatics metatheory criteria. In other words, it must score high on structure and specification, on testability and empirical support, and finally on richness and simplicity.

6.5.3   The Role of the Managerial and Systems Approach in a General Theory of Marketing

Merton (1957, p. 9) argued that the major task of sociology was to develop theories of the middle range. One can only speculate what he would recommend to his colleagues in sociology thirty years later. Our guess is that he would still urge a focus on middle-range theories.

We do not share the belief that marketing needs to focus primarily on theories of the middle range in the next few years. We have many concepts in marketing, some borrowed, some unique to marketing. We have different schools of thought that approach marketing from different perspectives and motives. Consequently, it seems appropriate to work toward integration and consolidation so that a general theory will have more solid blocks on which to build. The fact that we observe so little work on a general theory of marketing is less a criticism of marketing theorists than it is a criticism of the unsystematic and unintegrated body of knowledge that our metatheory evaluation revealed.

Will one approach to general theory development be more likely to emerge than others? To date, we have seen the systems approach of Alderson (1957, 1965) and the more managerial approaches of McInnes (1964) and Howard (1983) as the most likely approaches. There is a logical reason why a general theory of marketing will most likely come out of these two approaches. These are the only approaches that take, or have the capacity to take, a truly comprehensive view of marketing that includes the environment, and all relevant actors, as well as non-traditional elements like global competitors. Also, both approaches are able to incorporate the critical ingredients summarized in the previous section.

It is our hope that we will eventually have several general theories of marketing. But that seems a long distance into the future. We must not lose sight, however, of the fact that there is real value in working *toward* general theories of marketing. It is only by exploring the assumptions and linkages necessary to build such theories that we truly move toward marketing as a science.

We hope our colleagues and future scholars of marketing will take up this challenge. We also hope that the voyage through the history of marketing thought presented in this book will whet their appetites for development of a general theory of marketing.

Questions for Analysis and Discussion

1. To what extent have the various schools of marketing thought brought respectability to the marketing discipline? Which schools have contributed the most in this respect?

2. Can marketing be legitimately considered a science, or is it still a standardized art? What research philosophies have dominated the marketing investigation process? Has it helped or hurt the marketing discipline in establishing its legitimacy?

3. Some people argue that marketing academia developed a "physics envy" and made their research esoteric? According to them, premier marketing journals favor research and manuscripts for publication based on obscure models with a high level of mathematical sophistication, ignoring the pragmatics and business relevance. Examine the articles in the last two issues of the *Journal of Marketing Research* and *Marketing Science* to evaluate the integrity of the above statement.

4. Sheth and Sisodia (1999) revisited marketing's lawlike generalizations to conclude that prevailing generalizations centered around location, time, market, and competition were affected by at least one major contextual discontinuity challenging the relevance and validity of these well-accepted lawlike generalizations. Can you identify what factors in each category fundamentally change the marketing context, thus making previously established marketing theories or schools of thought irrelevant? What new approaches need to be developed in the evolving marketing context?

5. Which of the 12 schools of marketing discussed in this and previous chapters has the highest potential for providing the foundation for a general theory of marketing? If you believe that none of these 12 schools (or ideas therein) are likely to yield a general theory of marketing, then suggest an emergent school of marketing, or a specific idea therein, which has the highest potential to offer a general theory of marketing. Please justify your answer.

6. What is the prospect of an integrated marketing theory that brings all approaches and perspectives together to create a strong identity for the marketing discipline? What should be the key components and sub-components of such an integrated marketing theory?

CHAPTER

Marketing Strategy School of Thought

The marketing strategy lays out target markets and the value proposition that will be offered based on an analysis of the best market opportunities.

—Philip Kotler and Kevin Keller (2011)

An over-riding directional concept that sets out the planned path.

—David Aaker and Michael K. Mills (2001)

Essentially a formula for how a business is going to compete, what its goals should be and what policies will be needed to carry out these goals.

—Michael Porter (1980)

LEARNING OBJECTIVES

After reading this chapter, you will be able to:

- State the key concerns of the marketing strategy school of thought.
- Trace the contributions of marketing strategy thinking through various eras of the evolution of marketing discipline.
- Explain the taxonomical challenges of domain distinction between marketing strategy and strategic marketing.

- Enumerate the core ideas and theories developed by the marketing strategy school of thought.
- Determine new frontiers of research in marketing strategy.
- Evaluate the marketing strategy school of thought on specific metatheory criteria.

 ## 7.1 Introduction

The marketing strategy school of thought developed as an offshoot of the managerial approach to marketing in the 1970s (Shaw 2012) and further evolved into strategic marketing as a significant component of corporate strategic planning in the 1980s (Jain 1983; Wind and Robertson 1983; Varadarajan 2010, 2015). The marketing management perspective's fundamental concern was designing the marketing program or marketing mix, not the firm's mission or how to gain a competitive advantage. By contrast, the marketing strategy school of thought focuses explicitly on developing long-run competitive and consumer advantage (Anderson 1982; Wind and Robertson 1983; El-Ansary 2006). It has a high degree of overlap and is integral to business strategy. It provides inputs to corporate strategic planning through its unique ability to assess customer needs, perform market and competitor analysis, configure customer value through innovative offerings and partnerships, and evaluate the influence of other environmental factors impacting key stakeholders. Marketing strategy is combined with other strategic inputs (financial, technological, and human resources) to develop the integrated corporate strategy.

The critical concerns of the marketing strategy school of thinking are developing a long-term differential advantage for the corporation. These include:

1. variables of business growth (product and market development)
2. competitive strategies (market leaders, challengers, pioneers, cost vs. quality)
3. competitive effects (profits, survival, market share, and de-conglomeration)
4. portfolio management (product/customer portfolios and life-cycle management)
5. strategic differentiation (positioning and branding)
6. market planning (margin-returns and sequential vs. concurrent market entry)
7. strategic alignment (horizontal/vertical integration, networks, and partnerships)
8. value creation (brand and customer equity, market valuation)
9. capability enhancement (market process and knowledge sharing)
10. pursuing new opportunities (innovation and business model pivot), and
11. market disruptions (business model changes and transformative processes).

In essence, marketing strategy is focused on the future, on proactively seeking to change the conditions through strategic thrusts. These conditions may be market-related, customer-related, competition-related, or resource-related. Strategic marketing thrust aims to better position the firm to pursue opportunities, manage threats, become competitively superior, build better capabilities, offer superior value to customers, and be firmly poised for growth and profitability for the near- and long-term business operations. The terms marketing strategy and strategic marketing are often used interchangeably to emphasize marketing's role in the firm's strategic thrust. For example, while enumerating the foundational premises of marketing strategy, Varadarajan (2010, p. 119) states:

> The domain of strategic marketing is viewed as encompassing the study of organizational, inter-organizational and environmental phenomena concerned with (1) the behavior of organizations in the marketplace in their interactions with consumers, customers, competitors, and other external constituencies, in the context of creation, communication and delivery of products that offer value to customers in exchanges with organizations, and (2) the general management responsibilities associated with the boundary spanning role of the marketing function in organizations.

He proposes that strategic marketing fundamental issues include explanations in differences in competing firms' marketing behavior at the marketplace and the financial performance of competing brands/product lines/businesses (Varadarajan 2010, p. 133). He identifies 16 foundational premises of marketing strategy that Hunt (2018, p. 35) suggests could be grouped into four distinct areas addressing issues that focus on (a) *purposes* of marketing strategy; (b) *differentiation* strategy; (c) *cost-based* strategies; and (d) strategy *diversity*. Regarding marketing strategy purposes, Varadarajan (2010) contends that achieving a sustainable competitive advantage is *a* purpose of marketing strategy. However, it is not *the* purpose of marketing strategy, in a departure from the views espoused by some (e.g., Day et al. 1990). The other purposes of marketing strategy include: (a) creating market-based relational assets and market-based intellectual assets; (b) establishing and nurturing mutually beneficial exchange relationships; and (c) modifying/influencing/shaping the affect, cognition, and behaviors of customers and consumers (Varadarajan 2010, p. 135).

Varadarajan (2010, p. 128), thus drawing upon the AMA's 'official' definition of marketing, defines *marketing strategy* broadly as an:

> organization's integrated patterns of decisions that specify its crucial choices concerning products, markets, marketing activities and marketing resources in the creation, communication and/or delivery of products that offer value to customers in exchanges with the organization and thereby enables the organization to achieve specific objectives.

As a school of thought, marketing strategy has benefited from many seminal conceptual and empirical contributions in the past five decades. Still, it faces many challenges regarding its domain and different construct labels to refer to the same phenomenon (e.g., marketing strategy and strategic marketing). Varadarajan (2010, p. 138) points out that a proliferation of constructs has contributed to the prevailing confusion, and the contribution of some of these constructs to enhancing our understanding of the field is suspect.

7.2 Growth and Challenges of Marketing Strategy School of Thought

The marketing strategy school of thought emerged with the acceptance of the marketing concept (focus on serving customer wants and needs) as the *raison d'être* of corporate strategic goals and plans and not merely a functional purpose of the marketing department (Louth 1966). It led to a marketing school of thought to elevate marketing's role in the overall corporate strategic plan. A shift from consumers to competition started to emerge after the first energy crisis of 1972–1974. Competition became the focus because of the collapse of companies, especially in the airline and trucking industry. It led to many mergers and acquisitions, with private equity ruling the world and the emergence of billionaires, such as Warren Buffet (Sheth 2021). GE's PIMS database was shifted to Harvard and later to the Marketing Science Institute (MSI) and spurred hundreds of papers on competitive strategy rather than marketing operations (Szymanski et al. 1993).

Over the years, marketing strategy research expanded into services marketing and relationship marketing. Economic growth emerged from the service industries (e.g., cell phone networks, financial services, utility services, healthcare). The focus shifted from the acquisition of new customers to retaining existing customers. Loyalty programs, key account management, and customer centricity became the mantra. The most significant boost in the strategy area came from the market-orientation perspective (Kohli and Jaworski 1990; Narver and Slater 1990). It became a popular construct and generated substantial empirical research.

However, several marketing scholars have warned that marketing strategy thinking within the marketing discipline itself is troubled (Hunt 2018), has run its course, and now struggling with the midlife crisis (Sheth 2021). Some scholars observe that the development, testing, and dissemination of strategy theories and concepts within the academic marketing circles was marginalized (Day 1992). Many also decried the growing balkanization of academic marketing into quantitative modeling and consumer behavior, diminishing research on strategic marketing issues (Sheth and Sisodia 2006; Reibstein, Day, and Wind 2009; Clark et al. 2014). To add insult to injury, substantive confusion on the taxonomy and domain of marketing strategy remains. Varadarajan (2010) recognized the lack of clarity between marketing strategy and strategic marketing and a consequential identity crisis.

Similarly, Shaw (2012) noted the "semantic jungle" and the fundamental problem of lack of an integrating theoretical framework making the knowledge inconsistent at best and incoherent at worse. Houston (2016) warned that strategy might be becoming a 'taboo' topic or a dirty word. It appears that marketing strategy will have to go back to its roots and focus back on managerial marketing to get out of this trouble.

The following sections will first examine the taxonomical confusion between strategic marketing and marketing strategy. After that, we will trace the development and evolution of the marketing strategy school of thought, identify new frontiers of research that could revitalize marketing strategy contributions to the marketing discipline and beyond, and finally, evaluate the six metatheory criteria contributions as a school of thought.

7.3 Confusion Regarding the Domain and Taxonomy of Marketing Strategy

There are numerous points of confusion and debate in the literature about the domain and field of marketing strategy and the distinction between marketing strategy and strategic marketing (El-Ansary 2006; Hunt 2015; Shaw 2012; Varadarajan 2015). In the early managerial school writings, marketing strategy term meant normative decision policies and theories regarding specific aspects of marketing management, such as pricing, product, promotion, distribution, and their proportional use in marketing-mix for varying market demand or buyer behavior context (Allison 1961; Borden 1964; Brown 1957; Frey 1956; Howard 1957; Oxenfeldt 1958, 1960; Lipson 1962; Rathmell 1969; Wales 1957).

However, in the 1970s, when the firm's planning activity took center stage in business practice, a new field of endeavor emerged, called strategic marketing (Jain 1983; Wind and Robertson 1983). The acceptance of the marketing concept focusing the organizational processes towards identifying and fulfilling customer needs had given marketing the password to increase its influence on the more extensive corporate planning process. This cause was enhanced by Biggadike (1981), who highlighted the contributions of marketing to strategic management by explicitly arguing that marketing had made significant contributions to the choice of strategy.

> Marketing concepts and techniques, such as market segmentation, positioning, and perceptual mapping help define the environment and frame strategic choices in customer terms. The product life cycle concept helps dynamic analysis of the environment and different strategic options. Essentially, marketing sees strategic management as being market-driven, and provides aids for hypothesizing about customer needs and competitive behavior (Biggadike 1981, p. 621).

The dynamic business environment prompted adaptation involving the strategic market analysis and strategic market planning at corporate and strategic business unit (SBU) levels. However, Biggadike's observation that the marketing discipline was theoretically thin, with little hope for change in the future, was offensive to generations of marketing scholars.

Thus, marketing scholars began to distinguish between the marketing mix decisions and the strategic marketing process. However, as is familiar with most new schools of thought, this distinction has not been easy to make with taxonomy and clear genealogy that defines the marketing strategy domain and delineates it from other schools of thought. Several clarifying articles have been written on what constitutes marketing strategy or strategic marketing and how it differs from marketing management, but the confusion prevails (El-Ansary 2006; Germann, Ebbes, and Grewal 2015; Greenly 2007; Varadarajan 2010, 2015).

Thus, on the one hand, we have marketing-mix-related strategies, which according to some, belong to the managerial school of thought given its focus on marketing programs and strategy implementation within the marketing function. While on the other hand, we have strategic marketing planning that aims to drive a firm's competitive market position and overall corporate performance. It concerns issues at the firm or SBU level and sometimes at cross-functional groups, whereas marketing-mix strategies primarily address the marketing function's problems for implementing corporate strategy. So, the question remains whether we should consider it a 'School of Strategic Marketing' or a 'School of Marketing Strategy'?

Recognizing the scholarly arguments that marketing-mix decisions and policies are managerial issues best-considered matters of marketing program development or strategy implementation, one can say that it does not belong to the marketing strategy school of thought (El-Ansary 2006; Varadarajan 2015). In contrast, marketing research and theory addressing the firm's strategic posture, or its SBUs, including cross-functional considerations, belong distinctly to the marketing strategy school of thought.

7.4 Evolution of Marketing Strategy School of Thought

7.4.1 Early Thoughts on Marketing Strategy

The evolution of marketing strategy can be divided into two eras- before the 1980s and after that to the present. Although Wilkie and Moore (2003) classified the history of marketing thought into four eras, marketing strategy thinking developed in Era III (1950–1980) and was further advanced in Era IV (1980–present). Hunt (2018) has observed that some of the elements of marketing strategy thinking, including segmentation, differentiation, and competitive advantage, were implicitly mentioned by early marketing academic writers, such as Shaw (1912) and Alderson (1937). However, these concepts got more formally introduced in the marketing literature in the 1950s. For example, Smith (1956) made a case for product differentiation and market segmentation as alternative marketing strategies that either focused on bending of demand to the will of supply (product differentiation) or a rational and more precise adjustment of product and marketing effort to consumer or user requirements (segmentation). His strategies addressed demand heterogeneity, which was not adequately addressed by the economic theories of perfect competition and pure monopoly advanced by Robinson and Chamberlain in the 1930s. Similarly, Alderson (1957) answered the call for a marketing theory of competition with a differential advantage theory to solve strategic marketing problems (Hunt 2018).

Correspondingly, managerial economist Joel Dean (1950) articulated new product entry's strategic decision using skimming or penetration pricing strategies for market development. He also introduced the term "product life cycle" (PLC) through his descriptive model of "the cycle of competitive degeneration" (p. 53), emphasizing the perishable distinctiveness of products as competition increases. Subsequently, Levitt (1965) popularized the PLC concept and conceptualized its marketing strategy implications. Finally, Smallwood (1973) highlighted the value of PLC as key to strategic marketing planning, and Lambkin and Day (1989) used it to discuss a framework of market evolution cycles and competitive postures. Even though these concepts and strategies pertained to specific marketing mix elements, such as pricing and products, they have often been used as strategic approaches to a firm's competitive market positioning.

Howard (1957), Lipson (1962), and Oxenfeldt (1958) provided some formal thinking on marketing strategy as a planning process with a sequence of decision rules, order, and timing, which included the establishment of goals and a combination of instruments (called marketing mix or means) to design strategies. In addition, they highlighted specific strategic goals for marketing to accomplish, such as business survival, growth, profits, market position, and horizontal and vertical integration (Lipson 1962). These concepts laid the foundations of the early development of the marketing strategy school of thinking. The strategic marketing approach aimed to drive the marketing concept in corporate planning. It sought to develop strategies that establish a competitive advantage for its evolving marketing environment.

Consulting firms and their clients, such as the Boston Consulting Group (BCG), Stanford Research Institute (SRI), and General Electric (GE), shaped a significant portion of strategic marketing thinking in the 1970s. For example, the GE industry attractiveness-business strength screen and BCG product portfolio and market-share growth matrix were, for the most part, based on either an implicit cash flow maximization idea or some form of capital asset pricing model (Sheth and Gardener 1982). These consultants and corporate executives recognized the connection between market share and profitability. The same was discovered in the PIMS projects' results to identify and measure the significant determinants of return on investment (ROI) in individual businesses (Buzzell et al. 1975; Buzzell and Gale 1987). Despite its well-documented deficiencies (Jacobson 1988, 1990; Jacobson and Aaker 1985; Sheth and Frazier 1983), about two dozen doctoral dissertations and over 100 published articles and working papers relating to marketing strategy and firm performance have used the PIMS database (Buzzell 2004; Farris and Moore 2004).

At the theoretical level, El-Ansary (1979) initially suggested a framework integrating macro and micro marketing that would naturally lead to a theory of strategic marketing, which would be an integral part of a theory of corporate strategy integrating other business and management functions. Similarly, in a more Kuhnian-style paradigm (Kuhn 1970), Anderson (1982) proposed a guide to developing a theory of the firm that explicitly focuses on the role and constituency of marketing in setting corporate "goal structures" and strategic plans. Kotler (1987) later proposed a more broadened view of "mega marketing," suggesting that marketing strategies be applied to engage and cooperate with several parties outside the corporation, facilitate market entry, and create or alter the demand. This idea of engaging multiple external stakeholders is embraced by Sheth et al. (2016) in their elaboration of breakout strategies to achieve growth in emerging markets.

7.4.2 Contributions of the Early Marketing Strategy Thinking (Era I–III)

The beginnings of the marketing strategy school of thought fell into several overlapping categories. The first were those contributions that explicitly dealt with one aspect of a marketing strategy but with a strategic reference point (Thorelli 1977; Wind 1978; Pessemeir 1982). These included such concepts as market segmentation, positioning, product differentiation, product life cycle, and strategic pricing for market entry, which are all still widely used (Dickson and Ginter 1987).

The second category of contributions is on growth strategies that became popular due to the prevailing conditions of the post-war boom in demand in the fifties and sixties. Ansoff's (1957) growth matrix based on the growth vectors of market penetration, market development, product development, and diversification has been sustainably used in practice, teaching, and research for more than six decades now. Its simple yet conceptually powerful guide to business growth and expansion strategies is very appealing. Similarly, the Boston Consulting Group's (1970) product portfolio and growth-share matrix continue to be applied even today as a tool for strategic planning of product performance within an industry and at the company level. It guides resource allocation strategies among business units (Cardozo and Smith 1983). These frameworks made the growth and market share metrics integral to the strategic planning and performance evaluation of corporate SBUs.

Ideas of market share and relative growth were inherently rooted in competitive thinking. It got further accentuated with the increase in global competition intensity after the oil crisis of the 1970s that created an existential crisis for many companies and industries. Thus, competitive strategies became the focus of management and marketing strategy literature. Michael Porter's (1980) framework on competitive strategy influenced subsequent research and textbook content on strategic marketing (Henderson 1983; Phillips et al. 1983; Dickson 1992; Jayachandran et al. 1999; Varadarajan and Jayachandran 1999). Along with game theory, competitive strategy thinking led to marketing warfare contributions (Kotler and Singh 1981) and defensive marketing strategies (Hauser and Shugan 1983).

So, overall, one can say that the early thoughts on marketing strategy had a tremendous effect on the knowledge and development of marketing theory, thinking, and practice. Moreover, it laid the foundation for developing a strategic marketing approach that evolved since the 1980s and elevated the influence of marketing in designing and developing corporate strategies.

7.4.3 Development of the Marketing Strategy School of Thought in Era IV (1980–Present)

Since the 1980s, numerous articles have been published in marketing strategy, making it distinct marketing thought school. While the seventies' competitive concerns continued to occupy center stage in marketing strategy, a new strategic marketing orientation began to take grip. The realization that marketing literature had not focused on its mission to gain consumer and competitive advantage triggered it. However, such issues were implicit in the marketing management perspective. It was also oddly recognized that the marketing strategy literature until then had been developed primarily by nonmarketers (Wind and Robertson 1983). To rectify this, the *Journal of Marketing* (JM) published a special issue in Spring 1983 to focus attention on marketing strategy to encourage new research and new theoretical thinking in this area (Cunningham and Robertson 1983). Several papers from prominent marketing academics published in that issue presented a variety of strategic concepts and topics, both theoretical and empirical, related to common concern for competitive advantages, such as business definition, anatomy of competition, portfolio models, the experience curve, marketing/finance relationship, market selection, and the relationship between product quality, costs, and business performance. As expected, this provided the impetus and some coherence to the emerging literature in marketing strategy over the next couple of decades.

There were two perspectives on marketing strategy at that time. One viewed marketing strategy as an investment in marketing mix variables to serve a target market (Cook 1983). The second was that marketing strategy involved developing objectives and plans to achieve a long-run competitive advantage. This process view consisted of at least three steps:

1. assessing the organization's mission in the context of changing external factors,
2. developing a competitive strategy, and
3. organizing and delivering marketing resources.

Although most business strategy literature dealt with market share marketing variables, market growth, market development, and product differentiation, they generally ignored the fundamental marketing perspective of an empirical assessment and the integration of consumer responses to the strategic options. Strategic marketing thinking was eager to drive home this idea and establish a front-row role for itself in the corporate strategic planning process. Thus, strategic marketing concentrated on such aspects as market selection, competitive strategy formation, building relationships with important constituencies (customers, partners, and channel members), offering appropriate products/services, and determining the timing of changing relationships and product offerings, or the timing of market entry and exit (Jain 1983; Sudarshan 1995).

Varadarajan and Jayachandran (1999, p. 121), in their assessment of the state of the field of marketing strategy, distilled the contributions in extant literature into five broad research streams that addressed:

1. *Issues pertinent to marketing strategy* (e.g., branding, competitive behavior, positioning, and segmentation)
2. *Issues central to marketing strategy*, but with cross-functional implications (e.g., innovation and quality)

3. *Issues at the interface of corporate and marketing strategy* (e.g., synergy and horizontal integration), business and marketing strategy (e.g., the generic strategy of differentiation, market pioneering, and strategic alliances), or corporate, business, and marketing strategy (e.g., strategic market planning, global competitive strategy, and multimarket competition)

4. *Organizational-level phenomena* that affect marketing strategy and management in meaningful ways (e.g., corporate culture, market orientation, organizational learning, and strategy formulation processes)

5. *Outcomes of marketing and business strategy* (e.g., competitive positional advantages, market share, customer satisfaction, and market-based assets)

Thus, numerous articles have been published over the years on the strategic marketing planning process and the role and power of the marketing department in the overall firm performance (Menon et al. 1999; Feng et al. 2015).

Similarly, based on a review of research in marketing strategy published in the leading marketing academic journals during the most recent two decades, Morgan et al. (2018) classified the domain of most commonly studied topics into five sub-domains. These are:

A. **Strategy formulation-content research** – focused on the specific goals that a marketing strategy needs to deliver for the firm or the SBU and the broad strategic decisions towards its achievement. Almost a quarter of the 257 published articles they examined fell into this category. They observed that most of the studies in this category used existing strategy typologies from management literature (e.g., Miles and Snow's strategic archetypes or Porter's generic strategies) and primarily surveys (Chandy and Tellis 2000; Mizik and Jacobson 2003; Slater et al. 2007;). Morgan et al. (2018) observed that there had been less focus on studying the goals that marketing strategies are designed to achieve, except for the recent work of Spyropolou et al. (2018), who examined the extent to which an SBU's strategic goal of differential advantage determines subsequent positional advantages obtained subsequently.

B. **Strategy formulation-process research** – focusing on how managers develop marketing strategies and the mechanisms used to establish goals and broad strategic means (i.e., value proposition, positioning, timing). Morgan et al. (2019 found that only 6% of the published articles in their sample focused on this aspect of marketing strategy among the four sub-domains identified (Dickson et al. 2001; Menon et al. 1999). Montgomery et al. 2005 found relatively low use of strategic competitive reasoning in the MSM process.

C. **Strategy implementation-content research** – concerns the detailed integrated marketing program tactical decisions and resource deployments undertaken to achieve a concrete set of realized actions. According to Morgan et al. (2019, over the past two decades, more than half the published work in this sub-domain has focused on developing analytical models or using secondary data and marketing-mix modeling to understand the performance impact of marketing program decisions. Most of the studies are contingent and hence hard to synthesize them [e.g., optimal profit-maximizing decision models of Hauser and Shugan (2008); and dynamic linear model on effects of marketing program tactics of Bruce et al. (2012)]. In addition, most research in this sub-domain is empirical and focuses on the direct and interactive effects of marketing tactics and expenditures across multiple marketing program components. Few published papers examine all 4Ps simultaneously and dynamically to ensure relevant managerial insight (Ataman et al. 2010; Bolton et al. 2004).

D. **Strategy implementation-process research** – focuses on the mechanisms (e.g., budgeting, communication systems, performance monitoring, process alignment, organizational structure design) applied to deliver marketing strategy content decisions. Several topics explore this sub-domain. The most common is the marketing organization issue for accomplishing the marketing tasks. Both conceptual and research articles exist on this aspect (Homburg et al. 2000; Vorhies and Morgan 2003). In addition, some other studies have focused on marketing performance monitoring (O'Sullivan and Abela 2007; Homburg et al. 2012). In this context, Maltz and Kohli (2000) identify six integrating mechanisms that can reduce the inter-functional conflict in marketing strategy implementation, and there are differential effects across marketing's interactions with finance, manufacturing, and R&D.

E. Hybrid marketing strategy research – that covers more than one area. Morgan (2012) developed a macro-level conceptual framework that theoretically linked the firm resources and marketing capabilities to the firm's marketing strategy decisions and implementation to performance outcomes. Their article addresses issues relating to both strategy formulation-content and strategy implementation-content sub-domains. Varadarajan (2010) also provides a conceptual framework and domain statement on strategic marketing encompassing both formulation-content and implementation-content. And, in an empirical study, Krush et al. (2015) controlled business strategy type (formulation-content) to uncover that a firm's marketing capability dispersion within the firm (implementation-content) positively influences the firm, affecting customer responsiveness that drives marketing strategy implementation success and SBU performance.

Therefore, the assessment of recent marketing strategy research's domain content suggests that the core marketing strategy construct has received limited attention within strategic marketing literature. Recent research has focused more on individual marketing mix elements (individual tactics) than on marketing strategies and integrated marketing programs that focus on marketing strategy. Morgan et al. (2018) also observed that from theory building and theory use perspective, most papers published in the past two decades within the purview of marketing strategy had been logic- or data-driven in developing arguments. They recognize that such approaches are not necessarily wrong and that managers are interested in observed empirical relationships. However, these approaches are insufficient to understand the "why" aspect of the marketing strategy phenomena. They argue that this is problematic for the discipline since answering "why" is the *raison d'être* of any social science and for which managers seek valuable guidance.

7.4.4   Conceptual and Theoretical Contributions of Marketing Strategy School of Thought in Era IV

Despite the criticisms regarding the lack of integrated and more managerially relevant research on marketing strategy, the past four decades have witnessed the emergence of a rich body of research that has furthered scholarly and managerial understanding of marketing strategy (Varadarajan and Jayachandran 1999; Hunt 2018; Morgan et al. 2018; Varadarajan 2010). To summarize the contributions, one could look at the new strategic levers identified, and mechanisms developed that are now an integral part of the marketing and business literature lexicon, its applied frameworks, and theoretical foundations. Thus, the question is, what have we learned after 1980 that are beyond the core concepts of market segmentation, positioning, product differentiation, product life cycle, marketing mix, growth strategies, vertical and horizontal integration, and strategic pricing alternatives of skimming versus penetration? Below we identify the core ideas developed within the marketing strategy school of thinking or concepts that have become central tenets of developing marketing and business strategies.

Competitive Behavior and Action Planning

Identifying competitors' actions and reactions are central to marketing strategy research and practice. From planning simple tactical activities concerning specific marketing mix variables to planning more complex strategic market positioning, new product and technology development, and alliances and partnerships to gain competitive advantage, the theories and thoughts advanced during the current era are outcomes. The domain evolved into a more competition-centric strategic marketing process, considering organizational interdependencies beyond marketing strategies for products, markets, and marketing mix. Competitive analysis and game theory are applied to advance the knowledge on this aspect (Porter 1980; Moorthy 1985; Weitz 1985; Gatignon et al. 1989; Dickson 1992; Rao et al. 1995). Additionally, competitive signaling intended to convey information to competitors (or gain knowledge from competitors) is another strategy dimension that is now significantly used to preempt and establish norms of competitive conduct in the marketplace (Heil and Robertson 1991). Incorporating competitive approaches to marketing strategy planning, including multimarket competition, contributes to this school of thought (Jayachandran et al. 1999). Incidentally, the concept of "market share" as a strategic goal and performance metrics is inherently ingrained in the idea of relative competitive outcomes.

Innovation and Creative Destruction

The importance of innovation and R&D for long-term profitability and competitive advantage came to prominence in this era. It supported the "Austrian" school of strategy (Jacobson 1992), which suggests that the business environment is inherently dynamic, uncertain, and disequilibrium. Hence, profits and competitive advantages in such an environment result from the firm's discovery and innovation. Several articles in the marketing literature focused on innovation-related aspects, such as the timing of new product introductions and innovation investments in R&D leading to, and its consequent effects, on success or failure of new products or firm performance (Capon et al. 1990; Bayus et al. 1997; Boulding et al. 1997; Ittner and Larcker 1997). However, most marketing literature has primarily focused on product innovation, with scant attention given to the impact of innovation on other dimensions, such as channel structure and marketing process innovations (Varadarajan and Jayachandran 1999; Varadarajan 2010). However, some studies have emphasized the importance of innovation as a link between market orientation and organizational performance and learning (Han et al. 1998; Hurley and Hult, 1998).

Product and Service Quality

In the quest for overall superiority, excellence, and non-price ways to influence the demand curve of products, the marketing strategy literature has made tremendous contributions to the discipline through its explorations of product differentiation and service quality as generic strategies for competitive advantage (Phillips et al. 1983; Zeithaml 1988; Fornell 1995; Sharp and Dawes 2001). It has advanced the practical knowledge that businesses can achieve strategic value and returns by offering higher quality products and services. Higher quality can sustain higher prices and a larger market share (Buzzell and Gale 1987; Gale 1992). However, the ease with which consumers can determine the quality of the product or service influences their willingness to pay higher prices (Tellis 1987). Conversely, consumers use price as a surrogate to judge quality, especially when quality information is uncertain and hard to discern. In the case of services, matching and continuously exceeding customer expectations on various quality dimensions leads to stronger customer relationships and competitive advantage (Zeithaml et al. 1996; Bell et al. 2005).

Market Pioneers, Incumbents, and Challengers

Research relating to market pioneers' first-mover advantages in gaining market share and competitive advantage is another significant contribution during this era. The order of market entry, in terms of first movers, early followers, or late entrants, for new product introduction, entry into new markets, or deployment of a new process have been the subject of both conceptual and empirical research in this era (Lieberman and Montgomery 1988). Beyond the analytical-economic argument that market pioneers achieve substantial competitive advantage as a result of entry barriers, a new perspective that a pioneer, through its marketing efforts, can also favorably shape beliefs of consumers about ideal brand attributes and preferences and become the yardstick to evaluate later market entrants (Carpenter and Nakamoto 1989, 1990). However, if market pioneers do not have a significant asymmetric competitive advantage, later entrants may effectively challenge the pioneer, especially when the later entrants can successfully free ride on a pioneer's investments relative to a change in technology or the creation of potential consumer need (Kalyanaram et al. 1995). Some research also found that while being a pioneer helps a firm that is not an industry incumbent, an industry incumbent performs better as a later entrant (Mitchell 1991).

Market Orientation

Market orientation is the extent to which the firm's actions and culture are consistent with the marketing concept of creating better value for customers efficiently and effectively (Kohli and Jaworski 1990; Narver and Slater 1990). The idea of market orientation encompasses the three dimensions of customer orientation, competitor orientation, and inter-functional coordination. It explicitly advocates an organization-wide mechanism to generate market intelligence on tracking current and future customer needs, potential competitor strategies and actions, other environmental factors causing market disequilibrium, disseminating such intelligence across departments, and organization-wide responsiveness to it. In this world of hyper-competition characterized by market instability due to new product introductions, new technologies, new entrants, strategic moves of incumbents, and continually evolving consumer preferences, priorities, market boundaries, and competitive space, firms need to be more market-oriented to perceive the evolving market development forces and respond to it through strategic initiatives. The body of literature on market orientation has genuinely enriched the strategic marketing process and organizations' strategic planning process. It urges them to keep track of demand and supply variations in the marketplace and orchestrate appropriate responses to these changes through competitive action or innovation to gain a competitive advantage. Intelligence and company-wide knowledge management become critical as strategic levers for the firm's success. Extant research suggests that a firm's performance is positively related to its market orientation and is a source of sustainable competitive advantage (Hunt and Morgan 1995; Jaworski and Kohli 1996; Kirca et al. 2005; Siguaw et al. 1994).

Relationships and Strategic Alliances

With increasing recognition of marketplace interdependencies and the growth of the relationship marketing school of thought, inter-and intra-organizational cooperation and collaboration became the focus of numerous studies in business and marketing literature (Achrol 1991; Morgan and Hunt 1994; Sheth and Parvatiyar 1994; Varadarajan and Cunningham 1995). Marketing involves relationships, networks, and interactions (Gronroos 1996). Such thought has had a profound impact on marketing strategy literature and practice. Developing a conscious strategy of forming alliances and partnerships to pursue joint economic goals and sharing resources with value chain partners is now prevalent. It manifests itself in many forms, such as strategic alliances, cooperative marketing arrangements, co-branding, co-development, affinity marketing, ecosystem networks, and co-opetition. The pursuant strategy aims to incorporate customers, suppliers, and other infra-structural partners (even competitors) into the firm's developmental and marketing activities to develop combined capabilities for achieving the organizational mission and differential advantage. Even at consumer levels, marketing strategy increasingly sought long-term partnerships, loyalty strategies, and lifetime value relationships based on customer retention and engagement. Today, marketing and business strategy cannot be devoid of clear and articulate goals and processes for building customer relationships, channel partnerships, and other alliances.

Brand Equity, Customer Equity, and Market-Based Assets

Since a brand can be a primary source of competitive advantage if developed on the differential effect of brand knowledge on consumer response (Aaker 1991; Keller 1993, 2002), a consensus emerged that brands are a set of assets and liabilities that have a clear and measurable equity value (Kerin and Sethuraman 1998). The fundamental thesis of brand equity strategy is that to achieve a competitive advantage, thereby superior financial performance, firms should acquire, develop, nurture, and leverage an effectiveness-enhancing portfolio of brands (Hunt 2010, p. 415). Like brand equity, with the growing interest in customer relationships and understanding customers' lifetime value, the marketing strategy spotlight was also on customer equity (Rust et al. 2004; Vogel et al. 2008). The portfolio of profitable customers with significant lifetime value constitutes important market assets that could impact its market capitalization (Srivastava et al. 1998; Hanssens et al. 2009; Kumar and Shah 2009; Wiesel et al. 2008). Therefore, marketing strategy impact on shareholder value of the firm and Wall Street has been the focus of attention in recent times with special issues and dedicated conferences (see, for example, the Journal of Marketing special issue, November 2009).

Marketing Organization and Marketing Capabilities

The development of the resource-based view (RGV) within the strategic management field (Wernerfelt 1984) considerably influenced marketing strategy literature as well (Kozlenkova et al. 2014). Several scholars focused on studying marketing capabilities that enable organizations to achieve marketing excellence. Primarily marketing capabilities represent the sets of marketing skills and accumulated knowledge exercised through organizational processes to allow the firm to carry out its marketing activities with excellence. Day (1994) proposed specific capabilities to be mastered by market-driven organizations and ways to close the marketing capabilities gap (see Day 2011). In the literature, capabilities and competencies are often used interchangeably. The subset of corporate capabilities representing the firm's distinctive competencies, enabling it to make a disproportionate contribution to its competitive advantage, is often referred to as its "core competencies" (or core capabilities). Hamel and Prahalad (1991) suggested that core competencies are one prerequisite for creating new markets.

They argued that corporate imagination quickens when companies escape the trap of their served markets and follow expeditionary marketing of low-cost, fast-paced market incursions designed to bring the target quickly into view. The development of RBV paralleled the consensus within marketing that a firm's market orientation is the coordinated application of inter-functional resources to create superior customer value (Kohli and Jaworski 1990; Narver and Slater 1990).

Moorman and Day (2016), in their review of over two and a half decades of scholarship on marketing organization, examined the individual and integrative elements of the marketing organization—capabilities, configuration (including structure, metrics, and incentives), culture, and the human capital of marketing leadership and talent. They indicate that these four elements operate during the marketing strategy process through the activities of assessment (accountability), designing (anticipation and adaptation), resourcing (attraction and asset management), and implementing (alignment and activation). These activities enable the firm to anticipate market changes, activate effective implementation, ensure accountability for results, attract resources, and manage marketing assets. They further postulate that the firm's performance payoffs from the marketing organization depend on its handling of the marketing strategy process and integration. Therefore, studying marketing organization, capabilities, culture, and excellence offers many new research opportunities.

Resource-Advantage (R-A) Theory of Competition

In response to Alderson's (1937) call for a distinct *marketing* theory of competition, Hunt and Morgan proposed the resource-advantage theory (R-A Theory) of competition (Hunt and Morgan 1995; Hunt 2000). Hunt (2018, p. 38) points out R-A theory is "not a theory of strategy; it is a general theory of competition." However, he also notes that since successful strategies presume how competition works, the R-A theory provides a grounding in developing successful strategies. R-A theory of competition articulates the layers of business strategy and marketing strategy in an integrated framework (Hunt and Morgan 1995). At the business level, R-A theory identifies four strategic perspectives that drive business strategy:

1. *Industry-based strategy* – choose industries and competitive strategy-basis.
2. *Resource-based strategy* – seek resources that are valuable and inimitable.
3. *Competence-based strategy* – develop and leverage distinctive competence.
4. *Knowledge-based strategy* – gain and use knowledge to guide innovation.

The four specific theories of marketing strategy (Hunt 2010, p. 412) that purports to achieve a competitive advantage, and thereby superior performance for the firm, are:

1. *Market-segmentation strategy* – identify segments of demand, target specific segments, and develop specific marketing mixes for each target segment.
2. *Market-orientation strategy* – systematically gather market intelligence and use it in a coordinated way to guide and implement the strategy.
3. *Relationship-marketing strategy* – develop and nurture efficiency-enhancing and effectiveness-enhancing portfolio of relationships.
4. *Brand-equity strategy* – acquire, develop, promote, and leverage effectiveness enhancing portfolio of high-quality brands.

The resource-advantage theory is a general theory of competition that views competition as an evolutionary, disequilibrium-provoking process. Innovation and organizational learning are endogenous. Firms and consumers have imperfect information and in which entrepreneurship, institutions, and public policy affect economic performance (Hunt 2018, p. 40). Hunt has argued that his R-A Theory also provides the foundation for a General Theory of Marketing (Hunt 2010; Hunt and Arnett 2006).

Natural Market Structures and Rule of Three Theory

Sheth and Sisodia (2002) examined the market evolution and dynamics of competitive markets. They concluded that just like a living organism, competitive markets evolve in a highly predictable fashion, governed by the "Rule of Three." Considering these as natural market structures, they state:

> Simply put the Rule of Three states that naturally occurring competitive forces – if allowed to operate without excessive government intervention – will create a consistent structure across nearly all mature markets. In one group, three major players compete against each other in multiple ways: they offer a wide range of related products and services, and they serve most major market segments (Sheth and Sisodia 2002, p. 2).

Contrary to traditional economic theory, the "Rule of Three" (hereafter referred to as R3) implies that evolved markets are simultaneously oligopolistic and monopolistic. Suggesting a wide range of corporate, marketing, investment, and policy implications, some of which are at odds with the assumed buoyant linear market share-performance relationship established by PIMS data (Buzzell 2004; Buzzell and Gale 1987; Ramanujam and Venkatraman 1984), R3 states that:

> Through competitive market forces, markets that are largely free of regulatory constraints and major entry barriers (such as very restrictive patent rights or government-controlled capacity licenses) eventually get organized into two kinds of competitors: full-line generalists and product/market specialists. Full-line generalists compete across a range of products and markets and are volume-driven players for whom financial performance improves with gains in market share. Specialists tend to be margin-driven players, who actually suffer deterioration in financial performance by increasing their share of the broad market beyond a certain level (Sheth, Uslay, and Sisodia 2020, pp. 3–4).

According to R3, "full-line generalists" are typically the three major players (Big 3) that form the core, the inner circle, of the defined market they participate in. As the defined market matures, the Big 3 become better at solidifying their position. They set the play rules by which others wanting to join in that defined market must play. Because it is tough to face head-on competition from a full-line generalist, smaller players carve out those areas in which they can effectively specialize, usually as the product- or market-specialists targeting to serve some specific market needs or a specific group of customers. In some cases, a company becomes a "super-niche" specialist in both the product category and a market segment.

Furthermore, R3 postulates that as markets grow and mature, there exists yet a third group of participants (Sheth and Sisodia 2002). They are often too large and diverse to be considered specialists, yet not large enough to compete successfully against the Big 3. They cannot match and achieve the economies of scale and scope compared to any of the Big 3 players. They are also not as effective at meeting specific customer requirements as the specialists. As such, they may compete on price and try to reduce costs by cutting product quality and service, but their return on assets (ROA) remains low, if not negative. They are presumably in a "ditch" between Big 3 on one side and the product or market specialists on the other side. Usually, the Big 3 controls 70 to 90 percent of the market. Viable product or market specialists, appealing to smaller customers with specialized needs, own 1 and 5 percent of the market share. Those companies caught in the ditch typically capture only between 5 and 10 percent of a given market and find themselves unable to compete effectively against the Big 3 or the specialists.

Essentially, Sheth and Sisodia (2002) argue that an industry structure comprising three large generalists and numerous smaller specialists is "optimal" for firm stability and profitability in a competitive environment. Furthermore, they argue that the relationship between market share and profitability is non-linear in these structures, whereby small- and large-share firms can achieve high profitability, but midsized firms languish. The R3 theory can be summarized as follows:

1. industries tend to evolve toward a dynamic equilibrium with specific structure and distribution of firm sizes; and
2. a company's market share and degree of strategic focus are jointly related to its performance.

Uslay and colleagues (2010) empirically examined the "Rule of Three" theory by formally stating related hypotheses and empirically testing the idea's validity through data triangulation from Standard & Poor's COMPUSTAT, University of Chicago's CRSP database and the U.S. Census Bureau. They also examined the degree to which financial markets incorporate their implications in firm valuation. Their study supported the hypothesis that three generalists' industry structure is more prevalent in mature markets than other structures. When three main generalists exist in a market, industries' performance is superior to more than three or less than three generalists. They also found a non-monotonic convex function relationship between market share and profitability, supporting the R3 theory companies with mid-range market shares underperform both the specialists and the Big 3 generalists. Uslay and colleagues (2010) generally find strong support for the R3 theory. R3 theory suggests a curvilinear relationship with a convex function wherein market generalists with large market shares and specialist players with small market shares have better profitability than mid-size companies with market shares from 5–10%. However, they also find that generalists with excessive market shares (above 40%) perform worse than their smaller counterparts in the long run.

The R3 theory has many managerial implications for top management regarding how much growth strategy they should pursue, particularly for gaining market share. There are optimal market share levels for generalists and specialists for generating satisfactory shareholder returns, and assuming a linear or weak general relationship can lead to highly misleading conclusions (Uslay et al. 2017). For marketing professionals and theorists, the R3 theory is a valuable guide for the conditions in which a firm is better off growing primary demand for the product category versus aggressively pursuing market share, resulting in a loss in profitability. Sheth and colleagues (2020) have found supporting evidence to their Rule of Three in the global markets across industries, within Europe, Asia, and the emerging markets.

Concluding Remarks

Thus, despite its fragmentation, the marketing strategy school of thought made impressive contributions to the marketing discipline and business strategy practice in Era IV. However, several authors have recently pointed out that the drift in the norms of publication and the myopic approach in favor of rigor over relevance in academic marketing journals have made it increasingly challenging to publish traditional marketing strategy articles (Clark et al. 2014; Key et al. 2020; Lehmann et al. 2011; Sheth and Sisodia 2006). Given how closely intertwined is the future of marketing discipline to research on strategic marketing, it is necessary to overcome the academic irrelevance and the "identity crisis" currently plaguing marketing strategy research. Marketing strategy seems to have run out of tarmac in its current course. It needs to discover new areas of study and establish a new paradigm or perspective. Therefore, in the next section, we identify new promising research areas for revitalizing marketing strategy by shifting the focus back on customers. That also aligns with the emerging perspective of customer-centricity.

 ## 7.5 New Frontiers of Research in Marketing Strategy

It appears that marketing strategy will need to trace back to its roots and refocus on managerial marketing. There are six new areas of research that look very promising toward the revitalization of marketing strategy. All of them aim at shifting the focus back on customers. They are:

1. **Creating Value for Customers:** A customer is a buyer and a user. The buyer is looking for service value; a user is looking for performance value; a payer is looking for the price value. In other words, one can always win customers if one offers a superior product with a reasonable price in a customer-friendly service (Mittal and Sheth, 2001).

2. **Brand Value:** The second research area is developing the intangible asset (or goodwill) through brand value linked directly to the company's market value. Brands independent of the products are becoming more real, earning royalties by licensing the brand. Examples include Disney, Harley-Davidson, and most franchise brands.

3. **The Discipline of Selling:** Selling is gaining respect in marketing as a field of scientific inquiry. It is likely to range from behavioral experiments in campus laboratories to field experiments in cooperation with companies like Salesforce. Also, focus on key account performance and influencer marketing in social media. Selling as a persuasion process can learn from several disciplines, such as behavioral sciences, public opinion, and political sciences. The research on nudging by Thaler and Sustein (2008) represents an excellent example of this area's opportunities. Finally, we need a comprehensive model of selling as a process similar to the model of buyer behavior (Howard and Sheth 1969; Sheth 2020).

4. **Science of Pricing:** As mentioned before, the industry leads in research in pricing. It has resulted in psychological pricing concepts; price deals (two for one, for example); and dynamic pricing in many airlines and ridesharing services. In academic research, pricing has been anchored to economic theories of price elasticity (willingness to pay and ability to pay) and price as an entry barrier for customers wanting to make a purchase. More recently, pricing has focused on behavioral economics research, including risk-taking and price-quality relationships (Kahneman and Tversky 2000; Kahneman et al. 1982).

   Kent Monroe has been a pioneer in marketing on pricing research using Weber's concept of just noticeable difference (JND) in perception (Monroe 2003). However, more exciting research in pricing is possible today in the world of digital marketing and social media. Price as an indicator of quality is another central area of study. It is also possible to do macro-research at a national level to measure nations' price image. For example, China is perceived as a cheap goods manufacturer, as were Japan and South Korea at one time. An index of a price-based ranking of nations anchored to quality and performance is an excellent research opportunity at the macro level.

5. **Reverse Marketing:** The reverse marketing idea was introduced by Leenders and Blenkhorn (1989), Blenkhorn and Banting (1991), and Plank and Francis (2001) as a concept of demand-driven making (manufacturing). Today, with growing online procurement and shopping on Amazon, Alibaba, and Flipkart, and online sites of all major brick and mortar retailers (Macy's, J.C. Penney, Target), the process of buying is reversed. The purchase order is placed and paid for first, and then the product or service is configured or delivered to the home, office, or factory. It implies the need for marketing and supply chain to integrate in real-time (Sheth et al., 2009).

   Reverse marketing can be a rich area for developing theory. For example, is reverse marketing contextual or universal? What are the side effects, such as "stockout" or merchandise return? Should companies integrate the supply chain into the marketing function? What outcomes (cycle time, cost reduction, productivity gain, revenue growth, or cross-selling) help measure reverse marketing's efficiency and effectiveness? Finally, what impact is reverse marketing likely to have on advertising, promotion, and salesmanship?

6. **Role of Marketing in Society:** Interdependence between marketing and society is at the heart of macro marketing research, including the impact of public policy on consumption (demand) and production (supply). Examples include demarketing harmful products such as cigarette smoking and alcohol consumption through public policy and regulations. Indeed, most industries today face regulatory rules relating to product safety, product disclosure, product labeling, and truth in advertising and lending laws. On the other hand, marketing has an enormous impact on society through social and celebrity-led aspirations and peer group influences.

   The impact of marketing in encouraging overconsumption is a serious concern, especially concerning obesity and the environment. Social critics often blame marketing for climate change and lack of sustainability (plastic bottles and packaging materials). It has resulted in reviving research on marketing in society- can marketing be a force for a better world? What is marketing's role in creating value for all stakeholders, including the community and the planet, and delivering revenue growth and profitability for investors? As social activism for climate change and the environment grows worldwide, marketing strategy will likely revert to managerial marketing. The process will focus more on customers, community, and the planet and less on the competition.

7.6 Evaluation of Marketing Strategy School

The marketing strategy school of thought has made substantive contributions to the marketing discipline through seminal conceptual and empirical research over the past five decades. Given that strategy exists at multiple levels—corporate, business unit, and functional—of an organization, marketing research has advanced our knowledge on how marketing can contribute towards developing effective marketing strategies at all levels. At the corporate level, strategic marketing research develops frameworks for assisting business decisions and the broader goals to pursue the corporation and society's long-term sustainability. In a competitive arena, marketing strategy scholarship has enabled better decisions on business portfolios and investments relating to innovation, market growth, and market share acquisition at a business level. It also informs decisions on strategic positioning for market engagement, such as whether to be a specialist or a generalist and when to enter or exit specific markets. Furthermore, it provides theoretical guidance on the best ways to acquire and develop resources/competencies for competitive advantage and differentiation. Finally, at the functional level, marketing strategy research's centrality is on choices relating to the deployment of marketing resources to facilitate business goals and create a competitive advantage in the marketplace (Varadarajan and Yadav, 2002).

However, despite its impressive contributions, the marketing strategy literature has also generated dialog and debate on its very domain, particularly concerning the fundamental issues within its purview of study and the definition of marketing strategy as an organizational construct (Sheth 2021; Varadarajan 2015). Because this school of thought grew as an offshoot of managerial marketing, its initial concepts and constructs were rooted in managerial economics, such as response to heterogeneous markets, competitive differentiation, and pricing strategies. The strategy domain was concerned with product-market selections and choice of marketing-mix decisions. However, when marketing orientation became critical for defining corporate strategy, marketing strategy evolved into strategic marketing with consequent research focus on understanding, explaining, and predicting marketing's role in overall business performances. Thus, in the process, the extant research within the marketing strategy school of thinking got predominantly influenced by strategic management literature and inter-organizational economics.

Nevertheless, since marketing strategy is embedded in the industry structure and decisions related to the firm, products, buyers, customers, and the overall marketing environment, several construct labels also emerged within respective sub-domains, such as product management, channels, industrial marketing, buyer behavior, and relationship marketing. In turn, they have inadvertently contributed to the confusing vocabulary on marketing strategy. Varadarajan (2010, p. 138) provides an illustrative example of the proliferation of such constructs: "market strategy, marketing strategy, strategic marketing, strategic market planning, strategic marketing planning, strategic market management, customer-centric strategy, customer-driven strategy, customer-focused strategy, customer strategy, customer management strategy, customer relationship strategy, customer relationship management, and customer lifetime value management strategy." Although many strategy terms are operationalized in the marketing literature to specify specific managerial actions, for example, channel strategy, advertising strategy, customer acquisition strategy, customer retention strategy, partnering, and alliance strategy, the confusion persists.

This problem of proliferation of constructs, or terms, is not unique to the marketing strategy school of thought. As noted elsewhere in this book, it is evident in several schools of marketing thought and other business disciplines. Moreover, definitional ambiguities and potential conceptual overlap of meanings across terms are common problems for areas with considerable interest among business consultants, researchers, educators, and practitioners alike. Thus, we assess the marketing strategy school of thought on various metatheoretical criteria as follows:

STRUCTURE: **Are the concepts properly defined and integrated to form a strong nomological network?**

Marketing strategy school has provided many valuable concepts and constructs that guide managerial decisions and scholarly research. These include such concepts as market segmentation, product differentiation, strategic positioning, goods versus experiences, skimming versus penetration pricing strategies, brand equity and customer valuation, retention versus acquisition, full-line generalists versus specialists, niche marketing, market pioneers, incumbents, and challengers, concurrent versus sequential marketing, and market orientation and market-driving strategies. It has also provided the basis for determining growth strategies through market or customer penetration, product development and innovation, market and customer development, strategic alliances, market evolution cycles, and diversification ideas. Therefore, marketing strategy school is conceptually rich with tremendous practical concepts to advance marketing discipline knowledge.

However, there is substantial confusion regarding its domain and definition because of taxonomical problems in marketing strategy versus market strategy versus strategic marketing. Because of the marketing strategy's pervasiveness, several constructs appeared with overlapping concepts and operationally indistinguishable. As such, the nomological structure of the ideas is hard to follow. Moreover, it is pretty confusing because of the many interfacing layers of marketing strategy, such as market structures, competition, strategic business units, organizational hierarchies, product/service/experience designers, channels, customers, alliances, and other corporate stakeholders. The domain premise of marketing strategy is so broad that almost everything related to marketing decisions becomes its part.

The lack of conceptual distinction between corporate strategy (as in management literature) and marketing strategy (as in the purview of marketing research and literature) is another source of confusion within this school of thought. The limitations of some of the proposed conceptualizations of marketing strategy are evident. For example, conceptualizations of "where to compete" pertains to market strategy (and therefore should be considerations of corporate strategy), and "how to compete" pertain to marketing strategy (Varadarajan 2015). Similarly, the PIMS data-based research on market strategy applies to business strategy. It evaluates the business performance model as a function of industry structure variables from a competitive standpoint. Varadarajan (2010, 2015) provided an overall integrated framework of the marketing strategy domain and distinguished market strategy, marketing strategy, and strategic marketing. Still, no clear consensus on either the definitions or premises of inquiry has emerged. Therefore, from a structure point of view, the marketing strategy school of thought still lacks distinction and integration.

Our score on structure = 7

SPECIFICATION: Are the relationships specified in a manner to delimit hypotheses, or are they highly contingent?

In our assessment, the marketing strategy school has lost some of the specificity apparent in the early stages of this school's development. Concepts and hypotheses relating to specific aspects of strategy, such as market selection, segmentation and positioning, evolution and growth paths, competitive pricing models, market-share profitability relationship, market entries, and exit strategies, as well as innovation timing were delimited and generalizable in the earlier phases of its evolution. However, as marketing is getting fundamentally altered and established, the regularities and "lawlike generalizations" are considerably affected, challenging their validity. Marketing strategy school is struggling to develop delineable hypotheses that capture the altered phenomenon while allowing for the study of consequence variables. The debate on the conceptual distinction between marketing strategy and market strategy and whether strategic marketing is a separate concept remains unresolved.

The problem has been that marketing strategy concepts encompass a firm's crucial choices concerning markets to serve, market-entry mode, market entry timing, and other vital decisions concerning performing marketing activities, implying significant overlaps. Varadarajan (2015, p. 90) acknowledges that although the foundational premise of marketing strategy is generalizable across products, markets, and time horizons, the marketing strategy conducive to superior performance is contingent upon the internal organizational and external environmental factors.

Our score on specificity = 7

TESTABILITY: Are the operational definitions provided to ensure testability and intersubjective consensus?

There has been an epistemological concern on what should be measured and tested. Marketing strategy has traditionally been focused on singular outcome measures on financial performance. Still, recently, strong voices have been calling for measures that examine the social impact of marketing strategy, particularly for the triple-bottom-line of people, planet, and profits. Therefore, instead of stating marketing strategy issues only in specific reference to the marketplace and financial performance, it would be appropriate also to include ESG (economic, social, and governance) and sustainability-related performance goals and measures.

Our score on testability = 8

EMPIRICAL SUPPORT: What is the degree of confirmation in terms of empirical support?

Several underlying theses within the marketing strategy school of thought have empirical support. For example, postulations on organizational or functional performance due to specific strategies, such as market segmentation, targeting, positioning, growth strategies, innovation adoption, market leadership, niche marketing, skimming or penetration pricing strategies, as well as competitive differentiation, are all empirically supported. Similarly, developments in strategic marketing planning processes, including involving and engaging with various stakeholders in determining strategic marketing thrusts, have been empirically supported (Boyd et al., 2010; Homburg, Artz, and Wieseke, 2012; Homburg et al. 2014).

Overall, the marketing strategy school is quite strong on the criterion of empirical support. Nowadays, data on firm or SBU performance has become relatively easier to obtain from such sources as COMPUSTAT and the Sustainability Board. Thus, one can determine the impact of various marketing strategies on firm performance.

Our score on empirical support = 9

RICHNESS: **How comprehensive and generalizable is the theory?**

Over five decades of its continued evolution, the marketing strategy school has produced extensive knowledge to inform the marketing discipline. Evolving from its early focus on functional marketing strategies, marketing strategy school, since the 1980s, developed a broad construal of the field to engage in and chart the firm's strategic direction (Varadarajan 2010).

The marketing strategy examines several strategic aspects of value creation, including network strategies, alliances, capabilities, culture, resource deployment, and market engagement. Thus, marketing strategy school offers rich explanations for organizational and functional performance and has considerably influenced business practices and corporate strategy. It has led to value-creating transformations through market orientation, customer-centric organizations, and innovation strategies. Marketing strategy theories are generalizable beyond the marketing domain into other aspects of business practices, particularly strategic management (customer-centricity, alliances, and governance models); finance and accounting (brand equity and customer valuation); and human resources (capabilities, competencies, culture, and organizational learning). Marketing strategy theories are also generalizable across other social science disciplines, notably political science and public administration.

Our score on richness = 9

SIMPLICITY: **How easy is it to communicate and implement the theory?**

This school of thought's fundamental proposition is that specific marketing strategy processes such as STP, market orientation, customer focus, systematic innovation, orderly market entry, and nurturing the right partnerships to leverage resources contribute to superior firm performance. Some aspects of this school of study's broad construal are hard to comprehend and not relatively parsimonious, yet it is still quite elegant at its core. The marketing strategy school's critical goals are to infuse market and marketing thoughts and processes in the overall organizational strategy and design to achieve superior organizational performance. These are not everyday life experiences for most people, particularly those who have not been exposed to higher organization management levels. Therefore, they are not as easy to comprehend, relate, implement, or apply in the real world by those in the early stages of their career or have limited functional roles to play.

Developing a comprehensive or general marketing strategy theory is tricky due to too many variables and constructs. Although outcome variables are very well-defined, several constructs are process variables making them difficult to communicate and implement. The biggest drawback exists in the proliferation of constructs and complicated integration, making it more challenging to develop a comprehensive theory.

Our score on simplicity = 8

Table 7.1 summarizes our evaluation of the marketing strategy school of thought. This school is weak in syntax but quite strong in semantics and pragmatic aspects of theory building.

Table 7.1 Evaluation of the Marketing Strategy School*

Criterion	Rationale	Score
Structure	Somewhat confusing taxonomy and too many over-lapping constructs	7
Specification	A high degree of variance in specificity of constructs and concepts. Relationships between independent and outcome variables are sometimes contingent, affecting generalizability.	7
Testability	Many relationships are testable, but there is room for improvement due to the proliferation of constructs and confusing conceptualizations	8
Empirical support	Has a long history of research and empirical evidence. Availability of objective firm performance data makes model testing possible	9
Richness	A comprehensive and generalizable set of research issues offer vast potential for many mid-range theories	9
Simplicity	Some concepts are hard to communicate. Too many constructs affect parsimony, making it challenging to create an integrated general theory	8
	TOTAL	48

* Scores range from 1 (poor) to 10 (excellent).

Summary

The marketing strategy school of thought has made significant contributions to managerial thinking within the marketing discipline. It emerged with the acceptance of the marketing concept of fulfilling customer needs and wants as the central purpose of corporate strategic goals. It elevated marketing's role in the overall corporate strategic plan with a high degree of overlap with business strategy.

The critical concerns of the marketing strategy school of thinking have been about developing a long-term differential advantage for the corporation. It concerned itself with five primary domains of inquiry: (a) the variables of market growth and strategic differentiation, such as product and market development; (b) pursuing new opportunities through innovation and market disruptions; (c) portfolio planning and strategic alignment through alliances and vertical integration; (d) competitive strategies and effects on performance in terms of market share and profitability; and (e) capabilities enhancement for value creation, such as through brand and customer equity. In essence, marketing strategy is focused on the future – on proactively seeking to change the conditions through strategic thrusts, whether they are market-related, customer-related, competition-related, or resource-related. The terms marketing strategy and strategic marketing are often used interchangeably to emphasize marketing's role in the firm's strategic thrust.

Marketing strategy school has offered several new theories and constructs relating to organizational capabilities and competition that have strong potential to shape a general theory of marketing, for example, market orientation, resource advantage (R-A) theory, and the rule of three (R3). Market orientation advocates an organization-wide mechanism to generate market intelligence to track current and future customer needs, potential competitor strategies, and environmental factors causing market disequilibrium, linking them to the firm's performance and sustainable competitive advantage. The R-A theory articulates business strategy and marketing strategy layers in an integrated framework. It identifies strategic perspectives that drive business strategy to achieve competitive advantage through market segmentation, market orientation, relationship marketing, and brand equity strategies. Finally, the Rule of Three (R3) theory proclaims that competitive markets evolve in a highly predictable fashion as natural market structures, governed by the "Rule of Three."

Contrary to traditional economic theory, R3 implies that markets are simultaneously oligopolistic and monopolistic. Market share and profitability have non-linear relationships, suggesting a wide range of corporate, marketing, investment, and policy implications. Essentially, R3 argues that an industry structure comprising three large generalists and numerous smaller specialists is "optimal" for firm stability and profitability in a competitive environment. Thus, small- and large-share firms can achieve high profitability, but midsized firms languish.

Today, the marketing strategy school of thought is well-entrenched and is considered a subdiscipline of marketing encompassing several interest groups within its domain. For example, scholars interested in product management, branding, marketing communications, inter-organizational relationships and alliances, competitive strategies, pricing, marketing knowledge development, services marketing, relationship marketing, and those studying issues of marketing policies and macromarketing challenges all identify themselves within the overall ambit of marketing strategy subdiscipline. Thus, it has become the core of the marketing discipline. Yet it offers many new areas for research and knowledge development and has a solid potential to lay the foundations for a general theory of marketing.

Questions for Analysis and Discussion

1. Is it necessary to anchor marketing strategy on the competition? Why or why not?

2. Explain how the premise of marketing strategy evolved and expanded, including new strategic levers of marketing planning (from products, markets, and marketing mix to competition, customers, resources, capabilities, brand equity, and innovation).

3. To what extent are the central tenets of marketing strategy distinguishable from business strategy and strategic management? What are some of the distinctive contributions of marketing strategy school (compared to managerial marketing and strategic management)?

4. Is "market orientation" an aspect of a firm's *culture*, *strategy*, or both? What are the pros and cons of viewing market orientation as a culture versus strategy?

5. Shelby Hunt (2010) identified four specific marketing strategy theories that purport to achieve competitive advantage for the firm – market segmentation, market orientation, brand equity, and relationship marketing. Can you identify another type of marketing strategy beyond these four? Moreover, would the resource advantage (R-A) theory proposed by Hunt and Morgan (1995) still provide a positive foundation for the strategy you identified? Why, or why not?

6. Can the "Rule of Three" (R3) theory be considered a general theory of competition? Why, or why not? What aspects of R3 theory are specific to marketing strategy, and what aspects relate to overall business strategy?

7. Several scholars have observed that marketing strategy research is highly fragmented, lacking an integrated framework. How would you address this issue? Would you develop a new integrated marketing strategy theory or create a proper taxonomy? Is there a need to refocus the central tenets driving marketing strategy inquiry and practice?

CHAPTER

International Marketing School of Thought

LEARNING OBJECTIVES

After reading this chapter, you will be able to:

- Identify the key questions addressed by the international marketing school of thought.
- Explain the prevailing debate on standardization versus localization in international marketing practice.
- Answer if the effect of country of origin matters in marketing strategy.
- Assess the contribution of current models and frameworks in evaluating international market attractiveness and entry plans.

- Determine the value of global branding versus local branding.
- Recapitulate the value of cross-cultural research.
- Evaluate international marketing school of thought on specific metatheory criteria.

 ## 8.1 Introduction

As with many new schools of thought, the international marketing school grew out of a conceptual marriage between managerial and macromarketing schools of thought. The emergence of scholarly interest in international marketing can be traced to the aftermath of World War II.[1] Bradley (1987, p. 208) defined international marketing by augmenting the definition of marketing by stating it as "identifying needs and wants of consumers, producing assets to give a differential marketing advantage, communicating information about these assets and distributing and exchanging them internationally…." Albaum and Peterson (1984, p. 162) offered a similar definition: "influences on and activities involved in marketing not only to, but within foreign countries."

While international marketing's initial focus was on exporting, there was growing interest as large companies from developed markets increasingly became multinational corporations with a vested interest in foreign markets. Cavusgil and Nevin (1981) categorized early research efforts in this domain as follows:

1. *Macro-empirical* studies focused on aggregate trade flows between nations and their determinants.
2. *Macro-conceptual* studies sought to theorize the direction and magnitude of trade between nations, often utilizing a comparative advantage lens.
3. *Micro-empirical* studies focused on international marketing more than global business issues, using individual firms as the analysis unit.
4. *Micro-conceptual* studies made theoretical contributions by explaining the international marketing conduct of individual firms.

---

1. *Multinational Business Operations* by Sheth and Sethi (1973) with its four volumes on 1. Environmental Aspects of Operating Abroad, 2. Long Range Planning, Organization, and Management, 3. Marketing Management and 4. Financial Management represents one of the early treatises.

Due to the complexity of the perceived environment, interrelationships, and uncontrollable factors, micro studies were more popular and offered more relevance, whereas most macro-level research remained conceptual.[2] Even for micro-level empirical work, financial constraints of collecting data and data-comparability issues across cultures brought about significant challenges. Not surprisingly then, review studies of the period (e.g., Albaum and Peterson 1984, Boddewyn 1981; Bradley 1987) found international marketing to be "fragmentary and exploratory without a strong theoretical framework, and [lacking in] methodological rigor compared to the domestic U.S. marketing research" (Aulakh and Kotabe 1993, p. 5). For example. Albaum and Peterson (1984, p. 169) reviewed the empirical studies of international marketing from 1976–1982 and concluded that "research was predominantly descriptive or exploratory in nature, rather than analytical or normative... The empirical research... consisted of, for the most part, studies conducted in isolation and possessing no linkages to other studies; they did not possess either a sound conceptual or theoretical foundation."

Cavusgil and Nevin (1981) observed that the environment of international markets, regional studies of the international market, strategic international marketing management, and decision tools for international marketing were the broad topical areas that most scholars focused early on. They also assessed that strategic international marketing management was the topic that received the most attention. While the *Journal of International Business Studies* (JIBS) (e.g., Albaum and Peterson 1984; Boddewyn 1981, Parameswaran and Yaprak 1987; Walters 1986), and naturally the *Journal of Marketing* occasionally published relevant work, scholars of international marketing had to wait until 1983 for their first dedicated journal, *International Marketing Review*. The second one, *Advances in International Marketing,* would arrive in 1986, and the trifecta would be complete with the arrival of the *Journal of International Marketing* in 1993.[3] The fact that Aulakh and Kotabe (1993) identified some 720 published international marketing articles from 21 journals from 1980–1990 gives us a good indication of the growing body of the work during that period. Of the 720 articles, 37.5% were empirical, and about half (of both conceptual and empirical studies) dealt with marketing management issues such as marketing mix, market entry strategies, or foreign investment. Aulakh and Kotabe (1993) observed that pricing (understandably, due to the sensitive nature of pricing data), and somewhat surprisingly, market segmentation research, was lacking.[4] On the other hand, theory-based articles increased from 23.2% in 1980–1982 to 45.6% in 1989–1990, characterized as a welcome development.

Sheth (1997 p. 563) observed that "international marketing has predominantly remained a contextual practice and... it has been difficult to develop a theory of international marketing even based on contingency propositions." (also see Sheth and Eshghi 1989c). Sheth and Parvatiyar (2001, p. 26) noted: "international marketing has remained a contextual practice devoid of a well-accepted theory." They observed that markets are becoming borderless, proposed an emphasis on global marketing anchored to transnational similarities through eight processes: worldwide markets, mass customization, relationship management, trickle-up theory, global accounts, cross-functional consistency, value-based costing, and networked organization.

Notwithstanding, Czinkota and Ronkainen (2003, p. 13) proclaimed in their "International Marketing Manifesto" that "[today] might be called the triumph of international marketing... As a change agent, international marketing has brought important benefits to nation-states, firms, and their employees... Linked to this growth, these same countries have also achieved relatively greater gains of political freedom, greater increases

---

2. Interested readers may refer to Sheth and Eshghi (1989a, 1989b, 1989c, 1990, 1991) for macro and micro perspectives of global marketing and business.

3. For example, the *Journal of International Marketing* has become an academic outlet of high repute and impact factor (currently, 4.6 for annual impact, and 6.5 for 5-year impact). Griffith (2008, p. 1), as then editor-in-chief, characterized JIM as "a marketing strategy journal" and observed that JIM would be receptive to articles in two general domains: "(1) international—that is, when marketing activities occur across national boundaries—and (2) cross-cultural—that is, when comparisons regarding marketing-related issues are made across national boundaries." AMA Global Marketing SIG was founded in 1994, and its membership, not surprisingly, is from all around the globe. The Global Marketing SIG organizes a highly successful annual conference as well.

4. Alas, almost two decades later "research on export pricing [was] still characterized by the lack of a strong theoretical basis, the failure to agree on the relevant determinants of export pricing, and some weaknesses in research designs and analytical techniques, which may explain the many contradictory and confusing findings in the literature" (Tan and Sousa 2011, p. 1). Similarly, "segmentation and targeting research, which are central to IM strategy and whose pursuit was stressed by Aulakh and Kotabe (1993), remain in dire need of attention" (Samiee and Chabowski 2012, p. 383).

in life expectancy, higher literacy rates, and better overall standards of living… Consumers are the greatest beneficiaries of all. They are offered an unprecedented degree of product availability and choice." Their words encouraging managerial relevance were met with enthusiasm in three commentaries. International marketing scholars before and since have tended to focus on the following issues.

8.2 To Standardize or Localize, that is the Question

One of the longest-standing and influential debates in international marketing has been whether multinational firms should standardize or localize their global offerings (Solberg 2002; Zou and Cavusgil 2002). While the first proponents of standardization emerged from the domain of advertising (e.g., Elinder 1961; Killough 1978), the growing opportunities in foreign markets and the significant potential gains standardization promised led Theodore Levitt to argue powerfully in favor of it: "[S]uccess in a world of homogenized demand requires a search for sales opportunities in similar segments across the globe in order to achieve the economies of scale necessary to compete. Such a segment in one country is seldom unique—it has close cousins everywhere precisely because technology has homogenized the globe (Levitt 1983, p. 94)." Levitt made the case that consumers worldwide would be willing to live with standardization (less customization) to reap the benefits of lower prices and higher quality.

Jain (1989, p. 71), in a seminal article, made the following observations:

1. "There are two aspects of standardization, process and program (e.g., Sorenson and Wiechman 1975).

2. Across-the-board standardization is inconceivable (e.g., Killough 1978).

3. The decision on standardization is not a dichotomous one between complete standardization and customization (e.g., Quelch and Hoff 1986).

4. A variety of internal and external factors impinge on the standardization decision. Among these, product/industry characteristics are paramount (e.g., Wind and Douglas 1986).

5. Generally standardization is most feasible in settings where marketing infrastructure is well developed (e.g., Peebles, Ryans, and Vernon 1978)."

He, thus, identified target market (geographic area, economic factors), market position (market development, conditions, competition), nature of the product (type and positioning), environmental factors (physical, legal, political, infrastructure), and organization factors (corporate orientation, headquarters-subsidiary relationship, delegation of authority) as the determinants of marketing program standardization. In all, proponents of a global marketing approach argued for standardization of the marketing mix and programs across countries (Johansson 1997; Zou and Cavusgil 2002).

Nevertheless, the empirical evidence regarding performance gains of standardization remains mixed and inconclusive to this day. For example, Mandler et al. (2021, p. 417) cite some studies "offering evidence of positive (e.g., Alashban et al. 2002, Zou and Cavusgil 2002), non-significant (e.g., Chung 2003, Samiee and Roth 1992), and conditional (e.g., Katsikeas et al. 2006, Samiee and Chirapanda 2019) relationships, which also might be nonlinear (e.g., Sousa and Novello 2014). This fragmented picture seemingly results from the many varied conceptual and methodological considerations that provide the foundation for extant studies (Samiee and Chirapanda 2019)."

Ghemawat (2001) argued that psychic distance mattered and that most firms have misleadingly adopted a simplistic view of foreign operations' challenges. He pointed to drawbacks of country portfolio analysis, which focused on national wealth, consumer income, and propensity to consume as the root cause, and proposed the CAGE framework to overcome these challenges. The framework consisted of **C**ultural distance (religion, race, social norms, and language), **A**dministrative or political distance (colony heritage, currency, and trade agreements), **G**eographic distance (physical, size of the target, waterway access, topography, and infrastructures), and **E**conomic distance (gap in terms of wealth, income, cost, and resources). He warned against the perils of overestimating foreign market attractiveness (Ghemawat 2001).

While the debate was never fully settled, the adage "think globally, act locally" gradually became popular. A glocal marketing approach was adopted by several multinationals such as Honda, General Electric, General Motors, and General Dynamics (Sheth 2020). Schilke, Reimann, and Thomas (2009) reported that standardization led to higher profits when the products are homogeneous, global market penetration is high, cost leadership strategy is adapted, and strong coordination capabilities exist.

 ## 8.3 Country of Origin Effects

Country of origin (COO) has arguably been the most intensively studied research stream in international marketing, with roughly 600 refereed articles published over the last four decades (e.g., Lu et al., 2016). The vast majority of early studies on the country of origin reported that it matters (e.g., Cattin, Jolibert, and Lohnes 1982; Hampton 1977; Papadopoulos et al. 1987; Schooler 1965; Schooler and Sunoo 1971; White 1979) and that country stereotyping effect is indeed prevalent (Samiee 1994).

The literature suggests that COO serves as an extrinsic cue and can significantly influence consumers' perception of product quality and overall brand image (e.g., Verlegh and Steenkamp, 1999; Pharr, 2005). One of the key findings to date has been that consumers in advanced economies prefer products manufactured in their home countries and others whose cultures are perceived to be similar (Bilkey and Nes 1982; Elliott and Cameron 1994; Heslop, Papadopoulos, and Bourke 1998; Reierson 1967; Samiee 1994).

Consumer ethnocentrism (meaning, "beliefs regarding the appropriateness of purchasing foreign-made products" [Watson and Wright 2000, p. 1150]) has often been forth as an explanation for the COO impact on domestic purchase preferences where ethnocentric consumers display a tendency to buy domestic products over imported ones (Balabanis and Diamantopoulos 2004; Lantz and Loeb 1996). However, COO is a multidimensional construct. For example, consumers from developing economies favor foreign-sounding brands over those in their native tongue (Batra et al., 2000; Leclerc, Bernd, and Laurette, 1994).

Bayraktar, Uslay, and Ndubisi (2015, p. 354) presented "the following COO concepts and their definitions… *product origin*, which is communicated through the phrase 'made in …', refers to the country where the product is produced. *Brand origin* refers to the country in which the headquarters of the brand's parent firm is located, regardless of where the product is manufactured. *Ownership origin* refers to the nationality of those that own the brand. *Design origin* refers to the country where the product is designed. Finally, *parts origin* refers to the country(s) where the parts of the product come from. The prevalent finding in the studies examining the effects of partitioned COO (product origin, brand origin, ownership origin, design origin, and parts origin) on consumers' evaluations and judgments is that COO information, no matter how it is conceptualized, is used as an indicator of product quality (Jun and Choi 2007; Chao 1993; Srinivasan et al. 2004; Insch and McBride 1999; Chowdhury and Ahmed 2009; Paul 1993; Lee and Bae 1999; Thakor and Lavack 2003; Kim and Chung 1997)." Furthermore, COO has a significant and positive impact on consumer willingness to pay (Koschnate-Fischer, Diamantopoulos, and Oldenkotte 2012). Herz and Diamantopoulos (2017) found that a substantial proportion of consumers are influenced by COO even though they may claim the contrary.

On the other hand, it has been pointed out that brand recognition of COO tends to be low and that the importance and diagnostic value of COO may have been exaggerated (Balabanis and Diamantopoulos 2008; Liefeld 2004; Pharr 2005; Saimee, Shimp, and Sharma 2005). After all, in an increasingly global world, the distinctions between different aspects of the country of origin are blurring. Each element of COO listed above can take place in a different country or even continent. Therefore, while COO may be less influential in driving performance in a globalizing market, it can guide evaluations of needs and market entry decisions.

 ## 8.4 Market Attractiveness

When firms decide to globalize, the markets they should prioritize for expansion depend on the prosperity, size, infrastructure, and accessibility of the countries in consideration (Mitra and Golder 2002). To date, efforts to assess market attractiveness and country potential have predominantly utilized macro-economic and political factors. That was by and large necessitated because primary research in emerging markets was costly, challenging, and time-consuming. With the simplifying assumption that consumers in the same country set can be served effectively with a similar marketing mix, ranking or clustering techniques were utilized to identify the most attractive country-markets (Cavusgil and Nevin 1981; Sakarya, Eckman and Hyllegard 2007). Firms focusing on standardization would be better off using clustering, and ranking techniques better serve those trying to decide which market to enter next. Cavusgil, Kiyak, and Yeniyurt (2004) proposed a hybrid approach combining both techniques. Their tool used secondary data on country infrastructure, economic well-being, the standard of living, market size, and market dynamism.

Another critical aspect of a global marketing approach is the benefit reaped from coordinating value-chain activities. An optimal reconfiguration enables firms to specialize and take advantage of local resources (Craig and Douglas 1997; Roth, Schweiger, and Morrison 1991). Based on countries' unique comparative advantages, aka the Ricardian view, concentrating value chain activities that can be deployed most efficiently decreases total variable cost and redundancies across national or regional operations. For example, similar to how many manufacturing giants moved their manufacturing operations to China and Vietnam decades ago, Silicon Valley staples as well as many conglomerates are now moving more and more of their R&D centers or starting new ones in China and India (Sheth, Uslay, and Sisodia 2020; Yeniyurt, Cavusgil, and Hult 2005). Hence, the traditional R&D foci of multinationals' efforts (high quality, high margin) are quickly being replaced by affordability and accessibility foci of reverse innovation from emerging markets (Immelt, Govindarajan, and Trimble 2009; Ramamurti and Govindarajan 2018).

8.5   Market Selection and Entry Mode

The decision regarding market entry mode and operation in international markets has been "a consistent and persistent topic in business research generally and strategic marketing literature specifically for decades" since the entry mode is viewed as a critical determinant of foreign market performance (Schellenberg, Harker and Jafari 2018, pp. 601–602; Crick and Crick 2016). However, the traditional international marketing models suggested an escalation of commitment, such as exporting first, then creating subsidiaries, and ultimately establishing strategic partnerships (Malhotra, Agarwal, and Ulgado 2003; Townsend, Yeniyurt, and Talay 2009; Yeniyurt et al. 2009). Similarly, regional presence can give way to a multi-regional and ultimately global presence.

The extraordinary pace with which emerging markets are growing and the competitive path to globalization may increasingly necessitate bypassing the traditional framework. Thus, many businesses are increasingly "born global" (Knight and Cavusgil 1996, 2004). In contrast, even existing businesses may realize they are late to the game and become "born-again global" (Bell, McNaughton, and Young 2001). Availability of the internet and consequently mobile communications were critical catalysts for globalization and facilitated the diffusion of trends, brands, products, and services. E-commerce also enabled worldwide outreach without establishing proprietary global distribution networks, which significantly reduced capital requirements and further accelerated the formation of born-global and born-again global firms. As we will discuss later, the digital economy's concurrent rise in a global context is inevitable.

Crick and Jones (2000, p. 80) point out that technology-oriented, small and medium-sized enterprises might not follow Internationalization's traditional path: "Internationalization was much less deterministic than conventional wisdom suggests, for example, the export stage models. In several firms, there was evidence of an international orientation from the date they were founded, a rapid planned internationalization through several modes of market entry, and a concentration on major markets in the industrial sector through committed forms of entry strategy, such as subsidiaries. Firms balanced this rapid industrialization by attempting to obtain a competitive advantage internationally by using the available managerial and organizational competencies to exploit the proprietary technological know-how by exporting to several markets rather than relying on a few key ones."

Knight and Kim (2009) identified international orientation, international marketing skills, international innovativeness, and international market orientation as the four dimensions of international business competence, which they viewed as critical for the success of SMEs. Other key determinants of globalization are government/regulation, cost, markets, and competition (Yip and Hult 2011). But, of course, the journey does not end with the decision to enter and entry mode. For example, Griffith and colleagues (2017) demonstrated that brand equity, financial resources, and competitive intensity accelerate global rollout, improving global product performance. Nevertheless, Schellenberg and colleagues (2018) reviewed the literature on international market entry mode from the theoretical lens of the transaction cost approach, institutional theory, the eclectic paradigm, the Uppsala internationalization model, the resource-based view, and concluded that a detailed knowledge of how market entry decisions are made was still lacking.

This research stream has also been extended to market exit and, more recently, re-entry decisions. Crick (2004) reported that export readiness and entrepreneurial knowledge were critical in the decision to cease exporting. While a high level of foreign competition and strategic misfit can reduce the survival rate in international new ventures, high technological competence increases survival rates (Mudambi and Zahra 2007; Sousa and Tan 2015). More recently, scholars have focused on market re-entry. Javalgi and colleagues (2011) conceptualized that foreign market re-entry is tied to growth, diversification, sunk cost, and resource exploitation in the previously exited foreign market. Re-entry is associated with the rationale for an exit, and its likelihood is increased by the relational capital of the focal firm (Bernini, Du, and Love 2016; Yayla et al. 2018).

 ## 8.6 Global Branding

A corollary of global marketing was global brands, marketed across the world, which preserved the offerings' essence even as the marketing efforts may be adapted locally (Aaker and Joachimsthaler 1999; de Chernatony, Halliburton, and Bernath 1995). Global brands serve as a beacon of quality worldwide. Brand globalness, as a distinct brand attribute, can even help firms achieve higher status in emerging markets than they possess in their home markets (e.g., Jeep in China, McDonald's in Turkey) (Alden, Steenkamp, and Batra 1999; Batra et al. 2000; Steenkamp, Batra, and Alden 2003). Research on the waterfall (sequential market entry) versus sprinkler market entry (simultaneous entry) suggested that the latter is more appropriate for introducing a new product amidst intensive global competition (Kalish, Mahajan and Muller 1995), which also justifies investments in developing a global brand.

Ozsomer (2012) distinguished between brand "globalness" and "local iconness" and reported that while they are positively related in emerging markets, they tend to be negatively related in developed markets. Ozsomer and Altaras (2008) reviewed three consumer behavior theoretical streams consumer culture theory, signaling theory, and the associate network memory model. They proposed a model of global brand attitude and purchase likelihood. Their model includes international brand quality, prestige, global brand relative price, and notably global brand social responsibility as antecedents to global brand attitude, which drives purchases.

Douglas, Craig, and Nijssen (2001, p. 98) observed that "[j]ust as architectural plans provide the basis for a sound building, international brand architecture establishes the plan for developing a sound branding strategy." They proposed that firm-based drivers (administrative heritage, expansion strategy, corporate identity, and product diversity) lead to an international brand architecture (level in an organization, geographic scope, and product scope) and that this relationship is moderated by product-market drivers (target market, cultural embeddedness, and competitive market structure).

As aforementioned, an intensive academic debate regarding the extent of required standardization ensued, which settled on the notion of "be global, act local" (Wills, Samli, and Jacobs 1991). Hence, standardizing a marketing program does not require all marketing efforts and implementation to be identical. Firms operating in multiple countries can nevertheless accommodate flexibility to develop and alter plans on a country-by-country or region-by-region basis and benefit from common factors in their strategy and practice (Craig and Douglas 2000; Kotabe and Helsen 2010). Focusing on financial forecast measures, the brand's role, and brand strength, Interbrand has become prominent with its annual most valuable global brand rankings since 1988. Interestingly, the quintessential, most valuable global brand Coca-Cola is no longer considered among the top five. Currently, Apple is the leader with a $323B evaluation, followed by other tech-oriented juggernauts Amazon ($201B), Microsoft ($166B), Google ($165B), and Samsung ($62B) to round up the top 5 (https://www.interbrand.com/best-brands/). Samli and Fevrier (2008) observed that while global brands tend to preserve their equity in the short run, they tend to lose their value over more extended time frames.

Steenkamp (2020) identified the rise of the digital sales channels, cocreated global brand strategy, global transparency of brand activity needs, the global connectivity among the brand's consumers, and the Internet of

Things as five core underlying digital trends influencing global B2C brands. In addition, he observed that the marketplace was very dynamic and remained significantly ahead of international marketing researchers when it came to global brand building.

8.7 Cross-Cultural Research

Early international marketing researchers owe a great deal to Hofstede's (1980, 2001) seminal work on cultural dimensions and international differences. It is widely acknowledged as the most influential study of culture in international business. Hofstede (1980), utilizing an extensive database based on his work experience at IBM International and drawing from his subsequent work, introduced four cultural dimensions: power distance, individualism *vs.* collectivism, masculinity *vs.* femininity, and uncertainty avoidance. Subsequently, a fifth dimension, long-term orientation, was introduced (Hofstede and Bond 1984; Hofstede 1991, 2001).

Many researchers followed the stream Hofstede created and conducted research that compared consumers across cultures in a marketing context. They collectively demonstrated that globalization did not generate consumers with similar tastes or values and that cultural differences also mattered (Yeniyurt and Townsend 2003). For example, antecedents of market orientation may vary based on national culture, especially when individual actions and interpersonal relationships are concerned (Brettel et al., 2008). Similarly, Lee and Dawes (2005) examined Guanxi (i.e., the Chinese interpersonal business notion of passing the gate through connecting). They reported that Chinese industrial buyers' trust in a salesperson was more important than their trust in the sales organization for their long-term orientation towards the supplier.

Notably, most cross-cultural studies have focused on East-West differences, which have been taken for granted, whereas North-South has not received ample attention. Overall, genes and climate have arguably an outsized impact on culture and consumption patterns ranging from soft drinks, cheese, shoes, garments, and homes; that is, food, shelter, clothing choices and well as attitudes regarding time and space rely to a large extent on latitudes (Sheth 2017). Such differences can even be observed within the same country if it spreads far latitudinally (e.g., India). The shift of consumer preferences from unbranded to branded goods, faith-based consumption, diaspora markets, social media reach across borders, low-income consumers, and sustainability have been advanced as additional fertile areas for cross-cultural research (Sheth and Parvatiyar 2020).

Malhotra, Agarwal, and Ulgado (2003) reviewed various international product life cycle theories, market imperfections, strategic behavior, resource advantage, transaction cost, eclectic, Internationalization, and networks and advanced the understanding of the field with a unified conceptual framework that integrates entry modes and timing. They proposed that market risks' moderating role, global strategic, transaction-specific, and government-imposed factors can significantly influence foreign marketing performance. The word-of-mouth effect is prevalent; however, new products' diffusion speed tends to be faster in developed markets than developing ones (Talukdar, Sudhir, and Ainslie 2002). While there are differences based on product categories, the time to take off seems to be converging for developed countries over time, the S-shape of the diffusion curve has been flattening, and cultural orientation and income inequality remain significant predictors (Chandrasekaran and Tellis 2008; Griffith, Yalcinkaya, and Rubera 2014; Van den Bulte and Stremersch 2004).

8.8 Chindia and the Global Rule of Three

As emerging markets moved from the periphery and became central to the marketing discipline, such markets' study evolved from a fascinating hobby to absolute necessity. Leading scholars began to pay more attention to these markets, especially China and India. Similarly, multinationals' internationalization strategies from emerging markets have attracted more attention (e.g., Kumar et al. 2019; Sheth, Uslay, and Sisodia 2020). Sheth (2011a) suggested that heterogeneity of markets, sociopolitical governance, a chronic shortage of resources, unbranded competition, and inadequate structure are uniquely different for emerging markets and require rethinking marketing perspectives. Calantone, Griffith, and Yalcinkaya (2006) proposed and found empirical support for a modified Technology Adoption Model customized for the Chinese context. "[P]erhaps the biggest business strategy issue of our time [is] how competition between emerging market and established multinationals is likely to unfold with the big shift in many economic activities from advanced economies to emerging economies" (Ghemawat in Cuervo-Cazurra and Ramamurti 2014). Townsend, Yeniyurt, and Talay (2009) observed that multinational firms could create dominant global brands sooner if they emphasize building their presence in the three major continents as part of their early international expansion. Market size is a significant predictor of a brand's likelihood to launch in a new market, especially when market conditions are uncertain (Yeniyurt, Townsend, and Talay 2007). Therefore, the importance of Chindia will only increase as the center of gravity shifts from the Atlantic to the Pacific and concepts such as frugal innovation (serving subsistence markets [going back macro interface roots]), reverse brand lifecycle, and leveraging domestic scale advantages enabled by emerging markets come to the fore (Sheth and Sisodia 2006; Sheth 2011b; Sheth, Uslay, and Sisodia 2020).

Indeed, over half of the global growth is anticipated to be derived from just three countries: China (27.7%), India (13%), and the U.S. (10.4%), meanwhile the traditional sources of growth, Germany (1.9%), U.K. (1.5%), and France (1.5%), are anticipated to contribute less than 5% combined in 2025, using IMF purchasing power parity index (Tanzi and Lu 2020). Therefore, the new triad power will increasingly require a strong presence in China, India, and the U.S., and ultimately the continent of Africa over the traditional powerhouses of Europe (Sheth, Uslay, and Sisodia 2020).

Moreover, the digital economy is already on the rise, and it has vast potential to become global. When it comes to e-commerce, China already surpassed the U.S. in terms of size in 2013. Its $2 trillion e-retailing market is far bigger than American and European e-retail combined (The Economist 2021a). Chinese e-retailing is concentrated among three major players (where Alibaba, JD.com, and Pinduoduo account for over 90% of e-retail sales, whereas Amazon, Shopify, and eBay share of sales in the U.S. is less than 50% [The Economist 2021b]). However, it is also more dynamic than its Western counterparts and blends e-payments, group deals, flash deals, social media, instant messaging, short videos (e.g., Tiktok), and live streams via its "super-apps." Notably, the U.S. and its 330-million population is home to 30 times more (mostly struggling) malls than China's 1.4-billion population (The Economist 2021b). Thus, China that never anchored itself around costly high-end shopping malls has embraced e-commerce and benefits from delivery efficiencies in high-density areas. Interestingly, western e-tailing has more to learn from China than the other way around, and these lessons are replete with implications for global marketing.

As all marketing is contextual, Sheth (2020) offered a typology of international marketing context. He observed that macro and micro forces could influence global and domestic markets. While topics such as demographics and culture have been adequately covered, applying values, lifestyles, and unbranded competition (which makes 65% of consumption in emerging markets) continue to demand scholarly attention (Sheth 2011a; 2020). Even as the studies of international marketing school of thought are growing and becoming more sophisticated and complex (Samiee and Chabowski 2012), the examination of global topics such as global CSR, ethics, environmental sustainability, and capital markets in emerging markets can advance our understanding considerably. Similarly, the digital revolution and the resulting big data availability will leave no business area untouched (McKinsey Global Institute 2016), and international marketing is no exception. Sheth (2011a) proposed rethinking existing perspectives and practices in international marketing theory, strategy, policy, and practice, as illustrated in Figure 8.1.

As further evidence that the International Marketing School of Thought is maturing, recent literature reviews have focused on interface issues rather than central topics. For example, Yang and Gabrielsson (2018) reviewed the research at the interface of international marketing and entrepreneurship, Javalgi and Russell (2018) examined the literature on international marketing ethics, and Narayanan (2015) reviewed the literature regarding export barriers for SMEs. We envision that international marketing will continue to morph into global marketing in the coming decade and become even more central for scholarly pursuit in marketing.

8.9 Evaluation of the International Marketing School

STRUCTURE: **Are the concepts properly defined and integrated to form a strong nomological network?**

While the track record from earlier eras was much weaker, there has been some convergence regarding definitions over the last couple of decades, thanks to the efforts of an increasing number of scholars. However, there is a persisting taxonomical confusion between international and global marketing, affecting ontology and

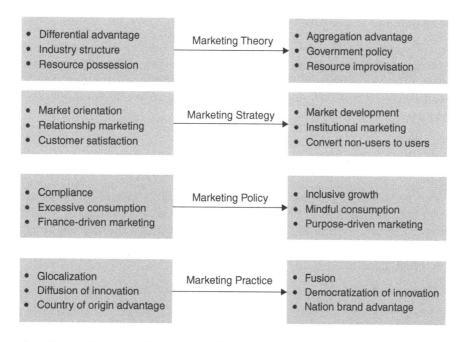

Figure 8.1 Rethinking existing perspectives and practices in international marketing.

nomological structure. Moreover, the demarcation between international marketing and international business has become less and less clear over time.

Our score on structure = 6

SPECIFICATION: **Are the relationships specified in a manner to delimit hypotheses or are they highly contingent?**

More effort is needed towards empirical generalizations; however, the theoretical basis for such work remains borrowed and patchy. Due to the inherent nature of culture, many cross-cultural studies have remained contextual. Overall, more macro-level work is necessary, which will lead to robust, generalizable results.

Our score on specification = 6

TESTABILITY: **Are the operational definitions provided to ensure testability and intersubjective consensus?**

While the field has suffered from a lack of data early on, prohibiting good proxies for variables of interest, many of the key variables of interest have been reasonably operationalized in more recent work. Unfortunately, much of the existing operationalization is still driven by (lack of) data availability. The proxies may have to be revisited in light of the digital revolution.

Our score on testability = 7

EMPIRICAL SUPPORT: **What is the degree of confirmation in terms of empirical support?**

International marketing has benefitted from the efforts of a large group of devoted scholars who have generated an impressive amount of empirical work. Some of the best examples of these empirical studies may escape the attention of mainstream marketing scholars since they are not published in the marketing journals but rather targeted at others such as the *Journal of International Business Studies*. There has been a significant increase in secondary data availability, engendering large-scale analyses across multiple markets and industries. Efforts to address measurement invariance and common method variance issues are ongoing. Nevertheless, there are still critical areas with mixed findings, such as the optima on the standardization-localization continuum subject to product category, cultural, and economic factors.

Our score on empirical support = 8

RICHNESS: **How comprehensive and generalizable is the theory?**

The complex nature of cross-cultural factors has constrained the number of universal findings and robust insights and guidance for practitioners. Cultural fusion, amplified and accelerated by social media, along with the notable increase in the availability of secondary data, may enable more generalizable results in the near future. However, it will also necessitate scholars to revisit global marketing's foundational premises (e.g., across-the-board standardization is inconceivable).

Our score on richness = 8

SIMPLICITY: **How easy is it to communicate and implement the theory?**

Beyond "think globally, act locally," international marketing scholars have not done a great job of distilling and marketing their main ideas and findings or creating landmark books. Moreover, the borders between international business and international marketing have also disappeared. As international business scholars creep more and more into marketing territory, this school also faces the danger of losing its identity. However, unlike the case of service marketing, the loss would be involuntary.

Our score on simplicity = 8

Table 8.1 Evaluation of the International Marketing School*

Criterion	Rationale	Score
Structure	Convergence in recent decades	6
Specification	More work remains to derive proper range for theory	6
Testability	Mature instruments and proven proxies finally available	7
Empirical Support	Great progress made; more work remains	8
Richness	Cultural fusion will further enrich global marketing	8
Simplicity	Need to diffuse more; seminal work from marketing is rare	8
	TOTAL	43

* Scores range from 1 (poor) to 10 (excellent).

▌Summary

International marketing has finally emerged from being a contextual practice to becoming a thought school. This is mainly due to globalization and the growth of emerging markets that strongly impacted the business world and the marketing discipline. Additionally, opportunities related to demographic diversity and the concurrent rise in the diffusion of digital technology, despite economic and institutional market disparities across nations, have added another impetus to the emergence and growth of the international marketing school of thought. Thus, in some ways, the regional marketing school of thought has been subsumed within international marketing thinking, along with the conceptual marriage of managerial marketing and macromarketing schools of thought.

International marketing manifesto has considered itself a change agent to bring essential benefits to nation-states, firms, and their employees and consumers with access to products, services, and technologies that would not be otherwise accessible to them. Accordingly, scholarly research in international marketing has focused on several domains: (a) standardization versus localization of marketing programs and marketing-mix variables; (b) country of origin effects; (c) market attractiveness; (d) market selection and entry mode; (e) global branding; (f) cross-cultural research; (g) globalization of markets; and (h) on the impact of emerging markets.

Current perspectives and practices in international marketing offer a very significant opportunity for rethinking in various terms of marketing theory (viz., differentiation advantage to aggregation advantage and resource improvisation); marketing strategy (e.g., market orientation to market development, and conversion of non-users to users); marketing policy (e.g., from compliance to inclusive growth, and mindful consumption); and of marketing practice (from globalization to fusion with local culture, a national brand advantage, and democratization of innovation). As the international marketing school of thought grows, more interface issues will be examined, such as international marketing and entrepreneurship and ethics. International marketing is anticipated to have a conceptual marriage with global marketing, and its importance for practice and scholarship will continue to grow.

Questions for Analysis and Discussion

1. Do international marketers have to choose between standardization and localization (either-or thinking), optimize on a continuum of the two, or can standardization and localization co-exist? Give examples to justify your rationale.

2. Is the country-of-origin less or more important in the digital age? For example, is product origin, brand origin, or design origin more critical in the digital age?

3. Can ownership origin still be relevant in a global market economy? Please give examples.

4. Which theories/concepts of mature markets fall short when applied to emerging markets? Conversely, which theories/concepts from emerging markets can be applied to mature markets?

5. Will international business and international marketing theories continue to converge? How can international marketing maintain its identity?

6. Can you draw parallels from the rise of US manufacturing and marketing power post-WWII to China's economic power post-Covid 19 pandemics?

CHAPTER

Services Marketing School of Thought

"There are no such things as service industries. There are only industries whose service components are greater or less than those of other industries. Everybody is in service. Often the less there seems, the more there is. The more technologically sophisticated the generic product (e.g., cars and computers), the more dependent are its sales on the quality and availability of its accompanying customer services (e.g., display rooms, delivery, repairs and maintenance, application aids, operator training, installation advice, warranty fulfillment). In this sense, General Motors is probably more service-intensive than manufacturing-intensive. Without its services its sales would shrivel."

—Theodore Levitt (1972)

LEARNING OBJECTIVES

After reading this chapter, you will be able to:

- Explain the factors that favored the emergence of the services marketing school of thought.
- Apply the service classification taxonomy to differentiate various types of services.
- Demonstrate the effect of SERVQUAL measures on consequent research in service quality.
- Describe the basic tenets of the Nordic School and its influence on services marketing thinking.

- State the fundamental premise and axioms of service-dominant (S-D) logic.
- Identify the emerging research perspectives in services marketing.
- Assimilate the metatheoretical evaluation of services marketing school of thought.

 ## 9.1 Introduction

The service sector has left no economy unimpacted. By the end of the last century, it had already claimed the lion's share of employment and value-add across all advanced economies in the world (Schettkat 2007; Witt and Gross 2020). First, businesses (e.g., professional services: accounting, IT, HR, advertising, and so on) and then households (e.g., cooking, cleaning, childcare, and so on) realized that outsourcing was a viable strategy, which provided a boon for the service economy (Malhotra and Uslay 2018; Sheth and Sisodia 1999).

Increasing quality of life around the world has also led to an increase in aggregate demand for services such as healthcare, education, and entertainment. Moreover, the proliferation of new technologies has propelled a gig economy of service workers and resulted in several mega-service platforms. As products, business environment, consumer expectations get more complex, the emphasis on services will continue to grow. Moreover, it will undergo significant transformation over the next few decades as artificial intelligence gets integrated into services.

However, while the notion that service is omnipresent in all business has been around for a long time, the message has taken even longer to sink in with business practice. For example, more than four decades after Levitt's seminal *Harvard Business Review* article cited above, Rust and Huang (2014, p.207) emphasized IT's role in the service revolution. They felt the necessity to observe that the "'products versus services' conceptualization of service is out of date and that service is everywhere, not just in the service sector. Of course, *service* is more than just 'services' (italics in original). However, rendering "service is everywhere" common wisdom will require getting to the next level of maturity in conceptual development.

For a school of thought to gain legitimacy, at least three conditions must exist: first, there is a need to establish that it is different from the general phenomenon; second, it needs to be shown that these differences are meaningful and relevant; and third, the availability of validated scale(s) or dominant research methodology enables scholars to carry on empirical inquiries to advance the field. A fourth condition, which is an outcome of the above three, is establishing a dedicated academic journal.[1] When the generic journals in a field cannot accommodate the volume of work generated, a dedicated journal usually follows. It also gains prestige as the studies in the sub-field become more rigorous.

This was precisely the pattern followed by the Services Marketing School of Thought. Unhappy with the rigid structures brought about by earlier schools such as the Commodity School and recognizing the growing importance of services in the aggregate economy, scholars began to argue that services were different from goods. They were intangible, heterogeneous, and inseparable from consumption (e.g., Bateson 1979; Berry 1980; Parasuraman, Zeithaml, and Berry 1985; Shostack 1977; Thomas 1978). The work then took the form of comparative studies to show how services were different from product markets and what must be done differently in different contexts (e.g., Donnelly 1976; Kotler and Conner 1977).

In his award-winning work, Lovelock (1983) demonstrated how services differed intrinsically by reviewing previously proposed classification schemes and diligently organizing them into five taxonomies, rich with managerial implications for new services and service extensions. Taxonomy 1 (2X2) focuses on the direct recipients of service and the nature of the service act and organized services as people vs. things and tangible vs. intangible dimensions. For example, healthcare is under the tangible-people category; freight transportation is under the tangible-things category; education in the intangible-people category; and accounting services is within the intangible-things category.

Taxonomy 2 (2X2) focuses on the relationship between the organization and its customers and the nature of service delivery, and organized services as membership vs. no formal relationship, and continuous delivery vs. discrete transaction dimensions. For example, telephone subscription is in the membership-continuous category; police protection is within the no formal relationship-continuous category; transit pass is in the membership-discrete transactions category, and restaurants are in no formal relationship-discrete category.

Taxonomy 3 (2X2) focuses on the extent to which service delivery is customized and the level of empowerment of front-line employees. For example, architectural design is in the high contact-personnel empowerment-high customization category; preventative health programs in the high contact-personnel empowerment-low customization category; retail banking in the low contact-personnel empowerment-high customization category; and spectator sports are in the low contact-personnel empowerment-low customization category.

Taxonomy 4 (2X2) focuses on the nature of demand relative to supply (demand fluctuations) and the extent to which supply is restricted (during peak demand). For example, natural gas is a low supply restriction (during peak)-wide demand fluctuations category; insurance is in the low supply restriction-narrow demand fluctuations category; passenger transportation is in the high supply restriction (during peak)-wide demand fluctuations category, and "services similar to [insurance, legal services, banking, and laundry and dry cleaning] but which have insufficient capacity for their base level of business" would be considered as high supply restriction (during peak)-narrow demand fluctuations category (Lovelock 1983, p. 17).

Finally, Taxonomy 5 (3X2) focuses on the method of service delivery (availability of service outlets) and the nature of interactions between the customer and the organization. For example, the barbershop is where the customer goes to service to a single site category; bus services are in the customer goes to service-multiple sets of sites category; lawn care is in the service comes to the customer-single site category; AAA emergency

---

1. A final outcome for sustaining the school is arguably through the formation of a growing and thriving special interest group among academics.

repairs are within the category of the customer comes to multiple sites; credits cards fall under the arm's length transactions-single site category; and broadcast network is under the arm's length transactions-multiple set of sites category. Lovelock (1985, 1988) also authored highly influential textbooks, which led to a proliferation of services marketing courses.

 ## 9.2 SERVQUAL

Much like the market orientation stream of research owes its tremendous spurt of growth in the nineties to the development and availability of rigorously validated measurement instruments, the explosion of research on the Services Marketing School of Thought can be traced to one fundamental scale: SERVQUAL.[2] Parasuraman, Zeithaml, and Berry (1985, p.47) had identified ten potentially overlapping dimensions of service quality as follows: tangibles, reliability, responsiveness, communication, credibility, security, competence, courtesy, understanding/knowing the customer, and access. Parasuraman, Zeithaml, and Berry (1988) followed up on their own work and utilized these ten dimensions to develop the 22-item SERVQUAL scale with the following five distinct dimensions: Tangibles, Reliability, Responsiveness, Assurance, and Empathy (observing that Assurance and Empathy encompassed the remainder of the original ten dimensions). They empirically examined the SERQVUAL scale qualities with data from four sectors (banking, credit cards, repair and maintenance, and long-distance telecommunications). They concluded: "[W]e hope the availability of this instrument will stimulate much-needed empirical research focusing on service quality and its antecedents and consequences" (Parasuraman, Zeithaml and Berry 1988, p.36). The authors' wish has certainly come true as their *Journal of Retailing* article can be credited for stimulating research in services and remains one of the highest cited scholarly articles of all time. Notably, the originators of SERVQUAL did not merely leave it to other scholars to put the scale to use and remained active contributors to the research stream.

Zeithaml, Berry, and Parasuraman (1988) suggested that the SERVQUAL scale could be used to examine the gaps in service quality they identified. Gap 1 referred to the difference between consumer expectations and management perceptions of these expectations. This gap was argued to be the result of firms' (lack of) marketing research orientation (−), upward communications (−), and numerous levels of management (+). Gap 2 referred to the difference between managerial perception and service quality specifications. This gap resulted from (lack of) management commitment to service quality (−), goal-setting (−), task standardization (−), and perception of feasibility (−). Gap 3 referred to the difference between the service quality specification and actual service delivery. This gap resulted from (lack of) teamwork (−), employee-job fit (−), technology-job fit (−), perceived control (−), supervisory control systems (−), role conflict (+), and role ambiguity of front-line employees (+). Gap 4 referred to the difference between service delivery and external communications. This gap resulted from horizontal communication (−) and propensity to overpromise (+).[3] Finally, Gap 5 can be viewed as the overall gap between customer expectations and perceptions, combining Gaps 1–4.

Parasuraman, Berry, and Zeithaml (1991) reassessed and refined the SERVQUAL scale further and concluded that their replication efforts and findings from extant studies collectively reinforced the reliability, face validity, and predictive/concurrent validity of the SERVQUAL scale, while results pertaining convergent and discriminant validity were mixed or inconsistent. They (1991) reiterated their confidence in the modified scale's usefulness for service quality research (also see Parasuraman, Zeithaml, and Berry 1994). Zeithaml, Berry, and Parasuraman (1993) focused on service quality antecedents and offered propositions regarding desired, adequate, and predicted expectations.

The cumulative progress was celebrated by Berry and Parasuraman (1993) and Fisk, Brown, and Bitner (1993), who reviewed the history of service marketing as an academic field of inquiry. Berry and Parasuraman (1993) attributed the explosion of services marketing research to demand factors (i.e., rapid growth in the service sector, deregulation of service industries), institutional production factors (i.e., Marketing Science

---

2. It is likely that the success of the SERVQUAL scale (Parasuraman, Zeithaml, and Berry 1988) even influenced the authors of the MKTOR (Narver and Slater 1990) and MARKOR (Kohli, Jaworski and Kumar 1993) scales as it predated the publications of these scales and was available in the form of an MSI report since 1986 (Parasuraman, Zeithaml, and Berry 1986).

3. + represents gap-increasing factors and − represents gap-reducing factors.

Institute,[4] American Marketing Association, and the Center for Services Marketing at Arizona State University [established in 1985]), and individual production factors (i.e., early dissertation based work [e.g., George and Barksdale 1974], the Nordic School [see subsequent section], the French connection, an American Network, Harvard Roots, and interdisciplinary influences), and acceleration factors (i.e., developments/events, publications). Their work chronicles the history of the services marketing literature and provides a thorough account of its early years in the nineties.

SERVQUAL was not without criticism (Smith 1995; Teas 1994). For example, Cronin and Taylor (1992) argued that the expectations-performance gap was not substantiated by conceptual and empirical evidence. They (1992, p. 56) noted service quality and customer satisfaction are distinctly different and suggested that perceived service quality is best conceived of as "a form of attitude, a long-run overall evaluation, whereas satisfaction is a transaction-specific measure," and offered an alternative scale, SERVPERF (also see Cronin and Taylor 1994).[5] Significant variations in the predictive validity of alternative measures have been observed, and more recently, it has been suggested that a weighted SERVPERF scale may provide the most diagnostic value (Andronikidis and Bellou 2010).

As aforementioned, SERVQUAL was nevertheless adopted widely, and due to an influx of interest, the services marketing discipline grew fast. The AMA held the first national conference focusing on services in Orlando in 1981. The *Journal of Services Marketing* was launched in 1987, and the *Journal of Service Research* was founded in 1998 with Roland Rust as founding editor and quickly became a high-impact outlet. Two other viable outlets, the *Journal of Service Management* (previously *International Journal of Services Management*) and the *Journal of Service Theory and Practice* (previously *Managing Service Quality*) rebranded themselves to signal their broad reception of service research. Moreover, SERVSIG (founded by Ray Fisk in 1993) has been one of the most active academic special interest groups of the AMA with its highly successful Frontiers in Service, QUIS, and SERVSIG conferences.

9.3 The Nordic School of Services

While the catalysts for the emergence of the Services School of Thought are multifaceted (Berry and Parasuraman 1993), the Nordic School's contributions have been especially noteworthy and deserve recognition. Christian Grönroos (e.g., 1978, 1982, 1984) and Evert Gummesson (e.g., 1978, 1979, 1981) are widely recognized as the chief proponents of the Nordic School; however, they have suggested that Richard Normann (e.g., 1984) and Bo Edvardsson (e.g., 1997) should also be recognized for their early contributions (Gummesson and Grönroos 2012). Starting in the late seventies, these scholars collectively recognized several tenets of what would come to be known as the service-dominant logic (Vargo and Lusch 2004) and explored the interdependency of service and relationship marketing, which culminated in the establishment of the Service Research Center (CTF) at Karlstadt University (Sweden) in 1986, and the Centre for Relationship Marketing and Service Management at Hanken School of Economics (Finland) in 1994. Gummesson (1995, pp. 250–251) observed: "Customers do not buy goods or services: they buy offerings which render services which create value…activities render services, things render services. This shift in focus to services is from the means and the producer perspective to the utilization and the customer perspective." Gummesson and Grönroos (2012, pp. 490–491) summarized the Nordic School contributions to service research as follows:

1. An evolving logic from goods towards a comprehensive view of services (Vargo and Lusch 2004) was advanced by the Nordic School decades earlier.
2. The Nordic school has focused on innovating thinking using case studies, action research, and interpretative methods over quantitative methods and offered conceptual guidance (opting for managerial relevance over extensive rigor).

---

4. The Marketing Science Institute also identified service quality a top research priority as early as 1982.

5. Another wildly popular gap measure of customer experience (including services), "the one number you need to grow," Net Promoter Score (which is simply calculated by subtracting detractors (0–6) from promoters (9–10) on a ten-point scale) (Reichheld 2003) has been discredited (Keiningham et al. 2007) yet still widely used in practice.

3. Maintained a focus on theoretical development to advance the discipline and viewed it as more than a precursor to empirical testing.

4. Offering normative and pragmatic guidance to practitioners.

5. Pointing out the limitations of narrowly conceived distinctions between goods and services such as intangibility.

6. "Services and service should not be defined as a goods anomaly but as something in its own right, representing a perspective and certain aspects on marketing. Service and goods should always be addressed as interdependent. In fact, goods have never been properly defined, and manufactured goods are also the outcome of processes, although the consumer is rarely present."

7. Observing the societal value of the service economy as a synthesis of goods and services.

8. The insistence that traditional marketing management thinking and marketing mix approaches need to be adapted to a relational perspective before applying it to service contexts.

9. Based on a stakeholder-view (e.g., marketing professionals, executives, customers, suppliers, intermediaries, and the media), service management and market-oriented management are more appropriate mindsets than service marketing and marketing management.

10. Services are combined into processes, and service production, delivery, and consumption are partly simultaneous processes where customers co-create value.

11. Customers' roles in services align with network thinking, and relationships, networks, and interaction are three core constructs.

12. C2C interactions have become central to marketing, where consumers play an increasingly more prominent role than marketers, thanks to social media and mobile, and the digital revolution.

In all, they observed that whereas the mainstream marketers asked the question as to "how do services fit in?" to marketing, the Nordic school had a more holistic point of departure and asked, "what should marketing concepts and models look like to fit in" to services in the marketing context (Gummesson and Grönroos 2012, p. 491). While the Nordic school has focused more on theoretical development, it has undoubtedly influenced empirical work. For example, Keillor, Hult, and Kandemir (2004) explicitly applied the Nordic School thinking to service encounters and reported significant differences among the service encounter's technical and functional aspects across eight countries, including emerging and developed markets.

9.4 Service-Dominant (S-D) Logic of Marketing

In their seminal article, Vargo and Lusch (2004) argued for a new "service-dominant" (S-D) logic. Drawing from extant research in services, relationship, managerial, and business-to-business marketing, they powerfully observed that an increasingly prevalent shift of scholarly and managerial focus away from products towards the process of service provision and value co-creation was taking place (Vargo and Lusch 2016). They (2004, p. 2) also distinguished between operand (finite and tangible) and operant (intangible) resources "which are employed to act on operand resources (and other operant recourses)" and espoused for the development of marketing capabilities enabled by services. As straightforward as the above arguments may sound today, the article took five years and three different editors to see it through publication. Such was the entrenchment of the goods-dominant logic in marketing academia. Vargo and Lusch (2004) put forth eight Foundational Premises (FPs):

1. FP1: The application of specialized skills and knowledge is the fundamental unit of exchange.
2. FP2: Indirect exchange masks the fundamental unit of exchange.
3. FP3: Goods are distribution mechanisms for *service provision.*
4. FP4: Knowledge is the fundamental source of competitive advantage.
5. FP5: All economies are *services economies.*
6. FP6: The customer is always a co-producer.

7. FP7: The enterprise can only make value propositions.
8. FP8: A *service-centered view* is customer-oriented and relational (italics added for emphasis).

Vargo and Lusch (2008) further refined the FPs proposed earlier (Vargo and Lusch 2004). In the process, they revised FP1 as "Service is the fundamental basis of exchange" while adding two more foundational premises (see S-D Logic Axioms 3 and 4 below). Finally, Vargo and Lusch (2016, p. 8) further refined the FPs, added another FP (see S-D Logic Axiom 5 below), and offered five axioms from which all previous FPs may be derived. These five axioms were:

1. S-D Logic Axiom 1: Service is the fundamental basis of exchange.
2. S-D Logic Axiom 2: Value is co-created by multiple actors, always including the beneficiary.
3. S-D Logic Axiom 3: All social and economic actors are resource integrators.
4. S-D Logic Axiom 4: Value is always uniquely and phenomenologically determined by the beneficiary.
5. S-D Logic Axiom 5: Value co-creation is coordinated through actor-generated institutions and institutional arrangements (Vargo and Lusch 2017, p. 47).

Marketing is a context-based discipline (Sheth and Sisodia 1999). Even as service is viewed as the fundamental basis of exchange as per axiom 1 of the S-D Logic, the value derived from an exchange is only one and often not the most important type of value. For example, consumers as users and payers may value performance, customization, and affordability more than value-in-exchange (Mittal and Sheth 2001; Sheth 2002; Sheth 2020). In that vein, the shift of focus away from value in exchange towards value-in-use and "value-in-context" (Chandler and Vargo 2011; Eggert et al. 2018; Payne and Frow 2017; Vargo, Maglio, and Akaka 2008) and extending its application to social and cultural contexts (Akaka, Schau, and Vargo 2013; Edvardsson, Tronvoll, and Gruber 2011) have been welcome developments. Similarly, Rust and Huang (2014, p. 207) observed that service does not necessarily need to be offered by front-line employees (e.g., automated services). Instead, they argued that purchase utility is derived from the consumption value rendered "from the service provided by the good."

Sheth and Uslay (2007, p. 305) observed that value co-creation could be construed as the foundation for a general theory of marketing:

> What if the foundation of marketing is defined as the co-creation of value rather than as value creation or value exchange?... Extending the value creation paradigm further, the need for and desire of actors to co-create value preempts and supersedes the need for exchange... Arguably, marketing is now amidst a paradigm shift from exchange (value in exchange) toward value co-creation (value for all stakeholders)... Just as the goods-dominant logic masks the fundamental process of service capabilities, in which goods are simply distribution mechanisms for service capabilities (Gutman 1982; Lusch and Vargo 2006; Vargo and Lusch 2004), exchange masks the value creation capabilities, and it is a distribution mechanism for value... Thus, all goods are (parts of) service solutions, and all exchange is part of a complex value co-creation process. As soon as we subscribe to the idea that value is determined/defined by the customer/end user, we need to submit that all value is created jointly.

Prahalad and Ramaswamy (2004) observed that value co-created in dialog, access, and transparency between customers and other agents is vital for competitive success. Sheth and Uslay (2007) noted that value co-creation extends to the entire value chain spectrum from co-conception to co-design, co-production, co-outsourcing, co-promotion, co-pricing, and co-distribution, co-consumption, co-maintenance, and co-disposal. The general importance of ascertaining and communicating the customer value proposition has been underlined in more recent work (Payne, Frow, and Eggert 2017).

While Grönroos and Voima (2013) distinguished between value creation in producer, customer, and joint spheres, Vargo and Lusch (2016, 2017) argued that the extent of value co-creation had been understated in their earlier work. They argued that value is co-created by many actors beyond producers and customers, proposed a growing emphasis on the service ecosystem, and acknowledged that value co-creation is the purpose of exchange and foundational to marketing.[6] While much work remains to be done, more scholarly efforts have recently been devoted to service ecosystems (e.g., Frow et al. 2014, 2019).

9.5 Beyond SERVQUAL and S-D Logic

We do not wish to convey the false impression that the vast literature on services marketing can be simply clustered around SERVQUAL and S-D Logic. On the contrary, many outstanding efforts have examined service topics and interfaces with marketing strategy, international marketing, relationship marketing, digital marketing, and consumer behavior contexts. For example, it has been shown that the relationships between service delivery quality, customer satisfaction, and customer loyalty are not linear, and returns to delighting customers may also not be universal (Oliver 1999; Olivia, Oliver, and MacMillan 1992; Rust and Oliver 2000).

9.5.1 Service-Profit Chain (SPC) Model

Heskett and colleagues (1994) put forth the service-profit chain model (SPC), which found broad practitioner support due to its simplicity. The unidirectional model suggested that internal service quality → employee satisfaction → employee retention and productivity → external service quality → customer satisfaction → customer loyalty → revenue and profitability (Heskett, Sasser, and Schlesinger 1997). Consequently, numerous scholars focused on augmented or different model sections in their work (e.g., Homburg, Wiseke, and Hoyer 2009; Hong et al. 2013).

Holgreve and colleagues (2017) recently brought these disparate studies together and conducted a meta-analysis of the SPC model. They reported that the original service-profit chain model is supported; however, they suggested considering additional effects and moderating factors to advance service theory and practice. For example, they observed that the SPC underestimates the impact of internal service quality; they found that in addition to its impact on employee satisfaction, internal service quality was also directly linked to employee productivity, external service quality, and profitability. Other findings included (a) direct effects of employee satisfaction on customer satisfaction and that of employee productivity on customer loyalty, (b) direct positive effect of external service quality on customer satisfaction and customer loyalty, but a negative effect on profitability; and (c) the direct positive impact of employee retention on revenue.

9.5.2 Customer Satisfaction and Services

Lariviere and colleagues (2014) examined the relationship of different types of commitment (affective, calculative, and normative) on customer loyalty in financial services; Kumar and colleagues (2013) offered a conceptual framework for data-driven services marketing, and Keiningham and colleagues (2014) examined the impact of the service failures of different severity on customer satisfaction and market share. Compensation for a service failure appears to be effective only if the service provider is responsible for the failure and frequently occurs (Grewal, Roggeveen, and Tsiros 2008).

Since 1994, the American Consumer Satisfaction Index (ACSI) has provided a substantive data source to test these and related relationships in services and other contexts (Fornell et al. 1996, 2006; Fornell, Morgeson and Hult 2016). A large sample ACSI-based study recently reported that recovery leads to loyalty more strongly in faster-growing economies, for luxurious offerings, for highly satisfied customers, and for customers with high customization expectations, and when the competition is more intense (Morgeson et al. 2020). The opposite was reported when the expectation of reliability was higher (as for manufactured goods) and for male customers.

Fang, Palmatier, and Steenkamp (2008) reported that transitioning from a product to a service-centric business (with a critical mass of 20–30% of revenue) enhances shareholder value. Dotzel, Shankar, and Berry (2013) differentiated between internet-based and people-based service innovations and concluded that non-human-dominated sectors should not use customer satisfaction to gauge the success of their innovations and be cautious in introducing people-based innovations. In contrast, it is more appropriate for high-margin players in small markets to focus on internet-based innovations.

---

6. A service ecosystem is a "relatively self-contained, self-adjusting system of resource-integrating actors connected by shared institutional arrangements and mutual value creation through service exchange" (Vargo and Lusch 2016, p. 161).

Aksoy and colleagues (2015) observed that relative measures might be more appropriate while most service research measurements have relied on absolute metrics. More recently, Berry and colleagues (2020) examined physical, emotional, financial, and information safety in the pandemic age and discussed the remarkable transformations that service organizations have adapted.

9.5.3 Eras and Evolving Focus of Services Research

Gummesson and Grönroos (2012, p. 482) observed that three eras defined by different paradigms could characterize services marketing: "the goods paradigm (pre-1970s); the services vs. goods paradigm with focus on differences (the 1970s–2000s); and the service paradigm based on goods/services integration and interdependency (2000s–)." It is noteworthy that the relationship between service technology use and average segment size appears to be related in an inverse-U-shaped manner (Rust and Huang 2014). With small segments, service delivery is typically one-to-one with little technology use. Technology enables mass customization and serves larger segments of customers. Yet, the mass-customization may lose its efficacy as segments grow further. However, as the technology used gets further sophisticated (such as using AI), customized solutions become feasible again and extend and skew the curve in favor of technology use (e.g., personalized recommendations). The fastest-growing businesses of our times have been service firms, i.e., Uber, Netflix, Airbnb, and even Tesla offer a service delivery platform. While there have been nascent efforts to bring service research to evolve to the reality of our times (for example, E-S-QUAL was proposed as a new scale to measure electronic service quality [Parasuraman, Zeithaml, and Malhotra 2005]), we need systematic efforts to revisit marketing theory and see how they hold up in digital environments (Yadav and Pavlou 2014). These efforts must begin with services since social media and all digital offerings are predominantly services.

Fortunately, service researchers have been getting periodical guidance regarding the research priorities derived from expert input (Ostrom et al., 2010; Ostrom et al., 2015). For example, Furrer and colleagues (2020) recently reviewed 3,177 service research articles published since 1993, identified the prevalent themes, and (using the BCG share-growth matrix) categorized them into stars, questions marks, cash cows, and pets, based on the growth rate and the number of articles for each theme. Their findings indicated that while the share of service quality research (cash cow) is declining, the growth of research on service-dominant logic (star) was off the charts. Other "star" service themes included emotions, technology/e-service, and relationship marketing. In fact, of the top 41 most influential service research articles (by citations per year) in their sample, eleven were focused on the theme of relationship marketing (also see the chapter on RM regarding overlap and confluence among service marketing and RM), six were focused on (e-) service quality, five were on the theme of S-D logic, four on co-creation, and three on customer satisfaction.

9.6 Concluding Remarks

As the Nordic School has correctly signaled early on, services and relationship marketing schools are closely aligned. Their domain identity will further converge as the S-D logic prevails. Despite the rich body of work on S-D logic, its one weakness has been a relative lack of empirical studies supporting it. The S-D logic claims to offer a foundation for a general theory of marketing (Lusch and Vargo 2006). Vargo and Lusch (2017) called for developing mid-range theory, frameworks, and models more amenable to empirical testing. There is a need to create and use scales for S-D logic to bring the services school to a new level of understanding.

Moreover, we must revisit our faith in "the religion of quality" as data (and increasingly big data) shows that investments do not always pay off. An optimal level of service quality is context-dependent (Rust, Zahorik, and Keningham 1995; Rust and Huang 2012). Nevertheless, such investments for quality must be made, and their trade-offs carefully examined. Therefore, the financial performance implications of varying magnitude and appropriate scope of investments are likely to remain viable avenues for future service research. After all, every offering, sector, and market involves some level of service, and all value is co-created.

A final closing point to ponder is whether services marketing will disengage from marketing like the functional school of thought has done recently by reinventing itself in the form of supply chain management and as it happened earlier with the buyer/consumer behavior school of thought, and subsequently by the research stream on consumer culture theory. The domain of services marketing has been expanding to include its interfaces (e.g., Service-H/R interface: customer contact employees), and consequently, its boundaries with management and operations have been quickly blurring. As noted previously, this broader conception of service has also been historically embraced by the Nordic School of Thought. As further evidence, of the eight specialty service research journals featured on the AMA SERVSIG website, only one includes "marketing" in its title. Finally, this trend is further reflected in AMA's Service Marketing SIG was renamed Service SIG in 2017. In its quest for interdisciplinarity, it is conceivable that service research will decouple from the S-D logic of marketing but may lose its marketing identity in the process.

9.7 Evaluation of the Services Marketing School

STRUCTURE: Are the concepts properly defined and integrated to form a strong nomological network?

The service marketing school is doing better than most previous schools in terms of definitions. Both SERVQUAL and S-D logic researchers have exerted considerable effort to define and refine the key concepts and factors. Nevertheless, there is an ongoing discussion of whether value co-creation should be restricted to interactions between consumers and producers or defined more broadly. For example, is simultaneity a requirement of value co-creation or not? These conversations will also have implications for testability. Thus, despite collective efforts to move beyond the distinguishing service IHIP characteristics, they are still embedded in services marketing practice (much like the 4Ps of marketing).

Our score on structure = 7

SPECIFICATION: Are the relationships specified in a manner to delimit hypotheses, or are they highly contingent?

While there is certainly room for more research to delineate moderating impacts and contextual differences exist, the fundamental relationships that have been advanced have been surprisingly resilient to contingency factors. Overall, most scholarly research in the services domain provides an impressive amount of specificity even though we have yet to agree upon general model specifications.

Our score on specification = 8

TESTABILITY: Are the operational definitions provided to ensure testability and intersubjective consensus?

One of the relative weaknesses of the S-D logic has been scant empirical research; meanwhile, SERVQUAL has been fully operationalized and subject to extensive testing and refinement, which substantially increases our average evaluation. Development of mid-range theories that focus on how different actors integrate resources in their service ecosystems would improve testability. As it matures, S-D logic will need testable propositions for each of its core tenets.

Our score on testability = 7

EMPIRICAL SUPPORT: What is the degree of confirmation in terms of empirical support?

As suggested by our explanation on testability, on the one hand, the fundamental axioms of S-D logic still lack empirical support, which implies a significant future research opportunity. On the other hand, SERVQUAL has been put to extensive use and garnered an impressive amount of empirical support. Hundreds of studies have also been published on different aspects of the service value chain.

Our score on empirical support = 7

RICHNESS: How comprehensive and generalizable is the theory?

It has been suggested that S-D logic can serve as the foundation of a general theory of marketing. Interestingly, Vargo and Lusch (2011) carried the S-D logic closer towards the systems school of thought and argued for actor-based service ecosystems, while Vargo and Lusch (2016) argued for its institutional aspects[7]. While SERVQUAL started its journey with "service" firms and retailers, it has found a broader purpose across sectors. Consequently, service marketing scholars have already delved into interdisciplinary research, which in some cases extends beyond the domain of marketing.

Our score on richness = 9

SIMPLICITY: **How easy is it to communicate and implement the theory?**

Despite their richness, from the S-D logic's axioms to the five factors of SERVQUAL and the unidirectional specification of the service-profit chain, the service marketing school's fundamental tenets are deceptively simple yet powerful. Citation counts can quickly demonstrate this ease of interpretation and implementation in scholarly research. For example, at the time of this writing, Parasuraman, Zeithaml, and Berry (1988) had close to 39,000 citations, Vargo and Lusch (2004) about 18,000, and Heskett et al. (1994) had received more than 6300 Google Scholar citations. In addition, there is a dedicated website for S-D logic (http://www.sdlogic.net/), which includes references to critical articles, presentations, teaching materials, and multimedia designed to disseminate S-D logic to scholars, practitioners and students.

Our score on simplicity = 9

Evaluation of the Service Marketing School*

Criterion	Rationale	Score
Structure	Consensus is finally emerging	7
Specification	Fundamental premises and axioms have been derived	8
Testability	S-D logic needs mid-range theories to improve testability	7
Empirical Support	The advancements have been lopsided	7
Richness	Some potential to serve as foundation for general theory	9
Simplicity	Simple but powerful	9
	TOTAL	47

* Scores range from 1 (poor) to 10 (excellent).

Summary

Services marketing thinking grew out of the commodities school due to the growth of the services sector and service-based economy. Scholars of services marketing school initially focused on the unique aspects of services marketing, compared to commodities and goods. They highlighted that services comprised unique characteristics of intangible, heterogeneous, inseparable from consumption, and perishable (IHIP). Achieving and measuring service quality and its consequences on customer satisfaction became a very significant domain of inquiry in marketing. Managing service quality as a continuous organizational process involving technology and human interactions became a key concern for this marketing school. It led to an explosion of research within the services marketing domain, particularly with the introduction of SERVQUAL – a rigorously developed and validated scale to measure service quality. SERVQUAL provided vital dimensions of service quality measurement and the linkage to customer expectations and satisfaction.

---

7. Vargo (2022, via email) noted that covering SDL under the umbrella of services marketing school may be misleading as S-D logic is more encompassing. Among other things, SERVQUAL is specific to services (intangible unites of output), whereas S-D logic has to do with value co-creation through the process of service exchange. It transcends many of the existing "schools," most notably systems and relationship marketing, but also the functional, institutional, managerial, macromarketing, and social exchange schools of thought.

Simultaneously, several scholars began to focus on comparative analysis between products and services to demonstrate the innate and contextual differences. These scholars collectively recognized several tenets of what would become known as the service-dominant (S-D) logic. The S-D logic argued that instead of a product perspective, all businesses should be viewed as predominantly providing services for which relationships and value creation processes become critical. They suggested a shift in focus to organizational competency instead of product outcomes for delivering customer value. It meant establishing institutions (norms and procedures) for value co-creation with customers and other marketing actors. The co-creation of value between institutions (or between an individual and an institution) is key to understanding market dynamics.

Like the marketing strategy school of thought, the services marketing school emphasized developing knowledge and specialized skills fundamental to achieving service success and competitive advantage. In addition, they argued that the customer is often a co-producer and co-creator of services working in collaboration with the marketing enterprise. In other words, the service-dominant view is primarily customer-centric and relational. From that perspective, the services and relationship marketing schools are closely aligned in their focus and approach.

The rise of services marketing led to the decline of the institutional marketing approach as services business fuelled the force of disintermediation and made direct-to-consumer marketing more ubiquitous. It also subsumed the tenets of the organizational dynamics school (for developing organizational capabilities for service delivery) and the systems school thinking (service organizations often operate in layers of ecosystems). Further, the services marketing school also incorporated ideas from the social exchange theories (engagements and interactions are common) and the managerial marketing school of thought (service positioning and competitive differentiation).

Thus, in many ways, the services marketing school of thought is an integrated view of several schools of marketing thought developed since the inception of the marketing discipline. It also represents the evolutionary effect of all the four megatrends of contextual forces discussed in the prologue of this book, particularly demographic shifts and the growth of digital media. However, the service-dominant (S-D) logic has remained a paradigm despite its appeal. Although several conceptual papers, and some empirical studies, have appeared on the service-dominant logic and its fundamental premise, it has yet to offer a full-blown general theory of marketing.

Questions for Analysis and Discussion

1. Is service *truly* everywhere? Can you identify a sector where the marketing of services is not important?

2. Which one of Lovelock's five services taxonomies has the most explanatory power? Which has the least?

3. In what ways would you update/adapt/extend Lovelock's taxonomies to incorporate the digital economy? How about the sharing economy?

4. In what ways would you update/adapt/extend the SERVQUAL framework to incorporate the digital economy? How about the sharing economy?

5. S-D Logic Axiom 1 stipulates that Service is the fundamental basis of exchange. Can exchange or value co-creation serve as the fundamental basis of marketing? Explain the pros and cons of your choice.

6. What makes services marketing scholarship distinguishable from service research? How would taking a Nordic School perspective influence your answer? Is it necessary or important to draw such boundaries? Why or why not?

10

Relationship Marketing School of Thought

Increasingly, a key goal of marketing is to develop deep, enduring relationships with all people or organizations that could directly or indirectly affect the success of the firm's marketing activities. Relationship marketing has the aim of building mutually satisfying long-term relationships with key parties—customers, suppliers, distributors and other marketing partners—in order to earn and retain their business.

—Philip Kotler (2006)

Relationship management is a special field all its own. It is as important in preserving and enhancing the intangible asset commonly known as "goodwill" as is the management of hard assets.

—Theodore Levitt (1983)

You're not just trying to create customers; you're trying to create fans. You do that by building a meaningful relationship.

—Philip Kotler (2018)

LEARNING OBJECTIVES

After reading this chapter, you will be able to:

- Identify the reasons for the rise of the relationship marketing school of thought.
- Explain the foundations of relationship marketing theory.
- Enumerate the reasons for the elevation and subsequent relegation of relationship marketing school of thought within the marketing discipline.

- Assess the potential of relationship marketing as the basis for developing a general theory of marketing.
- Recapitulate how relationship marketing school of thought can be revitalized.
- Critically evaluate the contribution of relationship marketing school on metatheoretical criteria.

10.1   Introduction

Over the past three decades, relationship marketing (RM) has witnessed spectacular growth as a marketing practice and a discipline (Hunt et al., 2006; Sheth 2017). It entered the business lexicon in the 1980s (Berry 1983) and quickly rose to the level of becoming a paradigm espousing the value of building, nurturing, and enhancing long-term relationships with customers and business associates. It was a paradigm shift away from the transactional marketing approach prevalent in the previous decades of economic liberalism and free-market capitalism, characterized by the competitive and sometimes adversarial stance between buyers and sellers (Brodie et al. 1997; Harker and Egan 2006; Parvatiyar and Sheth 1997). Instead, proponents of RM advocated close-cooperative and collaborative relationships among marketing actors to create and deliver personalized solutions and mutual value to all parties concerned. In addition, they emphasized a greater focus on customer retention, loyalty, and partnering programs to achieve efficiency and effectiveness in pursuing organizational goals and creating competitive advantage (Gruen 1997; Hunt 2010).

The principles of RM began to resonate with the broader marketing community in the 1990s and beyond, and its popularity among many levels of practitioners, consultants, and academics grew exponentially. RM practice quickly expanded into many business sectors, such as in banking and financial services, health care, hospitality, education, consumer goods, B2B, retailing, technology, software, tourism and travel, and even investor relations, talent management, and non-profit organizations (Arnett et al. 2003; Buttle 1996; Payne 2000). For example, a search of the term "relationship marketing" on Google search engine resulted in more than 1.17 Billion hits. On Google Scholar that primarily provides search results for academic articles, the total number of results with relationship marketing as "keywords" was more than 3.72 million results, including books and journal articles.

Today RM thinking is at the bedrock of new emergent approaches and models of customer-centricity (Shah et al. 2006; Palmatier et al. 2019), customer engagement (Harmeling et al. 2017; Verhoef et al. 2010), customer experience (Homburg et al. 2017; Verhoef et al. 2009), customer relationship management (Parvatiyar and Sheth 2001; Payne and Frow 2005), customer valuation (Kumar 2018; Kumar and Shah 2009), and value co-creation processes (Vargo and Lusch 2004, 2008; Lusch and Webster 2011; Malhotra, Uslay, and Bayraktar 2016). However, as Sheth (2017) points out, RM is experiencing a midlife crisis, similar to many other marketing schools of thought, despite its spectacular rise.

So, despite its short history, what led to RM's spectacular rise as a marketing practice and a discipline and its current midlife crisis? In the following paragraphs, we first examine the forces that led to RM's rise both as a marketing practice and a discipline. We then look at the factors that have somewhat relegated RM within the academic marketing discipline and suggest ways to revitalize and overcome RM's midlife crisis.

10.2 Why Did Relationship Marketing Rise?

10.2.1 Economic and Technological Shifts

Although the antecedents of the RM approach can be traced to the pre-industrial era wherein producers and consumers directly interacted with each other and artisans often made personalized items for the nobility (Sheth and Parvatiyar 1995a), the recent rise of relationship marketing can be attributed to a confluence of factors that became prominent in the early 1980s due to economic and technological shifts. On the one hand, the rise of the service economy served as a vital catalyst (Berry 1995; Grönroos 2000; Gummesson 2002) and, on the other hand, the application of semiconductor-based digital and computing technologies had substantial consequential effects on both production and marketing processes. It led to the rapid adoption of computers and information technology, flexible manufacturing, material resource planning (MRP), just-in-time delivery (JIT), total quality management (TQM), global alliances, industry convergence, and rapid introduction of new products. In turn, these processes necessitated partnering and collaborative relationships (Hunt et al. 2006; Palmatier 2008; Sheth et al. 2015; Wilson 1995).

Business practice in the 1980s and 1990s began to see "demassification" and "disintermediation" that once again brought producers and consumers together, facilitating "relational bonds" due to emotions and passions associated with production and consumption (Sheth and Parvatiyar 1995a). Relational emotion is more salient in the service-dominant world as production and consumption functions are not easily separable. Hence, knowing the preferences of repeat and most valuable customers becomes imperative to maintain their loyalty and business continuity. Furthermore, long-term relationship orientation became critical as more industries moved from just selling products to charging for services, leasing, or licensing their technology and know-how for monthly or annual utility-type fees. The role of marketing within the corporation thus began to change (Morgan 2000; Webster 1992).

The introduction of marketing automation systems and direct/database marketing approaches made addressable media for marketing communications more affordable for targeting niche markets. It led to one-to-one marketing and personalization (Peppers and Rogers 1993). With modular and flexible manufacturing, it was possible to do "mass customization" and present personalized offerings to customers (Pine 1999). Priorities shifted towards individualized marketing, customer retention, lifecycle management, and customer lifetime value instead of focusing on customer acquisition hitherto prevalent during the era of transactional marketing. The ethos of accountable marketing led to programs and processes of up-selling, cross-selling, membership marketing, affinity marketing, key account management, and precision targeting to ensure greater marketing productivity (Bhattacharya and Bolton 2000; Bowman and Narayandas 2001; Cannon and Narayandas 2000; Gruen 2000; Swaminathan and Reddy 2000).

Having solid relationships makes it easier for companies to offer product upgrades and newer generation products and services to their existing customer base, particularly in the digital technology world. Product lifecycles are considerably short, and products get obsolete even before they reach the customer premises. Therefore, instead of focusing on product marketing, it became more compelling to undertake relationship marketing wherein relationships could be leveraged to offer newer versions of products and services to help the customer stay up-to-date and become more productive. This phenomenon became pronounced in television, mobile phones, computers, software, personal gadgets, appliances, and even automobiles and home furniture (Sisodia and Wolfe 2000).

10.2.2 Partnerships for Efficiency and Effectiveness

In B-to-B marketing and industrial procurement, another force operated. Many companies began shifting towards strategic supplier partnering instead of the obsession for new vendor development to squeeze lower prices per transaction from them (Anderson and Narus 1990; Dwyer, Schurr, and Oh 1987). The driving force behind supplier partnering was the corporate mandate to achieve system-wide efficiencies and effectiveness by reducing uncertainties, opportunistic behavior, and overall transaction costs (Mentzer 2000; Williamson 1979). Long-term vendor agreements facilitated negotiations for lowering costs in subsequent years due to experience cost benefits. It became clear that TQM was possible only if vendors and dealers followed the same quality processes as in the focal manufacturing firm. In other words, partnering was essential for TQM and MRP practice implementation (Wilson 1995). Additionally, vendor partnering permitted the leverage of resources, experiences, and partners' competencies to develop new products/services and processes or enter new markets to gain effectiveness and competitive advantage (Hunt and Arnett 2003; Morgan and Hunt 1999).

Beyond the hierarchical efficiencies and effectiveness, relational partnering at the network level, such as those by the Japanese keiretsu, provided additional impetus to the rise of relationship marketing. According to Hunt et al. (2006, p. 75):

> Firm after firm is turning from discrete, short-term, arms-length, exchanges with a large number of suppliers toward long-term, relational exchanges with a smaller number of partners… the rise of strategic networks to compete with other networks has boosted the importance of relationship marketing.

Today, business ecosystem networks exist in many industries, including automotive, computers, software systems, space technology, telecommunications, or even health services and biotechnology industries. Prompted by Thorelli's (1986) seminal work, business and marketing academics began developing theories around networks and network-based competition. These networks were a group of independently owned and managed organizations that operated as partners rather than adversaries. The extent of partnership within the network is such that company boundaries often become fuzzy among the independent network firms. However, their relationships are permeable and include a complex set of inter-company connections (Cravens and Cravens 2000; Mattsson 1997; Piercy and Cravens 1995).

10.2.3 Global Phenomenon

Scholarly interest in these business networks and their web of relationships prompted a few Scandinavian marketing scholars to set up their research interest group, called the IMP Group (International Marketing and Purchase Group). This group, initially using an ethnographic methodology, developed an "interaction approach" between buyers and sellers based on the 878 interviews in 318 firms in several European countries. They came to believe that a model of buyer-seller cooperation better represented the data they had collected compared to the traditional view of buyers and sellers as adversaries. They conceptualized buyer-seller relationships as dyadic interactions both at individual and firm levels, often influenced by a multidimensional construct "atmosphere" involving power/dependence, cooperation, expectations, and closeness—and the environment of the interaction (Hakansson 1982; Hakansson and Wootz 1979).

Soon, the IMP Group's work became a research tradition that followed descriptive analysis of co-operative business and industrial relationships (Anderson et al. 1994; Hakansson and Snehota 2000). Unlike many North American researchers, the IMP Group was more interested in developing a holistic perspective of the full cooperation and collaboration network established by a select group of companies and conglomerate organizations. It provided a rich view of buyer-seller relationships and subsequently influenced many empirical studies on buyer-seller relationships in North America and elsewhere, sharing many common variables (Heide and John 1990; Noordewier et al. 1990). Several channel relationship models also use many of the same variables to predict channel relationships (Anderson et al. 1987; Andersson and Weitz 1989; Anderson and Narus 1984, 1990; Heide and John 1990, 1992).

Thus, as Sheth (2017, p. 2) points out, in contrast to other marketing schools of thought, RM became a global phenomenon all at once. In addition to the IMP Group, the Nordic school of services and relationship marketing made a very forceful argument for a paradigm shift from the marketing-mix approach to RM thinking (Grönroos 1994, 2000; Gummesson 1987, 2002). The Nordic School of RM's fundamental premise was that the general marketing-mix approach of 4Ps was passé, limiting, and reminiscent of the transactional marketing paradigm that was less relevant in the evolved context of service-based economies. Instead, they advocated a greater focus on long-term relationships, interactions with customers, improved technical quality, the establishment of customer information systems, cross-functional cooperation, and internal marketing to obtain commitment across the organization (Grönroos 2000). As a result, the IMP Group and the Nordic School and scholars from the UK, Australia, and New Zealand simultaneously offered their perspectives with empirical research with scholars from North America.

Another trigger for the rise of relationship marketing was the sudden rush to form international strategic alliances in anticipation of European integration in the early 1990s. Businesses worldwide were keen to partner with European companies to get a foothold in the large European Common market after the 1992 integration. These strategic alliances meant joint venture-type arrangements or cooperation between international organizations. Thus, many strategic marketing scholars theorized on the relational aspects of strategic alliances' formation, governance, and evolution. The relationship marketing perspective was integral to the strategic alliance's theoretical premise (Sheth and Parvatiyar 1992; Vardarajan and Cunningham 1995).

Takala and Uusitalo (1996) noted that this parallel development of the relationship marketing school of thought within separate research areas was far from coincidental. Aijo (1996) observed that these research streams emanated from within the specific business environment, similar to transactional marketing literature. Changes were happening in economic and technology applications in North America, significant alterations taking place in European industrial structures, concurrent with a rapid rise of service businesses in most developed nations. The other reason for the global interest in RM stemmed from Asia's high-context cultures, where personal relationships often intertwine with business relationships, such as guanxi, in China. The worldview of many people around the world did not align with the legalistic, adversarial, and competitive bedrock of transactional marketing. They found cooperation, collaboration, and long-term relationship perspective more natural to their societal upbringing and, hence, the proper axioms for developing marketing theories.

10.3 Foundations of Relationship Marketing Theory

Beyond a look at the forces that propelled the incredible rise of relationship marketing, it is essential to address three other vital questions:

1. What constitutes relationship marketing and what does not?
2. Why do firms and consumers engage in relationships with other firms and consumers? and
3. Why are some relationship marketing efforts more successful than others?

10.3.1 Relationship Marketing versus Marketing Relationships

El-Ansary (1997) raised an interesting question: what is the difference between "marketing relationships" and "relationship marketing"? Marketing relationships have existed even within the transactional marketing paradigm. They have been a topic of discussion for a long time in several contexts, such as channel relationships, agency-client relationships, buyer-seller relationships, and vendor or contractor relationships. Nevertheless, what distinguishes it from relationship marketing is its nature and specificity. Marketing relationships can take any form, including adversarial relationships, rivalry relationships, affiliation relationships, independent or dependent relationships, etc. However, relationship marketing constitutes only specific types of relationships that emphasize cooperation and collaboration between the firm and its customers and other marketing actors. Dwyer et al. (1987) characterized such cooperative relationships as interdependent and long-term oriented rather than concerned with short-term discrete transactions. Often long-term orientation is emphasized because of the belief that marketing actors will not engage in opportunistic behavior if they have long-term orientation and that such relationships seek mutual gains and cooperation (Ganesan 1994).

Thus, the terms relationship marketing and marketing relationship are not synonymous. Relationship marketing describes a specific marketing approach that is a subset or a particular marketing focus. Many have well acknowledged it as a paradigm shift in marketing approach and orientation (Brodie et al. 1997; Kotler 1990; Parvatiyar and Sheth 1997; Webster 1992). In the first edition of this book, Sheth and colleagues (1988) observed that the emphasis on relationships as opposed to transaction-based exchanges is very likely to redefine the domain of marketing (also see Sheth and Uslay 2007).

However, many scholars have also been hesitant in recommending the complete paradigm shift to a relationship marketing approach in all circumstances. They believe that there are various contextual reasons why some relationships need to be just transactional. They recommend adopting a marketing strategy continuum ranging from transactional to collaborative according to the context of the previous relationship with the customer, their orientation, or the market situation (Grönroos 1991; Aijo 1996; Brodie et al. 1997; Palmer 1994).

Relationship marketing is distinguishable from discrete transactions. According to Dwyer et al. (1987, p. 13), discrete transactions have a "distinct beginning, short duration, and sharp ending by performance." In contrast, relational exchange "traces to previous agreements [and] … is longer in duration, reflecting an ongoing process." Despite this clear distinction, relationship marketing has been defined in many different ways by scholars from various research perspectives (Harker 1999; Palmatier 2008).

10.3.2 Narrow versus Broad Views of Relationship Marketing

Nevin (1995) pointed out that relationship marketing reflected various themes and perspectives. Some of these themes offer a narrow functional marketing perspective, while others provide a broad and somewhat paradigmatic approach and orientation. Most practitioner definitions are narrow and contextual to a specific type of activity in our observation. In contrast, definitions offered by several marketing scholars who have studied the phenomenon in some depth are broader, more encompassing, and inclusive of various sub-fields or streams of research.

For example, one narrow perspective equates RM with database marketing to reach target customers and build campaigns utilizing individual information on purchase history and previous interactions with customers. This approach is a stimulus-organism-response (S-O-R) approach emphasizing the promotional aspect of marketing. Another narrow yet relevant viewpoint is to consider relationship marketing primarily for customer retention and loyalty. This viewpoint somewhat assumes the "Pavlovian" view of the customer wherein customers would act loyally, based on positive incentives, offerings, and dynamic interactions designed and stimulated by the marketer. Nowadays, some equate RM with software systems, such as customer relationship management (CRM) platforms, to manage individual or one-to-one customer relationships and integrate information technology and sales automation tools with customer retention and growth strategies. As valuable as these tools are for business functioning, definitions of relationship marketing anchored around them understate its core strategic premise (Szmigin and Bourne 1998; O'Malley and Prethora 2004). These narrow perspectives are still reminiscent of the transactional marketing paradigm and propagate a practice not as a customer-oriented approach to business but as a product-oriented philosophy that sought to "bend" the customer to fit the product (Grönroos 1994, 2019; Gummesson 1997; Veloutsou et al. 2002).

McKenna (1991) professed a more strategic view of relationship marketing by putting the customer first and shifting the role of marketing from manipulating the customer (telling and selling) to genuine customer involvement (communicating and sharing the knowledge). Morgan and Hunt (1994) drew upon the distinction between transactional and relational exchanges by Dwyer et al. (1987) to propose a more inclusive definition of relationship marketing. They categorized relational exchanges for a focal firm into four types: supplier partnerships, lateral partnerships, buyer partnerships, and internal partnerships. These types identify ten forms of relationship marketing depending upon the relational exchange activity domain, such as a just-in-time arrangement with suppliers, strategic alliances with competitors, lateral partnerships with non-profit or government agencies for joint R&D, etc. Morgan and Hunt (1994) propose that all ten are forms of relationship marketing. Therefore, they provide a 'broadened' view to suggest, "relationship marketing refers to all marketing activities directed towards establishing, developing, and maintaining successful relational exchanges" (Morgan and Hunt 1994, p. 22). This broad view echoed in the conclusive analysis of other definitions by Aijo (1996, p. 15):

> There is a growing consensus on the definition of RM as involving the following aspects: a close long-term relationship between various (network) participants involved in exchanging something of value (total market process).

Such a broadened definition of RM has come under attack by some scholars. For example, Peterson (1995) declared Morgan and Hunt's definition guilty of an error of commission that states that if their "definition is true, then relationship marketing and marketing are redundant terms and one is unnecessary and should be stricken from the literature because having both only leads to confusion" (Peterson 1995, p. 279). Other scholars who believe that relationship marketing is distinctly different from the prevailing transactional orientation of marketing would contest such an extreme viewpoint.

A broad stakeholder view of RM is supported as well as criticized by many (Ballantyne 1997; Christy et al. 1996; Gummesson 1996, 1999; Hunt 1997; Payne 1995; Tzokas and Saren 2000). For example, Sheth and Parvatiyar (1995b) consider RM as "attempts to involve and integrate customers, suppliers, and other infrastructural partners into a firm's development and marketing activities." However, they also observed that non-customer relationships are outside the marketing domain and that their inclusion in the marketing research agenda "risks the value and contributions of the marketing discipline in directing relationship marketing practice and research and theory development" (Parvatiyar and Sheth 2000, p. 7). Subsequently, Sheth et al. (2015, p. 122) observed that:

> For an emerging discipline, it is important to develop an acceptable definition that encompasses all facets of the phenomenon and also effectively delimits the domain to allow focused understanding and growth of knowledge in the discipline... limit the domain of relationship marketing to only those collaborative actions focused on serving the needs of customers. That would be consistent with marketing's customer focus and understanding that made the discipline prominent.

They argue that other aspects of organizational relationships, such as supplier relationships, internal relationships, and lateral relationships, are directly attended to by such disciplines as supply chain management, human resource management, and strategic management.

Therefore, relationship marketing has the most significant potential for becoming a discipline and developing its theory if it delimits its domain to the firm–customer aspect of the relationship. Of course, to achieve a mutually beneficial relationship with customers, the firm may have to collaborate with its suppliers, competitors, consociates, and internal divisions. The study of such relationships is a valid domain of relationship marketing if it studies how it enhances or facilitates customer relationships. Thus, Sheth et al. (2015) offer the following definition:

> Relationship marketing is the ongoing process of engaging in collaborative activities and programs with immediate and end-user customers to create or enhance mutual economic, social and psychological value, profitably (Sheth et al. 2015, p. 123).

The above definition is based on the axiom that collaborative relationships with customers lead to a more significant market value creation. Such value will benefit all parties engaged in the relationship. Designing and enhancing mutual economic, social, and psychological value is the purpose of relationship marketing. Their definition implicitly includes three underlying dimensions of relationship formation, i.e., purpose, parties, and programs. Accordingly, they present a process model of RM comprising four sub-processes of 'formation'; 'management and governance'; 'performance evaluation'; and 'relationship evolution or enhancement' (Sheth et al. 2015, 127–132). This process framework is consistent with the stages approach of Wilson (1995) and with the conclusion drawn by Palmatier (2008, p. 1) that a vast majority of RM definitions imply four general stages of identifying, developing, maintaining, and terminating.

10.3.3 Why Firms and Consumers Engage in Partnering Relationships or RM Programs?

Several authors have explored businesses' and consumers' motivations to engage in relational behavior and participate in partnering programs (Hunt et al., 2006). For businesses, the primary reason is to improve marketing productivity and enhance mutual value by increasing marketing effectiveness and marketing efficiencies (Sheth and Sisodia 1995; Sheth and Parvatiyar 1995b). Seeking and achieving strategic marketing goals, such as entering a new market, developing a new product or technology, serving new or expanded needs of customers, improved customer base with more high value and long-term customers, and better competitive position are examples of enhanced marketing effectiveness. Similarly, seeking and achieving operational goals, such as reducing distribution costs, lower cost of serving customers, streamlining order processing and inventory management, reducing the burden of high customer acquisition costs, and so on, are means of achieving marketing efficiencies (Sheth et al. 2015).

Hunt et al. (2006, p. 76) contend that competition is so central to market-based economies that firms engage in relational exchanges with other firms or consumers when such relationships enable them to compete better. In other words, RM involves a strategic choice made by firms to achieve competitive advantage and superior financial performance (Kalwani and Narayandas 1995). According to the resource-advantage theory (R-A theory), relationships provide a competitive advantage when they constitute relational resources—resources that contribute to the firm's ability to efficiently/effectively produce market offerings that have value for some customers or market segment(s) (Hunt 2002; Hunt and Derozier 2004).

Similarly, customers are also motivated to fulfill their goals related to efficiencies and effectiveness. It applies to both business customers and mass-market consumers. In their "commitment-trust" theory of RM, Morgan and Hunt (1994) identify relationship benefits as a critical antecedent for customers/consumers to engage in relational exchange. They contend that customers are motivated to reduce risk by engaging in relational interactions with partners they can trust regarding their reliability, integrity, and competence.

Sheth and Parvatiyar (1995b) suggest that consumers have a natural inclination towards engaging in relationships and reducing their choices as relational behavior provides psychological and sociological benefits. They draw upon various consumer and buyer behavior theories (such as Howard and Sheth 1969) to suggest that similar to "routinized buying behavior," when consumers choose to reduce their choices, they inadvertently also decide to reduce information search costs or new learning. They propose that:

> Consumers engage in relational market behavior to achieve greater efficiency in their decision-making, to reduce the task of information processing, to achieve more cognitive consistency

in their decisions, and to reduce the perceived risks associated with future choices (Sheth and Parvatiyar 1995b, p. 256).

Consumers thus gain more efficiency in their decision-making. Also, relational behavior helps the consumers in effective choice-making. They buy fewer brands or buy from fewer suppliers who have ample opportunity to learn and tailor personalized offerings to consumers, thus better fulfilling their needs. They benefit from the relational investments made by marketers (De Wulf et al. 2001). Moreover, consumers are also motivated to seek the rewards and benefits often promised in companies' RM programs, such as rewards, loyalty, or preferred customer programs.

Bagozzi (1995) believes that consumers are motivated by their goals, and engaging in relational behavior may be a means to fulfilling their end goals. He maintains that:

> The most common and determinative motive for entering in a marketing relationship is that consumers see the relationship as a means for the fulfillment of a goal to which one had earlier, and perhaps tentatively, committed. That is, people have goals to acquire a product or use a service, and a relationship then becomes instrumental in goal achievement (Bagozzi 1995, p. 273).

Thus, Bagozzi makes a case for thoroughly investigating consumers' goals in RM. In particular, he believes that "moral obligation" and "moral virtues" may play a vital motivational role for some consumers to engage in relational behavior. Altruistic and virtuous motivations go beyond seeking direct economic and sociological benefits of relational marketing programs.

Vargo and Lusch (2004) recognize that in the evolving new service-dominant marketing logic, the goal is to customize offerings. The consumer is always a co-producer and strives to maximize consumer involvement in customizing to fit their needs better. They state that the "focus is shifting away from tangibles and toward intangibles, such as skills, information, knowledge, interactivity and connectivity, and ongoing relationships" (Vargo and Lusch 2004, p. 15). Thus, their answer to why consumers engage in relational marketing processes contributes to producing goods and services customized to consumers' individual needs, wants, tastes, and preferences.

10.3.4 Factors that Drive RM Success

Since relationship marketing is more than a phenomenon—it is a business strategy that requires considerable time, effort, and resources for obtaining greater marketing productivity and mutual value—it is valuable to know the factors for its success. It is essential to understand what underlying characteristics, behavioral orientations, and governance and managerial processes determine RM's success or failure. Numerous research studies have been published that identify the outcomes, goals, or indicators of successfully designing and implementing RM strategies and programs. Hunt et al. (2006) report the success indicators to which RM has been linked as follows:

1. improvements in competitive advantage (Barclay and Smith 1997; Day 2000; Hunt 1997)
2. superior financial performance (Boles et al. 2000; Hunt 2000; Kalwani and Narayandas 1995; Walter and Gemünden 2000; Weber 2000)
3. improved customer satisfaction (Abdul-Muhumin 2002; Schellhase et al. 2000)
4. organizational learning (Selnes and Sallis 2003)
5. partners' propensity to stay (Gruen et al. 2000; Jap 2001; Verhoef 2003)
6. acquiescence by partners (Kumar et al. 1992; Morgan and Hunt 1994), and
7. a decrease in uncertainty (Achrol and Stern 1988; Morgan and Hunt 1994).

In a meta-analysis of the factors influencing relationship marketing's effectiveness, Palmatier et al. (2006) identify three types of relational outcomes: customer-focused outcomes, seller-focused outcomes, and dyadic outcomes. Within customer-focused outcomes are such measures as expectation of continuity of the relationship, word of mouth, and customer loyalty. Seller-focused outcomes essentially look at seller-objective performance, including sales, wallet share, profit performance, and other measurable changes to the sellers' business. Finally, the dyadic outcome primarily relates to cooperation characterized by coordination and joint actions. The relationship outcome variables (constructs) and representative papers are listed below:

1. the expectation of continuity (Crosby et al. 1990; Doney and Cannon 1997)
2. word of mouth, including referral (Hennig-Thurau et al. 2002; Reynolds and Beatty 1999)
3. customer loyalty (De Wulf et al. 2001; Hennig-Thurau et al. 2002; Srideshmukh et al. 2002)
4. seller objective performance, including sales, profit, and share of wallet (Reynolds and Beatty 1999; Siguaw et al. 1998), and
5. cooperation (Anderson and Narus 1990; Morgan and Hunt 1994).

Palmatier et al. (2006, p. 137) observe that while reviewing the RM literature related to relationship antecedents, mediators, and outcomes, many constructs with similar definitions operate under different aliases, i.e., constructs with similar names but different operationalizations. Thus, they used a single construct definition to code the existing research. However, they only included a construct in their conceptual framework if ten effects emerged to support its empirical analysis. Eighteen constructs were included in their conceptual model of relationship antecedents, mediators, and outcomes based on that criteria.

Four relationship mediators were identified as most significant in impacting relational outcomes (Palmatier et al. 2006):

1. commitment (Anderson and Weitz 1992; Jap and Ganesan 2000; Moorman et al. 1992; Morgan and Hunt 1994)
2. trust (Doney and Cannon 1997; Hibbard et al. 2001; Sirdeshmukh et al. 2002)
3. relationship satisfaction (Crosby et al. 1990; Reynolds and Beatty 1999), and
4. relationship quality (Crosby et al. 1990; De Wulf et al. 1999).

Similarly, support was also found for the following nine antecedents that determine RM effectiveness (Palmatier et al. 2006):

1. relationship benefits (Hennig-Thurau et al. 2002; Morgan and Hunt 1994; Reynolds and Beatty 1999)
2. dependence on the seller (Hibbard et al. 2001; Morgan and Hunt 1994)
3. relationship investment (De Wulf et al. 2001; Ganesan 1994)
4. seller expertise (Crosby et al. 1990; Lagace et al. 1991)
5. communication (Anderson and Weitz 1992; Mohr et al. 1996; Morgan and Hunt 1994)
6. similarity, including shared values (Crosby et al. 1990; Doney and Cannon 1997; Morgan and Hunt 1994)
7. relationship duration (Anderson and Weitz 1989; Doney and Cannon 1997; Kumar et al. 1995)
8. interaction frequency (Crosby et al. 1990; Doney and Cannon 1997)
9. manifest conflict — but not functional conflict (Anderson and Weitz 1992; Kumar et al. 1995).

The mediators of RM effectiveness factors and their influence on RM strategy success build on social exchange theory (Blau 1964; Homans 1958; Macaulay 1963) and relational contracting (Macneil 1980). Hunt et al. (2006) call these relationship mediators "relational factors" and note that most studies examining relational factors distinguish between discrete and relational exchanges (see distinction mentioned in the previous section; Dwyer et al. 1987; Macneil 1980). To sum it up, when relational parties know and trust each other, make adequate commitments to the relationship, keep promises, have shared values, frequently communicate, and cooperate to coordinate for joint actions, then relationship success is more likely.

10.4 Elevation of Relationship Marketing within Marketing Discipline and by the AMA

As we have seen in the preceding paragraphs, the fundamental premise of the relationship marketing school of thought is the normative perspective that developing and leveraging a long-term relationship with customers and other marketing stakeholders is the route to success in business. In their seminal article, Vargo and Lusch

(2004) recognizing the impact of many influential papers in this domain (e.g., Andersen and Narus 1990; Berry 1983, 1995; Dwyer et al. 1989; Grönroos 1994, 1995; Gummesson 1994, 2002; Morgan and Hunt 1994, 1999; Sheth and Parvatiyar 1995a, 1995b), identified relationship marketing among the seven research streams that emerged in the 1980s and continue through the 2000s as an essential social and economic process. Their contention (Vargo and Lusch 2004, p. 5) is that relationship marketing, along with other research streams, such as market orientation, quality management, services marketing, supply chain, network analysis, and resource management, are converging towards a "service-dominant logic," wherein "value is defined by and co-created in concert with the consumer." This customer-centric, market-driven, service-dominant logic strives to maximize consumers' involvement in developing customized offerings and seeks to be the predominant organizational philosophy in the current era (Vargo and Lusch 2008).

Despite its relatively short history, acknowledging relationship marketing as a mainstream discipline driver gave considerable impetus to this school of thought. It formed the bedrock for a more integrated and new dominant logic for marketing. Therefore, in 2004, when the American Marketing Association (AMA) officially announced a new marketing definition incorporating "managing customer relationships" as a central thrust of marketing processes, it generated considerable interest, both for and against it. The 2004 AMA definition stated that:

> Marketing is an organizational function and a set of processes for creating, communicating and delivering value to customers and for managing customer relationships in ways that benefit the organization and its stakeholders. (Keefe 2004)

The 2004 AMA definition generated many criticisms (in addition to positive comments) from scholars concerned about the very narrow characterization of the marketing domain and its perspective as an "organizational function and a set of processes" that excluded the systematic and aggregate features, or the societal role of marketing (Gundlach 2007; Gundlach and Wilkie 2009; Wilkie and Moore 2007; Zinkhan and Williams 2007). However, the definition also recognized the paradigm shift from short-term transactional thinking to a more useful relational perspective in modern marketing thinking. According to Gundlach (2007, pp. 247–248):

> Consider the paradigmatic recognition in marketing that, beyond transactions, relationships play an important role in marketing. This recognition has altered the scope and perspective of marketing from that of exchange involving discrete transactions bound temporally in time and space to relationships occurring over time and across space (Sheth and Uslay 2007). Similarly, as Vargo and Lusch (2004) observe, marketing is evolving from a state in which value in exchange is the dominant logic to a logic in which value in exchange and value in use dominates. Such an evolution further expands the necessary scope and perspective of marketing by broadening the concept of value to include individual, firm, stakeholder, and larger societal considerations and viewpoints (Lusch 2007).

Despite many voices that welcomed the shift in focus in AMA's definition of marketing away from the historical exchange paradigm to creating and delivering value through customer relationships (Lusch 2007; Sheth and Uslay 2007), several scholars were concerned about the elevation of "managing customer relationships" to such prominence that this one, particular, strategic thrust had become a part of the very definition of marketing. They were also unhappy about excluding the term "exchange" in the 2004 definition, a central construct of the 1985 AMA definition of marketing (Wilkie and Moore 2007, p. 275). Hence, responding to the considerable debate generated in conference sessions, book chapters, and a special section of JPP&M, the AMA constituted a committee and surveyed scholars to revisit its 2004 definition. Based on the recommendations of the select committee in 2007, a new definition of marketing was adopted that took away the explicit reference to customer relationships and reintroduced the construct of exchange perspective in the new definition as follows:

> Marketing is the activity, set of institutions, and processes for creating, communicating, delivering, and exchanging offerings that have value for customers, clients, partners, and society at large.

Indeed, not everyone will agree with the revised 2007 definition of marketing (as was the case for the 2004 definition); meanwhile, this definition was approved again in 2017 and continues to be the official AMA definition of marketing. Notwithstanding the controversy about the omission of customer relationship terminology, and reversal to the exchange focus in the definition of marketing, it is abundantly clear that the relationship marketing perspective is still prevalent within marketing practice, teaching, and scholarly activities.

At the beginning of the 21st century, scholars believed that relationship marketing had great promise and could rise to the level of becoming a discipline influencing other subdisciplines within the marketing area, such as consumer behavior and marketing strategy (Morgan 2000; Sheth and Parvatiyar 2002), as well as also other disciplines, including organization management, information systems, finance, entrepreneurship, psychology, economics, and sociology. However, recently, the relationship marketing school of thought seems to have lost its way and has been relegated to mere marketing practice. Competing ideas that germinated with relationship marketing thinking, such as customer engagement and customer-centricity, are staging their thought processes, building upon some of the concepts of relationship marketing school of thought, but at the same time, also chipping away the core philosophy considered as axioms of relationship marketing paradigm.

In the following paragraphs, we will first examine RM's theoretical roots and potential for forming a general marketing theory. After that, we will discuss the reasons for its relegation into a practice type by the AMA and its implications for a potential premature death of the relationship marketing school of thought. In doing so, we will first revisit the initial conceptualizations and theoretical propositions that had generated considerable excitement among scholars from many subdisciplines in the domain of relationship marketing leading to its rise in prominence within the first two of the preceding three decades. After that, we will examine the factors or forces that might have knowingly or unknowingly led to the hijacking and relegation of the relationship marketing school of thinking. For example, there could be either lack of fulfillment of the promise by this school or changing practices that made it less attractive to focus attention on this subject; or it could be variegated perspectives, theories, and research publications that drew the attention away from relationship marketing school of thinking. Therefore, in our final analysis, we will assess if and how relationship marketing could become a stand-alone discipline, similar to consumer behavior or marketing strategy.

10.5   RM's Identity Crisis and Relegation to a Marketing Type by AMA

The AMA on its website now lists relationship marketing as a type of marketing, in a very narrow perspective based on the definition provided by the Association of National Advertisers (ANA). They refer to relationship marketing as "strategies and tactics for segmenting customers to build loyalty." According to the AMA website:

> *Relationship marketing* leverages database marketing, behavioral advertising, and analytics to target consumers precisely and create loyalty programs.

It is an apparent relegation of relationship marketing from philosophy and school of thinking that drove new thought processes in marketing to mere practice; that is too centered around the narrow methods of database marketing and behavioral advertising to create loyalty programs. On the AMA website, below the definition of marketing (https://www.ama.org/the-definition-of-marketing-what-is-marketing/), six marketing types are listed, including influencer marketing, relationship marketing, viral marketing, green marketing, keyword marketing, and guerilla marketing. Relationship marketing equated with the other tactical activities signals that it is no more viewed as a paradigm, which is undoubtedly sad and a matter of great concern because much of the scholarly activities around the world that generated colossal enthusiasm and promise of a fundamentally changing academic and corporate thinking about the marketing function and its DNA, seems to have been lost. The unfortunate part is that instead of developing its definition of relationship marketing, the AMA has chosen to adopt a very narrow definition provided by the Association of National Advertisers (ANA). That is both amusing and shocking, reflecting a lack of disciplinary knowledge.

So, why has relationship marketing been relegated to this narrow practice-oriented and program type definition and puts it in the same league as "guerilla marketing," "keyword marketing," "influencer marketing," or "viral marketing"? How come, a school of thought that was emerging as a discipline, with theories, research, and scholarly contributions by some of the best-known marketing thinkers, and considered a paradigm shift by many just a decade and a half ago, and one that had become a critical thrust of the new marketing definition, suddenly become a pariah to be defined into a narrow practice type? We think several factors have led to this, for which perhaps, both marketing scholars and the AMA are responsible. We examine these factors below.

10.5.1 The Identity Crisis

Sheth (2016, p. 2) identifies the divergence, instead of convergence, of viewpoints regarding what constitutes RM among academics and practitioners as the key reason for the identity crisis. He observes that:

> Over the years, RM began to diverge rather than converge into a cohesive marketing practice or a discipline. While there were several efforts to identify key constructs such as trust and commitment, it did not evolve into a theory with empirically tested propositions in contrast to market orientation perspective in managerial marketing.

Unfortunately, research in RM currently resembles the proverbial five blind men and the elephant. It means different things to different scholars and practitioners. To many practitioners and scholars, RM still means managing loyalty programs and segmenting the market based on customer profitability analysis. For some others, RM is synonymous with CRM and database marketing. Even though the next generation of direct marketers have emerged, schooled in personalized marketing using predictive modeling, yield management methods, and web-based interactivity tools to engage with customers, they still have a tough time resisting the urge to push brand messages indiscriminately. Although CRM may have shed its discredited image from implementation failures in the early 2000s, due to process improvements and overcoming of the cultural resistance by salespeople, the psyche of most marketers is still tied to chasing sales, ignoring the most crucial aspect of RM of involving customers in collaborative efforts directed at co-creation of mutual value.

The other digital transformation tools, such as customer journey mapping, experience designs, customer lifecycle management, and multichannel integration powered by artificial intelligence (AI) and machine learning (ML), have tremendous, transformational value for customers and organizations desirous of efficiently implementing relational strategies. However, it has to be preceded by relational thinking and strategy that genuinely involves customers in the value creation process and builds emotional bonds. The problem is that most marketers have a one-sided view of what the organization can implement or leverage to push their sales agenda based on prevailing transactional marketing orientation. Without embracing the RM philosophy of collaboration and co-creation, all these tools, technologies, and methods will remain a push effort, devoid of an emotional bond with customers.

10.5.2 Academic Balkanization of RM

Perhaps one of the primary reasons for the RM identity crisis is its balkanization by academic scholars themselves. Despite its impressive growth in the 1990s and the first decade of this century, scholarly research and publications began to undermine the paradigm thrust of RM itself. A simple example of this lack of interest in theorizing RM's emerging discipline is that no new definition or research synthesis of the varied perspectives of relationship marketing was published in the last decade. Most RM-related publications are nowadays by econometric modelers who revel in applying their quantitative skills on available data. No wonder, therefore, RM and CRM became synonymous since the quantitative modelers could quickly access data in CRM and machine learning systems. Journal editors prefer research with high levels of quantitative rigor utilizing large datasets. Evolving attitudes have certainly tipped the scales away from new theoretical explorations based on psychological, sociological, and anthropological explanations of the phenomenon and its causes and consequences.

Because of this modeling bias, many researchers built their models with recommended practice strategies on observable and behavioral data available within information technology systems. For example, research publications on "customer engagement" have recently seen explosive growth since these can be defined in terms of observable activities on social media and other online technology systems. Subsequently, some scholars are pushing to replace RM with customer engagement as the new theoretical marketing paradigm.

Similarly, research and publications on loyalty and customer valuation models, including customer lifetime value (CLV), customer equity, and relationship equity, have been based on data-oriented quantitative modeling. Besides the temporal dimension of relationship duration between buyers and sellers, most of these models' underpinning is transactional activity driven, incorporating predictions of churn and relationship continuity or program profitability outcomes. These models are beneficial, but they have not advanced the theoretical premise of either relationship marketing or loyalty. Loyalty, by and large, has been constrained to a very narrow connotation in repeat buying instead of the mental and emotional commitment per its original ontology.

The other factor that has adversely impacted the relationship marketing school of thought is the strong allegiance to the exchange theory of marketing by many leading marketing academics. They are unwilling to make the paradigm shift away from the exchange perspective. The furthest they are willing to go is to acknowledge the phenomenon of relational exchange. Despite attempts by some scholars (Sheth and Uslay 2007; Vargo and Lusch 2004; Vargo 2008) to reorient the marketing discipline to value creation as the fundamental goal, many influential scholars are still propagating the exchange theory of marketing.

It is peculiar that while the balkanization of RM is taking place within the marketing discipline, other non-business fields have shown keen interest in what relationship marketing has to offer in the development of thoughts within their domain. A case in point is the discipline of economic sociology, which has acknowledged the parallel development of new economic sociology and relationship marketing (Kotelnikova 2012; Radadev 2012). They even published a special issue of the *economic sociology_the european electronic newsletter* (July 2012, vol. 13.3) and a special issue of Journal of *Economic Sociology = ekonomicheskaya sotsiolgiya* (2015, vol. 16.2), including review and synthesis articles on RM by Sheth, Parvatiyar, and Sinha (2012, 2015). It is interesting to note that economic-sociologist, Koelnikova (2012), in her commentary, observes that although relationship marketing articles define their subject matter as exchange relationships, new economic sociology has a much broader scope of interests. She states:

> Although both marketing scholars and economic sociologists argue that their focus is on studying relationships, both groups address a variety of relationships and the differences among them. In the economic field, two types of relationships co-exist. The first type includes relations that endure only within the time frame of a given transaction. The second type embraces relations that endure beyond the completion of a given transaction (Burt 2000); the existence of such relations implies that transactions can be based on already existing interpersonal relations or that, on the contrary, transactions can contribute to the formation of steady interpersonal relations. Each of these relationship types has different meanings and goals (Uzzi 1996). We would argue that marketing scholars tend to study the first type of relations, although they are increasingly devoting more attention to the customer life cycle models, which bring them closer to the second type. By contrast, economic sociologists are primarily interested in studying the second type of relationship, which is developed beyond transactions per se. Overall, marketing scholars typically prioritize formal contractual relationships, whereas economic sociologists devote more attention to informal interpersonal relations (Koelnikova 2012, p. 30).

In effect, relationship marketing as a discipline has a great promise to both explore new fundamental dimensions and influence and learn from other social sciences. It may be temporarily facing a mid-life identity crisis. However, as long as it does not get cast into a narrow practice type programmatic activity, it can impact the entire marketing thinking to become the dominant paradigm to form the basis for a new general marketing theory. There is an excellent opportunity to synthesize the divergent practices and perspectives into a comprehensive view of RM (Sheth 2016).

10.6   Can Relationship Marketing Become the Foundation of a General Theory of Marketing?

In their metatheoretical analysis, Moller and Halinen (2000) examined the propositions and the root traditions of relationship marketing research by separating the theoretical from its polemic perspectives. They refer to theoretical as the underlying disciplinary roots of RM and polemic as the critical stance towards the more extreme claims of its novelty and differentiation from existing marketing theory. So, instead of viewing it primarily as a business perspective or how it is practiced in various businesses, Moller and Halinen (2000) assess RM's theory development following certain research traditions. They compare and contrast the theoretical assumptions of different research traditions in defining the nature and context of marketing relationships. Such an analysis helps reveal both the potential differences and similarities of the premises under each root tradition. It enables us to discuss RM's possibility of forming a general theory within the marketing discipline.

Moller and Halinen (2000) identified four disciplinary roots of RM: services marketing, business marketing (or inter-organizational marketing), marketing channels, and ideas of database and direct marketing. However, they also acknowledge that:

> The Database Marketing and Direct Marketing tradition is perhaps best characterized as a practice, since it has no clear disciplinary background…. It has a strong managerial emphasis aiming at enhancing the efficiency of marketing activities, especially communication…. Relationships are seen as long-term in nature, but conceptual or other efforts to tackle the dynamism of customer relationships have been limited. The main focus is on how to keep customers loyal and profitable in an efficient way (Moller and Halinen 2000, p. 38).

Concerning RM studies in services marketing, they observe that no clear disciplinary background exists. In the early phase, services marketing was a contrarian response to "traditional marketing management." Subsequently, consumer behavior applications, service operations with human resources perspectives, and general management outlook were brought to bear to convey that relationship marketing is more an organizational philosophy that needs to be at the core of corporate decision-making and processes. Although both RM research and services marketing has been empirically and theoretically driven, service research has a hefty managerial orientation. With the introduction of the service-dominant logic by Vargo and Lusch (2004), relationship marketing and services marketing seem to converge on resource-advantage theory, value co-creation, and alliances. There began an evident commonality between relationship marketing theory and service-dominant logic, discussing alliances and partnerships for value co-creation.

We agree with Moller and Halinen (2000) about various research traditions that brought their interests and theoretical underpinnings to apply to the growing phenomenon of relationship marketing to provide a considerable theoretical base. In addition, services and database marketing approaches helped accentuate RM's importance as alternative practice frameworks to the traditional 4Ps and market segmentation approach. Still, they were limited in their contribution to advancing the theory on relationship marketing.

The RM school of thinking's most significant theoretical impetus came from research traditions in marketing channels and business-to-business/industrial marketing. These areas had emerged and developed within the marketing discipline, focused on a company's external relationships, particularly customer relationships. They were concerned about the most efficient and effective relationship arrangements and governance processes relating to channel partners and business customers. They drew upon literature and theories in economics and other social sciences to develop frameworks in the quest to create a deeper understanding and explanation of the underlying phenomenon in inter-organizational relationships. The political economy perspective, transaction cost economics, and social exchange theory (including social contracting) were among the most informative theoretical foundations of the relationship marketing school of thought.

10.6.1 Political Economy Perspective (PEP) as Foundation for RM

In the late 1970s, researchers interested in industrial marketing and marketing channels became interested in inter-organizational dyadic relationships between buyers and sellers (Bonoma and Johnston 1978; Frazier 1983; Zaltman and Bonoma 1977). It was new compared to the then prevalent marketing-mix approach, which considered exchange as transactional from a singular perspective of either the marketer or the buyer. They applied socio-economic theories, including political-economy perspective (PEP) of power-dependence as a guiding framework for the understanding of complex channel phenomenon (Achrol, Reve, and Stern 1983; Achrol and Stern 1988; Arndt 1983; Dwyer and Welsh 1985; Dwyer and Oh 1987; Heide and John 1990; Kumar et al. 1995; Stern and El-Ansary 1988; Stern and Reeve 1980). PEP "views a social system comprising interacting sets of major economic and sociopolitical forces which affect collective behavior and performance" (Stern and Reeve 1980, p. 53).

Accordingly, PEP suggests it may be helpful to analyze the economic and political factors impacting distribution channel relationships, such as internal economic forces, agreed trade terms, power-dependence balance among channel members, cooperation and conflict, external economic conditions in which channels exist, and the external sociopolitical system in which the channel members operate (Stern and Reeve 1980). This perspective generated substantial interest in developing new integrative frameworks to understand better the nature of long-term business relationships (Achrol 1991; Arndt 1983; Anderson and Narus 1990; Anderson and Weitz 1989; Heide and John 1990). The focus grew on efficient business relationships and governance mechanisms in the context of dyadic behavior and economic exchange between buying and selling organizations. Relationships were viewed as highly interdependent and reciprocal. Some research studies subsequently emphasized the economic aspects of channel relationships and others on social exchanges and norms.

10.6.2 Transaction Cost Economics and RM

The economic considerations led to an integration between PEP and transaction cost economics (TCE—also known as transaction cost analysis or TCA). TCE was first proposed by Coase (1937) and further developed by Williamson (1975, 1979, 1981, 1985), purported to explain the factors that determined the choice between arms-length market transactions and full forward integration as in hierarchical structures. TCE/TCA soon became a well-accepted paradigm in marketing for defining alternative forms of governance and suggests that exchange governance is driven by a firm's desire to minimize the direct and opportunity costs of exchange (Rindfleisch and Heide 1997). Several studies in marketing confirmed the core propositions of TCE concerning how efficiencies in transaction costs can be achieved based on chosen relational structure depending on the required frequency of interactions, need to protect specific assets, levels of uncertainty, and risks of partner opportunism (Anderson 1985; Anderson and Coughlan 1987; Anderson and Schmittlein 1984; Coughlan 1985; John and Weitz 1988; Klein et al. 1990).

The prevalence of hybrid channel arrangements also prompted several scholars to investigate and theorize partnering relationships using TCE/TCA (Heide and John 1990; Mudambi and Mudambi 1995; Noordewier et al. 1990; Rangan et al. 1993). TCA suggests that organizational performance is enhanced (i.e., transaction costs are lower) when the governance structure of the transaction is congruent with the underlying dimensions of the exchange (Robicheaux and Coleman 1994). Overall, the impact of TCE has been substantial in the development of relationship marketing literature, particularly for efficient buyer-seller partnerships and to advance theoretical propositions in marketing strategy and formation of business alliances (Chen and Chen 2003; Sheth and Parvatiyar 1992; Williamson and Ghani 2012). Relationship marketing has also conjunctively influenced TCE scholarship, as acknowledged by Williamson and Ghani (2011, p. 74):

> Scholarship at the intersection of transaction cost economics (TCE) and marketing has enjoyed an impressive record of growth over the past three decades, and the future promises more of the same…we advance the proposition that the relation between TCE and marketing has and should be a two-way street. In considering the scope for future research, we give special attention to the asymmetric costs, the dynamics of governance, and disequilibrium contracting.

10.6.3 Social Exchange Theory (SET) in RM

As Lambe et al. (2001, p. 3) point out, one of TCA's primary limitations is its limited capacity to explain relational exchanges' governance within conditions of varying risks of partner opportunism. Several studies have shown that relational control through norms or personal relations is often an effective means of governance (Anderson and Narus 1984, 1990; Dwyer, Schurr, and Oh 1987; Morgan and Hunt 1994; Wilson 1995). These studies suggest that partners can develop relationship-based governance over time. The core explanatory mechanism for such relationship governance has been drawn on social-exchange theory (SET), initially developed by Homans (1958), and intellectually contributed by researchers from sociology and social psychology (Blau 1960, 1964; Emerson 1962; Thibaut and Kelley 1959).

Scholars in sociology, psychology, and legal studies have developed a seminal body of research on SET. In essence, SET postulates that social exchange interactions involve expending economic and social resources, with associated perceived costs, by the parties involved in the social exchange. Over time, these costs and resources are weighed against the outcomes accruing to the exchange partners regarding economic and social rewards. They continue to engage in these exchange relationships if (a) their perceived economic and social reward outcomes outweigh the perceived costs; (b) it is perceived to be superior to other forms of exchange interactions; and (c) it is perceived that shared outcomes are fair and equitable among the exchange partners (i.e., procedural and distributive justice). SET further postulates that positive economic and social outcomes over time increase the trust between partners and their commitment to maintaining relational exchanges. Positive exchange interactions over time also produce relational exchange norms that govern the exchange partners' interactions (Lambe et al. 2001). These norms become the governance mechanism for interdependent relationships.

Most marketing studies utilizing SET have demonstrated that B2B relational exchange relies heavily on "relational contracts," or norms, to govern the relational exchange process (Heide and John 1992; Macneil 1980). Such relational contracts go beyond the formal written agreement, usually motivated by the parties' mutual recognition that the outcomes of such relational exchanges far exceed those that can be gained from another form of contractual arrangement or with a different partner. The relational contracts are contingent in their format when agreed terms and duties of parties and partners are less codifiable (Goetze and Scott 1981; Gundlach and Murphy 1993; Nevin 1995). They depend on norms. The norms (both explicit and tacit) are mutually agreed to rules of behavior developed over time as the parties in the relationship interact (Homans 1958; Blau 1964; Thibaut and Kelley 1959; Macneil 1980). Sometimes norms are established through learned behavior in other comparable relationships or by observing interactions in other exchange relationships.

In any case, relational norms increase relationships' efficiency because the agreed process of interactions reduces the exchange partners' uncertainty. It introduces regularity and control without contracts or legal mechanisms (Thibaut and Kelley 1959). Therefore, for these relational contracts to work, particularly in more complex arrangements, it requires high levels of cooperation, joint planning, mutual adaptations, process and goal alignments, and substantive communication between the parties involved in the relational governance process to meet the partnership objectives and needs (Gundlach and Murphy 1993; Hallen, Johanson, Seyed-Mohamed 1991; Nevin 1995). The utilization of SET to examine the process of relationship development has been supplemented by a substantial body of "research about the variables that make for a successful relationship" (Wilson 1995, p. 335). These include such variables and constructs as trust, commitment, cooperation, interdependence, relational norms, relational orientation, and satisfaction. Many empirical studies within the gambit of relationship marketing have applied TCA in conjunction with SET and PEP to develop a more integrated perspective on relationship development and governance, at least in channel and B2B relationships, and management and governance of strategic marketing alliances.

10.6.4 Resource Advantage (R-A) Theory of RM

In addition to drawing upon SET, Morgan and Hunt (1994) theory on relationship marketing identifies several distinct forms of intra- and inter-organizational relational partnerships, such as buyer partnerships (intermediate and ultimate customers), supplier partnerships (goods and service suppliers), lateral partnerships (with competitors, non-profit organizations, and government), and internal partnerships (various SBUs, functional departments, and employees of the firm), as pertinent to the study of relationship marketing. As for inter-organizational cooperation manifestations, these partnerships and strategic alliances have been a subject of inquiry and research tradition within strategic marketing and management literature (Varadarajan and Cunningham 1995). Lee Adler (1966) termed this phenomenon as "symbiotic marketing," and Johan Arndt (1979) conceptualized these long-lasting relationships with key customers and suppliers as "domesticated markets." Strategic alliances with customers, suppliers, and even competitors that pool the skills and resources of alliance partners for specific goals linked to strategic and operational objectives of effectiveness and efficiency, are pursued to develop a competitive advantage (Morgan 2000).

> In short, relationship marketing can be a major part of the firm's business strategy. Relationship marketing provides the firm with the guiding strategy for a wide variety of decisions, including (a) choices of transactional, recurrent, and relational exchange with customers, suppliers, and others; (b) methods for building competitive advantages based on relationships, where resources are shared through relationships; and (c) structure and selection of cooperative value nets that the

firm will participate in so that it may compete in increasingly competitive environments (Morgan 2000, p. 482).

Varadarajan and Cunningham (1995) observe that TCE and PEP's complementary perspectives (particularly, resource dependence concept) provide the theoretical explanations for structure and governance of partnership arrangements and strategic alliances. However, they are not the theoretical foundations for relationship marketing strategy (Heide 1994). From a strategy perspective, firms have to enter relationships more optimistically and access and leverage valuable resources that relationships often offer to be more competitive. This strategic orientation toward resources differentiates the resource-based theory approach to understanding relationships from TCE and resource dependence perspectives (Morgan and Hunt 1999).

> The focus of these theories is on the best responses to various environmental conditions, not on proactively seeking to change conditions through strategic thrusts…. Strategy … is a mechanism of change that reflects the power of idiosyncratic managerial intention and ability … which suggests that firms make conscious attempts to influence their environments through the exchange and interfirm relationships (Varadarajan and Cunningham 1995, p. 287).

Therefore, marketing scholars proposed relationship marketing models and conceptualizations based on the resource advantage view, which examined the link between firm resources and sustained competitive advantage (Barney 1991). It is assumed that firms as complex systems have a unique and heterogeneous set of strategic resources and abilities. Therefore through partnering or alliances, they can pool their distinct bundle of resources to create a competitive advantage in the marketplace. Under the resource-based view, the term *firm resources* are broadly construed to denote assets, capabilities, organizational processes, firm attributes, information, knowledge, etc., that are controlled by the firm and deployed to implement strategies that enhance efficiency and effectiveness (Daft 1983). Essentially, for sustained competitive advantage, firm resources must: be valuable, rare (among firm's current and potential competitors), imperfectly imitable, and not have strategically equivalent substitutes for it (Barney 1991). The resource-based strategy's argument was to focus on developing and acquiring rare, valuable, and inimitable resources as a means for achieving "rents," that is, profits above those achieved by a firm under the conditions of perfect competition (Hunt 2012). The resource-based view led to the Resource Advantage (R-A) theory of competition (Hunt and Morgan 1995, 1996, 1997) and subsequent grounding of relationship marketing in R-A theory (Hunt 1997; Morgan and Hunt 1999; Morgan 2000).

R-A theory is an "evolutionary, disequilibrium-provoking, process theory of competition, in which innovation and organizational learning are endogenous, firms and consumers have imperfect information, and in which entrepreneurship, institutions, and public policy affect economic performance" (Hunt 2012, p. 9). It combines the heterogeneous demand theory with the resource-based view of the firm. "R-A theory stresses the importance of market segments, heterogenous firm resources, comparative advantages/disadvantages in resources, and marketplace positions of competitive advantage/disadvantage… Resources are defined as the tangible and intangible entities available to the firm that enable it to produce efficiently and/or effectively a market offering that has value for some market segment(s)" (Hunt 2012, p. 10). In R-A theory, relationships are also considered resources like financial, physical, legal, human, organizational competencies, and information and knowledge resources.

RM strategy, whose fundamental thesis is that for competitive advantage, a firm should carefully develop and nurture a portfolio of relationships supported by the R-A theory of competition (Hunt and Morgan 1996; Hunt 2010). Despite being intangible, relationships can serve as a resource, even if they are not owned by the firm (belongs to partners), that can be accessed and leveraged to serve its customers. Also, these relationships have unique characteristics, meeting the criterion of being significantly heterogeneous. At the same time, they are imperfectly mobile with inherently varying degrees of cooperation that allow them to produce market offerings efficiently and effectively (Hunt 2010, 422–423).

Morgan and Hunt's (1994) commitment-trust theory of relationship marketing holds that commitment and trust are essential to developing cooperative and collaborative marketing relationships. However, Morgan (2000, p. 483) recognizes that this theory's explanatory power is limited in some respects, particularly the lack of a theoretical framework for the antecedents of commitment and trust. Thus, to more fully understand RM's strategic nature, an expanded theory of trust and commitment based on resource advantage theory is suggested that sheds light on the processes and motivations of relationship building. Morgan (2000) explains:

> The development of commitment, trust, and effective cooperation in marketing relationships depends on three intertwined sets of conditions. First, relationships that provide participants with superior economic benefits will foster effective cooperation and, thus, relationship perseverance and success… A second condition is that parties require the resources of their partners in order to achieve positions of competitive advantage. Indeed, the impetus for each party to enter relationships is to improve its competitiveness by obtaining resources that it does not already have or cannot acquire otherwise. (p. 484)

Relationship-based competitive advantage can be achieved by utilizing relational partnerships and networks to (a) efficiently acquire or develop resources that enhance efficiency; (b) combine primary resources or create complex resources; (c) position resource advantages in competitive situations; (d) maintain and protect resources (Morgan and Hunt 1999). However, managers are cautioned against two possible paths to relationship marketing misadventures. The first is to avoid allowing relationship-based resources from becoming a "strategic hindrance" (Barney 1991) due to poor decisions on its deployment. The second is to avoid allowing exchanges and interactions to become nonreciprocal, resulting in asymmetric dependence upon the relationship for resources and consequent relationship failure (Morgan and Hunt 1999, p. 288).

10.6.5 Consumer Motivation Theories in RM

Sheth and Parvatiyar (1995) (hereafter referred to as S&P) contend that consumers tend to engage in ongoing relationships with marketers due to psychological and sociological motivations of choice reduction. When consumers engage in relational arrangements, they implicitly or explicitly commit to the chosen marketing partner(s). Thus, they are willing to forgo other opportunities available in market-based transactions. Engaging in relationships is akin to making deliberate choice reduction decisions. Purposeful choice reduction is consumers' prevalent, natural, and expected behavior. It is seen in consumer tendencies for repeat purchase; brand and store loyalty; evoked or consideration sets; memberships in clubs or affinity groups; and even the decision to get married whereby one is precluded from seeking out other potential choices. Hence, S&P argue that choice reduction is the basic tenet of relationship marketing that should be considered axiomatic. A predisposition to get into relationships should be taken as axiomatic (Shrivastava and Kale 2003).

S&P invoke a vast array of consumer choice-decision theories—both psychological and sociological—to explain consumer motivations for engaging in relational market behavior. Within consumer behavior studies on consumers' brand loyalty or store loyalty, learning and information processing theories to understand customer repeat purchase and routinized buying behavior date back to the late 1960s and 70s (Hansen 1972; Howard and Sheth 1969; Jacoby and Chestnut 1978). Therefore, S&P contend that the same theories applied in consumer choice also explain choice reduction behavior since both are reductional. They propose that consumers engage in relationships because they want to reduce choices due to cognitive, learning, psychic comfort factors and facilitate:

1. *Simplified problem-solving* – "routinized buying" and "evoked set."
2. *Learning benefits* – "stimulus generalization" and "positive reinforcements."
3. *Information processing and memory* – "simplify" and "rehearse memory."
4. *Perceived risk* – "self-confidence" to reduce "perceived risk."
5. *Cognitive consistency* – reduce "psychic tension."

In essence, consumers engage in relationships in their self-interest to make life simpler and more accessible for them. Also, there are several sociological and institutional reasons for consumers to engage in relational market behavior. They are influenced by friends, family, and other societal institutions. Therefore, they choose to engage in specific relationships to conform to societal norms and expectations arising from:

1. *Family influences*– "power of the family over the individual."
2. *Social & influence groups*– "conforming to group norms."

3. *Reference groups* – "word-of-mouth" from opinion leaders.
4. *Government/civic responsibility* – "welfare expectations," "fear of law."
5. *Religious organizations* – "self-efficacy" and "fear of negative consequences."
6. *Employer influence* – "formal and informal" patronage.
7. *Marketer benefits* – rewards, recognition, experience, and value of programs.

Bagozzi (1995) acknowledges S&P's efforts as a tour de force in RM that lays the intellectual foundation for relationship ideas in consumer markets. He also notes that S&P's article makes several vital connections to ideas from basic research in psychology and sociology. Appraising S&P's propositions, he sums it up thus:

> …The authors advocate that the parties to the relationship should purposefully reduce choices and cultivate long-term relationships because they will improve effectiveness and efficiency of the parties in the relationship… S&P seem to be saying also that any theory of relationship marketing must integrate the psychological side of behavior with the sociological (or, more broadly, with the social). The consumer is both (a) pushed by the need to simplify and make sense of his/her consumption situation, avoid risk, and reduce psychological tension and cognitive dissonance, and (b) pulled by goals with global and local consequences for satisfaction. These motivational and purposive aspects of consumer behavior are inextricably embedded. S&P maintain, in a social context that contains well-defined inhibitors and facilitators, augmenting individual action. (Bagozzi 1995, 272–273)

While S&P's article is widely cited in the marketing literature and beyond, theoretically driven analysis of long-term relationships between consumers and marketers or distributors has remained scant (Moller and Halinen 2000). However, there is some promise in the future for consumer behavior theory-based relationship marketing studies within the services marketing domain, given several common research traditions.

In summary, it can be said that the fragmented nature of theories on the RM school of thinking that evolved within different research traditions poses several problems and also offers many opportunities. First, the multiple research approaches are partly independent and partly overlapping. Secondly, these approaches provide only partial theories or views of the relationship marketing phenomenon. Thirdly, they draw upon different theoretical sources and employ different conceptual frames of reference. And, fourthly, they often focus on issues at different aggregate levels and employ different analysis units.

Therefore, there is considerable opportunity for an integrated and general theory of relationship marketing that encompasses consumer and business relationships and builds upon the theoretical foundations employed by various research traditions. It would also lead to the revitalization of the RM school of thinking towards developing a general marketing theory.

10.7 Revitalizing RM School

To revitalize the RM school of thought, Sheth (2016) proposed a shift on two dimensions: from "share of wallet" to "share of heart" concerning the purpose of RM, and from "managing relationships" with customers to "managing contractual or virtual joint ventures" with customers as the process of RM.

10.7.1 From Share of Wallet to Share of Heart

Existing RM practices, including loyalty programs, bundled offerings, personalized services, KAM, and CRM efforts, have become universal and, therefore, commoditized. Therefore, marketing strategies and tactics designed to gain the share of customer's wallet as a critical metric for RM must give way to winning the "share of heart" as the new metric. It implies bonding with customers on an emotional plane beyond offering the economic or functional value of the product or service. The relationship transcends from business to friendship with customers. It also requires measuring the relationship's strength beyond numerical and financial outcomes. It also goes beyond the TCE as the basis of developing and maintaining the relationship and from a direct contractual relationship governed by contract laws to an implicit friendship governed by passion, purpose, and mutual respect. It will result in at least three new areas of research and practice in RM:

1. **Emotive feedback: the new listening post:** Past practice and research in measuring RM, such as customer lifetime value (CLV), has been numerical, mechanistic, and impersonal. We still do not know what makes consumers tick or their feelings, thoughts, and prejudices about the company and its offerings. It will require restoring emotive research techniques of the seventies such as motivation research (Zaltman 2003; Zaltman and Zaltman 2008; Levy 1985), or the use of brain research (Kenning et al. 2007; Chamberlain and Broderick 2007), storytelling (Brown et al. 2005), metaphor elicitation (Zaltman 1996), and science fiction, as depicted in movies such as Back to the Future and Minority Report.

2. **Purpose-driven: adding meaning in consumption:** A second significant way to win a share of the heart is to make products and brands more meaningful to customers above and beyond ingredients and benefits. Companies often attempt to win the share of heart by sponsoring social causes such as breast cancer, diabetes awareness, etc., but purpose-driven, mindful marketing relationship is much deeper and different than mere support of social causes (Sheth, Sethia, and Srinivas 2011; Malhotra, Lee, and Uslay 2012; Uslay and Erdogan 2014). It enables customers to achieve meaningful life by consuming a product or brand. It may even require encouraging reduced consumption instead of mindless consumption or reducing urban living's hectic pace (Cicek, Ulu, and Uslay 2020). It also requires educating customers about the impact of their choices on society and community and the moral and ethical dilemmas involved in choosing particular products and brands.

3. **Brand communities through social media:** The third area of future research in RM is social media use in developing and nurturing relationships within brand communities. The impact of social media on the development of brand communities have been dramatic (Kaplan and Haenlein 2010; Muniz and O'Guinn 2001). Its interactive nature allows users to be both consumers and producers of information, thus impacting brand assets and corporate reputation. However, there is also a dark side of both unintended and the intended consequences of social media, making it critical for marketers to channelize the customer-company relationship's emotive moods properly.

Social media are analogous to a potent drug that has excellent efficacy but significant side effects. It also has enormous reach with lightning speed that can spread like wildfire and quickly go out of hand, resulting in disastrous consequences. Therefore, being alert with ready responders to crisis management and disaster risk mitigation is critical in managing customer relationships in the age of social media. Developing and nurturing brand communities through social media will require a holistic approach and new capabilities.

10.7.2   From Managing Customers to Joint Venturing with Customers

A second dimension of the shift in revitalizing RM is the formation and governance to joint venturing with customers. A joint venture is a collaborative co-creation of value by all parties through a mutual commitment of resources and complementary capabilities. In a joint venture, the foundation of the relationship is anchored to mutual interdependence, commitment, and shared mission.

In traditional RM, it is usually the supplier who commits resources by investing in key accounts or relationship managers. Customers are free to walk away from the relationship, almost at will, unless they are bound by contracts such as mobile phone services or non-contractual exit barriers such as in installed technology, machines, processes, or people. However, in joint venturing, customers must commit resources (time, money, and capabilities). Also, both parties must accept interdependence instead of dependence in the relationship. Joint venturing with customers does not always require a legal entity formation. In many cases, just social contracts and norms govern the relationship. There are three ways to shift the process from managing customer relationships to joint venturing with customers.

1. **Co-creating value for end-users: the ultimate process:** Sheth et al. (2000) and Vargo and Lusch (2004) have suggested that co-creating value with customers is desirable and necessary as marketing becomes more customer-centric. Similarly, Prahalad and Rangaswamy (2004) assert that value co-creation is a pathway to creating a competitive advantage for a firm. When a firm joint ventures with its customers, co-creation of value becomes the critical mission or goal of the relationship. Formal metrics are needed to

measure its co-creation outcome. Depending on the objectives, they may include metrics relating to cost reduction, quality improvement, product development, or increased revenues and profits. Joint venturing with customers can also invoke the application of intangible resources such as co-branding, co-marketing, co-learning, and co-sharing.

The fundamental perspective in co-creating value is to focus on customer's customers or the ultimate end users. End users have three different customer roles. They are users, payers, and buyers. As users, they look for performance value; as payers, they look for price value; as buyers, they look for personalized service value. Mittal and Sheth (2001) have suggested several ways to create value for end-users. For example, performance value can be created through quality, innovation, and customization. Target costing and lean operations create price value. Easy access, rapid response, and nurturing relationships create service value. Co-creating value for end-users concerning performance, price, and personalization is a helpful framework.

2. **Cross-functional collaboration: hardest to implement:** To co-create value for end-users, cross-functional collaboration, both internal and external, is needed. Unlike the traditional approach of RM, wherein relational responsibilities are vested primarily in key account managers and customer support teams, cross-functional cooperation and collaboration transcend many functions such as legal, finance, IT, operations, engineering, human resources, supply chain, etc. They all have to learn to collaborate within and across the customer and supplier organizations, as was experienced in the transformative relationships between P&G and Walmart, Coca-Cola and McDonald's, and Sears and Whirlpool.

Team performance is assessed according to the objectives of the joint venture above and beyond performance appraisal by their functional supervisors. Like any joint venture, it requires executive sponsorship and a long-term commitment by both the supplier and the customer. In many cultures, the non-contractual relationship between a supplier and a customer often transcends several generations, particularly in family-owned businesses.

3. **Shared value: public-private partnership:** A third significant way to joint venture with customers is to focus on corporate social responsibility (CSR) and economic development (Porter and Kramer, 2006). This public-private partnership ranges from sustainability to micro-financing, education, nutrition, and public health to eradicating poverty and diseases. Large corporate and personal foundations, such as the Bill and Melinda Gates Foundation, McArthur Foundation, and Azim Premji Foundation, are partnering with governments and world agencies such as the World Bank and IMF to contribute toward economic development, especially in emerging markets of Africa, Asia, and Latin America. Such public-private partnerships require a good understanding of public policy as well as the ability to manage competing objectives of capitalistic private enterprises against public sector desire to serve a common cause (Uslay 2019). I requires a shared value mentality and measurement. Managing the triple-bottom-line (profit, people, and the planet) is the goal of both corporations and governments.

10.7.3 Concluding Remarks on Revitalizing RM School of Marketing Thought

Since its first formal appearance as a title of an academic article (Berry 1983), RM grew spectacularly both as a practice and a discipline. It became a major school of thought in marketing with numerous articles in academic journals providing the theoretical foundations of RM (Aijo 1996; Brodie 2016; Harker and Egan 2006; Morgan and Hunt 1994; O'Mailey and Prothero 2004; Bejou and Palmer 2005; Parvatiyar and Sheth 2000; Rao and Perry 2002; Samaha et al. 2014; Tadajewski and Saren 2009). Unfortunately, it has also become synonymous with CRM and database marketing. The focus on "relationship" in RM got relegated to just "marketing." It can be revitalized if it shifts focus from "share of wallet" to "share of heart;" and from "managing customer relationships" to "joint venturing with customers."

 ## 10.8 Evaluation of Relationship Marketing School of Thought

RM school of thought has made remarkable progress within such a short time of its historical evolution. Because of multiple research traditions converging on the core ideas and underlying philosophical underpinnings of RM thinking, it has captured the imagination of a vast number of scholars worldwide. As such, it has seen both a significant number of conceptual and empirical research studies to support various theoretical investigations on the motivations of formation, governance, evaluation, evolution, and dissolution of long-term marketing relationships. This school of thought has focused on the distinctive difference between relational and transactional-focused marketing and all arrangements in-between. Its influence on the overall marketing discipline has been tremendous, but not without controversies and criticisms. Below, we provide our summary evaluation of the RM school of thought.

STRUCTURE: **Are the concepts properly defined and integrated to form a strong nomological network?**

The RM school has relied on well-known concepts and theories from other behavioral sciences, including economics, political science, psychology, and sociology. As such, its theoretical foundations have been strong, particularly on the inter-organizational aspects of RM that are founded on theories in political economy, transaction cost economics, social exchange theory, and relational contracting. In addition, on the consumer relationship side and learning theories, information processing theories, memory, cognitive theories, and group conformance theories have contributed to its theoretical development. Therefore, the basic tenets of the RM school of thought seem to be well-defined and conceptually rich.

However, due to a lack of consensus on the definition of what constitutes relationship marketing, substantial confusion and controversy exist on its ontological stance. Being in a relationship has some broad consensus among scholars, but many cannot distinguish between marketing relationships and relationship marketing. Hence from an ontological point of view, RM school has not matured to create a shared understanding and distinction of the state of its being.

Similarly, from an epistemological position, RM school has considerable divergence. There are "objectivists" who would like to see RM-related measures in the form of observable and measurable behaviors. Simultaneously, many "instrumentalists" are concerned about the affective and emotive mental states of parties in a relationship who want to incorporate the unobservables in their scientific inquiry. There is also no agreement on whether RM outcomes must be measured in economic or non-economic measures.

Although most hypotheses and proposed theories integrate well within each research tradition to generate strong respective nomological networks across research traditions and inquiry domains, they are not integrated. Each has law-like generalizations that partially overlap with other areas and theoretical frameworks. Therefore, from a structure point of view, the RM school of thought could use more integration.

Our score on structure = 7

SPECIFICATION: **Are the relationships specified in a manner to delimit hypotheses, or are they highly contingent?**

Because RM School has emerged from several research traditions and marketing practices ranging from channels, industrial marketing, services marketing, marketing strategy, and database marketing, they do not have a core focus domain. The hypotheses have been quite scattered – specific within some areas but divergent across areas. RM studies on channel and industrial marketing relationships have the highest specificity but less so in services and consumer relationship studies. Many theories applied in relationship marketing are behavioral economics and social psychology; they are specified as contingency theories. Hence, relational behavior in those conditions may be driven by other contingency forces than those hypothesized by the RM school. It is particularly true for those proposed as general or comprehensive theories of relationship marketing.

Overall, many publications in relationship marketing are devoid of specificity in their hypothesis or propositions. Several terms used in the research studies are not specific and open to differing interpretations. It gets accentuated that the behavioral sciences from which many RM theories are drawn have their own specificity limitations.

Our score on specificity = 6

TESTABILITY: **Are the operational definitions provided to ensure testability and intersubjective consensus?**

The RM school is not as strong in this area because of the epistemological divergence on measuring and testing. There is no real consensus on what should be measured—behavioral or psychological, particularly about the outcome measures. Many have chosen to focus only on behavioral outcomes, drawing criticisms regarding whether the phenomenon's nuances have been ignored. Even for independent and mediating or moderating variables, there is a lack of consensus on many constructs' operationalization to explain the phenomenon. Perhaps only some intermediate variables, such as trust and commitment, have an intersubjective agreement. Still, even widely used constructs, such as cooperation and collaboration, have overlapping measurement scales, often confounding hypothesized results.

We believe that this relative lack of testability is because of this school's rapid development into multiple research traditions that developed their interpretations and operational definitions. Only a few constructs have standardized scales, but due to industry context changes and sectoral idiosyncrasies, even these standardized scales have to be adapted and operationally altered, making replicability difficult. The other problem is the proliferation of constructs applied within the RM school, which impacts the development of standardized scales and leads to a lack of parsimony in the theoretical explanations. It looks like everyone in RM school wants to explain everything therein. However, this may be due to the lifecycle of the RM School at this stage.

Our score on testability = 7

EMPIRICAL SUPPORT: **What is the degree of confirmation in terms of empirical support?**

The RM school is quite strong on this criterion. Because it has attracted many scholars from across marketing subdisciplines, extensive research and testing have been reported on the evidence of positive outcomes of RM activities. Also, because behavioral data is relatively more readily available in the current world of connectedness and extensive data systems, practitioners have been willing to share even proprietary databases with academics in the hope of receiving supportive empirical evidence for their activities and programs. The services and database-oriented research traditions of RM have been at the forefront of utilizing data models for empirical testing. It is similar to the trend in developing other disciplines, wherein empirical observations precede theory development. With overwhelming evidence and large-scale empirical research, we believe that relationship marketing is ready for more integrative and parsimonious theory development.

Our score on empirical support = 9

RICHNESS: **How comprehensive and generalizable is the theory?**

The RM school explains the antecedents, mediators, and outcomes of relationship phenomena and relationship partners' motivations. Because from the very beginning, the RM school of thought was interested in the entire process model from formation to governance to performance outcomes to its evolutionary development and exits and terminations in relational partnerships. It has a rich set of proposed theories conceptual models. It also has a very high degree of usefulness in explaining and manipulating the economic behavior of marketing entities considering relational arrangements (such as relationship reward structures, the extent of information sharing, frequency of interactions, role specification and planning processes, access and reconfiguration of resources, and incentive structures).

RM school is linked to the value co-creation process, value-chain and network relationships, and partnering and alliances that allow resource and asset sharing between partners and related entities. RM school is rich in providing explanations for alternative behavior when partners do not cooperate and engage in conflict and opportunistic behavior. RM school has led to many supportive business practices, corporate transformations towards a customer-centric approach, tools, and technologies that help measure various aspects of organizational performance and external partners' value, particularly its customers. RM theories are generalizable beyond the marketing domain into other aspects of business practices, such as strategic management (customer-centricity, alliances, and governance models); finance and accounting (customer valuation, cost of customer acquisition versus retention, relationship equity); and information systems (CRM systems, customer analytics, customer data platforms). RM theories are also generalizable across other social science disciplines and have been studied by behavioral economists, organizational psychologists, and economic sociologists.

Our score on richness = 9

SIMPLICITY: **How easy is it to communicate and implement the theory?**

The fundamental thesis of relationship marketing that to achieve superior economic performance and competitive advantage, firms should identify, develop and nurture relationships with select customers is quite simple and elegant. The key goals and relationship characteristics of customer retention, value, loyalty, trust, commitment, cooperation, interactions, collaboration, co-creation is commonly understood concepts both in organizational and personal settings. Many of these are experienced by individuals in their everyday life. Therefore, they are easy to understand, relate to, implement, and apply in the real world.

However, as was experienced in the early stages of the development of buyer behavior theories, developing a comprehensive or general theory of relationship marketing may be messy due to too many variables and constructs. The good part is that many of these constructs are not that abstract; they can be observed and measured. Nevertheless, numerous process variables make it difficult to communicate and implement. The prevailing lack of parsimony explains the lack of an elegant, comprehensive theory thus far.

Our score on simplicity = 8

Table 10.1 summarizes our evaluation of the RM school of thought. This school is weak in syntax but reasonably strong in semantics and pragmatic aspects of theory building.

Table 10.1 Evaluation of the Relationship Marketing School*

Criterion	Rationale	Score
Structure	It has benefitted from the well-defined concepts of the behavioral sciences from where it has borrowed. Lacks consensus on definition	7
Specification	Highly variant due to multiple research traditions	6
Testability	Specific definitions can be tested, but due to variance in industry context applications, scales are not standardized across domains	7
Empirical support	Extensive research across countries. Availability of objective practice data made model testing possible	9
Richness	Comprehensive process viewpoint and highly generalizable mid-range theories	9
Simplicity	Concepts are easy to communicate and experience but lacks parsimony and elegance for an integrated general theory	8
	TOTAL	46

* Scores range from 1 (poor) to 10 (excellent).

Summary

Over the past three decades, relationship marketing (RM) witnessed spectacular growth as a marketing practice and discipline. It was a paradigm shift away from the transactional marketing approach prevalent in the previous decades of economic liberalism and free-market capitalism, characterized by the competitive and sometimes adversarial stance between buyers and sellers. Instead, it emerged as a school of marketing advocating close-cooperative and collaborative relationships among marketing actors to create and deliver personalized solutions and mutual value to all parties concerned. In addition, it emphasized a greater focus on customer retention, loyalty, and partnering programs to achieve efficiency and effectiveness in pursuing organizational goals and creating competitive advantage. As a result, RM's principles began to resonate with the broader marketing community in the 1990s and beyond, and its popularity among many levels of practitioners, consultants, and academics grew exponentially.

Overall, relationship marketing school is a confabulation of ideas evolving from several traditional marketing schools of thought, including the institutional school, managerial marketing school, organizational dynamics school, social exchange school, functional school, and the buyer (consumer) behavior school of marketing thought. In that respect, it attracted attention from scholars across the spectrum of marketing subject interests, such as channels, business-to-business marketing, supply chain management, marketing strategy, direct and database marketing, product management, and consumer behavior. In addition, it brought to focus new thoughts and perspectives from social sciences, such as transaction cost economics, resource dependencies, resource advantage, social contracting, and socio-psychological considerations for long-term relationships. Thus, it was recognized as one of the major research streams that emerged in the 1980s and continued as an essential social and economic process through the 2000s. Today RM thinking is at the bedrock of new emergent approaches and models of customer-centricity, customer engagement, customer experience, customer relationship management, customer valuation, and value co-creation processes.

However, despite its meteoric rise and promise to significantly contribute to creating a general marketing theory, it got somewhat relegated from the central stage of reshaping the marketing discipline due to the fragmentation of its theories that evolved within different research traditions. This school's multiplicity of research approaches is partly independent and partly overlapping. Each provides only a partial theory or explanation of the phenomenon due to varied theoretical sources and different conceptual frames of reference. Also, they often focus on issues at different aggregate levels employing varying units of analysis. As a result, there appears to be an identity crisis within relationship marketing school, and it needs revitalization.

Therefore, considerable opportunity exists for developing an integrated and general theory of relationship marketing encompassing consumer and business relationships. Such an integrated theory would build upon the theoretical foundations of various research traditions and contribute toward creating a general marketing theory.

Questions for Analysis and Discussion

1. Is relationship marketing a philosophical thought or a narrow practice of "strategies and tactics for segmenting customers to build loyalty," as per the definition of relationship marketing stated on AMA's website? Please elaborate your answer with reasons for the elevation and subsequent relegation of relationship marketing within the marketing discipline.

2. On what aspects do relationship marketing and service-dominant logic converge? How do they complement each other in advancing the idea of transformative processes in an organization and the business ecosystem to create customer value?

3. Did relationship marketing change the dominant paradigm of marketing thinking regarding the centrality focus on market transactions and exchanges? Why are some scholars still unwilling to make value creation the central purpose of marketing instead of transactions and exchanges?

4. Why did several research traditions develop in relationship marketing within a short period? Which of the following theoretical foundations have the most significant impact on the development of relationship marketing theory and thought – (a) transaction cost economics, (b) social exchange and relational contracting, (c) political economy perspective, (d) resource advantage theory, (e) consumer behavior perspective, and (f) services marketing thinking?

5. Does relationship marketing have the potential to lay the foundation for a general theory of marketing? Why or why not?

6. Relationships traditionally involve several fundamental attributes endogenous to human psychology, such as memory (remembering people and events), learning, intelligence, emotions, interactions, and engagements. However, in the modern digital world, many of these endogenous attributes are becoming exogenous to humans, embedded in external devices, such as computers and smart phones, in the form of memory disk, machine learning, artificial intelligence, emoticons, and automated/synthetic engagements. How do these extensions of human attributes transposed into exogenous formats impact the nature of buyer-seller relationships? Will the role of humans diminish in customer relationship formation and consequent trust and commitment?

Epilogue

 ## What Have We Learned Now?

As mentioned in the Prologue, marketing practice and theory has had spectacular growth since the 1980s. Four new schools of thought emerged—services marketing, international marketing, marketing strategy, and relationship marketing. There was also renewed interest in theory development. Several scholars aspired to develop a general theory of marketing, especially after the emergence of relationship marketing.

Journal editors began to focus back on theory development as more and more empirical studies were getting published. Also, the search for law-like generalizations continued. However, major breakthroughs were far and few. Four notable exceptions of breakthrough concepts/theories with potential to form the foundation for a general theory of marketing were: (a) Market Orientation (Kohli & Jaworski 1990; Narver and Slater 1990); (b) Resource Advantage (R-A) Theory of Competition (Hunt & Morgan 1995; Hunt 2000, 2010); (c) the Rule of Three theory by Sheth and Sisodia (2002); and (d) the Service-Dominant (S-D) Logic by Vargo and Lusch (2004; 2017).

The spectacular acceptance of market orientation was contagious. It received universal appeal and acclaim. Hundreds of studies and local adaptations took place all over the world (Kirca, Jayachandran, and Bearden 2005). Similar to Porter's five forces of competition (Porter 1980), market orientation was quickly adopted by the management field and business strategy scholars who needed to go beyond the industrial organization (IO) thinking. Despite its exponential rise and wide acceptance as a construct, no one, including the authors, has attempted to develop a full-blown general theory of marketing or market orientation. It remains a construct and a normative perspective for the organization.

Similarly, the service-dominant (S-D) logic construct advocated focusing on value creation based on competency and not on the outcome, such as a product or service offering. For example, BF Goodrich decided that they are a specialty chemical company and not just a tire maker. This led to exiting the tire business and focusing on its core competency in the aerospace and defense market. Its shareholder value became bigger than Goodyear and Firestone combined. The S-D logic advocates that marketing is a value creation process among all market exchange actors, including the consumers. The co-creation of value between institutions is the key to understanding the market dynamics. Once again, the S-D logic is evolving from a paradigm toward becoming a grand theory given significant interest by other marketing scholars (Bolton 2020; Hunt 2020; Kotler et al. 2021; Ostrom et al. 2021). It quickly became an anchor to many conceptual papers and some empirical studies. There were several international conferences organized around the S-D logic (e.g., The Otago Forum 2005, 2008, 2011) as well as special issues of academic journals (e.g., *Industrial Marketing Management*, *Journal of Business Market Management*, *Journal of Business Research*, *Journal of Marketing Channels*, *Journal of Service Management*, *Marketing Theory*, *Service Science*). The continued stream of publications building the S-D logic toward a general theory of markets (Akaka, Koskela-Houtari, and Vargo 2021; Vargo 2018), promise that it has potential to develop into a full-blown general theory of marketing sometime soon. It transcends many schools of thought and offers a foundational premise to rethink marketing beyond the contours of competition and competitive advantage into processes and capabilities of creating strategic benefits and value co-creation.

The Rule of Three theory suggests that all industries, as they evolve from birth to growth to maturity, ultimately resemble a shopping mall. There are the anchor department stores such as Macy's, JC Penny, and Sears. They are full-line generalists with a one-stop shop. In between the full-line generalists are specialty retailers such as Footlocker, Zara, Lululemon, and many others. Specialists are of two types: those who specialize in a product category and those who specialize in a market segment. The full-line generalists make money through high volume and low margins. The product or market specialists make money through high margins and low volume.

Contrary to economic theory, each market is partly an oligopoly and partly a monopolistic competition. They coexist and complement each other in the short run. If a store has neither a differential advantage to command a high margin nor does it have the scale advantage to command high volume, it is likely to get stuck in the middle between generalists and specialists and fall into the ditch.

As the title of the theory implies, there is room for only three full-line generalists. On the other hand, there is no limit to how many specialists can coexist in a competitive market. The Rule of Three theory has been empirically tested (Uslay, Altintig, and Winsor 2010; Uslay et al. 2017). Findings were strongly supportive and showed that the industry reached an optimal point of profitability with three full-line generalists. The Rule of Three theory matches the consumer process of limiting choices to three brands or levels of quality such as good, better, and best. In other words, an equilibrium is established between the producer's profit motive and the public's welfare motive. It has been used as a framework in antitrust litigation (AT&T's acquisition of Time Warner) as well as mergers and acquisitions (T-Mobile's merger with Sprint).

Finally, the Rule of Three theory suggests that when markets become global, there is a further consolidation of large lateral competitors across the world into three global players, resulting in the Global Rule of Three (Sheth, Uslay, and Sisodia 2020). The Rule of Three theory can become a general theory of marketing from a competition perspective. However, it does not explain regulated monopolies and the lack of industry concentration for industry organized as partnerships or owner-managed businesses. It is, however, possible to examine the impact of regulation, ownership, changing demographics, and technology advances as moderators.

Compared to market orientation, service-dominant (S-D) logic, and the Rule of Three, the resource-advantage (R-A) theory proposed initially by Hunt and Morgan (1995) is far advanced toward becoming a general theory of marketing. Unlike the concepts of market orientation and Rule of Three, which are anchored to *competitive advantage*, R-A theory is anchored to *comparative advantage*, first advocated by David Ricardo (1821) in the context of a nation's advantage. It is also anchored to Edith Penrose's (1959) theory of the growth of the firm. The Hunt–Morgan theory of resource advantage accommodates most of the existing marketing concepts such as market heterogeneity, differential advantage, segmentation, positioning, and brand as an intangible asset. The R-A theory redefines the company's intangible assets, such as know-how, relationships with suppliers and customers, skills, and capabilities. It accommodates both market orientation and service-dominant logic concepts.

Also, the R-A theory integrates knowledge from economics, ethics, sociology, and psychology. Finally, it is very comprehensive. Indeed, Hunt (2010) has done a thorough job of summarizing how other theories and perspectives are incorporated or at least related to parts of the R-A theory (see pp. 394–395).

Finally, and most importantly, the R-A theory provides a framework for competitive strategy and strategic marketing. Despite its comprehensiveness and compelling arguments, the R-A theory is not widely studied. Many young scholars are not even aware of its existence. We think this is due to several reasons. In recent years, there has been a shift toward marketing analytics which relies on large-scale data mining, and through the sifting of a lot of dirt and debris, it finds a few gems of insights. At the same time, scholars in consumer behavior are conditioned by social psychology and lab experiments to test very focused and narrow hypotheses. Finally, most doctoral students are not required to study marketing theory and its evolution.

Unfortunately, marketing scholarship has become more nanoscopic. Younger scholars have the depth like the specialists in medicine but not the breadth of the discipline. However, great scholars are what we refer to as deep generalists. It is critical to know all aspects of marketing in addition to one's specialization.

Today's young scholars learn about the full spectrum of marketing only when they teach the core marketing management classes anchored to mainstream marketing textbooks such as Kotler and Keller (2016). It is compounded by the recent trend of fewer scholars who focus their doctoral dissertation on marketing management or marketing strategy. We sincerely hope that this book can serve as an impetus for the marketing discipline to embrace theory construction as necessary for marketing scholarship as modeling and laboratory experiments. In the table below, we provide a summary of our evaluation scores on metatheory criteria for all 16 schools of marketing thought developed since its inception.

Summary of metatheory evaluation of schools of marketing thought*

Schools of Thought	Metatheory Criteria						
	Structure	Specification	Testability	Empirical Support	Richness	Simplicity	Total
Commodity	3	4	3	6	8	8	32
Functional	5	3	7	7	8	8	38
Regional	7	6	7	7	4	7	38
Institutional	7	7	4	5	5	8	36
Functionalist	7	7	2	3	8	2	29
Managerial	8	7	8	9	9	9	50
Buyer behavior	8	8	6	8	9	8	47
Activist	5	5	4	7	5	6	32
Macromarketing	4	4	6	6	7	4	31
Organizational dynamics	8	8	4	3	5	4	32
Systems	5	8	6	5	8	8	40
Social exchange	8	4	5	5	9	9	40
Marketing strategy	7	7	8	9	9	8	48
Services marketing	7	8	7	7	9	9	47
International marketing	8	7	8	8	8	7	46
Relationship marketing	7	6	7	9	9	8	46

* Scores range from 1 (poor) to 10 (excellent).

References

Aaker, David A. (1991), *Managing Brand Equity: Capitalizing on the Value of a Brand*, New York, NY: The Free Press.

Aaker, David A. and Donald E. Bruzzone (1985), "Causes of Irritation in Advertising", *Journal of Marketing*, 49(Spring), 47–57.

Aaker, David A. and Michael Mills (2001), *Strategic Market Management*, Sydney: Wiley.

Aaker, David and Erich Joachimsthaler (1999), "The Lure of Global Branding", *Harvard Business Review*, November–December, 137–144.

Aaker, Jennifer (1991), "The Negative Attraction Effect? A Study of the Attraction Effect under Judgment and Choice", *ACR North American Advances*, 18(1), 462–469.

Abdul-Muhmin, Alhassan G. (2002), "Effects of Suppliers' Marketing Program Variables on Industrial Buyers' Relationship Satisfaction and Commitment", *Journal of Business and Industrial Marketing*, 17(7), 637–651.

Achrol, Ravi S. (1991), "Evolution of the Marketing Organization: New Forms for Turbulent Environments", *Journal of Marketing*, 55(4), 77–93.

Achrol, Ravi S., and Louis Stern (1988), "Environmental Determinants of Decision-Making Uncertainty in Marketing Channels", *Journal of Marketing Research*, 25(1), 36–50.

Achrol, Ravi Singh, Torger Reve, and Louis W. Stern (1983), "The Environment of Marketing Channel Dyads: a Framework for Comparative Analysis", *Journal of Marketing*, 47(4), 55–67.

Adler, Lee (1966), "Time Lag in New Product Development", *Journal of Marketing*, 30(1), 17–21.

Aijo, Tovio S. (1996), "The Theoretical and Philosophical Underpinnings of Relationship Marketing: Environmental Factors Behind the Changing Marketing Paradigm," *European Journal of Marketing*, 30(2), 8–18.

Akaka, Melissa Archpru, Kaisa Koskela-Huotari, and Steven L. Vargo (2021), "Formalizing service-dominant logic as a general theory of markets: taking stock and moving forward," *AMS Rev* 11, 375–389. https://doi.org/10.1007/s13162-021-00214-y

Akaka, M. A., H. J. Schau, and S. L. Vargo (2013), "The Co-Creation of Value-in-Cultural-Context." in R. W. Belk, L. Price, and L. Peñaloza (Eds.), *Consumer Culture Theory—Research in Consumer Behavior* Emerald Group Publishing Limited, 265–284.

Aksoy, Lerzan, Jens Hogreve, Bart Lariviere, Andrea Ordanini, Chiara Orsingher (2015), "Relative Measures in Service Research," *Journal of Services Marketing*, 29(6/7), 448–452.

Alashban, A. A., L. A. Hayes, G. M. Zinkhan, A. L. Balazs (2002), "International Brand-Name Standardization/Adaptation: Antecedents and Consequences," *Journal of International Marketing*, 10(3), 22–48.

Alba, Joseph W. and J. Wesley Hutchinson (1987), "Dimensions of Consumer Expertise", *Journal of Consumer Research*, 13(March), 411–454.

Albaum, Gerald and Robert A. Peterson (1984), "Empirical Research in International Marketing," *Journal of International Business Studies*, 15(Spring/Summer), 161–173.

Alden, Dana L., Jan-Benedict E.M. Steenkamp, and Rajeev Batra (1999), "Brand Positioning Through Advertising in Asia, North America, and Europe: The Role of Global Consumer Culture," *Journal of Marketing*, 63(January), 75–87.

Alderson, Wroe (1937), "A Marketing View of Competition," *Journal of Marketing*, 1(3), p. 189.

Alderson, Wroe (1945), "Factors Governing the Development of Marketing Channels", in *Marketing Channels*, R. M. Clewett, ed., Homewood, Illinois: Richard D. Irwin, Inc.

Alderson, Wroe (1948), "A Formula for Measuring Productivity in Distribution", *Journal of Marketing*, 12(April), 442–448.

Alderson, Wroe (1949), "Scope and Place of Wholesaling in the United States", *Journal of Marketing*, 14(September), 144–155.

Alderson, Wroe (1954a), "A Functionalist Approach to Competition", in *The Role and Nature of Competition in Our Marketing Economy*, Harvey W. Huegy, ed., Urbana: Bureau of Economic and Business Research, University of Illinois, 40–49.

Alderson, Wroe (1954b), "Factors Governing the Development of Marketing Channels", in *Marketing Channels for Manufactured Products*, Richard Clewett, ed., Homewood, Illinois: Richard D. Irwin, Inc., 5–34.

Alderson, Wroe (1956), "A Functionalist Approach to Consumer Motivation", in *Consumer Behavior and Motivation*, Robert H. Cole, ed., Urbana: Bureau of Economic and Business Research, University of Illinois, 7–24.

Alderson, Wroe (1957), *Marketing Behavior and Executive Action*, Homewood, IL: Richard D. Irwin.

Alderson, Wroe (1958), "The Analytical Framework for Marketing", in *Conference of Marketing Teachers from Far Western States Proceedings*, D. J. Duncan, ed., Berkeley: University of California Press.

Alderson, Wroe (1965), *Dynamic Marketing Behavior: A Functionalist Theory of Marketing*, Homewood, Illinois: Richard D. Irwin, Inc.

Alderson, Wroe and Miles W. Martin (1965), "Toward a Formal Theory of Transactions and Transvections", *Journal of Marketing Research*, 2(May), 117–127.

Alderson, Wroe and Reavis Cox (1948), "Towards a Theory of Marketing", *Journal of Marketing*, 13(October), 137–152.

Aldrich, Howard E. (1979), *Organizations and Environments*, Englewood Cliffs, New Jersey: Prentice-Hall, Inc.

Allport, Gordon W. (1961), *Pattern and Growth in Personality*, New York: Holt, Rinehart and Winston, Inc.

Alqahtani, Nasser and Can Uslay (2020), "Entrepreneurial Marketing and Firm Performance: Synthesis and Conceptual Development", *Journal of Business Research*, 113(May), 62–71.

Alqahtani, Nasser, Can Uslay, and Sengun Yeniyurt (2021), "Entrepreneurial Marketing and Firm Performance: Scale Development, Validation, and Empirical Test", working paper.

Amstutz, Arnold E. (1967), *Computer Simulation of Competitive Market Response*, Cambridge: Massachusetts Institute of Technology, The M.I.T. Press.

Amstutz, Arnold E. (1968), "Systems Analysis for Marketing Management", in *Changing Marketing Systems: Consumer, Corporate and Government Interfaces*, Reed Moyer, ed., Chicago: American Marketing Association, 300–306.

Anand, Punam (1987), "Inducing Franchisees to Relinquish Control: An Attribution Analysis", *Journal of Marketing Research*, 24(May), 215–221.

Anand, Punam and Louis W. Stern (1985), "A Sociopsychological Explanation for Why Marketing Channel Members Relinquish Control", *Journal of Marketing Research*, 22(November), 365–376.

Anderson, Erin M. (1985), "The Salesperson as Outside Agent or Employee: A Transaction Cost Analysis", *Marketing Science*, 4, 234–254.

Anderson, Erin, and Anne T. Coughlan (1987), "International Market Entry and Expansion via Independent or Integrated Channels of Distribution", *Journal of Marketing*, 51(1), 71–82.

Anderson, Erin, and Barton Weitz (1989), "Determinants of Continuity in Conventional Industrial Channel Dyads", *Marketing Science*, 8(4), 310–323.

Anderson, Erin, and Barton Weitz (1992), "The Use of Pledges to Build and Sustain Commitment in Distribution Channels", *Journal of Marketing Research*, 29(1), 18–34.

Anderson, Erin, and David C. Schmittlein (1984), "Integration of the Sales Force: An Empirical Examination", *The Rand Journal of Economics*, 15(3), 385–395.

Anderson, Erin, Leonard M. Lodish, and Barton A. Weitz (1987), "Resource Allocation Behavior in Conventional Channels", *Journal of Marketing Research*, 24(1), 85–97.

Anderson, Erin, Wujin Chu, and Barton A. Weitz (1987), "Industrial Purchasing: An Empirical Exploration of the Buyclass Framework", *Journal of Marketing*, 51(July), 71–86.

Anderson, James C. and James A. Narus (1984), "A Model of the Distributor's Perspective of Distributor-Manufacturer Working Relationships", *Journal of Marketing*, 48 (Fall), 62–74.

Anderson, James C. and James A. Narus (1990), "A Model of Distributor Firm and Manufacturer Firm Working Partnerships," *Journal of Marketing*, 54, 42–58.

Anderson, James C., Håkan Håkansson, and Jan Johanson (1994), "Dyadic Business Relationships within a Business Network Context", *Journal of Marketing*, 58(4), 1–15.

Anderson, Paul F. (1986), "On Method in Consumer Research: A Critical Relativist Perspective", *Journal of Consumer Research*, 13(September), 155–173.

Anderson, Paul F. and Terry M. Chambers (1985), "A Reward/Measurement Model of Organizational Buying Behavior", *Journal of Marketing*, 49 (Spring), 7–23.

Anderson, Paul F. (1982), "Marketing, Strategic Planning, and the Theory of the Firm", *Journal of Marketing*, 46(Spring), 15–26.

Anderson, Paul F. (1983), "Marketing, Scientific Progress, and Scientific Method", *Journal of Marketing*, 47(Fall), 18–31.

Andreasen, Alan R. (1965), "Attitudes and Customer Behavior: A Decision Model", in *New Research in Marketing*, Lee E. Preston, ed., Berkeley: Institute of Business and Economic Research, University of California, 1–16.

Andreasen, Alan R. (1975), *The Disadvantaged Consumer*, New York: The Free Press.

Andreasen, Alan R. (1977), "A Taxonomy of Consumer Satisfaction/Dissatisfaction Measures", in *Conceptualization and Measurement of Consumer Satisfaction and Dissatisfaction*, H. Keith Hunt, ed., Cambridge, Massachusetts: Marketing Science Institute, 11–35.

Andreasen, Alan R. (1982), "Disadvantaged Hispanic Consumers: A Research Perspective and Agenda", *The Journal of Consumer Affairs*, 16 (Summer), 46–61.

Andronikidis, Andreas, and Victoria Bellou (2010), "Verifying Alternative Measures of the Service-Quality Construct: Consistencies and Contradictions," *Journal of Marketing Management*, 26(5/6), 570–587.

Ansoff, H. Igor (1957), "Strategies for Diversification," *Harvard Business Review*, 35(5), 113–124.

Apte, Suhas and Jagdish N. Sheth (2016), *Sustainability Edge: How to Drive Top-Line Growth with Triple-Bottom-Line Thinking*, University of Toronto Press.

Armstrong, Gary M., C. L. Kendall, and Frederick A. Russ (1975), "Applications of Consumer Information Processing Research to Public Policy Issues", *Communications Research*, 2, 232–245.

Armstrong, Gary M., Metin N. Gurol, and Frederick A. Russ (1979), "Detecting and Correcting Deceptive Advertising", *Journal of Consumer Research*, 6(December), 237–246.

Arndt, Johan (1967), *Word of Mouth Advertising: A Review of the Literature*, New York: Advertising Research Foundation, Inc.

Arndt, Johan (1978), "How Broad Should the Marketing Concept Be?", *Journal of Marketing*, 42(January), 101–103.

Arndt, Johan (1979) "Toward a Concept of Domesticated Markets," *Journal of Marketing*, 43(4), 69–75.

Arndt, Johan (1983), "The Political Economy Paradigm: Foundation for Theory Building in Marketing", *Journal of Marketing*, 47(4), 44–54.

Arndt, Johan (1985), "On Making Marketing Science More Scientific: Role of Orientations, Paradigms, Metaphors, and Puzzle Solving", *Journal of Marketing*, 49(Summer), 11–23.

Arnett, Dennis, Steve German, and Shelby Hunt (2003), "The Identity Salience Model of Relationship Marketing Success: The Case of Nonprofit Marketing", *Journal of Marketing*, 67(2), 89–105.

Ashby, Harold J., Jr. (1973), "The Black Consumer", in *New Consumerism: Selected Readings*, William T. Kelley, ed., Columbus, Ohio: Grid, Inc., 149–176.

Aspinwall, L., (1958), "The Characteristics of Goods and Parallel Systems Theories", in *Managerial Marketing*, Eugene J. Kelley and William Lazer, Eds., Homewood, Illinois: Richard D. Irwin, Inc., 434–450.

Ataman, M. Berk, Harald J. Van Heerde, and Carl F. Mela (2010), "The Long-Term Effect of Marketing Strategy on Brand Sales," *Journal of Marketing Research*, 47(5), 866–882.

Aulakh, Preet S. and Masaaki Kotabe (1993), "An Assessment of Theoretical and Methodological Development in International Marketing: 1980–1990," *Journal of International Marketing*, 1(2), 5–28.

Bagozzi, Richard P. (1974), "Marketing as an Organized Behavioral System of Exchange", *Journal of Marketing*, 38(October) 4, 77–81.

Bagozzi, Richard P. (1975), "Marketing as Exchange", *Journal of Marketing*, 39(October) 4, 32–39.

Bagozzi, Richard P. (1977), "Marketing at the Societal Level: Theoretical Issues and Problems", in *Macro-Marketing: Distributive Processes from a Societal Perspective*, Charles C. Slater, ed., Boulder: Business Research Division, Graduate School of Business Administration, University of Colorado, 6–51.

Bagozzi, Richard P. (1978), "Marketing as Exchange: A Theory of Transactions in the Marketplace", *American Behavioral Scientist*, 21(March/April) 4, 535–556.

Bagozzi, Richard P. (1979), "Toward a Formal Theory of Marketing Exchanges", in *Conceptual and Theoretical Developments in Marketing*, O. C. Ferrell, Stephen W. Brown, and Charles W. Lamb, Jr., eds., Chicago: American Marketing Association, 431–447.

Bagozzi, Richard P. (1984), "A Prospectus for Theory Construction in Marketing", *Journal of Marketing*, 48(Winter), 11–29.

Bagozzi, Richard P. (1986), *Principles of Marketing Management*, Chicago: Science Research Associates.

Bagozzi, Richard P. (1995), "Reflections on Relationship Marketing in Consumer Markets", *Journal of the Academy of Marketing Science*, 23(4), 272–277.

Balabanis, George and A. Diamantopoulos (2004), "Domestic Country Bias, Country-of-Origin Effects, and Consumer Ethnocentrism: A Multidimensional Unfolding Approach", *Journal of the Academy of Marketing Science*, 32(1), 80–95.

Balabanis, George and Adamantios Diamantopoulos (2008), "Brand Origin Identification by Consumers: A Consumer Classification Perspective", *Journal of International Marketing*, 16(1), 39–71.

Balderston, F. (1964), "Design of Marketing Channels" in *Theory in Marketing*, Reavis Cox, Wroe Alderson, and Stanley J. Shapiro, eds., Homewood, Illinois: Richard D. Irwin, Inc., 163–175.

Baligh, Helmy H. and Leon E. Richartz (1967), *Vertical Market Structures*, Boston: Allyn and Bacon, Inc.

Banks, Seymour (1968), "A Non-Systematic Look at Systems: A Triumph of Optimism over Experience", in Robert L. King, ed., *Marketing and the New Science of Planning*, Chicago: American Marketing Association, 24–28.

Barclay, Donald W. and Brock Smith (1997), "The Effects of Organizational Differences and Trust on the Effectiveness of Selling Partner Relationships", *Journal of Marketing*, 61(1), 3–21.

Barksdale, H.C. (1980), "Wroe Alderson's Contributions to Marketing Theory", in *Theoretical Developments in Marketing*, Charles W. Lamb, Jr., and Patrick M. Dunne, eds., Chicago: American Marketing Association, 1–4.

Barney, Jay (1991), "Firm Resources and Sustained Competitive Advantage", *Journal of Management*, 17(1), 99–120.

Bartels, Robert (1951), "Can Marketing Be a Science?", *Journal of Marketing*, 15(January), 319–328.

Bartels, Robert (1962), *The Development of Marketing Thought*, Homewood, Illinois: Richard D. Irwin, Inc.

Bartels, Robert (1965), "Development of Marketing Thought: A Brief History", in *Science in Marketing*, George Schwartz, ed., New York: John Wiley & Sons, Inc., 47–69.

Bartels, Robert (1968a), "Are Domestic and International Marketing Dissimilar?", *Journal of Marketing*, 32(July), 56–61.

Bartels, Robert (1968b), "The General Theory of Marketing", *Journal of Marketing*, 32(January), 29–33.

Bartels, Robert (1970), *Marketing Theory and Metatheory*, Homewood, Illinois: Richard D. Irwin, Inc.

Bartels, Robert (1974), "The Identity Crisis in Marketing", *Journal of Marketing*, 38(October), 73–76.

Bass, Frank M. (1969), "A New Product Growth Model for Consumer Durables", *Management Science*, 15(January), 215–227.

Bass, Frank M., Robert D. Buzzell, Mark R. Greene, William Lazer, Edgar A. Pessemier, Donald L. Shawver, Abraham Shuchman, Chris A. Theodore, George W. Wilson, eds., (1961), *Mathematical Models and Methods in Marketing*, Homewood, Illinois: Richard D. Irwin, Inc.

Bateson, John E. G. (1979), "Why We Need Service Marketing," in *Conceptual and Theoretical Developments in Marketing*, O. C. Ferrell, S. W. Brown and C. W. Lamb, eds., Chicago, American Marketing Association, 131–146.

Batra, R., V. Ramaswamy, D.L. Alden, J-E.B.M. Steenkamp, and S. Ramachander (2000), "Effects of Brand Local/Non-Local Origin on Consumer Attitudes in Developing Countries", *Journal of Consumer Psychology*, 9, 83–95.

Bauer, Raymond A. (1960), "Consumer Behavior as Risk Taking", in *Dynamic Marketing for a Changing World*, Robert S. Hancock, ed., Chicago: American Marketing Association, 389–398.

Bauer, Raymond A. and Scorr M. Cunningham (1970), *Studies in the Negro Market*, Cambridge, Massachusetts: Marketing Science Institute.

Bauer, Raymond A. and Stephen A. Greyser (1967), "The Dialogue That Never Happens", *Harvard Business Review*, 45(November–December), 186–190.

Bayus, Barry L., Sanjay Jain, and Ambar G. Rao (1997), "Too little, Too Early: Introduction Timing and New Product Performance in the Personal Digital Assistant Industry," *Journal of Marketing Research,* 34(1,) 50–63.

Beem, Eugene R. (1973), "The Beginnings of the Consumer Movement", in *New Consumerism: Selected Readings*, William T. Kelley, ed., Columbus, Ohio: Grid, Inc., 13–25.

Beier, Frederick J. and Louis W. Stern (1969), "Power in the Channel of Distribution", in *Distribution Channels: Behavioral Dimensions*, Louis W. Stern, ed., Boston: Houghton Mifflin Company, 92–116.

Bejou, David and Adrian Palmer (2005), *The Future of Relationship Marketing*, Binghampton, NY: Best Business Books.

Belk, Russell W. (1974), "An Exploratory Assessment of Situational Effects in Buyer Behavior", *Journal of Marketing*, 38, 156–163.

Bell, Jim, Rod McNaughton, and Stephen Young (2001), "Born-Again Global Firms: An Extension to the 'Born-Global' Phenomenon," *Journal of International Management*, 7(3), 173–189.

Bell, Martin L. (1966), *Marketing: Concepts and Strategy*, Boston: Houghton Mifflin Company.

Bell, Simon J., Seigyoung Auh, and Karen Smalley (2005), "Customer Relationship Dynamics: Service Quality and Customer Loyalty in the Context of Varying Levels of Customer Expertise and Switching Costs", *Journal of the Academy of Marketing Science*, 33(2), 169–183.

Bennett, Peter D. (1965), *Marketing and Economic Development*, Chicago: American Marketing Association.

Bernini, M., J. Du, and J. Love (2016), "Explaining Intermittent Exporting: Exit and Conditional Re-Entry in Export Markets," *Journal of International Business Studies*, 47(9), 1058–1076.

Berry, Lenoard, Tracey S. Danaher, Lerzan Aksoy, Timothy Keiningham (2020), Service Safety in the Pandemic Age", *Journal of Service Research*, 23(4), 391–395.

Berry, Leonard (1980), "Services Marketing is Different," *Business*, 30(May–June), 24–29.

Berry, Leonard and A. Parasuraman (1993), "Building a New Academic Field – The Case of Services Marketing", *Journal of Retailing*, 69(1), 13–60.

Berry, Leonard L. (1980), "Services Marketing is Different", *Business*, 30(May–June), 24–29.

Berry, Leonard L. (1983), Relationship Marketing, In L. L. Berry, G. L. Shostack, and G. D. Upah eds., *Emerging Perspectives on Service Marketing*, 25–28, Chicago: American Marketing Association.

Berry, Leonard L. (1995), "Relationship Marketing of Services – Growing Interest, Emerging Perspectives", *Journal of the Academy of Marketing Science*, 23(4), 236–245.

Berry, Leonard L. (2002), "Relationship Marketing of Services Perspectives from 1983 and 2000", *Journal of Relationship Marketing*, 1(1), 59–77.

Bertalanffy, Ludvig Von (1968), *General System Theory*, New York: George Braziller, Inc.

Bettman, James R. (1979), *An Information Processing Theory of Consumer Choice*, Reading, Massachusetts: Addison-Wesley Publishing Company, Inc.

Bharadwaj, Sundar G. and P. Rajan Varadarajan (2005), "Toward an Integrated Model of Business Performance", *Review of Marketing Research*, 1(1), 207–243.

Bhattacharya, C. B., and Ruth N. Bolton (2000), "Relationship Marketing in Mass Markets", in *Handbook of Relationship Marketing*, Jagdish N. Sheth and Atul Parvatiyar (Eds.), 327–354.

Biehal, Gabriel and Dipankar Chakravarti (1986), "Consumers' Use of Memory and External Information in Choice: Macro and Micro Perspectives", *Journal of Consumer Research*, 12(March), 382–405.

Biggadike, Ralph (1981), "The Contributions of Marketing to Strategic Management", *The Academy of Management Review*, 6(4), 621.

Bilkey, W.J. and E. Nes (1982), "Country-of-Origin Effects on Product Evaluations", *Journal of International Business*, 13, 89–99.

Black, William C., Lyman E. Ostlund, and Robert A. Westbrook (1985), "Spatial Demand Models in an Intrabrand Context", *Journal of Marketing*, 49(Summer), 106–113.

Blair, Edward and Kenneth P. Uhl (1977), "Wroe Alderson and Modern Marketing Theory", in *Macro-Marketing: Distributive Processes From a Societal Perspective*, Charles C. Slater, eds., Boulder: Business Research Division, Graduate School of Business Administration, University of Colorado.

Blattberg, Robert C. and Subrata K. Sen (1976), "Market Segments and Stochastic Brand Choice Models", *Journal of Marketing Research*, 13(February), 34–45.

Blau, Peter M. (1960), "A Theory of Social Integration," *American Journal of Sociology*, 65(6), 545–556.

Blau, Peter M. (1964), "Justice in Social Exchange", *Sociological Inquiry*, 34(2), 193–206.

Blenkhorn, David L., and Peter M. Banting (1991), "How Reverse Marketing Changes Buyer-Seller Roles", *Industrial Marketing Management*, 20(3), 185–191.

Bloch, Peter H., D. Sherrell, and Nancy M. Ridgway (1986), "Consumer Search: An Extended Framework", *Journal of Consumer Research*, 13(June), 119–126.

Blozan, William and Paul Prabhaker (1984), "Notes on Aggregation Criteria in Market Segmentation", *Journal of Marketing Research*, 21(August), 332–335.

Boddewyn, Jean J. (1981), "Comparative Marketing: The First Twenty-Five Years", *Journal of International Business Studies*, 12(Spring/Summer), 61–79.

Boles, James, Thomas Brashear, Danny Bellenger, and Hiram Barksdale (2000), "Relationship Selling Behaviors: Antecedents and Relationship with Performance", *Journal of Business* and *Industrial Marketing*, 15(2–3), 141–153.

Bolton, Ruth N. (2020), First steps to creating high impact theory in marketing. *AMS Rev* 10, 172–178. https://doi.org/10.1007/s13162-020-00181-w

Bolton, Ruth N., Katherine N. Lemon, and Peter C. Verhoef (2004), "The Theoretical Underpinnings of Customer Asset Management: A Framework and Propositions for Future Research", *Journal of the Academy of Marketing Science*, 32(3), 271–292.

Bonoma, Thomas V. and Gerald Zaltman, Eds. (1978), *Organizational Buying Behavior*, Chicago: American Marketing Association.

Bonoma, Thomas V., and Wesley J. Johnston (1978), "The Social Psychology of Industrial Buying and Selling", *Industrial Marketing Management*, 7(4), 213–224.

Bonoma, Thomas V., Richard Bagozzi, and Gerald Zaltman (1978), "The Dyadic Paradigm with Specific Application Toward Industrial Marketing", in *Organizational Buying Behavior*, Thomas V. Bonoma and Gerald Zaltman, eds, Chicago: American Marketing Association, 49–66.

Borden, Neil H. (1964), "The Concept of the Marketing Mix", *Journal of Advertising Research*, 4(June), 2–7.

Boston Consulting Group (1970), *Perspectives on Experience*, Boston, MA: Boston Consulting Group.

Boulding, Kenneth (1956), "General Systems Theory — The Skeleton of Science", *Management Science*, 2(April), 197–208.

Boulding, William, Ruskin Morgan, and Richard Staelin (1997), "Pulling the Plug to Stop the New Product Drain", *Journal of Marketing Research*, 34(1), 164–176.

Bourne, Francis S. (1957), "Group Influence in Marketing and Public Relations", in *Some Applications of Behavioral Research*, Rensis Likert and Samuel P. Hayes, Jr., Eds., Paris: United Nations Educational, Scientific and Cultural Organization, 207–257.

Bourne, Francis S. (1965), "Group Influence in Marketing and Public Relations", in *Dimensions of Consumer Behavior*, J. V. McNeal, ed., New York: Appleton-Century-Crofts, 137–146.

Bowman, Douglas, and Das Narayandas (2001), "Managing Customer-Initiated Contacts with Manufacturers: The Impact on Share of Category Requirements and Word-of-Mouth Behavior", *Journal of Marketing Research*, (38)3, 281–297.

Boyd, Eric D., Rajesh Chandy, and Marcus Cunha Jr. (2010), "When Do Chief Marketing Officers Affect Firm Value? A Customer Power Explanation", *Journal of Marketing Research*, 47(August), 1162–1176.

Bradley, M. Frank. (1987), "Nature and Significance of International Marketing: A Review," *Journal of Business Research*, 15, 205–219.

Brandenburger, Adam M. and Barry Nalebuff (1996), *Co-opetition*, New York: Currency-Doubleday.

Brettel, Malte, Andreas Engelen, Florian Heinemann, and Pakpachong Vadhanasindhu (2008), "Antecedents of Market Orientation: A Cross-Cultural Comparison", *Journal of International Marketing*, 16(2), 84–119.

Breyer, Ralph F. (1934), *The Marketing Institution*, New York: McGraw-Hill Book Co.

Brien, Richard H. (1968), "Marketing Information Systems in Practice: The User's View", in *Marketing and the New Science of Planning*, Robert L. King, ed., Chicago: American Marketing Association, 172–175.

Brien, Richard H. and James E. Stafford (1968), "Marketing Information Systems: A New

Dimension for Marketing Research", *Journal of Marketing*, 32(July), 19–23.

Britt, Stewart Henderson (1974), "Standardizing Marketing for the International Market", *Columbia Journal of World Business*, (Winter), 39–45.

Brodie, Roderick J. (2016), "Enhancing Theory Development in the Domain of Relationship Marketing: How to Avoid the Danger of Getting Stuck in the Middle", *Journal of Services Marketing*, 31(1), 20–23.

Brodie, Roderick J., Nicole Coviello, Richard Brookes, and Victoria Little (1997), "Towards a Paradigm Shift in Marketing? An Examination of Current Marketing Practices", *Journal of Marketing Management*, 13(5), 383–406.

Brown, George H. (1952–1953), "Brand Loyalty — Fact or Fiction?", *Advertising Age*, 23(June 9), 53–55; (June 30), 45–47; (July 14), 54–56; (July 28), 46–48; (August 11), 56–58; (September 1), 44–48; (September 22), 80–82; (October 6), 82–86; (December 1), 76–79; 24(January 26), 75–76.

Brown, James R. and Ralph L. Day (1981), "Measures of Manifest Conflict in Distribution Channels", *Journal of Marketing Research*, 18(August) 3, 263–274.

Brown, John Seely, Stephen Denning, Katalina Groh, and Laurence Prusak (2005), *Storytelling in Organizations: Why Storytelling is Transforming 21st Century Organizations and Management*, New York: Routledge.

Brown, Stephen W. and Raymond Fisk (1984), *Marketing Theory: Distinguished Contributions*, New York: John Wiley & Sons, Inc.

Bruce, Norris I., Natasha Zhang Foutz, and Ceren Kolsarici (2012), "Dynamic Effectiveness of Advertising and Word of Mouth in Sequential Distribution of New Products", *Journal of Marketing Research*, 49(4), 469–486.

Bucklin, Louis P. (1962), "Retail Strategy and the Classification of Consumer Goods", *Journal of Marketing*, 27(October), 50–55.

Bucklin, Louis P. (1965), "Postponement, Speculation and the Structure of Distribution Channels", *Journal of Marketing Research*, 2(February), 26–31.

Bucklin, Louis P. (1966), *A Theory of Distribution Channel Structure*, Berkeley: Institute of Business and Economic Research, University of California.

Bucklin, Louis P. and James M. Carman (1974), "Vertical Market Structure Theory and the Health Care Delivery System", in *Marketing Analysis for Societal Problems*, Jagdish N. Sheth and Peter L. Wright, eds., Urbana-Champaign: Bureau of Economic and Business Research, College of Commerce and Business Administration, University of Illinois, 7–41.

Bullock, Henry A. (1961), "Consumer Motivations in Black and White", *Harvard Business Review*, 39 (May–June), 89–104; (July–August), 110–124.

Burrough, Bryan and John Helyar (1989), *Barbarians at the Gate: The Fall of RJR Nabisco*, New York, NY: Harper & Row.

Burt, Ronald S. (2000), "The Network Structure of Social Capital," *Research in Organizational Behavior*, 22, 345–423.

Butler, Ralph Starr (1923), *Marketing and Merchandising*, New York: Alexander Hamilton Institute.

Buttle, Francis (1996), Relationship Marketing: Theory and Practice, London: Paul Chapman.

Buzzell, Robert D. (1963), "Is Marketing a Science", *Harvard Business Review*, 41(January/February), 32–40, 166–170.

Buzzell, Robert D. (1968), "Can You Standardize Multinational Marketing?", *Harvard Business Review*, 46(November/December), 102–113.

Buzzell, Robert D. (1981), "Are There 'Natural' Market Structures?" *Journal of Marketing*, 45(Winter), 42–51.

Buzzell, Robert D. (2004), "The PIMS Program of Strategy Research: A Retrospective Appraisal", *Journal of Business Research*, 57(May), 478–83.

Buzzell, Robert D. and Bradley T. Gale (1987), *The PIMS Principles: Linking Strategy to Performance.* New York: The Free Press.

Buzzell, Robert D., Bradley T. Gale, and Ralph GM Sultan (1975), "Market Share-a Key to Profitability", *Harvard Business Review*, 53(1), 97–106.

Cadotte, Ernest R. and Louis W. Stern (1979), "A Process Model of Interorganization Relations in Marketing Channels", in *Research in Marketing*, Jagdish N. Sheth, Ed., Volume 2, Greenwich, Connecticut: JAI Press, Inc., 127–158.

Cadotte, Ernest R., Robert B. Woodruff, and Roger L. Jenkins (1987), "Expectations and Norms in Models of Consumer Satisfaction", *Journal of Marketing Research*, 24(August), 305–314.

Cady, John (1982), "Reasonable Rules and Rules of Reason: Vertical Restrictions on Distributors", *Journal of Marketing*, 46(Summer), 27–37.

Calantone, Roger, David A. Griffith, and Goksel Yalcinkaya (2006), "An Empirical Examination of a Technology Adoption Model for the Context of China, *Journal of International Marketing*, 14(4), 1–27.

Cannon, Joseph P., and Narakesari Narayandas, (2000), "Relationship Marketing in Mass Markets", in *Handbook of Relationship Marketing*, Jagdish N. Sheth and Atul Parvatiyar (Eds.), Thousand Oaks, CA: Sage, 407–430.

Caplovitz, David (1963), *The Poor Pay More: Consumer Practices of Low-Income Families*, New York: The Free Press of Glencoe.

Capon, Noel, John U. Farley, and Scott Hoenig (1990), "Determinants of Financial Performance: a Meta-Analysis", *Management Science*, 36(10), 1143–1159.

Cardozo, Richard N., and David K. Smith (1983), "Applying Financial Portfolio Theory to Product Portfolio Decisions: An Empirical Study", *Journal of Marketing*, 47(2), 110–119.

Carman, James (1973), "On the Universality of Marketing", *Journal of Contemporary Business*, 2(Autumn), 1–16.

Carpenter, Gregory S., and Kent Nakamoto (1989), "Consumer Preference Formation and Pioneering Advantage", *Journal of Marketing Research*, 26(3), 285–298.

Carson, Rachel L. (1962), *Silent Spring*, Boston, MA: Houghton Mifflin Company.

Cash, Harold C. and W.J.E. Crissy (1958), *A Point of View for Salesmen, The Psychology of Selling, Volume 1*, New York: Personnel-Development Associates.

Cattin, Phillippe. Alain Jolibert, and Colleen Lohnes (1982), A Cross-Cultural Study of "Made in" Concepts, *Journal of International Business Studies*, 13(3), 131–141.

Cavusgil, S. Tamer and John R. Nevin (1981), "State-of-the-art in International Marketing: An Assessment", in Ben M. Enis and Kenneth J. Roering, eds., *Review of Marketing*, Chicago, IL: American Marketing Association, 195–216.

Chamberlain, Laura and Amanda J. Broderick (2007), "The Application of Physiological Observation Methods to Emotion Research", *Qualitative Market Research*, 10(2), 199–216.

Chandler, Jennifer D. and Stephen L. Vargo (2011), "Contextualization and Value-in-Context: How Context Frames Exchange", *Marketing Theory*, 11(1), 35–49.

Chandrasekaran, Deepa and Gerard J. Tellis (2008), "Global Takeoff of New Products: Culture, Wealth, or Vanishing Differences?" *Marketing Science*, 27(5), 844–860.

Chandy, Rajesh K., and Gerard J. Tellis (2000), "The Incumbent's Curse? Incumbency, Size, and Radical Product Innovation", *Journal of Marketing*, 64(3), 1–17.

Chao, P. (1993) "Partitioning country-of-origin effects: consumer evaluations of a hybrid product", *Journal of International Business Studies*, 24(2), 291–306.

Chase, Stuart and F. J. Schlink (1927), *Your Money's Worth: A Study in the Waste of the Consumer's Dollar*, New York: The Macmillan Company.

Chen, Homin, and Tain-Jy Chen (2003), "Governance Structures in Strategic Alliances: Transaction Cost Versus Resource-Based Perspective", *Journal of World Business*, 38(1), 1–14.

Chicago: American Marketing Association, 116–119.

Childers, Terry L. and Robert W. Ruekert (1982), "The Meaning and Determinants of Cooperation Within an Interorganizational Marketing Network", in *Marketing Theory: Philosophy of Science Perspectives*, Ronald F. Bush and Shelby D. Hunt, eds.

Chowdhury, Humayun Kabir and Jashim Uddin Ahmed (2009) "An examination of the effects of partitioned country of origin on consumer product quality perceptions", *International Journal of Consumer Studies* 33 (July), 496–502.

Christy, Richard, Gordon Oliver, and Joe Penn (1996), "Relationship Marketing in Consumer Markets", *Journal of Marketing Management*, 12(1–3), 175–187.

Chung, H.F.L. (2003), "International Standardization Strategies: The Experiences of Australian and New Zealand Firms Operating in the Greater China Markets", *Journal of International Marketing*, 11(3), 48–82.

Cicek, Mesut, Sevincgul Ulu, and Can Uslay, (2020) "The Impact of the Slow City Movement on Place Authenticity, Entrepreneurial Opportunity, and Economic Development", *Journal of Macromarketing*, 39(4), 400–414.

Clark, Fred E. (1922), *Principles of Marketing*, New York: The Macmillan Company.

Clark, Lincoln H., Ed. (1954), *Consumer Behavior (Volume 1): The Dynamics of Consumer Reaction*, New York: New York University Press.

Clark, Lincoln H., Ed. (1955), *Consumer Behavior (Volume 2): The Life Cycle and Consumer Behavior*, New York: New York University Press.

Clark, Lincoln H., Ed. (1958), *Consumer Behavior (Volume 3): Research on Consumer Reactions*, New York: Harper and Brothers, Publishers.

Coase, Ronald (1937), "The Nature of the Firm", *Economica*, 4(16), 386–405.

Coase, Ronald H. (1937), "Some Notes on Monopoly Price," *The Review of Economic Studies*, 5(1), 17–31.

Collins, James C. (2001), *Good to Great: Why Some Companies Make the Leap… and Others Don't*, HarperCollins.

Converse, Paul D. (1943), *A Study of Retail Trade Areas in East Central Illinois*, Urbana: University of Illinois Press.

Converse, Paul D. (1949), "New Laws of Retail Gravitation", *Journal of Marketing*, 14(October), 379–84.

Converse, Paul D. (1959), *The Beginning of Marketing Thought in the United States*, University of Texas: Bureau of Business Research.

Converse, Paul D. and Harvey Huegy (1940), *The Elements of Marketing*, New York: Prentice-Hall, Inc.

Cook Jr, Victor J. (1983), "Marketing Strategy and Differential Advantage", *Journal of Marketing*, 47(2), 68–75.

Cooper, Lee G. (1987), "Do We Need Critical Relativism?" *Journal of Consumer Research*, 14(June), 126–127.

Copeland, Melvin T. (1923), "The Relation of Consumers' Buying Habits to Marketing Methods", *Harvard Business Review*, 1(April), 282–289.

Copeland, Melvin T. (1925), *Principles of Merchandising*, Chicago: A. W. Shaw Co.

Coughlan, Anne T. (1985), "Competition and Cooperation in Marketing Channel Choice: Theory and Application," *Marketing Science*, 4(2), 110–129.

Cox, Donald F., Ed. (1967), *Risk Taking and Information Handling in Consumer Behavior*, Boston: Division of Research, Graduate School of Business Administration, Harvard University.

Cox, Reavis, Charles S. Goodman, and Thomas C. Fichandler (1965), *Distribution in a High-Level Economy*, Englewood Cliffs, New Jersey: Prentice-Hall, Inc.

Craig, C. Samuel and Susan P. Douglas (1997) "Managing the Transnational Value Chain: Strategies for Firms from Emerging Markets", *Journal of International Marketing*, 5(3), 71–84.

Craig, Samuel C. and Susan P. Douglas (2000), "Configural Advantage in Global Markets", *Journal of International Marketing*, 8(1), 6–21.

Cravens, David W. and Karen S. Cravens (2000), "Relationship Marketing in Mass Markets", in *Handbook of Relationship Marketing*, in Jagdish N. Sheth and Atul Parvatiyar (Eds.), Thousand Oaks, CA: Sage, 431–456.

Crick, Dave (2004), "U.K. SMEs' Decision to Discontinue Exporting: An Exploratory Investigation into Practices Within the Clothing Industry", *Journal of Business Venturing*, 19(4), 561–587.

Crick, Dave and Marian V. Jones (2000), "Small High-Technology Firms and International High-Technology Markets", *Journal of International Marketing*, 8(2), 63–85.

Crick, Dave and Crick, J. (2016), The First Export Order: A Marketing Innovation Revisited," *Journal of Strategic Marketing*, 24, 77–89.

Cron, William L. and John W. Slocum, Jr. (1986), "The Influence of Career Stages on Salespeople's Job Attitudes, Work Perceptions, and Job Performance", *Journal of Marketing Research*, 23(May), 119–129.

Cronin, Joseph J. and Steven A. Taylor (1992), "Measuring Service Quality: A Reexamination and Extension", *Journal of Marketing*, 56(July), 55–68.

Cronin, Joseph J. and Steven A. Taylor (1994), "SERPERF Versus SERVQUAL: Reconciling Performance-Based and Perceptions-Minus-Expectations Measurement of Service Quality", *Journal of Marketing*, 58(January), 125–131.

Crosby, Lawrence A. and James R. Taylor (1982), "Consumer Satisfaction With Michigan's Container Deposit Law – An Ecological Perspective", *Journal of Marketing*, 46(Winter), 47–60.

Crosby, Lawrence A., Kenneth R. Evans, and Deborah Cowles (1990), "Relationship Quality in Services Selling: An Interpersonal Influence Perspective", *Journal of Marketing*, 54(3), 68–81.

Cuervo-Cazurra, A. and R. Ramamurti, (2014), *Understanding Multinationals from Emerging Markets*, Cambridge University Press.

Cunningham, Ross M. (1956), "Brand Loyalty-What, Where, How Much?" *Harvard Business Review*, 34(January/February), 116–128.

Cunningham, William H., and TS Robertson (1983), "Marketing Strategy-From the Editor," 47(2), 5–6.

Cyert, Richard M. and James G. March (1963), *A Behavioral Theory of the Firm*, Englewood Cliffs, New Jersey: Prentice-Hall, Inc.

Czepiel, John A., Larry J. Rosenberg, and Carol Suprenant (1980), "The Development of Thought, Theory and Research in Consumer Satisfaction," in *Theoretical Developments in Marketing*, Charles W. Lamb, Jr., and Patrick M. Dunne, Eds. Chicago: American Marketing Association, 216–219.

Czinkota, Michael R. and Ikka A. Ronkainen (2003), "An International Marketing Manifesto," *Journal of International Marketing*, 11(1), 13–27.

Daft, Richard L. (1983), "Learning the Craft of Organizational Research," *Academy of Management Review*, 8(4), 539–546.

Davidson, William R. (1961), "Channels of Distribution – One Aspect of Marketing Strategy," *Business Horizons* (February), 84–90.

Davis, Harry L. and Benny P. Rigaux (1974), "Perception of Marital Roles in Decision Processes," *Journal of Consumer Research*, 1(June), 51–62.

Dawson, Leslie (1979), "Resolving the Crisis in Marketing Thought," *Management International Review*, 19(3), 74–84.

Day, George S. (1994), "The Capabilities of Market Driven Organizations," *Journal of Marketing*, 58(October), 37–52.

Day, George S. (2000), "Managing Market Relationships," *Journal of the Academy of Marketing Science*, 28(1), 24–30.

Day, George S. (2011), "Closing the Marketing Capabilities Gap," *Journal of Marketing*, 75 (July), 183–195.

Day, George S. and Christine Moorman (2010), *Strategy from the Outside In: Profiting from Customer Value*, New York: McGraw Hill.

Day, George S. and Robin Wensley (1983), "Marketing Theory with a Strategic Orientation," *Journal of Marketing*, 47(Fall), 79–89.

Day, Georges and David A. Aaker (1970), "A Guide to Consumerism," *Journal of Marketing*, 34(July), 12–19.

Day, Georges. (1981), "The Product Life Cycle: Analysis and Applications Issues," *Journal of Marketing*, 45(Fall), 60–67.

Day, Georges. (1984), *Strategic Market Planning: The Pursuit of Competitive Advantage*, St. Paul, Minnesota: West Publishing Company.

Day, Ralph L. and E. Laird Landon, Jr. (1977), "Toward a Theory of Consumer Complaining Behavior," in *Consumer and Industrial Buying Behavior*, Arch G. Woodside, Jagdish N. Sheth, and Peter D. Bennett, eds., New York: Elsevier North Holland, Inc., 425–437.

Day, Ralph L. and H. Keith Hunt, Eds., (1983), *International Fare in Consumer Satisfaction and Complaining Behavior*, Bloomington: School of Business, Indiana University.

Day, Ralph L., Ed. (1977), *Consumer Satisfaction, Dissatisfaction and Complaining Behavior*, Bloomington/Indianapolis: Department of Marketing, School of Business, Indiana University.

De Chernatony, Leslie, Chris Halliburton, and Ratna Bernath (1995), "International Branding: Demand or Supply Driven Opportunity," *International Marketing Review*, 12/2, 9–22.

De Wulf, Kristof, Gaby Odekerken-Schröder, and Dawn Iacobucci (2001), "Investments in Consumer Relationships: A Cross-Country and Cross-Industry Exploration," *Journal of Marketing*, 65(4), 33–50.

Dean, Joel (1950), "Pricing Policies for New Products," *Harvard Business Review*, 28(November), 45–53.

Dean, Joel (1951), *Managerial Economics*, Englewood Cliffs, New Jersey: Prentice-Hall, Inc.

Dholakia, Nikhilesh, A. Fuat Firat, and Richard P. Bagozzi (1980), "The De-Americanization of Marketing Thought," in *Theoretical Developments in Marketing*, Charles W. Lamb, Jr. and Patrick M. Dunne, eds., Chicago: American Marketing Association, 25–29.

Dichter, Ernest (1947), "Psychology in Market Research," *Harvard Business Review*, 25(Summer), 432–443.

Dichter, Ernest (1962), "The World Consumer," *Harvard Business Review*, 40(July–August), 113–122.

Dichter, Ernest (1964), *Handbook of Consumer Motivation: The Psychology of the World of Objects*, New York: McGraw-Hill Book Company, Inc.

Dickson, Peter R., and James L. Ginter (1987), "Market Segmentation, Product Differentiation, and Marketing Strategy", *Journal of Marketing*, 51(2), 1–10.

Dickson, Peter R., and Philippa K. Wells (2001), "The Dubious Origins of the Sherman Antitrust Act: The Mouse that Roared", *Journal of Public Policy and Marketing*, 20(1), 3–14.

Dickson, Peter Reid (1992), "Toward a General Theory of Competitive Rationality." *Journal of Marketing*, 56(1), 69–83.

Donelly, James H. (1976), "Marketing Intermediaries in Channels of Distribution for Services," *Journal of Marketing*, 40(January), 55–57.

Doney, Patricia M., and Joseph P. Cannon (1997), "An Examination of the Nature of Trust in Buyer-Seller Relationships" *Journal of Marketing*, 61(2), 35–51.

Dongdae Lee and SangWook Bae (1999) ,"Effects of Partitioned Country of Origin Information on Buyer Assessment of Binational Products",in *NA – Advances in Consumer Research,* Volume 26, eds. Eric J. Arnould and Linda M. Scott, Provo, UT : Association for Consumer Research, 344–351.

Dotzel, Thomas, Venkatesh Shankar, Leonard L. Berry (2013), "Service Innovativeness and Firm Value," *Journal of Marketing Research*, 50(2), 259–276.

Douglas, Susan P., Samuel C. Craig, and Edwin J. Nijssen (2001), "Integrating Branding Strategy Across Markets: Building International Brand Architecture", *Journal of International Marketing*, 9(2), 97–114.

Dowling, Grahame R. (1983), "The Application of General Systems Theory to an Analysis of Marketing Systems", *Journal of Macromarketing*, 3(Fall), 22–32.

Doyle, Peter and John Saunders (1985), "Market Segmentation and Positioning in Specialized Industrial Markets", *Journal of Marketing*, 49(Spring), 24–32.

Drucker, Peter (1969), "The Shame of Marketing", *Marketing/Communications*, 297(August), 60–64.

Dubinsky, Alan J., Roy D. Howell, Thomas N. Ingram, and Danny N. Bellenger (1986), "Salesforce Socialization", *Journal of Marketing*, 50(October), 192–207.

Duddy, Edward A. and David A. Revzan (1947), *Marketing: An Institutional Approach*, New York: McGraw-Hill Book Company, Inc.

Duncan, C. S. (1921), *Marketing: Its Problems and Methods*, New York: D. Appleton and Co.

Dunn, S. Watson (1981), "Regulation in Advertising" in *Research in Marketing*, Jagdish N. Sheth, ed., Volume 4, Greenwich, Connecticut: JAI Press, Inc., 117–141.

Dwyer, F. Robert and M. Ann Welsh (1985), "Environmental Relationships of the Internal Political Economy of Marketing Channels", *Journal of Marketing Research*, 22(November), 397–414.

Dwyer, F. Robert and Orville C. Walker, Jr. (1981), "Bargaining in an Asymmetrical Power Structure", *Journal of Marketing*, 45(Winter), 104–115.

Dwyer, F. Robert, and M. Ann Welsh (1985), "Environmental Relationships of the Internal Political Economy of Marketing Channels", *Journal of Marketing Research*, 22(4), 397–414.

Dwyer, F. Robert, Paul H. Schurr, and Sejo Oh (1987), "Developing Buyer-Seller Relationships," *Journal of Marketing*, *51*(2), 11–27.

Edvardsson, B. (1997), "Quality in new service development: key concepts and a frame of reference," *International Journal of Production Economics*, 52(1/2), 31–46.

Edvardsson, B., B. Tronvoll, and T. Gruber (2011), "Expanding Understanding of Service Exchange and Value Co-Creation: A Social Construction Approach", *Journal of the Academy of Marketing Science*, 39(2), 327–339.

Edvardsson, Bo. (1997), "Quality in new service development: key concepts and a frame of reference", *International Journal of Production Economics*, 52(1/2), 31–46.

Edwards, Ward (1961), "Behavioral Decision Theory", *Annual Review of Psychology*, 12, 473–498.

Eggers, Fabian, Thomas Niemand, Sascha Kraus, and Matthias Breier (2020). "Developing A Scale For Entrepreneurial Marketing: Revealing Its Inner Frame And Prediction Of Performance", *Journal of Business Research*, 113, 72–82.

Eggert, Andreas, Wolfgang Ulaga, Pennie Frow, and Adrian Payne (2018), "Conceptualizing and Communicating Value in Business Markets: From Value in Exchange to Value in Use," *Industrial Marketing Management*, 69, 80–90.

El-Ansary, Adel (1979), "The General Theory of Marketing Revisited," in *Conceptual and*

Theoretical Developments in Marketing, O. C. Ferrell, Stephen W. Brown, and Charles W. Lamb, Jr., eds., Chicago: American Marketing Association, 399–407.

El-Ansary, Adel (1997), "Relationship Marketing: A Marketing Channel Context," in *Research in Marketing*, vol. 13, 33–46.

Eliashberg, Jehoshua, Stephen A. Latour, Arvind Rangaswamy, and Louis W. Stern (1986), "Assessing the Predictive Accuracy of Two Utility-Based Theories in a Marketing Channel Negotiation Context," *Journal of Marketing Research*, 23(May), 101–110.

Elinder, Erik (1961), "How International Can Advertising Be?," *International Advertiser* (December), 12–16.

Elliott, Gregory R, and Ross C. Cameron (1994), "Consumer Perception of Product Quality and the Country-of-Origin Effect," *Journal of International Marketing*, 2(2), 49–62.

Emerson, Richard M. (1962), "Power-Dependence Relations," *American Sociological Review*, 27(1) 31–41.

Emery, F. E. and E. L. Trist (1965), "The Causal Texture of Organizational Environments," *Human Relations*, 18(February), 21–32.

Engel, James F., David T. Kollat, and Roger D. Blackwell (1968), *Consumer Behavior*, New York: Holt, Rinehart and Winston, Inc.

Engel, James F., Roger D. Blackwell, and David T. Kollat (1978), "The Current Status of Consumer Behavior Research: Problems and Prospects (Chapter 21)," in *Consumer Behavior*, 3rd Edition, Hinsdale, Illinois: The Dryden Press, 564–584.

Engel, James F., Roger D. Blackwell, and Paul W. Miniard (1986), Consumer Behavior, 5th Edition, Chicago: The Dryden Press.

Enis, Ben M. (1974), *Marketing Principles: The Management Process*, Pacific Palisades, California: Goodyear Publishing Company, Inc.

Enis, Ben M. (1979), "Countering the Goods/Services Taxonomy: An Alternative Taxonomy for Strategy Formulation," *Proceedings of the Sixth International Research Seminar in Marketing*, Cordes, France.

Enis, Ben M. and E. Thomas Sullivan (1985), "The AT&T Settlement: Legal Summary, Economic Analysis, and Marketing Implications," *Journal of Marketing*, 49(Winter), 127–136.

Enis, Ben M. and Kenneth J. Roering (1980), "Product Classification Taxonomies: Synthesis and Consumer Implications," in *Theoretical Developments in Marketing*, Chicago: American Marketing Association, 186–189.

Enis, Ben M. and Kenneth J. Roering (1981), "The Marketing of Services: Different Product Properties, Similar Marketing Strategies," *Proceedings, Services Conference*, Chicago: American Marketing Association.

Erickson, Gary M. (1985), "A Model of Advertising Competition," *Journal of Marketing Research*, 22(August), 297–304.

Etgar, Michael (1978), 'Intrachannel Conflict and Use of Power," *Journal of Marketing Research*, 15(May), 273–274.

Evans, Kenneth R. and Richard F. Beliramini (1987), "A Theoretical Model of Consumer Negotiated Pricing: An Orientation Perspective," *Journal of Marketing*, 51(April), 58–73.

Executive Office of The President (1963), *Consumer Advisory Council, First Report*, Washington, D.C.: United States Government Printing Office (October).

Fang, Eric, Robert W. Palmatier, and Jan-Benedict E.M. Steenkamp (2008), "Effect of Service Transition Strategies on Firm Value," *Journal of Marketing*, 72(5), 1–14.

Farley, John U. (1967), "Estimating Structural Parameters of Marketing Systems: Theory and Application," in *Changing Marketing Systems . . . : Consumer Corporate and Government Interfaces*, Reed Moyer, ed., Chicago: American Marketing Association, 316–321.

Farley, John U., John A. Howard, and L. Winston Ring (1974), *Consumer Behavior: Theory and Applications*, Boston, Massachusetts: Allyn and Bacon, Inc.

Farris, Paul W., and Michael J. Moore (2004), *The Profit Impact of Marketing Strategy Project: Retrospect and Prospects*, New York: Cambridge University Press.

Fatt, Arthur C. (1967), "The Danger of 'Local' International Advertising," *Journal of Marketing*, January), 60–62.

Federal Trade Commission (1978), *FTC Staff Report on Television Advertising to Children*, Washington, D.C: Federal Trade Commission.

Feng, Hui, Neil A. Morgan, and Lopo L. Rego (2015), "Marketing Department Power and Firm Performance", *Journal of Marketing*, 79(5), 1–20.

Ferber, Robert, Ed. (1974), *Handbook of Marketing Research*, New York: McGraw-Hill Book Company.

Fern, Edward F. and James R. Brown (1984), "The Industrial/Consumer Marketing Dichotomy: A Case of Insufficient Justification", *Journal of Marketing*, 48 (Spring), 68–77.

Ferrell, O. C. and J. R. Perrachione (1980), "An Inquiry into Bagozzi's Formal Theory of Marketing Exchanges", in *Theoretical Developments in Marketing*, Charles W. Lamb, Jr., and Patrick M. Dunne, eds., Chicago: American Marketing Association, 158–161.

Ferrell, O. C. and Larry G. Gresham (1985), "A Contingency Framework for Understanding Ethical Decision Making in Marketing", *Journal of Marketing*, 49(Summer), 87–96.

Festinger, Leon (1957), *A Theory of Cognitive Dissonance*, New York: Row, Peterson and Company.

Fishbein, Martin (1963), "An Investigation of the Relationships Between Beliefs About an Object and the Attitude Toward That Object", *Human Relations*, 16(August), 233–239.

Fishbein, Martin and Icek Ajzen (1975), *Belief, Attitude, Intention, and Behavior: An Introduction to Theory and Research*, Reading; Massachusetts: Addison-Wesley Publishing Company.

Fishbein, Martin, Ed. (1967), *Readings in Attitude Theory and Measurement*, New York: John Wiley & Sons, Inc.

Fisk, George (1967), *Marketing Systems: An Introductory Analysis*, New York: Harper and Row.

Fisk, George (1981), "An Invitation to Participate in Affairs of the Journal of Macromarketing", *Journal of Macromarketing*, 1(Spring), 3–6.

Fisk, George and Robert W. Nason, Eds. (1979), *Macro-Marketing: New Steps on the Learning Curve*, Boulder: Business Research Division, Graduate School of Business Administration, University of Colorado.

Fisk, George, Ed. (1974), *Marketing and Social Priorities*, Chicago: American Marketing Association.

Fisk, George, Johan Arndt, and Kjell Gronhaug, Eds. (1978), *Future Directions for Marketing*, Cambridge, Massachusetts: Marketing Science Institute.

Fisk, George, Robert W. Nason, and Phillip D. White, Eds. (1980), *Macromarketing: Evolution of Thought*, Boulder: University of Colorado, Business Research Division.

Foote, Nelson N., Ed. (1961), *Consumer Behavior (Volume 4): Household Decision Making*, New York: New York University Press.

Ford, Gary T. and John E. Calfee (1986), "Recent Developments in FTC Policy on Deception", *Journal of Marketing*, 50(July), 82–103.

Fornell, Claes (1995), "The Quality of Economic Output: Empirical Generalizations about its Distribution and Relationship to Market Share", *Marketing Science*, 14(3), G203–G211.

Fornell, Claes, Forrest V. Morgeson III, and G. Tomas M. Hult (2016), "Stock Returns on Customer Satisfaction Do Beat the Market: Gauging the Effect of a Marketing Intangible" *Journal of Marketing*, 80(5), 92–107.

Fornell, Claes, Michael D. Johnson, Eugene W. Anderson, Jaesung Cha, and Barbara Everitt Bryant (1996), "The American Customer Satisfaction Index: Nature, Purpose, and Findings," *Journal of Marketing*, 60(4), 7–18.

Fornell, Claes, Sunil Mithas, Forrest V. Morgeson III, and M.S. Krishnan (2006), "Customer Satisfaction and Stock Prices: High Returns, Low Risk", *Journal of Marketing*, 70(1), 3–14.

Forrester, Jay W. (1958), "Industrial Dynamics: A Major Breakthrough for Decision Makers", *Harvard Business Review*, 36(July–August), 37–66.

Forrester, Jay W. (1959), "Advertising: A Problem in Industrial Dynamics", *Harvard Business Review*, 59(March/ April), 100–110.

Frank, Ronald E. (1962), "Brand Choice as a Probability Process", *Journal of Business*, 35(January), 43–56.

Frank, Ronald E. (1974), "The *Journal of Consumer Research*: An Introduction", *Journal of Consumer Research*, 1(June), iv–v.

Frazier, Gary L. (1983a), "Interorganizational Exchange Behavior in Marketing Channels: A Broadened Perspective," *Journal of Marketing*, 47(4), 68–78.

Frazier, Gary L. (1983b), "On the Measurement of Interim Power in Channels of Distribution", *Journal of Marketing Research*, 20(May), 158–166.

Frazier, Gary L. and Jagdish N. Sheth (1985), "An Attitude-Behavior Framework for Distribution Channel Management", *Journal of Marketing*, 49(Summer), 38–48.

Frazier, Gary L. and John O. Summers (1984), "Interfirm Influence Strategies and Their Application Within Distribution Channels", *Journal of Marketing*, 48(Summer), 43–55.

Frazier, Gary L. and John O. Summers (1986), "Perceptions of Interfirm Power and Its Use Within a Franchise Channel of Distribution", *Journal of Marketing Research*, 23(May), 169–176.

French, John R. P., Jr. and Bertram Raven (1959), "The Bases of Social Power", in *Studies in Social Power*, Dorwin Cartwright, ed., Ann Arbor: Research Center for Group Dynamics, Institute for Social Research, University of Michigan, 150–167.

French, Warren A., Hiram C. Barksdale, William D. Perrault, J.R., Johan Arndt, and Jehiel Zif (1983), "The Problems of Older Consumers: A Comparison of England, Israel, Norway and the United States", in 1983 AMA Educator' Proceedings, Chicago: American Marketing Association, 390–395.

Freud, Sigmund (1953), The Standard Edition of the Complete Psychological Works of Sigmund Freud, J. Strachy, ed., (24 Volumes), London: Hogarth Press.

Frow, Pennie, Janet R. McColl-Kennedy, Adrian Payne, and Rahul Govind (2019), "Service Ecosystem Well-Being: Conceptualization and Implications for Theory and Practice", *European Journal of Marketing*, 53(12), 2657–2691.

Frow, Pennie, Janet R. McColl-Kennedy, Toni Hilton, Anthony Davidson, Adrian Payne, and Danilo Brozovic (2014), "Value Propositions: A Service Ecosystems Perspective", *Marketing Theory*, 14(3), 327–351.

Fullbrook, Earl S. (1940), "The Functional Concept in Marketing", *Journal of Marketing*, 4 (January), 229–237.

Furrer, Olivier, Jie Yu Kerguignas, Cecile Delcourt, Dwayne D Gremler (2020), "Twenty-Seven Years of Service Research: A Literature Review and Research Agenda", *Journal of Services Marketing*, 34(3), 299–316.

Galbraith, John Kenneth (1958), *The Affluent Society*, Boston: Houghton Mifflin Company.

Gale, Bradley T. (1992), "Quality comes first when hatching power brands." *Planning Review*, 20(4), 4–48.

Ganesan, Shankar (1994), "Determinants of Long-Term Orientation in Buyer-Seller Relationships", *Journal of Marketing*, 58(2), 1–19.

Gardner, David M. (1973), "Dynamic Homeostasis: Behavioral Research and the FTC", in *Advances in Consumer Research*, Scott Ward and Peter L. Wright, eds., Urbana, Illinois: Association for Consumer Research, 1, 108–113.

Gardner, David M. (1976), "Deception in Advertising: A Receiver Oriented Approach to Understanding", *Journal of Advertising*, 5(Fall), 5–11, 19.

Gardner, David M. (1987), "The Product Life Cycle: A Critical Look at the Literature", in *Review of Marketing*, Michael J. Houston, ed., Chicago: American Marketing Association.

Gardner, David M. and Russell W. Belk, Eds., (1980), *A Basic Bibliography on Experimental Design in Marketing*, Chicago: American Marketing Association.

Gardner, David M., Ed. (1971), *Proceedings 2nd Annual Conference of the Association for Consumer Research*, College Park, Maryland: Association for Consumer Research.

Gardner, Edward H. (1945), "Consumer Goods Classification", *Journal of Marketing*, 9(January), 275–276.

Gardner, Meryl Paula (1985), "Mood States and Consumer Behavior: A Critical Review", *Journal of Consumer Research*, 12(December), 281–300.

Garrett, Dennis E. (1986), "Consumer Boycotts: Are Targets Always the Bad Guys?" *Business and Society Review*, 58(Summer), 17–21.

Garrett, Dennis E. (1987), "The Effectiveness of Marketing Policy Boycotts: Environmental Opposition to Marketing", *Journal of Marketing*, 51(April), 46–57.

Gaski, John F. (1984), "The Theory of Power and Conflict in Channels of Distribution", *Journal of Marketing*, 48(Summer), 9–29.

Gaski, John F. (1986), 'Interrelations Among A Channel Entity's Power Sources: Impact of the Exercise of Reward and Coercion on Expert, Referent, and Legitimate Power Sources", *Journal of Marketing Research*, 23(February), 62–77.

Gaski, John F. (1987), "The Inverse Power Source-Power Relationship: An Empirical Note on a Marketing Anomaly", in *Research in Marketing*, Jagdish N. Sheth, ed., Volume 9, Greenwich, Connecticut: JAI Press, Inc., 145–161.

Gaski, John F. and John R. Nevin (1985), "The Differential Effects of Exercised and Unexercised Power Sources in a Marketing Channel", *Journal of Marketing Research*, 22(May), 130–142.

Gaski, John F. and Michael J. Etzel (1986), "The Index of Consumer Sentiment Toward Marketing", *Journal of Marketing*, 50 (July), 71–81.

Gatignon, Hubert (1984), "Competition as a Moderator of the Effect of Advertising on Sales", *Journal of Marketing Research*, 21(November), 387–398.

Gatignon, Hubert and Thomas S. Robertson (1985), "A Propositional Inventory for New Diffusion Research", *Journal of Consumer Research*, 11(March), 849–867.

Gatignon, Hubert, Erin Anderson, and Kristiaan Helsen (1989), "Competitive Reactions to Market Entry: Explaining Interfirm Differences", *Journal of Marketing Research*, 26(1), 44–55.

Gelb, Betsy D. and Mary C. Gilly (1979), "The Effect of Promotional Techniques on Purchase of Preventative Dental Care", *Journal of Consumer Research*, 6(3), 305–308.

George, William R. and Hiram C. Barksdale (1974), "Marketing Activities in the Service Industries", *Journal of Marketing*, 38(October), 65–70.

Germann, Frank, Peter Ebbes, and Rajdeep Grewal (2015), "The Chief Marketing Officer Matters!", *Journal of Marketing*, 79(3), 1–22.

Ghemawat, Pankaj (2001), "Distance Still Matters: The Hard Reality of Global Expansion", *Harvard Business Review*, (September) (8), 137–147.

Goble, Ross and Roy Shaw (1975), *Controversy and Dialogue in Marketing*, Englewood Cliffs, New Jersey: Prentice-Hall, Inc.

Goetz, Charles J., and Robert E. Scott (1981), "Principles of Relational Contracts", *Virginia Law Review*, 67(6), 1089–1150.

Goldstucker, Jac L. (1965), "Trading Areas", in *Science in Marketing*, George Schwartz, ed., New York: John Wiley & Sons, Inc., 281–320.

Goldstucker, Jac L. (1966), "A Systems Framework for Retail Location", in *Science, Technology, and Marketing*, Raymond M. Hass, ed., Chicago: American Marketing Association, 412–429.

Graham, John L. (1987), "A Theory of Interorganizational Negotiations", in *Research in Marketing*, Jagdish N. Sheth, ed., Volume 9, Greenwich, Connecticut: JAI Press, Inc., 163–183.

Greene, C. Scott and Paul Miesing (1984), "Public Policy, Technology, and Ethics: Marketing Decisions for NASA's Space Shuttle", *Journal of Marketing*, 48(Summer), 56–67.

Greenly, Gordon E. (2007), "An Understanding of Marketing Strategy", *European Journal of Marketing*, 18(6–7), 90–103.

Grether, E.T. (1950), "A Theoretical Approach to the Study of Marketing", in *Theory in Marketing*, Reavis Cox and Wroe. Alderson, eds., Homewood, Illinois: Richard D. Irwin, Inc. 113–123.

Grether, E.T. (1983), "Regional-Spatial Analysis in Marketing", *Journal of Marketing*, 47(Fall), 36–43.

Grewal, Dhruv, Anne L. Roggeveen, and Michael Tsiros (2008), "The Effect of Compensation on Repurchase Intentions in Service Recovery", *Journal of Retailing*, 84(4), 424–434.

Griffith, David A., Goksel Yalcinkaya, and Gaia Rubera (2014), "Country-Level Performance of New Experience Products in a Global Rollout: The Moderating Effects of Economic Wealth and National Culture", *Journal of International Marketing*, 22(4), 1–20.

Griffith, David A., Goksel Yalcinkaya, Gaia Rubera, and Verdiana Giannetti (2017), "Understanding the Importance of the Length of Global Product Rollout: An Examination in the Motion Picture Industry", *Journal of International Marketing*, 25(4), 50–69.

Grönroos, Christian (1994), "From Marketing Mix to Relationship Marketing: Towards a Paradigm Shift in Marketing", *Asia-Australia Marketing Journal*, 2(1), 9–29.

Grönroos, Christian (1978), "A Service-Oriented Approach to Marketing of Services", *European Journal of Marketing*, 12(8), 588–601.

Grönroos, Christian (1982), "An Applied Service Marketing Theory," *European Journal of Marketing*, 16(7), 30–41.

Grönroos, Christian (1984), "A Service Quality Model and Its Marketing Implications," *European Journal of Marketing*, 18(4), 36–44.

Grönroos, Christian (1991), "The Marketing Strategy Continuum: Towards a Marketing Concept for the 1990s," *Management Decision*, 29(1), 7–13.

Grönroos, Christian (1994), "From Marketing Mix to Relationship Marketing: Towards a Paradigm Shift in Marketing," *Asia-Australia Marketing Journal*, 2(1), 9–29.

Grönroos, Christian (1995), "Relationship Marketing: The Strategy Continuum", *Journal of the Academy of Marketing Science*, 23(4), 252–254.

Grönroos, Christian (1996), "Relationship Marketing: Strategic and Tactical Implications," *Management Decision*, 34(3), 5–14.

Grönroos, Christian (2000), "Creating a Relationship Dialogue: Communication, Interaction and Value," *The Marketing Review*, 1(1), 5–14.

Grönroos, Christian (2019), "Are You Ready for Relationship Marketing? It is a Business Challenge," in *Handbook of Advances in Marketing in an Era of Disruptions: Essays in Honor of Jagdish N. Sheth*, Atul Parvatiyar and Rajendra Sisodia (Eds.), New Delhi: Sage Publications, 307–317.

Grönroos, Christian and Päivi Voima (2013), "Critical Service Logic: Making Sense of Value Creation and Co-Creation," *Journal of the Academy of Marketing Science*, 41(2), 133–150.

Grover, Rajiv and V. Srinivasan (1987), "A Simultaneous Approach to Market Segmentation and Market Structuring," *Journal of Marketing Research*, 24(May), 139–153.

Gruen, Thomas (1997), "Relationship Marketing: The Route to Marketing Efficiency and Effectiveness," *Business Horizons*, 40(6), 32–38.

Gruen, Thomas W., (2000), "Relationship Marketing in Mass Markets" in *Handbook of Relationship Marketing*, Jagdish N. Sheth and Atul Parvatiyar (Eds.), New Delhi: Sage Publications, 355–380.

Gruen, Thomas W., John O. Summers, and Frank Acito (2000), "Relationship Marketing Activities, Commitment, and Membership Behaviors in Professional Associations," *Journal of Marketing*, 64(3), 34–49.

Gummesson Evert and Christian Grönroos (2012), "The Emergence of the New Service Marketing: Nordic School Perspectives," *Journal of Service Management*, 23(4), 479–497.

Gummesson, E. (1978), "Toward a Theory of Professional Services Marketing," *Industrial Marketing Management*, 7, 89–95.

Gummesson, E. (1979), "The Marketing of Professional Services – An Organizational Dilemma," *European Journal of Marketing*, 13(5), 308–318.

Gummesson, E. (1981), "Marketing Cost Concepts in Service Firms," *Industrial Marketing Management*, 10, 175–182.

Gummesson, Evert (1978), "Toward a Theory of Professional Services Marketing," *Industrial Marketing Management*, 7, 89–95.

Gummesson, Evert (1987), "The New Marketing—Developing Long-Term Interactive Relationships," *Long Range Planning*, 20(4), 10–20.

Gummesson, Evert (1994), "Making Relationship Marketing Operational," *International Journal of Service Industry Management*, 5(5), 5–20.

Gummesson, Evert (1996), "Relationship Marketing and Imaginary Organizations: A Synthesis," *European Journal of Marketing*, 30(2), 31–44.

Gummesson, Evert (1997), "Relationship Marketing as a Paradigm Shift: Some Conclusions from the 30R Approach," *Management Decision*, 35(4), 267–272.

Gummesson, Evert (1999), "Total Relationship Marketing: Experimenting with a Synthesis of Research Frontiers," *Australasian Marketing Journal (AMJ)*, 7(1), 72–85.

Gummesson, Evert (2002), "Relationship Marketing in the New Economy," *Journal of Relationship Marketing*, 1(1), 37–57.

Gummesson, Evert and Christian Gronroos (2012), "The Emergence of the New Service Marketing: Nordic School Perspectives," *Journal of Service Management*, 23(4), 479–497.

Gundlach, Gregory T. (2007), "The American Marketing Association's 2004 Definition of Marketing: Perspectives on Its Implications for Scholarship and the Role and Responsibility of Marketing in Society," *Journal of Public Policy & Marketing*, 26(2), 243–250.

Gundlach, Gregory T., and Patrick E. Murphy (1993), "Ethical and Legal Foundations of Relational Marketing Exchanges," *Journal of Marketing*, 57(4), 35–46.

Gundlach, Gregory T., and William L. Wilkie (2009), "The American Marketing Association's New Definition of Marketing: Perspective and Commentary on the 2007 Revision," *Journal of Public Policy & Marketing*, 28(2), 259–264.

Gutman, Jonathan (1982), "A Means-End Chain Model Based on Consumer Categorization Processes," *Journal of Marketing*, 46(Spring), 60–72.

Haas, Raymond M., ed. (1966), *Science, Technology, and Marketing*, Chicago: American Marketing Association.

Haas, Robert W. (1986), *Industrial Marketing Management*, 3rd Edition, Boston: Kent Publishing Company.

Håkansson, Hårkan (1982), *International Marketing and Purchasing of Industrial Goods: An Interaction Approach,* New York: John Wiley & Sons.

Håkansson, Hårkan and Ivan Snehota (2000), *"The IMP Perspective: Assets and Liabilities of Business Relationships,"* in Handbook of Relationship Marketing, Jagdish Sheth and Atul Parvatiyar (Eds.), Thousand Oaks, CA: Sage Publications, 69–93.

Håkansson, Hårkan, and Björn Wootz (1979), "A Framework of Industrial Buying and Selling," *Industrial Marketing Management,* 8(1), 28–39.

Håkansson, Hårkan, Ed. (1982), *International Marketing and Purchasing of Industrial Goods: An Interaction Approach,* New York: John Wiley & Sons.

Halbert, Michael (1964), "The Requirements for Theory in Marketing", in *Theory in Marketing,* Reavis Cox, Wroe Alderson, and Stanley J. Shapiro, eds., Richard D. Irwin, Inc., 17–36.

Hall, A. D. and R. Z. Fagen (1968), "Definition of a System", in *Modem Systems Research for the Behavioral Scientist: A Sourcebook,* Walter Buckley, ed., Chicago: Aldine Publishing Company, 81–92.

Hall, Edward T. (1960), "The Silent Language in Overseas Business", *Harvard Business Review,* 38(May–June), 87–96.

Hallen, Lars, Jan Johanson, and Nazeem Seyed-Mohamed (1991), "Interfirm Adaptation in Business Relationships", *Journal of Marketing,* 55(2), 29–37.

Hamel, Gary and CK Prahalad (1991), "Corporate Imagination and Expeditionary Marketing," *Harvard Business Review,* 69(4), 81–92.

Hampton, Gerald M. (1977), "Perceived Risk in Buying Products Made Abroad by American Firms", *Baylor Business Studies,* 113(August), 53–64.

Han, Jin K., Namwoon Kim, and Rajendra K. Srivastava (1998), "Market Orientation and Organizational Performance: Is Innovation the Missing Link?" *Journal of Marketing,* 62(October), 30–45.

Hansen, Flemming (1972), *Consumer Choice Behavior: A Cognitive Theory,* New York: Free Press.

Hanssens, Dominique M., Roland T. Rust, and Rajendra K. Srivastava (2009), "Marketing Strategy and Wall Street: Nailing Down Marketing's Impact", *Journal of Marketing,* 73(6), 115–118.

Harker, Michael (1999), "Relationship Marketing Defined? An Examination of Current Relationship Marketing Definitions", *Marketing Intelligence and Planning,* 17(1), 13–20.

Harker, Michael and John Egan (2006), 'The Past, Present and Future of Relationship Marketing," *Journal of Marketing Management,* 22(1–2), 215–242.

Harmeling, Colleen M., Jordan W. Moffett, Arnold, Mark J., and Brad D. Carlson (2017), "Toward a Theory of Customer Engagement Marketing", *Journal of the Academy of Marketing Science,* (45)3, 312–335.

Hauser, John R. (1986), "Agendas and Consumer Choice", *Journal of Marketing Research,* 23(August), 199–212.

Hauser, John R., and Steven M. Shugan (1983), "Defensive Marketing Strategies", *Marketing Science,* 2(4), 319–360.

Hauser, John R., and Steven M. Shugan (2008), "Commentary: Defensive Marketing Strategies", *Marketing Science,* 27(1), 85–87.

Havlena, William J. and Morris B. Holbrook (1986), "The Varieties of Consumption Experience: Comparing Two Typologies of Emotion in Consumer Behavior", *Journal of Consumer Research,* 13(December), 394–404.

Heath, Robert L. and Richard Alan Nelson (1985), "Image and Issue Advertising: A Corporate and Public Policy Perspective", *Journal of Marketing,* 49(Spring), 58–68.

Heide, Jan B. (1994), "Interorganizational Governance in Marketing Channels", *Journal of Marketing,* 58(1), 71–85.

Heide, Jan B., and George John (1990), "Alliances in Industrial Purchasing: The Determinants of Joint Action in Buyer-Supplier Relationships," *Journal of Marketing Research,* 27(1), 24–36.

Heide, Jan B., and George John (1992), "Do Norms Matter in Marketing Relationships?", *Journal of Marketing,* 56(2), 32–44.

Heider, Fritz (1958), *The Psychology of Interpersonal Relations,* New York: John Wiley & Sons, Inc.

Heil, Oliver, and Thomas S. Robertson (1991), "Toward a Theory of Competitive Market Signaling: A Research Agenda," *Strategic Management Journal,* 12(6), 403–418.

Henderson, Bruce (1970), "Effects of Brand Local and Nonlocal Origin on Consumer Attitudes in Developing Countries," The Product Portfolio,

Boston Consulting Group (BCG), available at: www.bcg.com/publications/1970/strategy-the-product-portfolio, last accessed on January 19, 2022.

Henderson, Bruce D (1983), "The Anatomy of Competition," *Journal of Marketing*, 47(2), 7–11.

Hennig-Thurau, Thorsten, Kevin P. Gwinner, and Dwayne Gremler (2002), "Understanding Relationship Marketing Outcomes: An Integration of Relational Benefits and Relationship Quality," *Journal of Service Research*, 4(3), 230–247.

Herz, Marc and Adamantios Diamantoupulos (2017), "I Use It But Will Tell You That I Don't: Consumers' Country-of-Origin Cue Usage Denial," *Journal of International Marketing*, 25(2), 52–71.

Heskett, James L., Thomas O. Jones, Gary W. Loveman, W. Earl Jr. Sasser, and Leonard A. Schlesinger (1994), "Putting the Service-Profit Chain to Work," *Harvard Business Review*, 72(2), 164–174.

Heskett, James L., W. Earl Jr. Sasser, and Leonard A. Schlesinger (1997), *The Service Profit Chain, How Leading Companies Link Profit and Growth to Loyalty, Satisfaction, and Value*, New York: The Free Press.

Heslop, Louise A., Nicolas Papadopoulos, and Margie Bourke (1998) "An Interregional and Intercultural Perspective on Subcultural Differences in Product Evaluations," *Canadian Journal of Administrative Sciences*, 15(2), 113–127.

Hibbard, Jonathan D., Nirmalya Kumar, and Louis W. Stern (2001), "Examining the Impact of Destructive Acts in Marketing Channel Relationships," *Journal of Marketing Research*, 38(1), 45–61.

Hill, R. M., R. S. Alexander, and J. S. Cross (1975), *Industrial Marketing*, 4th Edition, Homewood, Illinois: Richard D. Irwin, Inc.

Hills, Gerald E. and Claes M. Hultman (2011), "Academic Roots: The Past and Present of Entrepreneurial Marketing," *Journal of Small Business and Entrepreneurship*, 24(1), 1–10.

Hills, Gerald E. and Claes M. Hultman (2013), "Entrepreneurial Marketing: Conceptual and Empirical Research Opportunities," *Entrepreneurship Research Journal*, 3(4), 437–448.

Hills, Gerald E., Claes M. Hultman, and Morgan P. Miles (2008), "The Evolution and Development of Entrepreneurial Marketing," *Journal of Small Business Management*, 46(1), 99–112.

Hirschman, Elizabeth C. (1980), "Innovativeness, Novelty Seeking, and Consumer Creativity," *Journal of Consumer Research*, 7(December), 283–295.

Hirschman, Elizabeth C. (1983), "Religious Affiliation and Consumption Processes: An Initial Paradigm," in *Research in Marketing*, Jagdish N. Sheth, Ed., Volume 6, Greenwich, Connecticut: JAI Press, Inc., 131–170.

Hirschman, Elizabeth C. (1986), "Humanistic Inquiry in Marketing Research: Philosophy, Method, and Criteria," *Journal of Marketing Research*, 23(August), 237–249.

Hofer, Charles W. and Dan Schendel (1978), *Strategy Formulation: Analytical Concepts*, St. Paul, Minnesota: West Publishing Co.

Hofstede, Geert (1980), *Culture's Consequences: International Differences in Work-Related Values.*, Newbury Park, CA: Sage Publications.

Hofstede, Geert (1991), *Cultures and Organizations: Software of the Mind*, New York, NY: McGraw-Hill.

Hofstede, Geert (2001), *Culture's Consequences: Comparing Values, Behaviors, Institutions, and Organizations across Nations*, 2d ed. Thousand Oaks, CA: Sage Publications.

Hofstede, Geert, and Michael H. Bond (1984), "Hofstede's Culture Dimensions: An Independent Validation Using Rokeach's Value Survey," *Journal of Cross-Cultural Psychology*, 15(4), 417–433.

Hogreve, Jens, Anja Iseke, Klaus Derfuss, and Tönnjes Eller (2017), "The Service-Profit Chain: A Meta-Analytic Test of a Comprehensive Theoretical Framework," *Journal of Marketing*, 81(May), 41–61.

Holbrook, Eds., Volume 12, Provo, Utah: Association for Consumer Research, 145–156.

Holbrook, Morris B. (1985), "Why Business is Bad for Consumer Research: The Three Bears Revisited," in *Advances in Consumer Research*, Elizabeth C. Hirschman and Morris B.

Holbrook, Morris B. and Elizabeth C. Hirschman (1982), "The Experiential Aspects of Consumption: Consumer Fantasies, Feelings, and Fun," *Journal of Consumer Research*, 9 (September), 132–140.

Holbrook, Morris B. and John A. Howard (1977), "Frequently Purchased Nondurable Goods and Services," in *Selected Aspects of Consumer Behavior: A Summary from the Perspective of Different Disciplines*, Robert Ferber, ed., Washington, D.C.: National Science Foundation, Directorate for Research Applications, Research Applied to National Needs, 189–222.

Holloway, Robert J. (1967b), "An Experiment on Consumer Dissonance", *Journal of Marketing*, 31 (January), 39–43.

Holloway, Robert J. and Robert S. Hancock, Eds (1974), *The Environment of Marketing Management: Selections from the Literature*, 3rd Edition, New York: John Wiley & Sons, Inc.

Holloway, Robert J., Ed. (1967a), A Basic Bibliography on Experiments in Marketing, Chicago: American Marketing Association.

Holton, Richard H. (1958), "The Distinction Between Convenience Goods, Shopping Goods, and Specialty Goods", *Journal of Marketing*, 23(July), 53–56.

Homans, George C. (1958), "Social Behavior as Exchange," *American Journal of Sociology*, 63(6), 597–606.

Homans, George C. (1961), *Social Behavior: Its Elementary Forms*, New York: Harcourt, Brace, and World, Inc.

Homburg, Christian, Alexander Hahn, Torsten Bornemann, and Philipp Sander (2014), "The Role of the Chief Marketing Officers for Venture Capital Funding: Endowing New Ventures with Marketing Legitimacy", *Journal of Marketing Research*, 51(October), 625–644.

Homburg, Christian, Danijel Jozic, and Christina Kuehnl (2017), "Customer Experience Management: Toward Implementing an Evolving Marketing Concept," *Journal of the Academy of Marketing Science*, *45*(3), 377–401.

Homburg, Christian, Jan Wieseke, and Wayne D. Hoyer (2009), "Social Identity and the Service–Profit Chain", *Journal of Marketing*, 73 (March), 38–54.

Homburg, Christian, John P. Workman, and Ove Jensen (2000), "Fundamental Changes in Marketing Organization: The Movement Toward a Customer-Focused Organizational Structure", *Journal of the Academy of Marketing Science*, 28(4), 459–478.

Homburg, Christian, Martin Artz, and Jan Wieseke (2012), "Marketing Performance Measurement Systems: Does Comprehensiveness Really Improve Performance?," *Journal of Marketing*, 76(3), 56–77.

Hong, Ying, Liao Hui, Jia Hu, and Kaifeng Jiang (2013), "Missing Link in the Service Profit Chain: A Meta-Analytic Review of the Antecedents, Consequences, and Moderators of Service Climate", *Journal of Applied Psychology*, 98(2), 237–267.

Houston, Franklin S. (1986), "The Marketing Concept: What It Is and What It Is Not", *Journal of Marketing*, 50(April), 81–87.

Houston, Franklin S. and Jule B. Gassenheimer (1987), "Marketing and Exchange", *Journal of Marketing*, 51(October), 3–18.

Hovland, Carl I. (1954), "Effects of the Mass Media of Communication", in *Handbook of Social Psychology*, Volume 2, Gardner Lindzey, ed., Cambridge, Massachusetts: Addison-Wesley Publishing Company, Inc., 1062–1103.

Howard, John A. (1957), *Marketing Management: Analysis and Decision*, Homewood, Illinois: Richard D. Irwin, Inc.

Howard, John A. (1963a), *Marketing: Executive and Buyer Behavior*, New York: Columbia University Press.

Howard, John A. (1963b), *Marketing Management: Analysis and Planning*, Revised Edition, Homewood, Illinois: Richard D. Irwin, Inc.

Howard, John A. (1977), *Consumer Behavior: Application of Theory*, New York: McGraw-Hill Book Company, Inc.

Howard, John A. (1983), "Marketing Theory of the Firm", *Journal of Marketing*, 47(Fall), 90–100.

Howard, John A. (1988), *Consumer Behavior in Marketing Strategy*, Englewood Cliffs, New Jersey: Prentice-Hall, Inc.

Howard, John A. and Jagdish N. Sheth (1969), *The Theory of Buyer Behavior*, New York, NY: John Wiley.

Howard, John A. and James Hulbert (1973), Advertising and the Public Interest: A Staff Report to the Federal Trade Commission, Chicago: Crain Communications, Inc.

Howard, John and Jagdish Sheth (1969), *Theory of Buyer Behavior*, New York: Wiley.

Howard, Ronald A. (1963), "Stochastic Process Models of Consumer Behavior", *Journal of Advertising Research*, 3(September), 35–42.

Huber, Joel, Morris B. Holbrook, and Barbara E. Kahn (1986), "Effects of Competitive Context and of Additional Information on Price Sensitivity",

Journal of Marketing Research, 23 (August), 250–260.

Huff, David L. (1964), "Defining and Estimating a Trading Area", *Journal of Marketing*, 28(July), 34–38.

Huff, David L. and Roland T. Rust (1984), "Measuring the Congruence of Market Areas", *Journal of Marketing*, 48(Winter), 68–74.

Hull, Clark L. (1952), *A Behavior System: An Introduction to Behavior Theory Concerning the Individual Organism*, New Haven, Connecticut: Yale University Press.

Hum, H. Keith, Ed. (1977), *Conceptualization and Measurement of Consumer Satisfaction and Dissatisfaction*, Cambridge, Massachusetts: Marketing Science Institute.

Hunt Shelby D. and Robert M. Morgan (1995), "The Resource-Advantage Theory of Competition: Dynamics, Path Dependencies, and Evolutionary Dimensions", *Journal of Marketing*, 60(October), 107–114.

Hunt, H. Keith and Ralph L. Day, Eds. (1979), *Refining Concepts and Measures of Consumer Satisfaction and Complaining Behavior*, Bloomington/Indianapolis: Department of Marketing, School of Business, Division of Research, Indiana University.

Hunt, Shelby (1997), "Competing Through Relationships: Grounding Relationship Marketing in Resource-Advantage Theory", *Journal of Marketing* Management, 13(5), 431–445.

Hunt, Shelby (2000), "A General Theory of Competition: Too Eclectic or Not Eclectic Enough? Too Incremental or Not Incremental Enough? Too Neoclassical or Not Neoclassical Enough?," *Journal of Macromarketing*, 20(1), 77–81.

Hunt, Shelby (2002), *Foundations of Marketing Theory: Toward a General Theory of Marketing*, New York: ME Sharpe.

Hunt, Shelby (2010), "Doctoral Seminars in Marketing Theory", *Journal of Historical Research in Marketing*, 2(4), 443–456.

Hunt, Shelby D. (1971), "The Morphology of Theory and the General Theory of Marketing", *Journal of Marketing*, 35(April), 65–68.

Hunt, Shelby D. (1976a), *Marketing Theory: Conceptualizations of Research in Marketing*, Columbus, Ohio: Grid Publishing.

Hunt, Shelby D. (1976b), "The Nature and Scope of Marketing", *Journal of Marketing*, 40(July), 17–28.

Hunt, Shelby D. (1977), "The Three Dichotomies Model of Marketing: An Elaboration of Issues", in *Macro-Marketing: Distributive Processes from a Societal Perspective*, Charles C. Slater, ed., Boulder: Business Research Division, Graduate School of Business Administration, University of Colorado, 52–56.

Hunt, Shelby D. (1983a), "General Theories and the Fundamental Explananda of Marketing", *Journal of Marketing*, 47(Fall), 9–17.

Hunt, Shelby D. (1983b), *Marketing Theory: The Philosophy of Marketing Science*, Homewood, Illinois: Richard D. Irwin, Inc.

Hunt, Shelby D. (2000), *A General Theory of Competition: Resources, Competences, Productivity, Economic Growth*. Thousand Oaks, CA: Sage Publications.

Hunt, Shelby D. (2010), *Marketing Theory: Foundations, Controversy, Strategy, Resource-Advantage Theory*. New York, NY: Routledge

Hunt, Shelby D. (2012), "Toward the Institutionalization of Macromarketing: Sustainable Enterprise, Sustainable Marketing, Sustainable Development, and the Sustainable Society", *Journal of Macromarketing*, 32(4), 404–411.

Hunt, Shelby D. (2018), "Advancing Marketing Strategy in the Marketing Discipline and Beyond: From Promise, to Neglect, to Prominence, to Fragment (to Promise?)", *Journal of Marketing* Management, 34(1–2), 16–51.

Hunt, Shelby D. (2020), "Indigenous theory development in marketing: the foundational premises approach," *AMS Rev* 10, 8–17. https://doi.org/10.1007/s13162-020-00165-w

Hunt, Shelby D. and Dennis B. Arnett (2006), "Toward a General Theory of Marketing: Resource-Advantage Theory as an Extension of Alderson's Theory of Market Processes", in B. Wooliscroft, R.D. Tamilia, and S.J. Shapiro (eds.), *A Twenty-First Century Guide to Aldersonian Marketing Thought*, Boston, MA: Springer, 453–471.

Hunt, Shelby D. and Dennis D. Arnett (2003), "Resource-Advantage Theory and Embeddedness: Explaining RA Theory's Explanatory Success", *Journal of Marketing Theory* and Practice, 11(1), 1–17.

Hunt, Shelby D. and John J. Burnett (1982), "The Macromarketing/Micromarketing Dichotomy: A

Taxonomical Model", *Journal of Marketing*, 46(Summer), 11–26.

Hunt, Shelby D. and John R. Nevin (1974), "Power in a Channel of Distribution: Sources and Consequences", *Journal of Marketing Research*, 11(May), 186–193.

Hunt, Shelby D. and Lawrence B. Chonko (1984), "Marketing and Machiavellianism", *Journal of Marketing*, 48(Summer), 30–42.

Hunt, Shelby D. and Robert M. Morgan (1995), "The Resource-Advantage Theory of Competition: Dynamics, Path Dependencies, and Evolutionary Dimensions," *Journal of Marketing*, 60(October), 107–114.

Hunt, Shelby D. and Scott Vitell (1986), "A General Theory of Marketing Ethics", *Journal of Macromarketing*, 6 (Spring), 516.

Hunt, Shelby D. James A. Muncy, and Nina M. Ray (1981), "Alderson's General Theory of Marketing: A Formalization", in *Review of Marketing 1981*, Ben M. Enis and Kenneth J. Roering, Eds., Chicago: American Marketing Association, 267–272.

Hunt, Shelby D., and Caroline Derozier (2004), "The Normative Imperatives of Business and Marketing Strategy: Grounding Strategy in Resource-Advantage Theory", *Journal of Business and Industrial Marketing*, 19(1), 5–22.

Hunt, Shelby D., and Dennis B. Arnett (2003), "Resource-Advantage Theory and Embeddedness: Explaining RA Theory's Explanatory Success," *Journal of Marketing Theory and Practice*, *11*(1), 1–17.

Hunt, Shelby D., and Robert M. Morgan (1995) "The Comparative Advantage Theory of Competition." *Journal of Marketing*, 59(2), 1–15.

Hunt, Shelby D., and Robert M. Morgan (1996), "The Resource-Advantage Theory of Competition: Dynamics, Path Dependencies, and Evolutionary Dimensions", *Journal of Marketing*, 60(4), 107–114.

Hunt, Shelby D., and Robert M. Morgan (1997), "Resource-Advantage Theory: A Snake Swallowing its Tail or a General Theory of Competition?," *Journal of Marketing*, 61(4), 74–82.

Hunt, Shelby D., and Scott J. Vitell (2006), "The General Theory of Marketing Ethics: A Revision and Three Questions," *Journal of Macromarketing*, 26(2), 143–153.

Hunt, Shelby D., Lawrence B. Chonko, and James B. Wilcox (1984), "Ethical Problems of Marketing Researchers", *Journal of Marketing Research*, 21(August), 309–324.

Hunt, Shelby, Michael Kleinaltenkamp, Michael Ehret, Dennis B. Arnett., and Sreedhar Madhavaram (2006), "The Explanatory Foundations of Relationship Marketing Theory", *Journal of Business and Industrial Marketing*, 21(2), 72–87.

Hurley, Robert F. and G. Tomas Hult (1998), "Innovation, Market Orientation, and Organizational Learning: An Integration and Empirical Examination", *Journal of Marketing*, 62(July), 42–54.

Hutchinson, Kenneth D. (1952), "Marketing as a Science: An Appraisal", *Journal of Marketing*, 16(January), 286–293.

Hutt, Michail D., Michael P. Mokwa, and Stanley J. Shapiro (1986), "The Politics of Marketing: Analyzing the Parallel Political Marketplace", *Journal of Marketing*, 50(January), 40–51.

Immelt, Jeffrey R., Vijay Govindarajan, and Chris Trimble (2009), "How G.E. is Disrupting Itself", *Harvard Business Review*, 87(October), 56–65.

Industrial Marketing Committee Review Board (1954), "Fundamental Differences Between Industrial and Consumer Marketing", *Journal of Marketing*, 19(October), 152–158.

Insch, G.S. and McBride, J.B. (1999) "Decomposing the Country-of-Origin Construct: An Empirical Test of Country of Design, Country of Parts, and Country of Assembly," *Journal of International Consumer Marketing*," 10(4), 69–91.

Ittner, Christopher D., and David F. Larcker (1997), "Product Development Cycle Time and Organizational Performance", *Journal of Marketing Research*, 34(1), 13–23.

Jackson, Donald W., Jr., Janet E. Keith, and Richard K. Burdick (1984), "Purchasing Agents' Perceptions of Industrial Buying Center Influence: A Situational Approach", *Journal of Marketing*, 48(Fall), 75–83.

Jacobson, Robert (1988), "Distinguishing Among Competing Theories of the Market Share Effect", *Journal of Marketing*, 52(4), 68–80.

Jacobson, Robert (1992), "The "Austrian" School of Strategy", *Academy of Management Review*, (17)4, 782–807.

Jacobson, Robert and David A. Aaker (1985), "Is Market Share All That it's Cracked Up to Be?", *Journal of Marketing*, 49(4), 11–22.

Jacobson, Robert. (1990), "Unobservable Effects and Business Performance," *Marketing Science*, 9(1), 74–85.

Jacoby, Jacob (1978), "Consumer Research: A State of the Art Review", *Journal of Marketing*, 40(April), 87–96.

Jacoby, Jacob and Constance Small (1975), "The FDA Approach to Defining Misleading Advertising", *Journal of Marketing*, 39(October), 65–68.

Jacoby, Jacob, and Robert W. Chestnut (1978), "Brand Loyalty: Measurement and Management",*Journal of Marketing Research*, 15(4), 659–660.

Jacoby, Jacob, Donald E. Speller, and Carol A. Kohn (1974), "Brand Choice Behavior as a Function of Information Load", *Journal of Marketing Research*, 11(February), 63–69.

Jagdish N. Sheth, Ed., New York: Harper & Row, Publishers, Inc., 347–362.

Jain, Subhash (1989),"Standardization of International Marketing Strategy: Some Research Hypotheses," Journal of Marketing, 53(January), 70–79.

Jap, Sandy D. (2001), "Perspectives on Joint Competitive Advantages in Buyer-Supplier Relationships", *International Journal of Research in Marketing*, 18(1–2), 19–35.

Jap, Sandy D., and Shankar Ganesan (2000), "Control Mechanisms and the Relationship Life Cycle: Implications for Safeguarding Specific Investments and Developing Commitment," *Journal of Marketing Research*, 37(2), 227–245.

Javalgi R. R., Seyda Deligonul, A. Dixit, T.S. Cavusgil (2011), "International Market Re-Entry: A Review and Conceptual Framework." *International Business Review*, 20(4), 377–393.

Javalgi, Rajshekhar G. and La Toya M. Russell (2018), International Marketing Ethics: A Literature Review and Research Agenda," *Journal of Business Ethics*, 148, 703–720.

Jaworski, Bernard J., and Ajay K. Kohli (1996), "Market Orientation: Review, Refinement, and Roadmap," *Journal of Market-Focused Management,* (1)2, 119–135.

Jayachandran, Satish, Javier Gimeno, and P. Rajan Varadarajan (1999), "The Theory of Multimarket Competition: A Synthesis and Implications for Marketing Strategy", *Journal of Marketing*, 63(July), 49–66.

Johansson, Johny K. (1997), *Global Marketing: Foreign Entry, Local Marketing, and Global Management*, Chicago: IL, Richard D. Irwin.

John, George, and Barton A. Weitz (1988), "Forward Integration into Distribution: An Empirical Test of Transaction Cost Analysis", *Journal of Law, Economics, and Organization*, 4(2), 337–355.

Johnston, Wesley J. and Thomas V. Bonoma (1981), "Purchase Process for Capital Equipment and Services" *Industrial Marketing Management*, 10(October), 253–264.

Judd, Robert C. (1964), "The Case for Redefining Services", *Journal of Marketing*, 28(January), 58–59.

Jun, J.W. and Choi, C.W. (2007), "Effects of Country of Origin and Country Brand Attitude on Nonprescription Drugs", *Journal of Targeting, Measurement and Analysis for Marketing*, 15(4), 234–243.

Kahle, Lynn R. (1986), "The Nine Nations of North America and the Value Basis of Geographic Segmentation", *Journal of Marketing*, 50(April), 37–47.

Kahneman, Daniel, D. Kahneman, and Amos Tversky (2000), *Experienced Utility and Objective Happiness: A Moment-Based Approach*, New York: Cambridge University Press.

Kahneman, Daniel, Paul Slovic, and Amos Tversky (1982), *Judgment Under Uncertainty: Heuristics and Biases*, New York: Cambridge University Press.

Kaish, Stanley (1967), "Cognitive Dissonance and the Classification of Consumer Coods", *Journal of Marketing*, 31(October), 28–31.

Kalish, Shlomo, Vijay Mahajan, and Eitan Muller (1995), "Waterfall and Sprinkler New-Product Strategies in Competitive Global Markets", *International Journal of Research in Marketing*, 12(2), 105–119.

Kallet, Arthur (1935), *Counterfeit—Not Your Money Buy What It Buys*, New York: The Vanguard Press.

Kallet, Arthur and F. J. Schlink (1933), *100,000,000 Guinea Pigs: Dangers in Everyday Food, Drugs, and Cosmetics*, New York: The Vanguard Press.

Kalwani, Manohar U., and Narakesari Narayandas (1995), "Long-Term Manufacturer-Supplier Relationships: Do They Pay off for Supplier Firms?", *Journal of Marketing*, 59(1), 1–16.

Kalyanaram, Gurumurthy, William T. Robinson, and Glen L. Urban (1995), "Order of Market

Entry: Established Empirical Generalizations, Emerging Empirical Generalizations, and Future Research", *Marketing Science*, (14)3, G212–G221.

Kangun, Norman (1974), "Environmental Problems and Marketing: Saint or Sinner?" in *Marketing Analysis for Societal Problems*, Jagdish N. Sheth and Peter L. Wright, eds., Urbana-Champaign: Bureau of Economic and Business Research, College of Commerce and Business Administration, University of Illinois.

Kangun, Norman, Ed. (1972), *Society and Marketing*, New York: Harper and Row, Inc.

Kaplan, Andreas M., and Micharl Haenlein (2010), "Users of the World, Unite! The Challenges and Opportunities of Social Media," *Business Horizons*, *53*(1), 59–68.

Karniouchina, Ekaterina V., Can Uslay, and Grigori Erenburg (2011), "Do Marketing Media Have Life Cycles? The Case of Product Placement in Movies", *Journal of Marketing*, 75(3), 27–48.

Kassarjian, Harold H. (1969), "The Negro and American Advertising, 1946–1965", *Journal. of Marketing Research*, 6(February), 29–39.

Kassarjian, Harold H. (1971), "Personality and Consumer Behavior: A Review", *Journal of Marketing Research*, 8 (November), 409–418.

Kassarjian, Harold H. and Thomas S. Robertson, Eds. (1981), *Perspectives in Consumer Behavior*, 3rd Edition, Glenview, Illinois: Scott, Foresman and Company.

Kasulis, Jack J. and Robert E. Spekman (1980), "A Framework for the Use of Power", *European Journal of Marketing*, 14(4), 180–191.

Katona, George C. (1953), "Rational Behavior and Economic Behavior", *Psychological Review*, 60(September), 307–318.

Katona, George C. (1960), *The Powerful Consumer: Psychological Studies of the American Economy*, New York: McGraw-Hill Book Company, Inc.

Katona, George C. (1964), *The Mass Consumption Society*, New York: McGraw-Hill Book Company, Inc.

Katona, George C. and Eva Mueller (1953), *Consumer Attitudes and Demand: 1950–1952*, Ann Arbor: Survey Research Center, Institute for Social Research, University of Michigan.

Katona, George C. and Eva Mueller (1956), *Consumer Expectations: 1953–1956*, Ann Arbor: Survey Research Center, Institute for Social Research, University of Michigan.

Katsikeas, C. S., S. Samiee, M. Theodosiou (2006), "Strategy Fit and Performance Consequences of International Marketing Standardization," *Strategic Management Journal*, 27(9), 867–890.

Katz, Daniel (1960), "The Functional Approach to the Study of Attitudes", *Public Opinion Quarterly*, 24(Summer), 163–204.

Katz, Daniel and Ezra Stotland (1959), "A Preliminary Statement to a Theory of Attitude Structure and Change", in *Psychology: A Study of Science*, Volume 3, Sigmund Koch, ed., New York: McGraw-Hill Book Company, Inc., 423–475.

Katz, Danjel and Robert L. Kahn (1966), *The Social Psychology of Organizations*, New York: John Wiley & Sons, Inc.

Katz, Elihu and Paul F. Lazarsfeld (1955), *Personal Influence: The Part Played by People in the Flow of Mass Communications*, New York: The Free Press.

Keefe, Lisa M. (2004), "What Is The Meaning of Marketing?," *Marketing News,* (September 15), 17–18.

Keillor, Bruce D., Tomas M. Hult, and Destan Kandemir (2004), "A Study of the Service Encounters in Eight Countries", *Journal of International Marketing*, 12 (1), 9–35.

Keiningham, Timothy L., Bruce Cooil, Tor Wallin Andreassen, and Lerzan Aksoy (2007), "A Longitudinal Examination of Net Promoter and Firm Revenue Growth", *Journal of Marketing*, 71(July), 39–51.

Keiningham, Timothy L., Forrest V. Morgeson, Lerzan Aksoy, and Luke Williams (2014), "Service Failure Severity, Customer Satisfaction, and Market Share: An Examination of the Airline Industry," *Journal of Service Research*, 17(4), 415–431.

Keith, Robert J. (1960), "The Marketing Revolution", *Journal of Marketing*, 24(January), 35–38.

Keller, Kevin L. (1993), "Conceptualizing, Measuring, and Managing Customer-Based Brand Equity", *Journal of Marketing*, 57(1), 1–22.

Keller, Kevin L. (2002), "Branding and Brand Equity", in *Handbook of Marketing*, eds., Bart Weitz and Robin Wensley, London, UK: Sage Publications, 151–178.

Keller, Kevin Lane (1993), "Conceptualizing, Measuring, and Managing Customer-Based Brand Equity," *Journal of Marketing*, (57)1, 1–22.

Keller, Kevin Lane (2002), "Branding and Brand Equity," *Handbook of Marketing*, 151.

Keller, Kevin L. (1993), "Conceptualizing, Measuring, and Managing Customer-Based Brand Equity", *Journal of Marketing*, 57(1), 1–22.

Kelley, William T., Ed. (1973), *New Consumerism: Selected Readings*, Columbus, Ohio: Grid, Inc.

Kelly, Eugene and William Lazer, Eds. (1958), *Managerial Marketing: Perspectives and Viewpoints*, Homewood, Illinois: Richard D. Irwin, Inc.

Kenning, Peter, Hilke Plassmann and Dieter Ahlert (2007), "Applications of Functional Magnetic Resonance Imaging for Market Research", *Qualitative Market Research: An International Journal*, 10(2), 135–152.

Kerin, Roger A. and Robert A. Peterson (1983), *Perspectives on Strategic Marketing Management*, 2nd Edition, Boston: Allyn and Bacon, Inc.

Kerin, Roger A., and Raj Sethuraman (1998), "Exploring the Brand Value-Shareholder Value Nexus for Consumer Goods Companies," *Journal of the Academy of Marketing Science*, (26)4, 260–273.

Key, Thomas Martin, Terry Clark, O. C. Ferrell, David W. Stewart, and Leyland Pitt (2020), "Marketing's Theoretical and Conceptual Value Proposition: Opportunities to Address Marketing's Influence," *AMS Review*, 10(3), 151–167.

Killough, James (1978), "Improved Payoffs from Transnational Advertising", *Harvard Business Review*, 56(July–August), 102–110.

Kim, Chung Koo, and Jay Young Chung. "Brand Popularity, Country Image and Market Share: An Empirical Study." *Journal of International Business Studies* 28, no. 2 (1997): 361–86.

Kirca, Ahmet H., Satish Jayachandran, and William O. Bearden (2005), "Market Orientation: A Meta-Analytic Review and Assessment of Its Antecedents and Impact on Performance," *Journal of Marketing*, 69 (April), 24–41.

Klein, Saul, Gary L. Frazier, and Victor J. Roth (1990), "A Transaction Cost Analysis Model of Channel Integration in International Markets," *Journal of Marketing Research*, 27(2), 196–208.

Knight, G.A. and S.T. Cavusgil (1996) "The Born Global Firm: A Challenge to Traditional Internationalization Theory", in S.T. Cavusgil and T. Madsen (eds.) *Advances in International Marketing*, Vol. 8, JAI Press: Greenwich, CT. 11–26.

Knight, G.A. and S.T. Cavusgil (2004) "Innovation, Organizational Capabilities, and the Born-Global Firm," *Journal of International Business Studies*, 35, 121–141.

Knight, Gary. A. and Daekwan Kim (2009), "International Business Competence and the Contemporary Firm," *Journal of International Business Studies*, 40, 255–273.

Kohli, A. K., and Bernard J. Jaworski (1990), "Market Orientation: The Construct, Research Propositions, and Managerial Implications", *Journal of Marketing*, 54(2), 1–18.

Kohli, Ajay K. (1985), "Some Unexplored Supervisory Behaviors and Their Influence on Salespeople's Role Clarity, Specific Self-Esteem, Job Satisfaction, and Motivation", *Journal of Marketing Research*, 22(November), 424–433.

Kohli, Ajay K., and Bernard J. Jaworski (1990), "Market Orientation: The Construct, Research Propositions, and Managerial Implications", *Journal of Marketing*, 54(2), 1–18.

Kohli, Ajay, Bernard J. Jaworski, and Aijith Kumar (1993), "MARKOR: A Measure of Market Orientation", *Journal of Marketing Research*, 30(4), 467–477.

Koschate-Fischer, Nicole, Adamantios Diamantopoulos, and Katharina Oldenkotte (2012), "Are Consumers Really Willing to Pay More for a Favorable Country Image? A Study of Country of Origin Effects on Willingness to Pay" *Journal of International Marketing*, 20(1), 19–41.

Koschmann, Anthony and Jagdish N. Sheth (2019), "Do Brands Compete or Coexist? How Persistence of Brand Loyalty Segments the Market", *European Journal of Marketing*, 53(1), 1–19.

Kotabe, Maaski and Kristiaan Helsen (2010), *Global Marketing Management: The International Business*, 5th Ed., John Wiley & Sons.

Kotelnikova, Zoya (2012), "New Economic Sociology and Relationship Marketing: Parallel Development," *Economic Sociology*, *13*(3), 27–33.

Kotler, Philip & Kevin Lane Keller (2016), *Marketing Management*, 15th ed., Upper Saddle River, NJ: Pearson.

Kotler, Philip (1967), *Marketing Management: Analysis, Planning and Control*, Englewood Cliffs, New Jersey: Prentice-Hall, Inc.

Kotler, Philip (1972a), "A Generic Concept of Marketing", *Journal of Marketing*, 36(April), 46–54.

Kotler, Philip (1972b), "What Consumerism Means for Marketers", *Harvard Business Review*, 50(May–June), 48–57.

Kotler, Philip (1975), *Marketing for Nonprofit Organizations*, Englewood Cliffs, New Jersey: Prentice-Hall, Inc.

Kotler, Philip (1986a), "Global Standardization—Courting Danger", *The Journal of Consumer Marketing*, 3(Spring), 13–15.

Kotler, Philip (1986b), "Megamarketing", *Harvard Business Review*, 64(March–April), 117–124.

Kotler, Philip (1987), "The Reemerging of Marketing Public Relations in Mega-Marketing Corporations", Remarks to the Corporate Associates Conference, Medill School.

Kotler, Philip (1990, November), Speech Presented at The Trustees Meeting of the Marketing Science Institute, Boston.

Kotler, Philip and Gary Armstrong (1987), *Marketing: An Introduction*, Englewood Cliffs, New Jersey: Prentice-Hall, Inc.

Kotler, Philip and Gerald Zaltman (1971), "Social Marketing: An Approach to Planned Social Change", *Journal of Marketing*, 35(July), 3–12.

Kotler, Philip and Kevin Lane Keller (2016), *Marketing Management*, 15th ed., Upper Saddle River, NJ: Pearson.

Kotler, Philip and Sidney J. Levy (1969), "Broadening the Concept of Marketing", *Journal of Marketing*, 33(January), 10–15.

Kotler, Philip T. and Kevin Lane Keller (2011), *Marketing Management*, (14th Edition), Upper Saddle River, NJ: Prentice Hall.

Kotler, Philip, and Ravi Singh (1981), "Marketing Warfare in the 1980s", *The Journal of Business Strategy*, (1)3, 30.

Kotler, Philip, and Richard A. Conner (1977), "Marketing Professional Services", *Journal of Marketing*, 41(January), 71–76.

Kotler, Philip, Waldemar Pfoertsch, and Uwe Sponholz (2021), "The Current State of Marketing," In: H2H Marketing: The Genesis of Human-to-Human Marketing: Springer, Cham, 1-28. https://doi.org/10.1007/978-3-030-59531-9_1

Kozlenkova, Irina V., Stephen A. Samaha, and Robert W. Palmatier (2014), "Resource-Based Theory of Marketing," *Journal of the Academy of Marketing Science*, 42 (1), 1–21.

Krapfel, Robert E., Jr. (1985), "An Advocacy Behavior Model of Organizational Buyers' Vendor Choice", *Journal of Marketing*, 49(Fall), 51–59.

Krugman, Herbert E. (1965), "The Impact of Television Advertising: Learning Without Involvement", *Public Opinion Quarterly*, 29 (Fall), 349–356.

Krush, Michael T., Ravipreet S. Sohi, and Amit Saini (2015), "Dispersion of Marketing Capabilities: Impact on Marketing's Influence and Business Unit Outcomes," *Journal of the Academy of Marketing Science*, (43)1, 32–51.

Kuehn, Alfred A. (1962), "Consumer Brand Choice as a Learning Process", *Journal of Advertising Research*, 2(December), 10–17.

Kuhn, Alfred (1963), *The Study of Society: A Unified Approach*, Homewood, Illinois: Dorsey Press.

Kuhn, Thomas S. (1962), *The Structure of Scientific Revolutions*, Chicago: University of Chicago Press.

Kuhn, Thomas S. (1970), Criticism and the Growth of Knowledge: Volume 4: in *Proceedings of the International Colloquium in the Philosophy of Science*, London, 1965. Vol. 4. New York: Cambridge University Press.

Kumar, Nirmalya, Lisa K. Scheer, and Jan-Benedict EM Steenkamp (1995), "The Effects of Perceived Interdependence on Dealer Attitudes", *Journal of Marketing Research*, 32(3), 348–356.

Kumar, V. (2018), "A Theory of Customer Valuation: Concepts, Metrics, Strategy, and Implementation", *Journal of Marketing*, 82(1), 1–19.

Kumar, V., and Denish Shah (2009), "Expanding the Role of Marketing: From Customer Equity to Market Capitalization", *Journal of Marketing*, (73)6, 119–136.

Kumar, V., Veena Chattaraman, Carmen Neghina, Berndt Skiera, Lerzan Aksoy, Alexander Buoye, and Joerg Henseler (2013), "Data-Driven Services Marketing in a Connected World", *Journal of Service Management*, 24 (3), 330–352.

Kumar, Vikas, Deeksha Singh, Anish Purkayastha, Manish Popli, and Ajai Gaur (2019), "Springboard internationalization by emerging market firms: Speed of first cross-border acquisition", *Journal of International Business Studies*, 51(2), 172–193.

Laczniak, Gene R. (1983), "Framework for Analyzing Marketing Ethics", *Journal of Macromarketing*, 5(Spring), 7–17.

Laczniak, Gener. and Patrick E. Murphy, Eds. (1985), *Marketing Ethics: Guidelines for Managers*, Lexington, Massachusetts: Lexington Books.

Lagace, Rosemary R., Robert Dahlstrom, and Jule B. Gassenheimer (1991), "The Relevance of Ethical Salesperson Behavior on Relationship Quality: The Pharmaceutical Industry", *Journal of Personal Selling and Sales Management*, 11(4), 39–47.

Lam, Wing and Michael J. Harker (2015), "Marketing and Entrepreneurship: An Integrated View from the Entrepreneur's Perspective", *International Small Business Journal*, 33(3), 321–348.

Lamb, Ruth Deforest (1936), *American Chamber of Horrors: The Truth About Food and Drugs*, New York: Farrar & Rinehart, Inc.

Lambe, C. Jay, C. Michael Wittmann, and Robert E. Spekman (2001), "Social Exchange Theory and Research on Business-to-Business Relational Exchange", *Journal of Business-to-Business Marketing*, 8(3), 1–36.

Lambkin, M., and George S. Day (1989), "Evolutionary Processes in Competitive Markets: Beyond the Product Life Cycle", *Journal of Marketing*, 53(3), 4–20.

Lantz, G. and Loeb, S. (1996), "Country-of-Origin and Ethnocentrism: An Analysis of Canadian and American Preferences Using Social Identity Theory," *Advances in Consumer Research*, 23, 374–378.

Lariviere, Bart, Timothy Keiningham, Bruce Cooil, Lerzan Aksoy, Edward C. Malthouse, (2014), "A Longitudinal Examination of Customer Commitment and Loyalty", *Journal of Service Management*, 25(1), 75–100.

Laurent, Gilles and Jean-Noel Kapferer (1985), "Measuring Consumer Involvement Profiles", *Journal of Marketing Research*, 22(February), 41–53.

Lavidge, Robert J. and Gary A. Steiner (1961), "A Model for Predictive Measurements of Advertising Effectiveness", *Journal of Marketing*, 25(October), 59–62.

Lazer, William (1966), "Education for Marketing in the 1970s", *Journal of Marketing*, 30(July), 33–37.

Lazer, William (1971), *Marketing Management: A Systems Perspective*, New York: John Wiley & Sons, Inc.

Lazer, William and Eugene J. Kelley (1962), "The Systems Approach to Marketing", in *Managerial Marketing: Perspectives and Viewpoints*, William Lazer and Eugene J. Kelley, Eds., Homewood, Illinois: Richard D. Irwin, Inc.

Leclerc F, Schmitt BH, Dubé L. Foreign Branding and Its Effects on Product Perceptions and Attitudes. *Journal of Marketing Research*. 1994; 31(2): 263–270.

Lee, Don Y and Philip L Dawes (2005), "Guanxi, Trust, and Long-Term Orientation in Chinese Business Markets", *Journal of International Marketing*, 13(2), 28–56.

Lee, Dondae and Sang Wook Bae (1999), "Effects of Partitioned Country of Origin Information on Buyer Assessment of Binational Products", *Advances in Consumer Research*, 26(3), 344–351.

Leigh, Thomas W. and Arno J. Retiians (1984), "A Script-Theoretic Analysis of Industrial Purchasing Behavior", *Journal of Marketing*, 48(Fall), 22–32.

Lele, Miijnd M. and Jagdish N. Sheth (1987), The Customer is Key: Gaining an Unbeaten Advantage Through Customer Satisfaction, New York: John Wiley & Sons, Inc.

Leong, Siew Meng (1985), "Metatheory and Metamethodology in Marketing: A Lakatosian Reconstruction", *Journal of Marketing*, 49(Fall), 23–40.

Levitt, Theodore (1958), "The Dangers of Social Responsibility", *Harvard Business Review*, 36(September/October), 41–50.

Levitt, Theodore (1960), "Marketing Myopia", *Harvard Business Review*, 38(July/ August), 45–56.

Levitt, Theodore (1965), "Exploit the Product Life Cycle", *Harvard Business Review*, 43(November/ December), 81–94.

Levitt, Theodore (1965), Exploit the Product Life Cycle, Graduate School of Business Administration, Harvard University, (43), 1–33.

Levitt, Theodore (1972), "Production-Line Approach to Service," *Harvard Business Review*, 50(5), 20–31.

Levitt, Theodore (1981), "Marketing Intangible Products and Product Intangibles", *Harvard Business Review*, 59(May/June), 94–102.

Levitt, Theodore (1983), "The Globalization of Markets", *Harvard Business Review*, 61(May/ June), 92–102.

Levy, Sidney J. (1985), "Dreams, Fairy Tales, Animals, and Cars", *Psychology and Marketing*, 2(2), 67–81.

Lewis, Richard J. and Leo G. Erickson (1969), "Marketing Functions and Marketing Systems: A Synthesis", *Journal of Marketing*, 33(July), 10–14.

Lieberman, Marvin B., and David B. Montgomery (1988), "First-Mover Advantages," *Strategic Management Journal*, (9)S1, 41–58.

Liefeld, John P. (2004), "Consumer Knowledge and Use of Country-of-Origin Information at the Point of Purchase," *Journal of Consumer Behaviour*, 4(2), 85–96.

Lipson, Harry A. (1962), "Formal Reasoning and Marketing Strategy," *Journal of Marketing*, 26(4), 1–5.

Lovelock, Christopher (1983), "Classifying Services to Gain Strategic Marketing Insights," *Journal of Marketing*, 47(Summer), 9–20.

Lovelock, Christopher (1984), *Services Marketing— Text, Cases, and Readings*, Englewood Cliffs, NJ: Prentice-Hall.

Lovelock, Christopher (1988), *Managing Services: Marketing, Operations, and Human Resources*, Englewood Cliffs, NJ: Prentice-Hall.

Lovelock, Christopher H. (1983), "Classifying Services to Gain Strategic Marketing Insights", *Journal of Marketing*, 47(Summer), 9–20.

Lu, Irene R.R., Louise A. Heslop, D. Roland Thomas, and Ernest Kwan (2016), "An Examination of the Status and Evolution of Country Image Research", *International Marketing Review*, 33(6), 825–850.

Lucas, George H., Jr., A. Parasuraman, Robert A. Davis, and Ben M. Enis (1987), "An Empirical Study of Salesforce Turnover", *Journal of Marketing*, 51(July), 34–59.

Luck, David J. (1959), "On the Nature of Specialty Goods", *Journal of Marketing*, 24(July), 61–64.

Luck, David J. (1969), "Broadening the Concept of Marketing-Too Far", *Journal of Marketing*, 33(July), 53–55.

Luke, Robert H., and E. Reed Doke (1987), "Marketing Journal Hierarchies: Faculty Perceptions, 1986– 87", *Journal of the Academy of Marketing Science*, 15(Spring), 74–78.

Lusch, Robert F. (1976), "Sources of Power: Their Impact on Intrachannel Conflict", *Journal of Marketing Research*, 13(November), 382–390.

Lusch, Robert F. (2007), "Marketing's Evolving Identity: Defining our Future," *Journal of Public Policy & Marketing*, 26(2), 261–268.

Lusch, Robert F. and James R. Brown (1982), "A Modified Model of Power in the Marketing Channel", *Journal of Marketing Research*, 19(August), 312–323.

Lusch, Robert F. and Frederick E. Webster Jr. (2011), "A Stakeholder-Unifying, Cocreation Philosophy for Marketing," *Journal of Macromarketing*, *31*(2), 129–134.

Lusch, Robert F. and Stephen L. Vargo (2006), "Service-Dominant Logic as a Foundation for a General Theory," *Marketing Theory*, 6, 281.

Macaulay, Stewart (1963), *Non-Contractual Relations in Business: A Preliminary Study*, Boulder, CO: Westview Press.

Mackenzie, Kenneth D. and Franceso M. Nicosia (1968), "Marketing Systems: Toward Formal Descriptions and Structural Properties", in *Marketing and the New Science of Planning*, Robert L. King, ed., Chicago: American Marketing Association, 14–23.

Mackenzie, Scott B., Richard J. Lutz, and George E. Belch (1986), "The Role of Attitude Toward the Ad as a Mediator of Advertising Effectiveness: A Test of Competing Explanations", *Journal of Marketing Research*, 23(May), 130–143.

Macneil, Ian R. (1980), *The New Social Contract*, New Haven, CT: Yale University Press.

Magee, John (1960), "The Logistics of Distribution", *Harvard Business Review*, 38(July/August), 89–101.

Magnuson Warren G. and Jean Carper (1968), *The Dark Side of the Marketplace: The Plight of the American Consumer*, Englewood Cliffs, New Jersey: Prentice-Hall, Inc.

Malhotra N. K., Agarwal J., and Ulgado F. M. (003), "Internationalization and Entry Modes: A Multitheoretical Framework and Research Propositions", *Journal of International Marketing*, 11(4): 1–31.

Malhotra, Naresh K. and Can Uslay (2018), "Make, Buy, Borrow or Crowdsource? The Evolution and Future of Outsourcing", *Journal of Business Strategy*, 39(5) 14–21.

Malhotra, Naresh K., Can Uslay, and Ahmet Bayraktar (2016), *Relationship Marketing Re-Imagined: Marketing's Inevitable Shift from Exchanges to Value Cocreating Relationships*. Business Expert Press: New York.

Malhotra, Naresh K., Olivia F. Lee, and Can Uslay (2012), "Mind the Gap: The Mediating Role of Mindful Marketing between Market and Quality Orientations, Their Interaction, and Consequences," *International Journal of Quality & Reliability Management*, 29 (6), 607–625.

Mallen, Bruce E. (1963), "A Theory of Retailer-Supplier Conflict, Control, and Cooperation," *Journal of Retailing*, 39(Summer) 24–32, 51.

Mallen, Bruce E. (1973), "Functional Spin-Off: A Key to Anticipating Change in Distribution Structure," *Journal of Marketing*, 37(July), 18–25.

Mallen, Bruce E., Ed. (1967), *The Marketing Channel: A Conceptual Viewpoint*, New York: John Wiley & Sons, Inc.

Maltz, Elliot, and Ajay K. Kohli (2000), "Reducing Marketing's Conflict with Other Functions: The Differential Effects of Integrating Mechanisms," *Journal of the Academy of Marketing Science,* (28)4, 479–492.

Mandler, Timo, Burcu Sezen, Jieke Chen, and Aysegul Ozsomer (2021), "Performance Consequences of Marketing Standardization/Adaptation: A Systematic Literature Review and Future Research Agenda," *Journal of Business Research*, 125(March), 416–435.

March, James G. and Herbert A. Simon (1958), *Organizations*, New York: John Wiley & Sons, Inc.

Markin, Rom J. (1969), *The Psychology of Consumer Behavior*, Englewood Cliffs, New Jersey: Prentice-Hall, Inc.

Martineau, Pierre (1958), "Social Classes and Spending Behavior," *Journal of Marketing*, 23(October), 121–129.

Maslow, Abraham H. (1954), *Motivation and Personality*, New York: Harper and Row, Inc.

Massy, William F. (1969), "Forecasting the Demand for New Convenience Products," *Journal of Marketing Research*, 6(November), 405–412.

Massy, William F., David B. Montgomery, and Donald G. Morrison (1970), *Stochastic Models of Buying Behavior*, Cambridge: Massachusetts Institute of Technology, The M.I.T. Press.

Matihews, J.B. and R. E. Shallcross (1935), *Partners in Plunder: The Cost of Business Dictatorship*, New York: Covici, Friede, Publishers.

Mattsson, Lars-Gunnar (1997). "Relationship Marketing" and the "Markets-as-Networks Approach Comparative Analysis of two Evolving Streams of Research," *Journal of Marketing Management*, 13(5), 447–461.

Mcaliter, Leigh, Max H. Bazerman, and Peter Fader (1986), "Power and Goal Setting Channel Negotiations," *Journal of Marketing Research*, 23(August), 228–236.

McCammon, Bert (1963), "Alternative Explanations of Institutional Change and Channel Evolution," in *Toward Scientific Marketing*, Stephen A. Greyser, ed., Chicago: American Marketing Association, 477–490.

McCammon, Bert (1965), "The Emergence and Growth of Contractually Integrated Channels in the American Economy," in *Economic Growth, Competition, and World Markets*, Peter D. Bennett, ed., Chicago: American Marketing Association, 496–515.

McCarthy, E. Jerome (1960), *Basic Marketing: A Managerial Approach*, Homewood, Illinois: Richard D. Irwin, Inc.

McClelland, David C. (1961), *The Achieving Society*, Princeton, New Jersey: D. Van Nostrand Company, Inc.

McCracken, Grant (1986), "Culture and Consumption: A Theoretical Account of the Structure and Movement of the Cultural Meaning of Consumer Goods," *Journal of Consumer Research*, 13(June), 71–84.

McGarry, Edmund D. (1950), "Some Functions of Marketing Reconsidered," in *Theory in Marketing*, Reavis Cox and Wroe Alderson, eds., Chicago: Richard D. Irwin, Inc., 263–279.

McGregor, Douglas (1960), *The Human Side of Enterprise*, New York: McGraw-Hill Book Company, Inc.

McInnes, William (1964), "A Conceptual Approach to Marketing," in *Theory in Marketing*, Reavis Cox, Wroe Alderson, and Stanley J. Shapiro, eds., Homewood, Illinois: Richard D. Irwin, Inc., 51–67.

McKenna, Regis (1991), *Marketing is Everything*, Boston, MA: *Harvard Business Review*.

McKinsey Global Institute (2016), Digital Globalization: The New Era of Global Flows, (March), available at https://www.mckinsey.com/~/media/mckinsey/business%20functions/mckinsey%20digital/our%20insights/digital%20globalization%20the%20new%20era%20of%20global%20flows/mgi-digital-globalization-full-report.ashx last accessed December 31, 2020.

McKiterick, John B. (1957), "What is the Marketing Management Concept," in *The Frontiers of*

Marketing Thought and Action, Frank Bass, ed., Chicago: American Marketing Association, 71–82.

McNeal, James U. (1987), *Children as Consumers: Insights and Implications*, Lexington, Massachusetts: Lexington Books.

McNiven, Malcolm A. (1968), "Marketing Research and Marketing Information Systems", in *Marketing and the New Science of Planning*, Robert L. King, ed., Chicago: American Marketing Association, 169–171.

Menon, Anil, Sundar G. Bharadwaj, Phani T. Adidan, and Steven W. Edison (1999), "Antecedents and Consequences of Marketing Strategy Making: A Model and a Test," *Journal of Marketing*, (63)2, 18–40.

Mentzer, John T. (2000), "Relationship Marketing in Mass Markets", in *Handbook of Relationship Marketing*, Jagdish N. Sheth and Atul Parvatiyar, Eds., Thousand Oaks, CA: Sage Publications, 457–480.

Merton, Robert K. (1957), *Social Theory and Social Structure*, New York: The Free Press.

Mick, David Glen (1986), "Consumer Research and Semiotics: Exploring the Morphology of Signs, Symbols, and Significance", *Journal of Consumer Research*, 13(September), 196–213.

Miller, Neal E. (1959), "Liberalization of Basic SR Concepts: Extensions to Conflict Behavior, Motivation, and Social Learning", in *Psychology: A Study of Science*, Volume 2, Sigmund Koch, ed., New York: McGraw-Hill Book Company, Inc., 196–292.

Miracle, Gordon E. (1965), "Product Characteristics and Marketing Strategy", *Journal of Marketing*, 29(January), 18–24.

Mitchell, Will (1991), "Dual Clocks: Entry Order Influences on Incumbent and Newcomer Market Share and Survival When Specialized Assets Retain Their Value," *Strategic Management Journal*, 12(2), 85–100.

Mitra, Debanjan, and Peter N. Golder (2002), "Whose Culture Matters? Near-Market Knowledge and Its Impact on Foreign Market Entry Timing," *Journal of Marketing Research*, 39(3), 350–365.

Mittal, Banwari, and Jagdish N. Sheth (2001), *ValueSpace: Winning the Battle for Market Leadership*. New York: McGraw-Hill.

Mizik, Natalie, and Robert Jacobson (2003), "Trading Off Between Value Creation and Value Appropriation: The Financial Implications of Shifts in Strategic Emphasis," *Journal of Marketing*, (67)1, 63–76.

Mohr, Jakki J., Robert J. Fisher, and John R. Nevin (1996), "Collaborative Communication in Interfirm Relationships: Moderating Effects of Integration and Control," *Journal of Marketing*, 60(3), 103–115.

Möller, Kristian, and Aino Halinen (2000), "Relationship Marketing Theory: Its Roots and Direction," *Journal of Marketing Management*, 16(1–3), 29–54.

Monieson, David D. and Stanley J. Shapiro (1980), "Biological and Evolutionary Dimensions of Aldersonian Thought: What He Borrowed Then and What He Might Have Borrowed Now", in *Theoretical Developments in Marketing*, Charles W. Lamb, Jr. and Patrick M. Dunne, eds., Chicago: American Marketing Association, 7–12.

Monroe, Kent B (2003), *Pricing: Making Profitable Decisions*, Boston, MA: McGraw-Hill.

Montgomery, David B. and Charles B. Weinberg (1979), "Toward Strategic Intelligence Systems", *Journal of Marketing*, 43(Fall), 41–52.

Montgomery, David B., Marian Chapman Moore, and Joel E. Urbany (2005), "Reasoning About Competitive Reactions: Evidence from Executives," *Marketing Science*, 24(1), 138–149.

Moorman, Christine, Gerald Zaltman and Rohit Deshpande (1992), "Relationships Between Providers and Users of Market Research: The Dynamics of Trust Within and Between Organizations," *Journal of Marketing Research*, 29(3), 314–328.

Moorthy, K. Sridhar (1985), "Using Game Theory to Model Competition," *Journal of Marketing Research*, (22)3, 262–282.

Morgan, Fred W. (1982), "Marketing and Product Liability: A Review and Update", *Journal of Marketing*, 46(Summer), 69–78.

Morgan, Neil A. (2012), "Marketing and Business Performance," *Journal of the Academy of Marketing Science*, (40)1, 102–119.

Morgan, Neil A., Hui Feng and Kimberly A. Whitler (2018), "Marketing Capabilities in International Marketing," *Journal of International Marketing*, (26)1, 61–95.

Morgan, Neil A., Kimberly A. Whitler, Hui Feng, and Simos Chari (2019), "Research in Marketing Strategy," *Journal of the Academy of Marketing Science*, (47)1, 4–29.

Morgan, Robert E., Tony McGuinness and Eleri R. Thorpe (2000), The Contribution of Marketing to Business Strategy Formation: A Perspective on Business Performance Gains, *Journal of Strategic Marketing*, 8, 341–362.

Morgan, Robert M., and Shelby D. Hunt (1994), "The Commitment-Trust Theory of Relationship Marketing," *Journal of Marketing*, (58)3, 20–38.

Morgan, Robert M., and Shelby Hunt (1999), "Relationship-Based Competitive Advantage: The Role of Relationship Marketing in Marketing Strategy," *Journal of Business Research*, *46*(3), 281–290.

Morgeson, Forest V. III, G. Tomas M. Hult, Sunil Mithas, Timothy Keiningham, and Claes Fornell (2020), "Turning Complaining Customers into Loyal Customers: Moderators of the Complaint Handling-Customer Loyalty Relationship," *Journal of Marketing*, 84(5), 79–99.

Morris, Michael H., Minet Schindehutte, and Raymond W. LaForge (2002), "Entrepreneurial Marketing: A Construct for Integrating Emerging Entrepreneurship and Marketing Perspectives," *Journal of Marketing Theory and Practice*, 10(4), 1–19.

Moyer, Reed (1968), *Changing Marketing Systems ...: Corporate and Government Interfaces*, Chicago, IL: American Marketing Association.

Moyer, Reed, Ed. (1972), *Macro Marketing: A Social Perspective*, New York: John Wiley & Sons, Inc.

Mudambi R. and Shaker A. Zahra (2007), "The Survival of International New Ventures," *Journal of International Business Studies*, 38(2), 333–352.

Mudambi, Ram, and Susan McDowell Mudambi (1995), "From Transaction Cost Economics to Relationship Marketing: A Model of Buyer-Supplier Relations," *International Business Review*, 4(4), 419–433.

Muncy, James A. and Raymond P. Fisk (1987), "Cognitive Relativism and the Practice of Marketing Science," *Journal of Marketing*, 51(January), 20–33.

Muniz, Albert M., and Thomas C. O'Guinn (2001), "Brand Community," *Journal of Consumer Research*, 27(4), 412–432.

Murphy, Patrick E. and Ben M. Enis (1986), "Classifying Products Strategically," *Journal of Marketing*, 50 (July), 24–42.

Myers, John G., William F. Massy, and Stephfn A. Greyser (1980), *Marketing Research and Knowledge Development: An Assessment of Marketing Management*, Englewood Cliffs, New Jersey: Prentice-Hall, Inc.

Nader, Ralph (1965), *Unsafe at Any Speed*, New York: Grossman.

Nagle, Thomas (1984), "Economic Foundations for Pricing," *Journal of Business*, 57(January), S3–S26.

Nalebuff, Barry and Adam M. Brandenburger (1996), *Co-opetition*. Crown Publishing Group.

Narayanan, Vijay (2015), "Export Barriers for Small and Medium Sized Enterprises: A Literature Review based on Leonidou's Model," *Entrepreneurial Business and Economics Review*, 3(2), 105–123.

Narver, J. C., & Stanley F. Slater (1990), "The Effect of a Market Orientation on Business Profitability," *Journal of Marketing*, 54(4), 20–35.

Nevin, John R. (1995), "Relationship Marketing and Distribution Channels: Exploring Fundamental Issues," *Journal of the Academy of Marketing Science*, 23(4), 327–334.

Newman, Joseph W. (1977), "Consumer External Search: Amount and Determinants" in *Consumer and Industrial Buying Behavior*, Arch G. Woodside, Jagdish N. Sheth, and Peter D. Bennett, Eds., New York: Elsevier North-Holland, Inc., 79–94.

Nickels, William (1974), "Conceptual Conflicts in Marketing," *Journal of Economics and Business*, 26(Winter), 140–143.

Nicosia, Francesco M. (1962), "Marketing and Alderson's Functionalism," *Journal of Business*, 35(October), 403–413.

Nicosia, Francesco M. (1966), *Consumer Decision Processes: Marketing and Advertising Implications*, Englewood Cliffs, New Jersey: Prentice-Hall, Inc.

Noordewier, Thomas G., George John, and John R. Nevin (1990), "Performance Outcomes of Purchasing Arrangements in Industrial Buyer-Vendor Relationships," *Journal of Marketing*, 54(4), 80–93.

Normann, R. (1984), *Service Management*, Wiley, Chichester.

Normann, Richard (1984), *Service Management: Strategy and Leadership in Service Business*, New York: John Wiley & Sons.

O'Shaughnessy, John and Michael J. Ryan (1979), "Marketing, Science and Technology," in *Conceptual and Theoretical Developments in*

Marketing, O. C. Ferrell, Stephen W. Brown, and Charles W. Lamb, Jr., Eds., Chicago: American Marketing Association, 577–589.

Ohlin, Bertil (1931), *Interregional and International Trade*, Boston: Harvard University Press.

Ohmae, Kenichi (1989), "Managing in a Borderless World," *Harvard Business Review*, 67 (May/June), 152–161.

Oliver, Richard L. (1999), "Whence Consumer Loyalty?" *Journal of Marketing*, 63(4), 33–44.

Olivia, Terence A., Richard L. Oliver, Ian C. MacMillan (1992), "A Catastrophe Model for Developing Service Satisfaction Strategies", *Journal of Marketing*, 56(3), 83–95.

O'Malley, Lisa, and Andrea Prothero (2004), "Beyond the Frills of Relationship Marketing", *Journal of Business Research*, 57(11), 1286–1294.

Osgood, Charles E. (1957a), "A Behavioristic Analysis of Perception and Language as Cognitive Phenomena", in *Contemporary Approaches to Cognition: A Symposium Held at the University of Colorado*, Cambridge, Massachusetts: Harvard University Press, 75–118.

Osgood, Charles E. (1957b), "Motivational Dynamics of Language Behavior", in *Nebraska Symposium on Motivation*, Marshall R. Jones, ed., Volume 5, Lincoln: University of Nebraska Press, 348–424.

Ostrom Amy L, Joy M. Field, Darima Fotheringham, Mahesh Subramony, Anders Gustafsson, Katherine N. Lemon, Ming-Hui Huang, and Janet R. McColl-Kennedy (2021), "Service Research Priorities: Managing and Delivering Service in Turbulent Times," *Journal of Service Research*, 24(3):329-353. doi:10.1177/10946705211021915

Ostrom, A. L., A. Parasuraman, D. E. Bowen, L. Patricio, and C. A. Voss (2015), "Service Research Priorities in a Rapidly Changing Context", *Journal of Service Research*, 18(2), 127–159.

Ostrom, A. L., M. J. Bitner, S. W. Brown, K. A. Burkhard, M. Goul, V. Smith–Daniels, H. Demirkan, and E. Rabinovich, E. (2010), "Moving Forward and Making a Difference: Research Priorities for the Science of Service", *Journal of Service Research*, 13(1), 4–36.

O'Sullivan, Don, and Andrew V. Abela (2007), "Marketing Performance Measurement Ability and Firm Performance," *Journal of Marketing*, (71)2, 79–93.

Oxenfeldt, A. R. (1960), "A Multi-State Approach to Pricing", *Harvard Business Review*, 38(July/August), 125–133.

Oxenfeldt, Alfred (1958), "A Dynamic Element in Consumption: The TV Industry," *Consumer Behavior: Research on Consumer Reactions*, New York: Harper and Brothers.

Oxenfeldt, Alfred (1958), 'The formulation of marketing strategy", in Eugene J. Kelley and William Lazer, eds., *Managerial Marketing: Perspectives and Viewpoints*, Homewood, IL: Richard D. Irwin, 264–272.

Özsomer, Ayşegül (2012), "Global Brand Purchase Likelihood: A Critical Synthesis and an Integrated Conceptual Framework", *Journal of International Marketing*, 16(4), 1–28.

Özsomer, Ayşegül and Selin Altaras (2008), "Global Brand Purchase Likelihood: A Critical Synthesis and an Integrated Conceptual Framework," *Journal of International Marketing*, 16(4), 1–28.

Packard, Vance O. (1960), *The Waste Makers*, New York: The David McKay Company, Inc.

Palmatier, Robert W. (2008), *Relationship Marketing*, Cambridge, MA: Marketing Science Institute.

Palmatier, Robert W., Christine Moorman, and Ju-Yeon Lee (2019), "Introduction to the Handbook on Customer Centricity," *Handbook on Customer Centricity*. Northampton, MA: Edward Elgar Publishing.

Palmatier, Robert W., Rajiv P. Dant, Dhruv Grewal, & Kenneth R. Evans (2006), "Factors Influencing the Effectiveness of Relationship Marketing: A Meta-Analysis," *Journal of Marketing*, *70*(4), 136–153.

Palmer, Adrian (1994), "Relationship Marketing: Back to Basics?" *Journal of Marketing Management*, *10*(7), 571–579.

Papadopoulos, Nicolas G., Louise A. Heslop, Francoise Garby, and George Avlonitis (1987), "Does Country of Origin' Matter? Some Findings from a Cross-Cultural Study of Consumer Views About Foreign Products," Report no. 87–104. Cambridge, MA: Marketing Science Institute.

Parameswaran, Ravi, and Attila Yaprak (1987), "A Cross-National Comparison of Consumer Research Measures." *Journal of International Business Studies*, 18(Spring), 35–49.

Parasuraman A., Valarie Zeithaml and Arvind Malhotra (2005), "E-S-QUAL: A Multiple-Item Scale for Assessing Electronic Service Quality", *Journal of Service Research*, 7(3), 213–233.

Parasuraman, A., Valarie A. Zeithaml, and Leonard Berry (1985), "A Conceptual Model of Service

Quality and Its Implications for Future Research," *Journal of Marketing,* (Fall), 41–50.

Parasuraman, A., Valarie A. Zeithaml, and Leonard Berry (1988), "SERVQUAL: A Multiple-Item Scale for Measuring Consumer Perceptions of Service Quality", *Journal of Retailing,* 64(Spring), 12–40.

Parasuraman, A, Valarie A. Zeithaml, and Leonard Berry (1994), Reassessment of Expectations as a Comparison Standard in Measuring Service Quality: Implications for Further Research, *Journal of Marketing,* 58(1), 111–124.

Parasuraman, Arun, Leonard L. Berry, and Valarie A. Zeithaml (1991), "Refinement and Reassessment of the SERVQUAL Scale," *Journal of Retailing,* 67(4), 420–450.

Park, C.W., Bernard J. Jaworski, and D.J. MacInnis (1986), "Strategic Brand Concept-Image Management", *Journal of Marketing,* 50(4), 135–145.

Parvatiyar, Atul and Jagdish Sheth (1997), "Paradigm Shift in Interfirm Marketing Relationships: Emerging Research Issues", *Research in Marketing,* 13, 233–255.

Parvatiyar, Atul, and Jagdish Sheth (2001), "Customer Relationship Management: Emerging Practice, Process, and Discipline," *Journal of Economic & Social Research,* 3(2), 1–34.

Paul, C. (1993), "Partitioning Country of Origin Effects: Consumer Evaluations of a Hybrid Product," *Journal of International Business Studies,* 24(2), 291–306.

Payne, Adrian (2000), Relationship Marketing: The UK Perspective, 39–67, In *Handbook of Relationship Marketing,* Jagdish Sheth and Atul Parvatiyar (Eds.), Thousand Oaks, CA: Sage Publications.

Payne, Adrian and Pennie Frow (2005), "A Strategic Framework for Customer Relationship Management", *Journal of Marketing,* 69(4), 167–176.

Payne, Adrian and Pennie Frow (2017), "Relationship Marketing: Looking Backwards Towards the Future", *Journal of Services Marketing,* 31(1), 11–15.

Payne, Adrian, Pennie Frow, and Andreas Eggert (2017), "The Customer Value Proposition: Evolution, Development, and Application in Marketing", *Journal of the Academy of Marketing Science,* 45(4), 467–489.

Peebles, Dean M., Jr., John K. Ryans, and Ivan R. Vemon (1977), "A New Perspective on Advertising Standardization," *European Journal of Marketing,* 11(8), 569–576.

Penrose, Edith (1959), *The Theory of the Growth of the Firm,* New York: John Wiley and Sons. Porter, Michael E. (1980), *Competitive Strategy,* New York: The Free Press.

Peppers, Don and Martha Rogers (1993), *The One to One Future: Building Relationships One Customer at a Time,* New York: Currency Doubleday.

Pessemier, Edgar A. (1982), *Product Management: Strategy and Organization,* New York: John Wiley & Sons.

Pessemier, Edgar and Moshe Handelsman (1984), "Temporal Variety in Consumer Behavior", *Journal of Marketing Research,* 21(November), 435–444.

Peter, J. Paul and Jerry C. Olson (1983), "Is Science Marketing?", *Journal of Marketing,* 47(Fall), 111–125.

Peters, Thomas J. and Robert H. Waterman, Jr. (1982), *In Search of Excellence: Lessons from America's Best-Run Companies,* New York: Harper and Row, Publishers, Inc.

Peterson, Robert A. (1995), "Relationship Marketing and the Consumer", *Journal of the Academy of Marketing Science,* 23(4), 278–281.

Peterson, Robert A. And Vijay Mahajan (1978), "Multi-Product Growth Models", in *Research in Marketing,* Jagdish N. Sheth, ed., Volume 1, Greenwich, Connecticut: JAI Press, Inc., 201–231.

Petroshius, Susan M. and Kent B. Monroe (1987), "Effect of Product-Line Pricing Characteristics on Product Evaluations", *Journal of Consumer Research,* 13(March), 511–519.

Pfeffer, J. and G. R. Salancik (1978), *The External Control of Organizations,* New York: Harper & Row.

Pharr, J.M. (2005), "Synthesizing Country-of-Origin Research from the Last Decade: Is the Concept Still Salient in an Era of Global Brands?" *Journal of Marketing Theory* and Practice, 13(4), 34–45.

Phillips, Lynn W. and Brian Sternthal (1977), "Age Differences in Information Processing: A Perspective on the Aged Consumer", *Journal of Marketing Research,* 14(November), 444–457.

Phillips, Lynn W., Dae R. Chang, and Robert D. Buzzell (1983), "Product Quality, Cost Position and Business Performance: A Test of Some Key Hypotheses", *Journal of Marketing,* (47)2, 26–43.

Phillips, Mary C. (1934), *Skin Deep: The Truth About Beauty Aids—Safe and Harmful*, New York: The Vanguard Press.

Piercy, Nigel F. and David W. Cravens (1995), "The Network Paradigm and the Marketing Organization: Developing a New Management Agenda", *European Journal of Marketing*, 29(3), 7–34.

Pine, Joe (1999), *The Experience Economy: Work Is Theatre and Every Business a Stage*, Boston, MA: Harvard Business School Press.

Pine, Joseph B. III (1999), *The Experience Economy: Work Is Theatre and Every Business a Stage*, Boston, MA: Harvard Business School Press.

Plank, Richard E., and Deborah Francis (2001), "Does Reverse Marketing Reduce Conflict in Buyer-Seller Relations?," *American Business Review*, (19)1, 76–83.

Pollay, Richard W. (1986), "The Distorted Mirror: Reflections on the Unintended Consequences of Advertising", *Journal of Marketing*, 50(April), 18–36.

Popper, Edward and Scott Ward (1980), *Children's Purchasing Requests and Parental Responses*, Boston: Marketing Science Institute.

Porter Michael E. (1980), Competitive Strategy. New York, NY: The Free Press.

Porter, Michael E. (1980), "Industry Structure and Competitive Strategy: Keys to Profitability", *Financial Analysts Journal*, (36)4, 30–41.

Porter, Michael E. (1980), *Competitive Strategy: Techniques for Analyzing Industries and Competitors*, New York: The Free Press.

Porter, Michael E. (1985), *Competitive Advantage: Creating and Sustaining Superior Performance*, New York: The Free Press.

Porter, Michael E., and Mark R. Kramer (2006), "The Link Between Competitive Advantage and Corporate Social Responsibility", *Harvard Business Review*, 84(12), 78–92.

Post, James E. (1985), "Assessing the Nestle Boycott: Corporate Accountability and Human Rights", *California Management Review*, 27(Winter), 113–131.

Prahalad, C.K. (2004), *Fortune at the Bottom of the Pyramid: Eradicating Poverty Through Profits*, Philadelphia, PA: Wharton School Publishing.

Prahalad, C.K. and Venkat Ramaswamy (2004), *The Future of Competition: Co-creating Unique Value with Customers*, Boston: Harvard Business School Press.

Prahalad, Coimbatore K., and Venkat Ramaswamy (2004), "Co-Creation Experiences: The Next Practice in Value Creation," *Journal of Interactive Marketing*, 18(3), 5–14.

Preston, Ivan L. (1976), "A Comment on 'Defining Misleading Advertising' and 'Deception in Advertising'", *Journal of Marketing*, 40(July), 54–57.

Preston, Ivan L. (1982), "The Association Model of the Advertising Communication Process", *Journal of Advertising*, 11(2), 3–15.

Punj, Girish and Richard Staelin (1983), "A Model of Consumer Information Search Behavior for New Automobiles", *Journal of Consumer Research*, 10(March), 366–380.

Puto, Christopher P., Wesley E. Patton III, and Ronald H. King (1985), "Risk Handling Strategies in Industrial Vendor Selection Decisions", *Journal of Marketing*, 49(Winter), 89–98.

Quelch, J. A. and E. J. Hoff (1986), "Customizing Global Marketing", *Harvard Business Review*, 64(May–June), 59–68.

Radadev, Vadim (2012), "Note from the Editor," *Economic Sociology*, 13(3), 1–49.

Ramamurti, R. and Vijay Govindarajan (2018), *Reverse Innovation in Health Care: How to Make Value-Based Delivery Work*, Boston, MA: Harvard Business School Press.

Ramanujam, Vasudevan and N. Venkataraman (1984), "An Inventory and Critique of Strategy Research Using the PIMS Database", *Academy of Management Review*, 9(1), 138–151.

Ramond, C. K. and Henry Assael (1974), "An Empirical Framework for Product Classification", in *Models of Buyer Behavior: Conceptual, Quantitative, and Empirical*.

Rangan, V. Kasturi, E. Raymond Corey, and Frank Cespedes (1993), "Transaction Cost Theory: Inferences from Clinical Field Research on Downstream Vertical Integration", *Organization Science*, 4(3), 454–477.

Rao, Ram C., Ramesh V. Arjunji, and B. P. S. Murthi (1995), "Game Theory and Empirical Generalizations Concerning Competitive Promotions," *Marketing Science*, 14(3), G89–G100.

Rao, Sally, and Chad Perry (2003), "Convergent Interviewing to Build a Theory in

Under-Researched Areas: Principles and an Example Investigation of Internet Usage in Inter-Firm Relationships", *Qualitative Market Research: An International Journal*, 6(4), 236–247.

Rao, Vithala R. (1984), "Pricing Research in Marketing: The State of the Art", *Journal of Business*, 57(January), S39–S60.

Rathmell, John M. (1969), *Managing the Marketing Function: Concepts, Analysis, and Application*, London: Wiley.

Read, Stuart, Nicholas Dew, Saras D. Sarasvathy, Michael Song, and Robert Wiltbank (2009), "Marketing Under Uncertainty: The Logic of an Effectual Approach", *Journal of Marketing*, 73(3), 1–18.

Reeves, Martin, Sandy Moose, and Thijs Venema (2014), "BCG Classics Revisited: The Growth Share Matrix," available at www.bcg.com/en-us/publications/2014/growth-share-matrix-bcg-classics-revisited, last accessed on January 30, 2021.

Reibstein, David J. and Hubert Gatignon (1984), "Optimal Product Line Pricing: The Influence of Elasticities and Cross-Elasticities", *Journal of Marketing Research*, 21(August), 259–267.

Reibstein, David J., George Day, and Jerry Wind (2009), "Guest Editorial: Is Marketing Academia Losing Its Way?", *Journal of Marketing*, 73(4), 1–3.

Reichheld, Frederick F. (2003), "The One Number You Need to Grow", *Harvard Business Review*, 88(12), 46–54.

Reidenbach, R. Eric and Terence A. Oliva (1981), "General Living Systems Theory and Marketing: A Framework for Analysis", *Journal of Marketing*, 45(Fall), 30–37.

Reidenbach, R. Eric and Terence A. Oliva (1983), "Toward a Theory of the Macro Systemic Effects of the Marketing Function", *Journal of Macromarketing*, 3(Fall), 33–40.

Reierson, C.C. (1967), "Attitude Changes Toward Foreign Products," *Journal of Marketing Research*, November, 4(4), 385–387.

Reilly, William J. (1931), *The Law of Retail Gravitation*, Austin, Texas: The University of Texas.

Resnik, Alan J. and Robert R. Harmon (1983), "Consumer Complaints and Managerial Response: A Holistic Approach", *Journal of Marketing*, 47(Winter), 86–97.

Rethans, Arno J. (1979), "The Aldersonian Paradigm: A Perspective for Theory Development and Synthesis", in *Conceptual and Theoretical Developments in Marketing*, O. C. Ferrell, Stephen W. Brown, and Charles W. Lamb, Jr., Eds., Chicago: American Marketing Association.

Review, 33(6), 825–850.

Revzan, David A. (1961), *Wholesaling in Marketing Organization*, New York: John Wiley & Sons, Inc.

Revzan, David A. (1965), *The Marketing Significance of Geographical Variations in Wholesale/Retail Sales Ratios*, Berkeley: University of California, Institute of Business and Economic Research.

Revzan, David A. (1967), *The Marketing Significance of Geographical Variations in Wholesale/Retail Sales Ratios, Part II: New and Supplementary Analysis and Revisions*, Berkeley: University of California, Institute of Business and Economic Research.

Reynolds, Kristy E., and Sharon E. Beatty (1999), "Customer Benefits and Company Consequences of Customer-Salesperson Relationships in Retailing", *Journal of Retailing*, 75(1), 11–32.

Rhoades, E. L. (1927), *Introductory Readings in Marketing*, Chicago: A. W. Shaw Company.

Ricardo, D. (1821). *On the Principles of Political Economy and Taxation*. Third ed. John Murray, Albemarle-Street, London.

Richins, Marsha (1983), "Negative Word-of-Mouth by Dissatisfied Consumers: A Pilot Study", *Journal of Marketing*, 47(Winter), 68–78.

Ricks, David A., Jeffrey S. Arpan, and Marilyn Y. Fu (1974), "Pitfalls in Advertising Overseas", *Journal of Advertising Research*, (December), 47–51.

Ridgeway, Valentine F. (1957), "Administration of Manufacturer-Dealer Systems", *Administrative Science Quarterly*, 1(March), 464–483.

Rindfleisch, Aric, and Jan B. Heide (1997), "Transaction Cost Analysis: Past, Present, and Future Applications", *Journal of Marketing*, 61(4), 30–54.

Robertson, Thomas S. (1971), *Innovative Behavior and Communication*, New York: Holt, Rinehart and Winston, Inc.

Robicheaux, Robert A. and Adel I. El-Ansary (1975–76), "A General Model for Understanding Channel Member Behavior", *Journal of Retailing*, 52(Winter), 13–30, 93–94.

Robicheaux, Robert A., and James E. Coleman (1994), "The Structure of Marketing Channel Relationships", *Journal of the Academy of Marketing Science*, 22(1), 38–51.

Robin, Donald P. (1978), "A Useful Scope for Marketing", *Journal of the Academy of Marketing Science*, 6(Summer), 228–238.

Robin, Donald P. and R. Eric Reidenbach (1987), "Social Responsibility, Ethics, and Marketing Strategy: Closing the Gap Between Concept and Application", *Journal of Marketing*, 51(January), 44–58.

Robinson, Patrick J., Charles W. Faris, and Yoram Wind (1967), *Industrial Buying and Creative Marketing*, Boston: Allyn and Bacon, Inc.

Rogers, Everett M (1983), Diffusion of Innovations, 3rd Edition, New York: The Free Press.

Rogers, Everett M. (1987), "The Critical School and Consumer Research", in *Advances in Consumer Research*, Melanie Wallendorf and Paul F. Anderson, eds., Volume 14, Provo, Utah: Association for Consumer Research, 7–11.

Rogers, Everett M. (1962), *Diffusion of Innovations*, New York: The Free Press of Glencoe.

Rook, Dennis W. (1985), "The Ritual Dimension of Consumer Behavior", *Journal of Consumer Research*, 12(December), 251–264.

Rook, Dennis W. and Sidney J. Levy (1983), "Psychosocial Themes in Consumer Grooming Rituals", in *Advances in Consumer Research*, Richard P. Bagozzi and Alice M., Tybout, Eds., Volume 10, Ann Arbor, Michigan: Association for Consumer Research, 329–333.

Roth, K., D. Schweiger, and A. Morrison (1991), "Global Strategy Implementation at the Business Unit Level: Operational Capabilities and Administrative Mechanisms", *Journal of International Business Studies*, 22(3), 369–402.

Ruekert, Robert W. and Orville C. Walker, Jr. (1987), "Marketing's Interaction with Other Functional Units: A Conceptual Framework and Empirical Evidence", *Journal of Marketing*, 51(January), 1–19.

Russo, J. Edard (1976), "When Do Advertisements Mislead the Consumer: An Answer from Experimental Psychology", in *Advances in Consumer Research*, Beverlee B. Anderson, ed., Volume 3, Ann Arbor, Michigan: Association for Consumer Research, 273–275.

Rust, Roland and Ming-Hui Huang (2012), "Optimizing Service Productivity", *Journal of Marketing*, 76(2), 47–66.

Rust, Roland and Ming-Hui Huang (2014), "The Service Revolution and the Transformation of Marketing Science", *Marketing Science*, 33(2), 206–221.

Rust, Roland and Richard L. Oliver (2000), "Should we Delight the Customer?" *Journal of the Academy of Marketing Science*, 28(1), 86–94.

Rust, Roland T., Anthony J. Zahorik, and Timothy L. Keiningham (1995), "Return on Quality (ROQ): Making Service Quality Financially Accountable," *Journal of Marketing*, 59(2), 58–70.

Rust, Roland T., Katherine N. Lemon, and Valarie A. Zeithaml (2004), "Return on Marketing: Using Customer Equity to Focus Marketing Strategy," *Journal of Marketing*, (68)1, 109–127.

Ryan, Franklin W. (1935), "Functional Concepts in Market Distribution", *Harvard Business Review*, 13(January), 205–224.

Sakarya, Sema, Molly Eckman, and Karen H. Hyllegard (2007), "Market Selection for International Expansion: Assessing Opportunities in Emerging Markets", *International Marketing Review*, 24(2), 208–238.

Samaha, Stephen A., Joshua T. Beck, and Robert W. Palmatier (2014), "The Role of Culture in International Relationship Marketing", *Journal of Marketing*, 78(5), 78–98.

Samiee, Saeed (1994), "Customer Evaluation of Products in Global Market", *Journal of International Business Studies*, 25(3), 579–604.

Samiee, Saeed and Brian R. Chabowski (2012), "Knowledge Structure in International Marketing: A Multi-method Bibliometric Analysis," *Journal of the Academy of Marketing Science*, 40, 364–386.

Samiee, Saeed and Kendall Roth (1992), "The Influence of Global Marketing Standardization on Performance", *Journal of Marketing*, 56(2), 1–17.

Samiee, Saeed and S. Chirapanda (2019), "International Marketing Strategy in Emerging-Market Exporting Firms," *Journal of International Marketing*, 27(1), 20–37.

Samiee, Saeed, Terence A. Shimp, and Subhash Sharma (2005), "Brand Origin Recognition Accuracy: Its Antecedents and Consumers' Cognitive Limitations," *Journal of International Business Studies*, 36(4), 379–397.

Samli, Coskun A. and Merici Fevrier (2008), "Achieving and Managing Global Brand Equity:

A Critical Analysis", *Journal of Global Marketing*, 21(3), 207–215.

Sarasvathy, Saras D. (2001), "Causation and Effectuation: Toward a Theoretical Shift from Economic Inevitability to Entrepreneurial Contingency", *Academy of Management Review*, 26(2), 243–263.

Sarasvathy, Saras D. (2008), *Effectuation: Elements of Entrepreneurial Expertise*. Cheltenham, U.K.: Edward Elgar Publishing.

Savitt, Ronald (1980), "Historical Research in Marketing", *Journal of Marketing*, 44(Fall), 52–58.

Savitt, Ronald (1981), "The Theory of Interregional Marketing", in *Regulation of Marketing and the Public Interest*, F. Balderston, James Carman, and Francesco M. Nicosia, eds., New York: Pergamon, 229–238.

Schellenberg, Michael, Michael John Harker, and Aliakbar Jafari (2018), "International Market Entry Mode – A Systematic Literature Review", *Journal of Strategic Marketing*, 26(7), 601–627.

Schellhase, Ralf, Petra Hardock, and Martin Ohlwein (2000), "Customer Satisfaction in Business-to-Business Marketing: The Case of Retail Organizations and Their Suppliers", *The Journal of Business and Industrial Marketing*, 15(2–3), 106–121.

Schettkat, R (2007), "The Astonishing Regularity of Service Employment Expansion," *Metroeconomica*, 58(3), 413–435.

Schewe, Charles D., Ed. (1985), *The Elderly Market: Selected Readings*, Chicago: American Marketing Association.

Schilke, Oliver, Martin Reinmann, and Jacquelyn S. Thomas (2009), "When Does International Marketing Standardization Matter to Firm Performance?" *Journal of International Marketing*, 17(4), 24–46.

Schlink, F. J. (1935), *Eat, Drink and Be Wary*, New York: Covici, Friede, Publishers.

Scholstak L. G. (1977), "Breaking Free from Product Marketing", *Journal of Marketing*, 41(2), 73–80.

Schooler, Robert D. (1965), "Product Bias in Central American Common Market," *Journal of Marketing Research*, 3(November), 394–397.

Schooler, Robert D. (1971), "Bias Phenomena Attendant to the Marketing to the Marketing of Foreign Goods in the U.S.," *Journal of International Business Studies*, 2(Spring), 71–80.

Selnes, Fred, and James Salis (2003), "Promoting Relationship Learning," *Journal of Marketing*, 67(3), 80–95.

Sethi, S. Prakash (1971), *Up Against the Corporate Wall: Modem Corporations and Social Issues in the Seventies*, Englewood Cliffs, New Jersey: Prentice-Hall, Inc.

Sethi, S. Prakash (1979), *Promises of the Good Life*, Homewood, Illinois: Richard D. Irwin, Inc.

Sethna, Zubin, Rosalind Jones, and Paul Harrigan (2013), *Entrepreneurial Marketing: Global Perspectives*, 1st ed. Bingley, UK: Emerald.

Sexton, Donald E., Jr. (1971), "Comparing the Cost of Food to Blacks and to Whites — A Survey", *Journal of Marketing*, 35(July), 40–46.

Shah, Denish, Roland T. Rust, Richard S. Parasuraman, and George S. Day (2006), "The Path to Customer Centricity," *Journal of Service Research*, (9)2, 113–124.

Sharp, Byron, and John Dawes (2001), "What is Differentiation and How Does it Work?" *Journal of Marketing* Management, (17), 7–8, 739–759.

Shaw, Arch W. (1912), "Some Problems in Market Distribution," *The Quarterly Journal of Economics*, 26(4), 703–765.

Shawver, Donald L. and William O. Nickels (1979), "A Rationalization for Macro-Marketing Concepts and Definitions", in *Macro-Marketing: New Steps on the Learning Curve*, George Fisk and Robert W. Nason, eds., Boulder: Business Research Division, Graduate School of Business Administration, University of Colorado.

Sheth Jagdish N., Nirmal Sethia, and Shanthi Srinivas (2011), "Mindful Consumption: A Customer-Centric Approach to Sustainability", *Journal of the Academy of Marketing Science*, 39(1), 21–39.

Sheth, Jagdish (2017), "Revitalizing Relationship Marketing," *Journal of Services Marketing*, 31(1), 6–10.

Sheth, Jagdish (2020), *The Howard-Sheth Theory of Buyer Behavior*, New Delhi: Wiley.

Sheth, Jagdish (2021), "New Areas of Research in Marketing Strategy, Consumer Behavior, and Marketing Analytics: The Future is Bright," *Journal of Marketing Theory and Practice*, 29(1). 3–12.

Sheth, Jagdish and Atul Parvatiyar (1992), "Towards a Theory of Business Alliance Formation," *Scandinavian International Business Review*, 1(3), 71–87.

Sheth, Jagdish and David Gardner (1982), "History of Marketing Thought: An Update," *Bureau of Economic and Business Research: University of Illinois-Urbana-Champaign,* 857, 1–26.

Sheth, Jagdish and Rajendra Sisodia (2002), *The Rule of Three: Surviving and Thriving in Competitive Markets,* New York: The Free Press.

Sheth, Jagdish N. (1967), "A Review of Buyer Behavior," *Management Science,* 13(August), B718–B756.

Sheth, Jagdish N. (1973), "A Model of Industrial Buyer Behavior," *Journal of Marketing,* 37(October), 50–56.

Sheth, Jagdish N. (1974a), "A Field Study of Attitude Structure and the Attitude Behavior Relationship," in *Models of Buyer Behavior: Conceptual, Quantitative, and Empirical,* Jagdish N. Sheth, ed., New York: Harper & Row Publishers, Inc., 242–268.

Sheth, Jagdish N. (1974b), "A Theory of Family Buying Decisions," in *Models of Buyer Behavior: Conceptual, Quantitative, and Empirical,* Jagdish N. Sheth, ed., New York: Harper & Row, Publishers, Inc., 17–33.

Sheth, Jagdish N. (1979a), "The Specificity of Industrial Marketing," *P. U. Management Review,* 2(December/January), 53–56.

Sheth, Jagdish N. (1979b), "The Surpluses and Shortages in Consumer Behavior Theory and Research," *Journal of the Academy of Marketing Science,* 7(Fall), 414–427.

Sheth, Jagdish N. (1985a), "History of Consumer Behavior: A Marketing Perspective," in *Historical Perspective in Consumer Research: National and International Perspectives, Proceedings of the Association for Consumer Research International Meeting in Singapore,* Chin Tiong Tan and Jagdish N. Sheth, eds., Singapore: School of Management, National University of Singapore, 5–7.

Sheth, Jagdish N. (1985b), "Presidential Address: Broadening the Horizons of ACR and Consumer Behavior," in *Advances in Consumer Research,* Elizabeth C. Hirschman and Morris B. Holbrook, eds., Volume 12, Provo, Utah: Association for Consumer Research, 1–2.

Sheth, Jagdish N. (1985c), *Winning Back Your Market: The Inside Stories of the Companies That Did It,* New York: John Wiley & Sons, Inc.

Sheth, Jagdish N. (1986), "Global Markets or Global Competition?," *The Journal of Consumer Marketing,* 3(Spring), 9–11.

Sheth, Jagdish N. (1997), "The Reincarnation of International Marketing," in *International Business: An Emerging Vision,* Brian Toyne and Douglas Nigh, eds. Columbia, SC: University of South Carolina Press. 561–567.

Sheth, Jagdish N. (2002), "A Generic Concept of Consumer Behavior," *Journal of Consumer Behavior,* 1(1), 7–18.

Sheth, Jagdish N. (2011a), "Impact of Emerging Markets on Marketing: Rethinking Existing Perspectives and Practices," *Journal of Marketing,* 75(July), 166–182.

Sheth, Jagdish N. (2011b), *Chindia Rising: How China and India will Benefit Your Business,* 2nd ed. Tata-McGraw Hill India.

Sheth, Jagdish N. (2017), *Genes, Climate, and Consumption Culture: Connecting the Dots,* Emerald Publishing.

Sheth, Jagdish N. (2020), "Customer Value Propositions: Value Cocreation," *Industrial Marketing Management,* 87, 312–315.

Sheth, Jagdish N. (2020), Borderless Media: Rethinking International Marketing, *Journal of International Marketing,* 28(1), 3–12.

Sheth, Jagdish N. (2020b), "Business of Business is More than Business: Managing During the Covid Crisis," *Industrial Marketing Management,* 88(July), 261–264.

Sheth, Jagdish N. (2020c), "Customer Value Propositions: Value Co-creation," *Industrial Marketing Management,* 87, 312–315.

Sheth, Jagdish N. and Abdolrezza Eshghi (1989a), *Global Accounting Perspectives,* Cincinnati: Southwestern Publishing Company.

Sheth, Jagdish N. and Abdolrezza Eshghi (1989b), *Global Financial Perspectives,* Cincinnati: Southwestern Publishing Company.

Sheth, Jagdish N. and Abdolrezza Eshghi (1989c), *Global Marketing Perspectives,* Cincinnati: Southwestern Publishing Company.

Sheth, Jagdish N. and Abdolrezza Eshghi (1990), *Global Macroeconomic Perspectives,* Cincinnati: Southwestern Publishing Company.

Sheth, Jagdish N. and Abdolrezza Eshghi (1991), *Global Microeconomic Perspectives,* Cincinnati: Southwestern Publishing Company.

Sheth, Jagdish N. and Atul Parvatiyar (2020), "Future Directions of Cross-Cultural Marketing Research," in *Handbook on Cross-Cultural Marketing,* Glen

H. Brodowsky and Camille P. Schuster (eds), Northampton, MA: Edward Elgar, 248–263.

Sheth, Jagdish N. and Atul Parvatiyar (2021), "Sustainable Marketing: Market Driving, Not Market-Driven", *Journal of Macromarketing*, 41(1), 150–165.

Sheth, Jagdish N. and Barbara L. Gross (1988), "Parallel Development of Marketing and Consumer Behavior: A Historical Perspective", in Historical Perspectives in Marketing, Ronald A. Fullerton and Terence Nevitt, eds., Lexington, Massachusetts: Lexington Books.

Sheth, Jagdish N. and Can Uslay (2007), "Implications of the Revised Definition of Marketing: From Exchange to Value Creation", *Journal of Public Policy and Marketing,* 22(2), 302–307.

Sheth, Jagdish N. and David M. Gardner (1982), "History of Marketing Thought: An Update" in *Marketing Theory: Philosophy of Science Perspectives*, Ronald Bush and Shelby Hunt, Eds., American Marketing Association, 52–58.

Sheth, Jagdish N. and Dennis E. Garrett (1986a), *Marketing Management: A Comprehensive Reader*, Cincinnati, Ohio: South-Western Publishing Company.

Sheth, Jagdish N. and Dennis E. Garrett (1986b), *Marketing Theory: Classic and Contemporary Readings*, Cincinnati, Ohio: South-Western Publishing Company.

Sheth, Jagdish N. and Gary L. Frazier (1982), "A Model of Strategy Mix Choice for Planned Social Change", *Journal of Marketing*, 46 (Winter), 15–26.

Sheth, Jagdish N. and Peter L. Wright, Eds (1974), *Marketing Analysis for Societal Problems*, Urbana-Champaign: Bureau of Economic and Business Research, College of Commerce and Business Administration, University of Illinois.

Sheth, Jagdish N. and Rajendra S. Sisodia (1999), "Revisiting Marketing's Lawlike Generalizations," *Journal of the Academy of Marketing Science*, 27(1), 71–87.

Sheth, Jagdish N. and Rajendra S. Sisodia (2006), *Tectonic Shift: The Geoeconomic Realignment of Globalizing Markets,* New Delhi: Sage Publications.

Sheth, Jagdish N. and Rajendra S. Sisodia (1999), "Outsourcing Comes Home", *The Wall Street Journal*, June 28, 16.

Sheth, Jagdish N. and Rajendra Sisodia Eds. (2006), *Does Marketing Need Reform? Fresh Perspectives on the Future.* Chicago: ME Sharpe.

Sheth, Jagdish N. and S. Prakash Sethi (1973), *Multinational Business Operations: Advanced Readings. Volume 1: Environmental Aspects of Operating Abroad, Volume 2: Long Range Planning, Organization and Management, Volume 3: Marketing Management, Volume 4: Financial Management*, Goodyear Publishing Company.

Sheth, Jagdish N. and S. Prakash Sethi (1977), "A Theory of Cross-Cultural Buyer Behavior", in *Consumer and Industrial Buying Behavior*, Arch G. Woodside, Jagdish N. Sheth, and Peter D. Bennett, Eds., New York: Elsevier North-Holland, Inc., 369–386.

Sheth, Jagdish N., and Atul Parvatiyar (1992), "Towards a Theory of Business Alliance Formation", *Scandinavian International Business Review*, 1(3), 71–87.

Sheth, Jagdish N., and Atul Parvatiyar (1995a), "The Evolution of Relationship Marketing", *International Business Review*, 4(4), 397–418.

Sheth, Jagdish N., and Atul Parvatiyar (1995b), "Relationship Marketing in Consumer Markets: Antecedents and Consequences", *Journal of the Academy of Marketing Science*, 23(4), 255–271.

Sheth, Jagdish N., and Gary L. Frazier (1983), "A Margin-Return Model for Strategic Market Planning," *Journal of Marketing*, (47)2, 100–109.

Sheth, Jagdish N., Arun Sharma, and Gopalkrishnan R. Iyer (2009), "Why Integrating Purchasing with Marketing is Both Inevitable and Beneficial", *Industrial Marketing Management*, (38)8, 865–871.

Sheth, Jagdish N., Atul Parvatiyar, and Mona Sinha (2012), "The Conceptual Foundations of Relationship Marketing: Review and Synthesis," *Economic Sociology: The European Electronic Newsletter*, 13(3), 4–26.

Sheth, Jagdish N., Atul Parvatiyar, and Mona Sinha (2015), "The Conceptual Foundations of Relationship Marketing: Review and Synthesis," *Journal of Economic Sociology = Ekonomicheskaya Sotsiologiya*, *16*(2), 119–149.

Sheth, Jagdish N., Can Uslay, and Rajendra S. Sisodia (2020), *The Global Rule of Three: Competing with Conscious Strategy*, New York, NY: Palgrave MacMillan.

Sheth, Jagdish N., David M. Gardner, and Dennis E. Garrett (1988), *Marketing Theory: Evolution and Evaluation*. John Wiley & Sons Incorporated.

Sheth, Jagdish N., Mona Sinha, and Reshma Shah (2016), *Breakout Strategies for Emerging Markets: Business and Marketing Tactics for Achieving Growth*, Old Tappan, NJ: Pearson Education.

Sheth, Jagdish N., N.K. Sethia, and S. Srinivas (2011), "Mindful Consumption: A Customer-centric Approach to Sustainability," *Journal of the Academy of Marketing Science*, 3 (9), 21–39.

Sheth, Jagdish N., Rajendra S. Sisodia, and Arun Sharma (2000), "The Antecedents and Consequences of Customer-Centric Marketing", *Journal of the Academy of Marketing Science*, 28(1), 55–66.

Sheth, Jagdish N., V. Jain, and A. Ambika (2020), "Repositioning the Customer Support Services: The Next Frontier of Competitive Advantage", *European Journal of Marketing*, 54(7), 1787–1804.

Sheth, Jagdish, and Atul Parvatiyar (2000), "The Domain and Conceptual Foundations of Relationship Marketing," *Handbook of Relationship Marketing*, 3–38.

Sheth, Jagdish, and Atul Parvatiyar (2002), "Evolving Relationship Marketing into a Discipline", *Journal of Relationship Marketing*, 1(1), 3–16.

Sheth, Jagdish, and Can Uslay (2007), "Implications of the Revised Definition of Marketing: From Exchange to Value Creation," *Journal of Public Policy & Marketing*, 26(2), 302–307.

Sheth, Jagdish, and Rajendra S. Sisodia (1995), "Feeling the Heat-Part 1", *Marketing Management*, 4(2), 8.

Sheth, Jagdish. N. and Atul Parvatiyar (2001), "The Antecedents and Consequences of Integrated Global Marketing," *International Marketing Review*, 18(1), 16–29.

Shrivastava, Samir, and Sudhir H. Kale (2003), "Philosophizing on the Elusiveness of Relationship Marketing Theory in Consumer Markets: A Case for Reassessing Ontological and Epistemological Assumptions," *Australasian Marketing Journal*, 11(3), 61–71.

Shugan, Steven M. (1987), "Estimating Brand Positioning Maps Using Supermarket Scanning Data", *Journal of Marketing Research*, 24(February), 1–18.

Shultz, Clifford (2007), "Marketing as Constructive Engagement: A Post AMA Synthesis," *Journal of Public Policy and Marketing*, 26(Fall), 293–301.

Siguaw, Judy A., Gene Brown, and Robert E. Widing (1994), "The Influence of The Market Orientation of the Firm on SalesForce Behavior and Attitudes," *Journal of Marketing Research*, (31)1, 106–116.

Siguaw, Judy A., Penny M. Simpson, and Thomas L. Baker (1998), "Effects of Supplier Market Orientation on Distributor Market Orientation and the Channel Relationship: The Distributor Perspective", *Journal of Marketing*, 62(3), 99–111.

Sinclair, Upton B. (1906), *The Jungle*, New York: The Jungle Publishing Company.

Sirdeshmukh, Deepak, Jagdip Singh and Barry Sabol (2002), "Consumer Trust, Value, and Loyalty in Relational Exchanges", *Journal of Marketing*, 66(1), 15–37.

Sisodia, Rajendra A., D. Wolfe and Jagdish N. Sheth, J. (2007), *Firms of Endearment: How World-Class Companies Profit from Passion and Purpose*. Wharton School Publishing/Pearson Education.

Sisodia, Rajendra S. and David B. Wolfe (2000), "Relationship Marketing in Mass Markets", in *Handbook of Relationship Marketing*, Jagdish N. Sheth and Atul Parvatiyar (Eds.), Thousand Oaks, CA: Sage, 525–564.

Slater, Charles C., Ed. (1977), *Macro-Marketing: Distributive Processes from a Societal Perspective*, Boulder: Business Research Division, Graduate School of Business Administration, University of Colorado.

Slater, Stanley F., Tomas M. Hult, and Eric M. Olson (2007), "On the Importance of Matching Strategic Behavior and Target Market Selection to Business Strategy in High-Tech Markets", *Journal of the Academy of Marketing Science*, 35(1), 5–17.

Smallwood, John E. (1973), *The Product Life Cycle: A Key to Strategic Marketing Planning*, New York: Routledge.

Smith, Anne M. (1995), "Measuring Service Quality: Is SERVQUAL Now Redundant?" *Journal of Marketing Management*, 11, 257–276.

Smith, Wendell R. (1956), "Product Differentiation and Market Segmentation as Alternative Marketing Strategies", *Journal of Marketing*, 21 (July), 3–8.

Solberg, Carl Arthur (2002), "The Perennial Issue of Adaptation or Standardization of International Marketing Communication: Organizational Contingencies and Performance", *Journal of International Marketing*, 10 (3), 1–21.

Sorenson, Ralph Z. and Ulrich E. Wiechmann (1975), "How Multinationals View Marketing Standardization", *Harvard Business Review*, 53(May/June), 38, 166–167.

Sousa, C. M. P. and Q. Tan (2015), "Exit from a Foreign Market, Do Poor Performance, Strategic Fit, Cultural Distance, and International Experience Matter? *Journal of International Marketing*, 23(4), 84–104.

Sousa, C.M., and S. Novello (2014), "The Influence of Distributor Support and Price Adaptation on the Export Performance of Small and Medium-Sized Enterprises," *International Small Business Journal*, 32(4), 359–385.

Spyropoulou, Stavroula, Constantine Katsikeas, Dionysis Skarmeas, and Neil A. Morgan (2018), "Strategic Goal Accomplishment in Export Ventures: The Role of Capabilities, Knowledge, and Environment", *Journal of the Academy of Marketing Science*, (46)1, 109–129.

Srinivasan, Narasimhan, Subhash C. Jain, and Kiranjit Sikand (2004), "An experimental study of two dimensions of country-of-origin (manufacturing country and branding country) using intrinsic and extrinsic cues," *International Business Review*, 13(1), 65–82.

Srivastava, Rajendra K., Tasadduq A. Shervani, and Liam Fahey (1998), "Market-Based Assets and Shareholder Value: A Framework for Analysis." *Journal of Marketing*, 62(1), 2–18.

Staudt, Thomas A. (1958), "Business Management as a Total System of Action and the Role of Marketing", in *Managerial Marketing: Perspectives and Viewpoints*, Eugene J. Kelley and William Lazer, eds., Homewood, Illinois: Richard D. Irwin, Inc.

Steenkamp, Jan-Benedict E.M. (2020), "Global Brand Building and Management in the Digital Age", *Journal of International Marketing*, 28(1), 13–27.

Steenkamp, Jan-Benedict E.M., Rajeev Batra, and Dana L. Alden (2003), "How Perceived Brand Globalness Creates Brand Value", *Journal of International Business Studies*, 34(1), 53–65.

Steiner, Robert L. (1976), "The Prejudice Against Marketing", *Journal of Marketing*, 40(July), 2–9.

Stern, Louis W. and Adel El-Ansary (1988), *Marketing Channels*, New Jersey: Prentice-Hall International Editions.

Stern, Louis W. And Ronald H. Gorman (1969), "Conflict in Distribution Channels: An Exploration", in *Distribution Channels: Behavioral Dimensions*, Boston: Houghton Mifflin Company, 156–175.

Stern, Louis W. and Torger Reve (1980), "Distribution Channels as Political Economies: A Framework for Comparative Analysis", *Journal of Marketing*, 44(3), 52–64.

Stern, Louis W., Ed. (1969), *Distribution Channels: Behavioral Dimensions*, Boston: Houghton Mifflin Company.

Sternthal, Brian, Alice M. Tybout, and Bobby J. Calder (1987), "Confirmatory Versus Comparative Approaches to Judging Theory Tests", *Journal of Consumer Research*, 14(June), 114–125.

Stewart, Paul W. and J. Frederic Dewhurst (1939), *Does Distribution Cost Too Much? A Review of the Costs Involved in Current Marketing Methods and a Program for Improvement*, New York: The Twentieth Century Fund, Inc.

Stigler, George J. (1951), "The Division of Labor is Limited by the Extent of the Market", *Journal of Political Economy*, 54(June), 185–193.

Sturdivant, Frederick D. (1968), "Better. Deal for Ghetto Shoppers", *Harvard Business Review*, 46(March/April), 130–139.

Sudharshan, Devanathan (1995), *Marketing Strategy: Relationships, Offerings, Timing, and Resource Allocation*, New Jersey: Prentice-Hall.

Sujan, Harish (1986), "Smarter Versus Harder: An Exploratory Attributional Analysis of Salespeople's Motivation", *Journal of Marketing Research*, 23(February), 41–49.

Swaminathan, Vanitha and Srinivas K. Reddy (2000), "Relationship Marketing in Mass Markets," in *Handbook of Relationship Marketing*, Jagdish N. Sheth and Atul Parvatiyar (eds.), Thousand Oaks, CA: Sage, 381–406.

Szmigin, Isabelle, and Humphrey Bourne (1998), "Consumer Equity in Relationship Marketing", *Journal of Consumer Marketing*, 15(6), 544–557.

Szymanski, David M., Sundar G. Bharadwaj, and Rajan P. Varadarajan (1993), "An Analysis of the Market Share Profitability Relationship", *Journal of Marketing*, 57(3), 1–18.

Tadajewski, Mark., and Michael Saren (2009), "Rethinking the Emergence of Relationship Marketing", *Journal of Macromarketing*, 29(2), 193–206.

Takala, Tuomo, and Outi Uusitalo (1996), "An Alternative View of Relationship Marketing: A Framework for Ethical Analysis," *European Journal of Marketing*, 30(2), 45–60.

Talukdar, Debabrata, K. Sudhir, and Andrew Ainslie (2002), "Investigating New Product Diffusion Across Products and Countries", *Marketing Science*, 21(1), 97–114.

Tan, Qun, and Carlos M.P. Sousa (2018), "Research on Export Pricing: Still Moving Toward Maturity", *Journal of International Marketing*, 19(3), 1–35.

Tanzi, Alex and Wei Lu (2020), "IMF Data Shows Coronavirus will Push China GDP Growth Well Beyond U.S.," available at https://economictimes.indiatimes.com/news/international/business/imf-data-shows-coronavirus-will-push-china-gdp-growth-well-beyond-us/articleshow/78686778.cms, last accessed December 20, 2020.

Teas, Kenneth R. (1994), "Expectations as a Comparison Standard in Measuring Service Quality: An Assessment of a Reassessment, *Journal of Marketing*, 58(January), 132–139.

Tellis, Gerard J. (1986), "Beyond the Many Faces of Price: An Integration of Pricing Strategies", *Journal of Marketing*, 50(October), 146–160.

Tellis, Gerard J. (1987), Consumer Purchasing Strategies and the Information in Retail Prices, *Journal of Retailing, 63*(3), 279–297.

Thakor, M.V. and Lavack, A.M. (2003), "Effect of perceived brand origin associations on consumer perceptions of quality", *Journal of Product & Brand Management*, 12(6): 394–407.

Thaler, Richard H., and Cass R. Sunstein (2009), *Nudge: Improving Decisions About Health, Wealth, and Happiness*, New York: Penguin.

The Economist (2021a), "Why Retailers Everywhere Should Look to China", available at www.economist.com/leaders/2021/01/02/why-retailers-everywhere-should-look-to-china, last accessed on January 25, 2021.

The Economist (2021b), "The Next Big Thing in Retail Comes with Chinese Characteristics," available at www.economist.com/business/2021/01/02/the-next-big-thing-in-retail-comes-with-chinese-characteristicsm, last accessed on January 25, 2021.

Thibaut, John W. and Harold H. Kelley (1959), *The Social Psychology of Groups*, New York: John Wiley & Sons.

Thomas, Dan R. E. (1978), "Strategy Is Different in Service Businesses," *Harvard Business Review*, 56(July–August), 158–165.

Thorelli, Hans B. (1986), "Networks: Between Markets and Hierarchies", *Strategic Management Journal*, 7(1), 37–51.

Thorelli, Hans B., and Sarah V. Thorelli (1977), *Consumer Information Systems and Consumer Policy*, Cambridge, MA: Ballinger Publishing.

Townsend, Janell D., Sengun Yeniyurt, and Mehmet Berk Talay (2009), "Getting to Global: An Evolutionary Perspective of Brand Expansion in International Markets," *Journal of International Business Studies*, 40, 539–558.

Tucker, W. T. (1974), "Future Directions in *Marketing Theory*", *Journal of Marketing*, 38(April), 30–35.

Tull, Donald S., Van R. Wood, Dale Duhan, Tom Gillpatrick, Kim R. Robertson, and James G. Helgeson (1986), "'Leveraged' Decision Making in Advertising: The Flat Maximum Principle and Its Implications", *Journal of Marketing Research*, 23(February), 25–32.

Tzokas, Nikolaos, and Michael Saren (1999), "Value Transformation in Relationship Marketing," *Australasian Marketing Journal*, 7(1), 52–62.

Uhl, Kenneth P. (1968), "Marketing Information Systems and Subsystems", in *Marketing and the New Science of Planning*, Robert L. King, ed., Chicago: American Marketing Association, 163–168.

Uhl, Kenneth P. and Gregory D. Upah (1983), "The Marketing of Services: Why and How is it Different?", in *Research in Marketing*, Jagdish N. Sheth, ed., Volume 6, Greenwich, Connecticut: JAI Press, Inc., 231–257.

Uslay, Can (2019), "The Next Frontier in Marketing: Self-Sustaining Marketing, Society, and Capitalism through Collaborative yet Disruptive Partnerships" in *Handbook of Marketing Advances in the Era of Disruptions – Essays in Honor of Jagdish N. Sheth*, A. Parvatiyar and R.S. Sisodia Eds., Sage, 490–500.

Uslay, Can and Emine Erdogan (2014), "The Mediating Role of Mindful Entrepreneurial Marketing (MEM) Between Production and Consumption", *Journal of Research in Marketing and Entrepreneurship*, 16(1), 47–62.

Uslay, Can, Ekaterina Karniouchina, Ayca Altintig, and Martin Reeves (2017), "Do Businesses Get Stuck in the Middle? The Peril of Intermediate Market Share," available at https://papers.ssrn.com/sol3/papers.cfm?abstract_id=3043330, last accessed April 9, 2021.

Uslay, Can, Z. Ayca Altintig, Robert D. Winsor (2010), "An Empirical Examination of the "Rule of Three": Strategy Implications for Top Management, Marketers, and Investors," *Journal of Marketing*, 74 (2), 20–39.

Uzzi, Brian (1996), "The Sources and Consequences of Embeddedness for the Economic Performance of Organizations: The Network Effect," *American Sociological Review*, 61(August), 674–698.

Vaile, Roland S., E. T. Grether, and Reavis Cox (1952), Marketing in the American Economy, New York: The Ronald Press Company.

Van den Bulte, Christophe, and Stefan Stremersch (2004), "Social Contagion and Income Heterogeneity in New Product Diffusion: A Meta-Analytic Test," *Marketing Science*, 23(4), 520–544.

Vanderblue, Homer B. (1921), "The Functional Approach to the Study of Marketing," *Journal of Political Economy*, 29(October), 676–683.

Varadarajan, P. Rajan, and Margaret H. Cunningham (1995), "Strategic Alliances: A Synthesis of Conceptual Foundations," *Journal of the Academy of Marketing Science,* 23(4), 282–296.

Varadarajan, P. Rajan, and Satish Jayachandran (1999), "Marketing Strategy: An Assessment of the State of The Field and Outlook," *Journal of the Academy of Marketing Science*, (27)2, 120–143.

Varadarajan, Rajan (2010), "Strategic Marketing and Marketing Strategy: Domain, Definition, Fundamental Issues, and Foundational Premises," *Journal of the Academy of Marketing Science*, 38(2), 119–140.

Varadarajan, Rajan (2015), "Strategic Marketing, Marketing Strategy and Market Strategy," *AMS Review*, 5(3), 78–90.

Vargo, Stephen L. (2018), "Service-Dominant Logic: Backward and Forward," in Vargo, Stephen L., and Robert F. Lusch, eds. *The SAGE handbook of service-dominant logic*. Sage, 720-739.

Vargo Stephen L. and Robert F. Lusch (2016), "Institutions and Axioms: An Extension and Update of Service-Dominant Logic," *Journal of the Academy of Marketing Science*, 44, 5–23.

Vargo, Stephen L. (2008), "Customer Integration and Value Creation: Paradigmatic Traps and Perspectives," *Journal of Service Research*, 11(2), 211–215.

Vargo, Stephen L. and Robert F. Lusch (2004), "Evolving to a New Dominant Logic for Marketing," *Journal of Marketing,* 68(1), 1–17.

Vargo, Stephen L. and Robert F. Lusch (2011). "It's all B2B…and Beyond: Toward a Systems Perspective of the Market," *Industrial Marketing Management*, 40(2), 181–187.

Vargo, Stephen L. and Robert F. Lusch (2016), "Institutions and Axioms: An Extension and Update of Service-Dominant Logic," *Journal of the Academy of Marketing Science*, 44, 5–23.

Vargo, Stephen L. and Robert F. Lusch (2017), "Service-Dominant Logic 2025," *International Journal of Research in Marketing*, 34(1), 46–67.

Vargo, Stephen L., and Robert F. Lusch (2004), "Evolving to a New Dominant Logic for Marketing, "*Journal of Marketing*, 68(1), 1–17.

Vargo, Stephen L., P. P. Maglio, and M. A. Akaka (2008), "On Value and Value Cocreation: A Service Systems and Service Logic Perspective," *European Management Journal*, 26(3), 145–152.

Veloutsou, Cleopatra, Michael Saren, and Nikolaos Tzokas (2002), "Relationship Marketing: What If…?," *European Journal of Marketing*, 36(4), 433–449.

Venkatesh, Alladi and Nikhilesh Dholakia (1986), "Methodological Issues in Macromarketing," *Journal of Macromarketing*, 6(Fall), 36–52.

Verhoef, Peter C. (2003), "Understanding the Effect of Customer Relationship Management Efforts on Customer Retention and Customer Share Development,"*Journal of Marketing*, 67(4), 30–45.

Verhoef, Peter C., Katherine N. Lemon, Ananthanarayanan Parasuraman, Anne Roggeveen Michael Tsiros, and Leonard A. Schlesinger (2009)," Customer Experience Creation: Determinants, Dynamics and Management Strategies," *Journal of Retailing*, 85(1), 31–41.

Verhoef, Peter C., Werner J. Reinartz, and Manfred Krafft (2010), "Customer Engagement as a New Perspective in Customer Management," *Journal of Service Research*, 13(3), 247–252.

Verlegh, P.W.J. and Steenkamp, J-B.E.M. (1999), "A Review and Meta-Analysis of Country-of-Origin

Research," *Journal of Economic Psychology*, 20(5), 521–546.

Vogel, Verena, Heiner Evanschitzky, and Balasubramani Ramaseshan (2008), "Customer Equity Drivers and Future Sales," *Journal of Marketing,* (72)6, 98–108.

Vorhies, Douglas W., and Neil A. Morgan (2003), "A Configuration Theory Assessment of Marketing Organization Fit with Business Strategy and its Relationship with Marketing Performance," *Journal of Marketing,* (67)1, 100–115.

Wales, Hugh and Lyndon E. Dawson, Jr. (1979), "The Anomalous Qualities Between Present-Day Conferences and Alderson's Marketing Theory Seminars," in *Conceptual and Theoretical Developments in Marketing*, O. C. Ferrell, Stephen W. Brown, and Charles W. Lamb, eds., Chicago: American Marketing Association, 222–227.

Walter, Achim, and Hans George Gemünden (2000), "Bridging the Gap Between Suppliers and Customers Through Relationship Promoters: Theoretical Considerations and Empirical Results," *Journal of Business* and *Industrial Marketing*, 15(2), 86–105.

Walters, Peter G. (1986), "International Marketing Policy: A Discussion of the Standardization Construct and its Relevance for Corporate Policy," *Journal of International Business Studies*, 17(Summer), 55–69.

Warner, W. Lloyd, Marchia Meeker, and Kenneth Eells (1949), *Social Class in America*, Chicago: Science Research Associates.

Watson, J.J. and Wright, K. (2000), "Consumer Ethnocentrism and Attitudes Toward Domestic and Foreign Products," *European Journal of Marketing*, 34(9/10), 1149–1166.

Weber, John A. (2000), "Partnering with Distributors to Stimulate Sales: A Case Study," *Journal of Business and Industrial Marketing*, 15(2/3), 154–162.

Webster Jr, Frederick E. (1992), "The Changing Role of Marketing in the Corporation," *Journal of Marketing*, 56(4), 1–17.

Webster, Frederick E., Jr. and Yoram Wind (1972), "A General Model for Understanding Organizational Buying Behavior," *Journal of Marketing*, 36(April), 12–19.

Weitz, Barton A. (1981), "Effectiveness in Sales Interactions: A Contingency Framework," *Journal of Marketing*, 45(Winter), 85–103.

Weitz, Barton A. (1985), "Introduction to Special Issue on Competition in Marketing," *Journal of Marketing Research*, (22)3, 229–236.

Weitz, Barton A., Harish Sujan, and Mita Sujan (1986), "Knowledge, Motivation, and Adaptive Behavior: A Framework for Improving Selling Effectiveness," *Journal of Marketing*, 50(October), 174–191.

Weld, L. D. H. (1917), "Marketing Functions and Mercantile Organization," *American Economic Review*, 7(June), 306–318.

Wells, William D. (1975), "Psychographics: A Critical Review," *Journal of Marketing Research*, 12(May), 196–213.

Westbrook, Robert A. (1987), "Product/Consumption-Based Affective Responses and Postpurchase Processes," *Journal of Marketing Research*, 24 (August), 258–270.

Whalen, Peter, Can Uslay, Vincent J. Pascal, Glenn Omura, Andrew McAuley, Chickery J. Kasouf, Rosalind Jones, Claes M. Hultman, Gerald E. Hills, David J. Hansen, Audrey.

Whalen, Peter, Can Uslay, Vincent J. Pascal, Glenn Omura, Andrew McAuley, Chickery J. Kasouf, Rosalind Jones, Claes M. Hultman, Gerald E. Hills, David J. Hansen, Audrey Gilmore, Joe Giglierano, Fabian Eggers, Jonathan Deacon (2016), "Anatomy of Competitive Advantage: Towards a Contingency Theory of Entrepreneurial Marketing," *Journal of Strategic Marketing*, 24(1), 5–19.

White, Philip D. and Charles C. Slater, Eds. (1978), *Macromarketing: Distributive Processes from a Societal Perspective, An Elaboration of Issues*, Boulder: Business Research Division, University of Colorado.

White, Phillip D. (1979), "Attitudes of U.S. Purchasing Managers Toward Industrial Products Manufactured in Selected Western European Nations," *Journal of International Business Studies*, 10(Spring/Summer), 81–90.

Whyte, William H., Jr. (1955), "The Web of Word of Mouth," in *Consumer Behavior (Volume 2): The Life Cycle and Consumer Behavior*, Lincoln H. Clark, ed., New York: New York University Press, 113–122.

Wiesel, Thorsten, Bernd Skiera, and Julian Villanueva (2008), "Customer Equity: An Integral Part of Financial Reporting," *Journal of Marketing,* (72)2, 1–14.

Wilkie, William L. and Edgar A. Pessemier (1973), "Issues in Marketing's Use of MultiAttribute Attitude Models", *Journal of Marketing Research*, 10(November), 428–441.

Wilkie, William L., and Elizabeth S. Moore (2003), "Scholarly Research in Marketing: Exploring The "4 Eras" of Thought Development," *Journal of Public Policy & Marketing*, 22(2), pp. 116–146.

Wilkie, William L., and Elizabeth S. Moore (2007), "What Does the Definition of Marketing tell us about Ourselves?", *Journal of Public Policy and Marketing*, 26(2), 269–276.

Williams, Kaylene C. and Rosann L. Spiro (1985), "Communication Style in the Salesperson-Customer Dyad", *Journal of Marketing Research*, 22(November), 434–442.

Williamson, Oliver (1981), "The Economics of Organization: The Transaction Cost Approach", *American Journal of Sociology*, 87(3), 548–577.

Williamson, Oliver (2002), "The Theory of the Firm as Governance Structure: From Choice to Contract", *Journal of Economic Perspectives*, 16(3), 171–195.

Williamson, Oliver E. (1975), *Markets and Hierarchies: Analysis and Antitrust Implications*, New York: Free Press.

Williamson, Oliver E. (1979), "Transaction-Cost Economics: The Governance of Contractual Relations", *The Journal of Law and Economics*, 22(2), 233–261.

Williamson, Oliver E. (1981), "The Economics of Organization: The Transaction Cost Approach," *American Journal of Sociology* 87(3), 548–577.

Williamson, Oliver E. (1985), *The Economic Institutions of Capitalism*, New York: Free Press.

Williamson, Oliver, and Tarek Ghani (2012), "Transaction Cost Economics and its Uses in Marketing", *Journal of the Academy of Marketing Science*, 40(1), 74–85.

Wills, James, Coskun A. Samli, and Laurence Jacobs (1991), "Developing Global Products and Marketing Strategies: A Construct and a Research Agenda," *Journal of the Academy of Marketing Science*, 19(1), 1–10.

Wilson, David T. (1995), "An integrated model of buyer-seller relationships", *Journal of the Academy of Marketing Science*, 23(4), 335–345.

Wind, Yoram (1978), "Issues and Advances in Segmentation Research," *Journal of Marketing Research,* (15)3, 317–337.

Wind, Yoram (1986), "The Myth of Globalization", *The Journal of Consumer Marketing*, 3(Spring), 23–26.

Wind, Yoram and R. Thomas (1980), "Conceptual and Methodological Issues in Organizational Buying Behavior", *European Journal of Marketing*, 14(5/6), 239–263.

Wind, Yoram and Susan P. Douglas (1986), "The Myth of Globalization", *Journal of Consumer Marketing*, 3(Spring), 23–26.

Wind, Yoram and Thomas S. Robertson (1983), "Marketing Strategy: New Directions for Theory and Research", *Journal of Marketing*, 47(Spring), 12–25.

Winter, Frederick (1984), "Market Segmentation: A Tactical Approach", *Business Horizons*, 27(January/February), 57–63.

Witt, Ulrich and Christian Gross (2020), "The Rise of the "Service Economy" in the Second Half of the Twentieth Century and Its Energetic Contingencies," *Journal of Evolutionary Economics*, 30, 231–246.

Woodside, Arch G., Jagdish N. Sheth, and Peter D. Bennett, Eds. (1977), *Consumer and Industrial Buying Behavior*, New York: Elsevier North-Holland, Inc.

Wright, Peter L. (1973), "Use of Consumer Judgment Models in Promotion Planning", *Journal of Marketing*, 37(October), 27–33.

Wu, Jie and Nitin Pangarkar (2006), "Rising to the Global Challenge: Strategies for Firms in Emerging Markets", *Long Range Planning*, 39(3): 295–313.

Yadav, Manjit and Paul A. Pavlou (2014), "Marketing in Computer-Mediated Environments: Research Synthesis and New Directions", *Journal of Marketing*, 78 (January), 20–40.

Yayla, Serdar, Sengun Yeniyurt, Can Uslay, and Erin Cavusgil (2018), "The Role of Market Orientation, Relational Capital, and Internationa-lization Speed in Foreign Market Exit and Re-Entry Decisions Under Turbulent Conditions," *International Business Review*, 27(6), 1105–1115.

Yang, Man and Peter Gabrielsson (2018), "The Interface of International Marketing and Entrepreneurship Research: Review, Synthesis, and Future Directions", *Journal of International Marketing*, 26(4), 18–37.

Yeniyurt, Sengun and Janelle D. Townsend (2003), "Does Culture Explain Acceptance of New Products in a Country? An Empirical Investigation," *International Marketing Review*, 20(4), 377–396.

Yeniyurt, Sengun, Janelle D. Townsend, Tamer S. Cavusgil, and P. N. Ghauri, (2009), "Mimetic and Experiential Effects in International Marketing Alliance Formations of U.S. Pharmaceuticals Firms: An Event History Analysis," *Journal of International Business Studies*, 40(2), 301–320.

Yeniyurt, Sengun, Janelle Townsend, and Mehmet Berk Talay (2007), "Factors Influencing Brand Launch in Global Marketplace", *Journal of Product Innovation Management*, 24(5), 471–485.

Yip George S. and Tomas M. Hult (2011), *Total Global Strategy*, 3rd ed., New Jersey: Prentice-Hall.

Zakia, Richard D. and Mihai Nadin (1987), "Semiotics, Advertising and Marketing", The *Journal of Consumer Marketing*, 4(Spring), 5–12.

Zaltman, Gerald (1996), "Metaphorically Speaking," *Marketing Research*, 8(2), 13.

Zaltman, Gerald (2003), *How Customers Think: Essential Insights into the Mind of the Market*, Boston, MA: Harvard Business Press.

Zaltman, Gerald and Robert Duncan (1977), *Strategies for Planned Change*, New York: John Wiley & Sons, Inc.

Zaltman, Gerald and Thomas V. Bonoma (1977), "Organizational Buying Behavior: Hypotheses and Directions," *Industrial Marketing Management*, 6(1), 53–60.

Zaltman, Gerald, and Lindsay H. Zaltman (2008), *Marketing Metaphoria: What Deep Metaphors Reveal About the Minds of Consumers*, Boston, MA: Harvard Business Press.

Zaltman, Gerald, Christian R. A. Pinson, and Reinhard Angelmar (1973), *Metatheory in Consumer Research*, New York: Holt, Rinehart and Winston, Inc.

Zaltman, Gerald, Karen Lemasters, and Michael Heffring (1982), *Theory Construction in Marketing*, New York: John Wiley & Sons, Inc.

Zeithaml Valarie, A. Parasuraman, and Leonard L. Berry (1990), *Delivering Quality Service—Balancing Customer Perceptions and Expectations*. New York: The Free Press.

Zeithaml, Carl P. and Valarie A. Zeithaml (1984), "Environmental Management: Revising the Marketing Perspective", *Journal of Marketing*, 48(Spring), 46–53.

Zeithaml, Valarie A. (1988), "Consumer Perceptions of Price, Quality, and Value: A Means-End Model and Synthesis of Evidence," *Journal of Marketing*, (52)3, 2–22.

Zeithaml, Valarie A., A. Parasuraman, and Leonard L. Berry (1985), "Problems and Strategies in Services Marketing", *Journal of Marketing*, 49(Spring), 33–46.

Zeithaml, Valarie A., Leonard L. Berry, and A. Parasuraman (1988), "Communication and Control Processes in the Delivery of Service Quality", *Journal of Marketing*, 52(April), 35–48.

Zeithaml, Valarie A., Leonard L. Berry, and A. Parasuraman (1996), "The Behavioral Consequences of Service Quality," *Journal of Marketing*, (60)2, 31–46.

Zeithaml, Valarie, Leonard Berry, and A. Parasuraman (1993), "The Nature and Determinants of Customer Expectations of Service," *Journal of the Academy of Marketing Science*, 21(1), 1–12.

Zielinski, Joan and Thomas S. Robertson (1982), "Consumer Behavior Theory: Excesses and Limitations", in *Advances in Consumer Research*, Andrew A. Mitchell, Ed., Volume 9, Ann Arbor, Michigan: Association for Consumer Research, 8–12.

Zif, Jehiel (1980), "A Managerial Approach to Macromarketing", *Journal of Marketing*, 44(Winter), 36–45.

Zikmund, William G. and William J. Stanton (1971), "Recycling Solid Wastes: A Channels of Distribution Problem", *Journal of Marketing*, 35(July), 34–39.

Zinkhan, George M., and Brian C. Williams (2007), "The New American Marketing Association Definition of Marketing: An Alternative Assessment", *Journal of Public Policy and Marketing*, 26(2), 284–288.

Zou, Shaoming and S. Tamer Cavusgil (2002), "The GMS: A Broad Conceptualization of Global Marketing Strategy and Its Effect on Firm Performance," *Journal of Marketing*, 66(October), 40–56.

Index